Handbook of Research on Foreign Language Education in the Digital Age

Congcong Wang
University of Northern Iowa, USA

Lisa Winstead
California State University, Fullerton, USA

A volume in the Advances in Educational
Technologies and Instructional Design (AETID)
Book Series

Published in the United States of America by
      Information Science Reference (an imprint of IGI Global)
      701 E. Chocolate Avenue
      Hershey PA, USA 17033
      Tel: 717-533-8845
      Fax: 717-533-8661
      E-mail: cust@igi-global.com
      Web site: http://www.igi-global.com

Library of Congress Cataloging-in-Publication Data

Names: Wang, Congcong, date- | Winstead, Lisa, 1960-
Title: Handbook of research on foreign language education in the digital age
 / Congcong Wang and Lisa Winstead, editors.
Description: Hershey, PA : Information Science Reference(an imprint of IGI
 Global), [2016] | Includes bibliographical references and index.
Identifiers: LCCN 2016003165| ISBN 9781522501770 (hardcover) | ISBN
 9781522501787 (ebook)
Subjects: LCSH: Language and languages--Study and teaching--Technological
 innovations. | Language and languages--Study and teaching--Computer
 network resources. | Second language acquisition--Study and
 teaching--Technological innovations. | Education, Bilingual--Technological
 innovations.
Classification: LCC P53.855 .H37 2016 | DDC 418.0078/5--dc23 LC record available at http://lccn.loc.gov/2016003165

This book is published in the IGI Global book series Advances in Educational Technologies and Instructional Design (AE-TID) (ISSN: 2326-8905; eISSN: 2326-8913)

British Cataloguing in Publication Data
A Cataloguing in Publication record for this book is available from the British Library.

All work contributed to this book is new, previously-unpublished material. The views expressed in this book are those of the authors, but not necessarily of the publisher.

For electronic access to this publication, please contact: eresources@igi-global.com.

Advances in Educational Technologies and Instructional Design (AETID) Book Series

Lawrence A. Tomei
Robert Morris University, USA

ISSN: 2326-8905
EISSN: 2326-8913

MISSION

Education has undergone, and continues to undergo, immense changes in the way it is enacted and distributed to both child and adult learners. From distance education, Massive-Open-Online-Courses (MOOCs), and electronic tablets in the classroom, technology is now an integral part of the educational experience and is also affecting the way educators communicate information to students.

The **Advances in Educational Technologies & Instructional Design (AETID) Book Series** is a resource where researchers, students, administrators, and educators alike can find the most updated research and theories regarding technology's integration within education and its effect on teaching as a practice.

COVERAGE

- Bring-Your-Own-Device
- Educational Telecommunications
- Classroom Response Systems
- Game-Based Learning
- Web 2.0 and Education
- Online Media in Classrooms
- Collaboration Tools
- Adaptive Learning
- Hybrid Learning
- Digital Divide in Education

IGI Global is currently accepting manuscripts for publication within this series. To submit a proposal for a volume in this series, please contact our Acquisition Editors at Acquisitions@igi-global.com or visit: http://www.igi-global.com/publish/.

Titles in this Series

For a list of additional titles in this series, please visit: www.igi-global.com

Knowledge Visualization and Visual Literacy in Science Education
Anna Ursyn (University of Northern Colorado, USA)
Information Science Reference • copyright 2016 • 431pp • H/C (ISBN: 9781522504801) • US $205.00 (our price)

Increasing Productivity and Efficiency in Online Teaching
Patricia Dickenson (National University, USA) and James J. Jaurez (National University, USA)
Information Science Reference • copyright 2016 • 327pp • H/C (ISBN: 9781522503477) • US $185.00 (our price)

Wearable Technology and Mobile Innovations for Next-Generation Education
Janet Holland (Emporia State University, USA)
Information Science Reference • copyright 2016 • 364pp • H/C (ISBN: 9781522500698) • US $195.00 (our price)

Creating Teacher Immediacy in Online Learning Environments
Steven D'Agustino (Fordham University, USA)
Information Science Reference • copyright 2016 • 356pp • H/C (ISBN: 9781466699953) • US $185.00 (our price)

Revolutionizing Education through Web-Based Instruction
Mahesh Raisinghani (Texas Woman's University, USA)
Information Science Reference • copyright 2016 • 391pp • H/C (ISBN: 9781466699328) • US $185.00 (our price)

Emerging Tools and Applications of Virtual Reality in Education
Dong Hwa Choi (Park University, USA) Amber Dailey-Hebert (Park University, USA) and Judi Simmons Estes
(Park University, USA)
Information Science Reference • copyright 2016 • 360pp • H/C (ISBN: 9781466698376) • US $180.00 (our price)

Handbook of Research on Cloud-Based STEM Education for Improved Learning Outcomes
Lee Chao (University of Houston - Victoria, USA)
Information Science Reference • copyright 2016 • 481pp • H/C (ISBN: 9781466699243) • US $300.00 (our price)

User-Centered Design Strategies for Massive Open Online Courses (MOOCs)
Ricardo Mendoza-Gonzalez (Instituto Tecnologico de Aguascalientes, Mexico)
Information Science Reference • copyright 2016 • 323pp • H/C (ISBN: 9781466697430) • US $175.00 (our price)

www.igi-global.com

701 E. Chocolate Ave., Hershey, PA 17033
Order online at www.igi-global.com or call 717-533-8845 x100
To place a standing order for titles released in this series, contact: cust@igi-global.com
Mon-Fri 8:00 am - 5:00 pm (est) or fax 24 hours a day 717-533-8661

We dedicate this book to world language educators and learners.

Editorial Advisory Board

List of Reviewers

Michael E. Everson, *University of Iowa, USA*
Kim Norman, California *State University, Fullerton, USA*
John J. Ivers, *Brigham Young University-Idaho, USA*
John Durham Peters, *University of Iowa, USA*
Timothy Church, *Washington State University, USA*
Marcia Katigbak Church, *Washington State University, USA*

List of Contributors

Table of Contents

Section 1
Commentary

Chapter 1
Jacques du Plessis, University of Wisconsin-Milwaukee, USA & University of KwaZulu-Natal, South Africa

Section 2
Technologies across Continents

Chapter 2
Carolin Fuchs, City University of Hong Kong, Hong Kong, China

Chapter 3
Geraldine Blattner, Florida Atlantic University, USA
Amanda Dalola, The University of South Carolina, USA
Lara Lomicka, The University of South Carolina, USA

Chapter 4
Eliane Thaines Bodah, Thaines & Bodah Center for Education and Development, USA
Josh Meuth Alldredge, Community Partnership for Child Development, USA
Brian William Bodah, Washington State University, USA
Alcindo Neckel, IMED University, Brazil
Emanuelle Goellner, Federal University of Rio Grande do Sul, Brazil

Section 3
Web Collaboration across Languages

Section 4
Less Commonly Taught Languages

Section 5
Teacher Education and Learning Strategies

Detailed Table of Contents

Section 1
Commentary

Chapter 1

>   *Jacques du Plessis, University of Wisconsin-Milwaukee, USA & University of KwaZulu-*
>   *Natal, South Africa*

This chapter is a commentary on the state of foreign language education in the digital age.

Section 2
Technologies across Continents

Chapter 2

>   *Carolin Fuchs, City University of Hong Kong, Hong Kong, China*

This case study contributes to the growing body of research on Language Massive Open Online Courses (LMOOCs) by examining their structural aspects (i.e., layout and format) and dialogic nature (i.e., interaction and negotiation) from the language learner's perspective. This exploratory study draws on data from 15 student teachers of English as a Second/Foreign Language at a private graduate institution on the East Coast of the U.S. As required by their technology elective, participants who were enrolled in a beginner-level LMOOC of their choice kept a log of their learning process/progress over a period of eight weeks. At the end of the course, they were invited to fill out a post-project questionnaire to reflect on their overall experience. The goal of the project was to educate student teachers on the pedagogical underpinnings of LMOOCs while exposing them to online language learning. In this study, the focus was primarily on self-reported system interaction and profile data since the Author was not involved in the design of any of the LMOOCs. Data collection instruments included a needs analysis, weekly LMOOC logs, and a post-LMOOC questionnaire. According to the questionnaire results, student-teachers' motivation was "satisfactory," and only four out of 15 student teachers completed their LMOOCs. Results further showed that structural aspects (i.e., content, materials, and procedures) rank higher than dialogic aspects (i.e., scaffolding and feedback). This questions the over-reliance on content transmission and instructivist (or teacher-instruction) approaches in LMOOCs, especially since MOOCs enrolment numbers rely heavily on learner's self-motivation to sign up and complete a course.

Chapter 3

Geraldine Blattner, Florida Atlantic University, USA
Amanda Dalola, The University of South Carolina, USA
Lara Lomicka, The University of South Carolina, USA

This chapter explores how French language learners in three different second and third year French courses (intermediate and advanced levels) understand and interpret hashtags using the popular microblogging tool Twitter. The present study highlights how this social media service may provide an authentic and dynamic platform that enhances the language learning experience, while developing students' multiliteracy skills in a second language (L2). Data from 18 students at a large southeastern university were examined via 579 analyzed tweets, 171 of which contained hashtags. In this project, we investigate the relationship between students' ability to access information in the hashtags and to understand the nature of the larger tweet in which it appears. The results of this study suggest that language learners have a tendency to glance over the hashtags and make guesses based on the information contained therein. The incorporation of cultural and linguistic elements linked to microbloggers' social tagging is an interesting and important aspect to add in foreign language classes. Learning about and understanding hashtags can promote the development of noticing cultural references, a skill that is indispensable for successful autonomous communication across national boundaries and for online communicative practices.

Chapter 4

Eliane Thaines Bodah, Thaines & Bodah Center for Education and Development, USA
Josh Meuth Alldredge, Community Partnership for Child Development, USA
Brian William Bodah, Washington State University, USA
Alcindo Neckel, IMED University, Brazil
Emanuelle Goellner, Federal University of Rio Grande do Sul, Brazil

Our chapter aims to explore the challenges, advances, and perspectives of language-education technology in Brazil. Language-education is an extremely important topic for Brazil because many indigenous languages are nearing extinction due to the legacies of colonization and the fact that Portuguese, the national language of Brazil, is the only official language and thus the single most utilitarian method of communication. This issue is further complicated by Brazil's increasingly globalized economy, which, for many individuals, demands the acquisition of a foreign language in order to compete. The English language has been introduced into the curriculum of the vast majority Brazilian public schools over the course of the past few decades. Additionally, several private, for-profit English learning enterprises now have widespread services throughout the country. But rates of English (and even Portuguese) fluency still vary greatly among the population. This raises a number of critical questions that will be discussed in this work. Why is learning a new language such a challenge? Which methodologies can be utilized to increase language acquisition and build fluency? What are the new technologies that are used in teaching a second language in Brazilian schools, and how is their impact being measured? Are Brazilian teachers prepared to integrate new technologies and innovative methods of teaching and learning? Our methodology involves bibliographical research including a literature review, a case-study, and participatory research through semi-structured interviews. Our results have shown that several technologies are being implemented in Brazil, and that as a theoretical framework, educational communication has been recognized as a powerful tool to incorporate such technologies in language education. Overall, the use of learning technologies is common and growing among students, while it is increasing at a more institutional pace among teachers.

Chapter 5

Many hybrid programs have been created in higher education institutions in the US for the last 15 years, most of them consisting of the combination of classroom instruction and an online platform. However, the flipped classroom has become very popular recently as a result of this hybrid model of instruction. The purpose of this chapter is to respond to the following questions: What is a more recommended model for teaching Spanish in the digital age? What kind of activities should we focus on, as instructors, in the classroom? What works best for students to study and practice outside of the classroom? Both models will be described with their advantages and disadvantages so that instructors can choose the one that better fits their courses.

Chapter 6

The explosive worldwide growth of the internet inspired the initial emergence and further implementation of distance teaching and learning in a multitude of areas, including languages. The change from the traditional classroom environment to a more diversified and flexible distance setting has been embraced by many educators, administrators, and students, yet it has also generated doubt and resistance from others. Students may potentially benefit from more efficient uses of multimedia resources with increased critical thinking, communication, and problem-solving skills. Meanwhile, critics also highlight the potential drawbacks for distance learning students, including isolation from peers, lack of engagement, and insufficient technical support. This chapter concerns the ways in which distance online learning content can be designed and developed through the utilization of multimedia and cultural-enriched materials for first-year-level College Chinese Foreign Language (CFL) courses. Discussions about employing virtual interaction, including student-content, student-instructor, and student-student interaction in course design and course design development. The chapter will end with discussions of the current challenges and new directions for a better practice of teaching and learning of Chinese language courses at a distance.

Section 3
Web Collaboration across Languages

Chapter 7

Tasha N. Lewis, Loyola University Maryland, USA

This chapter offers an innovative approach for implementing telecollaborative activities in order to enable students to connect with peers in real-time, with the goal of creating a micro-immersion experience called a "Virtual Language Exchange". This chapter describes and compares two intermediate Spanish classes participating in Virtual Language Exchanges via Skype: one paired with peers from the target language and culture, and one paired with peers from within the class itself. Students from both groups participate in meaningful interactions in the target language in order to complete the assigned task-based activities. The chapter argues that finding new ways to bring the target language to life by using technology, like the Virtual Language Exchange experience described here, can benefit students' foreign language development in multiple ways.

Chapter 8

Margarita Vinagre, Universidad Autónoma de Madrid, Spain

This study presents the findings from a group of forty-nine fourth year undergraduate students who were trained in a blended learning environment over two months in order to acquire base knowledge and hands-on experience about information and communication technologies (ICT) and their possible applications to the EFL classroom. The course was taught in English as a Medium of Instruction (EMI) and participants worked in a wiki designed specially to facilitate discussion and collaboration in the foreign language. Data were gathered from the participants' answers to an end-of-course questionnaire that featured eight five-point Likert-scale questions and five open-ended questions; quantitative and qualitative analyses were then performed upon the answers. Our findings and discussions elaborate on the impact the course had on the participants' perceptions regarding the acquisition of key competences for life-long learning.

Chapter 9

Sílvia Melo-Pfeifer, University of Hamburg, Germany

In this contribution, intercomprehension between Romance Languages (RL) will be analyzed as a particular setting of multilingual interaction in the globalized and digital world. Intercomprehension is a multilingual practice where interlocutors collaboratively achieve meaning through the use of typologically related languages and other semiotic resources, exploiting the similarities existing across languages and the opportunities of transfer they offer. The communicative contract underlying this particular typology of multilingual interaction stresses that each interlocutor should master at least one RL and use it productively and, at the same time, try to understand the RL of the other speakers. Through the analysis of multilingual exchanges in chat-rooms of the platform Galanet, the need to take a more open stance towards the communicative contract will be evinced. Particularly, three behaviors related to the breakdown of the communicative contract – and respective consequences – will be critically analyzed: the use of a taboo language (English), the use of other linguistic resources not included in the contract and the production of utterances in target languages. These communicative behaviors will justify the need to enrich the understanding of intercomprehension by adopting a translingual lens and, thus, by abandoning a still prevalent monoglossic orientation in research dealing with this multilingual communicative context.

Chapter 10

Ya Rao, Paul Valery University, France
Congcong Wang, University of Northern Iowa, USA
Jacob Bender, University of Iowa, USA

This qualitative study explores how a French-Chinese web collaborative blog-writing project provides a space for understanding the various metalinguistic approaches that foreign language learners' use to facilitate foreign language learning and intercultural communication. It adopts a multilingual-plurilingual approach, an interlingual approach and a web collaboration approach as a framework. Qualitative data was collected from the blogs and online interactions of 22 French Foreign Language (FFL) learners in China, and 24 Chinese Foreign Language (CFL) learners in France. The findings reveal the increased development of FFL and CFL learners' metalinguistic awareness, plurilingual competence, and bilingual skills that is accomplished through web collaboration. Implications regarding web-based tandem language learning and peer-assisted web collaboration are discussed.

Section 4
Less Commonly Taught Languages

Chapter 11

Agnieszka Legutko, Columbia University, USA

This chapter offers the first scholarly analysis of teaching the Yiddish language in the digital age, and argues that new media have a tremendous potential for rescuing endangered languages. It investigates the pedagogical advantages and disadvantages of using digital technologies in teaching languages, as well as the ensuing challenges for teachers and students. A brief overview of the history of the Yiddish language and culture is followed by examination of such new digital platforms as Yiddishpop.com, Mapping Yiddish New York, The Grosbard Project, Yiddish audio and visual materials available online, such as videos, sound archives, online newspapers and dictionaries, as well as distance learning opportunities.

Chapter 12

Byung-jin Lim, University of Wisconsin-Madison, USA
Danielle O. Pyun, Ohio State University, USA

This article presents intercultural and linguistic exchanges by foreign language learners in an exploratory study of Internet-based desktop videoconferencing between Korean learners at a university in the United States, and their counterparts at a South Korean college. The desktop videoconferencing project was designed for foreign language learners of Korean to assist in developing linguistic competence, as well as intercultural communicative competence, by providing the learners with the target language and culture through real-time, one-on-one communication. The study shows the emerging themes that recur in a video-chat. It also reports on the Korean language learners' self-rated proficiency in their target language. Challenges and difficulties in video-conferencing are examined, followed by a discussion of the effectiveness of synchronous one-on-one video-conferencing for language learning in general, and in Korean language education in particular.

Chapter 13

This case study explores the teaching and learning of Arabic at one Catholic university campus, with a focus upon the complex interactions between language and culture in a postmodern globalized context. Specifically, it examines the use of "multimodal culture portfolios" as a means to engage students both linguistically and culturally in classroom and community discourses. Through their interactions and co-construction of knowledge with other participants, these students are led to think about the multiple communicative contexts that are shaping and being shaped by them. Data collection was conducted through survey questionnaires and students' responses to the assigned culture portfolio. The participants were made up of students enrolled in first year Arabic courses during the 2012 spring semester. The purpose of this exploratory case is to attempt to understand students' investments in Arabic and their cultural knowledge of the Arab world pre and post their enrollment in the Arabic courses. It also seeks to understand their socialization into the culture assignment and the main challenges they faced in accessing, interacting with, and reflecting upon cultural aspects related to the Arab world. This study's findings are significant for enriching the general conversation on intercultural proficiency in classroom discourse, curricular decisions, roles and challenges of teachers, and the involvement in target language communities, particularly in less commonly taught languages such as Arabic.

Section 5
Teacher Education and Learning Strategies

Chapter 14

This chapter details a qualitative study conducted with pre-service elementary school student teachers enrolled in a Masters course on cultural and linguistic diversity at one university teacher education institute in France. The study aimed to evaluate the impact of the course on the student teachers' understanding of culturally and linguistically diverse classrooms and questioned whether the use of multi-media resources throughout the course could contribute to fostering a greater sense of empathy towards their future culturally and linguistically diverse students. The data analysis reveals that the use of video in particular, in combination with theoretical readings, was highly instrumental in helping the students to understand the concepts linked to second language acquisition and in providing them with strategies for their linguistically and culturally diverse classrooms. The authors question whether the use of multimedia is sufficient to foster a sense of empathy in students and suggest further pedagogical interventions.

Chapter 15

This study aims to investigate how English as a Foreign Language (EFL) teachers and students in China spontaneously use apps for smartphone and tablets to support their informal language learning. It also seeks to determine EFL teachers' perspectives on informal and formal Mobile Assisted Language Learning (MALL). A total of 240 smartphone and/or tablet users (186 students and 54 EFL teachers) from four colleges in Guangdong China participated in the survey. Twenty-eight teachers selected from the survey participants were interviewed afterwards. Analysis of the survey data showed that all participants were using apps to learn foreign languages informally. Survey data analysis also revealed that the most frequently used apps were based on form-focused behaviorist activities rather than learner-centered constructivist activities. A comparison of usage between EFL teachers and students revealed no significant difference in their choice of apps, yet students expected guidance from EFL teachers in using apps and resources to facilitate language learning. Finally, while the survey data indicated EFL teachers had positive attitudes towards informal MALL, the interviews revealed that many of them held negative sentiments toward MALL in the classroom. We interpret this difference in attitudes as a reflection of the teachers' concerns about learners' self-control and autonomous learning skills, as well as concerns about required teachers' knowledge and perceived changes to teachers' roles. We conclude by discussing the implications of MALL for language teacher education and professional development.

Chapter 16

This case study explores 1) the potential of a dual language program that provides an English Language Learner (ELL) and a Spanish Learner (SL) with opportunities to engage in authentic as well as mutual language exchange; and, 2) the multiple types of language strategies employed by adolescents to teach and learn language from one another in tandem learning situations. Findings from a transcription analysis of 12 English and Spanish videotaped sessions of one dyad reveal novel and in depth information about strategies utilized in compensatory, administrative, and social ways to extend the flow of communication in tandem learning. Findings indicate that tandem language learning not only provides a space for language learners to engage in plural strategies to promote teaching and learning, but also learner metacognition when peer learners employ interlingual and plurilingual measures to compensate for language gaps. Implications for the study of online tandem language learning are also highlighted.

Chapter 17
The Impact of Blog Peer Feedback on Improving Iranian English Foreign Language Students'
Writing 365
> *Mohsen Shahrokhi, Shahreza Branch, Islamic Azad University, Iran*
> *Shima Taheri, Shahreza Branch, Islamic Azad University, Iran*

The present study is an attempt to investigate (a) whether using blog peer feedbacks have any statistically significant effect on improving Iranian students' EFL writing skill, and (b) whether participants at different proficiency levels react differently to blog peer feedbacks, as far as their writing improvement is concerned. To this end, sixty Iranian female English Foreign Language (EFL) learners were selected based on their performance on the Oxford Placement Test (OPT) and were then divided into two groups. The first thirty-participant group was taught through the conventional face-to-face method; the second thirty-participant group, which consisted of the same proficiency level members as the first group, received blog peer feedbacks as the treatment. After three months of instruction, a post-test was administered and the results were subjected to statistical analysis. The ensuing analysis revealed that using blog peer feedbacks can have a statistically significant impact upon improving the writing skills of EFL learners.

Preface

Technology innovation has always been interrelated with human language evolution. From the most ancient clay tablets to the most current digital tablets, new technology has always empowered language communication and shaped culture. We can still examine today how innovative technologies can be adopted and advance their pedagogy and promote student learning.

Focusing on the current trends in digital technology and diversity within language education, this book overview echoes issues addressed in the introduction, while providing a global picture-of the highlights of the latest research in foreign language education in the digital age.

Section 1: Commentary

Opening with Chapter 1, "Reflection: How Now Shapes the Future – Emerging Trends from the Less Commonly Taught Languages Trenches," Dr. Jacques du Plessis proclaims a message centered on the world's responsibility to protect and foster the teaching of endangered languages. As President of the National Council of Less Commonly Taught Languages (LCTL), Dr. du Plessis shares his commentary upon and expertise about the challenges in the field of LCTL, in particular the case of Afrikaans. He cites some of the challenges for LCTL include budget problems and enrollment, which prevent adequate support for these languages in a digitalized world. He similarly calls on the community of language educators to engage in cross-collaboration and come up with solutions to counter the challenges facing LCTL programs, such as novel manners by which to world-connect online classes in a manner that promotes financial sustainability within these programs.

Given that all languages matter and reflect human heritage and identity, and further given that digital technology provide platforms, modes, and opportunities to engage in language practice, the chapters following Dr. du Plessis' provide a holistic and comprehensive review of current research and innovative pedagogy, trends, models, and approaches from multidisciplinary global perspectives, by which to engage with these issues. The chapters are grouped together in four categories: Technologies across Continents, Web Collaboration across Languages, Less Commonly Taught Languages, and Teacher Education and Learning Strategies.

Section 2: Technologies across Continents

In Chapter 2, "The Structural and Dialogic Aspects of Language Massive Open Online Courses (LMOOCs): A Case Study," Carolin Fuch provides an overview of the literature about the structural formats and interactive nature of LMOOCs as they engage with the learning process. This study of LMOOC satisfaction, which is based upon content, materials, and procedures, provides information about learner motivation for completing LMOOC courses

Chapter 3, "Mind Your Hashtags: A Sociopragmatic Study of Student Interpretations of French Native Speakers' Tweets," explores how social media such as Twitter is utilized in French language learning. Gerladine Blattner, Amanda Dalola, and Lara Lomicka, by means of a learner analysis of hashtags, examine how the use of the popular microblogger's metadata aggregator can be utilized to enhance second language multiliteracy and better promote online communication.

Chapter 4, "Challenges and Perspectives of Language Education Technology in Brazil: From Confronting Native Language Loss to Implementing EFL Classes," explores how Portuguese, the official language of Brazil, and English as a Foreign Language (EFL), continue to dominate language study in the South American country. Eliane Thames Bodah, Josh Meuth Alldredge, Brian William Bodah, Alcindo Neckel, and Emanuelle Goellner explore the uneven development of language study, acquisition, and development in Brazilian schools, and the challenge they face to integrate innovative technologies into language education. The authors examine how and why the educational institutions and teachers in Brazil continue to lag behind the pace of innovation.

For Foreign Language teachers who are not familiar with flipped and hybrid classroom, Clara Burgo in Chapter 5, "Teaching Spanish in the Digital Age: A Flipped Classroom or Just Hybrid?", provides a detailed overview of how these models can be employed to support in-class and outside-class support. She highlights the relative advantages and disadvantages of both flipped and hybrid classrooms, as well as provides recommendations for these two models' general pedagogical application and potential for improvement.

After discussing how technologies are used to facilitate a variety of alphabetical languages, authors Baily Li, Sijia Yao, and Wei Hong disclose the difficulties in applying an online format to non-alphabetical language courses. Chapter 6, "Beginning Chinese Foreign Language Online Course Design: Utilizing Multiple Digital Modes and Assessments," provides a thorough review of attempts to develop asynchronous and synchronous Chinese Foreign Language course design. They include a catalogue of challenges such as teaching logograph symbols, and discuss ways of engaging students with motivating multimedia materials. This information may prove beneficial and inspirational for instructors of eastern Asian languages, who may be considering developing their own web-based courses.

Section 3: Web Collaboration across Languages

The third section includes information about various types of web collaboration across different languages, such as Spanish, English, French, and Chinese. In recent years, web-based informal language learning environments have become more popular in regions such as Europe, which promote plurilingual approaches and methods. This new technological trend is drawing more attention towards less orthodox methods and approaches towards bridging language knowledge, and towards valuing prior language knowledge.

One of these less orthodox methods is the focus of Chapter 7, entitled "Creating a Micro-Immersion Environment through Telecollaboration." The micro-immersion environment in question provides an innovative approach that connect peers authentically in "real" time for virtual target language practice. Author Tasha Lewis provides detailed background about the benefits of virtual language exchange. In her study, native speakers of Spanish and English exchange languages while collaborating on mutual activities that benefit language development.

Chapter 8, "Developing Key Competences for Life-Long Learning in Online Collaboration: Teaching ICT in English as a Medium of Instruction," provides a basis for understanding how key competences benefit student learning. Margarita Vinagre explains how a blended learning environment that focuses on inquiry-based learning about information and communication technologies, such as wiki designed instruction, promote greater foreign language facilitated learning for undergraduate students studying English as a Foreign Language (EFL).

Foreign language and plurlingual language learning that is supported through online collaboration, wikis, and chats, allow learners to utilize prior language knowledge. As such, Chapter 9, "Translanguaging in Multilingual Chat Interaction: Opportunities for Intercomprehension between Romance Languages", challenges researchers and educators alike to look outside of traditional learning boxes. Sílvia Melo-Pfeifer describes how intercomprehension can occur when language learners engage in collaborative multilingual practice. Her study reveals how language users achieve meaning through the use of typologically related languages and other semiotic resources, and then transfer these similarities of knowledge towards the new languages that are being learned. Contrary to a monoglossic orientation, this research approach addresses how prior language knowledge can benefit learning in a plurilingual context online.

Chapter 10, "French-Chinese Dialogical Interaction via Web Collaborative Blog-Writing: Code-Switching to Extend Online Tandem Language Learning", is a translated chapter from French and Chinese into English by the research team. In this study, Ya Rao, Congcong Wang and Jacob Bender, in an effort to promote online tandem language learning, discuss a web-based blog-writing program for French Foreign Language learners in China, and a corresponding program for Chinese Foreign Language learners in France. The program provides a space for understanding metalinguistic awareness, plurilingual competence, and the bilingual skills that learners use to facilitate foreign language learning and intercultural communication. This chapter possesses broad implications for teachers who plan to design similar programs for extending students' language learning through web collaboration.

Section 4: Less Commonly Taught Languages

This section commemorates all of the instructors and professors involved in language fields across the world to retain these invaluable but often endangered/marginalized languages. Challenges in the maintenance, preservation, and the practice of languages such as Yiddish, Korean, and Arabic are illustrated. Also in this section, readers can ponder and reflect on the issues and approaches that best support LCTL speakers and children in our global community.

Chapter 11 begins with a historical review of the Yiddish language, providing the reader with information and statistics about a language considered by many to be dying. However, as Agi Legutko points out in "Yiddish in the 21st Century: New Media to the Rescue of Endangered Languages," that this language has re-emerged and been revitalized on social network sites. The author provides an overview and background of Yiddish language use, some of the challenges it currently faces, and the ways in which Yiddish is being revived through online interactions. The author discusses how Yiddish can be revitalized on campuses as a LCTL.

Another less commonly taught language is Korean, which is not widely offered outside of Asian countries. Nevertheless, LCTL language Korean language use has risen in popularity lately due to the Korean-wave, or K-wave, of dramas and songs enjoyed and consumed by fans globally. Byung-jin Lim and Danielle Pyun contribute to the primary research about "Korean Foreign Language Learning: Videoconferencing with Native Speakers." Chapter 12 emphasizes how synchronous real-time video-chat with native Korean speakers from a South Korean college helped American students develop linguistic and intercultural communicative competence in Korean.

Another LCTL that is often associated with more gross misconceptions than most is Arabic. In Chapter 13, Sawsan Abbadi addresses "Globalization and Possibilities for Intercultural Awareness: Multimodal Arabic Culture Portfolios at a Catholic University." The author had students develop and co-construct multi-modal culture portfolios that promoted opportunities that promoted greater understanding of the Arabic language and culture among diverse high school learners

Section 5: Teacher Education and Learning Strategies

What are the types of approaches that teachers can employ to help language learners' progress in targeted language study? How can instructors also promote language heritage pride and identity? The challenges of teacher education and the types of strategies utilized to bridge linguistic, cultural, and other borders are addressed in this section. In this section, we find that, from heritage language learners in France to heritage language learners in the United States and China, all benefit from culturally responsive and technological approaches that support their learning and language development.

We see these mutual benefits illustrated in Chapter 14, wherein Latisha Mary and Andrea Young detail "The Role of Multimedia in Expanding Pre-Service Teachers' Understanding of Culturally and Linguistically Diverse Classrooms and Furthering their Professional Identities." This study explores how multimedia can be utilized to promote greater empathy toward a diverse array of students' heritages.-

Moreover, Chapter 15, "Investigating Mobile Assisted English Foreign Language Teaching and Learning in China: Issues, Attitudes and Perceptions", investigates how English Foreign Language (EFL) teachers and students in China spontaneously use smartphone apps to support their informal language learning. Among other findings, Haizia Liu, Wenhao Tao, and William Cain find no significant difference in teacher-student choice of apps. Rather, in the use of app-assisted learning, what turns out to be most useful is how students expect guidance from teachers. The authors also explore the tensions between student self-discipline concerning the use of mobile devices and the teachers' desires to maintain positive attitudes towards the informal application of new technologies.

Closer to home, heritage language learners, such as Mexican English Language Learners in the United States, need to be provided with authentic opportunities to interact with English-speaking peers outside academic environments. In Chapter 16, "Mexican Heritage ELL and Native Speaker Interaction: A Case Study of Tandem Language Learning Strategies", Lisa Winstead provides a basis for analyzing the tandem language strategies used by peer learners to teach and learn language from one another. Findings from a transcription analysis of 12 English and Spanish videotaped sessions indicate that tandem language learning not only provides a space for language learners to engage in plural strategies to promote teaching and learning, but also learner metacognition, particularly when peer learners employ interlingual and plurilingual measures to compensate for language gaps.

With a similar interest in tandem language learning, Chapter 17, "The Impact of Blog Peer Feedback on Improving Iranian English Foreign Language Students' Writing", adopts a quantitative method to investigate (a) whether using blog peer feedbacks have any statistically significant effect on improving Iranian students' EFL writing skill, and (b) whether participants at different proficiency levels react differently to blog peer feedbacks, as far as their writing improvement is concerned. Mohsen Shahrokhi and Shima Taheri indicate that using blog peer feedback can have a statistically significant impact upon improving the writing skills of EFL learners.

From the various studies and chapters available within this book, we hope to be able to highlight both the challenges and opportunities afforded by emerging and new technologies within the ever-changing field of second-language acquisition studies. We likewise hope that the reader, whether they are an instructor or a researcher, may be able to glean fresh and innovative insights for navigating the ever-fraught world of foreign language instruction, no matter what situation they may be in, or whatever their circumstances may be.

Congcong Wang
University of Northern Iowa, USA

Lisa Winstead
California State University, Fullerton, USA

Acknowledgment

The goal of the *Handbook of Research on Foreign Language Education in the Digital Age* is to bring world language scholars together to share ideas about innovative ways to meet life-long language learning challenges in the digital age. Numerous individuals have supported us in this endeavor, including our reviewers, chapter authors, administrators, association leaders, copy-editor, colleagues, friends and families, to make this book come to life. This book commemorates the field's many efforts to improve world learners' intercultural communication and to make our world a more peaceful and inclusive place.

Our heartfelt appreciation for their support of this project is to Julie Husband, Chair of Languages and Literatures and Associate Professor of English, University of Northern Iowa, and Kim Norman, Chair of the Department of Elementary and Bilingual Education and Full Professor of Curriculum and Instruction, California State University, Fullerton.

We would especially thank the NCOLCTL president Jacques du Plessis and its previous president Michael E. Everson, as well as the CLTA-USA president Helen Shen, for their encouragement and invaluable feedback.

Deep gratitude goes out to the editorial board members and reviewers who voluntarily gave their time, expertise, and insights, which ensured the quality of this research book. Their detailed feedback helped each of the authors improve their research. Great appreciation is similarly extended to our numerous colleagues and friends for their support in providing in-depth review and feedback, which improved and refined our project: Joyce Chen, John Ivers, Jim O'Loughlin, Gabriela Olivares-Cuhat, Jennifer Cooley, John Durham Peters, Timothy Church, Marcia Katigbak Church, Sheila Benson, and Tom Zirker.

We acknowledge all of the leaders of academic associations, professors, and scholars who gave insightful feedback during the last-stage development of the *Handbook of Research on Foreign Language Education in the Digital Age*. Thank you for your invaluable insights throughout this process, which ensured the quality of this research publication.

Copy editor Jacob Bender, PhD Candidate in English, University of Iowa, could be depended on day or night, and even on weekends. We are immensely grateful for his diligent and concerted effort to proofread each chapter, provide feedback, review translated chapters multiple times, and copy edit word-by-word. His English expertise keeps the language of this book professional.

Finally, we would like to thank all professors, scholars, and doctoral students across 19 countries who submitted proposals and/or contributed to our chapters on 14 languages from around the globe. We appreciate the precious time doctoral advisors spent in supporting our future researchers who submitted and/or contributed to this volume. We are honored to learn about your research on language learning, especially research on endangered languages. In our opinion, all research has a potential and each study is valuable. We will always stand by your side and support you in a multilingual global community.

As a highly selective and refereed research book, the editors conducted careful initial screening, followed by a double-blind peer review. Each chapter was reviewed by two to three experts in the relevant research field. A second review was conducted for each chapter accepted. The acceptance rate for this book was just under 27%. Each chapter was copy-edited twice, first by a professional copy-editor of the book development team, and then by a copy-editor of the publisher.

Introduction:
Foreign Language Education in the Digital Age

How in the world can language instruction keep pace with technological change?

The rapid development of new technology and its worldwide application in education calls for innovative methods and approaches in teaching and learning language in the digital age. This introduction provides an overview of how technology has evolved over time and contributes to language communication alongside political, economic, and social lines.

1. UNDERSTANDING LANGUAGE COMMUNICATION AND TECHNOLOGICAL INFLUENCES

1.1 Language

Language is generally understood as the medium of communication of ideas and thoughts. Technological advances have assisted with language communication processes. When we speak about technology, we generally refer to computers and digital forms. However, technology refers to anything that is developed that makes life easier. Thus, technology can be a pencil with an eraser that makes writing and editing easier, or a candle utilized for evening reads by Abraham Lincoln.

Language communication has changed over the years in its audio form such as through word of mouth, oral storytelling and towards other modes. The historical development of asynchronous language communication over time is related to the physical, concrete, written purposeful, official, and historical communication on walls of Egyptian and Mayan pyramids as glyphs (Lawler, 2004) as well as in text form. There are even logographic symbols on bones in ancient China (Boltz, 1986; Lawler; 2004). Congruently, with the advent of more portable sources of communication matter such as hemp and paper, governments and business were able to communicate to one another through pamphlets, books, and bibles (Edwards, 2003; Gunaratne, 2001). These technologies sped up the dissemination of language through physical forms of technology, such as the advent presses developed across the world including block printing in China, Japan, in addition to the development of Korea's movable metallic type in 1377 (reaching its pinnacle in 1403) and the Gutenberg Press in Germany in 1440 (Friedman & Chartier, 1996; Gunaratne, 2001). Thus, official and formal business communication began with signs and later books, which increased the dissemination of ideas. Correspondingly, informal communication through letter writing similarly commenced and even signs such as graffiti sent more permanent text messages political and otherwise.

Technological advances in transportation, the building of roads, shipping as well aerial routes have contributed to the speed with which messages, ideas, and thoughts are delivered. Visual and oral synchronous communication emerged with the development of the telegraph and telephone. Similarly, online routes of communication have sped up the process of exchanging ideas across nations and across the globe at unprecedented speeds. Instant communication has fewer filters now as we are exposed to language and language ideas from other countries during internet and social media communication. Social media previously related through television sitcoms, movies, and commercial advertisement can now be easily accessed through mobile phones, computer devices, and video conferencing software. This visual, distant, and remote audio and video communication through technology is the closest we have come to having authentic conversations with the ability to interpret oral language but also gestures.

Immediate access to the internet provides us with opportunities to instantly access information and make connections with others and outside resources. Thus, virtual mediums allow us to permit more extensive research about language, including language words, phrases, logographs and other marks such as social pragmatics, captured and recorded online language interaction. For instance, language captured on streaming video permits our study of all aspects of language on grammatical as well as pragmatic levels about how learners learn language informally and in collaborative situations or how they might learn during online chat versus video. We can also delve further into the communication modes, strategies, and resources plurilinguals (as opposed to monolinguals) utilize during dual language learning and communication to acquire language (Winstead, 2013). Plurilinguals are individuals who know more than one language and can be considered polyglots. Educators can also determine how these interactions and ways of learning may contribute to formal learning situations.

1.2 Language Is a Comparable and Complex Term

Language is a comparable and complex term stemming from the different ways it is researched, learned, utilized in the digital age. Language reflects thought and can include any form of synchronous or asynchronous communication that leads to negotiation of meaning which may include not the only the words we speak, write or listen to but also language gestures, signs, and symbols in off-line or online communication in the digital age. Linguists examine the range of linguistic components including grammar, utterances, code-switching, or sociolinguistic discourse (Gumperz, 1982). Similarly, the paralinguistic aspects of language such as intonation and volume are examined for emotion and intent (Leeds-Hurwitz, 1990) and nonlinguistic forms of communication associated with the intended meaning of non-verbal behavior has also been explored (Baxter, 1984; Brown & Levinson, 1987). These modes of examination have been utilized in language as well as foreign language study to study various language learner discourses and speech patterns including the study of phatic digital text communication on Twitter (Schandorf, 2013) or segmentation of audio in nondigital vocalization (Pammi, Khemiri, Petrovska-Delacretaz, & Chollet, 2013).

How language, as well as foreign language, is understood depends on perspective. Foreign language and teaching has evolved in the digital age as we move from single language to an understanding of learners' language layer levels in a more plurilingual society. Foreign language similarly takes on new meaning in the digital age. Foreign language can be perceived as the outside language. In many societies, "foreign", in Chinese and in Japanese (外国), means outside. Thus, foreign language can be equated to the outside language. Note the same Chinese and Japanese logographs for a foreign person or alien: 外国人. This distinction of the "other" or "outsider" has a long history in the world and different terms are utilized to distinguish between citizens and others. Foreigners have often been considered barbarians or aliens in the past. Even in the present day, the term "illegal aliens" is utilized as a reference to some immigrants.

The scope of "foreign" is in comparison to what language counts as native. To understand what counts as foreign language, educators need to consider how contributions from first language (FL), second language (SL), heritage language (HL), as well as dual immersion (DI) and bilingual programs can contribute to a more holistic understanding of language learning. Similarly, in constructing our understanding of language categorizations, researchers should also consider language status, subordinance, and dominance in the field and in global societies as well as the consequences of such hierarchies in the digital age.

The first language is the inside language or the language of the community in which we live or are born. It is generally understood as the maternal language. However, plurilinguals can often speak more than one language that is learned and utilized in a neighborhood - early on. And it is possible that both parents may speak different languages and/or dialects that are learned simultaneously. Having plurilingual capability is not uncommon in some countries such as India or Spain. Individuals growing up in the Catalan area of Spain might consider their first language Catalan, and their second language Spanish. Although Catalan is an official language in Spain, the dominant language is Spanish. Catalan has a subordinate position and status despite measures recent to include Catalan on an equal level in schools. If the child from Catalonia moves to the United States, the first language may incorrectly be categorized as Spanish. Since Catalan is less well known, opportunities to receive primary language support would be limited in that language. As such, Catalan is again marginalized as a first language since it is less commonly known, used, or understood.

Thus, it is important to clarify what it means to be a second language, foreign language, heritage language or bilingual learner. Foreign language learners study a language outside of their own in the country of origin. For instance, an English foreign language (EFL) learner studies the target language as a foreign language in Japan, Peru, or another country. Second language learners, on the other hand, speak their maternal language first, for instance Spanish, in the country of origin, such as the United States. The second language is the language learned in the host country. It is generally, a language that a child may not want to learn, but has to because their parents immigrated to, say, the United States, France, or Japan. Thus, a native Spanish speaker who is a newcomer to the United States would be an English as a second language learner (ESL) in schools. In the United States, these students are also called English language learners (ELL). Thus, the designation depends on the context of the learner's situation as a foreign language or second language learner.

Similarly, a heritage language learner may be in the process of maintaining their primary language which could be their maternal as well as one of their heritage languages. The primary language and the heritage language may be one and the same, or they may be entirely different based on heritage language populations in schools with increasing linguistic and diversity. For instance, a Mexican immigrant to the United States picks up English in the context of living in the country. The Mexican student is not only a second language learner of English whose heritage language could be Spanish or possibly an indigenous language, e.g., Maya. Comparatively, an American student taking a Chinese Foreign Language (CFL) course in the United States is not studying the language in China. Thus, he or she is a CFL student, not a Chinese second language (CSL) student. Again, the context of the learner plays a role in language learner designations as well as pedagogical approaches. The second language learner, unlike his/her FL learner counterpart, has more possibilities of authentically using language on a daily basis. The foreign language learner who had little access to this type of authentic exchange before, can engage in language and collaborative practice with target language speakers. Unlike the second language learner, the FL learner does not have opportunities to be immersed in the country of the target language and must designate time for that purpose. More shaming occurs with second language learners than foreign language learners. Second language learners are often pushed to relinquish their primary language and learn the dominant language in the host state (Winstead, 2013; Helot & Young, 2005).

Government policies that globally promote official languages over others create language hierarchies either overtly or covertly. English only propositions, for example, can invalidate and devalue heritage and minority languages in mainstream society. For instance, Proposition 63 in California made English the official language of California (Padilla, Lindholm, Chen, Duran, Hakuta, et al. 1991). Similarly, other English-only initiatives in the United States include California's Proposition 227 and Arizona's Proposition 203 restrict and devalue native language use in states with high numbers of Latinos (Barker, 2001; Moreno, 2012). This type of language dominance is also seen in places such as France as well, where language hierarchies exist (Beardsmore, 2008; Young & Helot, 2003).

However, recent policy measures in countries around the world are promoting heritage and minority language revitalization. The European Union is promoting a more plurilingual approach that also recognizes regional languages (Beardsmore, 2008; Winstead, 2013). Policies in South America, such as the Declaration of Linguistic Rights in 1996, intend to preserve and maintain the preservation and maintenance of indigenous languages (Haboud, 2009), and policies in Australia include less commonly taught languages, preserving indigenous languages (Dunne & Palvyshyn, 2013). Despite worldwide efforts to preserve and value multiple languages, dominant versus subordinate language hierarchies continue to exist based on prior colonial situations and issues of territorial conflict, acquisition, and transnationalism.

The world has become a lot smaller through online communication, and our populations in schools and cities around the world have become more linguistically and culturally diverse. Researchers need to delve into various contexts and backgrounds of learners to understand the appropriate pedagogical approaches for learners that may fall under the multiple headings of not only foreign language learner but heritage and minority language learners as well. Congruently, the boundaries that researchers and educators have created between foreign language (FL), second language (SL), heritage language (HL), and dual language (DL) become blurry and often overlap. A student may be categorized under more than one heading.

In the field of foreign language, placement tests have been developed to assign students of diverse backgrounds into the appropriate levels of foreign language classes at universities. For example, with Chinese as an FL, surveys, interviews or proficiency assessments are used to determine the learners' native, or heritage language, or whether the student has participated in a dual immersion program. Examples of the possible backgrounds of the learner that can complicate appropriate instruction in the classroom include (1) a mainstream student from the host country who desires to learn Chinese as a foreign language, (2) an American-born Chinese student who speaks a Chinese dialect at home but studied in a Mandarin Chinese immersion school, (3) a student who was adopted from China and raised by an English-speaking couple, (4) a Cantonese-dialect speaking student who finished high school in Hong Kong as an English-speaking British colony prior to its transfer of sovereignty to China in 1997, (5) American students raised by English-speaking parents but who studied Chinese at international schools in China, and (6) Chinese-born ethnic minority students who studied Chinese at bilingual schools.

In understanding and recognizing the diverse language learner contexts, educators can become more informed to employ appropriate and differentiated pedagogical approaches associated with learners' plurilingual experiences and capabilities. Correspondingly, the gaps between various fields of study and approaches such as computer assisted language learning (CALL), which is geared toward communicative competence, might be shared and benefit disciplines such as ESL and EFL (Al-Hashash, 2007). It is imperative that digitally-oriented pedagogy is geared to enhance multiple literacies in face-to-face, hybrid, and online classroom learning environments.

2. TECHNOLOGY-ASSISTED FOREIGN LANGUAGE LEARNING (TALL) IN THE DIGITAL AGE

2.1 The Digital Age Is the Learner's Age: Teachers and Students as Digital Language Learners (DLLs)

In the United States, pre-school to high school language instruction and learning has declined in the last decade due to budget and other issues, causing a foreign language proficiency achievement gap (Pufahl & Rhodes, 2011). However, a report of opinion polls and surveys indicate increased U.S. interest in the value of learning world languages as part of 21st century goals (Rivers, Robinson, Harwood, & Brecht, 2013).

Free access to portable, global, cross-cultural, individualized and multilingual modes of chat, audio, and visual language interaction exist in most of the world. Similarly, multiple learning modes contribute to formal and informal language learning environments.

Broader and more equitable access levels the playing field for individuals who might otherwise, during non-digital times, have less contact with physical libraries and classrooms. Broader access to knowledge enables learners to learn independently from formal school education. Self-educated technological innovators, such as Microsoft's Bill Gates, Apple's Steve Jobs, and Facebook's Mark Zuckerberg reached their levels of success by following nontraditional career paths counter to those prescribed by the norms of society. Their successes in discovering, creating, and innovating prompt researchers, educators, and learners alike to consider whether schools are taking the appropriate approaches towards cultivating tech giants in the field of education.

Thus, a movement towards alternative patterns of learning and doing should be employed in order to move learning away from rigid boxes and enclosed spaces. Digital language learners (DLL) similarly should have opportunities to move beyond traditional and rigid barriers of traditional language teaching and learning. Instead language should mirror their informal learning modes as experienced via internet technology, computer games, social media, and mobile devices.

Advances in technology change and so does what counts as language learning and acquisition. The speed of this technological innovation makes it difficult for individuals to keep pace with novel technology, some of which becomes outdated before audiences can adapt to it. The role of the instructor is being challenged in academia (Jianli, 2012). Moreover, instructors across the globe feel less prepared and supported to teach with technology in classroom environments (Bilbatua & Herrero de Haro; 2014; Gallardo del Puerto & Gamboa, 2009; Jianli, 2012). Comparatively, instructors who feel more comfortable with digital media are more likely to utilize it (Bilbatua & Herrero de Haro; Wang, 2012).

Key aspects that promote a successful learning experience for the language student in a technology-enhanced environment, especially a web environment, include the following: (1) institutional support with appropriate technology to meet a learner's needs in the language learning environment (e.g., software and hardware requirements, high speed internet); (2) specific instruction and learner training to ensure continuous learning (e.g., technology software, trouble-shooting ability), (3) authentic digital opportunities for student-to-student language interaction; (4) student training and support to troubleshoot software and hardware technology failures. These aspects not only enhance the learning for the student but also are of benefit to the instructor. Additionally, institutional support should be available as well as release time for instructors to engage in digital language learning professional development that supports instruction and research in foreign language education.

2.2 Redefining Language Education in the Digital Age

From preschool up to university settings, technology is changing the way language is taught and learned as well as our perceptions and conceptual understandings. Technological change in the routes of language learning calls for new definitions in the field of language education. Similarly, possibilities created by innovations for the ways foreign language learning might be juxtaposed against the backdrop of second language, heritage language, as well as dual language online learning environments.

The transition from analog to digital prompted what many call the Digital Revolution. This revolution is characterized, in part, by the initial transition of television platforms in the 1980s and usage of digital television platforms in the 1990s (Dawson, 2010; McHale, 1995). Influences additionally contributing to the digital revolution are also associated with an increase in electronic media (Neuman, Park, & Panek, 2012), a leap in cell phone use from the 1980s and 1990s to the present (Blinn-Pike, 2009). The mobile phone usage has increased at even a higher rate than the internet usage (Aponte & Pessagno, 2009), as well as the rapid development of high-tech companies in the Silicon Valley (Berlin, 2003). Highly trained individuals in developing countries were also recruited as engineers and developers to work in the United States. Expatriate return and transnational exchanges of information contributed to the growth of technology and digital revolutions worldwide, especially in Asian countries (Kenney, Breznitz, & Murphree, 2013; Neuman, Park, & Panek, 2012; Ning, 2009). Correspondingly, the growth of the tech industry prompted more common use of the computer in the home, the workplace, and education globally (Gualerzi & Nell, 2010; Guilani, 2008; Tang, 1999).

Computer-Assisted Language Learning (CALL) was an appropriate and prominent term in the field of computer-mediated language study, but the term CALL might not be inclusive of other forms of technology in the digital age. Although many digital devices have a micro-computer such as s smartphone depending on how "computer" is defined, it has been suggested in the literature that the CALL term does not provide an overarching frame for understanding innovative and more nuanced contexts of language learning (Otto & Pusack, 2009; Andrews & Haythronthwaite, 2007). The creation of interactive web 2.0 technology, mobile technology, along with a series of new technologies (e.g., hologram, artificial intelligence), drives education to a new realm beyond desktop/laptop designations. Paradigmatic changes in conceptual designations of terms, such as CALL, need to be reviewed and updated. Instead, Technology-Assisted Language Learning (TALL) might be a more appropriate term that is broader and encompasses an entire group of technological possibilities beyond the computer. Furthermore, there may be a need to differentiate between TALL, Technology-Assisted Foreign Language Learning (TAFLL), Technology-Assisted Second Language Learning (TASLL), Technology-Assisted Dual Language Learning (TADLL), Technology-Assisted Heritage Language Learning (TAHLL) and Technology-Assisted Heritage Language Maintenance (TAHLM).

2.3 Technology-Assisted Language Learning (TALL)

2.3.1 Traditional Face-to-Face Classroom Evolution: Digital Support

Traditional face-to-face classes can be quite interactive or less so depending on the instructor's educational philosophical stance. Thus, should the instructor have a more progressivist (learner-centered) philosophy, the course will include some lecture but also social language interaction for language development. An instructor that is an essentialist might engage in more teacher-centered learning approaches of lecture, such as the audiolingual method, or focus on grammar, while providing fewer opportunities for social language interaction. In the traditional face-to-face classroom, the instructor lectures, writing on a white board. Students engage in physical note-taking, paper and pencil tests, and handwritten or typewritten work or homework. Instructors could utilize language dramas, the audiolingual method, and the study of language and literature through reading and writing with paper and pen, then typing, followed by computer use. When utilizing traditional approaches of the past, there were fewer opportunities for authentic exchange. Study abroad programs were the best venues for authentic interaction. Dual immersion schools also emerged with great success, e.g., Miami Dade County Schools employed dual immersion programs to address the influx of Cuban immigrants in schools in the 1970s; likewise, French-English dual immersion was also offered in Quebec, Canada to preserve the French language (Malakoff & Hakuta, 1990).

Advances in technology during the 1990s allowed for computer supported instruction, learning and games could be accessed via CDs and discs. Access to online digitalized materials in libraries began in the 1990s (Arms, 2012; Tenopir, 1999). However, wide-spread access to information and greater ability to communicate online became more available to the public in the mid-1990s (Zarotsky & Jaresko, 2000) and coincided with increased cell phone usage in the 2000s and greater smart phone use in the late 2000s. Similarly, changes in learning have occurred such as a move away from the overhead projector to multimedia presentation.

With increased computer access and the ability to go online, face-to-face classroom practice has changed. Increased usage of technology provides opportunities for multiple learning styles, and multiple modes of communication, interaction, and understanding. Research reveals that students exposed to multimedia materials are more apt to stop, reflect and edit their materials (Nutta, Feyten, Norwood, Meros, & Yoshii et al., 2002). Innovative digital devices and platforms are enhancing foreign language teaching and learning in classrooms as well as creating new spaces inside and outside of the classroom (e.g., hybrid, flipped, online, homeschool). Authentic language exchange has become available through present-day digital media and devices that provide windows into virtual realms. Different from the traditional classsrrom, novel features of Skype and other virtual face-to-face formats connect world learners through internet exchange.

Digital devices and digital media applied to note taking elevated the importance of typing skills over the writing tradition. Instead of merely emphasizing hand note-taking skills at the beginning of the course, teachers suggest optional methods for note-taking such as laptops, smartphones, recorders, or iPads. Students utilize laptop computers for group projects, presentations, and demonstations in classroom settings as well. With Web 2.0 technology, newly developed software and online chat room make telecollaboration possible (Richardson, 2007). By using Google Docs, students and teachers can edit the same document online simultaneously or asynchronously, saving time, energy and eliminating the need for physical meetings (Hubbard, 2009). With the affordability of digital and video cameras, as well as mobile phone cameras, students are creating movies and dramas. Video editing software also furthers their New Literacies skills as they create audio, video, and graphics, and add subtitles, transitions, and animations. A variety of websites and software, e.g., nawmal, Animoto, allows students to become 3D cartoon figures, or create personal animations and movies, respectively. These types of technologies are, however, underutilized in the foreign language classroom.

The Smartboard, an interactive whiteboard, motivates students' learning through interaction and promotes willingness to engage in classrooms. Its interactive projection display creates scenarios for language learning (Saine, 2012). Digital markers allow multiple learners to collaborate during storytelling. Notes on the smartboard can be saved on computer in digital format (Al-Saleem, 2012).

Content management systems (CMS) such as Moodle, Blackboard, E-learning, BrainHoney are widely utilized for middle school up to university language courses in the United States. These CMSs extend learning time and allow students to organize their assignments and track learning goals flexibly outside of class (e.g., taking online quizzes, using discussion boards, journals, and audio-visual-text materials). Moreover, these CMSs allow students to use laptop and smartphone to access course syllabi, calendars, discussion board, and their gradebook anywhere and anytime (Wang, 2012).

Mobile devices such as the iPad and software apps make language learning portable. Using Pleco apps on a smart phone, Chinese language learners, especially study abroad students, can handwrite unfamiliar Chinese characters on a touch screen and look up the meaning in an online digital dictionary. Online dictionaries (e.g., Pleco, PowerWord) allow students to hear how a new Chinese character is pronounced, see animation of how it is written, read examples of how it is used in sentences, as well as watch videos of how it is used in real life situations. Language cellphone games (e.g., ChineseSkill) enable students to learn vocabluary, pronunication and sentences, and entertain the learning experience. Game and quiz methods widely used in TV programs in the past are now being utilized to promote learning and assessment in language classrooms. Through smart phone text message polls and mobile voting (e.g., Kahoot), instructors can engage students in sharing their opinions about topics, quickly assess students' learning, and display percentage results on the screen for immediate feedback. With mobile voting, students can find out whether they answered the question correctly and the teacher can also review global classroom student performance results.

Social media (e.g., Facebook, Twitter, LinkedIn, Google Plus+), blogs, video-sharing websites (e.g., Vimeo, YouTube) and website builders enable students to absorb vast audio-visual information as well as display their creative work. The video chat and text chat function allows foreign language learners to partner with native speakers outside the country and practice speaking online. Wirelss internet and smart phone camera also allows learners to stream video images.

Website content builders such as Weebly, Wixs, Worldpress allows instructors and students to easily develop websites without programing skills. Embedded functions and templates for video, document, audio, discussion board, and text display enable users to develop personal websites based on their own ideas. Moreover, these sites can also be connected to and display online course content in a variety of formats except for some particular content management systems.

These types of digital software devices and apps also permit individualized and differentiated language instruction at the student's pace as well as in cooperative and collaborative formats, especially in mixed-level FL classrooms. The spaces for language learning have similarly expanded to hybrid, online, distance learning, and outside language class learning frontiers.

2.3.2 Online/Distance Learning

In the digital age, geographic distances, which were once barriers for face-to-face foreign language classes, can be bridged through online and distance learning. Teachers, students, and technology support staff can attend the same class without being at the same geographic location. Given that "in front of your teacher" can be interpreted as "in front of your computer screen," technology changes people's sense of distance and draws one another virtually closer. Prior definitions of classroom, whiteboard, and vocabulary may be interpreted differently by newer and younger DL learners in the digital age as a transition from the physical to virtual.

Videoconferencing software (Adobe Connect, Zoom, Skype) have revolutionized foreign language teaching and learning. Videoconferencing provides virtual platforms that can be utilized to practice and reinforce what is learned collaboratively in the classroom. It permits authentic tandem language learning with peers and overcomes the limitation of the traditional foreign langauge classroom—the ability to invite learners unable to attend face-to-face learning class (Hubbard, 2009; Zarotsky & Jaresko, 2000).

Whether an online course is delivered via content management systems or through synchronous video-conferencing, distance learning technology breaks down physical walls that separate local as well as global learners. Learners outside of formal learning channels (e.g., schools) can increase their social language learning through chat as well. From a cosmopolitan city such as New York to the remote countryside in places such as Timbuktu, online classes bring together culturally and linguistically diverse learners. Thus, videoconferencing expands the scope of cross-language communication and human interaction as well as increases the speed of language transfer (e.g. novel word and expression development, language borrowing, and gesture cognizance). These immediate technological connections promote classroom diversity and offer new approaches for working with diverse global learners.

Massive Open Online Courses (MOOCs) have been developed for network learning associated with self-regulated study, peer sharing, and collaboration (McAuley, Stewart, Siemens & Cormier, 2010). MOOCs allow unlimited users to get free access to the course online to support study specific topics as well as "offer extensive diversity, connectivity and opportunities for sharing knowledge" (Mackness, Mak, & Williams, 2010, p. 266). Although some MOOCs are attached to institutional settings, they can be quite independent as well. MOOCs provide a faster way of learning about concurrent and emerging knowledge, especially in the constantly changing field of technology.

2.3.3 Hybrid/Blended/Flipped

Combining the merits of face-to-face and online classrooms, hybrid or blended classrooms provides flexibility for instructors and their students. Hybrid or blended courses are delivered partially in classroom and partially online. The percentage variation between content delivered online or in-class is up to the institution and instructor. Instructors commonly utilize content management systems to organize teaching materials as well as provide grades and feedback to students.

Blended courses are generally intended to reduce instructor's workload in face-to-face time (Caulfield, 2011) in order to focus on course development of using synchronous and asynchronous media. Videotaped lectures, online resources, podcasts developed for outside-class learning, which are accessible online for student to preview or review (Educause Learning Initiative, 2012). The instructor, instead of introducing new content during class time, can better use class time for differentiating instruction and engaging students in meaningful collaboration on group projects. Thus, instructors can then re-allocate saved time for other academic activities and differentiate for individual students' needs. Blended formats are beneficial for small language programs that aim to recruit more students while at the same time reducing the face-to-face workload of the faculty.

With the flipped model, greater emphasis is placed on learners to self-regulate their learning as well as to collaborate with other students either face to face or online in order to be prepared for problem-solving and improvement before attending class (Educause Learning Initiative, 2012). Instructors are available for facilitating their learning and expanding upon this knowledge.

2.3.4 Homeschool and Informal Learning

Homeschool language learning has been similarly affected by digital technology. Individuals who have promoted language learning through homeschooling had fewer access to language resources. Digital sources became available but the interaction was primarily one-sided. Outside of language education, homeschoolers had access to DVDs or discs that had games, or language practice (Zarotsky & Jaresko, 2000). The 1990s were the beginning of games (e.g., matching words with pictures) in Spanish such as *Jump Start* for basic Spanish, and *Triple-Play* for more advanced Spanish language practice. One learning novel or soap opera called *Destinos* that was oriented towards learning Spanish vocabulary in a situated context. It was popular in the 1990s and is still being utilized as a teacher language resource for teaching Spanish in context (Annenberg Learner, n.d.). Students followed the episodes at the end and were required to answer questions related to the situations. Since that time, online language learning has expanded opportunities for homeschooled learners. Rosetta Stone was also a much more basic language learning material used in the 1990s and the early 2000, but there were few opportunities to authentically interact. However, now those who utilize Rosetta Stone have opportunities to speak with an interpreter online and can engage in online vocabulary recognition and practice. Other recent advances include the ability to choose a language, and with speech recognition, gauge one's pronunciation accuracy (Pitta, 2009).

Online gaming and the virtual world provide other venues for engaging students in learning language. Real-time strategy games and online role-playing games (e.g., *Age of Empires, World of Warcraft*) provide learner with scenarios, story plots and many language options. Multiple players have to comprehend the language plot in order to play the game. Online gaming promotes a willingness to communicate and lowers anxiety (Reinders & Wattana, 2014). In virtual worlds, *Second Life* is an example of how users create roles such as residents or avatars representing themselves to explore the virtual world and socialize with other users (Gee & Hayes, 2011). The virtual world approach enables users to become who they desire to be but cannot be in real life and to communicate with other users in different languages. While some games appear to be developed to fulfill people's needs for entertainment, online gaming foments unintentional learning (Reinhardt & Sykes, 2014; Theisen, 2013) and influences the acquisition of other skills such as the learning of foreign language vocabulary (Chik, 2014; Muhanna, 2012).

Virtual games and worlds appear to promote dominant languages, norms, and ideas. These multiple platforms, modes, and types of digital devices similarly have the potential to promote the preservation of minority and less commonly taught languages despite their uneven development over time.

3. ALL LANGUAGE MATTERS DESPITE UNEVEN DEVELOPMENT AND STATUS

Despite the various advantages and potentials of technology, language valuation and status is not shared globally. This section highlights the gaps existing in foreign language education and research advocates that all language matters from global perspectives and points of view, and encourages various methods and approaches within global and local contexts. Challenges to language education come in not only pedagogical forms but political forms as well including the uneven development and status of language. Thus, major gaps in the literature include complex issues such as uneven technology development and transferability issues in language study, uneven world language status and power, and inequitable access due to numerous digital divides.

3.1 Uneven Development and Transferability Issues among TALL Pedagogy

A historical review of languages reveals uneven language development and how some transferability occurs. Even when comparing languages, uneven development occurs when one language can be acquired more easily than another leading to literacy at a more advanced. With Italian, "spelling is transparent: every letter maps onto a single phoneme [...] This, gives Italians an enormous advantage" as their students' literacy skills advance much more quickly (Dehaene, 2009, p. 31).

In history, many languages have experienced some form of language transfer or borrowing with regard to writing. Koreans and Japanese have transferred and incorporated Chinese characters alongside the symbols that represent their written form of language because of the contact with China in the 4th and 5th centuries and the invention of metalic and block forms of printing in China (Zhang, 2010).

The language written in a nation's or culture's logographic forms is also representative of their cultural and linguistic identity. When symbols, glyphs, or other types of logographs are effaced, the evidence of culture is also eradicated. When reading Chinese and Japanese written languages, the combination of symbols creates new meaning and interpretations. The plural of trees 森 (forest) is more than one tree 木 (tree, wood). While that example is very simple, we can also see that the writing is also representative of the in depth social contextual understandings and meanings associated with pragmatics and the intent of the message. The significance of Chinese characters in Japan has changed historically and contextually over time from the original use of the logographs in China (Okimori, 2014).

In ancient China, literacy was a privilege of males and appears to reveal how the Chinese character woman when combined with other Chinese characters has taken on negative connotations. The representation for woman is 女 (woman) in its simplest form in both Chinese and Japanese. Should we take this same simple part of the logograph 女 and multiply the number of logographic representations of women? One would think that by doing so, the three characters 姦 would represent women; however, just combining these three female characters does not represent the plural of woman. Interestingly enough, this same logograph 姦 means women adulterers in traditional Chinese (Cherng, Chang, & Chen, 2009). The (1716) Kangxi Dictionary recorded the usage of 姦 (rape) in the Qing China (Zhang, 1933), which has been replaced by modern simplified Chinese character 奸 (rape) presently used in mainland China (Oxford Chinese Dictionary, 2010, p. 352). However, 姦 is still utilized in Taiwan and Japan for rape and adultery. Two characters for woman 奻 (quarrel) signifies argument in traditional Chinese but is no longer used by Eastern Asian countries (漢典, 2016). Changes of meaning over time reveal social positive or negative connotations but can also add to the richness of the dialogue and evolution of languages so important in understanding present-day communication. Specific language might die in the motherland but retain original meaning in countries where language is borrowed. Technological sharing between similar written language backgrounds has emerged between the Japanese and Chinese digital pedagogical systems.

Language reflects how nations view themselves as well as how they are viewed by others. The character国 kindom or country defines the meaning of country. The three horizontal strokes 三 from top to bottom respectively represents: sky or heaven, king, land and people. The vortical stroke 王connecting the top and bottom stroke indicates the king is the mediatator between heaven and people. The dot in玉 converts the king character into gade as jurals, jade as seals, representing supreme power and wealth. The square surroud the wealthy king indicates the king's ruling power over his territory, thus this character is a kindom or country国. People and their language outside this kingdom are considered foreign, 外国. Unlike how Chinese view their own nation, "China" in some slavic languages such as the Russian language is "Китай" (Khitan), a short-lived empire established by a non-Han Chinese ethnic minority after defeating the Han-Chinese majority. Western travelers introduced Khitan to Europe, which has been used by Russians to refer to China ever since. When a Chinese speaker introduces "I am from China" ("я из Китая" in Russian) he acturally says, "I am from the kindom of Khitan."

More recently, ancient Chinese characters, especially oracle bone inscripts, are often used as this basis for modern logo designs that integrate Chinese culture and art, such as Peking University's logo (Wusan, 2014). Ancient Chinese calligraphy also inspried Steve Jobs' innovative graphic design of icons and interfaces on Apple products, e.g., Mac, iPhone, iPad (Isaacson, 2011).

The rise of digital technology further drives language digitalized reformation. Due to unique features of world languages, technology-based pedagogy initiated by western notions may or may not transfer smoothly from one language to another. Seeking an easy input method, technology developers may choose to develop an alphabetic system or some sort of conversion method to input non-alphabetical written text into digital format. Few differences exist among alphabetic features of western languages such as English, Spanish, French, German, and Italian. These phonetic languages and their letters are quite similar with some variations. These variations affect the types of keyboards that are constructed within these countries; however, one can adapt fairly easily from one keyboard to another when learning and utilizing language. This Roman adaptation is not so evident for many eastern languages that employ different writing orientations, patterns, logographs or other types of symbols (e.g., Chinese, Japanese, Mayan). Western forms of technological pedagogy are considered a handicap for East Asians who utilize ideograms and generally have less familiarity with Roman alphabetic keyboards until they are in high school (Liu, Jaeger, Nakagawa, 2004; Nakayama, 2002).

Similarly, adopting technology-assisted Roman-oriented systems in language education first poses challenges to those teachers teaching other languages than English in the digital age. There are distinctive features of the reading, writing, listening, and speaking domains of language, including syntax, morphology, semantics, and phonology. Differences between alphabetical language and logographic language cause difficulty with inputing non-alphabetical symbols into computers (Liu et al., 2004, Nakayama, 2002).

Through language simplification of logographs or symbols, typing Chinese characters on an English keyboard becomes possible. Today, the most popular Chinese written text input methods is developed based on the Pinyin system, a Chinese alphabetical system created a half century ago in which the sound of Chinese characters can be spelled out by largely using English letters (Wong, Chai, & Ping, 2011).

Researchers have suggested that there be a delay in learning of of writing Chinese logographs. Some researchers have considered a focus on reading and symbol recognition (Allen, 2009) and other ways to delay the learning of writing Chinese logographs (Allen, 2009; Ye, 2013) to ease the cognitive load of the Chinese language learners. Pinyin provides a foundation for Chinese language learners to transit from learning the basic verbal phonetic pronunciation to recogning the actual Chinese characters. Just as the first- through third-grade native Chinese speakers learn Chinese, this approach is beneficial for new Chinese language learners, such as English and French speakers. The Pinyin approach helps them gain confidence in verbal practice and vocabulary knowledge before embarking solely on the written logographic form.

Since the written form of Chinese characters is associated with meaning while Pinyin is associated with sound, they can be viewed as two systems which require different skills to master. To type Chinese characters through Pinyin input method, learners need to be familiar with the Pinyin symbols. However, this method does not require learners to know Chinese logographs. While Pinyin contributes to simplified communication, it can be cumbersome due to numerous symbols. Being able to read Pinyin doesn't mean the learner can read online Chinese news written in Chinese characters.

Thus, teaching character writing online is a more formidable task for individuals who teach languages that are inherently different from western alphabetic languages. The writing is more complicated due to writing orientation and the multiple symbolic values and interpretations that emerge when combining characters. Therefore, teaching writing online is another example of uneven pedagogical transferability.

While using videoconferencing for verbal language learning across languages may be similarly effective for authentic language practice, videoconferencing software used for teaching writing is challenging. Unlike English FL peers, Chinese FL teachers face the challenge of teaching how to handwrite non-alphabetical symbols, take notes and use calligraphy brushes (Ramsey, Ong, & Chen, 1998). However, the newly developed online learning of Chinese characters can be more representative of how that language is learned, penned, painted, and/or communicated authentically through online pattern recognition (Liu et al., 2004).

3.2 Uneven World Language Status and Power

World language has nothing to do with the number of speakers. If so, Chinese would reign as the world's top language, especially with the rise of China economically. Almost 1,197,600 million people speak Chinese as compared with 355 million English speakers (Infoplease, 2014).

At this point in time, English has the highest status in the world and role as a dominant global language of communication (Dornyei & Ushioda, 2009; Lamb, 2004; Norton, 1997; Shimizu, Yashima, & Zenuk-Nishide, 2004). English is the language utilized worldwide for international business and consulting (Kordon, 2011) in the medical field in China (Zhang & Wang, 2015). Officials in Japan submitted a proposal to adopt English as the official language in 2000 (Kawai, 2009; Matsuura, Fujieda, & Mahoney, 2004). Although the proposal did not pass, it is an indication of the English language's dominance in the world.

Historically, the education systems of Japan and Singapore have been highly influenced by English (Sasaki, 2008). English has become the lingua franca in a number of intercultural contexts, e.g., intercultural counseling in Germany (Kordon, 2011) and interethnic communication with immigrants who work as transnationals in Singapore (Rubdy & McKay, 2013). Those who speak English have greater access to power of the written word, as much of what is written or developed digitally online and published in English. Voices of individuals who do not speak or write English fluently are silenced. Thus, there is an advantage for native speakers of English in a number of academic fields and businesses. Professors from other countries who may not read, write or speak English at highly proficient levels become disadvantaged in getting their work published. Moreover, research reveals that students with limited English language proficiency find themselves anxious and lack confidence (Wang, 2014; Winstead, 2013).

Thus, beginning with English, there is a hierarchy of world, minority, and regional languages. And even within countries, hierarchies exist based on historical positions of power of what language is considered official and is less commonly taught in schools. Minority language, regional language, and heritage language use has often been historically oppressed based on perceived status or importance in societies. Social Dominance Theory (SDT) provides a basis for understanding how historically one group can have social power and dominance over another group in a host society (Pratto, Liu, Levin, Sidanius, & Shih et al., 2000; Pratto & Stewart, 2011) such as Japanese over Koreans or French over North Africans.

3.2.1 Historical Influences Behind Language Status and Language Power

The ebbs and flows of language interest and status can be seen over time. Thus, in a global context, language status is related to perceptions of economic might, neighboring skirmishes, and exchanges of ideas through trade. Uneven language development is due, in part, to the military might such as encroachment on territories or due to economic exchange between neighbors. Some ethnic groups or nations might develop their written forms at a particular point in history. The exchange of ideas through trade and missionary exchange in Asia prompted the Koreans and Japanese to adopt aspects of the Chinese language beginning in the 6th century (Okimori, 2014).

Diplomatic and economic use of a particular language is related to military, economic, or more recently, technological might, and sometimes the numbers of individuals that speak the language globally. England, France, and Spain had colonies in the Americas and around the world, and these languages reigned globally from the 1500s until colonial independence. By the 18th century, French became the diplomatic language of the world (Giovanangeli, 2009). While French might be seen as slipping as a diplomatic language in the world, it is recognized as one of three working languages still utilized by the European Union alongside English and German. However, its diplomatic use around the world has diminished as more and more countries such as former French colony Vietnam, note their preference to utilize English as the diplomatic language of choice (Crosette, 2001).

Holocausts have also influenced language status through population elimination or policies, which have affected the use or study of particular languages (e.g., Armenian, Yiddish, indigenous languages during the WWII Japanese invasion). Thus, languages can be endangered and die through oppression, assimilation, or isolation (e.g., Native American languages in the United States and Canada as well as Quechua in Peru, and Maya in Guatemala). Extinct languages may no longer be spoken, but dead languages such as Latin may still be utilized in academic contexts.

Some ethnic minorities and indigenous cultures have passed down their legends and ideas from generation to generation over thousands years only through oral storytelling. Valid methods of communication of indigenous cultures including drawings, cave paintings, and Native North American smoke signals should not be ignored. The Navajo language, utilized as a code for synchronous American communication during World War II, was undecipherable by the Japanese and Germans. Despite this contribution to the war effort in the 1940s, Navajo remains a low-status and less commonly used language in the United States.

Territorial conflicts between rising powers and with neighbors of less economic might have influenced how not only one's national status is viewed but one's language status as well. Thus, an individual's language status is often derived from historical antecedents including post-colonial notions about particular groups behaviors and characteristics (Holland, Fox, & Daro, 2008), which has been described in the literature as linguistic imperialism (Modiano, 2001; Phillipson, 1998). Immigration and transnationalism have contributed to worldwide plurilingualism. These dominant and subordinant, oftentimes colonial, relationships are recreated in the countries that host this labor force. Prior conflicts lead to transnational exchange as those from third-world countries supply first-world countries with generally unskilled and cheap labor (Vertovec, 2001; 2004).

Hierarchies developed based on one's national and economic status also affect an individuals' language learner status in a host state (Beardsmore, 2008; Helot & Young, 2005; Winstead, 2013). Thus, while the host language is dominant, there is an often socially accepted understanding of the hierarchies of immigrants and their languages. Foreign transnational workers in Singapore provide unskilled labor. Yet, while English is used as their lingua franca, they are criticized by citizens of the host for their ability to use the language properly (Rubdy & McKay, 2013). In the examination of language categorizations and statuses worldwide, researchers should also consider issues of dominance and subordination of nation states and the consequences of language hierarchies among and within countries in the digital age.

3.2.2 Within-Country Language Status: From Language Dominance, Shame, and Loss to Revitalization?

Uneven transfer of language pedagogy is evident in recommendations for technological language innovations. To suggest that languages should be simplified and/or westernized becomes a political contention reflective of the status of world languages. Official country languages world-wide and within-country language hierarchies emerge based on perceived language status. Most countries push for homogeneity and assimilation which has led to language death (Khan, Humayun, Sajjad, & Khan, 2015). Issues of preserving linguistic integrity are related to language status hierarchies associated with language dominance, subordination, and oppression and guilty feelings of shame and language loss.

Territorial conquest of indigenous people's lands has led to conquering power language dominance across the world. The Cherokee language as well as a number of indigenous languages globally have become extinct or are near extinction (Crawford, 2004; Ostler, 2005; Zuo, 2007). Some indigenous groups have never developed the written form and, thus, any record of their linguistic contributions and legacies are lost. In North America, some Native Americans groups adopted the dominant language as a way to belong and fit into American society. In the 1800s, the Cherokee, who despite all of their efforts to belong in the United States, developed a writing system and a bilingual newspaper to communicate their ideas and economic success billingually. However, they were shunned, lost their lands and successful cotton plantation businesses, and were forced to migrate to reservations thousands of miles away from their homes in Florida to live on reservations in Oklahoma (Crawford, 2004).

Similarly in Latin America, Spanish is the dominant language based on prior colonialism. The Spanish burnt the codices of the indigenous populations of Mexico and Central America in order to promote new language and cultural world orders (Ostler, 2005). Native Americans such as the Maya have similarly lost their status. Indigenous languages are on the verge of extinction and rarely reach the status of less commonly taught languages (Hawkins, 1994; Yoshioka; 2010). Spanish has the highest status while minority languages such Inca or Mapuche are marginalized and close to the point of extinction.

Issues of homogeneity and national ideals and discourses of solidarity and assimilation made it difficult to ignore the dominant-subordinate language status paradigm within and across global societies. Thus, reasons for language status come from national discourses. A national goal of homogeneity can affect the positionality and success of minority groups such as multiple generations of Koreans in Japan (Matsunaga & Torigoe, 2008). France, which promotes the idea of oneness and being part of the whole, similarly affects the positionality and success of post-colonial non-European immigrants and transnationals in France. In France, first-world languages such as German and Spanish maintain higher status in the hierarchy of languages (Beardsmore, 2008, Young & Helot, 2003); however, the status of Arabic is lower (Winstead, 2013).

National English-only discourses in the United States similarly promote the theme of individual homogeneity, relinquishing home and heritage languages in societies as a way to belong. Language shame and loss has similarly been documented among bilingual individuals who speak a majority-minority language, such as Mexicans who also speak Spanish in the United States (Fitts et al., 2008; Flores & Murillo, 2001; Flores, 2005; Winstead, 2013). While numbers of Latinos have increased in the United States, so has the number of English-only policies that limit English use in the classroom (Barker, 2001; Valdez, 2001). Similarly, the status of Spanish-speaking heritage speakers in the United States is often associated with being a temporary migrant labor force that could be easily deported. Mexicans who were U.S. citizens during the 1930s, some of whom did not speak Spanish, were unconstitutionally deported in the Great Depression (Valenciana, 2006). In France, Arab-speaking North Africans make up a large part of the unskilled labor force who are still considered immigrants despite their citizenship status (Brinbaum & Kieffer, 2009).

Dominant and subordinate positioning in host societies appears to be related to minority achievement in schools. Subsequent generations of Latino children in the United States as well as later generations of North Africans in France have comparably lower achievement and greater dropout rates when compared with their mainstream counterparts (Alanis, 2010; Brinbaum & Bebolla-Boado, 2007). In addition, European immigrants, such as the Portuguese and Spanish, in France are perceived to have higher status than their non-European North African immigrant counterparts who speak Arabic (Brinbaum & Cebolla-Boado, 2007; Brinbaum & Kieffer, 2009). Stereotypes about minorities and their languages in society also contribute to their lower status, for example, Arabs pre- and post-9/11 who are depicted as terrorists (Derderian-Aghajanian & Wang, 2012) or when Latinos are similarly depicted as gangsters in movies (Mayer, 2004). Despite China's policy of minority language use, ethnic minorities in the vast republic still fall behind academically (Lam, 2007; Lundberg, 2009). Home-school language gap creates non-Chinese speaking children (e.g., Tibetans, Uyghurs) are have great difficulty understanding mainstream Mandarin instruction which results in low achievement and a corresponding low sense of well-being (Hansen, 1999; Lam, 2007). Post-colonial generations of Koreans in Japan are still not allowed to vote (Hanada, 2003; Ryang, 2012; Hayashi & Lee, 2007). The ethnic identity of children of Korean residents in Japan cause them to feel marginalized and have a sense of neither being from Korea or belonging to Japan (Matsunaga & Torigoe, 2008).

Acculturative or added approaches allow language learners to retain heritage languages while learning the dominant language in host societies. Researchers and educators globally push for additive approaches such as bilingualism, heritage language programs, and policies that protect ethnic minority rights as well as cultural and linguistic diversity (Helot & Young, 2005; Lundberg, 2009; Wang & Postiglione, 2008; Winstead, 2013; Zhu, 2014). Policy and efforts in South America to promote indigenous languages are commendable in maintaining as well as revitalizing heritage languages. The Universal Declaration of Linguistic Rights in 1996 is one such document intended to preserve indigenous and other languages and their cultures through bilingual minority language study alongside the mainstream study of Spanish, valuing both languages and multiculturalism (Haboud, 2009).

Ecuador follows the Intercultural Bilingual Education Model in Ecuador called MOSEIB which challenges mainstream curriculum and how it impinges on native indigenous populations' history, culture, and languages (Oviedo & Wildemeersch, 2008). In Europe, plurilingualism is being promoted to ensure that regional languages are similarly recognized (Beardsmore, 2008). Native American revitalization movements are supported by Native Americans and not necessarily by the government in the United States which has predominantly promoted assimilationist approaches in the curriculum (Vecsey, 2007; Warhol, 2011). However, to date, there are no policy statements or proposals to revitalize minority communities in ways that promote their cultural and linguistic integrity (Cohen & Allen, 2013; Warhol, 2011). Thus, the privilege of the dominant language and language marginalization are linguistic outcomes of economic and political conflicts associated with globalization. Interest in less commonly taught Asian languages has risen due to economic growth and the opening of their business markets to the world.

3.2.3 Recent Economic Growth and the Rise of Asian Language Statuses

The history of Asian countries and prior conflicts also affected language statuses in the Far East. In the grand global scheme, Asian countries and their languages have not been particularly popular with Westerners until the recent waves of economic growth that began after World War II. When particular Asian countries gained wealth, business increased globally due to trade relations and products sold which correspondingly influenced language status and global interest (Hyun, 2008).

Increased interest in Japan coincided with its economic rise in the 1980s. The United States influenced social and economic reconstruction occurred to boost the economy after World War II which also increased continued ties and trade between the two countries (U.S. Department of State, n.d.). Japan was best known initially for fuel-injection and small car manufacturing of fuel-injection cars at low prices at a time when gas prices were soaring in the 1970s (Wall St. Cheat, 2015), which led to greater popularity worldwide and their rise in the 1980s (Hyun, 2008). The *anime* (cartoon) *Speed Racer*, aired in the late 1960s, revealing a fast and furious car, which may have propelled Japanese car fame as well.

Japanese reliability became a global reputation. From car maufacturing and to speed racer types of car popularity, to technological innovations, e.g., camera making, and video games, Japanese culture also became popular world-wide as well (Toyoshima, 2008; Consalvo, 2009). The Japanese have contributed to video and digital entertainment, beginning with the videogram *Pac-Man* in 1980, then digital games such as *Dragon Quest*, as well as popular anime such as *Sailor Moon*. These among other popular titles that have emerged with recent global (Consalvo, 2009). The success of Sony was notable as well.

A reputation for quality and accuracy in building automobiles influenced consumer impressions and consumption of Japanese-made auto products, social media (e.g., anime and mangas), and technological devices and software contributed to the Japanese wave of global popularity in the 1990s. As neighboring Asians over the years became similarly enthralled with Japanese social media, South Korean melodramas became popular with the Taiwanese in the 1980s and the Japanese in 2004 (Hayashi & Lee 2007). International discussion between Asian members of various nationalities led to positive exchanges about the stars in online discussion boards with "real-time translations" (p. 210).

South Korea was not far behind Japan and began to develop its own car industry, camera, and video products in competition and often at lower prices than Japanese items in the United States; however, they have had less success in European markets. Koreans have successfully exported Korean-pop (K-pop) music videos and K-dramas around the world. Reasons for more dissemination of program are more accessible since all "major publications are digitalized and archived online" for easy retrieval (Hayshi

& Lee, 2007, p. 199). Korean television programs and social media have risen in stature in the United States and globally (Jung & Shim, 2014). One can see Mexican school girls dancing rhythmically to Gangnam style on Univision Spanish television. Korean programming is part of basic cable in places such as France. In California, Korean programming was offered as part of basic cable but that has now changed, and to get Korean programs costs more, possibly due to greater demand. Increased exposure to this Korean entertainment phenomenon has also prompted interest in Korean language study (Jung & Shim, 2014). And, although Korean is still considered a less commonly taught language alongside the numbers of individuals studying Japanese and Korean enrollment numbers have incresed significantly over the last 10 years (Goldberg, Looney, & Lusin, 2015). The "Korean Wave" similarly came to China during the late 1990s which also reveals the exchange of culture and information between Asian countries in the digital age (Hayashi & Lee, 2007; Shim, 2006).

China, one of the world's most ancient civilizations, with written records of language over 3,200 years old (Dong, 2014), largely influenced neighbors such as Korea and Japan with their language, writing, and religion (Louie, 2008). Gunpowder, papermaking, block printing, and the compass are a few of their ancient technological inventions and contributions (e.g., compass, block printing) that have influenced advances in other ideas globally. Despite a decline in contemporary China's sphere of infuence, it began opening its doors to the world in the 1980s with economic reforms despite some political hiccoughs. China's economic reform policy has contributed to the stimulation of high-tech products and the industry in general (Ebrey, 2006). Many technology companies established in the west (e.g., Adobe, Microsoft, Apple) have made inroads in the Chinese market, stimulating domestic innovation in language learning and communication technology. As such, the Chinese language has also become more influential in the digital community with a total of number of 649 million Internet users as of 2015 "outnumbering the entire U.S. population two to one" (Mckirdy, 2015). The rapid economic growth and increased rapprochement with western countries paralleled their ongoing business development, multilateral trade with western countries, and government supported international exchanges (Dillon, 2009), such as Obama's One Million Strong Initiative to encourage and support Chinese-American exchange and to achieve one million Americans engaged in language study by 2020 (Feldscher, 2015).

3.3 Inequitable Access to Technology: Implications of Socioeconomic, Corporate, and Other Digital Divides

Access to and the ability to disseminate language is power. Egyptian texts over thousands of years old are analyzed and read long after the language has died. Ancient nomadic cultures, e.g., Xionnu, are studied and preserved through Chinese written language scrolls (Ebrey, 2006). When no record exists for a particular language group in a historical period, such as the Huns, it is more difficult to reconstruct what happened historically. Just as "writing is not simply a storage device for speech; it is also a power technology" (Peters, 2013, p.4). Digital technology is power which affects the voices and messages that are delivered and heard in the digital age. However, national government restrictions, geographic isolation, or socioeconomically disadvantages limit opportunities to access wifi and social media.

Divides in technology development and dissemination are related to issues of access. Access to the internet in the United States is based on socioeconomics, demographics, ethnicity, and inequitable broadband access, as well as spatial divides (Warf, 2013). Other factors also associated with socioeconomic and spatial remoteness include government regulatory policies, corporate-created divides and class divides and voluntary non-involvement in technology due to religious or cultural beliefs that extend the gap between high-access and low-access groups. Religious and traditional beliefs and practices may cause low technology application even in technology-advanced countries. Religious groups such as the Amish have retained their traditional life style without cellphones, internet, cars, or electricity, and they kept a limited use of some modern amenities such as battery operated machineries and, thus, are not anti-technology (Brady, 2013).

Distance divides are also prominent and lead to inequitable access to technology-assisted learning which further expands the gap between fluent, less fluent, and non-fluent technology users. China has the largest population and rising middle class which creates a huge market for mobile technology in Chinese-speaking areas (Louie, 2008). In China, for example, corporate technological investment creates divisions based on socioeconomic status and due to geographic remoteness (Zhou, 2003). Due to small number of users and geographic isolated areas, technology investment in these languages is limited (Zhou, 2003). Comparatively, those who are multilingual, mutiethnic and who live in more remote areas have limited access to cell phones or computer systems in their villages (Louie, 2008). Moreover, the access is often not in their primary or heritage language (Hansen, 1999; Lam, 2007).

Government policy divides also contribute to differences between the haves and have-nots. For instance, there are a multitude of people in India who do not have access to basic apps. Most recently, India's government decided against utilizing Facebook as a source for access to basic apps and information via mobile phone devices (McCarthy, 2016; O'Brien, 2016). This decision may appear as censorship or possibly a question of control over whether Facebook should supply those ideals and norms that may run counter to Indian government policy and goals. Recent consolidations of information reflect privacy concerns. Google's convergence of information shared on its products, including one's web history or searches and visits happened in 2012 (Wall St. Cheat, 2015). Mobile and computer censorship in countries such as North Korea prevents populations from accessing worldwide information. Although improvements to provide greater accessibility in China exist, nevertheless current Internet censorship in mainland China, excluding Hong Kong and Macau, prevents certain western social media and search engines (e.g., Facebook, YouTube, and Google) from reaching broader Chinese audiences (Louie, 2008). A Chinese native in the mainland can enroll in an online course hosted in the United States but has no access to online resources which the American instructor might post on YouTube. Non-Chinese citizens such as visiting professors from the U.S. may be allowed to access broader TV channels and web-information and also some western Internet sites depending on the institution, region and citizenship. Similarly related, language dominance divides exist due to national language dominance over minority languages. Some minority languages lack language terms to describe new technological innovations in the west (Wang & Phillion, 2009). Thus, in some ways minorities not only have low status due to their lack of dominant language literacy but also their lack of access to digital literacy (Derderian-Aghajanian & Wang, 2012).

Subject matter divides and privilege exist in the realm of academic language study. For instance, English is the dominant language, thus more digital technology and other types of technological resources are available to support English language learning, yet this is less so for less commonly taught languages such as Korean in the United States. Low class sizes, especially for indigenous less commonly taught languages (LCTLs) is prominent, and schools with low budgets only manage to retain courses through online and self-directed language learning approaches (Dunne & Palvshyn, 2013; Godwin-Jones (2013).

3.4 TALL: Creating Access but Respecting Differences

When language classes become global through Internet technologies, course designers and instructors need to take accessibility factors in curricular design. Online technology has the potential to provide equitable access to language, heritage language, and dual language for remote and disadvantaged learners; access to learners in remote places via wireless network or Internet narrows the divide between those in privileged circumstances and others from disadvantaged situations. The mobile phone is the tool that is providing more access to people and information than other sources, such as computers (Blinn-Pike, 2009). Thus, a goal for educators would be to utilize this approach in formal face-to-face and online learning situations since the phone is generally the most accessible and affordable device for language learners. Informally, the cell phone connects learners with one another to maintain heritage language or learn others through free apps such as Skype.

Congruently, educators need to consider students' prior linguistic and cultural knowledge as potential and free resources for language maintenance and authentic interaction, which can supplement formal foreign language learning in and outside of the classroom (Young & Helot, 2003; Winstead, 2013). Heritage language speakers of Spanish may be able to contribute in Spanish in a foreign language setting in ways not previously imagined and possibly work in tandem on or offline with peers.

High demand for not only linguistic but cultural knowledge is being recognized in corporate industry (Grosse, 2004, 2010; Kramsch, 2005). Foreign language educators, correspondingly, need to recognize diverse students' prior language and cultural background knowledge as potential resources for language opportunities (Derderian-Aghajanian & Wang, 2012). Technology enhanced environments have expanded the way language learners background can be utilized as potential resources in technology-enhanced learning environments. Educators can create online liaisons, utilizing mobile devices, between these individuals to enhance language exchange. Providing native language speakers with online communicative practice leads to more accessible and more equitable opportunities for learners who are socioeconomically disadvantaged but want to learn a foreign language with a native speaker. Online technology provides tandem formats for dual and plurilingual language exchange that can even the playing field and provides opportunities for authentic interaction among native speakers. For instance, heritage language speakers of Spanish may be able to contribute in Spanish as a foreign language setting in ways not previously imagined and possibly work in tandem or offline with peers.

In order to facilitate all students' foreign language learning in the digital age, the trend of new technology development in the 21st century requires educators to be fluent in the use of technology but also in the knowledge and background of their learners (Wang, 2012; Wang, 2015). Technology should be a tool to enhance not a means to enforce how students learn.

4. THE RISE OF DIGITAL CULTURE AND LANGUAGE CROSS-POLLINATION: TRANSNATIONAL INFLUENCES

The digital age has sped communication to the point that information which may not exist in another language is adopted. Information is circulating at an unprecedented speed through the internet, leading to language evolutions and cross-pollination. From the creation of a new word in one language (e.g., internet phenomena) to the application of this word to a different language spoken on the other hemisphere, this neologism/newly-created word can skip several traditional steps (e.g., publication, translation, journalism, television) and become a popular word in another country through social media.

4.1 Digital Culture (D-Culture)

D-culture refers to *deconstructing* the old physical culture of socialization through *digital* technologies and *developing* a newer realm of online interaction and virtual reality that bypasses traditional gatekeepers of information. The D-Culture can challenge traditional modes, which avoids boycott by authority if the Internet and information remains accessible and is uncensored. The D-culturing process, thus, interferes with more traditional modes of communication as well as the traditional authoritative power.

In this model, technologies directly connect the knowledge creator (left) to the audience and the consumer (right) almost immediately. Through technologies (e.g., social media, MOOC, personal website, blog, mobile network), information flows from the creator to the audience without the interference of a traditional authority or gatekeeper of information (top). The model of D-Culture reveals the de-constructive and re-constructive power of technology in the circulation of information which challenges traditional channels of communication. The dotted arrow pointing from Authorities indicates how the gatekeepers try to block, interfere, control, or censor information. Creators of information have the choice of either going through authority channels to audiences or sending their information directly to audiences through free-access internet. Information that flows from the creator directly to the audiences is reflective of D-culture communication.

The power of authority can be reflected in many ways such as: a professor requires a student to revise a project prior to a public presentation, a journal reviewer rejects a manuscript for publication, a TV producer calls off a program to be aired, a video/image used for a news report gets cut off prior to broadcasting, or a parent sets a password to prevent a child from playing video games. In D-Culture, the virtual world has become a visionary place where knowledge creators do not go through authorities' regulated routes to gain fame.

Prensky (2001) who introduced the digital world to *Digital Natives, Digital Immigrants* caused an uproar in the learning community about the way we think and connect the conceptual understanding of the fluidity of technology-assisted learning with learners. This non-empirical publication with free downloadable copy reached 12,747 citation hits by early-March 2016 and this number is still growing.

Figure 1. The model of D-Culture
(Copyright The_Model_of D-Culture_Congcong Wang 2016, used with permission)

The Model of D-Culture

The Prensky phenomenon is an example of how the digital culture emerges in which digital natives and digital immigrants are not constrained to only use authoritative sources. By positioning new generations of students and old generations of educational authorities into this polarized-system, Prensky's claim challenged authority and revealed deeper language power issues, which will be analyzed in detail below.

Even in the realm of pop culture, music artists can become blocked from releasing their music. Cun Xue uploaded his Flash Music Video which became an internet sensation. With the success online, Cun Xue was then recognized by the China Central Television, the major Chinese television network. Similarly, the Chopsticks Brothers gained fame with the viral hits of a self-made film placed on the Internet. They wrote their own music and became Internet stars through primarily their own means. The Internet recognition and fame led to their recent American Music Award for *Little Apple* song that "[…] has generated more than 280,000 cover versions, in total racking up over 900 million views on Youku, China's largest online video portal" and is heard in public venues all over China (Sun, 2014).

While the ability to virtually bypass the conventional routes to stardom and disseminate ideas through digital means exists and the digital users appear to be grassroots (Gee & Hayes, 2011), questions remain about the power of virtual grassroots' sensation. One wonders whether a digital march or virtual protest would have the same effect? Could the advances gained in the U. S. civil rights movement have been achieved through virtual protest? What does a virtual world bode for the future of human's ability to gather, organize, and protest?

4.2 Language Status and Power: The Pyramid of Digital Language Status in D-Culture

Throughout the history of human civilization, language became power and literacy was the privilege of the elites as well a means of political control over the masses (Ebrey, 2006; Peters, 2013). China kept their logographic writing system despite exposure to phonetic languages (Ebrey, 2006). In this way, the Chinese government retained the ancient script among those privileged and educated who worked in government positions and aided to disseminate official ideals (Lung, 2008). Similarly, dominant religious ideals were disseminated throughout Europe via more affordable printing modes and increased literacy among its members.

Knowledge has become cheaper and been more easily accessed in the digital age. New Literacies (e.g., visual literacy, digital literacy, information literacy, media literacy) have been associated with a broader range of formats and ways to create and disseminate information whether it is with pen and paper or through digital means (Egbert & Hanson-Smith, 2007; Knobel & Lankshear, 2006; Leu, Kinzer, Coiro, & Cammack, 2004).

New Literacies as defined in this book refers to the skills of decoding and constructing meanings via digital language effectively for communication in the D-culture/digital world community (See Figure 2 for the Pyramid of Digital Language Status in D-Culture). Three key points should be considered with New Literacies: (1) proficiency levels, e.g., language proficiency, computer language proficiency; (2) individuals who access multiple literacies ranging from programmers and hackers to music downloaders and bloggers; and (3) multiple skills involved in information creation, digital movie/video editing, 3D modeling, animation, programming, video gaming, and digital music composing.

In the hierarchy/pyramid of D-culture, the highest proficiency of digital language provides programmers, hackers, technology giants (e.g., Apple, Google, Intel, Microsoft, Facebook) supreme power and dominance in the digital empire. The 2016 debate on whether Apple should create a backdoor program

Figure 2. The pyramid of digital language status in D-Culture
(Copyright The_Pyramid_of_Digital_Language_Status_in_D-Culture_Congcong Wang 2016, used with permission)

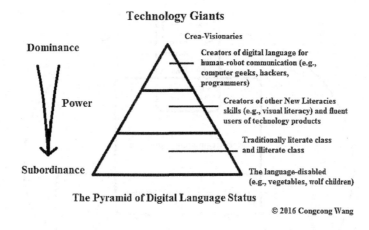

for authorities to extract data from locked iPhones is a good example (Selyukh & Domonoske, 2016). Comparatively, those who merely master lower-status New Literacies skills other than the digital language (e.g., visual literacy) seem to lack power (e.g., protecting their digital privacy from hackers). From a digital language power-influence perspective, the literate (e.g., reading and writing) in the non-digital world, to some extent, cannot be said to be "literate" and face marginalization as well as isolation in the digital age (e.g., deliver voice, acquire information, and protect their cultural integrity). Much as oral language was empowered by writing in ancient China and Egypt (Peters, 2013), or as high-status colonial languages had broader influence over population in physical colonies, advanced digital language skills empower high-status digital language groups to amplify their voices, colonize larger digital territory in global network and virtual world, attack low digital language status groups, as well as filter, mute, and erase certain voices in D-Culture communication.

4.3 Crea-Visionary Education

Access to technology and the ability to disseminate messages means power. From Bill Gates's vision of "computers in every home" to Steve Jobs's vision of "do what you believe is great work and love what you do" to Mark Zuckerberg's vision of "connect the world" (Beaumont, 2008; CBS News, 2014; Stanford Report, 2005), their quick elevation in the digital age reveals how digital technology can shift power from the privileged to the grassroot start-ups who become tech giants. In other words, riding a high-tech vehicle leads to a decline of traditional modes of communication, such as, television and print publications.

Language education in the digital age reflects a paradigm shift in which learners are given the tools to become visionaries and creators who foresee issues of the future and realize their vision through practice. Digital access allows these crea-visionaries to bypass the traditional gatekeepers of knowledge and create new knowledge. From mathmatical modeling, 3-D animations, games, to whatever one can dream of, there is no limit to a creator's potential except his/her own intellegence in building a virtual empire. Technological awareness and knowledge expands visions such as a D-language. This language can be "foreign" to most populations as well as reflect a trend of world language and culture emergence.

Figure 3. The Venn diagram of crea-visionary education
(Copyright The_Venn_Diagram_of_Crea-Visionary_ Education_Congcong Wang 2016, used with permission)

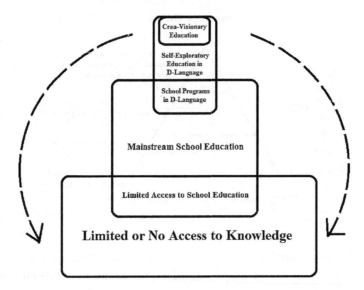

Currently, much of the world's population has limited access to formal schooling and resources due to remote geographical locations despite official goals of mandatory education. Some have cultural knowledge and traditions that can be valued and transmitted. Additionally, mainstream students in dominant schooling systems are not necessarily fluent in D-language, but some can develop digital language through self-exploratory learning. Among many self-explorers, some would not only develop profound D-language skills but create visions. These crea-visionaries have huge potential to influence the world by skipping the mainstream school systems and delivering their knowledge to the population with limited/no access to school knowledge.

With greater access to technology, third-world populations and those in remote areas can also participate in becoming crea-visionaries in their own communities. Access can empower learners to engage in self-exploratory types of learning even in situations where children have limited access to formal schooling. Gaining D-language through such access are steps towards becoming a crea-visionary.

4.4 Digital/Virtual Universal Language (D-Language)

The Digital/Virtual Universal Language or D-Language refers to a language that is effective for human interaction in the virtual world as well as a language that is easy, effective and efficient for human-robot and robot-robot communication, which includes but is not limited to current programming languages. This D-Language communication model below shows a conversation among four speakers: A speaker of human Language X, a speaker of human Language Y and two robots. The technology or D-Language (shown as the line) makes communication possible among different human speakers as well as robots.

Like D-culture, D-language may deconstruct and merge essences of many human languages. D-language can feature English as the current champion in a world language race and highlights its potential

Figure 4. The D-Language communication model
(Copyright The_D-Language_Communication_Model_Congcong Wang 2016, used with permission)

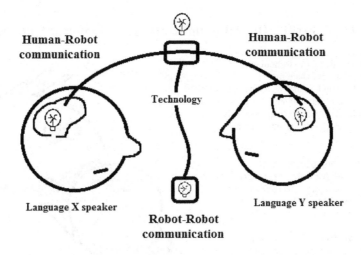

The D-Language Communication

© 2016 Congcong Wang

to be further simplified (e.g., "lol" means "laugh out loud"). D-language can also merge logographs and emoticons. Images empower D-language by increasing the quantity and accuracy of information delivered in ways that traditional oral or written forms cannot. Future image-transformative technology (e.g., chips built in the human brain for faster information transcription), may allow one (e.g., human or semi-robotic person) to visualize others' situational feelings without oral description. Programming humans may sound crazy; however, at a micro level, humans may have already been "programmed" in a natural language environment (e.g., a child's language acquisition through social language cultural immersion). While some researchers may think it impossible, history makes human language transition transition/emergence visible/observable.

At a macro level, the history of language simplification movements across continents reveals that technology has already reshaped human language, e.g., the 1900s simpler English terminology on American newspapers (Simplified Spelling Board, 1920), the 1930-1950s Chinese language simplification and Romanization in mainland China and Singapore (Perez, 2004), and the creation of Japanese Katakana for spelling western words such as "tennis" (テニス). More recent goals of simplification have emerged to make English writing more easily understood and acquired. A common complaint has been the French influence on English and varied pronunciation in addition to letters that can have multiple sounds, such as "c" and "s." Measures to adopt English for European communications in the European Union as well as simplify the language within five years to create Euro English (Dehaene, 2009).

Urgent demand for effective and efficient global web-communication speeds up human language evolution. Creation and updates of Google Translate and web-dictionaries, have challenged linguistic authorities. On February 24, 2016, the American Council on the Teaching of Foreign Languages (ACTFL) circulated the YouTube video *Why can't technology replace human teachers?* on social media. This video shows how several Google Translate attempts make Adele's song *Hello*, which do not make sense or reflect original meaning (Reese, 2016; ACTFL, 2016). However, the goal may not be to "replace"

Figure 5. Technological universals, digital colonization, and digital cultural integrity
(Copyright Technological_Universals,_Digital_Colonization,_and_Digital_Cultural_Integrity_Congcong Wang & Lisa Winstead 2016, used with permission)

Technological Universals, Digital Colonization, and Digital Cultural Integrity

Technological universals refer to technologies innovated in different areas but share similar functions (e.g., YouTube and YouKu as equivalent video sites in the U.S. and China) or any type of technology that is utilized universally (e.g., popularly branded products). It includes digital universals and virtual universals.

Technological colonization occurs when dominant ideas are digitally/virtually disseminated through technological universals. This digital/virtual information has the potential to replace and chip away traditional cultures and social ways of being.

Digital cultural integrity refers to moral/social obligation to preserve traditional cultures and languages for posterity. It is not just the recording of these minority cultures but also providing a breathing space which permits them to retain their authenticity in the digital age (e.g., Amish).

© 2016 Congcong Wang & Lisa Winstead

but "bypass" human routes. Thus, the status of human language in literature and communication is being challenged by "computing language" in engineering. Technology, not yet human's rival in artistic translation, but it may bypass official language gatekeepers by creating a currently unknown language. Alongside language emergence, indications of this rivalry can also be seen in digital cultural universals.

4.5 Technological Universals Influence Social Language Interaction

Cultural universals comprise what global societies, ethnic groups, and nations share and may include food, clothing, and more abstract concepts such as shelter, technology, government, and communication. These cultural universals have often been themes of study in the social studies that allows deeper inquiry into the whys and hows of societies' communication, traditions and governments (Alleman & Brophy, 2001, 2002, 2003; Winstead & Gautreau, 2014). While technology and communication are universal, in societies, the development of these communication technologies is different based on culture and location. For instance, technology and communication modes may look different for the Amish but also be quite different historically when making historical comparisons with ancient civilizations such as the Mayan culture. The telegraph and telephone was developed in North America, the Gutenberg press in Europe, and other types of printing comprise some of the technological advances that promoted greater dissemination and sharing of culture, politics, and ideas.

Technological universals have emerged in the digital age and represented by similar forms of technology for learning language. While a keyboard is a technological universal, the way it is used in China or Japan may be quite different due to alphabetic or logographic type. Video-sharing sites such as YouTube and YouKu are technological universals that are utilized respectively in the United States and China. However, due to the connectivity in the digital age, the boundaries between the technology universals as well as commonly known cultural universals are narrowing. At one time societies could be identified by their specific cultural and regional differences based on their diverse food, clothing, and communication modes. Digital bridges and access via online interaction leads to more common and dominant form of virtual communication that challenges traditional cultures and values.

New digital culture and language can influence face-to-face as well as online social interaction. Although netiquette exists, the speed of technology and the different modes, (e.g., Twitter versus face-to-face discussion), influence our interactions, and our formality in these types of learning situations. Children who have broad accessibility to technology (e.g., Warcraft, Wii, Facebook, YouTube, Youku) may spend most time socializing online instead of in real life (Gee & Hayes, 2011). From teenagers to adult couples, mobile devices allow users to enjoy digital intimacy near or far. Through the Internet, people may make friends globally with or without knowing the other party's identity. Technology allows shy learners to interact anonymously with humans and even robots in a virtual environment; addictions to video games, *anime* and social media may socially distance these users from family and friends. People from all cultural backgrounds may be fascinated by what innovative technology has brought to life yet may become bogged down in the ways digital culture overrides and sometimes replaces aspects of their traditional culture and socialization modes. How does technology impact language evolution?

Translanguaging in addition to language borrowing over the internet and mobile platforms becomes very active and causes language cross-pollinations. The shaping power of technology on interrelation in human society deconstructs our traditional cultural behaviors and interactions. Technology provides innovative means for communication and opportunities to mirror the cultural background of particular languages being learned. Translanguaging and code-switching languages have been utilized as a term to describe how speakers of two languages and bilinguals may insert words from two or more languages (Garcia & Wei, 2014). Code switching between Welsh and English was first described by Cen Williams as translanguaging as 'trawsieithu' in Welsh (The New York Times, 2010). Although described as writing in one language and speaking in another, translanguaging also reflects how bilingual and plurilingual speakers translanguage or interchange words, phrases, and complete interstitial sentences of one language with another

The English word "google" is originally a noun, but now can be used as a verb in "You can google it" which means "You can look it up on Google search engine." Since the English word "google" has been used by other language users before the company released an official translation, these non-English users often mix the English word "google" with words from their native languages. For example, in Chinese "你可以google一下" means "You can look it up on Google." After the company released their official Chinese name "谷歌", Chinese users still prefer to say "你可以google一下" to "你可以谷歌一下."

With the global popularization of K-pop Gangnam Style, its original Korean title "강남스타일 " (the style from the Gangnam area) has been translated into many different languages. Interestingly, its English translation adopts a transliteration of "Gangnam" and an English word "style." The Chinese translation "江南Style" adopts two Chinese characters "江南" based on the meaning of "강남" (Gangnam) and a non-translated English word "style" as well. To say "Gangnam Style is so cool" in Chinese "江南Style 太酷了", the speaker uses two languages no matter whether he/she knows English. Often, the youth in Eastern Asian countries consider it fashionable to mix English words with their mother tongue as well as the symbols of pop-culture.

4.5.1 Emoticon Culture: Logos and Symbol Co-Construction

As a new word combining "emote" and "icons", emoticons on the Internet were first created in the U.S. in the 1980s and are part of the Internet culture. ☺ ☹ :-):-(are the most commonly used emoticons to express happiness and sadness among Internet and mobile users.

As a uncommon character in modern Chinese, 囧 (pronounced as jiŏng and original means "window" or "bright") can date back to oracle bone inscript (Li & Li, 2014). Due to its shape of a face, 囧 has been given a different significance "embarrassment" "gloom" and has become a most popular emoticon in blogs and online chat rooms in Taiwan (Hammond & Richey, 2014; Ru, Lu & Li, 2010). From Taiwan the character was disseminated through Hong Kong and then mainland China via social media (Hammond & Richey; Ru, Lu, & Li).

Notably, unlike any language symbol, an emoticon can be recognized and used among any language users. Somehow, the popularization of emoticon culture reveals that such universal and cross-languaging symbols bridge languages and cultures globally. It further reveals a trend of world language emergence. Digital learners may then acquire such universal language and incorporate it into everyday speech. The question to ponder is whether this internet language is foreign or native for the digital learner in another country. Defeating many languages in their original forms, the emerging D-language co-constructs a fashion of language borrowing.

4.5.2 Digital Cultural Integrity

The consequences of such borrowing may be/become apparent as the world becomes smaller through technological global exchange. Measures have also been taken to retain languages within societies as a way of guarding linguistic and cultural integrity. It is interesting to note that the English cognate "word" *computer* is translated as *computadora* in Mexico. However, the Spanish utilize the term *el ordenador* for computer instead of *computadora*. Similarly, the French utilize the term l'*ordinateur* for that same concept and have historically been known to police their language and English equivalent intrusions of loan words that do not clearly translate from one language to another (Conlin, 2014). The two Chinese characters "电脑" respectively means "electronic" and "brain". Is this an effort by Europeans to retain their linguistic and cultural integrity? The Spanish and French have been known to exercise their rights to develop and maintain their language integrity through such language policing.

Language borrowing is a phenomenon of interaction. When language is borrowed, it also expresses the ideas and philosophies from the country where the language is borrowed. And, while borrowing is common, over the past four decades, there have been suggestions that the very foundation of ancient languages change due to the need for speed and efficacy, e.g., the attempt in 2001 to change Japan's official language to English (Kawai, 2009; Matsuura, Fujieda, & Mahoney, 2004). Access to English and English learning has been uneven as those who speak more mainstream languages such as Mandarin have greater access than minority counterparts (Feng, 2009). English language incursion in China has also created tensions with regard to the use and status of Mandarin over minority languages, but also English influence within the region has created tensions among minority and majority groups and concerning what language matters (Feng, 2009).

- **Digital Cultural Integrity:** Cultural integrity as described by Jagers (2001) is the value of the resources and knowledge of particular populations or groups. Digital cultural integrity refers to valuing and preserving culture and the cultural assets of individuals and minority populations and their languages. Language reflects cultural and social ideals. Language is a vital part of culture. When the origins, language, and culture of minorities are valued, this promotes student well-being and confidence (Phinney, Horencyzk, Liebkind, & Vedder, 2001; Jagers, 2001). For example, cultural integrity can be maintained in schools through Navajo storytelling by Navajos (Eder, 2007), and appreciation of native arts, such as Native American drumming (Moore, 2007). Similarly, digital oral history projects exist around the world to record and relate historical experiences. Educators have a moral role to ensure that we also promote digital linguistic integrity (Ishihara, Itoko, Sato, Tzadok, & Takagi, 2012; Yap, 2013).

- **Digital Linguistic Integrity.** Digital linguistic integrity refers to the sovereign right of a nation state as well as minorities to digitally record as well as learn and preserve their language through digital devices. Efforts to efface, erase, or quash particular language formats can represent attacks on the culture. Assimilation measures similarly affect linguistic integrity, in general. For instance, international pressures cause individuals in some in some countries such as Japan, to consider making English the official language (Kawai, 2009; Matsura, 2004). Although English has not become the official language in Japan, these types of propositions reveal the issues associated with language status and marginalization. Thus, linguistic integrity is also directly associated with retaining cultural integrity.

Western incursions and trade awakened Chinese and other Asian intellectuals to the need to speed communication and increase literacy. In the 1930s, mainland China began Western-influenced modernization and language simplification. By the 1950s, a large number of Chinese characters were simplified in mainland China to increase literacy rates through the ability to acquire the language faster (Perez et al., 2004). These characters were adopted by Singapore as well (Kane, 2006; Perez et al., 2004). Traditional Chinese characters are still in use in Taiwan and Hong Kong. Creation of the Pinyin system was intended to Romanize the Chinese language. The demand for Western spelling and Western words led to language reformations. For instance, the Japanese utilize katakana for the syllabic representation of foreign words for which there is, generally, no Chinese character equivalent. Computer is written as コンピュータ (computaa) in katakana. The Japanese did not borrow Chinese characters that represent this word, but instead utilize Katana to represent the computer phonetically and syllabically. Fettuccini, café, and other foreign terms are written in katakana as seen on menus in Italian and French restaurants in Japan.

Alternative forms other than Western forms for communication should be valued to maintain linguistic, cultural, as well as social integrity. Of course, all languages are influenced by other cultures and borrowed words. When one's language value is diminished, a sense of pride with which you are culturally as a person is diminished as well. Children whose language and cultural status is marginalized in society can lose their sense of well-being (Phinney et al., 2001; Jager, 2001). Well-being and pride can be diminished through dialogues in which the majority languages and cultures challenge minority domestically as well as globally. Thus, from a social justice perspective, in the digital age language educators have an important role to play within the struggle for language power and politics.

5. TECHNOLOGY AS BENIGN FACILITATOR OR HUMAN THREAT

The ancient Chinese game of Go is one of the last games where the best human players can still beat the best artificial intelligence players. (Mark Zuckerberg, Facebook post, January 26, 2016 in Palo Alto, CA)

However, in 43 days, history has been rewritten. On March 9, 2016, a Google A.I. beat Human world Champion Lee Sedol who said after the match, "I was very surprised. I didn't expect to lose. [But] I didn't think AlphaGo would play the game in such a perfect manner" (Sang-Hun & Markoff, 2016).

Currently, technologies are utilized as facilitators in various language learning and classroom contexts. In the future, will technologies replace the human language instructor? Where does technology drive humans' role in a technology-dominant society? With more human labor being replaced by machines to manufacture products, to help customers check out in stores, robots to monitor phone calls, software conducting translations, and virtual guides touring visitors at museums, concerns arise about how and where technology will drive the role of the human. Mark Zuckerberg's recently posted information (above) about Facebook AI researchers' advances in teaching computers to predict contextually.

Language is one of the most complex things for computers to understand. Guessing how to complete a sentence is pretty easy for people but much more difficult for machines [...] Mark Zuckerberg (Facebook post, February 18, 2016 in Palo Alto, CA).

Artificial intelligence researchers have found that a computer's AI memory has the ability to predict not only low frequency words such as "on" but also people's names and nouns that are missing in particular stories based on context, such as *Alice in Wonderland* (Hill, Bordes, Sumite, & Weston, 2016). Since language teaching and learning involves advanced skills as well as complex cognitive and emotional processes, language is a unique feature of human interaction and learning (Jagers, 2001; Phinney et al., 2001) that has not yet been fully duplicated by computers.

5.1 Digital Colonization: Replacement of Human Learning

While technology has not replaced humans in language education, the next generation of technology is under research and has the potential to replace human instructors. Hologram technology portrayed in *Star Wars* appears to be an inevitabilty. The maturity of hologram development has the potential to convert school language programs to language fast- food stores where a manager can manage multiple projected virtual scenarios to allow many human learners to immerse in virtual-authentic learning contexts.

With awareness and self-education in technology, some language educators may feel hesitant to adopt technology due to fear about being replaced by it. Schools and universities provide benign opportunities for technological professional development so that professors can convert their current on-campus courses into online formats. This reveals a new feature of technology-driven education. Developing an online language course requires a lot of expertise and effort in not just language but also technological know-how. The course might be equipped with vivid videos and animations, free resources for self-exploratary education and other engaging technologies. Once the course is developed, it requires less from the instructor who may only be needed to facilitate and manage the course when technologies fall short of human intelligence or aspects of the program become outdated, or where human technologies fall short of human intelligence, e.g., human interaction, problem solving, motivating, encouraging and comforting (Goodrich & Schultz, 2007; Goetz et al., 2003).

Since well-developed courses can be shared as well as assigned to those that have less experience (e.g., teaching assistants), and the university's ownership of intellectural property of the course has the potential to cause barriers in the language instructor or language developer's job relocation, those who invest huge amounts of time and knowledge to develop courses may begin to feel used and underpaid for their efforts. Course developers' intellectual rights are not addressed or protected and they may be considered obsolete once the course and format is in place, losing their position and the course they built. Technology course building benefits insititutions in a transition from education to business by reducing the budget of human labor. Since technology can be duplicated at low cost, time will only tell how positions might be eliminated.

The tech-industry dominated by corporation input and government decisions at the macro level drives education towards an unclear future. Artificial intelligence advances reveal, for the first time, how an AI machine can compete and even beat a human at a Go board game (Chappell, 2016; Shang-hun & Markoff, 2016) reflective of notions of more advanced robotic abilities as similarly suggested in the movie *Terminator*. While it takes humans many years to learn a language, it may take a robot just seconds to be programmed or reprogrammed. The learning speed of humans may fall behind that of future technologies. Robots are designed with efficiency, fast speed, and duration and even attractive appearance to overcome human shortcomings (Goodrich & Schultz, 2007; Russell & Norvig, 1995). From a robotic perspective, human time spent on rest, love, encouragement, and entertainment may be viewed as a waste or flaw in design. The danger of this machinery mindset is that society may become de-humanized when humans are expected to function efficiently as robots while robots function as autonomously and intelligently as humans. Should human and computer robots become rivals, a widening divide will emerge between TALL and human-facilitated language learning and technology-dominated instruction. The potential human-AI conflict is just a reflection of human society conflict. If humans cannot overcome their own shortcomings as a society, humans may carry the same mistakes to a new realm. When tension regarding resources and intelligence escalate, humans may lose more than they wagered.

5.2 While Robots Are Becoming Humanized, Humans Are Becoming Robotized

In the digital age, technology is power, capital, trend, fashion, identity, and finally D-culture. From programming to foreign languages, children can develop a variety of skills through web-surfing, bypassing parents' authority at home. Digital monitors used for baby-watching and children's learing software applications may reduce parent-children interaction. Consistently investing spare time on knowledge updates as well as attempts to catch up with the technology speed, parental and social time is sacrificed. Human relations in society are being digitalized in this very capital-driven world. In a materialist world, young people obsess much about enjoyment brought by technologies and chase it as a fashion. Some consumers are convinced and even misled by commercials that promote consumer culture and human desire for the "next-newer" the "next-better" without a limit.

When Apple products become a symbol representing a digital identity of many teenagers globally, some blind digital fashion chasers paid their costs for their digital ignorance. A Chinese teen Wang Shangkun, who sold a kidney to buy an iPad, became too weak to face alleged harvesters in trial (Bennett-Smith, 2012). When action deviates from actual need and financial affordability, it ends up with tragedies. Other cases reveal potential harm caused by the capital-driven technology industry and the global society's

Figure 6. Human-technology polarization
(Copyright Human-Technology_Polarization_Congcong Wang 2016, used with permission)

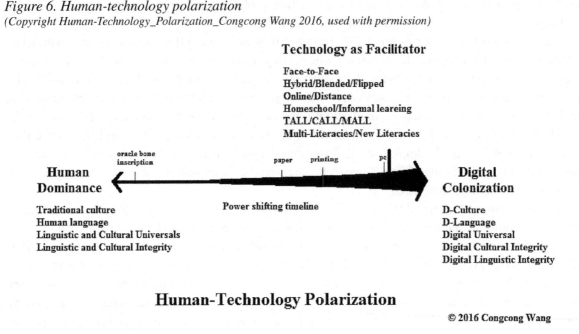

Human-Technology Polarization

© 2016 Congcong Wang

lack of knowledge and humanity. According to the New York Times, "137 workers at a factory here had been seriously injured by a toxic chemical used in making the signature slick glass screens of the iPhone" (Barboza, 2011). In a CNET report, "Benzene and n-hexane are chemicals thought to cause cancer and nerve damage, and they both have been used in the final assembly of Apple's iPhones, iPads, iPods, and Mac computers—until now" (Kerr, 2014). Thus, the capital-driven tech-industry has begun to treat humans as machines. The D-culture commercial colonization and enslavement of individuals reveals the D-Human aspect of how cultures and people's roles as laborers are deconstructed in society.

As social creatures, humans fear falling behind, being marginalized or becoming isolated. World cultures are melting into a virtual world with narrowed or even one way of thinking valued over another. What perspectives will be chosen? Will they be Eurocentric? Will these perspectives run counter to cultures? Where does technology lead us? What is considered important? By whom? The question is really not about whether we need technology, but what we create it for and what we expect our future to be. Is a classroom packed with technological media necessarily better than a non-tech classroom? It depends, but those who say "no" to technology seem to be out of date and very much out of style. Whether that out-of-datedness is a liability or a strength still remains to be seen.

6. THE GLORY OF HUMAN LANGUAGE AND CULTURE: WHAT ARE WE LOSING IN THE DIGITAL AGE?

After celebrating the surprises that technologies have brought to human society in the 21st century, educators and researchers should look back at the glory of the less digital side of human society. When humans are too busy learning new things, there is little time to think about the human aspects that may disappear in the digital age. Without reflection upon how digital technologies re-shape human society it is difficult to understand how aspects of language and culture might be lost or replaced.

6.1 Rethinking the Role of Technology in the Digital Age: Challenges to Traditions and Values

D-Culture and D-Language empower crea-visionaries in the virtual world. When virtual life dominates real life on a large scale, those whose voices are not heard in the virtual world appear to have lost their voices in the real world. But all voices matter. (Dr. Wang)

The digital age does not mean that traditional approaches are not utilized or even not beneficial, such as face-to-face learning and non-digital modes of learning. Instead, it is an era in which traditional and digital culture co-exist. Some people may argue that there is a way to duplicate a culture to retain human heritage. People may film a video or conduct a project with hologram images or even clone. But, really, can humans clone a culture? Culture is continuously evolving in contexts. As technology becomes more advanced, we can make duplicates which mirror our culture through filming and reactivation. However, from a philosophical stance, a duplicate is at most a copy that can never become the authentic or the original one. This is the uniqueness of human culture.

Humans appear to push traditional and indigenous culture to the brink of elimination while digital cultures dominate the world. Just because many cultures have been passed down orally does not mean that those forms are any less intrinsically important than those digital ones. Lacking technology, indigenous cultures and traditional culture are often labeled as "out of date" or "backward." Wise seniors in these cultures may never learn to use computers, but their histories without a digital format or a written text should not be ignored. So many ballads and dances can only be passed down authentically through human performances. People should stop using discriminatory eyes to view indigenous cultures, traditions, and religious practices.

The Amish towns known for their horse carriages and buggies which are representative of their culture, traditions, and beliefs (Amish American, n.d.). Tour groups visit nearby Amish towns bringing their digital and video cameras to capture the customs inherited since the 1800s and take photos with those Amish people whom they sometimes believe are actors. Tourists become upset when their photo-taking requests are denied. This is not Disneyland but living historical museums of authentic Amish who retain their culture and traditional past without digital erosion or invasion. Their traditional culture and language has neither been Americanized nor assimilated, nor digitalized. Their non-digital life should be respected in the digital age, and thus serve as an example that just because a group is out of step with current tech does not mean that their existence or methodologies are any less valid.

Rethinking the role of technology in a human society means to leave breathing space for individuals and groups from all walks of life by setting up boundaries rather than pushing everyone to accept new technologies or digital demands. Although having facilitated all levels of communication (e.g., individual, group, public and mass) and promotion of individualism online, digital technology in its present form also has the potential to erase individuality and promote commonality. Cultural and linguistic heritage has been replaced and assimilated under the heading of Americanism in the United States. Ethnic cultural pasts such as Irish and Scottish and respective languages, e.g., Gaelic, are forgotten. Heritages, ancestry, languages and oftentimes the struggles that brought immigrants to America are read about in textbooks. In China, ethnic minority children who have lost their heritage language and culture may say zhōng guó rén (中国人) or literally means the "middle kingdom people." When translated into English it means a "person from the country of China." Thus, if the minority culture, language, or history is retained, one is not of that nation. The underlying meanings are apparent and extend to one's sense of being an outsider or an insider, a true American or a true Chinese citizen that represents and speaks the dominant national language.

The name of the country becomes a symbol or a label that represents the brand of the product "human" who becomes digitally colonized. When humans are stripped off their cultural identities, awareness, humanity, they simply become empty vessels that can be filled with the new D-Culture. This reflects a form of human digital colonization. If humans only put forth replications instead of representing various aspects of human society, ways of thinking and whole cultures are marginalized. Thus, cultural and linguistic integrity is diminished or becomes extinct. Through this progression will insensitivity and apathy lead to a world where *Truman* exists, or that we wake up as duplicates as suggested in *Pendulum* or *Oblivion*? This is how human society is portrayed in Hollywood movies, but could these movies reflect a future reality in which eventually could humans lose control of themselves and the world they are living? Perhaps humans will gain an overreliance on technology-directed learning instead of human facilitation of instruction. Perhaps we will all speak one universal language and be just one and forget about our heritages, languages, and cultures. Yet again, perhaps one day the human empathy, and emotion will be most valued. If D-culture takes hold, maybe folks will have to buy tickets just to watch a real face-to-face human lecture.

6.2 What Can We Gain in the Digital Age?

Standing at the intersection of human language history, we readers should give language teachers credit for their time, effort, patience, care, love, and other emotional and intellectual investment in helping those who are disabled, newcomers, or just ordinary learners become who they did not dream to become. Those educators, teachers and language workers are the first people who welcome disadvantaged children such as refugees. Their effort to make those children feel home in a new community is invaluable, and, most importantly, human. These human aspects are what advanced technology can hardly surpass.

Eye-contact, a smile, face-to-face interaction, these simple moments bind the two individuals emotionally and nonverbally. The uniqueness of feeling cared and loved cannot be duplicated. This is the authenticity of human society as well as the originality of language learning.

Technologies can have the potential to promote human gain. The following chapters reveal how language teaching and learning supported by technology can provide authentic and real-time human-to-human scenarios that benefit and support language practice, development and acquisition. We just need to be mindful and not blind to the potential of technology to provide benefits to human learning, language preservation and maintenance. And, most of all, that we are still able to provide a human touch.

Congcong Wang
University of Northern Iowa, USA

Lisa Winstead
California State University, Fullerton, USA

REFERENCES

漢典. (2016, March 18). 奻. Retrieved from http://www.zdic.net/z/17/js/597B.htm

ACTFL. (2016, February 24). Why can't tech replace teachers? Here's what happens when you put Adele's "Hello" through Google Translate. *ACTFL*. Retrieved from https://twitter.com/search?q=Why%20 can%E2%80%99t%20tech%20replace%20teachers%3F%20&src=typd

Al-Hashash, S. (2007). Bridging the gap between ESL and EFL: Using computer assisted language learning as a medium. *Indian Journal of Applied Linguistics*, *33*(1), 5–38.

Al-Saleem, B. I. A. (2012). The interactive whiteboard in English as a foreign language (EFL) classroom. *European Scientific Journal*, 8(3).

Alanis, I. (2010). A Texas two-way bilingual program: Its effects on linguistic and academic achievement. *Bilingual Research Journal*, *24*(3), 225–248.

Alleman, J., & Brophy, J. (2001). *Social studies excursions, K-3. Book 1: Powerful units on food, clothing, and shelter*. Portsmouth, NH: Heinemann.

Alleman, J., & Brophy, J. (2002). *Social studies excursions, K-3. Book 2: Powerful units on communication, transportation, and family living*. Portsmouth, NH: Heinemann.

Alleman, J., & Brophy, J. (2003). *Social studies excursions, K-3. Book 2: Powerful units on childhood, money, and government*. Portsmouth, NH: Heinemann.

Allen, J. R. (2009). Why learning to write Chinese is a waste of time. *Foreign Language Annals*, *41*(2), 237–251.

Amish American. (2016, February 2). *Amish American: Iowa Amish*. Retrieved from http://amishamerica. com/iowa-amish/

Andrews, R., & Haythornthwaite, C. (2007). Introduction to E-learning research. In R. Andrews & C. Haythornthwaite (Eds.), *The SAGE Handbook of E-learning Research* (pp. 1–53). London, England: SAGE Publications, Ltd.

Aponte, R., & Pressagno, R. (2009). The communications revolution and its impact on the family: Significant, growing, but skewed and limited in scope. *Marriage & Family Review*, *45*, 576–586.

Arms, W. (2012). The 1990s: The formative years of digital libraries. *Library Hi Tech*, *30*(4), 579–591.

Barboza, D. (2011, February 22). Workers Sickened at Apple Supplier in China. *The New York Times*. Retrieved from http://www.nytimes.com/2011/02/23/technology/23apple.html?_r=0

Barker, V. (2001). The English-only movement: A communication analysis of changing perceptions of language vitality. *Journal of Communication*, *51*(1), 3–37.

Baxter, L. (1984). An investigation of compliance-gaining on politeness. *Human Communication Research*, *10*, 427–456.

Beardsmore, H. (2008). Language promotion by European supra-national institutions. In O. García (Ed.), *Bilingual education in the 21st century: A global perspective* (pp. 197–217). Chichester: Wiley-Blackwell.

Beaumont, C. (2008, June 27). Bill Gate's dream: A computer in every home. *The Telegraph*. Retrieved from http://www.telegraph.co.uk/technology/3357701/Bill-Gatess-dream-A-computer-in-every-home.html

Bennett-Smith, M. (2012, August 12). Wang Shangkun, Chinese teen who sold kidney to buy iPad, too weak to face alleged harvesters in trial. *The World Post*. Retrieved from http://www.huffingtonpost.com/2012/08/10/wang-shangkun-kidney-ipad_n_1764335.html

Berlin, L. (2003). Entrepreneurship and the rise of Silicon Valley: The career of Robert Noyce, 1956—1990. *Enterprise and Society*, *4*(4), 586–591.

Bilbatua, L., & Herrero de Haro, A. (2014). Teachers' attitudes towards computer-assisted language learning in Australia and Spain. *Círculo De Lingüística Aplicada a La Comunicación*, *57*(57), 3–44.

Blinn-Pike, L. (2009). Technology and the family: An overview from the 1980s to the present. *Marriage & Family Review*, *45*(6-8), 567–575.

Boltz, W. (1986). Early Chinese writing. *World Archaeology*, *17*(3), 420–436.

Brady, J. (2013, Spetember 2). Amish community not anti-technology just more thought. *NPR: All Tech Considered*. Retrieved from http://www.npr.org/sections/alltechconsidered/2013/09/02/217287028/amish-community-not-anti-technology-just-more-thoughful

Brinbaum, Y., & Cebolla-Boado, H. (2007). The school careers of ethnic minority youth. *Ethnicities*, *7*(3), 445–473.

Brinbaum, Y., & Kieffer, A. (2009). Trajectories of immigrants' children in secondary education in France: Differentiation and polarization. *Population-E*, *64*(3), 507–554.

Brown, P., & Levinson, S. C. (1987). *Politeness: Some universals in language usage*. New York: Cambridge University Press.

Caulfield, J. (2011). *How to design and teach a hybrid course: Achieving student-centered learning through blended classroom, online and experiential activities*. Sterling, Virginia: Publishing, LLC.

CBS News. (2014, February 24). Mark Zuckerberg on "connecting the world," and why he bought WhatsApp. Retrieved from http://www.cbsnews.com/news/mark-zuckerberg-on-connecting-the-world-and-why-he-bought-whatsapp-in-speech-at-world-mobile-congress/

Chappell, B. (2016, March 9). A.I. program from Google beats human world champ in game of Go. *NPR: The Two-Way*. Retrieved from http://www.npr.org/sections/thetwo-way/2016/03/09/469788814/ai-program-from-google-beats-human-world-champ-in-game-of-go

Cherng, R. J., Chang, C., & Chen, J. (2009). A new look at gender inequality in Chinese: A study of Chinese speakers' perception of gender-based characters. *Sex Roles*, *61*, 427–443.

Chik, A. (2014). Digital gaming and language learning: Autonomy and community. *Language Learning & Technology*, *18*(2), 85–100.

Cohen, E., & Allen, A. (2013). Toward an ideal democracy: The impact of standardization policies on the American Indian/Alaska native community and language revitalization efforts. *Educational Policy*, *27*(5), 743–769.

Conlin, J. (2014). The *Gazette Littéraire de l'Europe* and Anglo-French cultural diplomacy. *Études Épistémè*. Retrieved from http://episteme.revues.org/310

Consalvo, M. (2009). Convergence and globalization in the Japanese videogame industry. *Cinema Journal*, *48*(3), 135–141.

Crawford, J. (2004). *Educating English learners: Language diversity in the classroom*. Los Angeles: Bilingual Education Services.

Crossette, B. (2001). Diplomatically, French is a faded rose in an English garden. *The New York Times*. Retrieved from http://www.nytimes.com/2001/03/25/world/diplomatically-french-is-a-faded-rose-in-an-english-garden.html

Dawson, M. (2010). Television between analog and digital. *Journal of Popular Film & Television*, *38*(2), 95–100.

Dehaene, S. (2009). *Reading in the Brain: The Science and Evolution of a Human Invention*. New York, NY: VIKING.

Derderian-Aghajanian, A., & Wang, C. C. (2012). How culture affects on English Language Learners' (ELL's) outcomes, with Chinese and Middle Eastern immigrant students. *International Journal of Business and Social Science*, *3*(5), 172–180.

Dillon, M. (2009). *Contemporary China: An introduction*. New York, NY: Routledge.

Dong, H. (2014). *A history of the Chinese language*. New York, NY: Routledge.

Dornyei, Z., & Ushioda, E. (2009). Motivation, language identiteis and the L2 self: A theoretical overview. In Z. Dornyei & E. Ushioda (Eds.), *Motivation, language identity and the L2 self* (pp. 1–8). Bristol: Multilingual Matters.

Dunne, K., & Palvyshyn, M. (2013). Endangered species? Less commonly taught languages in the linguistic ecology of Australian higher education. *Babel*, *47*(3), 4–15.

Ebrey, P. B. (2006). *China: A cultural social political society*. Boston: Wadsworth Publishing.

Eder, D. J. (2007). Bringing Navajo storytelling practices into schools: The importance of maintaining cultural integrity. *Anthropology & Education Quarterly*, *38*(3), 278–296.

Educause Learning Initiative. (2012). 7 things you should know about flipped classrooms. *ELI Publications*. Retrieved from http://www.educause.edu/library/resources/7-things-you-should-know-about-flipped-classrooms

Edwards, L. (2003). Koscielniak, Bruce. Johannz Gutenberg and the amazing printing press. *School Library Journal*, *49*(9), 184.

Egbert, J., & Hanson-Smith, E. (2007). *CALL environments: Research, practice, and critical issues.* Alexandria, Virginia: Teachers of English to Speakers of Other Languages, Inc.

Feldscher, K. (2015, September 25). Obama wants 1 million Americans learnning Chinese by 2020. *Washington Examiner.* Retrieved from http://www.washingtonexaminer.com/obama-wants-1-million-americans-learning-chinese-by-2020/article/2572865

Feng, A. (2009). English in China convergence and divergence in policy and practice. *AILA Review, 22*(1), 85.

Fitts, S., Winstead, L., Weisman, E., Flores, S., & Valenciana, C. (2008). Coming to voice: Preparing bilingual-bicultural teachers for social justice. *Equity & Excellence in Education, 40*(3), 357–371.

Flores, S. (2005). Teaching Latino children and youth. *High School Journal, 88*(2), 1–2.

Flores, S., & Murillo, E. (2001). Power, language, and ideology: Historical and contemporary notes on the dismantling of bilingual education. *The Urban Review, 33*(3), 183–206.

Friedman, J., & Chartier, R. (1996). Gutenberg revisited from the east. *Late Imperial China, 17*(1), 1–9.

Gallardo del Puerto, F., & Gamboa, E. (2009). The evaluation of computer-mediated technology by second language teachers: Collaboration and interaction in call. *Educational Media International, 46*(2), 137–152.

García, O., & Wei, L. (2014). *Translanguaging: Language, bilingualism and education.* New York, NY: Palgrave Macmillan.

Gee, J. P., & Hayes, E. R. (2011). *Language and learning in the digital age.* New York, NY: Routledge.

Giovanangeli, A. (2009). Competing desires and realities: Language policies in the French-language classroom. *PORTAL: Journal of Multidisciplinary International Studies, 6*(1), 1–14.

Godwin-Jones, R. (2013). Emerging technologies: The technological imperative in teaching and learning less commonly taught languages. *Language Learning & Technology, 17*(1), 7–19.

Goetz, J., Kiesler, S., & Powers, A. (2003, October). Matching robot appearance and behavior to tasks to improve human-robot cooperation.*Proceedings of the 12th IEEE International Workshop on Robot and Human Interactive Communication ROMAN '03*(pp. 55-60). IEEE.

Goldberg, D., Looney, D., & Lusin, N. (2015, February 15). Enrollments in languages other than English in United States institutions of higher education. *The Modern Language Association.* Retrieved from https://www.mla.org/content/download/31180/1452509/2013_enrollment_survey.pdf

Goodrich, M. A., & Schultz, A. C. (2007). Human-robot interaction: A survey. *Foundations and Trends in Human-Computer Interaction, 1*(3), 203–275.

Grosse, C. (2010). Corporate recruiter demand for foreign language and cultural knowledge. *Global Business Languages, 3*(1), 2.

Grosse, C. U. (2004). The competitive advantage of foreign languages and cultural knowledge. *Modern Language Journal, 88*(3), 351–373.

Gualerzi, D., & Nell, E. (2010). Transformational growth in the 1990s: Government, finance and high-tech. *Review of Political Economy, 22*(1), 97–117.

Gumperz, J. J. (1982). *Discourse strategies*. New York: Cambridge University Press.

Gunaratne, S. (2001). Paper, printing and the printing press: A horizontally integrative macrohistory analysis. *Gazette, 63*(6), 459–479.

Haboud, M. (2009). Teaching foreign languages: A challenge to Ecuadorian bilingual intercultural education. *International Journal of English Studies, 9*(1), 63–80.

Hakuta, K. (1990). Language and cognition in bilingual children. In A. Padilla, C. Valdez, & H. Fairchild (Eds.), *Bilingual education: Issues and strategies* (pp. 47–59). Newbury Park, California: Sage Publications.

Hammond, K. J., & Richey, J. L. (2014). *The sage returns: Confucian revival in contemporary China*. Albany, New York, NY: State University of New York Press.

Hanada, T. (2003). Cultural diversity as social demand: The Korean minority and Japanese broadcasting. *Gazette, 65*(4-5), 389–400.

Hansen, M. H. (1999). *Lessons in being Chinese: Minority education and ethnic identity in southwest China*. Seattle, Washington: University of Washington Press.

Hawkins, J. A. (1994). *A performance theory of order and constituency*. New York, NY: Cambridge University Press.

Hayashi, K., & Lee, E. (2007). The potential of fandom and the limits of soft power: Media representations on the popularity of a Korean melodrama in Japan. *Social Science Japan Journal, 10*(2), 197–216.

Helot, C., & Young, A. (2005). The notion of diversity in language education: Policy and practice at primary level in France. *Language, Culture and Curriculum, 18*(3), 242–257.

Hill, F., Bordes, A., Sumite, C., & Weston, J. (2016, January). The Goldilocks Principle: Reading children's books with explicit memory representations. *Proceedings of the International Conference on Learning Representations ICLR '16*. Retrieved from http://arxiv.org/pdf/1511.02301v3.pdf

Holland, D., Fox, G., & Daro, V. (2008). Social movements and collective identity: A decentered dialogic view. *Anthropological Quarterly, 81*(1), 95–125.

Hubbard, P. (Ed.). (2009). Computer Assisted Language Learning: Vol. 1-4. (*Critical Concepts in Linguistics Series*). London, UK: Routledge.

Hyun, J. H. (2008). A comparative analysis of transplants and industrial location of Japanese and Korean automotive industries in Europe. *International Journal of Business, 13*(3), 215–235.

Infoplease (n. d.). Most widely spoken languages in the world. *Infoplease*. Retrieved from http://www.infoplease.com/ipa/A0775272.html

Isaacson, W. (2011). *Steve Jobs*. New York, NY: Simon & Schuster, Inc.

Ishihara, T., Itoko, T., Sato, D., Tzadok, A., & Takagi, H. (2012). Transforming Japanese archives into accessible digital books.*Proceedings of the 12th ACM/IEEE-CS Joint Conference on Digital Libraries* (pp. 91-100).

Jagers, R. T. (2001). Cultural integrity and social and emotional competence promotion: Work notes on moral competence. *The Journal of Negro Education, 70*(1-2), 59–71.

Jianli, W. (2012). Teachers' changing role in learning in higher education in China. *International Journal of E-Education, E-Business. E-Management and E-Learning, 2*(3), 223–226.

Jung, S., & Shim, D. (2014). Social distribution: K-pop fan practices in Indonesia and the 'Gangnam style' phenomenon. *International Journal of Cultural Studies, 17*(5), 485–501.

Kane, D. (2006). *The Chinese language: Its history and current usage*. Singapore: Tuttle Publishing.

Kawai, Y. (2009). Neoliberalism, nationalism, and intercultural communication: A critical analysis of Japan's neoliberal nationalism discourse under globalization. *Journal of International and Intercultural Communication, 2*(1), 16–43.

Kenney, M., Breznitz, D., & Murphree, M. (2013). Coming back home after the sun rises: Returnee entrepreneurs and growth of high tech industries. *Research Policy, 42*(2), 391–407.

Kerr, D. (2014, August 13). Apple halts use of two harmful chemicals in iPhone assembly: The tech giant bans the use of benzene and n-hexane in the final assembly of its devices and lowers the maximum use in early production phases. *CNET*. Retrieved from http://www.cnet.com/news/apple-halts-use-of-two-harmful-chemicals-in-iphone-assembly/

Khan, M. T., Humayun, A. A., Sajjad, M., & Khan, N. A. (2015). Languages in danger of death and their relationship. *Journal of Information. Business and Management, 7*(2), 239–254.

Kordon, K. (2011). Using English as a foreign language in international and multicultural consulting: Asset or hindrance? *Gruppendynamik Und Organisationsberatung, 42*(3), 285–305.

Kramsch, C. (2005). Post 9/11: Foreign languages between knowledge and power. *Applied Linguistics, 26*(4), 545–567.

Lam, A. (2007). The multi-agent model of language choice: National planning and individual volition in China. *Cambridge Journal of Education, 37*(1), 67–87.

Lamb, M. (2004). Integrative motivation in a globalizing world. *Synergy, 32*(1), 3–19.

Lankshear, C., & Knobel, M. (2006). *New literacies: Everyday practices & classroom learning* (2nd ed.). New York, NY: Open University Press and McGraw Hill.

Lawler, A. (2004). The slow deaths of writing. *Science, 305*(5680), 30–33.

Learner, A. (n. d.). Teacher resources and professional development across the curriculum. Retrieved from http://www.learner.org/series/destinos/

Leeds-Hurwitz, W. (1990). Notes in the history of intercultural communication: The Foreign Service Institute and the mandate for intercultural training. *The Quarterly Journal of Speech, 76*, 262–281.

Leu, D. J., Kinzer, C. K., Coiro, J. L., & Cammack, D. W. (2004). Toward a theory of new literacies emerging from the Internet and other information and communication technologies. In R. B. Ruddell & N. J. Unrau (Eds.), *Theoretical Models and Processes of Reading* (5th ed., pp. 1570–1613). Newark, DE: International Reading Association.

Li, Y., & Li, W. (2014). *The Language Situation in China* (Vol. 2). Boston, MA: Walter de Gruyter Inc.

Liu, C. L., Jaeger, S., & Nakagawa, M. (2004). Online recognition of Chinese characters: The state-of-the-art. *IEEE Transactions on Pattern Analysis and Machine Intelligence*, *26*(2), 198–213.

Louie, K. (2008). *The Cambridge companion to modern Chinese culture*. UK: Cambridge University Press.

Lundberg, M. (2009). Regional national autonomy and minority language rights in the PRC. *International Journal on Minority and Group Rights*, *16*(3), 399–422.

Lung, R. (2008). Translation officials of the Tang central government in medieval China. *Interpreting*, *10*(2), 175.

Mackness, J., Mak, S., & Williams, R. (2010). The ideals and reality of participating in a MOOC. In L. Dirckinck-Holmfeld, V. Hodgson, C. Jones, M. De Laat, D. McConnell, & T. Ryberg (Eds.), *Proceedings of the 7th International Conference on Networked Learning* (pp. 266-275). Lancaster, UK: University of Lancaster Press.

Matsunaga, M., & Torigoe, C. (2008). Looking at the Japan-residing Korean identities through the eyes of the "outsiders within": Application and extension of co-cultural theory. *Western Journal of Communication*, *72*(4), 349–373.

Matsuura, H., Fujieda, M., & Mahoney, S. (2004). The officialization of English and ELT in Japan: 2000. *World Englishes*, *23*(3), 471–487.

Mayer, V. (2004). Fractured categories: New writings on Latinos and stereotypes - A review essay. *Latino Studies*, *2*(3), 445–452.

McAuley, A., Stewart, B., Siemens, G., & Cormier, D. (2010). *The MOOC model for digital practice*. Retrieved from http://www.davecormier.com/edblog/wp-content/uploads/MOOC_Final.pdf

McCarthy, J. (2016, February 17). Should India's internet be free of charge or free of control? *NPR: All Tech Considered*. Retrieved from http://www.npr.org/sections/alltechconsidered/2016/02/11/466298459/should-indias-internet-be-free-of-charge-or-free-of-control

McHale, T. (1995). Digital spearheads the revolution: 1. *Electronic Buyers' News*, 38.

McKIrdy. E. (2015, February 4). China's online users more than double entire U.S. population. Retrieved from http://www.cnn.com/2015/02/03/world/china-internet-growth-2014/

Modiano, M. (2001). Linguistic imperialism, cultural integrity, and EIL. *ELT Journal*, *55*(4), 339–346.

Moore, R. (2007). An investigation of how culture shapes curriculum in early care and education programs on a Native American Indian reservation: "The drum is considered the heartbeat of the community. *Early Childhood Education Journal*, *34*(4), 251–258.

Moreno, J. B. (2012). Only English? How bilingual education can mitigate the damage of English-only. *Duke Journal of Gender Law & Policy*, *20*(1), 197–220.

Muhanna, W. (2012). Using online games for teaching English vocabulary for Jordanian students learning English as a foreign language. *Journal of College Teaching & Learning*, *9*(3), 235–244.

Nakayama, S. (2002). From PC to mobile internet—overcoming the digital divide in Japan. *Asian Journal of Social Science*, *30*(2), 239–247.

Neuman, W., Park, Y., & Panek, E. (2012). Tracking the flow of information into the home: An empirical assessment of the digital revolution in the United States, 1960-2005. *International Journal of Communication*, *6*, 1022–1041.

Ning, L. (2009). China's leadership in the world ICT industry: A successful story of its "attracting-in" and "walking-out" strategy for the development of high-tech industries? *Pacific Affairs*, *82*(1), 67–91.

Norton, B. (1997). Language, identity, and the ownership of English. *TESOL Quarterly*, *31*(3), 409–429.

Nutta, J., Feyten, C., Norwood, A., Meros, J., Yoshii, M., & Ducher, J. (2002). Exploring new frontiers: What do computers contribute to teaching foreign languages in elementary school? *Foreign Language Annals*, *35*(3), 293–306.

O'Brien, S. A. (2016, Feburary 10). Mark Zuckerberg reacts to board member's India comments. *CNN Money*. Retrieved from http://money.cnn.com/2016/02/10/technology/mark-zuckerberg-andreessen-india-facebook/index.html

Okimori, T. (2014). Korean and Japanese as Chinese-characters cultural spheres. *Acta Linguistica Asiatica*, *4*(3), 43–70.

Ostler, N. (2005). *Empires of the word: A language history of the world*. New York: HarperCollins.

Otto, S., & Pusack, J. (2009). Computer-assisted language learning authoring issues. *Modern Language Journal*, *93*(Suppl.), 784–801.

Oviedo, A., & Wildemeersch, D. (2008). Intercultural education and curricular diversification: The case of the Ecuadorian Intercultural Bilingual Education Model (MOSEIB). *Compare: A Journal of Comparative Education*, *38*(4), 455–470. doi:10.1080/03057920701860137

Oxford Chinese Dictionary. (2010). *Oxford Chinese dictionary*. New York, NY: Oxford University Press, Inc.

Padilla, A., Lindholm, K., Chen, A., Duran, R., & Hakuta, K. et al.. (1991). The English-only movement: Myths, reality, and implications for psychology. *The American Psychologist*, *46*(2), 120.

Pammi, S., Khemiri, H., Petrovska-Delacretaz, D., & Chollet, G. (2013). Detection of nonlinguistic vocalizations using ALISP sequencing.*2013 IEEE International Conference on Acoustics, Speech and Signal Processing*, 7557-7561.

Perez, B., McCarty, T. L., Watahomigie, L. J., Torres-Guzman, M. E., Dien, T., Chang, J.-M., & Nordlander, A. et al. (Eds.). (2004). *Sociocultural contexts of language and literacy*. New Jersey: Taylor & Francis.

Peters, J. D. (2013). Writing. In A. Valdivia & E. Scharrer (Eds.), *The International Encyclopedia of Media Studies: Media Effects/Media Psychology* (1st ed.). New Jersey: Blackwell Publishing Ltd.

Phillipson, R. (1998). Globalizing English: Are linguistic human rights an alternative to linguistic imperialism? *Language Sciences, 20*(1), 101–112.

Phinney, J. S., Horencyzk, G., Liebkind, K., & Vedder, P. (2001). Ethnic identity, immigration, and well-being: An interactional perspective. *The Journal of Social Issues, 57*(3), 493–510.

Pitta, D. A. (Ed.). (2009). Rosetta stone language training software: Spanish. Journal of Consumer Marketing, 26(5). Retrieved from edu/doi/full/ doi:10.1108/jcm.2009.07726eab.001

Pratto, F., Liu, J., Levin, S., Sidanius, J., Shih, M., Bachrach, H., & Hegarty, P. (2000). Social dominance orientation and the legitimization of inequality across cultures. *Journal of Cross-Cultural Psychology, 31*, 369–409.

Pratto, F., & Stewart, A. L. (2011). *Social dominance theory. The Encyclopedia of Peace Psychology.* New Jersey: Wiley-Blackwell.

Prensky, M. (2001). Digital natives, digital immigrants part 1. *On the Horizon, 9*(5), 1–6.

Pufahl, I., & Rhodes, N. (2011). Foreign language instruction in U.S. schools: Results of a national survey of elementary and secondary schools. *Foreign Language Annals, 44*(2), 258–288.

Ramsey, M., Ong, T., & Chen, H. (1998). Multilingual input system for the web-an open multimedia approach of keyboard and handwriting recognition for Chinese and Japanese.*Proceedings IEEE International Forum on Research and Technology Advances in Digital Libraries -ADL'98*, 188-194.

Reese, M. R. (2016, March 1). Google translate sings: "Hello" by Adele [Video file]. Retrieved from https://www.youtube.com/watch?v=GMi4MtyDg40

Reinders, H., & Wattana, S. (2014). Can I say something? The effects of digital gameplay on willingness to communicate. *Language Learning & Technology, 18*(2), 101–123.

Reinhardt, J., & Sykes, J. (2014). Digital game and play activity in L2 teaching and learning. *Language Learning & Technology, 18*(2), 2–8.

Report, S. (2005, June 14). "You've got to find what you love," Jobs says. *Stanford News.* Retrieved from http://news.stanford.edu/news/2005/june15/jobs-061505.html

Richardson, W. (2007). Teaching in a Web 2.0 World. *Kappa Delta Pi Record, 43*(4), 150–151.

Rivers, W., Robinson, J., Harwood, P., & Brecht, R. (2013). Language votes: Attitudes toward foreign language policies. *Foreign Language Annals, 46*(3), 329–338.

Ru, X., Lu, X., & Li, P. (Eds.). (2010). The China Society Yearbook: Vol. 4. *Chinese Academy of Social Sciences Yearbooks: Society.* Netherlands: Brill Academic Publishers.

Rubdy, R., & McKay, S. (2013). "Foreign workers" in Singapore: Conflicting discourses, language politics and the negotiation of immigrant identities. *International Journal of the Sociology of Language, 222*, 157–185.

Russell, S., & Norvig, P. (1995). Artificial Intelligence: A Modern Approach. New Jersey: Englewood Cliffs.

Ryang, S. (2012). The denationalized have no class: The banishment of Japan's Korean minority—a polemic. *CR (East Lansing, Mich.)*, *12*(1), 159–187.

Saine, P. (2012). iPods, iPads, and the SMARTBoard: Transforming literacy instruction and student learning. *New England Reading Association Journal*, *47*(2), 74.

Sang-Hun, C., & Markoff, J. (2016, March 9). Master of Go board game is walloped by Google computer program. *The New York Times*. Retrieved from http://www.nytimes.com/2016/03/10/world/asia/google-alphago-lee-se-dol.html?_r=0

Sasaki, M. (2008). The 150-year history of English language assessment in Japanese education. *Language Testing*, *25*(1), 63–83.

Schandorf, M. (2013). Mediated gesture: Paralinguistsic communication and phetic text. *Convergence*, *19*(3), 319–344.

Selyukh, A., & Domonoske, C. (2016, February 19). Apple, the FBI and iPhone encryption: A what's at stake. *NPR*. Retrieved from http://www.npr.org/sections/thetwo-way/2016/02/17/467096705/apple-the-fbi-and-iphone-encryption-a-look-at-whats-at-stake

Shaughnessey, E. L. (2006). The beginnings of writing in China. In C. Woods (Ed.), Visible Language: Inventions of writing in the Middle East and beyond. Chicago: University of Chicago Press; Retrieved from https://oi.uchicago.edu/sites/oi.uchicago.edu/files/uploads/shared/docs/oimp32.pdf

Shim, D. (2006). Hybridity and the rise of Korean popular culture in Asia. *Media Culture & Society*, *28*(1), 25–44.

Shimizu, K., Yashima, T., & Zenuk-Nishide, L. (2004). The influence of attitudes and affect on willingness to communicate and second language communication. *Language Learning*, *44*(1), 119–152.

Simplified Spelling Board. (1920). *Handbook of Simplified Spelling*. New York, NY: Simplified Spelling Board. Retrieved from https://archive.org/stream/handbooksimplif00boargoog#page/n6/mode/2up

Steinfeld, A., Fong, T., Kaber, D., Lewis, M., Scholtz, J., Schultz, A., & Goodrich, M. (2006, March). Common metrics for human-robot interaction. *Proceedings of the 1st ACM SIGCHI/SIGART conference on Human-robot interaction*. Retrieved from https://www.ri.cmu.edu/pub_files/pub4/steinfeld_aaron_m_2006_1/steinfeld_aaron_m_2006_1.pdf

Street, W. (2015). Wall St. cheat sheet: 7 reasons why we buy Japanese instead of American cars. Chatham: Newstex. Retrieved from http://search.proquest.com.lib-proxy.fullerton.edu/docview/1683369226?pq-origsite=summon

Sun, R. (2014). AMAs: China's Chopsticks Brothers win International song award. *The Hollywood Reporter*. Retrieved from http://www.hollywoodreporter.com/earshot/amas-2014-chinas-chopsticks-brothers-751585

Tang, J. (1999). The changing face of library and information science education in China in the 1990s. *Asian Libraries*, 8(1), 17–22.

Tenopir, C. (1999). Electronic reference and reference librarians: A look through the 1990s. *RSR. Reference Services Review*, 27(3), 276–280.

The New York Times. (2010, December 1). Translanguaging: An approach to bilingualism where speakers switch from one language to another. Retrieved from http://schott.blogs.nytimes.com/2010/12/01/translanguaging/?_r=0

Theisen, T. (2013). New spaces new realities: Expanding learning any time, any place. *Foreign Language Annals*, 46(2), 141–142.

Toyoshima, N. (2008). Longing for Japan: The consumption of Japanese cultural products in Thailand. *Sojourn: Journal of Social Issues in Southeast Asia*, 23(2), 252–282.

U.S. Department of State. (n.d.). U.S. Department of State: Office of the Historian. Retrieved from https://history.state.gov/milestones/1945-1952/japan-reconstruction

Valdez, E. O. (2001). Winning the battle, losing the war: Bilingual teachers and post-proposition 227. *The Urban Review*, 33(3), 237–253.

Valenciana, C. (2006). Unconstitutional deportation of Mexican Americans during the 1930's: A family history and oral history. *Multicultural Education Journal*, 13(3), 4–9.

Vecsey, C. (2007). Alfred A. Cave. Prophets of the Great Spirit: Native American revitalization movements in Eastern North America. *The American Historical Review*, 112(4), 1163–1164.

Vertovec, S. (2001). Transnationalism and identity. *Journal of Ethnic and Migration Studies*, 27(4), 573–582.

Vertovec, S. (2004). Migrant transnationalsim and modes of transformation. *International Migration Review*, 38(3), 970–1001.

Wang, C. (2012). Pre-service teachers' perceptions of learning a foreign language online: Preparing teachers to work with linguistic, cultural, and technological diversity. *International Journal of Computer-Assisted Language Learning and Teaching*, 2(2), 30–44.

Wang, C. (2015). From preservice to inservice: Can practicing foreign language learning online help teachers transfer linguistic, cultural, and technological awareness into teaching English Language Learners? *International Journal of Computer-Assisted Language Learning and Teaching*, 5(2).

Wang, J., & Postiglione, G. (2008). China's minorities without written scripts: The case of education access among the Dongxiang. *Journal of Asian Pacific Communication*, 18(2), 166.

Wang, M. (2014). An empirical study on foreign language anxiety of non-English major students: Take the sophomores in Inner Mongolia University of technology as an example. *Studies in Literature and Language*, 9(3), 128–135.

Wang, Y., & Phillion, J. (2009). Minority language policy and practice in China: The need for multicultural education. *International Journal of Multicultural Education*, 11(1).

Warf, B. (2013). Contemporary digital divides in the United States. *Tijdschrift voor Economische en Sociale Geografie, 104*(1), 1–17.

Warhol, L. (2011). Native American language policy in the United States. *Heritage Briefs Collection.* Retrieved from http://www.cal.org/heritage/pdfs/briefs/native-american-language-policy.pdf

Wenzhong, H., Grove, C., & Enping, Z. (2010). *Encountering the Chinese: A modern country, an ancient culture*. Boston: Intercultural Press.

Winstead, L. (2013). Apprehension and motivation among adolescent dual language peers: Perceptions and awareness about self-directed teaching and learning. *Language and Education, 27*(1), 1–21.

Winstead, L., & Gautreau, C. (2014). Cultural Universals as an integrated pedagogical approach for pre-service teachers. *Russian-American Education Forum: An Online Journal, 6*(2). Retrieved from http://www.rus-ameeduforum.com/content/en/?task=art&article=1001066&iid=19

Wong, L., Chai, C., & Ping, G. (2011). The Chinese input challenges for Chinese as second language learners in computer-mediated writing: An exploratory study. *TOJET: The Turkish Online Journal of Educational Technology, 10*(3), 233–248.

Wusan, D. (2014). Ancient Chinese thought of character formation and modern logo design. *Leonardo, 47*(2), 183–185.

Yap, C. (2013). Preserving the original layout of ancient Chinese texts using html5: Using Shuowen Jiezi as an example. *International Journal of Humanities and Arts Computing, 7*(supplement), 111–119.

Ye, L. (2013). Shall we delay teaching characters in teaching Chinese as a foreign language? *Foreign Language Annals, 46*(4), 610–627.

Young, A., & Helot, C. (2003). Language awareness and/or language learning in French primary schools today. *Language Awareness, 12*(3 & 4), 234–246.

Zarotsky, V., & Jaresko, G. S. (2000). Technology in education—Where do we go from here? *Journal of Pharmacy Practice, 13*(5), 373–381.

Zhang, X. (2010). The formation of East Asian world during the 4th and 5th centuries: A study based on Chinese sources. *Frontiers of History in China, 5*(4), 525–548.

Zhang, Y. (1933). *Kangxi Zidian* (Tong ban ying yin). Shanghai: Shanghai wu yin shu guan.

Zhang, Z., & Wang, Y. (2015). English language usage pattern in China mainland doctors: AME survey-001 initial analysis results. *Quantitative Imaging in Medicine and Surgery, 5*(1), 174.

Zhou, M. (2003). *Multilingualism in China: The politics of writing reforms for minority languages 1949-2002* (Vol. 89). New York, NY: Walter de Gruyter.

Zhu, G. (2014). The right to minority language instruction in schools: Negotiating competing claims in multinational china. *Human Rights Quarterly, 36*(4), 691–721.

Zuo, X. (2007). China's policy towards minority languages in globalizing age. *Transnational Curriculum Inquiry, 4*(1), 80–91.

Section 1
Commentary

Chapter 1
Reflection:
How Now Shapes the Future – Emerging Trends from the LCTL Trenches

Jacques du Plessis
University of Wisconsin-Milwaukee, USA & University of KwaZulu-Natal, South Africa

ABSTRACT

This chapter is a commentary on the state of foreign language education in the digital age.

INTRODUCTION

When it comes to learning a foreign language, Spanish makes sense as a prominent foreign language in the United States. The fast-growing population of native Spanish speakers has set a foundation for an increasingly bilingual future for the country. Recent surveys of US education indicate that Spanish has over six million learners, while French has only around one million learners, and German has close to 400,000 learners. Also, Spanish enrollments are steadily increasing, while French and German have experienced decreasing enrollments. As for other languages such as ASL, Russian, Arabic, Mandarin Chinese, and Japanese, there is either an increased or sustained interest (ACTFL Report Summary, 2011).

Given that there are over 7,000 languages in the world, it is important to ask: how should these other 99.9% of world languages feature in our education system? Why is it that, with the large number of speakers of Hindi, Javanese, Portuguese, we still face such a limited offering of foreign languages at our schools and universities?

Less-commonly taught languages (LCTLs) face the same fate – they are largely financially unsustainable (see Dunn, Kerry, and Palvynshyn, 2013; and Trotman, 2010). Excluding the elite universities that possess sufficient endowments to sustain such discretionary linguistic activities, it is not a viable option overall to broaden or even to sustain such LCTL offerings. It is important to understand why these languages are, by implication, not well positioned to survive in today's academic context in the United States. This chapter will explain how we got into this situation and it will address how the realities of today can be exploited to turn this around to alter the perspective of diversity and how to help LCTLs thrive in the current climate.

DOI: 10.4018/978-1-5225-0177-0.ch001

WHO SURVIVES?

The dramatic shift in revenue streams for public education impacts the very purpose of what a university education will be in the future. In the 1960s, state support for public higher education was around 80%. That has dwindled to below 20% today (2015). The unavoidable result has been a greater dependence on tuition dollars to sustain the enterprise, leading to greater scrutiny of the financial sustainability of every course and program. As a rather typical example, the University of Michigan explains the need to raise tuition as follows: "For the coming fiscal year (FY2016) state funding will increase 1.4 percent, which helped to keep the increase in tuition at less than the rate of inflation for in-state students. However, in the 1960s, state funding made up 80 percent of the U-M's general fund budget – the budget that pays for the university's core academic programs. In the coming year, the state appropriation will be around 16 percent of the general fund budget" (University of Michigan, 2014). The website includes the following graph to visualize this reality (see Figure 1).

While the government was a steady and reliable funder of higher education, the mission of the university offered the "universe" of knowledge for learning, exploration and research. Although the university trained students in specialization fields, there was a strong focus on critical thinking and intentional exposure to a broad diversity of ideas and thought about the cultural and intellectual richness of humanity. As the Physics Department chair at University of Wisconsin-Milwaukee so aptly put it to me, the most common profession students graduating in the physics department go into is the stock market. Their skills in forecasting, building models, and thinking critically prepares them well for this field.

When public education was largely state funded, tuition was reasonable and students felt more inclined to include courses for personal enrichment or to explore fields of interest. That is no longer the case; Vogel (2015) states that student loan debt has tripled since 2005 to $1.19 trillion. She further reports

Figure 1. State support vs. tuition and fees, 1960 - 2012

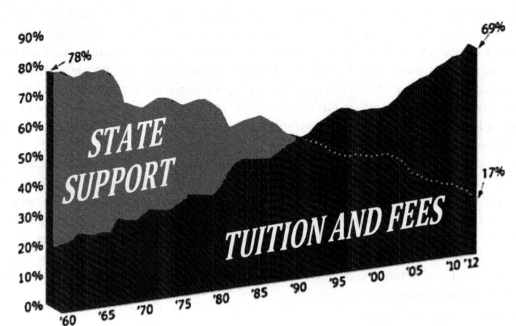

the findings that most students have no other option than to borrow money to attend college. The high cost to the student puts them under pressure to get in and out. This changed context of financial risk has consequently altered the options and focus for students.

On the university side, the change in revenue streams makes many institutions largely tuition driven. This dependence on the revenue stream alters the mission. The strength of the decision of what is being taught is influenced by what is profitable. The rounding and refinement of the student takes a back seat to concrete skills for specific jobs. The direct link between professional jobs and specific studies becomes dominant, e.g. a legal degree, or a degree in physical therapy, or in nursing, etc. Courses in the arts and humanities and elsewhere that bring sophistication to the reasoning of the students and broadening of their perspectives and ethical base have to bow to skill-based courses that directly prepare the student as a graphic designer, the teacher, the social worker, etc.

This altered context seems to be a gloomy environment for LCTLs to thrive in. Even in the traditional model it was already the case that few LCTLs had dedicated faculty lines. Teaching was, and still is, commonly performed by adjunct faculty, graduate students, or native speakers tenured in another department. Mostly large research universities were able to support some LCTLs. To find a good hour and day to teach was another difficulty. Larger, more popular courses would get the best times during the day and LCTLs would have to be taught in the late afternoon or early evenings, which created a disincentive for some students to take the class.

In this environment where tuition becomes a significant debt incursion for the student, and where budgetary woes makes it more difficult to courses with an expected low enrollment, it seems clear that only the foreign language courses with higher enrollment would remain. This chapter explores how we can reverse this unwelcome trend.

VIRTUAL WORLDS, REAL POSSIBILITIES

As a case study I will present the journey of Afrikaans, a less-commonly taught language, to show the future potential for most LCTLs in both the K-12 system as well as in higher education. This is a personal and professional reflection of what is possible in the light of the current budgetary challenges and technological possibilities.

As a child in Africa, I believed Afrikaans was big – it was my world. It serves a community from cradle to grave. In education, Afrikaans delivers from the 1st grade to PhD. Notable Afrikaans speaking public figures are Field Marshal Jan Smuts, a key figure behind the formation of the League of Nations and later the United Nations; the Nobel Peace Laureate F.W. de Klerk; the billionaire Dr. Anton Rupert; Hollywood actress Charlize Theron. Afrikaans speaker Dr. Christiaan Barnard is who performed the world's first heart transplant, while Prof. Herman Steyn recently lead the team that developed the momentum wheel for the Rosetta Philae probe that landed on a comet (Lamprecht, 2014). But the world hardly noticed Afrikaans then, nor do they notice it today. Afrikaans is part of that 99% of languages that are seen as having a "mostly-local" impact along with languages, such as Bemba, Catalan, Dutch, Estonian, Zulu, and etc. Is there a realistic alternative for most of the world's 7,000 languages that face the reality of limited interest?

I came to the USA in 1984 and started teaching Afrikaans at BYU in 1985. I taught Afrikaans there for 15 years and noticed that (as elsewhere) LCTLs stood in the back of the line when it came to the allocation of time slots. I had to teach between 4pm and 9pm. This time slot limited the interest. After my PhD in Instructional Technology, I took a tenure track position at the University of Wisconsin-Milwaukee in 2002. With my tenure line in the School of Information Studies, I was able to teach Afrikaans as needed at the college level without that enrollment affecting my employment, but other Afrikaans instructors have not been as fortunate, which threatens the overall health of the field of Afrikaans instruction in America.

Openlanguages.net: The Pantry vs. The Menu

In 2002, Open Courseware was an emerging field in academia (Wikipedia: OpenCourseWare) and I decided to port my many years of materials development into an open courseware Web offering. This resulted in the launch of www.openlanguages.net in 2004. As an open courseware platform, openlanguages' design differed from the most common designs of the time. The approach chosen is what I call the "pantry approach". The most common approach then and now is the "menu approach". With a menu approach, the content is ordered according to the expected progression of learning from beginner to advanced topics. This approach is well suited for beginners. The drawback is that there are many sequences possible as one progresses from beginner to advanced topics, so a chosen sequencing is baked into the DNA of the offering with the hope that it will be well received, now and in the future. But a drawback is that random access is not the objective of the design. If learners, because of unique life experiences, have varying abilities, the menu design does not accommodate the customized needs very well. The pantry approach on the other hand clusters the content around logical gravitational points; and within each gravitational point, a logical flow is created to order and to expand the area to a more complete offering. Openlanguages developed five key gravitational concentrations: pronunciation, vocabulary, grammar, culture, and communication, and each can be described as follows:

- Pronunciation divides into specific and holistic. The Specific section addresses all vowels, consonants, diphthongs, and diacritics individually. The Holistic section offers text and audio for songs, poems, short stories, fables, and readings.
- Vocabulary divides into many umbrella topics, with smaller subtopics, ending in a specific vocabulary list. An example of topic substructures are *People > At Home > The House – Furniture*.
- Grammar was designed as a holistic blueprint of all the major grammar features, showing the interactive potential of each. As an add on, a grammar generator was developed to allow users to practice and develop the fluid generation of grammar (http://ow.ly/U72RR).
- Culture offers information about the language, the music, history, food, humor, and etc., as well as a section in Afrikaans, including an encyclopedia of Western Music, a music section with links to many music videos on YouTube, choirs, folk songs and a list of contemporary artists. The section also contains Afrikaans readings, poetry, fables, short stories, and rhymes.
- Communication covers spoken and written communicative competencies to focus on oral and written proficiency. It is divided by topic for beginner through intermediate levels.

This design is not meant to be a linear offering. It allows for many curricula, even with divergent approaches to be layered over the same content. Should there be content that is not yet covered, it can then be added to more fully "stock the pantry". Any and all curricula could then integrate new content. Furthermore, as new educators come on board, they could peruse existing curricula and either adopt one, or modify an existing curriculum or build their own, based on their own philosophies and draw from the strengths of any of the other curricula. All items are supported with instructional modules to promote learning. Competing modules could be developed to constantly refine the best delivery of instruction and learning objects.

This open learning environment is an important infrastructure component to support the bigger vision. We will return to this development within the context of the next point which holds the key to resolving the growth of LCTLs.

Transcend the Campus

For LCTLs to be financially viable, the offering of a language has to transcend the boundaries of the campus. This proves to be a difficult obstacle to overcome. Objection to this idea is strong for predictable reasons from faculty and administrators.

The tradition of an onsite university is to develop everything in house. It is precisely the selection of what the university offers that makes it more or less attractive to prospective students. In fact, within the university this mindset is perpetuated and colleges, schools, and departments often replicate courses to compete with each other. A change to include other campuses means administration would need to think differently to be able to figure out the transfer of credit, the arrangements to pay for classes, and how to collaborate with administrators at other universities to make this a reality. The responses often heard serves the comfort and convenience of the administrator's job and does not focus on the best interests of the students. The answer might be, if they want to take a course from us, let them enroll as a non-degree seeking student, and then work with their home institution to transfer the credit. This moves all the work of figuring it out to the student and seems like an answer because it theoretically solves the problem. The truth is, this option has always existed and it has failed to deliver because the onus rests on every student over and over to figure out the bureaucracy and to manage it. Consequently, students hardly ever pursue this option. Whereas, if the administration had paved the way by addressing the administrative hurdles by creating partnerships with a plan in place, this would be an attractive and viable option for consideration and student interests would be well served.

Faculty often resist an intercampus partnership as well. This predictable resistance once again speaks of self-interest, rather than serving the best interest of the student. I have had the following feedback regarding this design to transcend campus boundaries. Let's say campus X teaches Spanish, German, and French and that their French program is not strong. The suggestion that their students could take a LCTL from another campus would not interest them. They would want to protect their French program and this intercampus partnership would be perceived as a threat to their own enrollments. Although this is a legitimate reason, the bigger question is, would you actively want to force all your students to choose between Spanish, German, and French because you perceive more options as a threat, or could you see the wider choice as an opportunity in what you could then develop on top of that? Is it our role as educators to intentionally limit the interest and academic pursuits of our students? The better next step might be to see how these new languages could be used to strengthen and add to our offering of certificates, minors, or majors.

A New Vision

The best way to describe the potential of LCTLs in the future is to simply move ahead in time and to describe the future as if it has been in place for years, rather than to suggest critical considerations to improve the current system. Once a vision is in place, the critical considerations will speak for themselves.

The new model below is based on some assumptions. Easy access to broad band internet is expected. An adequate level of computer literacy is needed. The student needs to be comfortable enough to learn and work in a paperless environment and have a familiarity with social media. Finally, it is very important for the student to be self-driven and a successful learner outside of a bricks and mortar classroom.

The model would look as follows: Sarah Samuels is about to start her freshman year and she shows up at Ruth Cohen's office. Ruth is the college's academic advisor assigned to work with prospective and new students. Sarah tells the advisor she wants to design fashions one day and that she wants to do a business degree in merchandizing and a minor in fashion design. However, she has a fascination for the cultures of south and south-east Asia, and she would first like to learn the Malay language and then learn Indonesian. The advisor says, "let me text you the link to the foreign language options you can consider" and then she asks Sarah to look over the options and to come talk with her later in the week.

Sarah goes home and she is amazed at what she finds in the south-east Asian region. Her college offers Thai, Lao, Burmese, Indonesian, Malay, Javanese, Vietnamese, and Tagalog. There are videos posted by faculty and students, talking about their experiences and what they have done with their language. There is a network of students currently enrolled, as well as past graduates, where she can ask questions about their academic path and their recommendations and caveats to her. It is important to note that the student body comes from many universities and her network reaches far wider than her college campus. She is exposed to the possibilities of study abroad, internships, teaching English in these countries, and entrepreneurial partnerships with young entrepreneurs from overseas. This leads her to surf the web some more and to do research about the other language offerings. She finally feels drawn to Javanese, spoken by close to a 100 million speakers.

She engages online with those who are in the Javanese program and she makes the connections she was hoping for, to connect her to the cultural richness of the island of Java and the traditions of their textile designs and use of color. She is excited to find the social support network and the prospects to immerse in the culture and to actually have opportunities to go to Java and experience the Javanese world intimately. She decides to pursue this language and cultural journey and returns with excitement to go talk with her adviser.

Two years later Sarah had taken four semesters of Javanese and she is about to spend six months on the island of Java. She has expanded her interests to sustainable architecture and design, and at the end of her six-month study abroad, she is signed up to do an internship with a company headquartered in Bangkok. During her study abroad she is planning to expand her language learning to include Malay and basic Thai.

Her college reports that for the past five years their alumni do far better in post-graduation placement and that more companies are eager to recruit their graduates. Because of their global connectedness, their branding has improved significantly and the success of their students tell the story for them.

That World Is Already Here

The ability and concept to transcend the campus with academic programs already exist. Study abroad is a good example. For many years there have been numerous companies specializing in offering well-designed programs all over the globe, and many universities send their students on these programs for credit without having to hire faculty and staff to develop or manage them.

Another interesting development is within virtual high schools. In Wisconsin, every school district has the option to set up a virtual high school, and students from across the state is eligible to enroll in any of the more than 30 virtual high schools (Evers, 2015). The initial expectation was for virtual high schools to be an alternative for some students, which it is. I am on the board of one of these virtual schools and they have experienced an increase in part time enrollments from students who opt to selectively take virtual courses like Chinese that are not available in their high school. Because the virtual schools can enroll students from outside of their school districts, this virtual school model is constantly adapting to inform the state leadership in K-12 education about how to lead and guide the future of education in the state. Virtual schools now have layered a new infrastructure over the traditional bricks-and-mortar schools to transcend the boundaries of traditional schooling and to avail themselves of new opportunities that are not available otherwise.

CONCLUSION

It seems like universities, with their alleged ivory tower mentality, might be late to embrace this opportunity. There is a pressing need to reform. On the one hand the costs of tuition and textbooks is unsustainable (Rogers, 2015; and Rogers, 2013). On the other hand, the opportunities that technology offers compels academia to respond to the pressing needs and to create viable opportunities for their students. This is the chance for the university to embrace the idea to become a receiver institution, to list courses that are received from elsewhere where there is not the capacity to create or sustain such courses. It is time as well for the university to become a sender institution of courses where there is capacity or the potential capacity within the framework of an intercampus inclusion of courses. This can be a win-win situation to develop a culture to serve a wider audience. In taking this step, the potential of MOOCS (Massively Open and Online Courses) can be better integrated into the bigger whole of a fast changing higher education landscape. Furthermore, the emergence of self-instructional learning should be accommodated with test-out options and courses that are based on the self-instructional model.

At this point, let us take up the discussion about the development of LCTL courses on www.openlanguages.net. This environment does not prescribe the role of the learner and attempts to make the material as friendly as possible to learners in diverse contexts. For example, such open courseware learning environments could serve the need of traditional F2F courses or online courses, as well as the needs of self-instructional learners. The argument for open courseware is compelling. Development could be a collective effort among many individuals or institutions and be kept up to date and expanded like Wikipedia is today. It also would reduce the cost to study for students internationally. Textbook prices have risen by 142.5% between 1998 and 2014, whereas recreational books have risen by 1.6% (Perry, 2013). From another perspective, consumer prices have risen by 266% from 1978 till 2015. Over the same period, textbook prices have risen by 987% (Perry, 2015). Thus, for an inter campus course to use open courseware, would enhance the value to the students served. This model enhances the branding of the program and university without incurring new financial commitments.

The future of LCTLs can be bright if we are able to respond to the fiscal realities in Higher Education today and to more fully exploit the affordances of cyberspace. Open courseware, the use of online technologies, and embracing the new mission to collaborate across campuses are vital actions in this climate to stay relevant. Institutions who effectively succeed in this new era first will be the pioneers of the face of Higher Education of the future. The deep cuts in state contributions to Higher Education have made universities far more dependent on enrollment (Strahler, 2015). This context frames universities to see each other as "the competition". Rather than undercutting each other and being locked into a competitive model, maybe reframing the vision to develop a collaborate model would offer a more sanguine and sensible solution to the difficulties of the day, for both LCTLs, but more importantly, for universities as a whole.

REFERENCES

Dunne, K., & Palvyshyn, M. (2013). Endangered Species? Less Commonly Taught Languages in the Linguistic Ecology of Australian Higher Education. *Babel, 47*(3), 4–15.

Evers, T. (2015). 2014-2015 Virtual Charter Schools. Retrieved from http://sms.dpi.wi.gov/sites/default/files/imce/sms/pdf/cs_2015_VirtualSchs.pdf

Lamprecht, S. (2014). SU Engineer helped to land Philae on comet. *Stellenbosch University*. Retrieved from http://www.sun.ac.za/english/Lists/news/DispForm.aspx?ID=1996

Oliff, P., Palacios, V., Johnson, I., & Leachman, M. (2013). Recent Deep State Higher Education Cuts May Harm Students and the Economy for Years to Come. *Center on Budget and Policy Priorities*. Retrieved from http://www.cbpp.org/research/recent-deep-state-higher-education-cuts-may-harm-students-and-the-economy-for-years-to-come

Perry, M. (2013). Chart of the day: The college textbook bubble. *AEI.org*. Retrieved from https://www.aei.org/publication/chart-of-the-day-the-college-textbook-bubble/

Perry, M. (2015). Monday night links. *AEI.org*. Retrieved from http://www.aei.org/publication/monday-night-links-10/

Rogers, J. (2015). American higher education is one of the greatest bubbles of our time. *BusinessInsider.com*. Retrieved from http://www.businessinsider.com/jim-rogers-higher-education-is-a-bubble-2015-1

Rogers, K. (2013). Did the college textbook bubble burst? *Fox Business*. Retrieved from http://www.foxbusiness.com/personal-finance/2013/10/10/college-textbooks-next-bubble-to-burst/

Strahler, S. R. (2015). Are Illinois Public Universities Doomed? *Chicago Business*. Retrieved from http://www.chicagobusiness.com/article/20150815/ISSUE01/308159989/are-illinois-public-universities-doomed

Trotman, W. (2010). The Handbook of Language Teaching. *ELT Journal, 64*(3), 342–344. doi:10.1093/elt/ccq028

University of Michigan. (2014, June). Additional Q&A About Tuition. Public Affairs & Internal Communications. Retrieved from https://publicaffairs.vpcomm.umich.edu/key-issues/tuition/additional-qa-about-tuition/

Vogel, P. (2015, October 2). Myths and Facts About the College Debt Crisis. Media Matters for America. Retrieved from http://mm4a.org/1WC9ii2

Wikipedia. (2015, November 2). OpenCourseWare. Retrieved from https://en.wikipedia.org/wiki/OpenCourseWare

Section 2
Technologies across Continents

Chapter 2
The Structural and Dialogic Aspects of Language Massive Open Online Courses (LMOOCs):
A Case Study

Carolin Fuchs
City University of Hong Kong, Hong Kong, China

ABSTRACT

This case study contributes to the growing body of research on Language Massive Open Online Courses (LMOOCs) by examining their structural aspects (i.e., layout and format) and dialogic nature (i.e., interaction and negotiation) from the language learner's perspective. This exploratory study draws on data from 15 student teachers of English as a Second/Foreign Language at a private graduate institution on the East Coast of the U.S. As required by their technology elective, participants who were enrolled in a beginner-level LMOOC of their choice kept a log of their learning process/progress over a period of eight weeks. At the end of the course, they were invited to fill out a post-project questionnaire to reflect on their overall experience. The goal of the project was to educate student teachers on the pedagogical underpinnings of LMOOCs while exposing them to online language learning. In this study, the focus was primarily on self-reported system interaction and profile data since the Author was not involved in the design of any of the LMOOCs. Data collection instruments included a needs analysis, weekly LMOOC logs, and a post-LMOOC questionnaire. According to the questionnaire results, student-teachers' motivation was "satisfactory," and only four out of 15 student teachers completed their LMOOCs. Results further showed that structural aspects (i.e., content, materials, and procedures) rank higher than dialogic aspects (i.e., scaffolding and feedback). This questions the over-reliance on content transmission and instructivist (or teacher-instruction) approaches in LMOOCs, especially since MOOCs enrolment numbers rely heavily on learner's self-motivation to sign up and complete a course.

DOI: 10.4018/978-1-5225-0177-0.ch002

BACKGROUND

Massive open online courses (or MOOCs) are an offspring of open educational resources (OERs). OERs, such as the OER Commons (https://www.oercommons.org/), offer an abundance of freely accessible learning, teaching, and testing materials for learners and teachers. MOOCs, on the other hand, are free online courses developed by start-ups or universities for anyone with Internet access. Popular providers include Coursera, edX, Khan Academy, and Udemy. Language massive open online courses (or LMOOCs) have also been developed by a number of universities (e.g., University of Pennsylvania and Carnegie Mellon University).

While MOOCs have been around since 2008, their coverage in public media had decreased by almost 50% by mid- 2014 from the peak of their media popularity in 2013 (Kovanović, Joksimović, Gašević, Siemens, & Hatala, 2015); nevertheless, language education research has recently become increasingly interested in language massive open online courses or "LMOOCs" (see edited volumes by Bárcena & Martín-Monje, 2014 and Dixon & Thomas, 2015). This is due to the potential of LMOOCs in providing more learners with free access to language education and with increasing opportunities for interactions among other learners and speakers of the target language (with the latter being the subject of communicative language teaching). By the same token, the nature of existing LMOOCs and their potential for language learning have remained underexplored. This study thus aims to advance our understanding of the structural aspects (i.e., layout and format) and dialogic nature (i.e., interaction and negotiation) of LMOOCs from the language student-teachers' perspective. More specifically, this exploratory case study investigates how language student-teachers (STs) at a private graduate school in the U.S. experienced beginner-level language MOOCs. 15 STs of English as a Second/Foreign language tracked their learning process/progress in weekly LMOOC logs as part of their spring 2015 technology elective's requirement. In this study, the focus was primarily on self-reported system interaction and profile data, since the Author was not involved in the LMOOCs' designs. Data collection instruments included a needs analysis, weekly MOOC logs, and a post-LMOOC questionnaire. The study draws on the structure and dialogue components of the transactional distance model (see Shearer, Gregg, Joo, & Graham, 2014). The structure of the course encompassed course design elements such as learning objectives, activities, assignments, and assessments. The dialogue aspects of the course refer to the meaningful interactions between teachers and learners, or among learners themselves in the distance educational context. While MOOCs can be approached from the transactional distance model in a general sense, the "massive" and "open" factors may change the dynamics of participant interactions and can also have an impact on learning outcomes (Shearer, Gregg, Joo, & Graham, 2014).

The next section will briefly review the first MOOCs, the difference between cMOOCs and xMOOCs, and prior studies on student MOOC enrollments and attrition, and their related challenges.

MOOC Types

cMOOCs vs. xMOOCs

It is important to highlight the traditional distinctions between cMOOCs and xMOOCs because of their different structural set-ups, and the interactions these differences afford language learning and teaching. Connectivist MOOCs (the "c" in cMOOC) have been considered as distributed networks in the sense that they do not run on a single website or with a centralized core of content; the content in cMOOCs is networked. In cMOOCs then, participants are encouraged to meet in locations of their choice and self-organize (Mackness, 2013). Connectivism was coined by George Siemens a little more than a decade ago, and it includes some of the following principles: Learning and knowledge are based on a diversity of opinions; learning is a process of connecting nodes or information sources; continuous learning is facilitated through nurturing and maintaining connections; decision-making is itself a learning process; and choosing what to learn and the meaning of incoming information is seen through the lens of a shifting, transient reality (Siemens, 2005). cMOOCs thus focus on principles of autonomy, diversity, openness, and interactivity (Rodriguez, 2012). In contrast, xMOOCs (the "x" comes from the open course model originally formed as MITx, which was then joined by other universities, and has evolved into edX.org) are centralized networks on one designated main platform, and interaction takes place in discussion forums (Mackness, 2013; Sokolic, 2014).

Another distinction has been made between content-based, task-based, and network-based MOOCs. Characteristics of content-based MOOCs include acquisition as instructivist (i.e., focusing on teacher instruction and on content transmission, information transmission, and (pre-) commercial), while those of task-based MOOCs focus on skill development through task completion, the success of which is dependent on collaboration. In connection with this, community creation is not necessarily the underlying goal. Network-based MOOCs are connectivist and have as their goals socially constructed knowledge and community creation (Beaven, Hauck, Comas-Quinn, Lewis, & de los Arcos, 2014).

According to Teixeira & Mota (2014), another early cMOOC, the first institutional or "iMOOC," was developed at Universidade Aberta (UAb.pt) and stressed "learner-centredness, flexibility, interaction and digital inclusion." The designers' goal was to combine autonomy and self-directed learning with a heavy focus on the interactional and social components of learning. They aimed at articulating the flexibility that distance online learners need, especially flexible pacing for adults with demanding professional and personal lives. The designers further wanted to help bridge the digital divide by making learning available to as many people as possible in the hopes that more people, in turn, would take advantage of the digital affordances (Teixeira & Mota, 2014, pp. 35).

Since the first MOOCs were cMOOCs, the bulk of early MOOC publications between 2008 and 2011 dealt with themes such as agency, connectivism, actor network theory, dangers, learner experience, pedagogies, technology, and trends. (Liyanagunawardena, Adams, & Williams, 2013). According to Teixeira & Mota's review (2014, pp. 33-34), the first non-language MOOC "Connectivism and Connective Knowledge" course (CCK08) came out from the University of Manitoba in 2008 and was based on connectivist principles (Teixeira & Mota, 2014, p. 33-34). Primary focus was placed upon participatory pedagogy, networked learning, and content-through-artefacts, rather than the transmission of a fixed body of knowledge. Resources were shared, interacted with, and reflected on in collaboration with others in the same learning community. The course organizer assigned took on the role of the facilitator and took part of that learning community: "[W]hile there was a course site, with the relevant information (weekly topics, list of suggested resources, synchronous session schedule, etc.) and Moodle forums where people could interact, the conversation was distributed by the participants' own spaces (mostly individual blogs) and several social spaces (Twitter, Facebook, Second Life, etc.)" (Teixeira & Mota, 2014, p. 33-34). Later research on discourse in the 2011 iteration of the cMOOC Connectivism and Connective Knowledge (CCK11) looked at how social media platforms (blogs, Twitter, and Facebook) affect the learning processes that shape learners' interests and the topics to which they devote significant attention (Kovanović et al., 2015).

Community and Interaction in LMOOCs

Some have argued that when "compared to cMOOCs, xMOOCs have a community problem" (Caulfield, 2013), but that students seem to self-organize in discussion groups outside of the xMOOC platform to achieve more of a cMOOC approach to discussions (Sokolic, 2014, p. 22). A recent study comparing Spanish blended, online, and MOOC courses found that higher levels of any type of interaction (learner-content, learner-learner, and learner-instructor) directly correlated with higher grades: "[Learner-learner] interaction shows the weakest, often negligible, correlation with final grades, and it is only significant in the case of the MOOC." By the same token, learner-content interaction was the strongest predictor in the MOOC course (Rubio, 2015, p. 79). Lewis, Comas-Quinn & Hauck (2015) have analyzed learner collaboration via forum postings, networking, and clustering in a translation MOOC. The authors draw on sociality theory to explain how concepts of empathy and altruism result in learners collaborating rather than engaging in individual learning styles. While cMOOCs (or network-based MOOCs) have great potential in terms of the connectivist principles that underlie this approach, this can be problematic for lower-level language learners unless the MOOC offers appropriate scaffolding (e.g., Teixeira & Mota, 2014). Scaffolding and instruction must include both the structure and dialogue of MOOCs, i.e., automated system feedback in combination with instructor feedback. Both were somewhat problematic in the beginner-level MOOCs in this study, as will be seen below.

Prior MOOC research has also focused on learning experiences and influence of learning style preferences on user intentions regarding MOOCs (Chang, Hung, & Lin, 2015, p. 528). Terras & Ramsay (2015) stressed the importance of considering the psychosocial and cognitive profiles of learners especially with regard to digital literacy skills, individual differences in motivation, and self-regulation.

Furthermore, while some researchers have pointed out that new engagement strategies are needed for face-to-face and online learners to improve course retention (de Freitas, Morgan, & Gibson, 2015; Toven-Lindsey, Rhoads, & Berdan Lozano, 2014), Sokolic (2014) stressed that goals and planning are more important than the actual MOOC platform. While instructor presence is important (Rubio, 2015; Sokolic, 2014, p. 22), it is not feasible due to the massive number of students enrolled in MOOCs. Consequently, Teixeira and Mota have argued that "learning support has to rest in the learning community, through collaboration, dialogue, peer feedback, and active engagement from participants in the learning process" (Teixeira & Mota, 2014, pp. 36).

Beaven et al. (2014) analyzed the Open University's OT12 translation LMOOC, which was not primarily a content-based MOOC since learners had to engage with its participatory elements, even if only by taking part in the group translation activities designed to use open translation tools. Beyond these tasks, however, OT12 also included "genuine opportunities for networking, which for some participants was an important aspect of the learning experience" (Beaven et al., p. 41). This points to the motivational force of learner engagement and interaction and other important dialogic aspects.

An additional challenge in MOOCs is the concept of negotiating the learning process with learners in an effort to cater to individual needs and differences. Educators have pointed out that learners create their own learning agenda, which tends to differ from the teacher's syllabus, and that the notion of the process syllabus provides a basis for jointly negotiating a learning agenda with the learner (e.g., Benson, 2011; Breen & Littlejohn, 2000). Similarly, learners need to be part of the assessment in order to empower and motivate students. This can be done through negotiating the assessment with the learner, and through providing ongoing evaluation of student progress, self-assessments, and peer reviews (e.g., Chao, 2007).

Enrolments, Motivation, and Attrition

MOOC Enrolments

According to a recent study, the highest number of participants enrolled in MOOC courses is in the sciences. For instance, a large-scale report by the MIT and Harvard on findings from two years of hosting 68 MOOCs for 1.7 million participants who logged 10 million "participant hours" of activity found that Computer Science courses had average participation numbers almost four times higher than other subjects (68,000 vs 19,000) but lower certification rates (Ho et al., 2015). In the Principles of Written English course (College Writing 2x, BerkeleyX on the edX platform), for instance, enrollment averaged about 50,000 participants per five-week segment of the course (Sokolic, 2014, p. 21).

With regard to MOOC participant profiles, Seaton, Coleman, Daries, and Chuang's (2015) study stressed the importance of integrating MOOCs into teacher education in one form or another. The authors found that a large proportion of edX learners were teachers, and that 28% of edX survey respondents identified themselves as past or present teachers. The authors questioned whether opportunities were being missed to engage teachers with MOOCs since 54% were interested in accreditation opportunities and more than 70% desired greater access to MITx materials for use in their own courses. The authors suggested that MOOC providers should include opportunities such as offering professional development for teachers, providing tools that allow teachers to customize MOOC content into "personal online courses," and providing profiling facilities so experienced teachers could identify themselves and be paired with novices to promote greater dialogue and learning.

MOOC Motivation

Intrinsic motivation goes hand in hand with learners' need to master tasks and learn different skills or competences, their need to experience a sense of belonging and relatedness to other people, and their need to feel autonomous in that they are in control of their own behaviors and goals (van Lier, 1996). While it is difficult to explore these notions in MOOCs since dissatisfied students simply drop out, some studies have tackled these issues. For instance, Sokolic (2014) included learning specific vocabulary or structures to communicate while traveling, or pursuing higher education as reasons for learners to enroll in LMOOCs. Other studies have found that learning about content ranks high among learners' motivation. For instance, learners in the "German for Spanish Speakers: Fundamentals" LMOOC included learning more about the course content and their own professional development as the main reasons for their motivation (de Larreta-Azelain, 2014, p. 77). In a similar vein, Beaven et al. found that reasons for students to join the Open University's OT12 translation LMOOC included learning more about the content (i.e. translation) and translation skills (73%), an interest in open tools and educational resources or in second language learning (29%), an opportunity for professional or work-related development (18%), and an adjunct to or a continuation of a formal course of study (16%) (Beaven et al., p. 37-38). The authors concluded that learning about the content (i.e. translation) was the main driver for joining the MOOC, and that the prospect of acquiring translation skills motivated participants to engage with a relatively unfamiliar environment (Beaven et al., 2014).

Additionally, Murray (2014) has stressed the importance of considering the social dimension: "As a part of the reflection process, learners need to have opportunities to talk about their learning. It is in small group discussions about learning that educators can begin to address the emotional dimension, and perhaps even the political dimension, by working on discursive resources" (p. 333). Formative assessment in most LMOOCs comes in the form of self-correction tests or peer feedback on course products. Participants have also been provided activity feedback in the form of different recommender systems or badges for the completion of tasks, or for relevant contributions to the community (Teixeira & Mota, 2014, pp. 37). Sokolic, on the other hand, has argued for structured self-assessment instead of peer assessments in LMOOCs (2014, p. 25). This would foreground teacher-learner dialogue.

MOOC Attrition

Despite the affordances of MOOCs (i.e., free of charge, convenience, possibility of interaction with a massive amount of other learners), some of the most frequently cited MOOC challenges include "low course completion rates, high degree of learner attrition, and the lack of a theoretical framework that would allow for better understanding of learning processes in networked learning" (Kovanović et al., 2015). Other issues include participants' (dis)satisfaction, learning support, technological environment, and the quality of the learning experience (Daniel, 2012; Holton, 2012; Kop, Fournier & Mak, 2011; Sokolic, 2014). For instance, a recent comparative study between xMOOC versus cMOOC course models showed relatively low levels of student participation in both formats (Dawson, Joksimović, Kovanović, Gašević, & Siemens, 2015). The authors concluded that the cMOOC's level of autonomy (or self-regulation) requires a high degree of intrinsic motivation and maturity from the learner to result in assessment completion. This has led others to compile a list of variables that can predict student MOOC drop-out rates, e.g., the amount of time spent per correct homework item and the amount of time spent on learning resources such as video lectures, and the proportion of time that students spend on the course that falls on the weekend (Boyer & Veeramachaneni, 2015).

Research Questions

Against the backdrop of the constraints and affordances outlined above, the next section will identify some structural and dialogic aspects of LMOOCs as experienced by language student teachers. More specifically, student teachers rated items such as content, layout, materials, feedback, interaction, and negotiation of meaning (based on SLA criteria such as interaction and negotiation of meaning, interaction in the target language with an authentic audience, involvement in authentic tasks, exposure to and encouragement to produce varied and creative language, enough task time and feedback, meaningful guidance to the learning process, an atmosphere with ideal stress and anxiety levels, and the support of learner autonomy) (see Egbert, Hanson-Smith, & Chao, 2007). Research questions were as follows:

1. How do language student teachers perceive their overall experience in beginner-level LMOOCs of their choice?
2. What structural aspects do they find conducive/not conducive to language learning? Why?
3. What is the dialogic nature of their LMOOCs?

RESEARCH DESIGN

Participants

Participants included 15 student teachers of English as a Second/Foreign Language at a private graduate institution on the East Coast of the U.S. As part of their coursework in a Spring 2015 technology elective, students enrolled in a beginner-level language MOOC of their choice kept a log of their learning process/progress over a period of eight weeks and evaluated their overall experience at the end. Their MOOC participation, weekly MOOC reflection logs, and a final analysis/evaluation questionnaire constituted 30% of their grade. The researcher-instructor (hereinafter the Author) taught the course in spring 2015.

While the teacher takes on a wide range of roles before, during, and after the MOOC, e.g., designer, organizer, facilitator, evaluator, and researcher (de Larreta-Azelain, 2014, p. 72), the focus here will be on the researcher role since she did not design the MOOCs that her STs enrolled in. Table 1 shows participants (names are pseudonyms), their language backgrounds, and the beginner-level language MOOCs they chose. It should be noted that a course such as Spanish B (see Table 1) can be defined as a MOOC

Table 1. LMOOCs and participants

LMOOCs*	Student	Program/ Semester	First Language	Other Languages
Hindi (switched from Russian)	Danu	MA TESOL K-12 2nd semester	English	Bengali, Spanish, Italian
Spanish B (switched from Spanish A)	Liam	MA TESOL K-12 2nd semester	English	Chinese, Russian
Spanish B	Aadya	MA TESOL K-12 2nd semester	Bangla	Limited Hindi and Spanish
Spanish A	Ellen	MA TESOL 2nd semester	English	Turkish
Spanish A	Yanyu	MA Bilingual Bicultural Education	Chinese	English
Italian A	Arthur	MA Applied Linguistics 2nd semester	English	Some Spanish/Korean/ Italian
Italian B	Kelly	MA TESOL 2nd semester	Chinese	English, German, Slovenian
Chinese	Si-yeon	MA Applied Linguistics 2nd semester	Korean	English, beginning Japanese, Spanish
Chinese	Billy	MA TESOL K-12 2nd semester	English	Basic Spanish, Japanese
Chinese	Padraig	MA TESOL 2nd semester	Thai	English, French
Casual Japanese Conversation	Angus	MA TESOL 2nd semester	English	Japanese, Chinese
Casual Japanese Conversation	Jenny	MA TESOL 2nd semester	English & Korean	Casual Japanese Conversation
Advanced Placement (AP) Spanish Language and Culture	Megan	MA TESOL K-12 2nd semester	English	French, Spanish, beginning Arabic
AP Spanish Language and Culture (switched from Chinese)	Ally	MA Applied Linguistics 2nd semester	English	
AP Spanish Language and Culture (switched from Russian)	Kira	MA TESOL 4th semester	English	Beginning German, Spanish

Note. *all LMOOCs are beginner-level unless otherwise noted in that it is "massive" (an unlimited number of students can enroll), "open" (in that it is freely available to anyone), 'online' (in that it is offered online), and a "course" in that the designers have laid out a pedagogical rationale as well as a course sequence for the materials. These features will be discussed in more detail below. Moreover, as discussed above, most language MOOCs do not necessarily provide for learner-learner interactions (which would place them on the cMOOCs end of the continuum), but deliver content and information for self-study purposes (which would place them on the xMOOCs end of the continuum).

As shown from Table 1, one student (Danu) enrolled in the beginner-level Hindi LMOOC, two students in Spanish B (Liam, Aadya), two students in Spanish A (Ellen, Yanyu), three students in Chinese (Si-yeon, Billy, Padraig), two students in Italian A (Arthur, Kelly), two students in Casual Japanese Conversation (Angus, Jenny), and three students in Advanced Placement (AP) Spanish Language and Culture (Megan, Ally, Kira – initially, only Megan was signed up for this course; Ally had started in the Chinese MOOC course, and Kira in the Russian MOOC but both switched to AP Spanish later).

The Spanish MOOCs were the most popular among participants. This does not seem surprising provided that Spanish MOOCs rank second (Bárcena & Martín-Monje, 2014). English, the top language, was not an option for students in this study because participants had either native or near-native proficiency. Although the main focus was on beginner-level LMOOCs, one student, Megan, wanted to take the Advanced Spanish Language and Culture course. In addition to Megan, two more STs (Ally, Kira) switched to the AP Spanish Language and Culture MOOC (Log 7) when they heard in class from Megan how well-designed the course was.

The LMOOCs: A Brief Description

The nature of the LMOOCs will be laid out briefly here before turning to the data collection and analysis procedures.

Hindi MOOC

The Hindi LMOOC is primarily a content-based MOOC in that acquisition is first and foremost instructivist with a focus on teacher instruction and content transmission (see Beaven et al.). Topics focus on introductions, greetings, getting around, shopping, and getting help. The *culture* example in the introductory video focuses on pragmatics, i.e., how not to sound rude in a different country. The *grammar* focus is on identifying masculine/feminine endings and using the demonstratives and possessives. Additionally, the Hindi MOOC shares characteristics of task-based MOOCs in that skill development is achieved through task completion. For instance, conversational goals include asking someone's name, introducing yourself and others, responding to introductions, and talking about Hindi names and famous people. However, task success does not rely on collaboration since learners work individually through a system of flashcards, nor is community creation a goal (cf. Beaven et al.). However, collaboration, engagement, and community creation are crucial factors in language learning.

Chinese

According to the Chinese for Beginners website, this MOOC is taught by an Associate Professor at the School of Chinese as a Second Language at Peking University. The course provides learners with a "basic understanding of Chinese Mandarin" (e.g., personal information, daily life, food, price, city, weather, and hobbies) needed for traveling in China for leisure or business purposes. The website promises dialogues in combination with selected reading materials and practice activities with rich and varied content to "stimulate the learners' interests." While this MOOC does not focus on the study of Chinese characters, it does provide an introduction to phonetics. This Chinese MOOC also shares characteristics of task-based MOOCs in that speaking skill development is achieved through task completion. For instance, learners participate in dialogues from real-life scenarios found in everyday communications. The course contains six hours of video and quizzes (with subtitles in English, Serbian, Urdu, and Marathi).

Casual Japanese Conversation

The Casual Japanese Conversation course focuses on casual Japanese conversation delivered via video and PDF files. Requirements include "great motivation," and students will be able to learn the Japanese alphabet (e.g., Hiragana and Katakana), how to pronounce the characters, and how to say daily phrases in casual and polite ways. The instructor describes himself as a "traveler, translator, aspiring web/mobile app developer."

Spanish A and Italian A

Spanish A, a content-based MOOC in beta version, focuses on Spanish pronunciation, introductions, pronouns, common verbs, and describing actions and activities using the present tense. According to their "Learning Methodology" website, Spanish A includes a pretest ("you'll be given an objective and you'll start trying to understand native content"), adaptive exercises ("Spanish A will identify your strengths and weaknesses, and give you exercises you need" and "Spanish A will continually adapt to your needs and help you solidify your understanding"), grammar instruction (learning the grammar principles needed for the objective through video instruction), writing assignment completion and recording, quizzes similar to the pretests, and hangouts ("Spanish A will automatically pair you with a classmate so you can practice the objective together"). (*There was no information on the Italian A LMOOC to be found on their website.)

Spanish B MOOC

According to the Spanish B website (which has been designed for English speakers who want to learn Spanish), MOOC participants will learn a version of Spanish closer to what they would hear in Latin America rather than in Spain, but the site claims that differences were "relatively small" and that everybody would be able to understand the language learner's speech. The site further lists a number of Spanish-speaking (native speaker-level) contributors to the MOOC.

AP Spanish Language and Culture

The Advanced Placement Spanish Language and Culture MOOC prepares learners for the AP Spanish Language and Culture Exam. According to publicly available information, the course is an interactive online course run by Boston University, and conducted entirely in Spanish by two Ph.D. faculty members and one M.A. lecturer. Materials include authentic written and audio texts, and students will be able to speak conversational and formal Spanish (oral presentations). Themes include contemporary life, families and communities, personal and public identity, science and technology, beauty and aesthetics, and global challenges.

DATA COLLECTION AND ANALYSIS

Data Collection

In this study, the focus was primarily on self-reported system interaction and profile data since the Author was not involved in the LMOOCs' designs (see de Larreta-Azelain, 2014). Data collection instruments include a needs analysis, weekly MOOC logs, and a post-MOOC questionnaire (all administrated via Qualtrics).

The needs analysis served the purpose of finding out about participants' prior experience and expertise with MOOCs and social networking tools as well as their experience in using technology in language teaching. In addition to demographic information about participants (e.g., linguistic, cultural, and educational backgrounds), open-ended questions elicited information regarding prior technology experience and proficiency (on a 4-point Likert Scale with 1=insufficient, 2=satisfactory, 3=good, 4=very good). These factors were deemed important because "digital literacy skills, individual differences in motivation and self-regulation are key learner attributes in the context of MOOC-based learning" (Terras & Ramsay, 2015, p. 472).

Questions in the weekly logs centered around structural aspects (such as language/skill/content foci of the MOOC activities, the content support for the activity's pedagogical goal, the use of technology to support the pedagogical goal, the clarity of activity procedures, and the use of authentic materials), as well as the dialogic nature of the MOOC (including communication/interaction/self-reflection opportunities, peer-to-peer interaction, instructor/TA feedback/error correction, self-assessments, and motivation to participate). STs were further asked to identify conditions of optimal language learning such as learner autonomy, authentic task, and optimal time and feedback based on Egbert et al. (2007).

Post-MOOC questions asked participants about whether they completed the MOOC, their top three experiences, and their overall impression of the success of their MOOCs for language learning purposes.

Data Analysis

The Likert scale items generated descriptive quantitative results, while the qualitative data (participants' open-ended questionnaire responses) were coded according to meaning units (words or phrases) that capture action and provide a "summative, salient, essence-capturing, and/or evocative attribute for a portion of language-based or visual data" (Saldaña, 2009, p.3). Egbert et al.'s optimal conditions for language learning (2007) provided the initial coding criteria, which were later categorized. The first step was to sort out the posts indicative of the optimal conditions. During the initial open coding of the qualitative data, all logs were coded based on indicators for the optimal conditions for language learning (e.g., "authentic/ity,"). Additionally, the Author identified *in vivo* codes generated by the subjects (e.g., Strauss & Corbin, 1998), e.g., "struggl/e/ing," "confus/ed/ion/ing," "difficult/y," or "impress/ed/ive." For each code, the Author judged whether the indicator represented a positive or negative conception (see Shearer et al., 2014). The following was indicated through +/- and/or if the participants used an adverb added to further define the degree (i.e., *very, quite, rather*). This example was coded *feedback (+)*: "Embedding videos and having instant feedback quizzes are good uses of tech tools (Billy, Log 2). In contrast, this was coded *feedback (–)*: "I think the lesson lacks instantaneous feedback" (Padraig, Log 2). These codes (scaffolding, feedback) were then grouped thematically to form categories under structural or dialogic aspects.

RESULTS AND DISCUSSION

Overall LMOOC Experience

With regard to the first research question (i.e., How do language student teachers perceive their overall experience in beginner-level LMOOCs of their choice?), the following was found. According to the post-MOOC questionnaire results, four of the 15 participating STs completed their MOOCs (Billy, Padgraig, Ellen, and Megan), while the majority (nine) completed their MOOC courses of choice partially, and two (Aadya and Liam) did not complete their MOOCs. The four completed MOOC courses were Chinese for Beginners (Billy and Padraig), Spanish A(Ellen), and Advanced Placement Spanish Language and Culture (Megan). The two MOOC courses that were not completed by student teachers were Spanish A (Liam), and Spanish B (Aadya).

Overall, participants' prior experience and self-rated proficiency with MOOCs ranked between "insufficient" and "satisfactory" (1.86). This is along the lines of the Open University's study on their open translation MOOC, which found that only three out of 196 respondents had prior experience with online courses, but not with MOOCs (Beaven et al., p. 4).

Structural Aspects of LMOOCs

In terms of the second research question (i.e., What structural aspects do language student teachers find conducive/not conducive to language learning? Why?), the following items were ranked the highest (between "good" and "satisfactory"): *Structure of layout* (2.74), and *structure of content* (2.65), *authentic language materials* (2.63), *theme-based curriculum* (2.56), *opportunities for self-assessment* (2.40), *size of the MOOC* (2.29), and *opportunities for reflection* (2.25). According to their weekly MOOC logs, STs ranked items relating to the structural nature higher (e.g., layout and content of the MOOC, authenticity of materials, as well as opportunities for self-assessment/self-reflection) than items relating to the dialogic nature (e.g., the structure of the /interaction/communication, as well as their overall motivation to complete the MOOC). In order to explore these aspects further, the following sub-sections will explore participants' qualitative comments with regard to the different LMOOCs by drawing on STs' reflections regarding their LMOOCs' structural aspects (i.e., content and layout) and dialogic nature (i.e., interaction and negotiation).

Hindi MOOC

The Author first draws on data from Danu, a second-semester K-12 student teacher with prior teaching and technology experience, and one of the few students who rated her prior MOOC proficiency as "good" (3.0) - in contrast to the participants' mean of 1.86 (N=14). Danu initially starts out taking a beginner Russian MOOC, about which she comments in her Log 1: "the most boring thing ever." She then switches to the Hindi MOOC (beginning Hindi), for which she completes a total of two logs (Logs 2, 3), and which she partially completes.

In her first weekly log regarding her enrolment in the Hindi MOOC, Danu mentions that the language focus is on basic questions and answers for common scenarios, e.g., weather, and introductions (in formal/informal contexts). Danu thinks the procedures of the activity are very clear ("[j]ust click the arrow to move forward," Log 2). Danu further believes not only are the technology tools easy to use, but also the user interface is pleasant to look at and easy to navigate. Each lesson is presented in the form of a series of digital flashcards with content ranging from teaching and practicing a new phrase or word to providing grammatical or historical information. The content is transmitted in small chunks through flashcards and a voice saying the word, so learners are not overwhelmed with information and can slowly build up their skills and knowledge. Every lesson has several flash cards that allows students to review contents from previous lessons through random pop-ups before quizzing the learner (Log 3).

In both logs, Danu rates the authentic materials "very good." She also feels that learners are involved in authentic tasks and that learners work in an environment with an ideal stress/anxiety level; however, the latter is not specified further. She points out in Logs 2 and 3 that the voices reading everything out loud (in English or in Hindi) are authentic recordings of real people (varying between male and female). She finds them very friendly, clear to understand, easy to listen to, and encouraging; except she is unclear whether learners are to record themselves speaking out loud the sample dialogue they heard or not. "Although I speak everything aloud, I can imagine other learners just flipping through the cards quickly, reading and listening without speaking aloud" (Log 3).

Additionally, in her logs, opportunities for reflection change positively from "satisfactory" to "good," whereas opportunities for self-assessment turn from "very good" to "good."

In sum, it seems that the Hindi MOOC tasks allow learners to review and proceed at their own pace and work in a self-directed manner and that the flashcard delivery breaks down the content into manageable chunks which allows for recycling of materials. The final comment, however, implies that the system allows for 'cheating' in cases where learners are not intrinsically motivated to complete the speaking-aloud task.

Chinese MOOC

According to Padraig (with prior teaching experience and a self-reported prior MOOC proficiency of "satisfactory"), the content focus is on helping learners with proper pronunciation of Chinese sounds (Log 3). One focus is on describing and asking about the kinship titles of family members, the vocabulary words for counting, asking about time (What time is it now?), and talking about different times during the day and daily arrangements (your daily routines). The content focuses on building a stronger knowledge and getting an idea of how sentences are constructed in Chinese in a variety of daily situations (and mostly popular conversational topics). He feels that the content supports the goal of this activity of both understanding contents in Chinese and being able to properly construct language to successfully communicate: "The content presented efficiently illustrates how Chinese is used compared to English in these situations" (Log 3). Padraig further states that the slides enhance the lectures because they include Chinese characters that learners can match with the English equivalents. The audio recordings also support the self-evaluation test at the end of the activity since it allows for learners to replay. The procedures of the activity are well-constructed. Si-yeon (with prior teaching experience and a self-reported prior MOOC proficiency of "very good") and Billy (with prior teaching experience and a self-reported prior MOOC proficiency of "good") agree as well: "I think the procedure is very clear. It felt intuitive," Billy, Log1). Topics are relevant and build on previous content; however, Padraig feels there is not enough time to practice. In terms of authentic materials, he thinks that since the content focuses on vocabulary that students are likely to encounter, the words are relevant and meaningful for enhancing communicative skills (e.g., food, dishes). However, Billy thinks there is not enough time for learners to repeat after the instructor (Log 1). Like the Hindi MOOC, this LMOOC is content-based in that acquisition is instructivist and focuses on content transmission through lectures and slides. While procedures are clear, there does not seem to be enough scaffolding and practice time.

Casual Japanese Conversation MOOC

Angus (with prior teaching experience and a self-reported prior MOOC proficiency of "insufficient") and Jenny (who has no prior teaching experience and does not provide any self-rating for prior MOOC proficiency) both take this course. In his Log 4, Angus provides feedback on the program's missing support, scaffolding and feedback: "Lectures do not support language learning. Students need to practice using the language. You can repeat after the instructor but do not get any feedback." In his Log 6, Angus further mentions that the procedures given are not very clear, and that "the content on [this MOOC] is very basic and does not include enough information, examples, or models" (Angus, Log 8).

This MOOC also seems to prioritize the structural aspects (i.e., content transmission) through video lectures and supporting text materials.

Spanish A and Italian A

With regard to the Spanish A procedures, Liam (with prior teaching experience and a self-reported prior MOOC proficiency of "insufficient") finds the procedures of the exercises clear, but the interface of Spanish A confusing (Log 1).

Ellen (with prior teaching experience and a self-reported prior MOOC proficiency of "insufficient") believes the Spanish A procedures are clear. However, she concedes that this might have been simply due to the fact that the procedures were always the same and that she must have gotten used to them: "No instructions again. The procedures are clear to me as I've gotten used to the program, however there is no follow- up with the meaning of the contexts. Each context seems to be quite different than the next" (Ellen, Log 5).

Yanyu (with prior teaching experience and a self-reported prior MOOC proficiency of "insufficient") has mixed feelings about the Spanish A course. She thinks that the interface is "really good" in her first log:

As Egbert points out, the students need to be mindful/motivated about performing the task in order to have any sort of language learning success (condition 6). I would say the user interface of [Spanish A]is really good, and the designer make the language learning more like a game by asking students to unlock different chapters (Yanyu, Log 1).

In her second log, Yanyu expresses some confusion about the content, though: "Honestly speaking, though the course represents the content twice, once with English translation, and once simply Spanish. I still feel very confused to understand the meaning of the content" (Log 2). In a subsequent log it is unclear whether she considers the "super long conversation" a constraint or an affordance: "The Spanish A program presents a super long conversation presenting how different Spanish speakers would act when they start communicating. Typically, everyone starts with the same language structure. The repetitive greetings do help learners to familiarize the key vocabulary and language structure (Yanyu, Log 5). While it seems that the repetitive nature of Spanish A can aid with rote memorization, there appears to be a lack of feedback.

In a similar vein, with regard to format, instructions, and procedures of the Italian A, Arthur (with prior teaching experience and a self-reported prior MOOC proficiency of "insufficient") thinks the Italian A course is set up well due to the intuitive content, clear directions, and through target sentences and language in a number of different contexts by different people in the video:

At the beginning of the section videos of Italian speakers were used to present the target sentences. Also when the user clicks on any word in a written sentence (besides the blank) an immediate English translation is presented to help the user determine what the missing word might be. There are also scales on the screen that show you how many questions you have gotten right (in terms of stars) and how many questions you have gotten wrong (in terms of loosing "lives" or "hearts"). These were effective motivators for not just clicking random answers until you get the correct one as you cannot complete a level unless you get a certain score (Arthur, Log 1).

Later on, however, Arthur feels that verbs such as "muffle, evade, unscrew" are "far too obscure" for teaching beginners (Arthur, Log 6). Moreover, in his Log 8, Arthur points out the malfunctioning of one listening comprehension activity that automatically yielded a score of 0% for the user. Arthur complains about this via the "send a comment" function.

Kelly likes that the Italian A MOOC allows "users to work on their own, and at their own pace" (Log 2), and Ellen also enjoys the fact that she can work at her own pace:

I also appreciated the fact that I could listen and work on my own (at my own pace) in the comfort of my apartment while doing this work--if I had been in a classroom and given this task, I think I would have completely given up. So I think there is great value in learning about pronunciation features of a language in a language learning environment such as this, however the complete lack of guidance is overwhelming (Ellen, Log 1).

However, Ellen stresses on several occasions that there are not enough instructions and that there is not enough guidance:

This is the area where this activity really needs improvement. There were no instructions so the first few seconds of the activity I had no idea what I was doing. Second, [Spanish A's] listening activities have this intense time-limit aspect where you must select the correct answer within maybe 10 seconds or you 'loose points'-- for such an activity like this, more think time is needed and this needs to be considered. Also, there was no follow up to clarify the meanings of the words that I missed (again 75%) so I was left wondering what words I had learned (Ellen, Log 3).

In terms of authenticity, a number of STs provide positive examples. Arthur primarily writes about the Italian children's songs and videos he engages in. He enjoys the "somewhat authentic" materials, which is supported by Kelly, who agrees on the "authentic input" of the Italian song (Kelly, Log 2). Arthur states the following with regard to what he likes about the Italian A MOOC:

The music video section was created very well as it used authentic Italian music videos to teacher vocabulary and get the learner familiar with listening and pronunciation. [...] It was also helpful to have the easily accessible direct translation function during every activity in the mooc as I could look up the meaning of any familiar words on the spot without leaving the page (Arthur, Post-MOOC Q.).

While Arthur emphasizes the "catchy chorus" of the songs (Arthur, Post-MOOC Q.), he also feels that three music videos in a row are "annoying" (Arthur, Log 5). Liam also starts out enjoying the videos on the Spanish A because the song is "quite catchy," but he also feels that it gets "annoying after a while" (Liam, Log 1).

By the same token, Arthur writes that "the least engaging and least authentic portion of the mooc" is the song in the absence of an activity. The directive asks to "'listen to the song and your ear will tune to the language.'" But, according to Arthur, there is no motivation to listen to the song as there is no task related to it. He thinks it is "frustrating and boring at the same time," and that it "would have been nice to put the sounds in the context of words to make it a little more interesting" (Arthur, Log 2).

Spanish B MOOC

The "interactive game format" (Log 5) eventually triggers Liam's switch from Spanish A to Spanish B. He finds the interactive game format motivating and it makes him "want to keep getting correct answers." He likes the game-like structure of Spanish B and wishes that more language courses were structured in that way and that the sounds, graphics, and the game format all come together "in a great way" (Liam, Log 5). The language focus of Spanish B includes different conjugations for personal pronouns and verbs in Spanish and the possessive case for personal pronouns in Spanish (Liam, Log 6). What Liam likes in particular is that the games focused on an integrated approach for testing, i.e., on all four skills: "The games in [Spanish B] support the pedagogical goal by testing all four modalities - speaking, reading, writing, and listening. The learner must use all four modalities if he wants to progress to the next level" (Liam, Log 7). In addition to the interactive nature of the games on the Spanish B, Liam also thinks the layout is better compared to Spanish A. He believes that Spanish B is more appropriate for beginner-level learners:

Overall, I find that [Spanish B] is a huge improvement from [Spanish A]. The layout is uncluttered, and it is easy to understand. Also, it is much more fun to complete. Compared to the [Spanish A] exercises (listen to a song and fill in the blank), the [Spanish B] exercises seem to be much more targeted at beginners and fun, to boot" (Liam, Log 5). [...] I have found using this mobile app to be pleasant and fun. It is a great choice to put this language learning app on the cellphone. It is easy to click 3 buttons and form a sentence. (On the computer, I would have to point and click with a mouse, but here, selecting an answer is just a thumbprint away.)" (Liam, Log 7).

Throughout their logs, both Aadya (with prior teaching experience and a self-reported prior MOOC proficiency of "insufficient") and Liam mention that the procedures of the Spanish B MOOC are "clear," "very clear," or "extremely clear." According to Liam, "[t]he procedures are formatted like a game. They are so simple that I believe a child could do it" (Liam, Log 5).

Aadya also comments on the lack of feedback of the Spanish B MOOC in an activity asks learners to identify animals through pictures:

The strength bars of the previously learned words were low so I had to study the flashcards and test myself on them. Then I had to redo the lessons with those words in them to strenghten [sic] the bars. [...] Reviewing with the flashcard had no interactive sounds like the other activities I did so it felt like there was no feedback, which was not motivating. I felt like I was just using a deck of vocabulary words instead of using a piece of technology to learn (Aadya, Log 3).

Finally, Liam expresses concerns about long-term language learning when comparing the two Spanish MOOCs, Spanish A and Spanish B:

Overall, I think that I have experienced all that [Spanish B] has to offer. I've now spent about the same amount of hours on [Spanish B] than I have on [Spanish A]. The problem with [Spanish A] was that the layout was hard to use and the exercises - especially the guess the words in the song game - became tedious quickly. Meanwhile, with [Spanish B], the layout is clear and the games are addicting. However, because of the game format, I don't think that i'm retaining as much information as I would if I were viewing the video lectures on [Spanish A]. It seems that both platforms have their drawbacks. I am considering switching into another language MOOC for the next log (Liam, Log 7).

In sum, with regard to Spanish A and Italian A, the use of videos and songs seems attractive at first but feels monotonous after a while. In a similar vein, the game-like formats such as in Spanish B seem attractive to learners at first, but can leave them wondering about the overall learning outcome.

AP Spanish Language and Culture

The AP Spanish Language and Culture MOOC receives high ratings (between "good" and "very good") from Megan for all items throughout. For instance, in her Log 8, she underlines the high quality of the videos and the content-based approach to teaching the language: "It was really cool to see the MOOC teacher and her spanish [sic] speaking colleagues discussing the art in a way that seemed complex but linguistically clear to model as a student." Megan also feels the questions in the quiz about the cultural video are very clear, and points out on several occasions that the procedures are "clear." She enjoys the fact that they can choose a work of art from a region of their choice and that "the task of analyzing art itself was very authentic." Moreover, she feels "the content was really focused on the discussion of art itself but through the vehicle of Spanish," and that materials cater to laypeople without an art history background (Log 8). This seems to be along the lines of Rubio's research findings (2015), which discovered that a (mixed-level) Spanish MOOCs focused less on language development and more on the acquisition of content knowledge.

Dialogic Nature of the LMOOCs

In terms of the third research question (i.e., What is the dialogic nature of their MOOCs?), STs rated the following dialogical aspects of their LMOOCs low (between "satisfactory" and "insufficient"): *Opportunities for intercultural interaction* (2.03), *opportunities for authentic communication* (1.99), *peer-to-peer negotiation* (1.72), *instructor feedback and error correction* (1.64), *instructor collaboration* (1.62), and *TA feedback and error correction* (1.53). Finally, motivation of participants to engage with the content, participate in the course discussion, and complete the course for the benefit of all was ranked "satisfactory" (2.05). There were 52 negative and 43 positive comments regarding feedback, and this section will look more closely at participants' qualitative comments.

Hindi MOOC

In the Hindi MOOC, opportunities for authentic communication fall from "very good" to "good" in both of Danu's logs, and instructor collaboration and peer-to-peer negotiation are rated "insufficient" in both logs. Intercultural interaction also drops from "satisfactory" (Log 2) to "insufficient" (Log 3), even though Danu feels that learners have opportunities to interact and negotiate meaning (Log 2), she does not specify this further, however. There is no evidence of learner-learner interaction in any of her MOOC logs.

Danu further reports practicing speaking out loud after listening to the website's program. She stresses in both logs that although learners have enough time, there is "no feedback whatsoever." This is also reflected in her ratings, in which instructor feedback and error correction turn negatively from "satisfactory" to "insufficient," and in which TA feedback and error correction is "insufficient" on both occasions. Her motivation to engage with the content, participate in the course discussion, and complete the course for the benefit of all, change positively from "insufficient" in her initial log to "very good" in her subsequent log. However, it is not clear what causes Danu to not complete the Hindi MOOC.

Chinese MOOC

Si-yeon points out that the presentation in lecture format does not provide opportunities for interaction or negotiation of meaning. Even though the Chinese MOOC has a comment section for each lecture where learners could post questions about the content, that comment section is in English rather than the target language, which precludes interaction in the target language with an authentic audience (Si-yeon, Log 1). Padraig, on the other hand, attributes the lack of interaction to the fact that the course is delivered online ("on-line learning do [sic] not support interactions, found in the classroom," Log 2). In a similar vein, Billy concedes that "the ability to speak and interact in authentic environments is limited. This makes sense, given the nature of the MOOC," (Log 2). Even though it seems understood that the MOOC should be treated as a different instructional format from in-class or online due to its unique features "massive" and "open," Si-yeon points out that the lack of interaction seems inherent, but that personalization and feedback could compensate for this shortcoming: "The course could require us to record our voices about our own daily life (with relation to culture) and upload it so that we can receive feedback. It would personalize the experience so that I could relate to the content more easily" (Si-yeon, Log 4).

In the Chinese MOOC, task success does not seem to rely on collaboration since learners work through quizzes on their own, nor does community creation seem to be a goal (cf. Beaven et al.).

Casual Japanese Conversation MOOC

Angus' comments regarding level of difficulty and instructor collaboration and feedback are particularly self-evident provided that he has some background in Japanese:

I wanted to see how this course was, even though I have some background in Japanese, I think this course could serve as a good refresher but to learn as it is designed, from a total beginners perspective I would find it very challenging. I do not think it meets the optimal conditions for language learning. I checked to see if students were willing to post and there seems to be several that do post but the most recent reply from the instructor was about 7 months ago (Angus, Log 4).

He underlines that the Japanese MOOC is not conducive to language learning in a subsequent log ("As with all content-based MOOCs I have seen on [this provider] I find that this course does not meet the conditions for optimal language learning," Angus, Log 5). In his final log, Angus mentions that even though he understands that the course is directed at beginners, "the information provided does not really allow students to do much with the language" (Log 8). It seems that the dialogic nature of this MOOC is also limited, and that the learner-content interaction in this MOOC cannot seem to compensate for this to facilitate his language learning (cf. Rubio, 2015).

Spanish/Italian A and Spanish/Italian B MOOCs

As with the other LMOOCs discussed so far, most STs point out issues with interaction and negotiation in the case of the Italian A and Spanish A MOOCs. For instance, Ellen highlights that the most interesting activity allows her "to interact with the language" by ordering syllables in Spanish words, and that this is the most negotiated meaning she has done. "This activity, compared to the many activities I've completed, seemed to be the most interesting and really allowed me to interact with the language – especially the fact that I had to order the syllables in Spanish words. I think this is really the most I've negotiated meaning, hands on, in this MOOC" (Ellen, Log 6). Here, it appears as if negotiation of meaning is perceived as interacting with the task or program as opposed to interacting with another speaker. However, negotiation of meaning generally requires another interlocutor or person to interact with (Egbert et al.).

Overall, there the dialogic nature of the Spanish/Italian A and Spanish/Italian B MOOCs seem to fall short in that there is no interaction involving instructor or peers. Like in the other MOOCs, task success does not rely on collaboration since learners work individually through the exercises and quizzes. Despite the "hangouts" function, community creation does not seem to be a goal (cf. Beaven, et al.).

AP Spanish Language and Culture MOOC

With regard to the AP Spanish Language and Culture MOOC, Megan stresses that she has to negotiate meaning and interact with the material, but does not mention if this includes any interactions with other learners of the target language. However, in the same log, she mentions that they have "the most interaction with [their] teacher," which she appreciates a great deal. She does not go into detail, however, in terms of the nature of the interaction. Kira finds it very helpful to watch the professor pronounce the sounds "because I am able to mimic how her face looks when she makes the sounds" (Log 8). Megan further states that it is "cool to see her not just giving us directions, but facilitating a discussion of art." In addition to praising for the structural aspects of this AP Spanish MOOC as discussed above, the dialogic elements especially with regard to teacher interaction were also valued highly. Nonetheless, it is unclear if peer interaction occurs and to what extent.

CONCLUSION AND RECOMMENDATIONS

This study set out to explore student teachers' experience in (beginner-level) language MOOCs. First, the overall experience was explored by looking at completion rates. Second, structural aspects such as content, layout, and procedures as well as feedback functions were analyzed. Third, the dialogic nature of LMOOCs was examined since interaction and negotiation of meaning with other speakers of the target language play a vital role in language learning.

With regard to the overall MOOC experience, according to the post-MOOC questionnaire results, four of the 15 participating STs completed their MOOCs, while the majority (nine) completed their MOOC courses partially, and two did not complete their MOOCs.

Furthermore, the structural aspects of the LMOOCs (i.e., procedures and content) were ranked higher than the dialogic features (i.e., interaction and negotiation) of the beginner-level LMOOCs - with the exception of the AP Spanish course. For instance, it seems that a game-like course format can be advantageous for language learning but that there is also a need for more differentiation and individualized feedback in order to effectively recycle materials. But this may be difficult to achieve in a course with a "massive" number of students – especially at the beginner levels due to learners' limited linguistic proficiency. It appears that this has been achieved more successfully in the AP Spanish LMOOC. By the same token, an over-reliance on content is counter to SLA-grounded research on language learning and best practices in language teaching (cf. Egbert et al.).

The general lack of interaction and negotiation is evidenced in the low ratings of the dialogic aspects of the majority of LMOOCs. To this end, STs seemed rather dissatisfied with the learner-teacher/TA interaction ("the instructor prepared a lot of drilling sessions […] the instructor was too ambitious" Yanyu, Log 8; "lectures do not support language learning," Angus, Log 4). The number of positive versus negative comments regarding feedback/correction was balanced, however it becomes evident that the feedback/correction did not involve human but machine interaction. While this may not be an issue since learner-content interaction seems to be the strongest predictor for student success in MOOCs (Rubio, 2015), these findings may have impacted student motivation and resulted in the rather low completion rate of the LMOOCs in this study (only 4 out of 15). This is particularly interesting given that enrolment was not optional but a mandatory part of the technology elective for STs. In order to tap into learner motivation more, MOOC designers would thus need to combine the philosophy of cMOOCs and the structure in the xMOOCs since "engagement, community, membership, communication and creativity are highlighted as key features for effective LMOOCs" (Bárcena & Martín-Monje, 2014, p.8).

One limitation of the study was that MOOC enrolment and documentation were required elements of STs' elective course. This may have prevented participants to set "real" initial goals for why they wanted to participate in their particular MOOCs of choice, and what specifically they wanted to learn. In contrast, Beaven et al. (2014), Teixeira & Mota (2014), and Sokolic (2014) have all highlighted the importance of goal-setting because MOOCs are very different learning environments and they do not mean the same thing to everyone. Nonetheless, participants in this study explicitly stated their reasons for dropping out or for switching their MOOC (which is something that seems to have been underexplored in LMOOCs to this date).

Another limitation is how the actual elective and the in-class MOOC discussions may have shaped participants' perception of their LMOOC experiences. It is also unclear if/how results improved or did not improve as STs were getting more comfortable with the language. This might have been the case in the AP Spanish MOOC since it was not a beginner-level MOOC. It could be the case that STs enrolled in that course were already able to understand what was going on in the MOOC.

Future research should entail further in-depth case studies of student teachers taking different LMOOCs. Student teachers would need to provide a detailed profile of themselves, i.e., their prior teaching and learning experience (with/without technology), their teaching beliefs and approaches, as well as their attitudes and experiences toward online learning. Ideally, they would also be able to state their motivation for enrolling in an LMOOC and set language learning goals, which they regularly revisit. Additionally, large-scale survey studies would allow for covering and comparing a wider number of LMOOCs. It would be interesting to see if participants end up taking the same LMOOC, and if/how their experiences differ especially with regard to the dialogic nature of the course.

ACKNOWLEDGMENT

I wish to thank all project participants for their time, effort, and dedication. I would also like to thank Cameron Lee as well as two anonymous reviewers for their insightful comments on a previous draft of this paper.

REFERENCES

Bárcena, E., & Martín-Monje, E. (2014). Introduction. LMOOCs: An emerging field. In E. Martín-Monje & E. Bárcena (Eds.), *Language MOOCs: Providing Learning, Transcending Boundaries* (pp. 1–15). Warsaw: De Gruyter Open.

Beaven, T., Codreanu, T., & Creuzé, A. (2014). Motivation in a MOOC, Issues for course designers. In E. Martín-Monje & E. Bárcena (Eds.), *Language MOOCs: Providing Learning, Transcending Boundaries* (pp. 48–66). Warsaw: De Gruyter Open.

Beaven, T., Hauck, M., Comas-Quinn, A., Lewis, T., & de los Arcos, B. (2014). MOOCs: Striking the right balance between facilitation and self-determination. *MERLOT Journal of Online Learning and Teaching*, *10*(1), 31–43.

Benson, P. (2011). *Teaching and researching autonomy* (2nd ed.). London, UK: Longman.

Boyer, S., & Veeramachaneni, K. (2015). Transfer learning for predictive models in massive open online courses. In C. Conati, N. Heffernan, A. Mitrovic, & M. F. Verdejo (Eds.), Artificial Intelligence in Education, LNCS (Vol. 9112, pp. 54-63). Switzerland: Springer International. doi:10.1007/978-3-319-19773-9_6

Breen, M., & Littlejohn, A. (Eds.), (2000). *Classroom decision-making: Negotiation and process syllabuses in practice*. Cambridge, UK: Cambridge University.

Caulfield, M. (2013). *xMOOC Communities Should Learn From cMOOCs*. Retrieved from EduCause Review website: http://www.educause.edu/blogs/mcaulfield/xmooc-communities-should-learn-cmoocs

Chang, R., Hung, Y., & Lin, C. (2015). Experiential online development for educators: The example of the Carpe Diem MOOC. *British Journal of Educational Technology*, *46*(3), 528–541. doi:10.1111/bjet.12275

Chao, C. (2007). Theory and research: New emphases of assessment. In J. Egbert & E. Hanson-Smith (Eds.), *CALL environments: Research, practice, and critical issues* (2nd ed., pp. 227–240). Alexandria, VA: TESOL.

Colpaert, J. (2014). Conclusion. Reflections on present and future: Towards an ontological approach to LMOOCs. In E. Martín-Monje & E. Bárcena (Eds.), *Language MOOCs: Providing Learning, Transcending Boundaries* (pp. 161–170). Warsaw: De Gruyter Open. doi:10.2478/9783110420067.10

Daniel, J. (2012). Making sense of MOOCs: Musings in a maze of myth, paradox and possibility. *Journal of Interactive Media in Education*. Retrieved from http://www-jime.open.ac.uk/jime/article/viewArticle/2012-18/html

Dawson, S., Joksimović, S., Kovanović, V., Gašević, D., & Siemens, G. (2015). Recognizing learner autonomy: Lessons and reflections from a joint x/cMOOC. *Proceedings of HERDSA conference*. Retrieved from http://www.sfu.ca/~dgasevic/papers_shared/herdsa15.pdf

de Freitas, S., Morgan, J., & Gibson, D. (2015). Will MOOCs transform learning and teaching in higher education? Engagement and course retention in online learning provision. *British Journal of Educational Technology*, *46*(3), 455–471. doi:10.1111/bjet.12268

de Larreta-Azelain, M. (2014). Language teaching in MOOCs: The integral role of the instructor. In E. Martín-Monje & E. Bárcena (Eds.), *Language MOOCs: Providing learning, transcending boundaries* (pp. 67–90). Warsaw: De Gruyter Open. doi:10.2478/9783110420067.5

Dixon, E., & Thomas, M. (Eds.). (2015). *Researching Language Learner Interactions Online: From Social Media to MOOCs*. San Marcos, TX: CALICO.

Egbert, J., Hanson-Smith, E., & Chao, C. (2007). Foundations for teaching and learning. In J. Egbert & E. Hanson-Smith (Eds.), *CALL environments: Research, practice, and critical issues* (2nd ed., pp. 1–14). Alexandria, VA: TESOL.

Ho, A., Chuang, I., Reich, J., Coleman, C., Whitehill, J., Northcutt, C.,... Petersen, R. (2015). *HarvardX and MITx: Two Years of Open Online Courses Fall 2012-Summer 2014*. Retrieved from Social Science Research Network website: http://ssrn.com/abstract=2586847

Holton, D. (2012). *What's the "problem" with MOOCs?* Retrieved from EdTechDav website: https://edtechdev.wordpress.com/2012/05/04/whats-the-problem-with-moocs/

Joksimović, S., Kovanović, V., Jovanović, J., Zouaq, A., Gašević, D., & Hatala, M. (2015). What do cMOOC participants talk about in Social Media? A Topic Analysis of Discourse in a cMOOC. *Paper presented at the5th International Conference on Learning Analytics & Knowledge* (pp. 156-165). New York, NY: ACM.

Kop, R., Fournier, H., & Mak, S. (2011). A pedagogy of abundance or a pedagogy to support Human beings? Participant support on Massive Open Online Courses. *International Review of Research in Open and Distance Learning (Special Issue - Emergent Learning, Connections. Design for Learning)*, *12*(7), 74–93.

Kovanović, V., Joksimović, S., Gašević, D., Siemens, G., & Hatala, M. (2015). What public media reveals about MOOCs: A systematic analysis of news reports. *British Journal of Educational Technology*, *46*(3), 510–527. doi:10.1111/bjet.12277

Lewis, T. Comas-Quinn, & Hauck, M. (2015). Clustering, collaboration, and community: Sociality at work in a cMOOC. In E. Dixon & M. Thomas (Eds.), Researching language learner interactions online: From social media to MOOCs (pp. 45-61). San Marcos, TX: CALICO.

Liyanagunawardena, T., Adams, A., & Williams, S. (2013). MOOCs: A systematic study of the published literature 2008-2012. *International Review of Research in Open and Distance Learning*, *14*(3). Retrieved from http://www.irrodl.org/index.php/irrodl/article/view/1455/2531

Mackness, J. (2013). *cMOOCs and xMOOCs - key differences*. Retrieved from https://jennymackness.wordpress.com/2013/10/22/cmoocs-and-xmoocs-key-differences/

Murray, G. (2014). The social dimensions of learner autonomy and self-regulated learning. *Studies in self-access learning journal, 5*(4), 320-341.

Read, T. (2014). The archetectonics of language MOOCs. In E. Martín-Monje & E. Bárcena (Eds.), *Language MOOCs: Providing learning, transcending boundaries* (pp. 91–105). Warsaw: De Gruyter Open.

Rodriguez, C. (2012). MOOCs and the AI-Stanford like Courses: Two Successful and Distinct Course Formats for Massive Open Online Courses. *European Journal of Open, Distance and E-Learning, II*, 1–13.

Rubio, F. (2015). The role of interaction in MOOCs and traditional technology-enhanced courses. In E. Dixon & M. Thomas (Eds.), *Researching language learner interaction online: From social media to MOOCs* (pp. 63–88). San Marcos, TX: CALICO.

Saldaña, J. (2009). *The coding manual for qualitative researchers*. Los Angeles, CA: SAGE.

Seaton, D., Coleman, C., Daries, J., & Chuang, I. (2015). Enrollment in MITx MOOCs: Are we educating educators? *EduCause Review*. Retrieved from http://er.educause.edu/articles/2015/2/enrollment-in-mitx-moocs-are-we-educating-educators

Shearer, R., Gregg, A., Joo, K., & Graham, K. (2014). Transactional Distance in MOOCs: A critical analysis of dialogue, structure, and learner autonomy. *Paper presented at the 55th Adult Education Research Conference*, Middletown, PA, Penn State Harrisburg.

Siemens, G. (2005). Connectivism: A learning theory for the digital age. *Instructional Technology & Digital Learning, 2*(1).

Sokolic, M. (2014). What constitutes an effective language MOOC? In E. Martín-Monje & E. Bárcena (Eds.), *Language MOOCs: Providing learning, transcending boundaries* (pp. 16–32). Warsaw: De Gruyter Open.

Strauss, A., & Corbin, J. (1998). *Basics of qualitative research: techniques and procedures for developing grounded theory* (2nd ed.). London, UK: SAGE.

Teixeira, A., & Mota, J. (2014). A proposal for the methodological design of collaborative language MOOCs. In E. Martín-Monje & E. Bárcena (Eds.), *Language MOOCs: Providing learning, transcending boundaries* (pp. 33–47). Warsaw: De Gruyter Open. doi:10.2478/9783110420067.3

Terras, M., & Ramsay, J. (2015). Massive open online courses (MOOCs): Insights and challenges from a psychological perspective. *British Journal of Educational Technology*, *46*(3), 472–487. doi:10.1111/bjet.12274

Toven-Lindsey, B., Rhoads, R., & Lozano, J. (2015). Virtually unlimited classrooms: Pedagogical practices in massive open online courses. *The Internet and Higher Education*, *24*, 1–12. doi:10.1016/j.iheduc.2014.07.001

van Lier. (1996). *Interaction in the language curriculum: Awareness, autonomy, authenticity*. New York, NY: Longman.

KEY TERMS AND DEFINITIONS

Affordance: A feature or characteristic of something that makes it easier for its users to perform an action.

Blog: A website (originally "web log") that functions like a journal or diary where people share their personal experiences.

cMOOC: Connectivist MOOC (based on connectivist principles) does not run on a single website and allows its participants to meet elsewhere and self-organize.

Connectivism: A new theory of learning for the digital ages coined by George Siemens (2005) that integrates principles of different theories such as chaos, network, complexity and self-organization theories.

Constraint: A feature or characteristic of something that makes it harder for its users to perform an action.

iMOOC: Institutional MOOC.

Instructivism: Teacher-fronted instruction (vs. learner-centered).

LMOOC: Language Massive Open Online Course.

MOOC: Massive Open Online Course.

OER: Open Educational Resources.

xMOOC: Formerly the MITx model, now: edX.org (content-transmission model).

Chapter 3
Mind Your Hashtags:
A Sociopragmatic Study of Student Interpretations of French Native Speakers' Tweets

Geraldine Blattner
Florida Atlantic University, USA

Amanda Dalola
The University of South Carolina, USA

Lara Lomicka
The University of South Carolina, USA

ABSTRACT

This chapter explores how French language learners in three different second and third year French courses (intermediate and advanced levels) understand and interpret hashtags using the popular microblogging tool Twitter. The present study highlights how this social media service may provide an authentic and dynamic platform that enhances the language learning experience, while developing students' multiliteracy skills in a second language (L2). Data from 18 students at a large southeastern university were examined via 579 analyzed tweets, 171 of which contained hashtags. In this project, we investigate the relationship between students' ability to access information in the hashtags and to understand the nature of the larger tweet in which it appears. The results of this study suggest that language learners have a tendency to glance over the hashtags and make guesses based on the information contained therein. The incorporation of cultural and linguistic elements linked to microbloggers' social tagging is an interesting and important aspect to add in foreign language classes. Learning about and understanding hashtags can promote the development of noticing cultural references, a skill that is indispensable for successful autonomous communication across national boundaries and for online communicative practices.

DOI: 10.4018/978-1-5225-0177-0.ch003

INTRODUCTION

Following the social networking media explosion, online communities have been the focus of a variety of applied linguistic and second language acquisition (SLA) studies. Scholars have attempted to integrate these new communicative platforms into both teaching and learning in higher education. One tool that has grown in popularity over the last decade is Twitter. This tool allows people to tweet short text messages, often from a mobile device, in order to disseminate a thought, opinion, or a feeling. Lakarnachua and Wasanasomsithi (2014) note that Twitter blends features of both blogging and social networking. It is often utilized for short spontaneous communication. In educational research, Twitter's role as a learning tool has shown potential in myriad ways over the last few years. Microblogging can provide opportunities for learning to take place out of the classroom, and it can serve as a tool for collaborating with experts (Lord & Lomicka, 2014; Wesely, 2013). It also offers both access and mobility (Antenos-Conforti, 2009), provides authenticity in learning (Lomicka & Lord, 2012), fosters student engagement and involvement (Ragueso, 2010), serves as a knowledge-sharing tool (Dennen & Jiang, 2012), and is participatory, authentic, and immediate (Antenos-Conforti, 2009).

In order to grow the current body of literature on Twitter, we explore a less researched area of this microblogging tool – the use of hashtags and how learners of French understand the ways in which native speakers employ them. Hashtags were first used in chat forums in the 1990's in order to categorize items into groups. While Twitter did not invent hashtags (they first appeared on Twitter in 2007), the microblogging tool did help hashtags to reach surprising levels of popularity, meriting further study (D'Cunha, 2014). After much success on Twitter, other digital platforms, such as Instagram, Facebook, Google+, and Pinterest adopted hashtags for both personal and professional ventures. Users now tag keywords, phrases and strings of text to search for and track conversations and topics. Hashtags can also be used to show humor, sarcasm and to assign meaning to a post. When using hashtags, it is important to be specific and to cater hashtags to the corresponding social media network. Hashtags should be relevant, not too long, and they should not consume the message. We chose to explore hashtags using Twitter because hashtags were linked to this tool before other social networking platforms. To that end, the present chapter focuses on the incorporation of the microblogging platform Twitter in the context of second language (L2) classes, and addresses the potential linguistic benefits of such an addition from a teaching and learning perspective.

REVIEW OF THE LITERATURE

Social Media in Language Teaching and Learning

There is evidence that the use of social media is helpful and provides much needed resources in the context of language teaching and learning. For instance, scholars have investigated the potential of electronic discussion forums as a tool to develop intercultural communicative competence and digital literacy (see for example: Farrell Whitworth, 2009, Hanna & de Nooy, 2003; 2009), and found that integrating a task that forces learners to interact in an authentic communicative setting with native speakers was a linguistically constructive improvement to their L2 education. In a similar vein, Sotillo (2009) and Lee (2009) both conclude that chat-based activities help to increase learners' awareness of linguistic L2 forms, especially less standard varieties, such as abbreviations and colloquial expressions.

In addition to chat and forums, Facebook has been the focus of a number of investigations. Some of these studies have looked at the language learners' ability to communicate and interpret meaning in social interactions. Mills' (2011) work, for example, illustrates that using Facebook can facilitate the development of a sense of community, and create both a positive and dynamic engagement between learners. Integrating this social media has also proven to be beneficial for enhancing socio-pragmatic features that L2 learners studied even at the beginning level (Blattner & Fiori, 2009; Blattner & Fiori, 2011; Blattner, 2011; Reinhardt & Zander, 2011Blattner & Lomicka, 2012). Recently, Wang and Vasquez (2014) investigated the impact of using Facebook as a writing platform, and suggested that there was a significant difference in terms of the quantity of writing, as students made more updates to their assignment on the social media than in a traditional environment. Across social media, there seems to be a consensus that electronic and social tools are invaluable for various reasons for the apprenticeship of foreign languages. Our particular study looks at the microblogging tool Twitter and students' understanding of hashtags in the language learning context.

FEATURES OF TWITTER AND ITS ACADEMIC POTENTIAL IN L2 ACQUISITION

The social networking tool that continues to gain popularity and is, consequently, becoming the focus of more educational research is Twitter. Butler (2010) defined this microblogging service as a communication platform, as well as a personal and professional outlet; it has also been identified as an environment where information is shared and relationships are built (Trubitt & Overhotlzer, 2009). Aydin (2014) explains that higher education institutions use Twitter regularly to engage alumni, students and faculty or to inform them of closings, emergencies, and other public safety issues on campus. This trend illustrates the fact that many educators and students have a Twitter account and are already familiar with this online social tool. Shweiki media confirms that 80% of college students use Twitter, which comes in just behind Facebook (95%). In that respect, the use of Twitter is on the rise in academia, even among university professors, who, according to Rogers (2013) are increasingly using Twitter in education because it contributes to a more engaging learning environment. However, Symmons (2013), for example, in a study conducted on how professors use Twitter, finds that as a teaching tool, Twitter was not as popular as other social media tools in the classroom. She indicates that professors prefer to use Twitter as a source for gaining knowledge, accessing external information and staying up to date in their respective fields of study and expertise. However, Symmons also suggests that Twitter's use in the classroom is steadily on the rise. It is not surprising then that in the past few years, scholars have begun to conduct studies to investigate the potential of Twitter as an instructional tool. Considering Twitter's social goal, and its penetration into the educational setting, studies (e.g. Dunlap & Lowenthal, 2009; Ferguson, 2010) have discovered that Twitter, within an educational context, can extend the space limitation of physical classrooms, encourage participation, promote knowledge sharing, and facilitate informal learning within the community.

In microblogging platforms such as Twitter, early developments have primarily examined tweets at the surface level, through frequency counts as a way to develop competence and also through opportunities to build community. For example, Antenos-Conforti (2009) suggested that the incorporation of Twitter can extend the physical L2 classroom, as it provides a space that encourages participation and fosters a sense of community. In another early L2 study, Perifanou (2009) conducted research using Edmodo (as a microblogging tool) in an Italian language class with 10 second-year students. Using sociocultural theory to frame the study, tweets were analyzed for frequency counts. Other studies using Twitter in

L2 contexts have generally focused on the areas of student production of tweets and student analysis of tweets. While the production of tweets may increase students' L2 output, the analysis of tweets exposes students to L2 input, which are both vital to L2 learning.

The first study to explore Twitter within an L2 context was Antenos-Conforti (2009). Twenty-two participants enrolled in university-level intermediate Italian tweeted for one semester. Her data, documenting frequency and distribution of tweets, were analyzed in addition to a Likert questionnaire and a follow-up free-response questionnaire. Results suggested that the use of Twitter helped to create a virtual extension of the physical classroom, fostered community, and encouraged participation among students. Likewise, Hattem (2012) used structured grammatical tasks to encourage noticing using the Twitter. Forty-nine students participated in the seven-week study, where more than 3500 tweets were collected and analyzed. Results suggested that microblogging can help students to notice target language structures. Lomicka and Lord (2012) examine the role of communicating with native French speakers in the context of an intermediate French class. Their findings reveale that the students rapidly created a collaborative community in which they shared valuable and constructive information, illustrating how this microblogging tool can become an appropriate venue for language practice and cultural exchange outside the classroom. Castrillo de Larreta-Azelain (2013) investigated learner attitudes toward using Twitter in collaborative writing in German classes. Using a mixed-methods study, Castrillo de Larreta-Azelain used various sources of data, including tweets and a pre- and post-questionnaire. Findings suggest that students were able to create a new learning community, and that the Twitter task allowed students to practice writing competence. More recently, Fornara (2015) examined whether an instructor modeling L2 usage could affect students' use of the L2 on Twitter. Ninety-three students taking Italian 2 were included in a control and experimental group, who tweeted during an academic semester. Tweets were tallied and analyzed via tweetdownload.net (easily downloads all of your data from Twitter) and pre and post surveys were administered. Results included both the number of new vocabulary items and the grammar structures used in tweets. There were no significant findings across the two groups; however, students indicated that they believed that Twitter was a useful tool, and that it provided them with additional opportunities for practicing vocabulary and grammar. Results also found that the presence of a co-tweeting instructor did not significantly influence student use of these features.

In addition to studies in which students produced tweets, other work has outlined ways in which students can benefit from analyzing native speaker tweets. For example, Blattner, Dalola and Lomicka (2015; 2016) investigated the benefits of integrating Twitter in first-year French classes as a tool to expose L2 learners to authentic and culturally rich linguistic input. The focus of their analysis was on how learners understood the tweets of well-known French speakers, emphasizing particular linguistic elements, such as the interpretation of English words and abbreviations. The results suggested that their participants did not become "tweetsmart" when it came to identifying English borrowings and abbreviations; however, their project gave these beginning L2 learners an enriching opportunity to better understand an L2 in an authentic and informal context. They discovered that students became aware of widespread use of the English language in this microblogging tool, which is an accurate representation of the prolific lexical borrowing happening at present in French-speaking countries. In addition, they noted that their participants struggled to accurately identify and interpret most of the abbreviations they encountered, highlighting their challenge with interpreting language they have never or rarely encountered in their language textbooks, despite its popularity in authentic language and electronic social media environments, such as Twitter. All in all, their findings in both studies underscored that the act of analyzing these tweets assisted students in developing their comprehension of cross-cultural pragmatics and enhanced their digital literacy skills.

These studies suggest that Twitter has positive effects on the learning process of socio-pragmatic elements, and also exposes students to an array of lexical items, such as borrowings and abbreviations, which are typically omitted from language textbooks due to their judged informality or substandard nature. While many aspects of Twitter have been investigated, other aspects such as hashtags, have been less common in the L2 setting. While much research explores the potential of new instructional methods using technology and mobile learning, our project adds to the scope of L2 sociopragmatic teaching and research on the microblogging tool Twitter, which has also been the focus of recent investigations.

Hashtags in Twitter

In the past few years, a new social process has emerged to make discourse readily findable by others –the process of hashtagging. A small number of scholars have investigated the function and role of hashtags from linguistic or communication perspectives (Bastos et al. 2012; Kehoe & Gee, 2011; Scott, 2015; Zappavigna, 2012; 2015a). These studies have identified that a hashtag is a label for content that is marked with a # symbol and may include a word, initialism, concatenated phrase (a series of linked words), or an entire clause (Zappavigna, 2015b, p.1). Tags have several key functions that include the ability 1) to assist one in locating a target audience; 2) to send high volumes of information and content to a select group; 3) to categorize tweets, and 4) to participate in chats based on shared interests. Tweets containing hashtags typically receive more engagement than those that do not. Hashtags can be a key semiotic resource supporting searchability in social media discourse (Zappavigna, 2015a). Twitter is thus seen as a movement towards "searchable talk" (Zappavigna, 2012), which enables individuals to search social media discourse and give them an ability to find similar tweets in quasi 'real-time' (Zappavigna, 2015a). In other words, social affiliation can equate to large-scale practices and social tagging, if the L2 hashtag is understood.

L2 learners need to understand not only the words in the hashtags themselves, but also be able to identify the boundaries when they are attached in a longer string. In addition, as Zappavigna (2015a) underscores, hashtags perform different types of meaning. Hashtags typically indicate the semantic domain of a post (e.g. *#meteo* (gloss: weather)), link a post to an existing collective practice (e.g. *#vacances* (gloss: vacation)) or make: "an emotionally charged metacomment" (p.275) (e.g. *#jecroisquejepreferefumer* (gloss: I think I'd rather smoke)). Clearly, tags are more than an inherent part of a tweet; these keywords are often essential to a post and to extending a discussion on a particular topic. Since the origin of hashtags in the microblogging service Twitter, Zappavigna (2015b) explains that they have since spread to other forms of social media and mediated contexts such as television and advertising, highlighting how linguistically preeminent they have become. In her work on the pragmatics of hashtags, Scott (2015) argues that while they are important to search functionality, they are also appropriated by users to perform other roles in the communicative process. She concludes that by allowing tweeters to make intended contextual assumptions accessible to readers, "hashtags facilitate the use of an informal, casual style, even in the unpredictable and largely anonymous discourse context of Twitter" (p. 8). In other words, hashtags seem to bring us closer to bridging the gap between the formal language taught in foreign language classrooms and the informal colloquialisms frequently used, not only in social media, but also in casual spoken communication among native speakers.

All things considered, the role of hashtags in language learning has remained relatively untouched. To our knowledge, only one study, Solmaz (in press), has examined the role of hashtags in the language learning context. Hashtags can be used in myriad ways, such as to help connect learners with each other and with the content material, to examine the engagement rate of tweets, to model authenticity and to promote communication. In this recent study, Solmaz uses an ecological framework to explore the potential of hashtags, in situations where hashtags are convention markers for annotating the content of tweets. Using an autoethnographic approach, he analyzes his own Twitter experiences in his target language during a six-month period. He examines hashtags both qualitatively and quantitatively and suggests that they can create affiliation with target language speakers and allow students to better reach out to them in their communities and join in on authentic conversations. Our study builds upon Solmaz's work by looking at another unique aspect of hashtags: how native speaker hashtags are understood by language learners.

RESEARCH QUESTIONS

The research questions of the present study explore the following areas:

1.   What are the different structural and functional types of hashtags in French, and how well do L2 learners understand them?
2.   What types of information can L2 learners infer and extract from L2 hashtags?
3.   What types of information are L2 learners unable to infer and extract from L2 hashtags?

METHODS

Participants

Participants were recruited on a voluntary basis from three second- and third-year French courses (intermediate and advanced levels) at a southeastern university in the United States during the fall semester of 2015. 25 students participated in a series of guided tasks using Twitter—only 18 analyzed tweets that contained hashtags. Information on the participants' demographics, linguistic background and experience with social media was solicited via a short background survey (see Appendix A). Of the 18 participants, there were seven males and eleven females, ranging in age from 16-72 years (mean = 24.9; mode = 21). Eight in the group were new to Twitter, while the other ten had been regular users for a range of 3-72 months (mean = 33.9; standard deviation: 19.7). Ten of the participants were enrolled in second-year French studies (7 in third semester, 3 in fourth semester), while eight were enrolled in third-year French studies (all in fifth semester).

Materials

Similar to grammatical and lexical knowledge, pragmatic competence appears to benefit from the SLA framework of noticing. Schmidt's (1993, 2001) noticing hypothesis is viewed as "the strongest impetus for pragmatic intervention" (Taguchi, 2011, p. 291). That said, a learner's first step to acquiring L2 pragmatic features is to notice linguistic forms, functional meanings, and relevant contextual structures in the input. In other words this project aims to provide input and practice opportunities to learners who can develop an implicit understanding of pragmatic forms and their uses in the selected electronic medium: Twitter.

Tasks

Guided by the theoretical concept of noticing (Schmidt 1993; 2001), this study explores the effectiveness of an instructional approach (through guided tasks) to develop sociopragmatic awareness in French learners, by specifically involving learners' engagement with hashtags. The project consisted of a weekly linguistic analysis of tweets: students were instructed to join or log into their pre-existing Twitter account, and select three personalities to follow for the duration of the project. These personalities came from a list of pre-selected French native speakers, divided into two categories: "Entertainment", composed of comedians, sports figures and musicians, of which the students chose two to follow, and "News groups", of which the students chose one to follow. Each week, participants completed the questionnaire for each tweet that they chose to analyze, resulting in three tweets per week (one for each personality they followed) for a period of 10 weeks (=30 analyses total). They documented each analyzed tweet by capturing it in a screenshot (see Appendix B for an example) and submitting the image with their analysis (see Appendix C for a copy of the linguistic questionnaire students completed for each tweet). A number of questions in this analysis addressed students' recognition and understanding of hashtags, by asking them to first identify each hashtag and then make sense of them in the context of the larger tweet in which they were embedded. Once the task had been completed, students shared their reactions to it in a short post-task questionnaire (see Appendix D).

Analysis

Our analysis investigates the relationship between students' ability to access information embedded in hashtags, as a function of the content of the larger tweet. We measure this skill via their ability to parse and contextualize hashtags at the micro and macro levels. Each of the 579 French-language tweets and its corresponding analysis was inspected individually for the presence of hashtags. 171 of the tweets contained 245 hashtags that were further examined. Questions from the guided linguistic task pertaining to these hashtags were then scored for correctness and evaluated according to the following parameters:

1. Did the participant correctly identify each and all of the tweet's hashtags?
2. Did the participant over-identify material in the tweet as hashtags?
3. Did the hashtag(s) contain any iconic cues, e.g. acronyms, capital letters delineating word boundaries, numbers, abbreviations, emoticons, etc.?
4. Were participants able to click on a hashtag and correctly classify its following as small, medium or large?
5. Were participants able to translate the content of each hashtag into English?
6. Were participants able to explain why the tweeter had included the hashtag(s)?
7. Did the hashtag(s) directly reinforce any supplemental visual cue presented in the tweet, e.g. an attached picture or video?
8. What was the nature of any comprehension errors that occurred? Token counts and percentages for each subgroup were tabulated alongside textual examples from the tweets.

In the sections that follow, we will discuss the nature of the hashtags in our corpus, cite the numbers and types of success and failures, and then examine the relationship between the comprehension of hashtags and the comprehension of the larger tweet.

RESULTS

The following sub-sections present the results of the hashtag analysis of native French speaker tweets, carried out by intermediate and advanced L2 French learners. The components that will be discussed cover questions 15-19 in Appendix C. Due to space limitations, the other components are not within the scope of this chapter.

Collection of Hashtags

Table 1 shows a classification of each hashtag based on following size. Participants determined this information by clicking on each hashtag and observing the number of tweets that contained it. "Small" followings were those that yielded a short, finite list of tweets containing it; this was typical of comments, reactions and other novel and unestablished creations. "Medium" followings contained longer, finite lists, typical of events and places that were less well-known and/or had a spelling in French that was different in other languages. "Large" followings were identified by an infinite list that kept populating after several scrolls; this was typical of well-known events and places, and/or those whose name was spelled the same way in French as in other languages.

Hashtag following size is of interest in this study because the linguistic questionnaire asked participants to explain the content and motivation of each hashtag in a tweet, only after having clicked on it to observe its distribution in the larger Twitter medium. Given that hashtags with larger followings tend to index subjects that are common (e.g. *#meteo, #litterature*), visible on an international level, e.g. *#newyork, #Lufthansa*, or depicted by the same word(s) across several languages (e.g. *#MissionImpossible, #audiences*), we would expect French learners to have a higher success rate in this category. This is because they are likely to be familiar with common French words, international themes and items that are cognates with English, their first language. Conversely, given that hashtags with small followings tend to index unique reactions, e.g. *#jecroisquejepreferefumer*, and unestablished responses crafted in the moment, e.g. *#departpourlanorvege*, we would expect French learners to have a lower success rate in this category. This is because the ability to make sense of the hashtag not only requires the ability to know the meaning of the words appearing in it, but also to know where to draw the boundary between several words that run together. These predictions were borne out, as shown in the "percent correct"

Table 1. Hashtags organized by following size

Following Size	% of Total HTs	% Correct	Examples
Small	56/245 (22.9%)	39/56 (69.6%)	*#fiertépuissancemille, #entomologie, #NeLesOubliezPas*
Medium	2/245 (1%)	1/2 (50%)	*#JourdeSouvenir, #gadaucine*
Large	187/245 (76%)	152/187 (81.3%)	*#Paris, #DALS, #KohLanta, #TV5Monde, #newyork, #NRJ*

column in Table 1. See Figure 1 for an example where a participant had no iconic cues, i.e. capital letters, to help them determine word boundaries, and ended up misparsing the individual elements of an unestablished hashtag. As Zappavigna (2015b) explained, this misparsing phenomenon is not unusual with native speakers (and sometimes even challenging), especially if the latter are relatively new to the microblogging sphere. In fact, similar to ambiguous sentences (i.e., high attachment, low attachment, garden path constructions), there are ambiguous hashtags that can lead to multiple interpretations depending on how one identifies possible word boundaries (i.e., #nowthatcherisdead →1. Now Thatcher is dead 2. Now that Cher is dead).

- **Actual Hashtag Translations:** #Hollande (=French president), *#SansDents* (=how Hollande referred to the poor in private, due to their bad hygiene), *#Trierweiler* (Hollande's ex-partner), *#paspuresister* (=*pas pu résister*, "I couldn't resist" (here, making this joke))
- **Participant's Hashtag Translations:** *#Hollande* (=French president), *#SansDents* (=without teeth), *#Trierweiler* (=another person), *#paspuresister* (=pas pure sister, "There is a woman (maybe his real sister?) and she must have done something wrong.")

Structural Typology of Hashtags

The corpus of 245 hashtags exhibited three recurring structural patterns, shown in Table 2. Table 3 displays the five recurring iconic features that were observed, i.e. typeface, letter size, and presence of accent marks, numbers, abbreviations and acronyms. All 245 of the tweets can be described by one, or a combination of two or more, of the features listed in Tables 2 and 3. In the case where hashtags were missing accents in the orthography (Table 3), the relevant letter(s) appear underlined and in boldface.

A large percentage of the hashtags in the corpus were single grammatical words, as revealed in Table 2; however, similar correctness percentages were attested across all four structural types. Table 3 reveals a small number of accented letters written without their accent, yet shows that participants were rarely thrown off by their absence (for similar findings in other electronic media, see van Compernolle

Figure 1. Hashtag with small following and no iconic cues leads to misparse

Table 2. Structural features of NS French tweets

	% of Total HTs	% Correct	Examples
One Grammatical Word	65/245 (26.5%)	52/65 (80%)	*#montréalaise,#respect, #allez, #innovateur, #fun*
Article + Noun	11/245 (4.5%)	8/11 (72.7%)	*#LesStagiaires, #laquotidienne, #LesInfiltres, #TaFête, #LesMiller*
Short phrases	29/245 (11.8%)	23/29 (79.3%)	*#quellelionne, #CourageJules, #SansDents, #paspuresister, #greatestalltime, #oupresque, #departpourlanorvege, #gadaucine*
Full sentences	4 /245 (1.6%)	3/4 (75%)	*#Elleladore, #NeLesOubliezPas, #jecroisquejepreferefumer, #PartageonsDesOndesPositives*

Table 3. Iconic features of NS French tweets

	% of Total HTs	% Correct	Examples
Using caps to delineate word boundaries	54/245 (22%)	49/54 (90.7%)	*#CoupeDavis, #InfoDuJour, #ChansonPourUneAutre*
(Containing) Acronyms	42/245 (17.1%)	31/42 (73.8%)	*#ASIAM, #confJDCV, #RDS, #LNH, #JO*
(Containing) Abbreviations	2/245 (1%)	2/2 (100%)	*#mtl, #confJDCV*
(Containing) Numbers	31/245 (12.7%)	23/31 (74.2%)	*#15x15, #TV5MONDE, #20ansF5, #Gad20ans, #20livresF5*
Lacking accents found in standard French orthography	23/245 (9.4%)	20/23 (87%)	*#b e b e , #gadaucine, #quellelecondevie, #departpourlanorvege, #jecroisquejepreferefumer*
Emoticons	2/245 (1%)	2/2 (100%)	*#<3*

and Williams, 2007; 2011; van Compernolle, 2011). High comprehension rates are noted here among hashtags using capital letters to overtly mark word boundaries and those containing emoticons and abbreviations. Of all the forms of iconicity manifested by hashtags, the participants had the most difficulty making sense of acronyms, a finding previously identified in a similar study examining the behavior of first-year French learners (Blattner, Dalola & Lomicka, 2015; 2016). For example, the French hashtag #JO, an acronym for for *Jeux Olympiques* 'Olympic Games', was often mistaken for a single word or a proper noun, further obstructing or misleading subsequent interpretation.

Hashtags with Visual Cues

Many of the analyzed hashtags were reinforced with visuals that assisted in or fully communicated some part of all of their meaning. These visual cues could be found in an attached photo, video, profile picture or name. In the case of hashtags containing acronyms, for example, the full name of the person/event/ show indicated by the acronym was often written out elsewhere in the tweet or as a caption to a linked picture/video. This behavior represented 27/245 (11%) of the hashtags in this collection, which participants correctly identified 21/27 (77.8%) of the time. See Figure 2 for two instances of these hashtags with larger textual support.

Figure 2. Different kinds of hashtags presented in tandem with visual cues

Functional Typology of Hashtags

The 245 hashtags can be divided into three recurring structural groupings (see Figure 3). These largely reflect the taxonomy put forth by Zappavigna (2015a). See Table 4 for examples and comprehension rates.

The hashtags in this dataset were largely used to index specific events, places, and shows (66.1% of the time), followed by general themes (27.4%) and metacommentary on something indicated in the larger tweet (6.5%). Participants' comprehension rates were comparable across each of these functional types (77.6% vs. 85.8% vs. 75%). The slightly higher rates observed in the Event/Place/Show category can be explained by the additional textual support readers received in the larger tweet from the account name, and the @tagging of involved parties and organizations, e.g. *@TF1, @Stromae, @RFI,* and so forth.

Types of Comprehension Errors

A taxonomy of the types of errors participants made when parsing hashtags is presented in Table 5. Similar rates are attested for literal interpretations, incorrect event/object types, unknown vocabulary

Figure 3. Breakdown of hashtag functional types

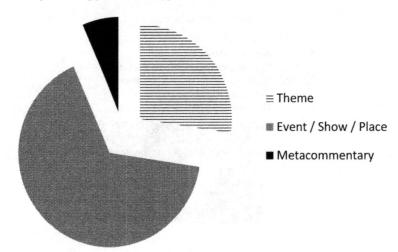

≡ Theme

▓ Event / Show / Place

■ Metacommentary

Table 4. Functional types of hashtags in NS French tweets

Functional Type	% of Total HTs	% Correct	Examples
Theme	67/245 (27.4%)	52/67 (77.6%)	*#changement, #coiffure, #moto, #cordeur, #couture*
Event / Place / Show	162/245 (66.1%)	139/162 (85.8%)	*#OnTheRunTour, #JamelComedyClub, #metz, #Musikelles*
Metacommentary	16/245 (6.5%)	12/16 (75%)	*#greatestalltime, #jecroisquejepreferefumer, #<3, #halluncinationmatinale*

Table 5. Taxonomy of hashtag errors

Error Type	Occurrences	P's French Level	Examples
Literal HT meaning instead of figurative	4	3,4,5	*#montréalaise, #JamelComedyClub (tv show), Africanités (tv show)*
Acronyms	6	5	*#200mdc, #MDR (Marrakech du rire), #LCDLJS, #DPDA, #FOG*
Guessed wrong type of event/object	3	4,5	*#64Minutes (tv show), #fiertépuissancemille (metacommentary)*
Unknown vocabulary	5	3	*#cordeur, #universalisme, #beauparcours*
Mislead by some other part of tweet	3	3,4	*#hallucinationmatinale (metacommentary), #ace (tennis), #NormanSurScene*
Unknown cultural reference	10	3,4,5	*#copainsdabord (song), #lebefore (tv show), #SansTambour (comedy tour), tristitude (song), #bessis (political figure), #larochesuryon (town), ConversationSecrete (tv show), #Lille (city)*

and following misleading information elsewhere in the tweet. Unknown vocabulary is only documented here among the least experienced learners, i.e. those in the third semester, while acronyms appear most problematic among the most experienced group of users. Favoring literal interpretations over figurative ones is found at all levels. The most common error of all types and among all French levels is that of the unknown cultural references. The problematic forms here included references to entertainment, politics, and geography that learners without much first-hand exposure to the language in everyday contexts would be unlikely to know, given the limited material related to current popular culture and popular expressions in traditional foreign language textbooks. (Blattner, 2014; Hassal, 2008; Vellenga, 2004).

Comprehensibility of Hashtags vs. Comprehensibility of Larger Tweet

In several cases, participants in this study easily parsed a tweet's hashtag(s) to answer the various questions of the current study without ever breaking the surface of the larger tweet in which they were embedded. The end result consisted of a translation of the overall tweet that was devoid of all detail and, in some cases, disjointed from or skewed by the nature of the hashtags it contained. This trend was observed in 48/171 (28.1%) tweets. See examples in Figures 4a-b.

Figure 4. Understood hashtags, misunderstood tweet #1

a. disjointed tweet translation, caused by hashtags

Rose ✔
@rosekeren

Arrêtez de fumer sans grossir? C possible avc Nico pass. Gerbe assurée.
#jecroisquejepreferefumer
9/2/14, 5:18

b. skewed tweet translation, caused by hashtags

Rose ✔   ✿   +⚏ Follow
@rosekeren

Plus facile de toucher le ciel a la marelle qu en jeûnant j imagine... #yomkippour #courage

↩ Reply   ⇄ Retweet   ★ Favorite   ••• More

- **Actual Tweet Translation**: Stop smoking without gaining weight? It's possible with Nico Pass. Vomiting guaranteed. #IthinkI'drathersmoke
- **Participant's Translation**: Stop smoking without getting fat? It's possible that Nico will be sick. #IthinkIprefertosmoke
- **Actual Tweet Translation**: I bet it's easier to reach heaven by playing hopscotch than by fasting. #YomKippur #GoodLuck
- **Participant's Translation**: I imagine that it is easier to hit hopscotch heaven while fasting #YomKippur #ShowCourage

DISCUSSION

While we did not see results similar to Solmaz (in press) where hashtags created a strong affiliation with target language speakers, the current study points to some interesting trends. Results indicate that most hashtags contain 1-word structures and/or acronyms. The meaning of these acronyms was contextually bound and reinforced by cues provided in either the account name or accompanying image. The present data suggest that these contextual cues generally assisted students in comprehending hashtag use. The instances of miscommunication that occurred were mainly due to lesser-known hashtags, hashtags without accompanying visual cues, and hashtags with acronyms that were not easily linkable to text in the larger tweet. To that end, Zappavigna (2015b) also reports that the meaning of particular hashtags can be difficult to interpret for "those who fall outside its community of use since they often include forms of abbreviation or concatenation [linking together several words]" (p. 2).

Participants at all levels had little difficulty understanding the hashtags. On the contrary, the more surprising result was that the hashtags served as a summary of the larger tweet, a modern-day, electronic "cliff notes," providing the gist, without requiring more involved textual interaction from the reader. If students simply read the hashtag, they could gain a simple understanding of the topic, without tackling any of the difficult content. This created the tendency to make educated guesses based on a superficial glance of the hashtags, a technique that learners may also apply when following tweets in their native language. Kramsch's (2014) work echoes this argument by claiming that students who are digital natives are driven by the conventions of communication of new fast-paced media, and consequently no longer try to understand every word of a text; they instead skim and scan the text for information, satisfied with just the gist of its message.

As a result, two clear comprehension issues surfaced affecting the overall comprehension of the tweet itself:

1. Participants had difficulty understanding the more nuanced prose of the tweets, and based their global understanding of it on what they had understood from the hashtags; and
2. Participants thought they understood more about the larger tweet than they actually did from their understanding of the hashtags, and made erroneous associations, assumptions and translations.

These two findings highlight the importance of preparing and guiding students in interpreting and using electronic social media such as Twitter, as they do not master all linguistic aspects of these forms of communication in an L2 (for similar findings with forums, see Hanna & DeNoy, 2003; Blattner and Williams, 2009).

As Kramsch (2014) recently points out, the prolific semiotic activity, disrespect for academic authority (orthographic grammatical and lexical rules and conventions), hybridities and code-switchings are all common aspects of microblogging spheres that language learners need to experience in the L2 before attempting to participate in such electronic forms of communication. The predictable convention of communication addressed in a typical classroom does not introduce these multimodal outbursts of creativity and innovation. However, Kramsch also mentions that dealing with multiple semiotic modalities has become a crucial element of acquiring communicative competence in an L2. Thus, hashtags with visual cues represent another example of multimodalities and they can help language learners become more familiar with acronyms. They also develop an ability to later infer meaning of other acronyms in an L2. This type of input provides learners with culturally rich examples that rarely appear in foreign language textbooks. Therefore, the best way to familiarize language learners with new modes of communication and develop their multiliteracy is to introduce activities with social media where deterritorialized culture is embedded in social media users, and, as such, does not become fossilized in the typical stereotypes of language textbooks (Kramsch, 2014).

Furthermore, results point to the utility of hashtags as valuable landmarks that are used to comment on a tweet theme, event and the tweeter's reactions to them. In several cases where the prose in the tweet body contained difficult structures, uncommon vocabulary, oblique cultural references or inside jokes, participants were able to extract a general sense of what the tweet was trying to convey just from the included hashtag(s). In the absence of hashtags, participants were forced to rely more on accessing the larger structures of the prose in the body of the tweet, which they were not always successful at doing.

Finally, participants in this study were administered an exit survey to gauge their general level of satisfaction and likeliness to continue following NS French personalities on Twitter. Fourteen of eighteen students completed the survey, reporting an average satisfaction score of 6.3/7 (mode: 7), an average likeliness score to keep following the same NS French personalities that they began following for this project of 5.9/7 (mode: 7) and an average likeliness score to follow other L1 French personalities after the project is over of 5.1/7 (mode: 7). These findings suggest that the students enjoyed participating in the overall tweet analysis task and being exposed to the popular language therein, as they deemed it to reflect both authentic present-day forms and usage in French.

While hashtags can be used in myriad ways, both in the classroom and in research—to present cultural information, assist with multiliteracy skills, connect learners, and engage students in tweets, modeling authenticity and promoting communication—this study provides another way of using hashtag research, that of analyzing how students understand and interpret native speaker tags.

CONCLUSION

In sum, this chapter helps us to shed new light on how L2 learners understand and interpret hashtags in an L2 environment. The results of the present study indicated that students were able to achieve an understanding of NS hashtags, which was often facilitated by visual cues, acronyms, or short summary phrases. Without these contextual markers, we speculate that students would have been more challenged to understand hashtags appropriately. However, the nature of social media implies the ability to use multiple indexicalities; students at institutions of higher education still need to work on developing the ability to interpret messages regardless of the language in which they are written.

Given the results obtained, we argue that students are able to make better sense of linguistic L2 references in the hashtag when they receive priming/scaffolding from the tweet. The specific linguistic task also directs them to be more aware of elements of the tweet and to notice certain aspects (Schmidt, 1993; 2001). Further, we argue that Twitter is an appropriate medium for introducing students to such components in the L2 (like we have many times before), because it allows them to interpret in the most authentic way possible, then leaves certain ambiguous components open for interpretation. If students encountered hashtags in any other context, like a book or article, they would likely not be able to infer their meaning as well because the context would not be as tightly constrained. Rather, it is only by repeated exposure and practice that they will develop this ability to interpret implied messages in an L2.

PEDAGOGICAL IMPLICATIONS

Moreover, after reviewing numerous studies using Twitter in educational settings, Aydin (2014) noted that Twitter can definitely be used to improve collaboration, develop reflective and critical thinking and encourage learners to share information and knowledge. In addition, Twitter also facilitates informal learning, which is not often the focus of classes in higher education, yet positively impacts attention and network awareness, ultimately leading to multiliteracy. D'Cunha (2014) highlighted the importance of understanding and using hashtags appropriately, as they can be detrimental if used incorrectly, causing a tweet to be perceived as rude or ignorant, revealing oftentimes that one is simply inexperienced at using Twitter. Embracing and promoting contemporary and popular modes of expression enable language learners to become active members of different global learning communities and use a foreign language in innovative ways (Kasper, 2000).

As we look to the future of hashtag research and how these tags may impact language learning tasks in and out of the classroom, the present study points to several areas that merit further exploration. There is a need to look at native speaker hashtags and further analyze what type of hashtags are the most difficult to interpret for L2 learners. As previously established, hashtags can take up the full range of experiential and interpersonal linguistic functions, and are not uniformly understood in all languages. The size of the sample of hashtags did not allow for such an extensive type of analysis and is beyond the scope of this paper. However, identifying whether experiential and interpersonal hashtags or topic-marker hashtags are problematic may help us further develop techniques of vocabulary acquisition based on its usage in social media. As Kramsch (2014) explained, the meaning of words in social media go beyond simple referential and denotative meaning, often pushing users to innovative and creative interpretations that are a new challenge for language learners. These tags should also be explored on different social networking tools (in addition to Twitter), and studies should examine how students understand and interpret the tags both with and without contextual tools. There is also a need to explore student-generated hashtags and how students are able to use target language hashtags that they produce.

This study suggests that social media services may provide an authentic and dynamic context that enhances the cultural enrichment of language learners. While we are not questioning the continuation of teaching L2 linguistic standards in the context of the L2 classroom, the amount of SLA research that has investigated the impact of social media on the development of communicative competence, and more specifically, the sociopragmatic aspects of an L2, points to the necessity of sensitizing learners to the stylistic choice that must be made to respect communicative conventions associated with particular electronic media.

REFERENCES

Antenos-Conforti, E. (2009). Microblogging on Twitter: Social networking in intermediate Italian classes. In L. Lomicka & G. Lord (Eds.), *The next generation: Social networking and online collaboration in foreign language learning* (pp. 59–90). San Marcos, TX: Computer Assisted Language Instruction Consortium.

Aydin, S. (2014). Twitter as an educational environment. *Turkish Online Journal of Distance Education*, *15*(1), 10–21.

Bastos, M. T., Raimundo, R. L. G., & Travitzki, R. (2013). Gatekeeping Twitter: Message diffusion in political hashtags. *Media Culture & Society*, *35*(2), 260–270. doi:10.1177/0163443712467594

Blattner, G. (2011). Web 2.0 Technologies and Foreign Language Teaching. In V. Wang (Ed.), *Encyclopedia of E-Leadership, Counseling and Training* (pp. 89–107). Hershey, PA, USA: IGI Global.

Blattner, G. (2014, October). Communicative competence in L2: The invisible culture is invisible in textbooks. *Paper presented at the FFLA*, Miami, FL.

Blattner, G., Dalola, A., & Lomicka, L. (2015). Tweetsmart: A pragmatic analysis of well-known native speaker Tweeters. In E. Dixon, & M. Thomas (Eds.), Researching Language Learner Interactions Online: From Social Media to MOOCs (pp. 213-235). San Marcos, TX: CALICO.

Blattner, G., Dalola, A., & Lomicka, L. (2016). Twitter in foreign language classes: Initiating learners into contemporary language variation. In V. Wang (Ed.), *The Handbook of Research on Learning Outcomes and Opportunities in the Digital Age* (pp. 769–797). Hershey, PA, USA: IGI Global. doi:10.4018/978-1-4666-9577-1.ch034

Blattner, G., & Fiori, M. (2009). Facebook in the Language Classroom: Promises and Possibilities. *Instructional Technology and Distance Learning*, *6*(1), 17–28.

Blattner, G., & Fiori, M. (2011). Virtual social network communities: An investigation of language learners' development of socio-pragmatic awareness and multiliteracy skills. *CALICO Journal*, *29*(1), 24–43. doi:10.11139/cj.29.1.24-43

Blattner, G., & Lomicka, L. (2012). A sociolinguistic study of practices in different social forums in an intermediate French class. *International journal on instructional technologies and distance education* *9*(9), 3-24.

Blattner, G., & Williams, L. F. (2009). Teaching and Learning Linguistic and Social Dimensions of French-Language Discussion Fora. In L. Abraham, & L. Williams (Eds.), Electronic Discourse in Foreign Language Learning and Teaching (pp. 263-289). Series: Language Learning & Language Teaching. Amsterdam: John Benjamins.

Butler, K. (2010). Tweeting your own horn. *District Administration*, *46*(2), 41–44.

Castrillo de Larreta-Azelain, D. (2013). Learners' attitude toward collaborative writing in e- language learning classes: A twitter project for German as a foreign language. *Revista Española de Lingüística Aplicada*, *26*, 127–138.

D'Cunha, R. (2014, March 7). Semiotics and the #Hashtag. Digital Marketing Blog. Retrieved from http://www.gravytrain.co.uk/blog/semiotics-hashtag/

Dennen, V. P., & Jiang, W. (2012). Twitter-based knowledge sharing in professional networks: The organization perspective. In V. P. Dennen & J. B. Myers (Eds.), *Virtual professional development and informal learning via social networks* (pp. 241–255). Hershey, PA: IGI. doi:10.4018/978-1-4666-1815-2.ch014

Dunlap, J. C., & Lowenthal, P. R. (2009). Tweeting the night away: Using Twitter to enhance social presence. *Journal of Information Systems Education, 202*, 129–135.

Farrell Whitworth, K. (2009). The discussion forum as a locus for developing L2 pragmatic awareness. In L. Abraham & L. Williams (Eds.), *Electronic Discourse in Foreign Language Learning and Teaching* (pp. 263–289). Amsterdam: John Benjamins. doi:10.1075/lllt.25.20whi

Ferguson, H. (2010). Join the flock! *Learning and Leading with Technology, 37*(8), 12–15.

Fornara, F. (2015, June). Micro-Input: Effects of an Instructor Model on L2 Student Practice on Twitter. Paper presented at the Computer-Assisted Language Consortium Conference, Boulder, CO, USA.

Hanna, B. E., & de Nooy, J. (2003). A funny thing happened on the way to the forum: Electronic discussion and foreign language learning. *Language Learning & Technology, 7*(1), 71–85.

Hanna, B. E., & de Nooy, J. (2009). *Learning Language and Culture via Public Internet Discussion Forums*. New York, NY: Palgrave Macmillan. doi:10.1057/9780230235823

Hassal, T. (2008). Pragmatic performance: What are learners thinking? In E. Alcón Soler & A. Martínez Flor (Eds.), *Investigating pragmatics in foreign language learning, teaching and testing* (pp. 72–93). Buffalo: Multilingual Matters.

Hattem, D. (2012). The Practice of microblogging. *The Journal of Second Language Teaching and Research, 1*(2), 38–70.

Kasper, L. (2000). New technologies, new literacies: Focus discipline research and ESL learning communities. *Language Learning & Technology, 4*(2), 105–128.

Kehoe, A., & Gee, A. (2011). Social tagging: A new perspective on textual aboutness. Methodological and historical dimensions of corpus linguistics. In P. Rayson, S. Hoffman, & G. Leech (Eds.), Studies in Variation Contacts and Change in English (pages). Helsinki: Research Unit for Variation, Contacts, and Change in English. Retrieved from http://www.helsinki.fi/varieng/series/volumes/06/kehoe_gee/

Kramsch, C. (2014). The challenge of globalization for the teaching of foreign languages and cultures. *Electronic Journal of Foreign Language Teaching, 11*(2), 2249–2254.

Lakarnchua, O., & Wasanasomsithi, P. (2014). L2 student writers' perception of microblogging. *Electronic Journal of Foreign Language Teaching, 11*(2), 327–340.

Lee, L. (2009). Exploring native and nonnative interactive discourse in text-based chat beyond classroom settings. In L. Abraham, & L. Williams (Eds.), Electronic Discourse in Foreign Language Learning and Teaching (pp. 263-289). Series: Language Learning & Language Teaching. Amsterdam: John Benjamins. doi:10.1075/lllt.25.10lee

Lomicka, L., & Lord, G. (2012). A tale of tweets: Analyzing microblogging among language Learners. *System, 40*(1), 48–63. doi:10.1016/j.system.2011.11.001

Mills, N. (2011). Situated learning through social networking communities: The development of joint enterprise, mutual engagement, and a shared repertoire. *CALICO Journal, 28*(2), 345–368. doi:10.11139/cj.28.2.345-368

Perifanou, M. A. (2009). Language micro-gaming: Fun and informal microblogging activities for language learning. *Communications in Computer and Information Science, 49*(1), 1–14. doi:10.1007/978-3-642-04757-2_1

Raguseo, C. (2010). Twitter Fiction: Social Networking and Microfiction in 140 Characters. *The Electronic Journal for English as a Second Language, 13(4).* Retrieved from http://www.tesl-ej.org/wordpress/issues/volume13/ej52/ej52int/

Reinhardt, J., & Zander, V. (2011). Social network¬ing in an intensive English program classroom: A language socialization perspective. *CALICO Journal, 28*(2), 326–344. doi:10.11139/cj.28.2.326-344

Rogers, M. (2013). Wired for teaching. Inside Higher Education. Retrieved from https://www.inside-highered.com/news/2013/10/21/more-professors-using-social-media-teaching-tools

Schmidt, R. (1993). Awareness and second language acquisition. *Annual Review of Applied Linguistics, 13*, 206–226. doi:10.1017/S0267190500002476

Schmidt, R. (2001). Attention. In P. Robinson (Ed.), *Cognition and second language instruction* (pp. 3–32). Cambridge: Cambridge University Press. doi:10.1017/CBO9781139524780.003

Scott, K. (2015). The pragmatics of hashtags: Inference and conversational style on Twitter. *Journal of Pragmatics, 81*, 8–20. doi:10.1016/j.pragma.2015.03.015

Shweiki Media. Social Networking: College Students and Social Media Statistics. Retrieved from http://www.shweiki.com/blog/2014/02/social-networking-college-students-social-mediastatistics/

Solmaz, O. (in press). Autonomous Language Learning on Twitter: Performing Affiliation with Target Language Users through #Hashtags. In *The Handbook of Research on Digital Tools for Self-Directed Language Learning.*

Sotillo, S. (2009). Learner noticing, negative feedback, and uptake in synchronous computer mediated environments. In L. Abraham & L. Williams (Eds.), *Electronic Discourse in Foreign Language Learning and Teaching* (pp. 87–110). Amsterdam: John Benjamins. doi:10.1075/lllt.25.08sot

Symmons, J. (2013). An Exploration of Professors' Use of Twitter in Higher Education. Retrieved from http://www.dr.library.brocku.ca/bitstream/handle/10464/4960/Brock_Symmons_Janet2013.pdf?sequence=1

Taguchi, N. (2011). Teaching pragmatics: Trends and issues. *Annual Review of Applied Linguistics, 31*, 289–310. doi:10.1017/S0267190511000018

Trubitt, L., & Overholtzer, J. (2009). Good communication: The other social network for successful IT organizations. *EDUCAUSE Review, 44*(6), 90–98.

vanCompernolle, R. A. (2011). Use and variation of French diacritics on an Internet dating site. *French Language Studies, 21*(02), 131–148. doi:10.1017/S0959269510000293

vanCompernolle, R. A., & Williams, L. (2007). De l'oral a l'électronique: La variation orthographique comme ressource sociostylistique et pragmatique dans le français électronique. *Glottopol, 10*, 56–69.

vanCompernolle, R. A., & Williams, L. (2010). Orthographic variation in electronic French: The case of l'accent aigu. *French Review (Deddington), 83*, 820–833.

Vellenga, H. (2004). Learning pragmatics from ESL and EFL textbooks: How likely? *TESL-EJ, 8*(2). Retrieved from http://www.tesl-ej.org/wordpress/issues/volume8/ej30/ej30a3

Wang, S., & Vasquez, C. (2014). The Effect of Target Language Use in Social Media on Intermediate-level Chinese Language Learners' writing performance. *CALICO Journal, 31*(1), 78–102. doi:10.11139/cj.31.1.78-102

Zappavigna, M. (2012). *Discourse of Twitter and Social Media, Continuum Discourse Series*. London: Continuum.

Zappavigna, M. (2015a). Searchable talk: The linguistic functions of hashtags. *Social Semiotics, 25*(3), 274–291. doi:10.1080/10350330.2014.996948

Zappavigna, M. (2015b). Searchable talk: The linguistic functions of hashtags in tweets about Schapelle Corby, *Global Media Journal, 9*(1). Retrieved from http://www.hca.westernsydney.edu.au/gmjau/?p=1762

ADDITIONAL READING

Cunha, E., Magno, G., Comarela, G., Almeida, V., Gonçalves, M. A., & Benevenuto, F. (2011, June). Analyzing the dynamic evolution of hashtags on twitter: a language-based approach. In *Proceedings of the Workshop on Languages in Social Media* (pp. 58-65). Association for Computational Linguistics.

Fewell, N. (2014). Social networking and language learning with Twitter. *Research Papers in Language Teaching and Learning, 5*, 223–234.

Ishihara, N., & Cohen, A. (2010). *Teaching and learning pragmatics: Where language and culture meet*. New York, NY: Routledge.

Leis, A. (2014). Encouraging autonomy through the use of a social networking system. *The JALT Call Journal, 10*(1), 69–80.

Liu, K. L., Li, W. J., & Guo, M. (2012, July). *Emoticon Smoothed Language Models for Twitter Sentiment Analysis*. AAAI.

Mompean, J. A., & Fouz-Gonzales, J. (2016). Twitter based EFL pronunciation instruction. *Language Learning & Technology, 20*(1), 166–190.

Page, R. (2012). The linguistics of self-branding and micro-celebrity in Twitter: The role of hashtags. *Discourse & Communication, 6*(2), 181–201. doi:10.1177/1750481312437441

Taguchi, N., & Sykes, J. (Eds.). (2013). *Technology in Interlanguage Pragmatics Research and Teaching*. John Benjamins Language Learning and Teaching Series. doi:10.1075/lllt.36

KEY TERMS AND DEFINITIONS

Hashtag: Word or phrase preceded by a hash or pound sign (#) and used to identify messages on a specific topic, or facilitate a search for it.

Hybridities: Words or sentences that contain elements from two or more languages, e.g. *franglais, trop awesome*.

Indexicalities: The use of signs to point out any linguistic or social identity.

Metacommentary: Commentary about other commentary. In the context of Twitter, hashtags are often employed with this function, as a way of categorizing or reacting to the comments made in the tweet.

Microblogger: A person who engages in the act or practice of posting brief entries on a blog or social-media website.

Misparsing: Incorrectly placing word boundaries in a contiguous sequence of letters. For example, #FATALBERT may be parsed correctly as FAT_ALBERT or misparsed as FATAL_BERT. Because hashtags do not allow for spaces between words, this is a common outcome in the Twitter environment.

Multiliteracy: In our technologically-saturated society, being *literate* does not only imply being able to read and write, but also knowing how to interact in a variety of electronic media. In other words technology users must rapidly identify the discursive and interactional norms in a particular medium in order to communicate with other users in an appropriate and expected manner.

Searchable Talk: Online discourse where the primary function appears to be affiliation via 'findability'.

Socio-Pragmatic Competence: An ability to recognize the effect of context on strings of linguistic events and to use language appropriately in specific social situations. In romance languages a typically difficult socio-pragmatic competence for language learners is to master the pronouns of address (i.e.: tu/vous in French, tu/usted in Spanish).

Tweetsmart: A term used to describe someone who is a savvy user of Twitter.

APPENDIX A

Metalinguistic Survey

This is a quick survey designed to let us know about your online habits. Your answers will remain confidential. Thank you for your participation.

1. Please type your initials below.
2. What is your age?
3. What is your gender?
4. What do you consider your first language?
5. What do you consider your second language?
6. Do you speak any other languages? Please indicate them below.
7. How long have you been exposed to the French language?
8. How old were you when you first used Twitter?
9. How old were you when you first used Facebook?
10. How old were you when you first used Instagram?
11. On average, how many hours per week do you spend on Twitter?
12. On average, how many hours per week do you spend on Facebook?
13. On average, how many hours per week do you spend on Instagram?
14. What kinds of people and groups do you follow and interact with on Twitter in your FIRST LANGUAGE?
15. What kinds of people and groups do you follow and interact with on Twitter in your SECOND LANGUAGE?
16. What kinds of people and groups do you follow and interact with on Twitter in ANY OTHER LANGUAGES you speak?
17. What kinds of people and groups do you follow and interact with on Facebook in your FIRST LANGUAGE?
18. What kinds of people and groups do you follow and interact with on Facebook in your SECOND LANGUAGE?
19. What kinds of people and groups do you follow and interact with on Facebook in ANY OTHER LANGUAGE you speak?
20. What kinds of people and groups do you follow and interact with on Instagram in your FIRST LANGUAGE?
21. What kinds of people and groups do you follow and interact with on Instagram in your SECOND LANGUAGE?
22. What kinds of people and groups do you follow and interact with on Instagram in your ANY OTHER LANGUAGE you speak?
23. Have you previously used social media IN FRENCH?
24. If you use it or have used it in French, is it a PASSIVE use (i.e. reading, liking other posts) or an ACTIVE use (i.e. posting, commenting)?
25. Rate the social networks from your preferred (1) to your least preferred (3).
26. Do you use any other social networks?

APPENDIX B

Anatomy of a Tweet

Alex Bilodeau = full name of person/organization whose account is tweeting
@ABilodeau_ski = Twitter handle associated with this person/account
"Je vous…artiste d'ici" = body of tweet
#montréalaise = hashtag
@airborne = Twitter handle of another Twitter user that is being tagged in this discussion

Figure 5. Screenshot of a Tweet

Alex Bilodeau ✔
@ABilodeau_ski

Je vous amène avec moi dans
une escapade #montréalaise via
l'application @airborne Plein de
place à découvrir à Mtl avec vos
artiste d'ici

8/28/14, 3:14 PM from Montréal, Québec

3 RETWEETS **8** FAVORITES

APPENDIX C

You will complete this questionnaire for each tweet that you analyze.

1. Please select 2 tweets a week for each of the 3 personalities you chose to follow. Be sure to select tweets that are not just lists of people or hashtags, but that also contain a linguistic message (aim for ~7+ non-hashtag/@people words).

DO NOT USE THE TRANSLATE BUTTON THAT TWITTER HAS RECENTLY INTEGRATED WHEN YOU ARE ANALYZING YOUR TWEETS. If you need to look words up, please use a dictionary (e.g. print or Wordreference.com) to do so. We will ask you to share with us exactly what words and expressions you looked up.

2. Save a screenshot of the actual tweets (instructions here: http://www.take-a-screenshot.org/).
3. Complete this 'Linguistic Questionnaire' for each tweet. You should complete 6 questionnaires per week, for 5 weeks.
4. When you have finished with each tweet, paste the screenshots into a single word document that you will hand in to your teacher.

Linguistic Questionnaire for Each Tweet

1. Please enter your initials.
2. Type the name and twitter handle of the person who wrote this tweet, e.g. Firstname Lastname @ twitterhandle.
3. Please enter the date this tweet was posted, e.g. month/day/year.
4. Please rate on a scale of 1 (not at all) to 7 (completely) HOW WELL YOU UNDERSTOOD THIS TWEET.
5. Do you notice any misspellings, ungrammatical constructions or unconventional punctuation in this tweet? If YES, please explain each instance you found. If NO, type NA.
6. Are there any English words used in the tweet? If YES, which one(s)? If NO, type NA.
7. Are you able to tell what this English word means in this tweet? If YES, what does it mean? If NO, type NA.
8. Would you use this English word this way in English? If NO, how is it different? If YES, type SAME.
9. Are you surprised to see this English word has been borrowed into French? If YES, why? If NO, type NA.
10. Are there any greetings in this tweet? If YES, which one(s)? If NO, type NA.
11. In your opinion, what is the nature of this greeting? Formal, Informal, Neutral.
12. Are there any abbreviations used in the tweet? If YES, which one(s)? If NO, type NA.
13. Can you write the full corresponding French word and English translation of these abbreviations or acronyms? If YES, please write it here. If NO, type NA.
14. Do you use the English equivalent abbreviation? YES, NO.
15. Are there any hashtags in this tweet? If YES, which one(s)? If NO, type NA.

16. Click on the tweet in your feed, then click on the hyperlinked hashtags(s) or look them up in the search function. How large is the hashtag's following? (You can determine this by seeing how many other people are tagging it. If the list keeps going and going as you scroll, it has a large following. If you reach the end of the list of tweets tagging it in a few scrolls, it has a small following.) Please indicate each hashtag and following as such: total # of hashtags in tweet, names of hashtags with large followings(L), names of hashtags with small followings(S).

17. What does each hashtag mean in French? / Why do you think the tweeter has included it/them in the tweet?

18. Examine each of the hashtags. Are any of them written in the same way as words in other languages? YES, NO, NA.

19. If YES, look at how others have tagged them (by clicking on the hashtag and examining the list of tweets it appears in). Are all of the speakers tagging it also speaking French? Does the tag indicate the same thing as in your original tweet? Please specify any other languages/meanings, etc. below. Type NA if no hashtags.

20. Can you guess the mood of the tweeter? If YES, what is it? If NO, type NA.

21. What words, punctuation, capitalization, hashtags, etc. helped you identify the mood? Specify each individual item separately. Type NA if none.

22. What register do you think is being used in the tweet? Formal, Informal.

23. What words, punctuation, capitalization, hashtags, etc. helped you identify the register? Specify each individual item separately. Type NA if none.

24. Are any other people/groups ADDRESSED in the body of this tweet? People / groups being addressed will appear in the @username sequence. If YES, type their usernames here. If NO, type NA.

25. Do you know who this person/these people are? If YES, specify each below. If NO, type NA.

26. Quickly google this person's / group's identities. Does their involvement in this tweet now make sense? Explain who each addressee is and why you think they are addressed. If you are unsure, type UNSURE.

27. Are any other people / groups MENTIONED in the body of the tweet? People / groups being mentioned will just have their names typed in plain text without being addressed with an @ symbol. If YES, type their names here. If NO, type NA.

28. Do you know who this person/these people are? If YES, specify each below. If NO, type NA.

29. Quickly google this person's / group's identities. Does their involvement in this tweet now make sense? Explain who each addressee is and why you think they are addressed. If you are unsure, type UNSURE.

30. Quickly google this person's / group's identities. Does their involvement in this tweet now make sense? Explain who each addressee is and why you think they are addressed. If you are unsure, type UNSURE. If you are unsure of some part of the tweet, you can say that in your translation or guess at what it might mean.

31. Which word(s) / expressions(s) did you need to look up in the dictionary in order to translate it for the previous question? If none, type NA. Otherwise, please indicate the word(s) in French and the translation for each you got from the dictionary.

APPENDIX D

Post-Task Exit Survey

Thank you for your participation in the French Twitter project! Please rate the statements below on a scale of 1 to 7 (where 1 is "not at all" and 7 is "completely") based on your experience in this project. This survey should take 5 minutes or less to complete. We welcome any and all of your feedback. Thank you.

1. Please indicate your initials below.
2. I liked participating in this Twitter project in French.
3. I have a better understanding of greetings in French because of my participation in this project.
4. I have a better understanding of abbreviations in French because of my participation in this project.
5. I have a better understanding of English borrowings in French because of my participation in this project.
6. I have a better understanding of hashtags in French because of my participation in this project.
7. I have a better understanding of speaker emotions in French because of my participation in this project.
8. I have a better understanding of register (= level of formality) in French because of my participation in this project.
9. I have a better understanding of cultural nuances in French because of my participation in this project.
10. I think Twitter is a worthwhile place for learners to study the French language.
11. I used Twitter regularly (in any language) before this project.
12. I will use Twitter regularly (in any language) after this project.
13. I will continue to follow the same French speakers that I followed for this project now that this project is over.
14. I will follow other French speakers on Twitter now that this project is over.
15. Please leave any additional comments you have about this experience here.

Chapter 4

Challenges and Perspectives of Language Education Technology in Brazil: From Confronting Native Language Loss to Implementing EFL Classes

Eliane Thaines Bodah
Thaines & Bodah Center for Education and Development, USA

Josh Meuth Alldredge
Community Partnership for Child Development, USA

Brian William Bodah
Washington State University, USA

Alcindo Neckel
IMED University, Brazil

Emanuelle Goellner
Federal University of Rio Grande do Sul, Brazil

ABSTRACT

Our chapter aims to explore the challenges, advances, and perspectives of language-education technology in Brazil. Language-education is an extremely important topic for Brazil because many indigenous languages are nearing extinction due to the legacies of colonization and the fact that Portuguese, the national language of Brazil, is the only official language and thus the single most utilitarian method of communication. This issue is further complicated by Brazil's increasingly globalized economy, which, for many individuals, demands the acquisition of a foreign language in order to compete. The English language has been introduced into the curriculum of the vast majority Brazilian public schools over the course of the past few decades. Additionally, several private, for-profit English learning enterprises now have widespread services throughout the country. But rates of English (and even Portuguese) fluency still vary greatly among the population. This raises a number of critical questions that will be discussed in this work. Why is learning a new language such a challenge? Which methodologies can be utilized to

DOI: 10.4018/978-1-5225-0177-0.ch004

increase language acquisition and build fluency? What are the new technologies that are used in teaching a second language in Brazilian schools, and how is their impact being measured? Are Brazilian teachers prepared to integrate new technologies and innovative methods of teaching and learning? Our methodology involves bibliographical research including a literature review, a case-study, and participatory research through semi-structured interviews. Our results have shown that several technologies are being implemented in Brazil, and that as a theoretical framework, educational communication has been recognized as a powerful tool to incorporate such technologies in language education. Overall, the use of learning technologies is common and growing among students, while it is increasing at a more institutional pace among teachers.

1. INTRODUCTION

Brazil is the largest country in South America and contains the largest portion of the Amazon rainforest of any country within its national borders. It also has a unique and exemplary role as a post-colonial multicultural developing nation, one that can raise important questions for the world in terms of the contemporary intersection of language and technology. Our work aims to explore the challenges and perspectives of language-education technology in Brazil. Our methodology involves a bibliographical research including a literature review, a case-study, and participatory research through semi-structured interviews.

The need for presenting a case-study and a participatory research emerges from the contrasting educational realities found across the country. For instance, in the north, where the Amazon rainforest is located, many indigenous languages are nearing extinction, there are few resources to preserve what is left, and technologies to learn a new language or revitalize an indigenous one are scarce. In the South, the native forest of the so-called Atlantic Jungle slowly gave space to development. Currently, only 8% of it remains, and is found in state parks or areas of conservation. Such development not only dramatically impacted the environment, it also brought major changes and new technologies to the developed communities, including tools to learn a second language.

Portuguese, the national language of Brazil, is the only official language recognized by the government and thus the single most utilitarian method of communication. However, Brazil is home to approximately 200 distinct indigenous groups who collectively speak 170 different languages (IBGE, 2007). For these groups, the need to communicate in Portuguese for economic survival brings forth simultaneous challenges of learning a second language and maintaining the primary indigenous language. These challenges will be presented here in this chapter through a case-study conducted in 2011 in a Northern Brazilian indigenous community. This section explores trends in local autochthonous languages and the threats manifested by globalized "Brazilian" culture, which inundates indigenous communities and replaces traditional language use with necessarily utilitarian linguistic choices (Meuth Alldredge, 2011).

To address the situation in Southern Brazil, we will consider ways in which language learning is influenced by our increasingly globalized economy and highly competitive job market. The acquisition of a foreign language as a personal asset can become of great interest to citizens in the South. By and large, English is the most popular second language among Southern Brazilians. It has been introduced into the curriculum of the vast majority of public schools over the course of the past few decades. Additionally, several private, for-profit English learning enterprises now have widespread services throughout the country. Nonetheless, it has been observed that the availability of English classes is not necessarily proportional to fluency. To illustrate this situation, we present participatory research conducted in Southern Brazil that includes the formal system of Brazilian education. Our conclusions are that all teachers utilized the following basic tools for teaching a foreign language: computer for presentations and internet access; TV and DVD; other electronic frameworks; and other basic audiovisual tools that aid in communication processes for information exchange and knowledge acquisition.

These two contrasting studies situate the perspective of this chapter, and make the case that Brazilian diversity adds to the complexity of language-education in that country. It further confirms access disparities: while some schools only have books (or copies of the books) to use in classroom, others capitalize on the use of live social media, internet, and other recent technological tools.

1.1. Review of Technologies Applied to Education

Although there are numerous technologies applied to education, especially in the field of language learning, this topic is commonly associated with the use of a computer. Computer-Assisted Language Learning (CALL) was introduced in the 1960s, when language education was simply understood as language learning, and not language acquisition. It was assumed that the computer's primary contributions to second-language acquisition were programs based on traditional language learning (Jarvis & Krashen, 2014).

Some alternative terms such as Technology Enhanced Language Learning (TELL), Mobile Assisted Language Learning (MALL), and Mobile Assisted Language Use (MALU) were proposed later on. Each of these areas presents both challenges and opportunities for teachers and students. For instance, Brown (2014) observed that while the opportunity for communicative language teaching with MALL is viable, the question of how to best design MALL environments for this purpose is still undetermined.

When discussing the current state of the use of new technologies in the foreign language classrooms, Ruschoff and Ritter (2001) point out that the effects of traditional instructivist theories of language learning with their transmission-based modes of learning are still present in both CALL and TELL. On another note, Jarvis and Achilleos (2013) suggest a need to move education from CALL towards MALU because there is a potential alignment of MALU with the notion of the digital resident and a newly emerging educational theory of connectivism.

Language education technological tools vary greatly, for example, from basic computer usage to mobile devices. Both offline and online software tools offer exciting opportunities for the language classroom but e-learning technology has been increasingly employed in instruction to enhance teaching and learning (Ruschoff & Ritter, 2001; Riasati et al, 2012). Social network sites for language learning to facilitate English as a Second Language (ESL) classes are also beneficial and should be as easy to use and as intuitive to navigate as possible (Lui et al, 2015). A successful example is web-based writing instruction, which has proved to be an important factor in enhancing the writing quality of low-ability ESL students (Wang, 2005).

Wang (2014) proposed a study in which a group of students carried mobile devices to complete ESL writing assignments within specific and familiar subject environments, stimulating real-life situations or contexts. Activities presented within familiar contexts, and supported by their proposed ESL writing system, inspired students to not only write more sentences, but to describe the target objects clearly and thoroughly. Furthermore, Liu et al (2014) investigated a mobile learning initiative by a large school district in the United States to provide iPod touch devices 24/7 to teachers and students of ESL learners. Their results revealed that the iPod touch was used to support language and content learning, that it provided differentiated instructional support, and that it extended learning time from classroom to home.

On a larger scale, technology has made a measurable impact in language learning mostly through computer-assisted pronunciation training, and in particular, automatic speech recognition that can facilitate the improvement of pronunciation and can provide immediate, effective feedback (Golonka et al., 2014). Yet throughout the globalized world, issues of accessibility to the web and to technological devices have not been eradicated (Ene, 2014).

There are still concerns about practicality of technology activities (Cviko et al, 2014). Involving teachers in the design of technology-rich activities could improve their relevance. It could also positively affect teachers' perceptions and further technology implementation, but some teachers and students may still prefer traditional language-teaching and -learning styles, despite ready access to technology (Yeung et al, 2015).

Zhao (2003) finds that existing literature on the effectiveness of technology uses in language education is very limited in four aspects: a) The number of systematic, well-designed empirical and evaluative studies of the effects of technology uses in language learning is very small; b) the settings of instruction where the studies are conducted are limited to higher education and adult learners, excluding child learners; c) the languages studied are limited to common foreign languages and ESL; and d) the experiments are often short-term, involving only one or two aspects of language learning (e.g., vocabulary or grammar).

1.2 Theoretical Background: Educommunication

Educational communication, or educommunication, is a theory that emerged from the relationship between education and technology. It has been found to be a powerful tool to incorporate technologies into language education. Educommunication can be defined as every communication action developed in an educative space that is aimed at producing a system that could empower its participants (Soares, 2000).

The educommunication theory is opposed to the idea of maintaining segregation of knowledge, focusing instead on originating new socially-based fields of intervention. Teachers can, for example, promote reading activities as a method to show the media's capability to distort certain facts in order to satisfy special interests. Instructors may also offer creative conditions to assignments, where in addition to learning how to read media texts, students learn to produce their own messages and reflect upon them. This theoretical framework has various interdisciplinary implications and opportunities.

In some European countries such as Spain (Aguaded-Gomez, 2011), educommunication first appeared under the name of media education. Furthermore, there are records showing it as a discipline in the 1920s in Russia, when the film industry was developing rapidly (Fedorov, 2001). Currently, in Latin America, educommunication is a popular subject. In Brazil, many children see themselves as having the right to access new technologies that enable them to produce their own messages according to their own creativity, interests, and social participation (Soares, 2008).

Brazil's 1996 Law for Educational Guidelines and Bases (Lei de Diretrizes e Bases) encouraged the introduction of education around communication in the public school curricula (Soares, 2001). This same legislation also declares the need to incorporate the technologies applied to learning processes, including language learning.

There is also a strong component of social transformation in educommunication. For instance, a project of educommunication conducted at the Centre of Community Media Sao Miguel, in Brazil, was attributed to having contributed to local development and social change, and was acknowledged as a communication system for development strategy (Souza, 2013). It is also based on the premise that the process of dialogue should be built on the authentic exchange of viewpoints, on real intent and on interdisciplinary thinking, consequently culminating in joint reflections (Melo, 2011).

Important educommunication principles are alterity, social awareness, inclusion, citizenship, shared learning spaces, and access to communication. Alterity is understood here as the exercise of a new insight by adopting the viewpoint of another person. Schaun (2000) states that alterity is the substrate where educommunication grows. In this sense, it can help with the establishment of more humanitarian relationships. Social awareness refers to the development of critical knowledge of the media and other communication means that deliver information about society. Inclusion here aims at inserting diverse groups in the discussions mediated by edocummunication, through which each individual can become more familiar with his or her duties and rights as a citizen. Citizenship, shared learning spaces, and access to communication depend on the local reality where educommunication takes place.

Overall, educommunication practices have three important components: education, communication, and action. In other words, the instructor aims to create democratic and communicative spaces through action and practice. It is a field that emerged from new needs to organize knowledge and information where education and communication converge into a new meaning, not only in the interpersonal sphere but also in the spheres mediated by new technologies (Barbero, 2000).

2. CASE STUDY: INDIGENOUS LANGUAGE LOSS AND OPTIONS FOR REVITALIZATION THROUGH TECHNOLOGY IN NORTHERN BRAZIL, 2011

Josh Meuth Alldredge

Note: Informally cited statistics and quotes are sourced from the researcher's primary data collection, interviews, and participant-observation in Nova Esperança. All community members have been given pseudonyms in this chapter.

2.1 Introduction

It is possible that ever-improving models of second-language learning can be effectively applied in indigenous culture preservation programs. If there is localized social support for and investment in such preservation, all options (including novel technologies and methods) should be explored. However, it is critical that application of such technologies to indigenous language revitalization projects is directly informed by an understanding of the context, challenges, and depth of loss inherent to culture disappearance. This section aims to illuminate these issues by examining, first, a case study of indigenous culture loss and resuscitation in *Nova Esperança*, and second, by exploring how technology can be utilized to provide motivated learners with tools for indigenous language acquisition and revitalization.

Nova Esperança is an indigenous village in the northernmost municipality of Roraima, which is the northernmost state in Brazil. The community is composed of three distinct ethno-linguistic groups: the Macuxi, Wapixana, and Taurepang. This diversity is no surprise, as Brazil is home to 170 distinct living languages and bore witness to the death of countless others during colonization (Grinevald, 1998). Around 60% of the village's 29 families identify as members of the Macuxi ethnic group, 30% as Wapixana, and 10% as Taurepang. Historically, each group has had its own language, dance, music, food preparation, and spirituality (Tuxaua, personal communication, 2011). This is both a positive and a negative aspect of the village in the sense that it increases cultural diversity and awareness, but fractures the cohesive identity of the village and precludes the use of an indigenous language as the principal medium of communication within the community.

2.2 History and Conditions

Historically, in their relations with the dominant society, the indigenous peoples were victims of an atrocious and systematic process of decimation in all aspects: physical, moral, spiritual and cultural. (Tuxaua, personal communication, 2015)

As with colonized groups throughout the world, the tribes that now live in *Nova Esperança* have been victims of stigma for hundreds of years. Portuguese missionaries and settlers vilified indigenous spirituality, taught that speaking the native language was shameful and absurd, and began to categorize and make a spectacle of indigenous identity with pejorative rhetoric and policies (Metcalf, 2005). Further, greater Brazilian society gradually embedded itself in a market economy that enforced linguistic uniformity, a singular value system based on currency, accumulation of assets, and division of labor (rather than a localized economy that prized self-made goods and mutual generosity) (Tuxaua, personal communication, 2011).

With the flow of international capital increasing, Brazil launched into the global economy. However, the country underwent what can be defined as "pocket" development: much of the progress that the capital economy brought to the country was concentrated in bubbles of wealth in the higher classes in urban areas. Indigenous land reaped very few of the beneficial effects of that development, but the negative aspects certainly reached the tribes (Becker & Egler, 1992). They suffered relative poverty and stigmatization of language, culture, and their subsistence sharing economy. Critically, the indigenous peoples of Roraima, as in many cases of cultural domination, began to internalize the discourse of stigma, according to the Tuxaua (chief) of *Nova Esperança*. He mentioned that this absorbed stigma has effectively rooted out traditional indigenous spirituality. The cosmology, as he called it, has been stamped out by Catholicism and now by evangelical Protestantism (Tuxaua, personal communication, 2011).

Though rich in resources, the population of *Nova Esperança* is classified as poor, given their small monetary incomes and relative lack of commercial and infrastructure development. Families with financial means tend to avoid endemic and nutritious *mandioca* (cassava) and wild pig, and instead choose to spend their income on packaged foods, white rice, spaghetti, and beef. In a very real way, cultural pride in subsistence food systems has been damaged. One could identify an array of causes: colonialism, federal domination, cultural stigmatization, and the ever-widening gap between the greater Brazilian progress and tribal development.

In a larger scope, cultural protagonism, or enthusiastic and proud action to promote and maintain one's culture, is absent or significantly diminished in all generations. That is not to say that indigenous elders are not proud. But combating the erasure of indigenous identity by the greater Brazilian value systems requires more pronounced resistance than local cultural pride; it demands action. The leadership of *Nova Esperança* has hosted indigenous entrepreneurial fairs, but these events are insufficient in helping many individual community members feel ownership over their traditions, cultural identity, and their future. Now, the Tuxaua explained how since the 1980s, the Brazilian federal government has prioritized the *"resgate da identidade indígena,"* or the rescue of indigenous identity. In the governmental rhetoric and policy, there is a discourse of cultural preservation, interchange, and mutual respect between "Brazilian identity" and the multitudes of indigenous identities. But underneath the political discourse, the main cultural current still stigmatizes indigeneity (Tuxaua, personal communication, 2011).

A narrative intertwining themes of wealth, success, whiteness, intelligence, and global access has steadily gained credence in the community, which has disrupted local value systems and promotes assimilation into greater Brazil. Of course, some aspects of indigenous tradition remain. Complex understandings of plant medicine, animal behavior, agriculture, and food preservation are still held by many adults and elders. Vital to the maintenance of this localized knowledge is the continued sovereignty of the indigenous peoples over their land and resources. But even more important are the successful teaching and learning processes that transfer knowledge through generations. According to members of the community, the cultural interfaces between elders, parents, youth, and children are changing more rapidly than ever before, and most families are experiencing some sort of generational dissociation. On a larger scale, such changes jeopardize indigenous culture and allow language loss, transformations which are illustrated in the following sections.

2.3 Education

To succeed, the children and youth will need to learn to think critically, not just methodically. (Tuxaua, personal communication, 2011)

The village has a preschool and an elementary school (Escola Estadual Indígena Arturo Pinto Da Silva), which are housed in a building constructed by the state of Roraima six years ago. Before, the school was in a one-room house. Currently, two teachers instruct some 50 children (separated into preschool and elementary rooms) from 8 to 11:30 am, Monday through Friday, covering topics such as geography, mathematics, and Portuguese. The elementary school teacher holds field trips and special workshops to help the children learn about local concepts, such as plant medicine. No indigenous language classes are currently taught at the village school, though every student, parent, and teacher involved with the school is indigenous. The state and federal governments send Portuguese-language textbooks and instructional videos to the school, which the elementary teacher uses as teaching aids. Fifth through eighth grades and the following three years of high school are not offered in *Nova Esperança*, and older students take a bus to the nearby village of *Sorocaima* to attend classes (Anna, personal communication, 2011).

Though the new school building, which dominates the view of the village from the adjacent highway, satisfies the basic space and amenity needs of the community, its sturdy presence masks other problems with the local education system. The school is vastly understaffed, and with two teachers attempting to instruct five grades (one exclusive to preschool), many children are falling through the cracks. The older students (in fourth grade) seemed bored in class and unengaged from their work, while the youngest pupils struggled intensely with the challenging material.

The elementary school teacher, Anna, did break down exercises into advanced and beginning sections, but even that failed to give each grade, let alone each student, adequate and appropriate support. Several parents complained that they had seen children move on to fifth grade without knowing how to read. Anna confirmed that some students were failing, and pointed to both a lack of parent support for studying and the understaffing problem; further, when she is only paid for 25 hours a week, she cannot afford to spend all day teaching and then coaching each student individually. She argued that many parents, having never experienced a good education, do not understand the value of studying hard to pursue a career (Anna, personal communication, 2011). The Tuxaua informed the researcher that some parents view the school as a formal, white, outside institution as well, which does not make them apt to support it as their children's medium of instruction (Tuxaua, personal communication, 2011).

Parent reluctance is also one of the main reasons why children are not exposed to the Wapixana and Macuxi languages in the local school system, with the exception of rudimentary Macuxi taught in the neighboring community of *Sorocaima*. Many *Nova Esperança* parents do not want children taught indigenous languages in the school because it seems paternalistic: a state institution mostly teaches native children about native culture, essentially making Macuxi language a foreign idiom as opposed to their maternal tongue. This is a critical point, because indigenous culture is most often carried through the generations by familial connections; as the group's identity, it is conveyed socially, organically, and naturally. Language is the medium through which an identity and localized knowledge are expressed; thus, for a student to fully engage with her or his culture, language arguably cannot be taught by force or by anyone who does not share that identity.

Further, designations of groups and belonging are integral to language. For example, Macuxi speakers group people into "us," "white," and "civilized" (Portuguese-speaking Brazilians) (Beto, personal communication, 2011). When parents stop speaking Macuxi to their children, or those children choose to reject their maternal language, their framework for understanding where they fit in the world also changes. They lose solidarity with their culture and local society, and tend to struggle in finding a new sense of belonging. Those are consequences that the lectured instruction of language in a traditional school setting cannot address. Linguists Mark Warschauer and Keola Donaghy (1997) argue that if language revitalization is to be pursued, organizers and instructors must create "authentic opportunities to communicate outside of the classroom" with the language in question (p. 358). Given these realities, traditional second-language teaching methods in schools may be inadequate for cultural revitalization. In order to understand the potential value of applying technology to language education, we must understand the full scope of culture loss in *Nova Esperança*.

2.4 Culture Loss

While Macuxi, Wapixana and Taurepang are not classified as endangered or dying languages by most linguistic organizations (which tend to focus documentation efforts on populations of living speakers of a given language numbering in the tens or hundreds), they are nevertheless disappearing at an alarming rate. *Nova Esperança* is an urgent case because of its small size, linguistic diversity (with no common language apart from Portuguese), and its proximity and assimilation to greater Brazil because of its location along a federal highway.

Unfortunately, *Nova Esperança* provides an example of localized language death, occurring noticeably over the course of the three most recent generations. For the most part, the eldest generation of *Nova Esperança* speaks their indigenous language amongst themselves and sometimes to their children (the middle generation) who understand (but rarely respond in Wapixana or Macuxi), and whose own offspring barely understand their grandparents and speak solely Portuguese. While other communities have thousands of Wapixana and Macuxi speakers, *Nova Esperança* risks permanently losing these languages, and along with them, fundamentals of its community identity that cannot be easily revitalized through basic language classes.

When transmitted familiarly, languages carry associations, experiences, memories, histories, intimacy, and solidarity. If these indigenous languages are acquired as a second tongue, as the young students of *Nova Esperança* would learn Macuxi or Wapixana if they were taught by traditional methods only in school, the languages might feel forced, foreign, and dissociated from the meaning and warmth they inherently contain when spoken by a mother to a child, between families, or amongst elders. Many members of the community have realized that the implication of this language loss could be a permanent relinquishment of cultural ownership, and thus there is local motivation to create language preservation programs. For Vona, language preservation would be the most important type of project any organization could implement. "When you stop speaking your language, you lose a big part of your identity. People are ashamed of being indians so they don't speak" (personal communication, 2011). Helena, a visiting teacher in training and language researcher, said that a language dies because people don't speak to their children or don't speak to them early enough. She stated that she made that mistake and now her children do not want to learn Macuxi (personal communication, 2011).

When Aline, a Wapixana elder, was asked what she thought about language loss in the community, she said with evident pride, "*Eu não deixo a minha cultura* (I don't leave my culture)." She estimated that of the 50-65 people of the village who identify as Wapixana, around 40 do not speak the language. These are mostly the younger family members and, surprisingly, the village leadership. She asked, "How can they fully represent the interests of those who *do* consider Wapixana language as a crucial part of their identity?" (Aline, personal communication, 2011).

Beto, Tainara, and Sara, Macuxi parents and elders, agreed that traditional language is disappearing. Other, larger communities speak Macuxi almost exclusively, Beto explained, but *Nova Esperança* and many other villages have fallen behind. He noted that indigenous language has almost no economic utility in larger cities or in *Nova Esperança*. Because the village is linguistically diverse, no single indigenous language can be used to communicate with between families of different tribal origin, while Portuguese is almost guaranteed to be understood. Language disappearance is only one aspect of cultural loss. For example, Tainara, in her mid-nineties, is the only member of the community who still remembers how to sing *Parixara*, a Macuxi song and group dance, though she cannot dance *Parixara* by herself.

When Tainara was asked about one of the younger members of the household who had walked by without greeting her, she said, "He does not speak Macuxi, he only speaks the *língua emprestada* (or the 'borrowed' language, Portuguese)" (Beto, Tainara, Sara, personal communication, 2011).

As Wayt W. Gibbs writes in his Scientific American article *Dying Languages*,

...one factor that always seems to occur in the demise of a language is that the speakers begin to have 'collective doubts about the usefulness of language loyalty.' Once they start regarding their own language as inferior to the majority language, people stop using it for all situations. Kids pick up on the attitude and prefer the dominant language. In many cases, people do not notice until they suddenly realize that their kids never speak the language, even at home. (2002, p. 85)

This is a crucial point: there is often no conscious decision to stop using the language, but rather a slow silencing caused by its lack of utility in the greater world.

The Tuxaua, or village leader, told the researcher that the pejorative rhetoric that was used by missionaries, settlers, and landowners for centuries still operates today, and is even internalized and used by the indigenous people. For example, the Tuxaua's mother, Renata, called the Macuxi language "*gíria*," which literally means "slang." She learned Macuxi as a young woman and can still understand the language. However, she chose to never speak it, dismissing it: "No, I don't speak that slang." As village matriarch, she is unusual in that she does not actively support cultural preservation, as do most of the other elders. But Natalia, her daughter-in-law, whose own parents refused to speak Macuxi with her, understood

Renata's situation: how could you justify re-learning your maternal language if the culture with power told you your whole life it was just babble? The implications of Renata's language loss are significant. Because her children—the village leadership (the Tuxaua, his wife Juliana, and his sister Anna)—don't speak Wapixana or Macuxi, they tend to treat that aspect of their culture more as an artifact than a way of life (Tuxaua, Renata, Beto, Tainara, Sara, Natalia, Juliana, Anna), personal communication, 2011).

Gabriella, a Macuxi woman who recently moved into the community, understands Macuxi but cannot speak it. According to her, the loss of language is much more severe and rapid in *Nova Esperança* than in other villages. In *Nova Esperança*, she thought, children and youth are not as interested in learning indigenous language or learning about anything "cultural" (personal communication, 2011). The Tuxaua summed up the crisis well when he asserted that "we're losing our respect for traditional morals, our elders, their unique knowledge, and ourselves; especially the youth. We need to correct that loss" (personal communication, 2011). In a recent interview, the Tuxaua indicated that revitalization efforts are already moving forward; there is a larger plan to incorporate language and cultural resuscitation into the development of regional ethnotourism, which itself constitutes part of the Multi-year Plan of Roraima, a statewide development initiative. Ethnotourism, argues the Tuxaua, creates a concrete motivation to revive and add value to the indigenous culture (personal communication, 2015). Using economic incentives may be an effective mechanism to promote cultural regrowth, which raises questions of utility: why do indigenous languages atrophy, and how can communities foster their usefulness in the eyes of younger generations?

2.5 Discussion of Theoretical Contributions

The threads of youth disengagement, culture clash, and language loss are intimately interwoven. Many linguistic theorists and anthropologists agree that the most serious blows to an indigenous language occur when parents stop speaking it in front of their children. This generally happens as a result of decades, if not centuries, of exposure to an imposed language and the stigma that flows from the dominant society and inundates the minority culture. Over time, this stigma gains traction and manifests itself in disutility, which is what the Macuxi and Wapixana refer to when they note that no one speaks indigenous language in the towns and cities. Few people now use these indigenous languages for trade or business, and it is rarely used outside the village (if it is used there at all). Naturally, if all the members of the household already speak Portuguese and it is the preferred language in school and work, it eventually pushes the mother tongue out of use in the home.

Linguist David Dalby (2003) explains that there are around 5,000 languages globally that are the dominant or mother tongue for someone (other estimates put the total number of languages around 7,000), and most studies point to an accelerated death rate that will leave humanity with a maximum of 2,500 languages by the end of the century. The world is losing a language as often as every 2 weeks, according to Dalby's estimate. English and "national languages" dominate media and public discourse (2003, ix). This is largely because of colonial legacies of English, combined with globalization, two factors which leave many indigenous youth thinking that the largest languages of the world are paths to success. Theorist Ngugi Thiong'o calls this phenomenon an "imperialist bomb," an internalization that pervades a society that has been dominated for hundreds of years by another culture and over time causes oppressed people to reject their own language and culture in favor of that of their oppressors (1986, p. 3).

So what is lost when those youths choose to join another language and culture? Marianne Mithun explains,

...when a language disappears, the most intimate aspects of culture can disappear as well: fundamental ways of organizing experience into concepts, of relating to each other, of interacting with other people. The more conscious genres of verbal art are usually lost as well: traditional ritual, oratory, myth, legends, and even humor. Speakers commonly remark that when they speak a different language, they say different things and even think different thoughts. (Mithun and Dalby, 2003, p. 252)

Her point illuminates the void that could grow between a *Nova Esperança* elder who processes in Wapixana and her grandchild, who may only think about the world in Portuguese.

Language scholars agree that the accelerated language death to which we are now bearing witness is completely unprecedented. David Crystal, one of the most renowned linguists of our time, argues that these rapid disappearances are not to be taken lightly. He posits all people should be concerned about this crisis of silence for a series of reasons. First, human diversity supports human stability (allowing cross-fertilization of thought). Second, language supports identity, the core meaning-maker for humans. Third, languages are vaults filled with exclusive and subjective histories. Fourth, languages add to the sum of human understanding (which we all are arguably striving to augment). Lastly, and perhaps most bluntly, Crystal argues we should be concerned with language death because languages are inherently fascinating (2000). Ken Hale, another prominent language theorist, explains how linguistic diversity (specifically, varying grammar dealing with subjects, verbs and tenses) proves and supports the adaptability and multifaceted nature of the human mind.

For example, our dominant-language views on the separation of singular and plural subjects limit the potential understanding of grouping (Hale, 1992). What could we understand or imagine if we were to learn a language with completely different grouping categories, spaces, and descriptors? What will humanity lose when such a language disappears?

Crystal puts forth a set of criteria for evaluating language health and stability. If we apply it to the overall, regional health of the Wapixana and Macuxi languages (which correspond with the two main indigenous groups of *Nova Esperança*), they are "potentially endangered: socially and economically disadvantaged, under heavy pressure from a larger language, and beginning to lose child speakers" (2000, p. 21). However, *within* the community, the languages are near "moribund," one step above extinct. This means there are a handful of fluent speakers remaining, and most of these are old and unlikely, if the status quo continues, to transfer their knowledge to the younger generations. Why have language preservation programs not taken off here, and everywhere else mother tongues are threatened?

In *The Significance of Diversity in Language Endangerment and Preservation,* Mithun (1998) argues one problem with language preservation efforts is that few people recognize the astounding diversity of languages that exist globally, and the associated importance of that diversity. She argues that all communities must come to grips with this threat against our human variety, and, though one cannot completely remove the economic and social conditions that threaten languages, one *can* give full support to bilingual education programs and the promotion of localized languages as viable and useful equals of the dominant language (Mithun, 1998).

It is important to note that successful endangered language revitalization cannot be imposed from outside the given culture. This raises the question of how speakers of an endangered language are motivated to preserve it. Jeanette King (2009) addresses this issue in the case of Māori second-language speakers in New Zealand. As many individuals are learning Māori for the first time (not having had generational transmission of the language), they are internally motivated to revitalize the language because it means they can claim autonomy of their cultural well-being, reconnect with their heritage, and redefine their individual identity. Because of these robust individual motivators (and the strong number of living speakers), Māori revitalization has largely been successful. However, revival efforts for moribund languages tend to be fueled by motivations that are external: a sense of responsibility towards the society's past, the community, and the future of the culture. "However," King notes, "it is unclear whether invoking a moral imperative towards the language which the speaker may not share may be as effective as appealing to more internally focused motivations already held by the speakers" (2009, p. 105). Thus, efforts to revitalize Wapixana, Macuxi, or Taurepang in *Nova Esperança* should capitalize on, if not be principally fueled by, internal motivations of the individuals. The question that follows, then, is how technology can be utilized to provide the motivated participants with tools for localized language acquisition and revitalization.

Linguist Candace Galla, writing on the resurgence of Hawaiian language use, notes that a serious difficulty in any revitalization is creating "authentic materials that depict the language and culture in a non-stereotypical way" (2009, p.169). This is especially the case because technology tends to codify and regularize the language in question. For example, who, in a revitalization-oriented Hawaiian-language radio show, defines *the* indigenous culture? Who has access to radio technologies, and who has the ability to express their personal representation of the culture? Though these issues can pose problems for a fully "democratic" cultural resurgence, diverse technologies do provide meaningful, individualized, and creative opportunities for revitalization. Galla indicates that the "Hawaiian Renaissance" is successful because of easy access to a plethora of language-use avenues: elder groups, inspiring educators, radio programming, immersion programs, music and podcasts, online libraries and dictionaries, digitized archives, and Hawaiian-language news. From Galla's case study, we can conclude that an array of accessible technologies can offer a creative space for participating endangered-language learners to utilize their linguistic heritage in their environment and their daily lives.

But as Mark Warschauer (1998) points out in *Technology and Indigenous Language Revitalization: Analyzing the Experience of Hawai'i*, the debate around the impact of technology use in language revitalization is hardly resolved. Some may view communications technology as a homogenizing global force that diminishes the relevance and prevalence of indigenous languages. In other cases, technology is seen as a neutral medium for communication that does not damage heritage languages, but rather provides a space for free discourse. Still others view the technological opportunities for language revitalization as the sole means of effective resuscitation. Technology simultaneously plays all of these roles, and appears to create one additional and profound impact on language: it offers a dynamic space of struggle. Because technology use is becoming a part of daily life around the world (and endangered-language areas are no exception), engaging new language technologies is one of the only effective ways to "compete" with dominant cultures and languages. The strength of technology use for language acquisition and revitalization lies in its "multiplicative effect," a term utilized by Warschauer (2004) to indicate simultaneous outcomes: reconnection to individual and collective cultural resources, an increased sense of agency, power, and thus motivation, a stronger grasp of real technological skills, and a more robust self-expression. Naturally, technology (for example, Navajo or Māori language keyboards) use will alter the context, delivery, and significance of the language for learners, but the modern evolution of an indigenous language is often seen as a small sacrifice to make for its overall resuscitation. Further, it is possible that technology can actually support the emotional and historical associations (as well as the solidarity) that an indigenous language creates organically as it transfers from one generation to the next.

If, in the case of *Nova Esperança*, revitalization efforts prove possible and promising, technology use must be chosen and initiated (not necessarily designed) by the constituents of the language. This is important for two reasons: it guarantees appropriate access for the indigenous participants, and it improves the relevance, significance, and purpose of the language within the technology. When asked about the role technology can play in indigenous language acquisition and revitalization, the Tuxaua indicated that the community "will use technology because our principal audience, children and youth, use technology frequently today. The question now is how to crate pedagogical methodologies that incentivize their participation…" (Tuxaua, personal communication, 2015). The process of developing these methodologies must be a dialogue with those who will participate; namely, young people. Reversing the perceived disutility of indigenous languages in the minds of youth must be preceded by the creation of accessible and intuitive interfaces through familiar technological mediums. This could be as simple as a small documentary project, or as complex as the design of an app to switch one's smartphone keypad to the indigenous alphabet. The Tuxaua noted the key aspect of this revitalization strategy: it must reflect the technological experiences and desires of its participants and embed language acquisition moments in real-world projects. This aim is congruent with the principles of educommunication, namely, the idea that the educational experience should provide avenues of communication that empower participants (Soares, 2000).

Keeping in mind the "imperialist bomb" theory that Thiong'o proposes and the stigma of indigenous language that native youth have internalized, we must also consider the ability of technology to provide forward-facing avenues of learning. That is, can technology use in *Nova Esperança* create mechanisms for language acquisition that are not tainted by historically negative perceptions of indigenous languages as "backwards" and "slang"? The answer is likely affirmative: the Māori and Hawaiian case studies demonstrate that technology can provide dynamism, ownership, and practicality that overcome legacies of stigma and empower learners with purpose.

Despite the reluctance of *Nova Esperança* community members to accept indigenous language education in traditional schools (and Warschauer and Donaghy's insistence on creating learning opportunities *outside* of the classroom), the potential contributions of public education must be recognized. The Tuxaua, in fact, indicates that the ethnotourism project (which is constituted in part by community-based cultural revival work) and "will have a partnership with the school." He notes that "in this case, we will have to build a partnership with the state as well as with private institutions" (Tuxaua, personal communication, 2015). Necessarily, the educational strategies to foster indigenous cultural awareness and linguistic familiarity among youth will be determined by the local community, with implementation support from the state, the schools, and private organizations. Funds to invest in such programs and technological tools will be available through the Multi-year Plan of Roraima (Tuxaua, personal communication, 2015).

2.6 Section Conclusion

While many indigenous leaders in Brazil, including those in *Nova Esperança*, are organizing to fight for autonomy and cultural preservation, innumerable young indigenous people are losing their cultural bearing and rejecting their heritage. This is a critical moment: either the implementation of relevant technologies and strategies will help youth reconnect with their cultural resources and cultivate purpose and pride through their indigeneity, or these living cultures will be ruptured and considered only artifacts in a matter of generations. *Nova Esperança* characterizes this turning point, and could benefit from technology-based cultural preservation efforts. Though we know technology can alter the indigenous language it helps to teach, such changes must be seen as necessary outcomes of maintaining linguistic relevance and utility. In the case of *Nova Esperança*, the community and their partner stakeholders will be required to deploy varied technologies in the effort to reengage youth in cultural practice and to build a sustainable economy.

3. PARTICIPATORY RESEARCH IN SOUTHERN BRAZIL

3.1 Introduction

As mentioned in the introduction to this book chapter, English is a popular second language in both the public and private school systems in Brazil. The analysis of language policies in Brazil suggests that English can be seen as a foreign language in public schools but as an international language in private language institutes. These two divergent views of English reflect a social separation between those who can afford private institutions with important technological tools to learn English and those who cannot (Finardi, 2014).

There is a great disparity among public school systems. Stanek (2013) stated that the primary challenge for public schools in Brazil is how to improve basic education. For example, at the end of the 9th grade, only 27% of students achieve the expected skills and competencies in Portuguese, which is the official language. This scenario is even worse for second language education, where teachers are hard to find or may not even have the proper qualifications. In fact, the Brazilian Ministry of Education reported that a significant number of high school teachers lack specific qualification in the subject that they teach (MEC, 2010).

In the public school system, there is also a shortage of materials, and textbooks (or copies made of textbooks) are the most commonly used tool to teach a language in Brazil. Most of these textbooks are out of date and not situated in the student's current reality. Santos (1997) analyzed the content of English in Brazilian textbooks for elementary schools, identifying three themes: representations of a world devoid of problems, representations of a fragmented world, and representations of learning as an individual process. These authors found out that textbook messages reinforced a conservative educational trend in Brazil. The messages suggested a simplistic and non-critical view of the subject. If the student is not involved with the subject or the contents are disconnected from the student's reality, there may be an increase of academic failure. Working with the local reality has the much-needed quality of offering an accessible and well-known universe to the student, keeping them interested (PCN, 1997).

There is an attempt to change this out-of-date method of teaching a second language in the public system and recent government programs are trying to insert computers in target schools to better align them with the global use of technology in language-education. Braul (2006) shows that using computers in language classrooms brought variety into the classroom atmosphere, developed learners' particular language skills, and increased autonomy.

The private school system is already ahead in the use of technology in language-education. A previous investigation conducted by Neckel et al. (2014) showed that instructors at a private University in Southern Brazil utilized several computer-derived technological tools in their classrooms. Instructors pointed out that the internet, information and communication technologies in the classroom can be positive, but that their efficacy depends on the student involvement. Some common tools listed in order of preference are: (i) computer and presentation software, (ii) internet, TV and DVD, (iii) radio, and (iv) overhead projector. There was a consensus about the effectiveness of using these tools to aid teaching process and the majority of these instructors (59%) continue to seek formal training in technology use.

3.2 *Vox Populi*: From the Student's Perspective

Aiming to investigate language learning from the student perspective, a participatory study focused on challenges and benefits of the use of technologies in language learning was conducted in the city of Passo Fundo, Rio Grande do Sul, southern Brazil. Semi-structured interviews were applied during the first semester of 2014 to a senior class in the private university listed in the previous section.

A total of nineteen college students participated in this research. Data was collected for social and demographic information, second language learning, challenges on learning a new language, the use of technologies to mediate the educational process, and suggestions on how to improve second language educational methods. The Method of Content Analysis (MCA) was used to evaluate the data. Students were 20 to 39 years old, and the majority of them (74%) were female. Most of them were full-time students and only 31% were working while going to school. Their occupations included internships, government work, project assistantships, and self-employment.

When participants were asked which foreign language they had learned, 22% stated that they never took classes in a foreign language. For the ones who did, Spanish (40%) and English (33%) were the most cited languages, followed by Italian (11%) and French (6%). Regarding the time spent on learning a second language, 22% had never participated in formal classes, 33% had less than two years of classes, 23% had between two and four years, and 17% had five years or more of classes. However, from all the interviewees, only one considered himself fluent, and emphasized that such fluency came from social media interactions rather than from formal classes.

When asked about the challenges they face while learning a second language, the majority (44%) mentioned shortage of time as the main reason, while 11% mentioned costs and language structure. The remaining participants identified other challenges such as balance between work and study, writing and grammar, vocabulary, pronunciation, verbal tenses that vary from one language to another, and structure that can to be intimidating and complex. Interviewees also reported that there are not enough videos used in classes or ways to continue practicing the language after class.

Students were also asked how technology could help them learn a new language. Their answers varied greatly. Online classes, videos, research, and distance education were the most popular answers, but quick dissemination of knowledge, alternative learning methods, and rapid access were also listed as benefits of using technology. Some students mentioned research through ethernet (local area network), downloadable books and online kits as important language learning tools. Social media applications were said to encourage them to study at home, in a non-formal setting, and in conversation via Facebook and Skype with people from other countries. More music and other innovative methods were reported as a need. Among the suggestions, students listed the possibility of bringing a foreign student to class so they could learn about culture and customs of other countries through face-to-face interaction. Watching a foreign TV series with daily conversations was also pointed out as a good learning method.

It is important to note that even students who took formal classes were not able to communicate in English; only two interviewees answered questions in English. Power and Erling (2014) observed a similar situation in Bangladesh, suggesting that training has failed to provide teachers with the necessary skills for effective classroom practice because student participation in lessons is usually passive. In the same perspective, Lai (2015) highlighted the importance of raising teachers' awareness of the different roles they can play and of enhancing their abilities to promote learner-directed use of technology for learning outside the classroom.

3.3 Technological Intervention in Education: Perspectives for Language Education

Communication is an important building block of the human society, one that in recent decades has been developed through tools such as graphic language, film production, radio, and television to make it more effective (Cordova, 2008). Currently, technological intervention in education (TIE) can be considered as one of the top trends in education that makes use of different tools, especially in regard to distance education. Technological intervention implies a relationship between pedagogical practices and actions, and it can be seen as a bridge to fill the gap between these practices and their social applications.

TIE also makes use of educommunication as mentioned in the theoretical frame of this chapter. In Brazil, educommunication gained strength in the 20th century and still plays a role within the communication spaces in informal education through the use of media. Educommunicaton aims to increase the capacity of expression of individuals while multiplying knowledge and spreading awareness on relevant issues (Barreto, 2004). It can be flexible to both public and private school systems on language-education. Although oral communication and books are valued means of knowledge acquisition, audiovisual resources are gaining popularity, given that they require no reading to transmit messages and that they capitalize on their attractiveness to our senses.

Audiovisual teaching methods and procedures include educational film, television, film devices, recording and artwork. We can divide the resources into those that appeal to vision and those that appeal to our aural sense. Visuals are those elements that are written, analogue, iconic, schematic, and abstract-emotional, with the materials presented via blackboard, posters, pictures, museums, photos, movies, flipcharts, diagrams, graphics, maps, objects, and slides. The audio resources are those utilizing radio, tapes, disks, and others. According to Cordova (2008), the audiovisual resources are divided into three categories: designed materials, audio materials, and non-designed. This new category of non-designed materials includes illustrative materials, such as photographs, charts and graphs, objects, models, maps and such activities as documentaries or professional visits, theater performances and exhibitions, and others.

It is essential to emphasize that for educommunication, technological resources are used in a very important way (Almeida, 2006). The use of the internet is increasing in school systems as we seek improvement in pedagogical practices. Schools go beyond information and become responsible for the social inclusion of students and their success in the competitive job market and in other aspects of life.

According to Oliveira (2001), the use of new technologies, especially computer-based systems, ensures improvement in learning and development of students. New technologies can aid in skill development for the new economy. In this sense, education is viewed as a process for developing an individual's citizenship. Such a process requires access to information as well as the critical capacity of analyzing it. The availability of information and communication technologies has brought new opportunities for distance education and universities, schools, other educational institutions, and professional and business organizations. The development of distance learning courses based on digital learning environments that can be accessed via the internet is a leading trend.

Beyond expanding possibilities of academic success, the incorporation of alternative technological resources into distance learning education is presented as a strategy to democratize and raise the standard of training quality for Brazilian professionals in many areas. This means that distance education is growing at a fast pace, and so is the use of technology in education (Almeida, 2006). Education as a whole, in particular for teacher training, can benefit from information and communication technologies (ICT). ICT has been applied for multiple purposes, ranging from overtaking the limits set by "old technologies" such as blackboard and printed materials, to solving the most varied educational problems (and even to socioeconomic and political issues).

In this informational era, the term "teacher" has been giving way to other educator terms such as "facilitator", "animator", "tutor", "instructor", and even "monitor" in Brazil. Monitor, in its multiple meanings, may be an image-synthesis of the *casualization* of teaching. By referring to the meaning of the word in dictionaries, we can summarize it as: one who gives advice, lessons, or warns, or a student who assists the teacher in the teaching of the subject, in application of exercises, to clarify doubts, etc., outside of regular classes. If the teacher could become a monitor, who then would occupy the traditional position of the teacher?

The answer to this question is fully evident in reference to distance education. Technological systems are becoming cheaper, more available, and easier to handle. They can utilize current practices to optimize teaching potential, familiarize citizens with the technology that is in their daily lives, provide individuals with means to quickly update knowledge, and motivate students and staff to continuously learn at any stage of their lives. It is the technology (specifically, that is cheap and accessible) that occupies the position of the subject capable of developing strategic actions, in other words, the teacher.

There is an urgent need to insert various information and communication technologies in the development of teacher's training courses. This will prepare them for the noblest purpose of education: definition and management of ethical, scientific, and aesthetic references for sharing and negotiation (Andre, 2004: 25).

So far, connecting devices like television have been the root of training and programming that are promoted at the national level. For instance, in Brazil the top hits are TV school and PROINFO. At the state level, even at the elementary level (as in the case of Ceara and Maranhao), tele-classes can provide radical technological substitution. It is necessary to reform the education from top to bottom, making it more flexible and capable of increasing national competitiveness. Inclusion via technology is one of the most effective mechanisms in creating a competitive, integrated global economy.

In the globalized world, technologies are inserted every day and everywhere. Yet despite its positive impact in the educational system, technology is not yet as ubiquitous there as in other areas of daily life. As we move forward, it is important not to let the use of technologies dominate classrooms entirely, since the relationship between student and teacher is still very important, and it is up to us to know what the limits of technology are (Consani, 2008).

In the past few years, the Brazilian government has been investing in education technology. Training teachers in new technologies through government programs can substantially upgrade what currently exists in Brazil for language learning. There are still many challenges due to accessibility, and the use of technologies is increasing at a more institutional pace among teachers than it is among students.

3.4. A Non-Native Experiential Overview of Portuguese Language-Education

There is a variety of resources for learning Portuguese as a second language for the purpose of tourism. These range from common textbooks and books on tape to language immersion and interactive software with online programs that involve conversations with native speakers. The cost for these programs can be significant, putting them out of reach of the majority of Brazilians. These highly interactive methodologies of language learning are largely geared toward foreigners who visit Brazil for business or tourism.

Portuguese is a challenging language to learn if one is not a native speaker (Thaines and Bodah, 2008). The nasal sounds required to properly speak the language are difficult for a non-native speaker to pronounce correctly, which tends to reinforce a practice common to apprehensive students of any language: deliberate avoidance of certain words in order to prevent misunderstandings.

While language immersion has largely been touted for quite some time as the fastest, easiest, and most complete way to learn a language, unique complexities exist for this practice within Brazil. As discussed in Section 3, less than 30% of the Brazilian population is considered fluent in "proper" Portuguese by the time they complete the 9th grade. This lack of proper grammar and pronunciation may cause individuals to maintain their use of incomplete Portuguese into their adult life.

This could be the environment to which the non-native speaker is introduced through language immersion when visiting Brazil. If the visitor underwent preparation through formal language classes or language learning software prior to traveling to the county, their arrival in Brazil could be their first exposure to a regional slang, dialect, or incomplete language, which can present a tremendous challenge. It is not uncommon for completely different words to be utilized for the same meaning in different regions of Brazil.

Once in Brazil, many beginning second-language learners are incapable of listening to a radio broadcast and gaining anything useful from it due to the speed of speech among native speakers. For this same reason, radio broadcasts can prove to be an invaluable resource for intermediate and advanced students as a way to practice their comprehension of the language at a pace which is common among native speakers. This effect is applicable to nearly every language, and certainly not restricted to Portuguese. The same can be attributed to the spoken dialog of a television program. However, with TV, the visual aspects in addition to the use of subtitles can greatly help to convey the intended meaning to early learners.

Strong regional accents further complicate radio and television broadcasts. A majority of national Brazilian news broadcasts originate from Rio de Janeiro, an area with a very distinct and strong regional accent that can sound foreign to anyone who has studied Brazilian Portuguese outside of that area. When immersed in Brazil, it is noticeable that the Rio de Janeiro regional accent is aspired to within Brazil and connotes the desired wealth and culture associated with the greater Rio region as a whole, but the dialect can appear nearly indecipherable to a foreign student of Portuguese.

This increases the use of technology and social media platforms (if one can resist the "translate this" icon), as users can approach messages at their own pace, and can look up words they may not understand. Social media introduces the language learner to the use of a word or phrase in a certain context. Visual clues again can help to associate specific vocabulary with certain situations (for example, when reading a post connected to a certain photograph, video, or article).

Perhaps social media's greatest asset is its ability to evolve and reflect current trends in real time. Movies or novellas exist in a single context or time frame--that in which they were recorded or that which they were meant to emulate. Social media adapts to trends as they evolve, and students can get a sense of the current meaning of words and phrases. This helps them to avoid awkward misuse of yesterday's (or yesteryear's) terminology and helps them develop a modern vernacular that is relevant, which strengthens their interactions with native speakers and further increases their word bank.

The divide between the largely ineffective textbook-based learning style of Portuguese among Brazilians (evidenced by the significant percentage non-fluent Portuguese speakers in Brazil), and the technology-based systems of foreign learners can prevent communication. Brazilians who rely on tourism for their income are understandably very eager to effectively communicate with their visiting guests. All too often, this results in the use of other languages, such as English, Spanish, German, or French to communicate in areas where foreign tourists are numerous. This is understandable, but it lessens or even prevents the facilitation of productive Portuguese-language experiences among foreign visitors to Brazil. While this certainly bolsters tourism and lessens the burden on the foreign traveler, it undoubtedly also weakens the Portuguese-language structure in those regions, leading to the adoption of language hybrids such as "Portunhol" (a mixture of Portuguese and *Espanhol/* Spanish), and creating yet another impediment to correct Portuguese acquisition and usage.

4. FINAL CONSIDERATIONS

Our chapter proposes to explore the challenges and perspectives of language-education technology in Brazil by presenting information on distinct realities manifested throughout the country. We conclude that indigenous language loss poses a unique educational challenge and may be best addressed with the use of modern, relevant, and accessible technology tools. We also found that the lack of teacher training in operational systems and even in class content can be a debilitating obstacle in itself, as pointed out by student participants in Southern Brazil.

In addition to more investment in technologies and teacher training, we suggest a reflection on the basis of education practices. When the technology is available, teaching and learning of languages should be multidisciplinary and optimized through partnership among a variety of educators, students, parents, and other community members (Thaines and Rodrigues, 2007). In most cases, education that includes technology must still be performed through dialogues, and these dialogues should encourage critical thinking and acknowledge solidarity between the participants (Freire, 2005).

While our work presented specific information on the intersection of education technologies, indigenous language loss and revitalization, and second-language acquisition through a theoretical and case-study framework, we also aimed to provide an informative reference for curricular designers. The educational challenges and perspectives that we presented in this chapter, though situated in the realities of Brazil, will help to inform the globally-minded decisions of language educators seeking innovative solutions for student growth, today and tomorrow.

REFERENCES

Aguaded-Gómez, J. I. (2011). Media Education: An International Unstoppable Phenomenon. The Work of the UN, Europe and Spain in the Field of Edu-communication. *Comunicar, 37,* (7-8).

Almeida, M. E. B. (2006). Technology and distance education: Approaches and contributions of digital and interactive learning environments. *Revista Educação e Comunicação, São Paulo, 1*(16), 1–23.

Andre, M. (2004). A survey of teachers to assess teacher training. In *Romanowski et al. (Org.). Local knowledge and universal knowledge: research, teaching and teacher action* (pp. 205–218). Curitiba: Champagnat.

Martin-Barbero, J., & Barcelos, C. (2000). Comunicação e mediações clutrais [Communication and cultural mediations (Interview)]. *Revista Brasileira de Ciências da Comunicação, 23*(1), 151-163.

Barreto, R. G. (2004). Technology and education: Work and teacher training. *Educação & Sociedade, Campinas, 25*(89), 1–15.

Barros, D. M. V., & Amaral, S. F. (2006). Emotional intelligence in learning mediated virtual space. *Educação Temática Digital, Campinas, 8*(2), 152–161.

Becker, B. K., & Egler, C. A. G. (1992). *Brazil: a new regional power in the world economy.* New York, New York: Cambridge University Press Archive.

Bejarano, P. A. C., & Chapeton, C. M. (2013). The role of genre-based activities in the writing of argumentative essays in EFL. *Profile Journal, Colombia, 15*(1), 26–85.

Braul, B. (2006). *ESL teacher perceptions and attitudes toward using computer-assisted language learning (CALL): recommendations for effective CALL practice* [MA dissertation]. Department of Secondary Education, Edmonton, Alberta, Canada.

Brown, D. B. (2014). *Mobile learning for communicative language teaching: An exploration of how higher education language instructors design communicative mall environments* [Doctoral dissertation]. The University of Memphis, Memphis, TN, USA.

Chen, C. M., Wang, J. Y., & Chen, Y. C. (2014). Facilitating English-language reading performance by a digital reading annotation system with self-regulated learning mechanisms. *Journal of Educational Technology & Society, 17*(1), 102–114.

Consani, M. A. (2008). Technological mediation in education: concepts and applications [Master's thesis]. Universidade de São Paulo, São Paulo, Brazil.

Cordova, S. T. (2008). Use of visual aids in teaching of veterinary medicine. *Revista Eletrônica Lato Sensu, São Paulo, 3*(1), 1–15.

MCC Costa. (2001). *Educomunicar é Preciso!* Retrieved from http://www.ups.br/educomradio/café/café.asp?editora=TSUPH&cod=377

Crystal, D. (2000). *Language Death.* New York, NY: Cambridge University Press. doi:10.1017/CBO9781139106856

Cviko, A., McKenney, S., & Voogt, J. (2014). Teacher roles in designing technology-rich learning activities for early literacy: A cross-case analysis. *Computers & Education, 72,* 68–79. doi:10.1016/j.compedu.2013.10.014

Dalby, A. (2003). *Language in danger: The loss of linguistic diversity and the threat to our future.* New York, NY: Columbia University Press.

Delors, J. et al.. (2004). *Education: The treasure within. Report to UNESCO of the International Commission on Education for the XXI. 9* (p. 80). São Paulo: Cortez.

Ene, E., & Connor, U. (2014). Technological applications for language teaching: ICT and equipment use in teaching & learning foreign languages. National Foreign Languages 2020 Project, Hanoi, Vietnam.

Fazenda, C.A.I. (1993). *Interdisciplinaridade: história, teoria e pesquisa* (2nd ed.). Campinas, SP: Loyola.

Fedorov, A. (2001). A Russian Perspective. *Educommunication (Belgium)*, *55*, 92–95.

Finardi, K. (2014). The slaughter of Kachru's five sacred cows in Brazil: Affordances of the use of English as an international language. *Studies in English Language Teaching*, *2*(4), 401.

Freire, P. (2005). *Teachers as cultural workers: Letters to those who dare teach.* Boulder, CO: Westview Press.

Galla, C. K. (2009). Indigenous language revitalization and technology: From tradition to contemporary domains. In J. Reyhner & L. Lockard (Eds.), *Indigenous language revitalization: Encouragement, guidance & lessons learned* (pp. 167–182). Flagstaff, AZ: Northern Arizona University Press.

Gibbs, W. (2002) Saving dying languages. *Scientific American*, August, 79-85. Retrieved from http://www.language-archives.org/documents/sciam.pdf

Golonka, E. M., Bowles, A. R., Frank, V. M., Richardson, D. L., & Freynik, S. (2014). Technologies for foreign language learning: A review of technology types and their effectiveness. *Computer Assisted Language Learning*, *27*(1), 70–105. doi:10.1080/09588221.2012.700315

Grenoble, L., & Whaley, L. (Eds.). (1998). *Endangered languages: Current issues and future prospects.* New York, NY: Cambridge University Press. doi:10.1017/CBO9781139166959

Grinevald, C. (1998). Language endangerment in South America. In L. Grenoble & L. Whaley (Eds.), *Endangered languages: Current issues and future prospects.* New York, NY: Cambridge University Press. doi:10.1017/CBO9781139166959.007

Hale, K. (1992) Endangered languages. *Linguistic Society of America*, *68*(1). Retrieved from http://www.jstor.org/pss/416368

Hebrard, J. (2000). The goal of the school is culture, not the same life. *Presença pedagógica, Belo Horizonte, 6*(33), 5-17.

Hwang, W. Y., Chen, H. S., Shadiev, R., Huang, R. Y. M., & Chen, C. Y. (2014). Improving English as a foreign language writing in elementary schools using mobile devices in familiar situational contexts. *Computer Assisted Language Learning*, *27*(5), 359–378. doi:10.1080/09588221.2012.733711

Instituto Brasileiro de Geografia e Estatística. (2007). *Brazilian statistics.* Retrieved from www.ibge.gov.br

Jarvis, H., & Achilleos, M. (2013). From Computer Assisted Language Learning (CALL) to Mobile Assisted Language Use (MALU). *Tesl-Ej*, *16*(4), n4.

Jarvis, H., & Krashen, S. (2014). Is CALL obsolete? Language acquisition and language learning revisited in a digital age. *TESL-EJ*, *17*(4), n4.

King, J. (2009). Language is life: The worldview of second language speakers of Māori. In J. Reyhner & L. Lockard (Eds.), *Indigenous language revitalization: Encouragement, guidance & lessons learned* (pp. 97–108). Flagstaff, AZ: Northern Arizona University Press.

Lai, C. (2015). Modeling teachers' influence on learners' self-directed use of technology for language learning outside the classroom. *Computers & Education, 82,* 74–83. doi:10.1016/j.compedu.2014.11.005

Liu, M., Abe, K., Cao, M., Liu, S., Ok, D. U., Park, J. B., & Sardegna, V. G. et al. (2015). An analysis of social network websites for language learning: Implications for teaching and learning English as a Second Language. *CALICO Journal, 32*(1), 114–152.

Liu, M., Navarrete, C. C., & Wivagg, J. (2014). Potentials of mobile technology for K-12 education: An investigation of iPod Touch use for English language learners in the United States. *Journal of Educational Technology & Society, 17*(2).

Maffi, L. (Ed.). (2001). *On biocultural diversity: Linking language, knowledge, and the environment.* Washington, DC: Smithsonian Institution Press.

Maffi, L., & Woodley, E. (2010). *Biocultural diversity conservation.* Washington, DC: Earthscan LLC.

Mello, L. (2011). Communication management and the dialogue in education: An educommunication theme. In T. Bastiaens & M. Ebner (Eds.), *Proceedings of World Conference on Educational Media and Technology 2011* (pp. 2490-2496). Waynesville, NC: Association for the Advancement of Computing in Education (AACE).

Metcalf, A. C. (2005). *Go-betweens and the colonization of Brazil: 1500-1600.* Austin, TX: University of Texas Press.

Meuth Alldredge, J. R. (2011). An analysis of social, environmental, and cultural problems in a northern Amazonian indigenous community. In E. T. Bodah (Ed.), *Conversas entre educadoras: novos dialogos / Conversations among educators: new dialogues.* Pullman, WA: Thaines & Bodah Center for Education and Development.

Ministério da Educação do Brasil. (2010). Retrieved from http://mec.gov.br

Mithun, M. (1998). The significance of diversity in language endangerment and preservation. In L. Grenoble & L. Whaley (Eds.), *Endangered Languages: Language Loss and Community Response.* New York, NY: Cambridge University Press. doi:10.1017/CBO9781139166959.008

Oliveira, M. R. N. S. (2001). From the myth of technology to the technological paradigm: Technological mediation in didactic and pedagogic practices. *Revista Brasileira de Educação, Caxambu, 2*(18), 1–16.

Power, T., & Erling, E. (2014). Supporting development through improving English language teaching and learning in Bangladesh. *The Open University/UKAID.* Retrieved from http://oro.open.ac.uk/41532/1/Power2014ba.pdf

Riasati, M. J., Allahyar, N., & Tan, K. E. (2012). Technology in language education: Benefits and barriers. *Journal of Education and Practice, 3*(5), 25–30.

Rüschoff, B., & Ritter, M. (2001). Technology-enhanced language learning: Construction of knowledge and template-based learning in the foreign language classroom. *Computer Assisted Language Learning, 14*(3-4), 219–232. doi:10.1076/call.14.3.219.5789

Santos, D. M. D. (1997). *Learning English as a foreign language in Brazilian elementary schools: Textbooks and their lessons about the world and about learning* [Master's thesis]. University of Oklahoma, Norman, OK.

Schaun, A. (2002). *Educomunicação: reflexões e princípios*. Rio de Janeiro, Brazil: Mauad.

Secretaria de Educação Fundamental. (1997). *Parâmetros curriculares nacionais: meio ambiente, saúde*. Retrieved from http://portal.mec.gov.br/seb/arquivos/pdf/livro01.pdf

Soares, I. D. O. (2001). *Caminhos da educomunicação*. São Paulo, Brazil: Salesiana.

Soares, I. D. O. (2008). The right to screens: From media education to educommunication in Brazil. *Comunicar*, *30*(30), 87–92. doi:10.3916/c30-2008-01-013

Soares, I. D. O.,.... (2000). *O projeto Educom: Formação de professores on line numa perspectiva educomunicativa*. Retrieved from http://www.ups.br/educomradio/cafe/textos/educom_puc.doc

Souza, C. (2013). *The combination of educommunication and community media as a development communication strategy: a case study of the Centre of Community Media São Miguel on Air in São Paulo, Brazil*. (Master's thesis). Malmö University, Malmö, Sweden.

Stanek, C. (2013). The educational system of Brazil. *IEM Spotlight.*, *10*(1), 1–10.

Survival International. (2012). *Brazilian indians*. Retrieved from http://www.survivalinternational.org/tribes/brazilian

Sykes, J. M., Oskoz, A., & Thorne, S. L. (2013). Web 2.0, synthetic immersive environments, and mobile resources for language education. *CALICO Journal*, *25*(3), 528–546.

Thaines, E., & Bodah, B. (2008). *E.E. from Brazil to the U.S.: an invitation to the practical diversity on environmental education*. Passo Fundo, Brazil: Berthier.

Thaines, E., & Rodrigues, L. D. (2007). Educação ambiental: potencialidades e desafios da pratica pedagogica no cotidiano escolar. In *Teoria e pratica pedagogica*. Passo Fundo, Brazil: Universidade de Passo Fundo.

Thiong'o, N. (1986). *Decolonizing the mind: The politics of language in African literature*. Nairobi, Kenya: Oxford Publishing Company.

Wang, L. (2005). The advantages of using technology in second language education: Technology integration in foreign language teaching demonstrates the shift from a behavioral to a constructivist learning approach. *T.H.E. Journal* [Technological Horizons in Education], *32*(10), 38.

Wang, Q. (2014). A study of the relationship between foreign language teachers' TPACK and their self-efficacy on technology integration. *Computer-Assisted Foreign Language Education*, 4, 003.

Warschauer, M. (1998). Technology and indigenous language revitalization: Analyzing the experience of Hawai'i. *Canadian Modern Language Review*, *55*(1), 139–159. doi:10.3138/cmlr.55.1.139

Warschauer, M. (2004). *Of digital divides and social multipliers: Combining language and technology for human development. Information and communication technologies in the teaching and learning of foreign languages: State of the art, needs and perspectives* (pp. 46–52). Moscow: UNESCO Institute for Information Technologies in Education.

Warschauer, M., Donaghy, K., & Kuamoÿo, H. (1997). Leokī: A powerful voice of Hawaiian language revitalization. *Computer Assisted Language Learning, 10*(4), 349–362. doi:10.1080/0958822970100405

World Wildlife Foundation. (2012) *Amazon: world's largest tropical rainforest and river basin.* Retrieved from http://www.worldwildlife.org/what/wherewework/amazon/index.html#

Yeung, A. S., Chen, Z., & Li, B. (2015). Maximizing the benefit of technology for language learning. In C. Koh (Ed.), *Motivation, Leadership and Curriculum Design* (pp. 185–199). Singapore: Springer. doi:10.1007/978-981-287-230-2_15

Zhao, Y. (2013). Recent developments in technology and language learning: A literature review and meta-analysis. *CALICO Journal, 21*(1), 7–27.

Chapter 5
Teaching Spanish in the Digital Age:
A Flipped Classroom or Just Hybrid?

Clara Burgo
Loyola University Chicago, USA

ABSTRACT

Many hybrid programs have been created in higher education institutions in the US for the last 15 years, most of them consisting of the combination of classroom instruction and an online platform. However, the flipped classroom has become very popular recently as a result of this hybrid model of instruction. The purpose of this chapter is to respond to the following questions: What is a more recommended model for teaching Spanish in the digital age? What kind of activities should we focus on, as instructors, in the classroom? What works best for students to study and practice outside of the classroom? Both models will be described with their advantages and disadvantages so that instructors can choose the one that better fits their courses.

INTRODUCTION

In 2012 there were over five million college students in the U.S. taking at least one hybrid or online course (Russell, 2012). The typical hybrid course consists of face-to-face interaction and the use of an online component. That is, it is a form of classroom instruction that incorporates both face-to-face instruction with web-based multimedia instruction. There are several factors to consider when designing a hybrid course. According to Sitter, Carter, Mahan, Massello, and Carter (2009), there should be a careful balance between both face-to-face and online components, with clear objectives and elements to engage students in deep critical thinking and learning. In order to do so, it is important to make a good selection of the best assignments for the face-to-face classroom and the best to do online. One of the main goals of hybrid instruction can be exposing students to structured input activities based on the theoretical framework of VanPatten's (1996, 2000) input processing model, essential for second language acquisition. Usually, these activities are done online before coming to class via an electronic platform, in

DOI: 10.4018/978-1-5225-0177-0.ch005

contrast to the traditional classroom. There is a time management system so that instructors can set up deadlines in order to make sure students finish the activities on time and come ready to class. This way, instructors can maximize their face-to-face class time with communicative activities. The benefits of using a technology-enhanced teaching approach are supported in this chapter based on the effectiveness of hybrid and flipped models according to classroom-based research, specifically in foreign language instruction in higher education for small or medium size classes. In a nutshell, this new learning environment is a combination of face-to-face interaction with an online component.

Research has shown the benefits of using this hybrid model compared to the traditional model of all face-to-face classroom instruction (Caulfield, 2011; Koller, 2011; Ng, 2009; Rubio & Thoms, 2012). According to the research cited here, instructors spend less time lecturing as students spend more time engaged in task-oriented activities in a hybrid course. Thus, students become engaged as producers of their own learning outcomes, they develop more autonomy, and are provided with communicative tools to make the language meaningful in the Spanish classroom (Hermosilla, 2014). It is a model that provides beneficial results since it combines the best of both types of instructional delivery (Presby, 2001). As is widely known, hybrid courses are now very common at the college level.

Usually, grammar lessons are taught in the classroom because of their learning complexity, while practice is done online, especially input activities. However, as Hermosilla argued, there are also challenges for both students and instructors in this hybrid model. One challenge for many instructors is allowing students be in control of their own learning. Students can advance at their own pace and the instructor role would be more that of support, clarification, and reinforcement via practice. In general, hybrid courses do not always require the same amount of time in the classroom (2/3) as online (1/3). That is, two thirds of the course time is delivered face-to-face while the remaining one third is delivered online. This could become a problem with regards to university administrations that might not financially compensate for the online section of the course and only quantify the in-class time, usually the majority of the course time. However, it could impact instructors' workload (Godev, 2014). Godev conducted a study in which she compared a basic Spanish hybrid course with a traditional one. Twice the enrollment of students was in the hybrid rather than the traditional course. One of the main benefits of this hybrid model revealed that the amount of time spent by instructors in grading was the same as the traditional course that had half the number of students.

Flipped courses, on the other hand, were introduced as an innovative and alternative version of hybrid courses. The flipped classroom is a form of hybrid learning in which students learn new content online by watching video lectures before class. In this model, the activities that used to be homework are now done in class with teachers offering more personalized guidance and interaction with students, instead of providing them with lectures of the material. Students' first exposure to the language takes place mainly outside of the classroom through lecturing videos, podcasts, media, readings, or online activities; the class time is exclusively relegated to the processing and assimilation of knowledge via peer interaction, cooperative learning, or as a support to the "individual" learning outside of the classroom. Overall, it is an inverted classroom, in which instructional materials are delivered online prior to class and class time is dedicated to practice (e.g. problem solving, discussion, or debates). Sink (2008) claimed that the main goal of the flipped classroom was to make the course reflect real-life experiences and transfer what they learned to their jobs. The role of the instructor changes from that of a lecturer to a facilitator (Stutzmann, Colebech. Khalid, Chin, & Sweigart, 2013); the student changes from a passive to an active learner. As they claimed, there are many benefits of using this technique, but the main one is that classrooms became more active, engaging, interactive, and fun than the traditional classroom.

In order to describe how this technique works, Bloom's revised Taxonomy needs to be examined (Anderson & Krathworl, 2001). Brame (2013) summarized the top five benefits of the flipped classroom: to give students the opportunity to gain first exposure to the language prior to class, to provide them with an incentive to come ready to class, to assess student understanding, and to spend class time with activities that focus on higher levels of cognition. In sum, this model is a way to maximize class time (Jacot, Noren, & Berge, 2014). Nevertheless, there are also some drawbacks to choosing this model. According to a study conducted by Johnson (2013), students enjoyed self-pacing but they also experienced some problems with this model since it was very easy to fall behind and difficult to stay motivated. Another issue was the immediacy of the classroom. Some students complained about having to wait in order to receive feedback, answers to their questions, and/or clarification. Roehl, Reddy, and Shannon (2013) added other disadvantages, such as the time students took to adapt to this new learning environment. Thus, the instructor's role as a mediator plays a crucial role in this process. Throughout this chapter, the following research questions will be answered:

1. What kind of activities should instructors do in class in the flipped classroom?
2. What works best for students to study and practice outside of the classroom in the flipped model?
3. What are the main advantages of each model (hybrid and flipped)?
4. What is the most recommended model for teaching Spanish in the digital age?

This chapter advises the implementation of the model that best adapts to instructors and students' specific needs. Some important factors have to be taken into consideration: the enrollment of the course, time and technology issues (e.g. the amount of time dedicated to creating videos or podcasts for the flipped classroom versus the online platform already provided by many current textbooks typically used in most hybrid courses), or the degree of autonomy that instructors are willing to give the students. After responding to the research questions stated above, examples of activities that can be implemented within each model will be provided, along with a few tips to overcome the challenges faced by instructors and students in both cases.

BACKGROUND

Research suggests that hybrid or blended teaching might be effective in the foreign language classroom with regard to oral proficiency (Blake, Cetto, Pardo-Ballester, & Wilson, 2008) and online interaction and discourse, due to the addition of the online platform as an important component of the course (Meskill & Anthony, 2005). A hybrid model has been described as a face-to-face and technology-enhanced instructional component (Neumaier, 2005). Quantitatively speaking, 30% to 80% of the class was usually offered online (Allen & Seaman, 2011). Studies showed that students' progress in the target language (Spanish or French) was similar to that in traditional face-to-face classes (Chenoweth, Ushida, & Murday, 2006). However, students preferred the hybrid design rather than the traditional one because of its flexibility and the autonomy they were allowed (Cubillos, 2007). Some of the advantages of adding an online component to face-to-face instruction are the following: increasing students' time on tasks, making students independent learners, giving students the opportunity of tailoring their practice to their own needs and pace, providing immediate feedback for students so that instructors can track their progress, increasing student motivation, offering alternative and multidimensional teaching resources, and increasing students' exposure to authentic materials and contexts (Cubillos, 1998; Frommer, 1998).

Grgurovic (2011) established a division between comparative and non-comparative empirical studies in the use of hybrid models of language learning. Comparative studies examined the effectiveness of hybrid learning by comparing it to traditional instruction. Non-comparative studies examined the design and implementation of a hybrid program and student-teacher attitudes towards it. Murday, Ushida, and Chenoweth (2008) found that students showed increased satisfaction over time, from first through fourth semester language courses.

Most of the research in Spanish has been done in language courses. The typical hybrid course consists of twice a week face-to-face instruction and the equivalent of one class/hour online. This hour is usually dedicated to online homework (e.g. the online workbook instead of the hard-copy workbook) that needs to be completed before or after the face-to-face class. Nevertheless, the online component could be administered in alternative formats. Arispe and Blake (2012), for example, used a weekly chat session via SCMC (Synchronous Computer Mediated Communication) apart from the online platform of the textbook. In this hybrid course, the role of the instructor was scaffolding students in planned classroom lessons and becoming a mediator during the chats. In these chat sessions, students had to negotiate meaning through task-based activities within the following structure: warm ups, information-gap activities, and cool-downs. Arispe and Blake wanted to study the social and cognitive qualities in a successful hybrid learner. Results found that conscientious learners were the ones that benefited the most from the hybrid model, since these type of learners typically make goals and have a clear study plan. Therefore, conscientiousness was the most important indicator of success, as is usually the case in any learning setting. Then, low-verbal learners benefited more from online instruction than high-verbal students, since they appreciated the self-paced nature of this model. In another alternative format, Cubillos (2007) implemented a hybrid third-semester Spanish language course that employed the online system WebCT to deliver the lessons and *Quia* for practice activities. He encountered that hybrid courses were more appealing to more experienced college learners (sophomores, juniors and seniors) than all face-to-face instruction. Moreover, these learners also showed increased self-motivation and autonomy because of their experience with language courses. That is, personality type and learning style might determine teaching style. In another study by Schwieter (2011), instructors and students' positive and negative feedback on the use of this model of instruction in a Spanish program was reported. Instructors appreciated counting on an online system that graded students' activities and provided students with immediate feedback. Additionally, assigned grades were directly transferred to the grade book. In terms of sources of input, technology provided access to assorted videos, materials, and samples of dialectal variation in the Spanish-speaking world. On the negative side, instructors complained about the reduced class time for interaction and how students complained about the overload of online homework for students. Students, however, appreciated meeting fewer days a week and completing online activities for practice.

In short, hybrid instruction turned out to be as effective as face-to-face instruction but with both higher levels of satisfaction for students and better individualization of instruction, suggesting that this model was a valuable asset for language instruction, at least at the university level.

Furthermore, this model is not only appropriate for language courses but also for content-based courses. Despite the lack of research in content-based courses at the university level, there are only a few studies that favored this model. Jochum (2011) showed the effects of a hybrid model used in a Latin American culture course with 23 participants. According to this study, students loved the online component and reported gains in self-confidence with the language and with speaking Spanish with their classmates. More recently, Jochum (2013) studied students' opinions on a hybrid Spanish grammar course with a medium class size (19). The class met for 75 minutes once a week (face-to-face-interaction) and the rest of the time online via Blackboard. During face-to-face instruction, there was interaction with the instructor and the rest of the students, and a focus on the main objectives of the course. Individual and group activities, however, were assessed online. Students' surveys showed that they really enjoyed hybrid instruction since they had the opportunity to work online at their own pace. Class time was dedicated to expanding upon what they had learned online and to answering students' questions. They reported that the online design helped students feel more comfortable with their literacy skills in Spanish. Jochum interpreted these results as supportive of online instruction. Regarding the main objective of the course, improving their Spanish grammar, the majority of them thought that their grammar improved due to online interaction. They found beneficial two specific aspects: working independently on the online assignments, and the feedback they received from their peers. In sum, they considered the hybrid model an opportunity to be exposed to the best of both worlds; the environment of the online component, and the face-to-face interaction of the traditional classroom.

Recently, a new version of the hybrid model (the flipped classroom) has become a source of interest among educators. In the flipped classroom, students see online a pre-recorded lecture while class time is exclusively dedicated to active learning (Houston & Lin, 2012). One of the main purposes of flipping the classroom is humanizing it (Kahn, 2011). As Kahn explains, in a traditional college classroom, 95% of the time is spent lecturing while only 5% is actually spent working with students. This newer model allowed for opportunities to change this dynamic (lecture as homework) so that 100% of the class time is actually spent working with students. The flipped (or inverted) classroom can be defined as a class in which, what was traditionally done in class is done at home now, while the homework (that was traditionally done at home) is done in class (Bergmann & Sans, 2012). But, what is a flipped classroom on a day-to-day basis? As a warm-up activity, they proposed to start the face-to-face class with a discussion about the video students had watched before class. Then, an assignment was created for a day (e.g. a lab or a problem-solving activity).

Lage, Platt, and Treglia (2000) conducted a survey with students in a flipped microeconomic class at Miami University. At home, students had to review videos with the lectures, read power point slides with audio, and perform online quizzes. In class, students used the first 10 minutes to ask questions for clarification purposes and then they spent the rest of the class completing activities and experiments. At the end of the semester, students took the survey and rated the course very favorably, highlighting the fact that they especially enjoyed working in groups. They seemed more motivated with this format since they were allowed to have ownership of their own learning. Moreover, instructors also rated this course as a stimulating learning environment with active involvement of the students.

In Foertsch, Moses, Strikwerda, and Litzkow (2002), students rated very positively a flipped model called eTEACH (a streaming video and multi-media application) that was used at a university with large engineering classes. They rated this model at 4 levels: lectures, instructor's responses, course and instructor. As a typical flipped class, students watched the lectures at home at their own pace, and class time was relegated to small group problem-solving activities.

Another case study of a successful engineering flipped class took place in another university in 2008 (Zappe, Leicht, Messner, Litzinger, & Lee, 2009). Students considered this class to be very helpful, especially in how they primarily spent class time solving problems instead of being lectured. Zappe et al. offered three tips that were key to success: giving online quizzes before class, keeping the videos short (20 to 30 minutes), reviewing the content before in-class activities, and adding multimedia to the online lectures.

As has been shown, most research on classroom flipping has focused on general subjects rather than on language learning (Han, 2015). Increasingly, this model has lately become more and more popular as applied to language programs.

A FLIPPED CLASSROOM OR JUST HYBRID?

After describing both models via case studies and their applications in the classroom, the research questions can now be addressed:

1.   What kind of activities should instructors do in class in the flipped classroom?

Witten (2013) flipped her Spanish classroom by spending her class time doing activities interactively such as presentations, conversations, and projects that increased students' interest. In the same line, Bell (2015) proposed the following activities: group and pair work, games, task-based activities to apply what they learned to real-life situations, and/ or problem-solving tasks. Learning objectives were the same as those in the traditional classroom: ACTFL proficiency guidelines for speaking, reading, listening, and writing were achieved via activities, assignments, and projects. These activities were learner-centered and designed in order to conduce learners into critical thinking, exploration, discussion, and collaborative learning. In order to hold students accountable, Henshaw (2014) proposed student response systems such as I-Clicker and free-writing activities. There are other activities that would work better in large classes such as brainstorming of ideas, debates, discussion, and questions, think-pair-share (posing a problem to the class, discussing it in pairs, and sharing it with the rest of the class), one sentence summary (at the end of the class to enhance writing skills) or a one-minute paper (to assess comprehension and writing). The class, then, becomes the conversation and creation space where teachers can behave as facilitators of learning (Valenza, 2012). The purpose of the in-class activities should be to support student understanding of the learning objectives, help students process what they learned, and to be engaged and flexible (Spencer, Wolf, & Sams, 2011). They proposed using student-content or project-based learning to obtain these outcomes.

On the other hand, Janson, Ernst, Lehmann, & Leimeister (2014) conducted a study on peer assessment for a large lecture class using the flipped model. The authors proposed watching a video or script-based learning units outside of the classroom first. Then, students prepared a solution for a text assignment within an allocated group. Every group engaged in a collaborative clarification process by preparing power point slides with their solutions. Finally, the discussion of students' solutions was held in class considering further aspects of the findings and emphasized their strengths. Using a collaborative application dedicated to tutorials, learners elaborated a common solution. The researchers concluded, then, that peer assessment resulted in a useful method to improve the learning process and increasing learning outcomes.

2.   What works best for students to study and practice outside of the classroom in the flipped model?

Students are introduced to content prior to class so that they are able to practice what they have learned in a guided setting (Muldrow, 2013). The focus of language courses is usually on vocabulary and grammar learning outside the class (Bell, 2015). However, there are other components such as culture or other skills (such as reading, writing, and listening) that can be done outside of the classroom. In the flipped classroom, instructors assign the lecture as homework in form of a video, narrated PowerPoint, screencast, podcast, readings, simulations, or online discussions as warm-up activities for what will be practiced in class. It would be helpful to offer instructors guided and reflective questions or prompts to help them recognize the objectives and an online means so that students can submit questions. Henshaw (2014) suggested the use of web 2.0 tools such as TalkAbroad, WeSpeke or Blackboard Collaborate for interactional exchanges. By using these tools, students can chat on their own and lines can get automatically recorded. If using screencasts (recordings with audio narration and screen images), then these resources should last a maximum of 15 minutes in order to not exhaust students' attention (McKeachie & Svinicki, 2006). Under this model, the home represents the lecture space since the frontal teaching model has flipped (Valenza, 2012). Lectures have to be effective so it is important to choose an engaging video that you can create or take from YouTube or assorted websites, since students appreciate variety. In order for instructors to make sure students perform these tasks before coming to class, instructors can require them to take notes while watching the assignments or, alternately, conducting quizzes to assess their understanding of the material. Over all, students have to be prepared and held accountable to make the flipped model work. Therefore, students have to be prepared to make the flipped model work.

3.   What are the main advantages of each model (hybrid and flipped)?

There is evidence that hybrid instruction can positively impact students' achievement, decrease students' attrition, and facilitate an increase in students' performance (López-Pérez, Pérez-López & Rodríguez Ariza, 2011). It is a redesign of the traditional model with a shift from lecture-centered to student-centered instruction, where students become active and interactive learners. Benefits of this model affect both students and institutions: the improvement of learning outcomes, allowing more flexibility, improving autonomy and research skills, creating a sense of community, the cost and its effectiveness, and student satisfaction. This flexibility can accommodate a diverse student population with different learning styles and paces (Poon, 2013). In Poon's study, students reported positive remarks on hybrid learning since they enjoyed having more independence in their own learning and being able to study off-campus. They insisted on the importance of training in order to fully understand this model. It is a good mix of delivery methods that suit a greater spectrum of students than the traditional method. However, students still insisted on the importance of face-to-face interaction. As mentioned, institutional support is crucial. Institutions have to be ready to invest time and money in making these courses work successfully. Hybrid learning creates opportunities for students' understanding of topics through their own research and exploration (Sharpe, Benfield, Roberts, & Francis, 2006). According to Scida and Saury (2013), the key to success of the hybrid model is realistically assessing the areas in which computers can have the most positive benefit and how it can be used to save instructors' time.

Flipped classrooms also use a student-centered approach since they place more responsibility on students' shoulders (Sams, 2011). This model promotes personalized learning for students who can then watch the videos at their own pace (Danker, 2015). But it is not only at that level that students are responsible of their own learning as expected; they are also responsible for their mastery of content and for coming prepared to class, since videos are required to be watched before (Alvarez, 2011; Fulton, 2012).

Switching from a traditional to a flipped classroom brings many benefits for students: they become active learners instead of passive learners; technology facilitates learning and the order of class time and homework is inverted since homework comes first and class time offers more personalized instruction, support for challenging subject matter, and a focus on higher order cognitive critical thinking tasks (Bergmann, Overmyer, & Wilie, 2012). Technology can facilitate learning predominantly in two ways: presenting content, and assessing achievement (Davies, Dean, & Ball, 2013). As Marwedel and Engel (2014) explained, in the era of the digital age, class time should be spent using teaching strategies that would take advantage of the physical presence of the students, since standard lectures have failed to do so. Actually, this approach trains students to perform teamwork and stimulates more interaction among them.

On the other hand, attendance by both the instructor and the student is not as important as in the traditional or typical hybrid classroom. That is, students who are absent can study the notes at home and instructors, when they have to be absent, can find a substitute teacher to assist students during class time. In terms of students' feelings, they did not feel as frustrated as in the traditional classroom, since the form of this course allowed many opportunities for one-on-one instruction when needed. They saw or read the lecture with a focus on the basics of the material and they worked on challenging and high-cognitive tasks in the classroom, the actual opposite of the traditional classroom (Talbert, 2012). Finally, there were also positive results with respect to productivity: assignments were completed at a higher level of quality (Alvarez, 2011).

Then, what is the main innovative difference between the hybrid model and the flipped classroom? The latter establishes free time for hands-on work. Learning is based on asking and responding to questions and helping each other, where the instructor is guiding on the side and the interaction with and among students increases. The hybrid model helps students to feel less intimidated at participating, and encourages them to ask question, whereas in the traditional classroom, questions are usually asked at the end of the class.

Scullen (2014) explains three important reasons why she decided to use a flipped model in a French class:

1. The students do most of the learning outside of the class. At the beginning of each class, students take a quiz to demonstrate what they learned and to provide feedback to the instructor
2. Teaching time is limited. This is especially beneficial for student teachers so that they can focus on practice.
3. Class time is focused on student learning since there is more in-class interaction and engagement with students.

One of the main advantages of this model in a college classroom is how effective it is for learning. In Danker (2015), students were able to make connections with previous knowledge to build an understanding of what they were taught. A key component for success in a flipped classroom might be the amount of peer cooperation it required. Cooperation resulted in higher achievement and productivity, more engagement in the learning process, and greater social competence (Smith & Kampf, 2004). There is also increased instructor-student and student-student interaction despite the class size. As a consequence, there is increased time for feedback as well. Thanks to the in-class activities, students also developed soft skills such as communication skills (Danker, 2015).

Can it be concluded that flipping works? Janson et al. (2014) proposed an application of a technology-enhanced peer assessment for large-scale information system lectures. This didactic method enhanced interaction and feedback and addressed high cognitive levels of educational objectives without increasing the workload of lecturers much. It aimed to make learners aware of their learning behavior and empowered them in creating their own learning environments with individual resources while discovering their particular learning patterns. E-learning tools were used to personalize their learning processes for awareness support. Regarding reflection, it was a meta-cognitive process described by Janson et al. (2014) as a conscious re-evaluation of their learning experiences with the objective of guiding future behaviors. Learners were able to communicate through several platforms to share their problems and solutions with their peer work. Thus, this exchange allowed them to learn from their peers and to contribute to their own work. Peer assessment helped learners become experts and provided them with a deeper understanding of the learning content (Sadler & Good, 2006). They argued that there were four main advantages of this method: logistical, pedagogical, metacognitive, and affective. It saved time for lecturers (logistical), learners obtained a deeper understanding of the learning contents by assessing their peers (pedagogical), students increased their awareness of their own strengths and weaknesses (metacognitive), and they valued their peers' feedback more than that of their lectures (affective). In short, Janson et al.'s findings showed that peer feedback was very positive for their learning processes.

4.   What is the most recommended model for teaching Spanish in the digital age?

In order to select the best model for a Spanish course, the limitations of each model (developed in the following section) have to be taken into consideration. The most common controversies that these models cause are explained and some solutions are also suggested in the following section.

The flipped classroom blends direct instruction with a constructivist approach (Bergman et al., 2012). Even though, as it has been shown, it offers many advantages, such as personalized instruction and increased interaction, technological support and maturity are required for active and autonomous learning to be effective. Therefore, using this model at a higher education institution that can provide institutional support for its successful implementation is strongly recommended. On the other hand, even a typical hybrid course (more and more common for basic language courses) may not be the best fit for all learners (especially for beginners) since it is necessary for students to have a high degree of self-motivation and to be able to work more independently (Blake et al., 2008). Therefore, educators should examine carefully the relationship between the characteristics of the language learning and the format of instruction before going hybrid (Gascoigne & Parnel, 2014).

Issues, Controversies, Problems

Despite all the advantages shown by both models, there are also some challenges to face. Regarding the disadvantages of the hybrid model, the first potential problem to consider is the lack of understanding of the new roles of instructors and students (LaMance, 2012). Students must assume their new role as self-disciplined independent learners and instructors as facilitators. As a consequence, students sometimes face some challenges derived from its implementation, such as feelings of isolation and unrealistic expectations. These reactions are legitimate, above all if instructors are not successful in engaging students, who might experience a culture shock if they are used to traditional instruction and are not well trained in these models (Talbert, 2012).

Added to the expected technology issues, students might feel invaded in other areas of their lives due, in part, to the time commitment this model requires. As Cubillos (2007) found in his study comparing traditional instruction and hybrid instruction in an introductory Spanish course, there is a direct correlation between student success in hybrid or traditional instruction and the type of student personality. On the other hand, institutions also faced time and support issues for the redesign of these courses (Poon, 2013).

The disadvantages of using the hybrid and flipped models are usually related to the careful preparation they require and the limited access to internet that some students might have. In fact, even though students might feel comfortable using technology for personal use, they might not have the competence to use the tools needed for computer-assisted language learning instruction such as microphones or webcams, according to Winke, Goertler and Amuzie (2010). This could also be the case for the instructors, who need the appropriate training and equipment.

Therefore, this is even more challenging in the case of the flipped model since recording lectures requires a significant amount of skill and time. In fact, lectures and in-class activities have to be well connected so that the course flows. Regarding the disadvantages that both models share, there is a higher probability of students not doing their homework compared to the traditional classroom. The consequences for this are more serious in the flipped model since students have to take more responsibility for their own learning but this issue is a real problem in both cases (Danker, 2015).

As was mentioned earlier, many institutions have gone through serious budget cuts for some years and they were obligated to reduce costs, especially in the humanities. Thus, class sizes have increased and courses have been cancelled. This financial situation made institutions rethink alternatives for instruction such as hybrid, flipped, or online courses. Technological advances, then, have been envisioned as a viable pedagogical tool under these circumstances in order to move along a continuum from the traditional to the online course (Hokanson, 2000; Kinney & Robertson, 2003; Tunison & Noonan, 2001). The hybrid classroom results in a compromise position for many institutions, which makes it a very attractive alternative to both traditional and online instruction across disciplines (Carroll, 2003; Hopper, 2003; Oblender, 2002; Patterson, 2004). In order to implement an effective hybrid program, there should be institutional support for the redesign of these courses with clear objectives, considering what objectives are best achieved online and what objectives can work better in the classroom in a way that these two learning environments are well integrated (Dziuban, Hartman, Juge, Moskal, & Sorg, 2006). An important institutional challenge is the difficulty in acquiring new technology learning skills (Dziuban & Moskal, 2013; Voos, 2003).

On another hand, Manjinder (2012) argues that the way flipped classrooms were used in many higher education institutions did not manage to replace teacher-centered with student-centered instruction. The teacher sometimes still had an expert role and had to communicate it to the learners, using the same teaching philosophy as the traditional classroom (Tucker, 2012). If the model is not well implemented, although students may still get the content from other sources, they still learn from the words of experts, either from the textbook or from the instructor (Hoffman, 2014).

Nonetheless, more research is needed on the actual benefits or shortcomings on the typical hybrid or flipped model.

The basis for the flipped model divided educational learning objectives into the cognitive, affective, and psychomotor domains (Krathwohl, Bloom, & Masia, 1973; Pohl, 2000; Simpson, 1972). In Bloom (1984), he argued that if a student receives individual attention, he could achieve a high attainment of proficiency via constant feedback corrective process. Unfortunately, this one-to-one ideal learning situation is not very realistic for many institutions since it is very expensive (Thomson, 2011).

In the same vein, the flipped classroom can particularly be an issue for beginners or for an instructor's first flipped course (Collins, 2011). Milman (2012) also added that students with disabilities might also struggle with this model.

SOLUTIONS AND RECOMMENDATIONS

Creating a hybrid course implies developing suitable online materials. These supplements could be pricey and time-consuming, above all if both the online workbook and additional materials are employed. Nevertheless, publishers are making electronic resources available for students and instructors (e.g. test banks, extra activities, tutorials, lesson plans…). There are student and institutional factors that play a key role so that these courses can succeed. Student-related factors are: management of their expectations (the wrong assumption being that a traditional face-to-face class involves less work), training students so that they are ready to use the new technology (Beadle & Santy, 2008; Harris, Connolly, & Feeney, 2009), and consideration of their needs (Bliuc, Goodyear, & Ellis, 2007; Harris et al., 2009; Mitchell & Honore, 2007). Mitchell and Honore emphasized that student motivation was particularly important with e-learning since it directly affects their participation. Thus, students have to be encouraged to take responsibility for their own learning (Tabor, 2007; Vaughan, 2007). Additionally, instructors usually struggle to make students excited and engaged in language courses. It is a long process to get students on board (leaving the traditional model behind), requiring a significant investment of time, and marketing. Therefore, instructors have to be clear and enthusiastic about this model (Demski, 2013). LaMance (2012) proposed adding more meaningful interaction in the hybrid activities such as setting up video-conferences or chats with native speakers. In order for them to do so, instructors had to plan learning experiences (Honeycutt & Garrett, 2014).

Instructor-related complications include using resources on communication to assist students and facilitators (Garrison & Kanuka, 2004; Harris et al. 2009). Even though the good use of technology is a given for this kind of courses, the focus should be on teaching and learning methods; technology is just a means to facilitate student learning (Sloman, 2007). Instructors should focus on what activities students need to do in order to achieve the learning goals of this model.

Poon (2013) advised using a flexible approach to match students' expectations and to preserve a simple teaching style. Institutions should have a realistic idea of the time, cost, and support this model involves; this includes student training and professional development opportunities for instructors for the effective use of technology. Training becomes a never-ending process so instructors and students should get trained regularly; instructors need to give students resources to become independent learners. Thus, LaMance (2012) suggests reserving a computer lab as a workspace for the hybrid assignments. If there are personnel running the lab, students also have the opportunity of looking for help regarding technology issues. This way, students' anxiety and the extra burden on instructors are reduced. Moreover, students could develop a sense of community and participation could be increased (Beauvois, 1999; Beauvois & Eledge, 1995-1996; Grgurovic, 2011). Another proposal for student training would be that of Henshaw (2014): orientation sessions (virtual or in person) and course quizzes. On the other hand, students might complain about how busy they get when taking a hybrid or flipped course. LaMance (2012) proposed changing the activities into more meaningful activities or changing how students saw said activities. These two proposals are interrelated: changing the way activities are presented will possibly change students' attitudes towards them.

In the same vein, Lage, et al. (2000) acknowledge the intensive work that flipping a class involved, e.g., creating and uploading videos, power point lectures, and online quizzes. Even though the amount of work might seem overwhelming at times, they also propose some recommendations to reduce the workload for instructors; for example, using online activities or altering previously used materials. Furthermore, they argue that since there were no lectures in class, preparation time dropped drastically. However, it is advisable to customize materials and not to rely entirely on publisher-ready materials since they sometimes lack interactive instruction and feedback, essential for successful technology enhanced courses (Henshaw, 2014).

There exists simple and accessible technology for recording and sharing videos. Instructors can set up a camera or use a screen casting software such as Jing to record videos or upload the videos to YouTube. This technology is easy to learn and mostly cost free (Talbert, 2012).

Another drawback that has been noticed is that students had to take responsibility for their own learning but this model offered instructors the possibility of engaging students who need a different style or more one to one interaction (Houston & Lin, 2012).

Even though students cannot receive immediate answers to their questions (unless there is an online chat or regularly scheduled office hours), at the beginning of the course instructors must train the students to watch the videos effectively. That is, students should have no distractions when they are watching the videos, and they should pause and rewind them at times; they also proposed recording their questions and writing a summary of their learning. This way, students come to class with appropriate questions and instructors can assess the efficiency of their videos (Bergmann & Sams, 2012).

Khan (2012) explains that teachers become even more necessary after online exposure by students. This contradicts one of the basic arguments against the hybrid or flipped models: computer-based instruction might eventually replace teachers.

Common obstacles for blended or flipped classrooms have to do with the access to technology for some students. Therefore, instructors should offer assorted resources to compensate for this problem, e.g. downloading the lessons onto DVDs, or making computers available in the lab or in the library (Danker, 2015).

For unprepared students (those feeling behind for not completing their homework), it is recommended that instructors implement a few strategies: homework can be tracked and class activities adjusted for unprepared students (Kachka, 2012). They can even be allowed to watch the video (in case they had not watched it at all) at the beginning of the class.

In short, Bennett, Kern, Gudenrath, & McIntosh (2011) conclude that in order to have an effective flipped course, there were some characteristics that have to be met. These were the most crucial: that discussions be led by students with material previously prepared outside of the classroom, that collaborative work be fluid, that content be given context, and that students challenge each other on content, take ownership of their learning, ask exploratory questions and be actively engaged in problem solving and critical thinking.

FUTURE RESEARCH DIRECTIONS

According to Halverson, Graham, Spring, and Drysdale (2012), there has been limited empirical research on hybrid learning. As a starting point, Poon (2013) conducted a study of academics' and students' perspectives in a UK institution. However, more research is needed in this direction in more universities and in particular more subjects. Regarding instructors' and students' perceptions in language courses, it would be interesting to find out whether students feel more enthusiasm for the subject when they perceive they gained more mastery of grammar and vocabulary. In the same line, instructors' opinions should be considered in order to know whether they enjoyed more teaching hybrid courses since they did not have to deal with the same issues as in a traditional course. That is, class time is employed in more creative and flexible ways rather than lecturing (Scida & Saury, 2013).

Most of the research to date has focused on how technology can facilitate language learning but there are not many studies on how language instructors use technology. In this line, Murday et al. (2008) have called for qualitative assessments of technology by students. More research is needed to explore how to present materials so that students can understand the pedagogical rationale behind this instructional model and to select effective activities for both instructors and students (LaMance, 2012). Focus groups could determine what students want from hybrid courses, specifically how activities can be presented so that students do not feel overwhelmed but engaged and motivated instead (Bañados, 2006).

Another factor to keep in mind for future research is the effect of learning and personality styles on the success of the hybrid programs, and how to make the necessary changes to accommodate most or all learning styles (Beauvois & Eledge, 1995-1996). Burston (2003) emphasized the need for changes in learning strategies and teaching practices in order to do so. A research project with interview data and classroom observation could help to shed more light on this issue.

On another note, Danker (2015) suggests further development of the instructional design for the flipped classroom, including hybrid learning with active learning experiences such as experiential and project-based learning, so that students become more engaged in their own learning. Instructors should work towards motivating students and creating peer interactions in order to accomplish a task or achieve a common goal. Regarding the peer assessment method by Janson et al. (2014), Janson et al. (2014) suggest further research into peer assessment as an individual learning success verification method during the learning process. That is, it should be investigated as a manner of saving time and resources to measure learning success. More work is needed to assess technology-enhanced peer assessment effects on awareness, reflection, and learning outcomes.

Halili and Zainuddin (2015) proposed implementing the flipped classroom in areas with limited access to Internet, for example, conducting a case study with an experimental and a control group in order to investigate the efficiency of this model compared to the traditional or control group.

CONCLUSION

The purpose of this chapter was to present an overview of the hybrid and flipped classroom models as emerging forms of instruction of Spanish in the digital age. The author attempted to describe the main advantages and disadvantages of each model for both instructors and students so that instructors can make a decision about what model to choose in a technology-enhanced Spanish course. In the flipped model, tips were offered about what activities can be implemented in the classroom (e.g. pair work and problem-solving tasks) and outside the classroom (e.g. online discussions and reflective questions), and what resources can be used at a low price (e.g. WeSpeke, Jing, YouTube). These findings recommend the implementation of the model that works better for the instructors and students considering the degree of autonomy instructors want to give their students, the enrollment of the course, and the institutional support they can receive. Then, some challenges to these models were provided, followed by some solutions and recommendations for how to overcome them. Finally, the chapter ends with some suggestions for future research and gaps in the literature. Since there is not much research on the benefits and shortcomings of the hybrid or flipped model, it is still too early to draw clear conclusions.

REFERENCES

Allen, I. E., & Seaman, J. (2011). *Going the distance: Online education in the United States.* Babson Survey Research Group and Quahog Research Group, LLC.

Alvarez, B. (2011). Flipping the classroom: Homework in class, lessons at home. *Learning First.* Retrieved from http://www.learningfirst.org/flipping-classroom-homework-class-lessons-home

Anderson, L. W., & Krathwohl, D. R. (Eds.), (2001). *A taxonomy for learning, teaching and assessing: A revision of Bloom's taxonomy of educational objectives.* New York: Longman.

Arispe, K., & Blake, R. J. (2012). Individual factors and successful learning in a hybrid course. *System,* 4(40), 1–27.

Bañados, E. (2006). A blended-learning pedagogical model for teaching and learning EFL successfully through an online interactive multimedia environment. *CALICO Journal, 23*(3), 533–550.

Beadle, M., & Santy, J. (2008). The early benefits of a problem-based approach to teaching social inclusion using an online virtual town. *Nurse Education in Practice, 8*(3), 190–196. doi:10.1016/j.nepr.2007.07.004 PMID:17855168

Beauvois, M. (1999). Computer-mediated communication: Reducing anxiety and building community. In D. J. Young (Ed.), Affect in foreign language and second language learning: A practical guide to creating a low-anxiety classroom atmosphere (pp. 144-165). Boston, MA: McGraw Hill College.

Beauvois, M. H., & Eledge, J. (1995-1996). Personality types and megabytes: Student attitudes toward computer mediated communication (CMC) in the language classroom. *CALICO Journal,* 13(2 & 3), 27-45.

Bell, T.R. (2015). The flipped German classroom. *Proceedings of the Central States Conference in the Teaching of Foreign Languages Report* (pp. 17-38).

Bennett, B., Kern, J., Gudenrath, A., & McIntosh, P. (2011). *The flipped class revealed.* The Daily Riff.

Bergmann, J., Overmyer, J., & Wilie, B. (2012). The flipped class: Myths versus reality. *The Daily Riff.* Retrieved from http://www.thedailyriff.com/articles/the-flipped-class-conversation-689.php

Bergmann, J., & Sams, A. (2012). *Flip your classroom: Reach every student in every class every day.* International Society for Technology in Education.

Blake, R., Cetto, M., Padro-Ballester, C., & Wilson, N. L. (2008). Measuring oral proficiency in distance, face-to-face, and blended classrooms. *Language Learning & Technology*, *12*(3), 114–127.

Bliuc, A. M., Goodyear, P., & Ellis, R. A. (2007). Research focus and methodological choices in studies into students' experiences of blended learning in higher education. *The Internet and Higher Education*, *10*(4), 231–244. doi:10.1016/j.iheduc.2007.08.001

Bloom, B. (1984). The 2 sigma problem: The search for methods of group instruction as effective as one-to-one tutoring. *Educational Researcher*, *13*(6), 4–16. doi:10.3102/0013189X013006004

Brame, C. (2013). Flipping the classroom. Vanderbilt University Center for Teaching. Retrieved from http://cft.vanderbilt.edu/guides-sub-pages/flipping-the-classroom/

Burston, J. (2003). Proving IT works. *CALICO Journal*, *20*(2), 219–226.

Carroll, B (2003). Going hybrid: Online course components increase flexibility of on-campus courses. *Online Classroom*, February, 4-7.

Caulfield, J. (2011). *How to design and teach a hybrid course: Achieving student-centered learning through blended classroom, online, and experiential activities*. Sterling, VA: Stylus.

Chenoweth, N., Ushida, E., & Murday, K. (2006). Student learning in hybrid French and Spanish courses: An overview of language online. *CALICO Journal*, *24*(1), 115–146.

Collins, P. T. (2011). An insider's view to meeting the challenges of blended learning solutions. T + D, *65*(12), 56-61.

Cubillos, J. H. (1998). Technology: A step forward in the teaching of foreign languages? In J. Harper, M. Lively, & M. Williams (Eds.), *The coming of age of the profession: Issues and emerging ideas for the teaching of foreign languages* (pp. 37–52). Boston: Heinle and Heinle.

Cubillos, (2007). A comparative study of hybrid versus traditional instruction in foreign languages. *NECTFL Review*, *38*, 20-38.

Danker, B. (2015). Using flipped classroom approach to explore deep learning in large classrooms. *The IAFOR Journal of Education*, *3*(1), 171–186.

Davies, R. S., Dean, D. L., & Ball, N. (2013). Flipping the classroom and instructional technology integration in a college-level information systems spreadsheet course. *Educational Technology Research and Development*, *61*(4), 563–580. doi:10.1007/s11423-013-9305-6

Demski, J. (2013). 6 expert tips for flipping the classroom. *Campus Technology*, *25*(5), 32–37.

Dziuban, C., Hartman, J., Juge, F., Moskal, P., & Sorg, S. (2006). Blended learning enters the mainstream. In C. J. Bonk & C. R. Graham (Eds.), *Handbook of blended learning: Global perspectives, local designs* (pp. 195–208). San Francisco, CA: Pfeiffer.

Dziuban, C., & Moskal, P. (2013). Distributed learning impact evaluation. Retrieved from http://cdl.ucf.edu/research/rite/dl-impact-evaluation/

Foertsch, J., Moses, G., Strikwerda, J., & Litzkow, M. (2002). Reversing the lecture/homework paradigm using eTEACH® web-based streaming video software. *The Journal of Engineering Education, 91*(3), 267–274. doi:10.1002/j.2168-9830.2002.tb00703.x

Frommer, J. G. (1998). Cognition, context, and computers: Factors in effective foreign language learning. In J. Muyskens (Ed.), *New ways of learning and teaching: Focus on technology and foreign language education* (pp. 199–223). Boston: Heinle and Heinle.

Fulton, K. P. (2012). Ten reasons to flip. *Phi Delta Kappan, 94*(2), 20–24. doi:10.1177/003172171209400205

Garrison, D. R., & Kanuka, H. (2004). Blended learning: Uncovering its transformative potential in higher education. *The Internet and Higher Education, 7*(2), 95–105. doi:10.1016/j.iheduc.2004.02.001

Gascoigne, C., & Parnel, J. (2014). Hybrid language instruction: Finding the right fit. *Proceedings of the Central States Conference on the Teaching of Foreign Languages Report* (pp. 53- 64).

Godev, C. (2014). First-year hybrid Spanish courses: How instructors manage their time. *Hispania, 97*(1), 21–31. doi:10.1353/hpn.2014.0020

Graham, C. R. (2006). Blended learning systems: definition, current trends, future directions. In C. J. Bonk & C. R. Graham (Eds.), *Handbook of Blended Learning: Global perspectives, local designs*. San Francisco, CA: Pfeiffer Publishing.

Grgurovic, M. (2011). Blended learning in an ESL class: A case study. *CALICO Journal, 29*(1), 100–117. doi:10.11139/cj.29.1.100-117

Halili, S.H. & Zainuddin Z. (2015). Flipping the classroom: What we know and what we don't. *The Online Journal of Distance Education and E-learning, 3*(1), 28-35.

Halverson, L. R., Graham, C. R., Spring, K. J., & Drysdale, J. S. (2012). An analysis of high impact scholarship and publication trends in blended learning. *Distance Education, 33*(3), 381–413. doi:10.1080/01587919.2012.723166

Han, Y. J. (2015). Successfully flipping the ESL classroom for learner autonomy. *NYC TESOL Journal, 2*(1), 98–109.

Harris, P., Connolly, J., & Feeney, L. (2009). Blended learning: Overview and recommendations for successful implementation. *Industrial and Commercial Training, 41*(3), 155–163. doi:10.1108/00197850910950961

Henshaw, F. (2014). *Do's and Don'ts of Flipped, Hybrid and Online Courses. American Association of Teachers of Spanish and Portuguese (AATSP)*. Conference Talk.

Hermosilla, J. (2014). Hybrid Spanish programs: A challenging and successful endeavor. *Hispania, 97*(1), 1–4. doi:10.1353/hpn.2014.0010

Hoffman, E. (2014). Beyond the flipped classroom: Redesigning a research methods course for e3 instruction. *Contemporary Issues in Education Research, 7*(1), 51–62. doi:10.19030/cier.v7i1.8312

Hokanson, S. G. (2000). Distance education in foreign languages. *Rocky Mountain Review of Language and Literature, 54*(2), 85–93. doi:10.2307/1348122

Honeycutt, B., & Garrett, J. (2014). Expanding the definition of a flipped learning environment. *Instructional Design: Faculty focus.*

Hopper, K. (2003). *Reasons to go hybrid. Distance Education Report, 7*(24), 7.

Houston, M., & Lin, L. (2012). Humanizing the classroom by flipping the homework versus lecture equation. In Society for Information Technology and Teacher Education International Conference (pp. 1177-1182).

Jacot, M. T., Noren, J., & Berge, Z. L. (2014). The flipped classroom in training and development: Fad or the future? *Performance Improvement, 53*(9), 23–28.

Janson, A., Ernst, S. J., Lehmann, K. &Leimeister, J. M. (2014). Creating awareness and reflection in a large-scale IS lecture—the application of a peer assessment in a flipped classroom scenario. *Proceedings of the 4th Workshop on Awareness and Reflection in Technology-Enhanced Learning (ARTEL 2014) to be held in the context of EC-TEL* (pp. 35-50).

Jochum, C. J. (2011). Blended Spanish instruction: Perceptions and design. *Journal of Instructional Psychology, 38*(1), 40–46.

Jochum, C. J. (2013). Analyzing student perceptions of a blended Spanish grammar course. *Tarptautinis psichologijos žurnalas: Biopsichosocialinis požiūris, 12*, 105-116.

Johnson, G. B. (2013). Student perception of flipped classroom [Master's thesis]. The University of British Columbia, Canada.

Kachka, P. (2012). Educator's voice: What's all this talk about flipping. Retrieved from https://tippie.uiowa.edu/faculty-staff/allcollege/kachka.pdf

Khan, S. (2011). Salman Khan talk at TED 2011 [Video webcast]. Retrieved from http://youtube/gM-95HHI4gLk

Khan, S. (2012). *The one world schoolhouse: Education reimagined.* New York: Twelve.

Kinney, D. P., & Robertson, D. F. (2003). Technology makes possible new models for delivering developmental Mathematics instruction. *Mathematics and Computer Education, 37*(3), 315–328.

Koller, D. (2011, December 11). *Death knell for the lecture: Technology as a passport to personalized education. The New York Times.* Retrieved from http://www.nytimes.com/2011/12/06/science/daphne-koller-technology-as-a-passport -to-personalized-education.html?pagewanted=all&_r=0

Krathwohl, D. R., Bloom, B. S., & Masia, B. B. (1973). *Taxonomy of educational objectives, the classification of educational goals. Handbook II: Affective domain.* New York: David McKay Co., Inc.

Lage, M. J., Platt, G. J., & Treglia, M. (2000). Inverting the classroom: A gateway to creating an inclusive learning environment. *The Journal of Economic Education, 31*(1), 30–43. doi:10.1080/00220480009596759

LaMance, R. A. (2012). *Say hello to hybrid: Investigating student and instructor perceptions of the first hybrid language courses at UT* [Master's Thesis]. University of Tennessee.

López-Pérez, M. V., Pérez-López, M. C., & Rodríguez-Ariza, L. (2011). Blended learning in higher education: Students' perceptions and their relation to outcomes. *Computers and Education*, *56*(3), 818–826. doi:10.1016/j.compedu.2010.10.023

Manjinder. (2012). Before we flip classrooms, let's rethink what we're flipping to. *TechEdBlog*. Retrieved from http://techedblog.tumblr.com/post/34356480070/before-we-flip-classrooms-lets-rethink-what-were

Marwedel, P., & Engel, M. (2014). *Flipped classroom teaching for a cyber-physical system course-An adequate presence-based learning approach in the internet age. Proceedings of the 10th European Workshop on Microelectronics Education (EWME)*, (pp. 11-15). IEEE. doi:doi:10.1109/EWME.2014.6877386 doi:10.1109/EWME.2014.6877386

McKeachie, W., & Svinicki, M. (2006). *McKeachie's teaching tips: Strategies, research, and theory for college and university teachers.* (12th ed.). Boston: Houghton-Mifflin.

Meskill, C., & Anthony, N. (2005). Foreign language learning with CMC: Forms of online instructional discourse in a hybrid Russian class. *System*, *33*(1), 89–105. doi:10.1016/j.system.2005.01.001

Milman, N. B. (2012). The flipped classroom strategy: What is it and how can it best be used? *Distance Learning*, *9*(3), 85–87.

Mitchell, A., & Honore, S. (2007). Criteria for successful blended learning. *Industrial and Commercial Training*, *39*(3), 143–149. doi:10.1108/00197850710742243

Muldrow, K. (2013). A new approach to language instruction: Flipping the classroom. *Language and Education*, *8*, 28–31.

Murday, K., Ushida, E., & Chenoweth, N. A. (2008). Learners' and teachers' perspectives on language online. *Computer Assisted Language Learning*, *21*(2), 125–142. doi:10.1080/09588220801943718

Neumeier, P. (2005). A closer look at blended learning: Parameters for designing a blended learning environment for language teaching and learning. *ReCALL*, *17*(2), 163–178. doi:10.1017/S0958344005000224

Ng, E. M. W. (Ed.). (2009). *Comparative blended learning practices and environments.* China: Hong Kong Institute.

Oblender, T. E. (2002). A hybrid course model: One solution to the high online drop-out rate. *Learning and Leading with Technology*, *29*(6), 42–46.

Patterson, J. (2004). For quality and cost-effectiveness build a hybrid program. *Distance Education Report*, *8*(21), 1–2.

Pohl, M. (2000). *Learning to think, thinking to learn: Models and strategies to develop a classroom culture of thinking.* Cheltenham, Vic.: Hawker Brownlow.

Poon, J. (2013). Blended learning: an institutional approach for enhancing students' learning experiences, *Journal of Online Learning and Teaching, 9(2)*, 271-288.

Presby, L. (2001). Seven tips for highly effective online courses. *Syllabus*, *14*(11), 17.

Roehl, A., Reddy, S. L., & Shannon, G. J. (2013). The flipped classroom: An opportunity to engage millennial students through active learning strategies. *Journal of Family and Consumer Sciences, 105*(2), 44–49. doi:10.14307/JFCS105.2.12

Rubio, F., & Thoms, J. (Eds.). (2012). *Hybrid language teaching and learning: Exploring theoretical, pedagogical and curricular issues. AASC.* Boston: Heinle.

Russell, V. (2012). Learning complex grammar in the virtual classroom: A comparison of processing instruction, structured input, computerized visual input enhancement, and traditional instruction. *Foreign Language Annals, 45*, 42–71.

Sadler, P. M., & Good, E. (2006). The impact of self and peer grading on student learning. *Educational Assessment, 11*(1), 1–31. doi:10.1207/s15326977ea1101_1

Sams, A. (2011). The flipped class: Shedding light on the confusion, critique, and hype. The Daily Rift. Retrieved from http://www.thedailyriff.com/articles/the-flipped-class-shedding-light-on-the-confusioncritique-and-hype-801.php

Schwieter, J. W. (2011). Preparing students for class: A hybrid enhancement to language learning. *College Teaching Methods and Styles Journal, 4*(6), 41–50.

Scida, E. E., & Saury, R. E. (2013). Hybrid courses and their impact on student and classroom performance: A case study at the University of Virginia. *CALICO Journal, 23*(3), 517–531.

Scullen, M. E. (2014, November 14). Flipping and blending the language classroom: Experiment or new standard? Pearson online webinar.

Sharpe, R., Benfield, G., Roberts, G., & Francis, R. (2006). The undergraduate experience of blended e-learning: A review of UK literature and practice. York, UK: The Higher Education Academy. Retrieved from http://www.heacademy.ac.uk/assets/documents/teachingandresearch/Sharpe_ Benfield_Roberts_Francis.pdf

Simpson, E. J. (1972). *The classification of educational objectives in the psychomotor domain.* Washington, DC: Gryphon House.

Sink, D. L. (2008). Instructional design models and learning theories. In E. Biech (Ed.), *The ASTD handbook for workplace learning professionals* (pp. 195–212). Alexandria, VA: ASTD Press.

Sitter, V., Carter, C., Mahan, R., Massello, C., & Carter, T. (2009). Faculty and student perceptions of a hybrid course design.*Proceedings of the ASCUE*, Myrtle Beach. ASCUE.

Sloman, M. (2007). Making sense of blended learning. *Industrial and Commercial Training, 39*(6), 315–318. doi:10.1108/00197850710816782

Smith, K., & Kampf, C. (2004). Developing writing assignments and feedback strategies for maximum effectiveness in large classroom environments. *Proceedings of the International Professional Communication Conference IPCC '04* (pp. 77-82). IEEE. doi:doi:10.1109/IPCC.2004.1375279 doi:10.1109/IPCC.2004.1375279

Spencer, D., Wolf, D., & Sams, A. (2011). Are you ready to flip? Retrieved from http://www.thedailyriff. com/articles/are-youready-to-flip-6891.php

Stracke, E. (2007). A road to understanding: A qualitative study into why learners drop out of a blended language learning (BLL) environment. *ReCALL, 19*(1), 57–78. doi:10.1017/S0958344007000511

Stutzmann, B., Colebech, D. Khalid, A., Chin, C. & Sweigart, J. (2013). Flipped classroom or flipped out?: Professors attitudes towards online learning. SoTL Commons Conference Paper.

Tabor, S. W. (2007). Narrowing the distance: Implementing a hybrid learning model for information security education. *Quarterly Review of Distance Education, 8*(1), 47–57.

Talbert, R. (2012). Inverted classroom. *Colleagues,* 9(1). Retrieved from http://scholarworks.gvsu.edu/ colleagues/vol9/iss1/7

Thompson, C. (2011). How Khan Academy Is Changing the Rules of Education. *Wired.* Retrieved from http://www.wired.com/magazine/2011/07/ff_khan/

Tucker, C. (2012). Flipped classroom: Beyond the videos. *CatlinTucker.com.* Retrieved from http:// catlintucker.com/2012/04/flipped-classroom-beyond-the-videos/

Tunison M., & Noonan, B (2001). On-line learning: Secondary students' first experience. *Revue Canadienne de l'Education [Canadian Journal of Education],* 26(4), 495-511.

Valenza, J. K. (2012). The flipping librarian. *Teacher Librarian, 40*(2), 22–25.

VanPatten, B. (1996). *Input processing and grammar instruction: Theory and research.* Norwood, NJ: Ablex.

VanPatten, B. (2000). Processing instruction as form–meaning connections: Issues in theory and research. In J. F. Lee & A. Valdman (Eds.), *Form and Meaning in Language Teaching* (pp. 43–68). Boston: Heinle & Heinle.

Vaughan, N. D. (2007). Perspectives on blended learning in higher education. *International Journal on E-Learning, 6*(1), 81-94.

Voos, R. (2003). Blended learning – what is it and where might it take us? Sloan-C View, 2 (1), 3-5. Retrieved from http://www.sloan-c.org/publications/view/v2n1/blended1.htm

Winke, P., Goertler, S., & Amuzie, G. L. (2010). Commonly taught and less commonly taught language learners: Are they equally prepared for CALL and online language learning? *Computer Assisted Language Learning, 23*(3), 199–219. doi:10.1080/09588221.2010.486576

Witten, H. (2013). World languages. In J. Bretzman (Ed.), *Flipping 2.0: Practical strategies for flipping your class* (pp. 265–280). New Berlin, WI: The Bretzman Group.

Zappe, S., Leicht, R., Messner, J., Litzinger, T., & Lee, H. (2009). *"Flipping" the classroom to explore active learning in a large undergraduate course.* American Society for Engineering Education.

KEY TERMS AND DEFINITIONS

Cooperative Learning: A mode of learning based on the concept that knowledge is a social construct.

Face-to-Face Interaction: A traditional form of classroom instruction, in which the instructor spends most of the class time lecturing students.

Facilitator: An instructor role of a discussion leader guiding students to accomplish a task instead of being a mere lecturer.

Input Activities: Assignments in which students are only assessed on comprehension of a particular form after being exposed to the target language in a communicative context.

Learning Environment: A combination of qualities that create the classroom experience.

Learning Outcomes: Statements that identify what students will know or will be able to do at the end of the course.

Online Component: A form of instruction that is delivered entirely via technology.

Task-Oriented Activities: Assignments that are goal oriented as a measure of success.

Chapter 6
Beginning Chinese as a Foreign Language Online Course Design:
Utilizing Multiple Digital Modes and Assessments

Bailu Li
Purdue University, USA

Sijia Yao
Purdue University, USA

Wei Hong
Purdue University, USA

ABSTRACT

The explosive worldwide growth of the internet inspired the initial emergence and further implementation of distance teaching and learning in a multitude of areas, including languages (Harasim, 2000; Holmberg et al., 2005; White, 2003, 2006; Blake & Delforge, 2007; Hampel & de los Arcos, 2013). The change from the traditional classroom environment to a more diversified and flexible distance setting has been embraced by many educators, administrators, and students, yet it has also generated doubt and resistance from others. Students may potentially benefit from more efficient uses of multimedia resources with increased critical thinking, communication, and problem-solving skills (Tricker et al., 2001; Felix, 2002; Spangle, Hodne & Schierling, 2002; Levy & Stockwell, 2006). Meanwhile, critics also highlight the potential drawbacks for distance learning students, including isolation from peers, lack of engagement, and insufficient technical support (Shield 2000; Muilenburg and Berge, 2005; Simonson et al., 2009; Berge 1999; Hara and Kling 2000; Bower, 2001; Wang & Chen 2013). This chapter concerns the ways in which distance online learning content can be designed and developed through the utilization of multimedia and cultural-enriched materials for first-year-level College Chinese Foreign Language (CFL) courses. Discussions about employing virtual interaction, including student-content, student-instructor, and student-student interaction in course design and course design development. The chapter will end with discussions of the current challenges and new directions for a better practice of teaching and learning of Chinese language courses at a distance.

DOI: 10.4018/978-1-5225-0177-0.ch006

REVIEW OF THE LITERATURE

Distance Language Learning

Distance education has expanded rapidly in the last two decades to solve campus problems such as budget cuts, overcrowding, and student demand for flexible schedules (Bates, 1997; Furstenberg, 1997; Joliffe & Stevens, 2001; Collis & Moonen, 2001; Fleming et al., 2002; Garbett, 2011). This type of course has been defined as a learning environment in which students and teachers are separated by distance and sometimes by time (Moore & Kearsley, 1996, p.1). Extensive efforts are currently being invested in developing distance-learning environments. Distance course offerings are increasing at a faster rate than their traditional counterparts, with the number of higher-education distance courses nearly tripling between 1995 and 2003 (Beck, 2010), and almost 100% of public institutions claim distance instruction as a strategic section of their long-term plans (Major, 2010).

Flexibility is no doubt a significant advantage of distance courses for students. Flexibility attracts learners to distance-learning programs more than any other aspect (Schoech, 2000). In the distance environment, students have control over time, pace, and modality of material access (Egbert & Jessup, 1996), while instructors can tailor instruction, facilitate understanding, and provide feedback to each student (Easton, 2003).

As distance-learning practice and research proliferate over time, language learners, instructors, and researchers also sense the flexibility and potential of the new distance language environment (White, 2006). The acquisition of a foreign language requires a language-rich environment in which learners are continuously exposed to productive skills. McDonough (2001) catalogs the extensive variety of approaches in online programs that provide engaging multiple-format methodologies to language learning, e.g., applications entail colorful graphics, motion pictures, video, and sound, all integrated into real-life settings. Additionally, McDonough refers to how language learners have unlimited access to videotaped instructional sessions, notes, PowerPoint presentations, podcasts, tutorials, practice exercises, and assessments.

Compared to more "content-based" academic subjects, the challenges for teaching language at a distance, in particular, the acquisition and practice of the four primary skills of listening, speaking, reading, and writing, are magnified to a much greater extent on in distance learning. It has been acknowledged that for language acquisition to occur, learners should be exposed to a sufficient amount of comprehensible input, both oral and written (Krashen, 1982), and need opportunities to produce comprehensible output; that is, to offer oral and written forms in the target language (Swain, 1985). This requirement is not easy to satisfy in any language learning setting, but it is particularly more complex in a distance language-learning context, given the geographic distance between learners and instructors, and the often asynchronous communication and feedback among them. A number of scholars question less listening and speaking opportunities that challenge the development of oral proficiency (Felix, 2001; Hurd, 2005, 2007; Jaggars, 2014). Affective factors, including learning anxiety with isolation from a language learning group (Brown, 2006), and lack of instant feedback (Hurd, 2007), are also subject to extensive criticism toward distance language learning.

Chinese Courses at a Distance

With the growing economic status of China and the identification of Mandarin Chinese as a critical language, the learning of Chinese as a foreign language (CFL) has become a global trend. However, despite substantial research and empirical studies on distance education, the development and implementation of Chinese language courses at a distance are still in their infancy. Challenges in the field include instructor overload and insufficient proficiency and staff development to support students in classrooms (Xie, 2003), as well as the ever present question of how effective well developed, interactive courses can be in supporting student perceptions of learning success (Cheng, 2011; Kan, 2013; Sun, Chen & Olson, 2013)

Xie (2003) explored how much the potential challenges of distance Chinese language courses in U.S. higher education have to do with instructor overload. Xie suggests that learner misuse of technology, lack of technical training and distance teaching experiences, and overload of designing and maintaining distance course materials are the primary frustrations instructors might confront, while insufficient oral opportunities and lack of autonomous strategies might account for the deficiency and even failure of students.

Moreover, Cheng (2011) examined the perceptions of six advanced and 18 second-year Chinese language learners' perceptions, as well as performance, over a period of four semesters. Results from a questionnaire he administered indicated that 78% of the students preferred the in-class versus online environment, noting that they preferred a more natural and familiar environment. In terms of performance, Cheng found that while listening, speaking, and reading skills were comparable between students in both groups, the online class students had issues with grammar and sentence patterns.

Having some face-to-face contact online and how supportive content delivery format positively affect how students perceive their language learning experience and overall course quality. Li and Hong (2014) in their study of first-year Chinese distance courses write about the importance of presented content design, and discuss future directions and suggestions in developing and maintaining a sustainable Chinese distance course, with a focus on material selection, modes of interaction, student motivation, and assessment.

Unlike Cheng (2013), Kan (2013) found that entry-level Chinese students who participated in a blended entry level course in the United Kingdom had high positive attitudes towards on-line blended learning, which was due to the interactivity of the course, based on the end-of-the-course survey. Kan explained how the online study planner, the synchronous online conference tool (*Elluminate*), the interactive online language exercises for all four skills, and online discussion forums were adopted in the design and delivery of the course. Kan contended that integrating various learning resources to maximize learning outcomes without overloading students is the biggest challenge for future program applications.

Sun, Chen, and Olson (2013) propose a prototype to develop and implement a fully online beginners Chinese language classes in another Midwest university in the U.S. Similarly, Sun, Chen, and Olsen (2013) found that addition to the utilization of a variety of technological tools and activity, curriculum redesign and content development, as well as the establishment of online learning communities, was essential in online course effectiveness. For instance, they demonstrated a hybrid of asynchronous instruction (i.e. a 15-30-minute video-based daily instruction, a private Facebook group with students at all levels) and synchronous interaction (i.e. optional on-campus office hours and online Skype video chat) as the key components for a successful online Chinese language course.

In a study of 35 English native speaking pre-service teachers' experience of learning Chinese as a foreign language online, Wang (2012) found that most participants initially perceived that Chinese was a difficult language and fewer than half expressed interest in studying Chinese as a foreign language in the first place. However, after taking a 10-week Chinese Moodle online course, which entailed multiple language and culture sections, most participants expressed more positive attitudes towards Chinese language learning. The study indicated that interactive tasks and various online materials (e.g., videos, voice recorders, writing demos) promoted positive perceptional change about learning Chinese. By switching teachers' roles to Chinese language learners, participants affirmed that their Chinese online learning experience increased their linguistic, cultural, and technological awareness, as well as empathy for diverse students. To explore whether and how participants actually applied the awareness into teaching practice, Wang (2015) conducted a follow-up study and found that most in-service teachers confirmed that learning Chinese online courses helped them understand potential difficulties diverse students faced and thus transfer their awareness into teaching. Proposing a model, Wang (2015) indicated that teachers' awareness development and transfer is "a complex and dynamic process" (p.16) in which contextual factors and personal factors (e.g. teachers' efforts and beliefs) may affect how teachers apply their awareness developed during the Chinese course to their teaching practice. These two studies reveals that Chinese online learning experience not only benefits teachers with developing their foreign language skills, but also increases their awareness of how to work with diverse students.

Thus, motivation about language learning can be associated with providing engaging opportunities to explore language and culture as supported by technology, to also change language as well as cultural perceptions. With the inspiration from the research referenced above and a strong attempt to further examine the effectiveness of distance Chinese language courses, Li and Hong (2014) launched first-year distance Chinese courses in Fall 2013. The authors presented content design, and discussed future directions and suggestions on developing and maintaining a sustainable Chinese distance course, with a focus on material selection, modes of interaction, student motivation, and assessment. Yao and Hong's (2015) ongoing study focused on the assessment of two online test tools, *Respondus* (Foster & Layman, 2013) and *Speak Everywhere* (Li, Fukada & Hong, 2012), when evaluating students' task-based linguistics skills, along with cultural and communicative skills.

UTILIZING INTERACTIVE LEARNING MODES AS PROGRAM THEORETICAL FRAMES FOR COURSE DESIGN

In the framework of distance education, there are three types of interactive learning modes that need to be considered: student-content interaction, student-instructor interaction, and student-student interaction (Moore, 1989, Moore and Kearsley, 1996). According to the authors, all three types of interactions must be equally present throughout courses.

Miller, et al. (1996) emphasize that students desire personal contact with their instructors and peers, along with high-quality technology in the distance education environment. New techniques must be constructed to facilitate interactions, since the three types of interactions directly relate to course satisfaction. Naidu (2013) also pointed out that the objective learning outcomes depend a great deal on the quality of the communication between learners and teachers, as well as among learners.

As Osman & Herring (2007) contended, multiple methods of content exploration and transmission should be designed for the online language courses, including synchronous and asynchronous learning activities, technology-advanced content design, and multiple communication methods, such as e-mail, webcam conversations, and discussion forums.

Student-Content Interaction

According to Moore (1989), it is the first type of interaction that takes place between the student and the content. Such interaction takes place when the learner, with the help of the instructor or the teaching institution, obtains new knowledge and combines it with the body of his or her pre-existing knowledge. Moore postulates that, without this type of interaction, there could be no education, since the educational process entails the learner's intellectual interaction with content and changes the cognitive structure of the learner's mind.

Student-Instructor Interaction

Moore (1989) contends that the instructor is especially valuable in responding to the listener's application of new knowledge, by permitting and guiding students to interact with the content most effectively. Chang, Chen, & Hsu (2011) also point out that the most important role of an online instructor is to ensure the participation of students online. Gilson et al. (1998) suggest that long-distance teachers need to encourage their students frequently to express their opinions and give feedback. Timeline for feedback is also critical for successful learning experiences (Herring & Smaldino, 2001). Students need to be informed as quickly as possible regarding how well they are doing.

Synchronous Meetings

Moore & Kearsley (1996) pointed out that long-distance videoconferencing more closely resembles traditional classroom education than any other form of long-distance education. Research shows that synchronous communication can overcome some of the limitations associated with the asynchronous distance learning environment, such as providing opportunities for immediate feedback and helping to build connections between the instructor and students (Hines & Pearl, 2004). Synchronous communication has also been found to have a positive impact on other aspects of distance education, as compared to asynchronous communication, such as a better understanding of students' learning attitudes (Hwang & Yang, 2008) and increased student satisfaction with web-based courses (Cao, et al., 2009). The authors find that practice and revision in the implementation of synchronous meetings are in agreement with the research results presented above. In addition, according to the observation, synchronous meetings facilitate the students to be more committed and extrinsically motivated in learning the language.

THE DEVELOPMENT AND IMPLEMENTATION CFL COURSE DESIGN

The literature available for the Chinese language online distance language courses is dearth. This chapter is based on the first distance language courses on campus which contributes to a U.S.-initiative intended to promote more Chinese language learning in the United States. Researchers were interested in finding out what are the best methods and approaches that can promote Chinese foreign language (CFL) proficiency in reading, writing, listening, and speaking.

Context of Course Design and Development

The Chinese courses were exposed to reading, vocabulary, grammar, and Chinese culture through multimedia materials in this distance course. The authors introduce how an interactive and community-based distance-learning environment was developed to ensure the three types of interactive modes:

1. Student-content interaction,
2. Student-instructor-interaction, which is supported through
3. Synchronous meetings.

The authors also promoted small groups and partner activities so that students could utilize Chinese in meaningful communicative contexts. After completing the second semester of the distance Chinese course, students were expected to understand/produce simple conversations and read/write short paragraphs with Chinese characters. Considering the development and course design, the authors had students regulate their learning pace, as well as interact with peers and the instructor, who acted as a facilitator online. Thus, students primarily completed the assignments on their own. Quizzes and tests were performance-based and were offered online.

The goals of developing and delivering distance Chinese language courses were three-fold:

1. To maximize the existing university technology in order to serve the language curriculum, which has been otherwise regarded as applicable only in traditional classrooms;
2. To provide expanded learning opportunities of core courses to students who are unable to take the classroom courses due to internships, studies abroad, and summer sessions; and
3. To provide empirical research results on distance courses in Chinese language education, which are currently lacking in the field nationwide.

Since Fall 2013, there has been a total of 93 students (one student took CHNS102Y twice) who have enrolled in the first-year entry-level distance Chinese courses in the institute. At this time, 82 students have completed this online distance CFL course.

The students involved during the implementation of course design were comprised of 45 male and 37 female students; 53 students have an Asian background, including 33 South Korean, 7 heritage, 7 Japanese, 1 Indonesian, 3 Malaysian, and 1 Thai student. Another 30 students were from the U.S. (27), Germany (1), Peru (1), and Mexico (1). The majors of the students varied, and included engineering, liberal arts, chemistry, math, and pharmacy.

The retention rate was relatively low for the first semester. Five students withdrew from the classes and the study. Another four students in the following semesters dropped the classes later in the semesters due to personal or health issues, which prevented them from obtaining further academic achievement in the language. Summer CHNS101 and CHNS102 in the Fall 2015 semesters experienced relatively low enrollment. In fact, moderate student attrition of Chinese language study has been noted across the United States as of late (Goldberg, Looney, & Lusin, 2015).

Table 1. Enrollment information for distance Chinese courses

Semester	Course	Initial Enrollment	Final Enrollment
Fall 2013	CHNS101Y	12	7
Spring 2014	CHNS102Y	14	14
Summer 2014	CHNS101Y	10	9
Fall 2014	CHNS101Y	8	7
Fall 2014	CHNS102Y	5	5
Spring 2015	CHNS102Y	15	14
Summer 2015	CHNS101Y	6	6
Summer 2015	CHNS102Y	5	4
Fall 2015	CHNS101Y	14	13
Fall 2015	CHNS102Y	5	4
		Total: 94(-1)	Total: 83(-1)

COURSE CONTENT, DEVELOPMENT, AND IMPLEMENTATION: HOW TO

The content development and learning activities are in accordance with successful achievement in reading, writing, listening, and speaking. Despite the high dependency on technology in the delivery of distance and less commonly taught courses, Palloff and Pratt (1999) contend that "technology does not teach students; effective teachers do" (p. 4). In other words, how the instructor constructs and delivers the course content is one of the fundamental effective elements of distance learning.

In this section, multimedia materials, including PowerPoint Presentations, mini video grammar lectures, daily theme videos, Fun Hanzi (Hanzi, or 汉字, which in this chapter refers to characters, simplified or traditional in Mandarin Chinese), and Fun Reading, are developed exclusively for the online version of first-year Chinese courses. The following sections are the descriptions of each multimedia material employed in this CFL course.

Vocabulary and Text Presentations

The widespread adoption of PowerPoint Presentations (PPTs) in higher education makes it an effective tool when textbook knowledge is delivered and extended to distance learners. A wealth of accessible multimedia materials embodied in the PPTs are collected and compiled to elaborate the contents in and beyond the textbook. The students were expected to study these materials on their own.

Goals

When designing PPTs for text and vocabulary sections, the authors consider the following goals. Such goals are developed to be compatible with the traditional face to face curriculum.

- **Hanzi Etymology**: To recognize 20-30 high-frequency radicals and to identify the semantic and phonetic components of a compound character.

- **Pinyin:** To produce basic sounds with correct tones and to strengthen the correct pronunciation by enforcing tone precision at sentence levels.
- **Reading:** To recognize about 100-150 high-frequency characters, to look up the meaning and pronunciation of characters using a dictionary, and to read simple messages, personal notes, holiday cards, and short letters.
- **Structures:** To produce the basic structure of Mandarin Chinese, including verbal, adjectival, and nominal predicates; common interrogatives; time adverbials; and prepositional phrases.
- **Language Use:** To perform culturally appropriate functions such as greetings, requests for directions, apologies, and family and other daily activities, and to handle and perform successfully a limited number of simple communicative tasks pertaining to topics that meet survival needs, such as time telling, performing daily routine tasks, hosting guests, shopping, renting, and seeing a doctor.
- **Culture:** To become familiar with the basic assumptions of Chinese culture and contemporary Chinese society.

Practices

In order to achieve the goals above, the authors designed the following contents in the PPTs.

- **Explain Hanzi Etymology:** Offer explicit explanations of the morpheme and phonetic structures for typical characters (Figures 1 and 2).
- **Record Audios for Every New Word from the Textbook:** Insert audio files for supplementary words and extra sentences. Add audio and video links for pinyin tutoring.

Figure 1. Examples of Hanzi etymology in PPTs

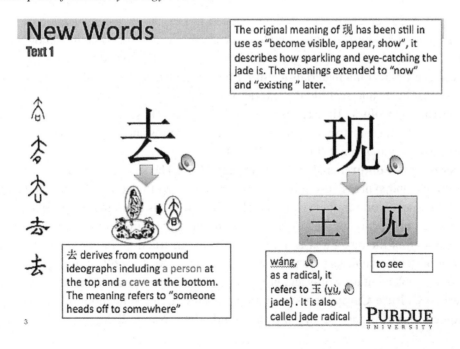

Figure 2. Examples of Hanzi etymology in PPTs

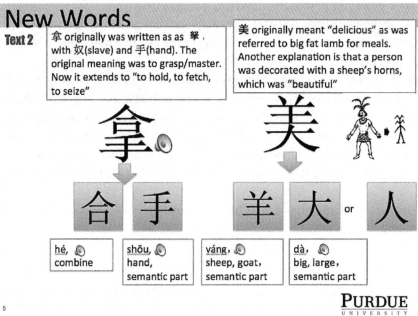

- **Provide Multiple Exposures of Context-Based Reinforcement**: Often the dialogues are culturally enriched with phrases first and then with a short dialogue. For example, when the new word "年 (nián, year)" was introduced in Lesson 9, a short dialogue on the topic of "中国人都回家过新年 (zhōngguó rén dōu huíjiā guò xīnnián, Chinese people all tend to go back home and celebrate the Chinese New Year with their families)" is composed, followed by a photo that shows masses of people rush onto the train stations before the Chinese New Year. When the new word "睡觉 (shuìjiào, sleep/go to bed)" was introduced in Lesson 11, a conversation of "应该早点睡觉 (yīnggāi zǎodiǎn shuìjiào, should go to bed early)" was developed in the dialogue, with a brief introduction and extensive links regarding the benefits of going to bed early from a Chinese health perspective. Extra reading materials featuring further lexical and cultural messages were also provided to consolidate and scaffold the text delivery (Figures 3, 4, and 5).
- **Use Contrasting Colors, Tables, Notes, and Examples:** These are designed to explain the similarities and differences between Chinese grammar structures and English ones, followed by exercises for each grammar point (Figures 6, 7, and 8)
- **Emphasize Text Comprehension and Language Use:** The strategies of metacognition, answering questions, and synthesizing/summarizing are provided to deepen students' understanding of the text. Learners work on their own to tackle the questions/tasks that arise first and then move to the explicit instruction of the key sentences and grammar points of the text. The well-rounded comprehension of the target text is not the end of the instruction; rather, learners are challenged with brief performance tasks to make connections to real world application. Learners will also be exposed to supplementary words and phrases with the context provided (Figures 9, 10, and 11).
- **Connect to Culture Components:** Culture issues are highly influential in language and cannot be divorced from it in the learning process (Zaid, 1999, Nault, 2006). Therefore, cultural topics

Figure 3. Examples of culture-enriched short dialogues and reading

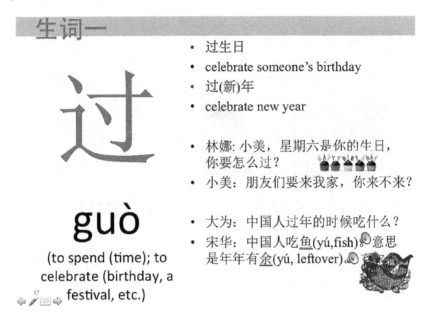

Figure 4. Examples of culture-enriched short dialogues and reading

and information are embedded in the explanations and extensions of vocabulary and texts. Extra links for texts and videos are also included at the end of each lesson. Figures 12-13 show AV links to Chinese zodiac signs, story, and associated personal traits. Birthdays expressions are taught. Online images of the Beijing Opera are used for students to practice the pattern "Who are they?" in Chinese, with the intent that as they both practice the language and also acquire the cultural knowledge (Figures 12 and 13).

Figure 5. Examples of culture-enriched short dialogues and reading

Figure 6. Examples of grammar PPTs

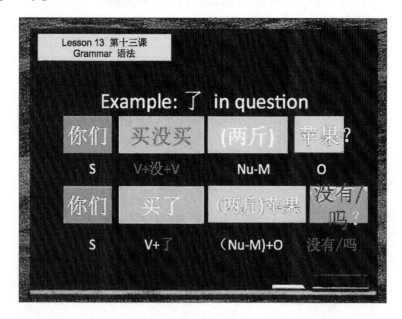

Mini Video Grammar Lectures

The major goal of the mini video grammar lectures is to help facilitate students' efficient understanding of the relatively difficult grammar topics. Students are expected to use the grammar structures correctly, meaningfully, and socially appropriately after watching the videos. The videos then draw learners' attention to the grammatical forms they see and hear. In addition, the appearance of the instructor relieves the

Figure 7. Examples of grammar PPTs

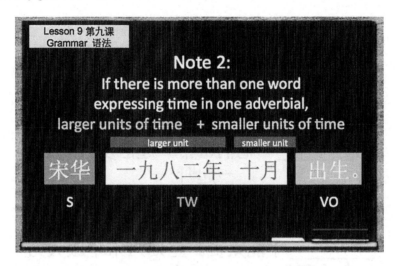

Figure 8. Examples of grammar PPTs

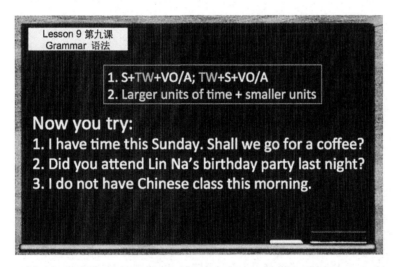

feelings of anxiety and isolation that online students usually experience and thus increases teacher-learner interactions (Miller 1996; Naidu, 2013). The grammar topics are selected based on students' feedback and the instructor's observation. The topics include the usage of "很 (hěn, very)", the interrogative pronouns, words expressing time as adverbials, the particle "了 (le, a modal particle, aspect particle)", and the difference between "几 (jǐ, how many, how much)" and "多少 (duōshǎo, how many, how much)", etc.

The outline of the grammar lecture video is as follows: the instructor first greets the students and introduces the grammar topic. The instructor follows with PowerPoint presentations to exhibit the basic grammatical structure and provides multiple examples. They are designed with enlarged fonts and color codes to bring about students' attention (Figure 13-14). The video lecture ends with a real-life question to personally connect with students. For example, when the difference between "几"and "多

Figure 9. Examples of text comprehension and language usage

课文一- Read text 1 and fill in the blanks

宋华听说大为_____了感冒。大为说他现在还有点儿头疼。大为想_____宋华一件_____。大为认识了一个漂亮的_____。他们常常一起散步，一起看_____，一起听_____。可是他的宿舍太小了。大卫想租一间有_____和_____的房子。_____不能太贵。星期六宋华跟大为一起去租房_____看看。

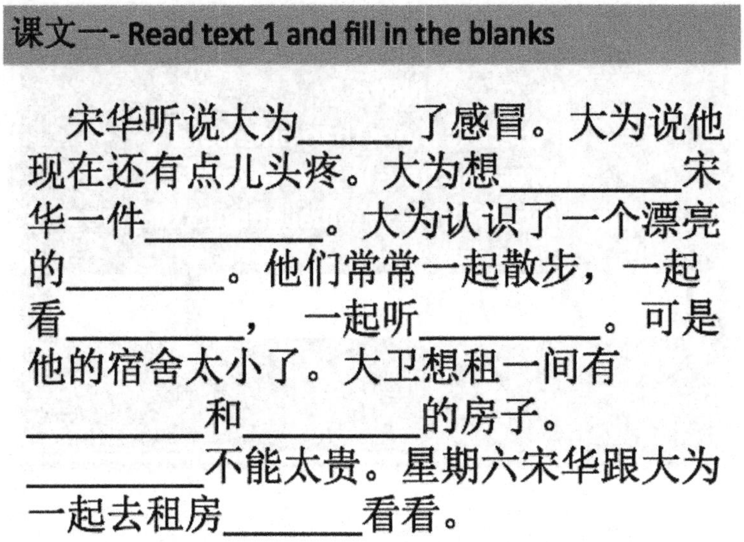

Figure 10. Examples of text comprehension and language usage

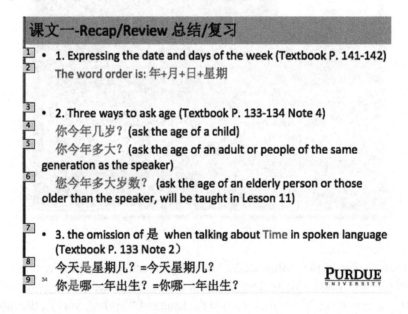

课文一-Recap/Review 总结/复习

- 1. Expressing the date and days of the week (Textbook P. 141-142)
  The word order is: 年+月+日+星期

- 2. Three ways to ask age (Textbook P. 133-134 Note 4)
  你今年几岁？(ask the age of a child)
  你今年多大？(ask the age of an adult or people of the same generation as the speaker)
  您今年多大岁数？ (ask the age of an elderly person or those older than the speaker, will be taught in Lesson 11)

- 3. the omission of 是 when talking about Time in spoken language (Textbook P. 133 Note 2）
  今天是星期几？=今天星期几？
  你是哪一年出生？=你哪一年出生？

PURDUE UNIVERSITY

少" is taught,the instructor asks the students "你们家有几口人? (nǐmen jiā yǒu jǐ kǒu rén, how many people are there in your family)" and expects the students to answer. Following the grammar lecture is a mini video segment that records a Chinese student's life on campus, in order to review the grammar previously presented in the lecture. The goal is to immerse the students in a meaningful context while grammar is taught (Figures 14 and 15).

Figure 11. Examples of text comprehension and language usage

Figure 12. Examples of culture extension

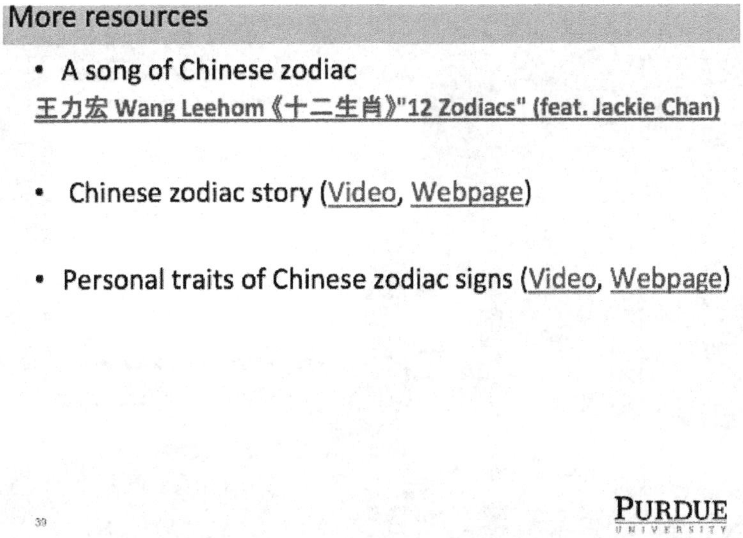

Themed Videos

Comprehension was perceived as the first step for language learning. Research has demonstrated that repetition of comprehensible information, delivered in varying forms, especially video, is associated with greater rates of measurable learning and comprehension (Brindley and Nunan, 1992; Wetzel et. al, 1994, Gruba, 1999). Video can be controlled at the students' pace and will, and it presents not only images but

Figure 13. Examples of culture extension

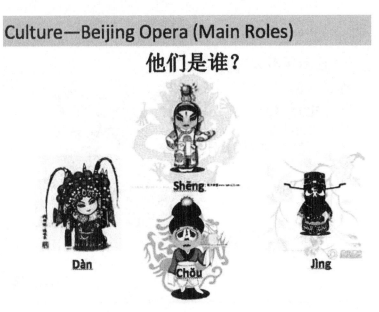

Figure 14. Examples of mini grammar lectures

also "real language that is not simplified and is spoken at a normal speed with genuine accent" (Burt, 1999, p.2). It also provides contextualized information, including non-verbal cues and non-lexical cues (Bello, 1999) and context (Fazey, 1999) to generate or validate student hypotheses.

In the courses, nine comprehensive videos are provided to the students on a storyline featuring four students' daily lives. The length of each video varies from three to five minutes. Three Chinese native speakers and one advanced-level non-native Chinese student play the roles of 小美 (Xiǎoměi, female name), 大国 (Dàguó, male name), 苏世 (Sū shì, male name) and 魏凯 (Wèi kǎi, male name) in the vid-

Figure 15. Examples of mini grammar lectures

eos and act out various scenarios, e.g. greetings, ordering food, introduction, shopping and bargaining, being sick, all of which are concurrent with the topics in the textbook.

The corresponding worksheets are composed of five to six open questions related to the main idea, comprehension of key sentences, meanings of new vocabulary, and a cultural compare-and-contrast question to be answered in English. The intention is to motivate students to meet the ACTFL Connections and Comparison goals while learning a foreign language. The compare-and-contrast question asks students to reflect on the similarities and differences related to the specific topics between their own cultures and the Chinese culture presented in the videos. By engaging in these questions, students can better reflect on their own cultures from a global perspective, while increasing their intercultural awareness (Figures 16 and 17).

Figure 16. Examples of themed videos on campus

Figure 17. Examples of themed videos on campus

Fun Hanzi and Fun Reading

Fun Hanzi and Fun Reading, as culturally enriched and entertaining activities, are designed to provoke students' learning interest while reading. Motivation, according to White (2006), is still a significant but under-analyzed field. These two activities are piloted as extra exercises to use culture and entertainment to increase students' motivation. That is why we use "fun" in the titles of these two activities: Fun Hanzi and Fun Reading, in the hopes that students will have fun while they engage in these activities. Additionally, given the absence of direct mediation of the learning process by instructors, the distance course emphasizes the learner-course content interface, an approach to encourage the constructive, dynamic, and mutual interrelation between learners and the course content.

Fun Hanzi, as a supplementary exercise, is developed to stimulate their interest in hanzi. "Fun Hanzi" attempts to include the concepts of "Hanzi are fun to learn" ("学汉字很有趣") and "Hanzi are interesting" ("有趣的汉字"). The supplementary Hanzi are carefully selected not only to refresh students' memory of the current Hanzi in the textbook, but more importantly, to motivate their interest in Hanzi learning. The new Hanzi selected are all closely related to the Hanzi in the textbook, in order for the students to effectively review them within a new context. Moreover, students can expand their Hanzi inventory by learning the extra Hanzi closely associated with the textbook Hanzi. Fun Hanzi assignments require students to seek out the connection between the textbook Hanzi and the new Hanzi, for example, to recognize the same radical from two different Hanzi, or find stroke differences of Hanzi within the same radical. Students actively engage in discovery and exploration, which attempts to feel more like a game than a tedious exercise. Several categories of Hanzi were selected in a Fun Hanzi activity as follows.

1. The new Hanzi are several strokes different from the textbook Hanzi. For instance:
    Adding strokes to form new Hanzi:
    十 (shí, ten) → 干(gān, dry); 王(wáng, king); 玉(yù, jade) ↘ 千 (qiān, thousand); 禾 (hé, young crop); 和 (hé, and)

2. The new Hanzi share the same radicals with the textbook Hanzi. For instance:
   清 (qīng, clear) vs. 情 (qíng, feeling)
3. The Hanzi combination that is formed with two textbook Hanzi. For instance:
   Can you guess what 生气 means based on what we have already learned--生 (in 学生 of Lesson Four) and 气 (in 天气 of Lesson Six) ?
   It means "angry." e.g. 我很生气 (I am angry) 。

The authors try to introduce the Hanzi that college students may relate to, or popular in daily life, such as 爱 (ài, love) and 生气 (shēngqì, angry). Each Fun Hanzi section has 2-3 exercises where students are asked to find Hanzi connections or to guess the meaning of new Hanzi based on their current knowledge. The number of new Hanzi in each section are no more than eight, in order to reasonably maximize students' progress while avoiding overwhelming them.

Fun Reading, similarly, demonstrates another effort to motivate students' learning through reading. Reading is a substantial component in the learner-course content communicative mode. To engage students in an entertaining way, as in "Fun Hanzi," the authors created a romantic story between two Chinese students, 田田 (tiántian, female name) and 不不 (bùbu, male name). Students read a part of the story every two lessons with comprehension questions. The story was written in a way that keeps students reading until the end, to achieve the goal of developing their initial reading skills, as well as learning about Chinese dating culture, a topic familiar to college students. The Hanzi in Fun Reading are carefully selected to fit the content and level of students' comprehension. Fun Hanzi and Fun Reading, along with their worksheets, provide ample opportunity to allow reviews of previous materials, and at the same time expand vocabularies and develop reading skills in a meaningful context.

Synchronous Meeting Challenges

Over the past few semesters, the synchronous meetings have seen some major changes. First, the frequency of the meetings change from once a week to once every two lessons, and finally settle down to once per lesson, as the best result for both the instructor's workload and the students' self-evaluation/communication. Second, the number of students participating in one synchronous meeting varies from one to more; however individual meetings are the ultimate choice, since personal needs and style can be fulfilled, and personal feedback can be delivered to the maximum. Third, the online meeting tool switched from Adobe Connect to WebEx, due to the strategic change in the university levels in the Spring of 2015. The sequence of events in a typical synchronous meeting usually consists of an announcement section, error correction for the previous lesson, a mini lecture, oral practice, and timed dictation at the end. Students are encouraged to ask questions at any time during the meeting. Each meeting takes 30-60 minutes, depending on the content difficulty and students' proficiency levels. Immediate feedback is provided throughout the meeting.

Despite technological improvements, interaction between the instructor and students is challenged by technical difficulties such as slow internet connections, time lags, slow transmission speed that leads to the screen freezing, and interrupted connections. This impeded communication and interaction between the instructor and students made students "frustrated" and "anxious," as reflected in the students' feedback. Nevertheless, the technical issues should not obscure the virtue of synchronous meetings that bridge the gap between the isolated instructor and students, and provide instant feedback on both sides.

Speak Everywhere

Speak Everywhere (SE), an in-house oral practice software, is designed and developed specifically as a foreign language oral practice/assessment platform. It consists of three sub-systems: author, instructor, and student (Author, 2012). Instructors and/or material designers use the author sub-system to create oral exercises, using video, audio, graphics, and/or text. Students then access the student sub-system to work on the exercises. As they speak, their oral response is recorded, which they can listen to immediately afterwards. They can also compare the pre-recorded sounds with their own pronunciation simultaneously by clicking the comparison icon on the SE platform (see figure 17). They can repeat each audio item as many times as they wish. When they are satisfied with their oral production, they can submit it to the system. When instructors log into the instructor sub-system, they can find which students have done which exercises and listen to each audio recording. They can choose to grade the exercises and/or give feedback via written/audio comments, or both.

Exercises in SE are assigned to students twice per lesson. By the first due date, students must complete the read and repeat exercises for pinyin and new vocabulary; when the lesson is approaching to the end, students are required to complete more comprehensive and interactive exercises, including Q&A, picture description, grammar drills, oral reading, and short speech.

Students perceive SE as a useful and flexible tool for practicing oral exercises at their pace while the instructor monitors and measures the students' speaking and listening outcomes through SE. The newly released feedback notification function allows the students to check the instructor's feedback in a timely manner before the errors are fossilized (Figures 18, 19, and 20).

Figure 18. Examples of Speak Everywhere exercises and feedback

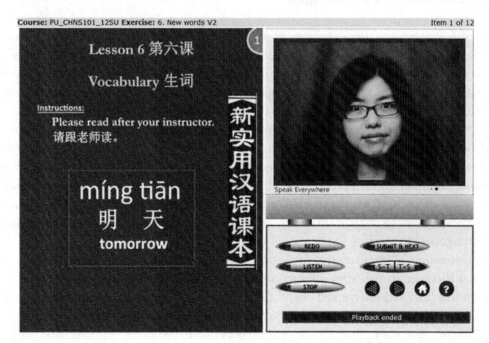

Figure 19. Examples of Speak Everywhere exercises and feedback

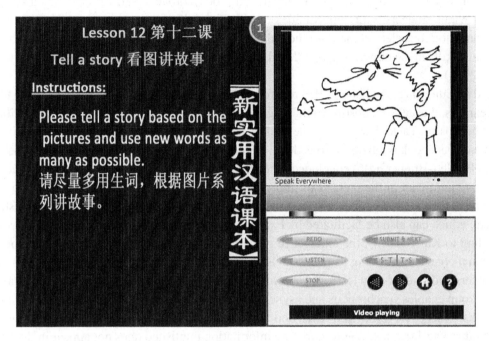

Figure 20. Examples of Speak Everywhere exercises and feedback

(Charles)	1☑ 2☑ 3☑ 4☑ 5☑		Play all	Delete all
(Marquette)	0☑ 3◉ ☑ 3☑ 0◉ ☑ 3☑		Play all	Delete all
(Raymond)	0☑ 3☑ 3☑ 3☑ 3◉ ☑		Play all	Delete all

Student-Student Interaction

Research has revealed that collaboration among students does provide learning benefits (Tee & Karney, 2010). Tee and Karney contend that online discussions can yield information and insights that students cannot have learned from more formal sources, and at the same time, establish a sense of community through which members "share divergent world views, opinions and experiences, develop trust, and make decisions based on a growing common understanding" (p. 405). Among all student-student interaction modes in the distance courses, discussion group seems to have one of the most influential features in encouraging active participation and outreaching to international/Chinese-speaking communities (Buckley, 2011; MacDonald & Caverly, 2001; Kan, 2013). Teamwork, on the other hand, has caught increasing attention in distance language contexts (Lou et al., 2001; Beldarrain, 2006; Rennie & Morrison, 2012).

Private Facebook Groups

In general, online asynchronous discussions benefit students by promoting student-centered learning, encouraging wider student participation, and allowing students to interpret and produce more in-depth and reasoned discussion (Buckley, 2011). Allowing students to select their own contributions and commentary to online discussion questions encourage more autonomous learning and provoke more critical thinking (Cole & Kritzer, 2009). According to Breault (2003), broader, self-reflective, and self-selected response provides students with opportunities to identify problems that interest them and then result in their connection to society at large. In the online language domain, online discussions also facilitate better writing skills in the target language (MacDonald & Caverly, 2001) and stimulate cultural interaction (Kan, 2013).

Inspired by Sun, Chen, & Olson (2013) regarding the creation of a private Facebook group for online Chinese learners, the authors substituted the original discussion forum in Blackboard Learn with private Facebook groups for each class during the Fall of 2014, and received highly positive feedback from most students. Facebook is currently considered the most popular platform for online social networking in the U.S. Bartlett-Bragg (2006) concluded that integrating social networks into learning practices has become very significant in the process of improving learning and teaching opportunities. In addition, students tend to feel safe and comfortable communicating with their peers in a relaxed and less structured atmosphere, which can also be facilitated by Facebook implication in the distance language courses.

According to Kurtz (2014), the emergence of Facebook groups in which participation does not require personal connection among its members has created the opportunity for a learning community in which teachers and students can learn and communicate together without sharing their personal lives. A Facebook group enables synchronous and asynchronous interactions and information sharing (statuses) through links, videos, surveys, files, texts, and photos. Any Facebook member may open a group and invite any other Facebook member to join. The information published does not appear in the members' logs. It is visible only to other group members (Meishar-Tal, Kurtz, & Pieterse, 2012). Petrovic et al. (2014) also contended that students find Facebook better for data search/revisit and has a much more user-friendly interface when compared to the course management system Moodle. The feedback is echoed by students' reflection that they prefer to use Facebook group for discussion, rather than the inherent discussion forum in the course management system—e.g. Blackboard Learn—for similar reasons.

Kurtz (2014) stresses that the heart of a Facebook group is the wall, on which members of the group can share content, comment on each other's posts, provide links to websites, insert videos, and etc. Providing a sense of ownership of the learning process, the course website offers more top-down content imposed by the instructor. In the private Facebook discussion group, students are required to post their original thoughts on each discussion topic and reply to at least one other person's post. The first topic in each lesson usually asks students to respond with a short paragraph regarding the topic of the texts, and the second topic is designed for cultural exploration and comparison. The purpose is not only to develop the students' L2 linguistic skills, but also to provide an opportunity to share cultural values and beliefs by interviewing Chinese native speakers, watching videos, searching information online, and discussing their findings and observations with peers in the Facebook groups. This exposure to diverse points of view builds understanding and fosters the capability to respect other perspectives of community members from diverse backgrounds (MacKnight, 2000). The instructor can be engaged in the development of student community by promoting active interaction among various viewpoints and contact students individually.

Small Group Activities

Group work is another key pedagogical tool to facilitate student-student interaction in a distance context. Prior literature suggests that group work could arouse students' learning interests, cultivate their exploring ability and creative thinking (Davidson & Worsham, 1992; Johnston & Miles, 2004), and improve their team spirit and social communication skills (Fearon, McLaughlin, & Eng, 2012; Olivera & Straus, 2004). In the current courses, a small group is formed of two or at most three students to ensure everyone has sufficient speaking opportunities. Meanwhile, collaboration and interaction facilitate their individual learning process. The oral tasks consist of textbook exercises, reading the texts, interviewing each other, and engaging in task-based small talks with the given scenarios. Students practice and record their audio/video files, and then upload the files to YouTube.com or submit them directly to Blackboard Learn. According to this researcher's observation and student feedback, the ones who share similar cultural background or proficiency levels are more motivated and actively involved in the group work. Students also value oral group work as an important asset for increasing oral practice opportunities, which in turn increases a critical life skill necessary for future careers.

In addition, small group oral practice also helps the instructor evaluate the ongoing instruction for individual students. Distinct from individual oral practice in Speak Everywhere, the small group work focuses more on the student's individual linguistic competence when communicating with the group. The instructor gives written comments to each student in a timely manner that includes grammar errors and pragmatic inappropriateness. Correct forms and pragmatic usage are explicitly elaborated in the synchronous meetings, followed by similar tasks to be completed by the students. The student-student and student-instructor interactions in small group work have been essential for learners to construct a supportive social environment, to overcome the loneliness of the long-distance language learner (Shield, Hauck, & Kotter, 2000), and provide much-needed speaking opportunities to language learners.

COURSE ASSESSMENT IMPLEMENTATION

Over the course of three-year trials, in addition to course development and delivery, alternative means to assess distance students' performance was also taken into consideration. After experimental explorations and comparison of the capacities and limitations of different assessment tools, the authors came to the point of adopting a hybrid of projects, performance-based tests, written tests, and timed dictations to optimize the learning outcome. In the following sections, each assessment tool employed in the last two semesters will be discussed in detail.

Culture-Focused Projects

Immensely different from the traditional course, the distance course requires a new standard to examine students' language competence. Due to logistical, technical, and administrative limitations, the assessment has to be adjusted by emphasizing oral skills and cultural competence. A great amount of oral tasks and culture-focused projects have been included in the evaluation of student performance, such as video projects that focus on the cultural enrichment, including working with a Chinese friend and online oral practices with peers.

In the newly developed assignment, the cultural project, students are required to complete an individual three-minute video clip with topics of their choosing that are related to aspects of Chinese culture that interest them. For example, in the topic of "米 (mǐ, rice)", students need to introduce the cultural concept of "米" through visuals or motions such as grains in general, farm land with rice, rice culture and production in China, and the dietary preference of Asians towards rice. At the end of the video, students also need to demonstrate how to write "米" in a correct stroke order and its combinations with other words such as "米饭 (mǐfàn, cooked rice)" or "大米 (dàmǐ, husked rice)."

Based on field notes, students appeared to be highly motivated and interested exploring topics such as festivals, art, transportation, cities, educational system, and emperors, to name a few. After making their own videos, students were asked to upload them to YouTube and share the links on the private Facebook group. They are also asked to watch their peers' productions and comment on at least one project. Grades were based on students' understanding of the vocabulary in its cultural context, organization of the video, comments from their peers, and the visual aids they have applied.

In addition to the cultural project, a comprehensive final oral project is also assigned to the learners with their partners. Unlike the cultural project, this project intends to focus on oral linguistic performance that is somewhat comparable to the oral exam in the traditional classroom. It is composed of a one-minute self-introduction of each student in the team and a three-minute skit collectively that needs to cover the materials (vocabulary and patterns) they have learned in the semester. Students work together to write up the script, practice, and record their production. Creativity in script writing and performance is strongly encouraged with extra points. Grading is based on originality of content, grammar, fluency, and performance.

Performance-Based Oral Tests

From the experiences trying out different tools for on-line testing, the authors are facing the challenges both from logistic and pedagogical perspectives. The conventional written exams are not ideal for the distance-learning mode where students are supposed to be physically off campus. Moreover, it is impractical and inconvenient to maintain the traditional paper test within a fixed time frame and physical space, even if a few of the distance students happen to be on campus.

In searching for optimal means of assessment, the authors found that performance-based assessments have been used for the evaluation of second languages for over two decades. McNamara (1996) argues that one of the key factors for the development of performance-based assessments originates from the increasing focus on the ability to use language communicatively and appropriately in different contexts. Thus, performance-based assessment much more highly emphasizes language skills rather than traditional means of the more typical paper-and-pencil-based tests, which may put more weight on writing skills.

With an attempt to identify the best combination of tools, the authors studied two online test platforms, *Respondus* and *Speak Everywhere* (SE), to evaluate students' task-based linguistic skills, along with their cultural and communicative skills.

While online tests offer students great flexibility in time and place for taking exams, they do impose some restrictions. Without a proctor during the test, it is highly likely that students will rely on books or online resources to complete tests. They may achieve high scores without diligently and actively learning the required material. To restrict such possibilities, the online test software, *Respondus*, was the first option to be considered to replace the conventional paper test. *Respondus* has the ability to block external Internet communications, as well as the ability to record the students' webcam while they are in the process of the exam. Another feature of *Respondus* is that the instructor has the ability to design a multitude of questions in addition to the standard multiple-choice questions. The students' capability of writing Hanzi can also be tested by *Respondus*. In addition, questions appear one by one, such that a leaking of the exam questions is not possible. With these positive and intriguing features, however, it was also noted that *Respondus* required an impeccable Internet connection in order to function properly, and it turned out that the students' Internet connectivity was not sufficient to proceed with *Respondus* Lockdown. Furthermore, it took the instructor a tremendous amount of time to monitor the live video to prevent cheating and to design questions for the test pool.

After a semester trial of *Respondus*, the authors decided to go ahead and explore another option with the hope of finding a task and performance-based testing tool. *Speak Everywhere* (SE) thus came into being. SE, as introduced in Section 5.2.2, has the capability of delivering reliable and efficient online exercises. Different from the paper exam, the task and performance-based test primarily assesses students' pragmatic competence in target language. Task and performance-based tests require frequent and effective practices by the students in order to achieve accuracy, fluency, and ultimately the best performance on linguistically as well as culturally appropriate tasks. Cheating is not an issue, because student performance is evaluated based on instant oral tasks.

Types of exercises in SE practice bank include picture and word, translation, dialogue, paragraph reading, and situational dialogue. In picture and word, students have to say the word with the limited time after the picture of the word is presented (Figure 20). Translation exercises include words, phrases, and sentences. For dialogue, students need to complete a dialogue exercise with the instructor (Figure 21). Paragraph reading is designed to test students' pronunciation and fluency. Students are required to read a paragraph within a required time frame.

The online assessment presents gains and losses due to its virtual nature. On one hand, students enjoy the convenience and flexibility of online assessment that may result in their increasing interest to continue Chinese language learning. Compared to those who take traditional Chinese classes, distance students are exposed to more task-based language materials and various online resources related to Chinese culture as a required part of their courseware. On the other hand, the lack of Hanzi handwriting is perceived as a loss in the online assessment. The disadvantages of online assessment are remedied by the complementary written assessment, as discussed below (Figures 21 and 22).

Figure 21. Examples of oral assessment in Speak Everywhere

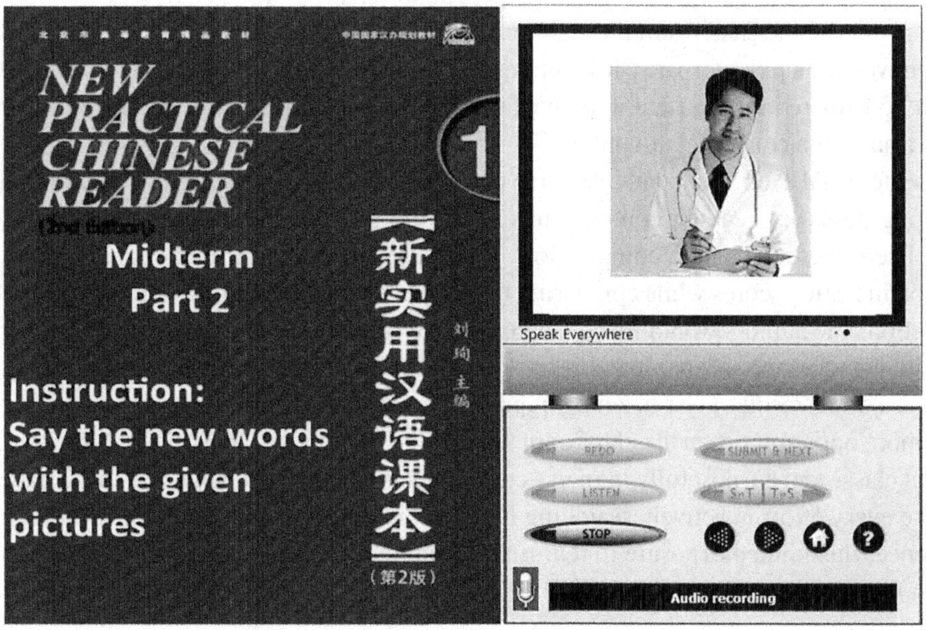

Figure 22. Examples of oral assessment in Speak Everywhere

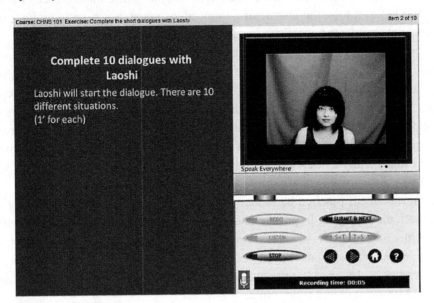

Written Assessment Design

Even though the focus of the courses shifted to a more performance-based assessment modality, the authors still found the traditional written tests and quizzes to be an inevitable component to evaluate students' overall competence and learning outcomes, especially for Chinese that employs a logographic writing system. The written assessment is composed of two parts: a formative timed dictation and a summative written final exam. The purpose of a written final exam is twofold. First, writing proficiency, especially handwriting, is essential for the logographic language system. The written final is intended to compensate for the lack of a written assessment; second, by sharing the same format with the traditional classes, the results of the final exam may demonstrate if distance students' writing skill is comparable with their conventional counterparts. It is interesting to note that logistically, the distance students on campus can be gathered for the final written exam. In the near future, effort needs to be committed to convert the final exam completely to online.

The semester final exam is a comprehensive one that usually includes a listening comprehension of short and long passages, reading comprehension, fill-in-the-blank exercises of situational dialogues, grammar-related questions, and a composition. While the individual differences should be taken into consideration in testing scores while comparing the results between the two groups of learners, there are two observations the authors would like to share in the written results of the distance learners.

First of all, the scores of distance learners are lower on average in the listening comprehension portion. This could be a direct result of less listening opportunities than the conventional learners who have been exposed to more opportunities in the classroom with the instructors and their peers. Moreover, while the conventional classroom purposefully immerses the students in the target language, the distance students have to make every effort in actively searching for such "immersion" that is often times very limited in real life. Hence, this limited exposure to real-time listening for distance learners may account for their weakness in listening scores.

Second, some distance learners show less proficiency in Hanzi writing in the timed final exam. On one hand, the logographic nature of the Chinese Hanzi and the disconnection between Hanzi and its pronunciation make it challenging to memorize, especially for learners from alphabetic-language backgrounds. On the other hand, the only requirement for the distance learners to use handwriting is the "copy vocabulary and text" homework while the traditional students do all other homework by hand. Thus, the deficit of handwriting skill of the distance students could be partially a result of the performance-based approach of assessment, and partially due to insufficient effort and lack of effective strategies from the students.

To make up this obvious loss in the distance course, and in order to increase the opportunities for handwriting practice and to provide formative assessment in the written form, the authors tried out timed dictation in Spring 2015, a new attempt at assessing students' handwriting accuracy and fluency in a distance environment. Instructional preparation for this activity is as follows.

First, the instructor selects the vocabulary to make up ten key sentences from the lesson currently being taught. The length of sentences is controlled at 10-15 characters. Next, in order to determine how much time is reasonable to assign to students, the instructor works with two native speakers of Chinese to write down each sentence and record the time of completion.

Using the average time recorded and multiplying it by three, the length of time would be the time frame within which the distance students are required to complete the sentence dictation. The three-time writing speed allows adequate time for completion while preventing a slower speed that may undermine the performance and achievement in the examinations. The key sentences, along with the audios and instructions, would then be uploaded to Blackboard Learn at the beginning of the lesson for students to listen and practice. They would have plenty time to do so before the actual timed dictation during the synchronous WebEx meeting at the end of each lesson.

Ideally, writing accuracy and fluency are assessed while the listening input is also increased, as students may repeatedly listen to the audio files when they practice writing. However, in reality, from what the authors have observed and interviewed, not all students made good use of the audio files throughout the span of the lesson. Many of them only worked on the written key sentences versus their accompanying audio files before dictation to make sure they at least will not lose points toward their writing grade. In any case, it is noted that, if nothing else, students definitely practiced Hanzi writing more than before. They also benefited from the instant feedback from the instructor when explicit explanation and demonstration of the correct written forms took place. Some of the students do report the benefit from the audio files, although not extensively used, as is hoped for.

UTILIZING STUDENT PERSPECTIVES FOR CFL COURSE DESIGN

In the development of the course, students' perspective is seen as one of the key variables in determining the success or failure in distance courses, including their needs, expectations, and satisfaction (Owens, et al., 2009). Understanding students' perceptions regarding distance education is an integral part for developing and implementing a successful distance learning environment. A course that fails to meet students' expectations and needs may lead to low levels of student involvement (Hall, 2001).

Analysis of Student Perceptions of Course Design and Delivery

The authors utilized course evaluation data as well as student comments to further their understanding of CFL course effectiveness. Over the span of three years, the authors have adopted different measures to elicit students' first-hand feedback. For the first three semesters, data was collected from course evaluations and discussion questions. In Fall 2014, two reflection journals were integrated each semester. Reflections are rich sources for documenting students' narratives about what they are learning in a course and how critically they are thinking about it.

Participants

There are in total of 58 students who participated in the course evaluation in the form of online questionnaire and anonymous responses. 78 students were involved in discussion or submitted pre- and post- reflection journals as parts of their course assignments. The 78 participants included 6 graduate students and 72 undergraduates, in the distribution of 35 female and 43 male students. Nine participants noted that they had previous online learning experiences, while others had never taken an online course. Fifty participants had Asian backgrounds, including 7 heritage learners, 31 South Korean, 7 Japanese, 1 Indonesian, 3 Malaysian, and 1 Thai student.

Data Sources

The data of the study were primarily from two major sources—anonymous course evaluation results, and students' reflections. The latter consisted of online discussion, both pre-journal and post-journal. These sources are explained.

Course Evaluation

The university-level course evaluation was conducted at the end of the semester. It was strongly encouraged but was not mandated to be completed. The reports of the evaluation were released after the grades had been submitted and finalized. The questionnaire contains Likert scale survey questions in general-specific order concerning students' satisfaction of the course and the instructor. For example, participants first rated "Overall, I would rate this instructor as" and then rated "My instructor uses various activities that involve me in learning" in Likert scales. The evaluation ended with written comments for things were expected to be continued and things to be improved. The course evaluation helped obtain general impression of the course and the instructor, and to some extent compile suggestions for further revision and enrichment.

Online Discussion

From the Fall semester of 2013 to the Summer semester of 2014, some discussion questions were designed as a supplementary source to reflect on participants' own learning process and to provide suggestions for the course. For example, "Please list the most engaging activity(-ies) you have had in the course, and state why you like them." and "Please summarize the most challenging aspect(s) in the course. Discuss and share with your classmates how you handle the challenge(s)."

Pre-Journal

Extended from online discussion questions and started from the fall semester of 2014, participants were asked to complete a paper pre-journal to gather demographic information of participants. In addition, questions such as "What skill(s) would you like to spend more time on?" and "What types of interaction will you expect to work with your classmates?" were asked to obtain initial expectation and perception of the participants. The pre-journal also included a brief survey on their initial attitudes towards interaction, Hanzi writing, and performance-based assessment.

Post-Journal

In order to compare participants' initial and closing perception of the course and learning process, a post-journal was given to retrieve first-hand reflections and feedbacks on the curriculum design, oral and written assignments, and assessments. The post-journal consists of 12 open-ended questions and 3 parallel questions, with respect to the attitudes in the pre-journal.

Data Analysis

Data were collected through course evaluations and written documents. In the course evaluation, the mean value and standard deviation of the quantitative data were analyzed to demonstrate the central tendency and variances of participants' general satisfaction towards the course and the instructors. The written comments in the course evaluation and discussion, and the reflection journals were entered into the NVivo (NVivo for Mac) software system and coded according under the headings of distance learning, curriculum design, interaction and support, and/or challenges. The program analyzed the codes according to the noted themes, thus allowing a large amount of qualitative data to be organized, examined, and analyzed (Bourdon, 2002).

FINDINGS

Feedback from Learners for Ongoing Course Design and Use

Since student evaluations are used by 75% of colleges and universities to assess teaching effectiveness (Laverie, 2002), it is believed that there is positive value in using this instrument. The table below demonstrates the satisfaction rate of participants with the course and the instructors since its inception (Table 2).

The evaluation of CHNS101Y in Summer 2015 is an exceptional case. Evaluation from only one of the six students was received, which could not be seen as representative to the overall measurement of the courses. Despite the unrepresentative data from Summer 2015, overall, students were satisfied with their distance course experiences, with a mean ranging from 3.7 to 5 on a five-point Likert scale. They were also satisfied with the instructional quality with a mean ranging from 3.8 to 5. From the past six semesters, the mean of Spring 2014, when CHNS102Y was first launched, was rated the lowest. Students in that semester complained about the length and format of the homework, lack of grammar lectures, and the efficiency of team meetings instead of individual meetings. Those particular suggestions lead the revision of the curriculum and pedagogy after Spring 2014.

Table 2. Mean of course satisfaction and instructor satisfaction

	Mean of the Course satisfaction	Mean of the Instructor satisfaction
Fall, 2013-CHNS101Y	4.8/5 (SD=0.43)	4.8/5 (SD=0.43)
Spring, 2014-CHNS102Y	3.7(SD=0.94)	3.8 (SD=0.63)
Summer, 2014-CHNS101Y	4.5/5 (SD=0.90)	4.8/5 (SD=0.76)
Fall, 2014-CHNS101Y	4.8/5 (SD=0.43)	4.8/5(SD=0.43)
Fall, 2014-CHNS102Y	5/5 (SD=0)	5/5 (SD=0)
Spring, 2015-CHNS102Y	4.5/5 (SD=0.56)	4.8/5 (SD=0.47)
Summer, 2015-CHNS101Y	2/5	3/5
Summer, 2015-CHNS102Y	4.3/5(SD=0.47)	4.8/5(SD=0.47)

Findings Based on Qualitative Reflections and Comments

During the course, students commented in their reflections about the benefits and challenges of online distance CFL learning. Similarly, they were asked to reflect about their own experiences. Please note that all names of participants shown below have been replaced with non-identifying pseudonyms.

1. **Comprehensive Course:** "The course was as comprehensive as a live classroom would be" (Ann, from post-journal, Spring 2015).
2. **Motivating Materials, e.g., Multimedia:** "This is great for distance learning as you need a lot of motivation to work through everything! Having different and interesting material makes this much easier" (John, from post-journal, Fall 2015).
3. **Flexibility with Distance Learning:**
   a. "The possibility to study at your own pace is wonderful" (Julie, from course evaluation, Fall 2013).
   b. "The freedom the distance learning course is providing you is exceptional and perfect for motivated students. For me the course was the perfect mix of freedom and pressure" (Mary, from online discussion, Spring 2014).
   c. "I enjoy the speaking everywhere the most. Since we're not in a classroom environment, we have less opportunities to actually speak the language. But I think speaking everywhere allows to overcome this problem. I like how I can listen to myself before submitting, because the sound for when you're just saying and sound from a recording is different. It is easier to tell the mistake and try to fix" (Sam, from post-journal, Spring 2014).
4. **Authentic Communication Opportunities:** "I especially like the videos created by the professors. It helps to hear Chinese people talk at their usual speed and leaves a great feeling if you can actually understand them" (Jenny, from post-journal, Fall 2014).
5. **Instructor-Student Support:**
   a. "The instructor was extremely communicative and quick to respond to questions and concerns, as well as participating fully in student discussions to give us a thorough perspective on all lessons and all possible learning opportunities" (John, from course evaluation, Summer 2014).
   b. "The teacher is extremely approachable and enhanced the learning experience. The WebEx meetings are a great way to check if you actually understand the content. It is also great that

the teacher provides a document to go through in these meetings to have it more structured. Furthermore, feedback on assignments is always extremely fast, which helps the learning" (Chole, from course evaluation, Spring, 2015).

6. **Opportunities for Teamwork:**
   a. "The teamwork is probably my favorite thing in this class. I feel that learning in group is extremely beneficial and helps me improve. My teammate is knowledgeable, smart and friendly" (Daisy, from post-journal, Spring 2014).
   b. "I enjoy teamwork and I am encouraged to keep doing it in the future. This assignment allows you to group with other people who are around your level in terms of Chinese, and work together and we really get to learn more from one another" (Tim, from post-journal, Summer 2015).
   c. "The Facebook group was a great way to get everyone in participating in the discussion questions" (Smith, from post-journal, Fall 2015).
   d. "My best takeaway from CHNS 101 online at Purdue was the way in which it helped me directly engage in my international community" (Jenny, from post-journal, Fall 2014).

In spite of the above, the authors realize that a great amount of drawbacks and issues exist and still await optimal improvement. The current issues include:

Technical Difficulties

Network, equipment, and software malfunctions can be detrimental to the effectiveness of distance learning. Among all of the technical issues students have confronted over the semesters, the network connection during synchronous meetings is the most troublesome, due to the importance of high-quality video and audio. While alternative options are always available, a suboptimal technological experience hinders students' confidence in the distance learning framework.

Online meeting sometimes are laggy. (George, from discussion, Spring 2014)

It was annoying when the audio or video quality was low during the online meeting. (Stacy, from post-journal, Fall 2015)

Communication Among Distance Students

Unlike in a traditional classroom setting where group work is easily achieved, the communication dynamics amongst the members of a distance course are significantly different. Due to the virtual nature of such an environment, groups are formed without prior interactions between the team members. Personality issues, combined with lack of productive real time discussion opportunities, resulted in misunderstandings and an overall less than satisfactory team experiences in the distance courses.

The online interactions with my instructor and team member were helpful, however given my non-traditional schedule, it was slightly difficult to find time to meet with my team member and the instructor during the time slots available. (Brian, from post-journal, Summer 2015)

As I chose this class because of the time flexibility, I felt it's hard to meet up with team member every other week. (Zoe, from post-journal, Fall 2015)

Limitations in Program Design and Implementation

Due to the initial stage of development and instructional trial, distance Chinese could not fully resolve the deep-seated doubt over the students' oral and aural proficiency without substantial data-supported evidence. However, oral and written performance data of the students have been intentionally collected over the past seven semesters with the hopes that the next step of the research would focus on experimental study to compare oral proficiency level between distance and conventional classroom students. Furthermore, although subsequent modifications, such as video grammar lectures in the second semester, more synchronous meetings in the third semester, and time-dictation in the fifth semester, have been included in the content development based on the observations from previous semesters, more attention needs to be given to core curriculum changes of distance Chinese if data-supported research indicates a substantial deficit of distance students from classroom ones in all areas of learning.

CHALLENGES AND FUTURE DIRECTIONS

The adventures in developing and delivering distance Chinese courses have generated new challenges and hence have become new directions in experiment and research. First, with the tendency to evaluate students' output in a more performance-based approach, the issue over whether Hanzi handwriting is still among the key elements in instruction and assessment is debatable. On one hand, as the prevalent and dominated method of teaching and learning Hanzi domestically and in CFL context, repeated handwriting and dictation are deemed to having a positive effect on mediating Hanzi reading (Tan et al., 2005), and in creating a long-lasting image in the brain (Longcamp et al., 2008). Not only do instructors and researchers believe in the benefits Hanzi handwriting brings, but students are also reported to associate strong handwriting Hanzi ability with better Hanzi reading and reading comprehension, as well as enhancing the understanding of Chinese culture (Morgan, 2012). On the other hand, scholars also postulate the negative effects with the emphasis of Hanzi writing and production.

There is no doubt that Hanzi handwriting is a time-consuming process, especially for those with an alphabetic-language background. Xu and Jen (2005) contended that the requirement of Hanzi production slowed down the speed of vocabulary acquisition, thus the development of other skills including speaking and listening had to follow the same slow pace. In the real-life application, as Allen (2008) argued, there is very little need to handwrite Hanzi for CFL learners, even when they are in a native speaking environment where writing is still produced by keyboarding. Electronic communication, including email and social network sites, has been dominant in social and organizational communication. Therefore, redesigning a balanced distance CFL curriculum that keeps the essentials of traditional classroom instruction and technology enhancement becomes emergent. More empirical research is needed to examine how to carefully select and efficiently utilize the new technology to facilitate Hanzi acquisition at a distance.

Second, the issue of improving oral and listening skills in the distance setting deserves further investigation. Despite a wealth of instructional effort, including synchronous meetings, video grammar lectures and exercises, Speak Everywhere, collaborative learning and etc., the authors still recognize the challenges of distance students when producing longer conversations and spontaneous oral responses. Looking ahead, while intending to provide more support and guidance to the less independent students, the authors are also looking into more flexibility and opportunities to accommodate different learning styles, interests, and skill levels. Learning opportunities may include extended synchronous meetings, more level-appropriate multimedia resources (e.g. songs, movie clips, and online speeches), and eTandem language learning, as discussed below.

Third, it is worth considering how to incorporate more interactive tasks and enhance interpersonal communication in the distance courses. Empirical research reveals that increased interaction in distance courses is associated with higher achievement and student satisfaction (Zirkin and Sumler, 1995). Interaction occurs not only in the virtual classroom context; rather, it can take place through the global communication network (Belz, 2002). eTandem language learning, which pairs language learners with different native languages over global communication network or in-house language exchange, is another promising tool for the future development of distance language courses.

Tian and Wang (2010) examined eTandem learning via synchronous communication in Skype between English and Chinese speakers. The finding indicates a consensus from both groups of students that the language exchange had enhanced their linguistic and intercultural competence. Wang, Szilas, et al. (2013) also reported students' reflection on a three-year eTandem course between Chinese and French, and concluded with positive feedback from the students regarding linguistic and cultural enhancement. Kan et al. (2013) carried out a small-scale project to pair up 10 beginning Chinese learners with blended instruction in Open University, UK, and 10 on-campus students and staff from Beijing Jiao Tong University. The study also revealed linguistic, cultural, professional, and interpersonal advantages through a nine-week program. The above findings will be considered as distance curriculum improvement continues.

Last but not least, it is essential to consider the impact of other variables on learners' academic achievement, including learners' personality, motivation, self-regulation, and technical sophistication. According to Oxford (1990), the affective factors of the learner, such as beliefs, motivation, and anxiety, are one of the biggest influences on language learning success or failure. Kim and Schniederjans (2004) pointed out that students' personality characteristics can be strong indicators of the resulting grade achievement in web-based instruction, with the indication of a number of personality characteristics that entail "commitment to work" and "positive learning orientation" "compliantly cooperative," and "self-confident" to be highly related to grade performance. Successful online students are also highly self-regulated (Holmberg, 1995; Jung, 2001; Kearsley, 2000). Lynch and Dembo (2004) discussed five self-regulatory attributes that are selected as being especially important for distance learner success, including motivation (self-efficacy and goal orientation), internet self-efficacy, time management, study environment management, and learning assistance management. Future empirical studies of these attributes on CFL distance learner performance would be interesting to find correlation between non-language learners and language ones. From the instructor point of view, however, attention needs to be given to look into the balance (or imbalance) of effort, experiences, qualification and training of instructors and the quality and operation of distance courses. In sum, as the authors move on with teaching and scholarship in distance Chinese, the authors anticipate more sophistication in curriculum design, as well as in future assessment on distance and conventional students' output, technology, and increased experiences of the instructions. In fact, plans are currently being developed to conduct a pilot study on performance-based assessment on conventional classroom students' oral and aural skills, in order to compare with that of the distance students.

REFERENCES

Allen, J. (2008). Why learning to write Chinese is a waste of time: A modest proposal. *Foreign Language Annals, 41*(2), 237–251. doi:10.1111/j.1944-9720.2008.tb03291.x

Bartlett-Bragg, A. (2006). Reflections on pedagogy: Reframing practice to foster informal learning with social software. Retrieved from http://matchsz.inf.elte.hu/tt/docs/Anne20Bartlett-Bragg.pdf

Bates, A. W. (1997). The impact of technological changes on open and distance learning. *Distance Education, 18*(1), 93–109. doi:10.1080/0158791970180108

Beck, V. S. (2010). Comparing online and face-to-face teaching and learning. *Journal on Excellence in College Teaching, 21*(3), 95–108.

Beldarrain, Y. (2006). Distance education trends: Integrating new technologies to foster student interaction and collaboration. *Distance Education, 27*(2), 139–153. doi:10.1080/01587910600789498

Bello, T. (1999). New avenues to choosing and using videos. *TESOL Matters, 9*(4), 20.

Belz, J. A. (2002). Social dimensions of telecollaborative foreign language study. *Language Learning & Technology, 6*(1), 60–81.

Berge, Z. L. (1999). Interaction in post-secondary, Web-based learning and teaching. *Educational Technology, 39*(1), 5–11.

Bernard, R. M., Abramia, P. C., Loub, Y., & Borokhovski, E. (2004). A methodological morass? How we can improve quantitative research in distance education. *Distance Education, 25*(2), 175–198. doi:10.1080/0158791042000262094

Blake, R., & Delforge, A. (2007). Online Language Learning: The Case of Spanish Without Walls. In B. Lafford & R. Salaberry (Eds.), *The art of teaching Spanish: Second language acquisition from research to praxis* (pp. 127–147). Georgetown: Georgetown University Press.

Blake, R. J. (2009). The use of technology for second language distance learning. *Modern Language Journal, 93*(1), 822–835. doi:10.1111/j.1540-4781.2009.00975.x

Bourdon, S. (2002). The integration of qualitative data analysis software in research strategies: Resistances and possibilities. *Forum Qualitative Sozial Forschung, 3*(2), 1–10.

Bower, B. L. (2001). Distance education: Facing the faculty challenge. *Online Journal of Distance Learning Administration, 4*(2).

Bown, J. (2006). Locus of learning and affective strategy use: Two factors affecting success in self-instructed language learning. *Foreign Language Annals, 39*(4), 640–659. doi:10.1111/j.1944-9720.2006.tb02281.x

Bransford, J. D., Brown, A. L., & Cocking, R. R. (2000). *How people learn: Brian, mind, experience, and school*. Washington, D.C.: National Academy Press.

Breault, R. A. (2003). Dewey, FreJre, and a pedagogy for the oppressor. *Multicultural Education, 10*(3), 2–6.

Brindley, G., & Nunan, D. (1992). *Draft Bandscales for Listening. IELTS research projects: project 1 NCELTR*. MacQuarie University.

Buckley, F. (2011). Online discussion forums. *European Political Science, 10*(3), 402–415. doi:10.1057/eps.2010.76

Burt, M. (1999). *Using videos with adult English language learners*. East Lansing, MI: National Center for Research on Teacher Learning.

Chen, C. (2011). Online Chinese teaching and learning: A case study. *Journal of Technology and Chinese Language Teaching, 2*(2), 50–68.

Cole, J. E., & Kritzer, J. B. (2009). Strategies for success: Teaching an online course. *Rural Special Education Quarterly, 28*(4), 36–40.

Collis, B., & Moonen, J. (2001). *Flexible Learning in a Digital World: experiences and expectations*. London: Kogan Page.

Davidson, N., & Worsham, T. (1992). *Enhancing thinking through cooperative learning*. New York: Teachers College Press.

Easton, S. S. (2003). Clarifying the instructor's role in online distance learning. *Communication Education, 52*(2), 87–105. doi:10.1080/03634520302470

Egbert, J. L., & Jessup, L. M. (1996). Analytic and systemic analyses of computer-supported language learning environments. *TESL-EJ, 2*(2), 1–24.

Fazey, M. (1999). *Guidelines to help instructors help their learners get the most out of video lessons*. Unpublished manuscript. Lexington, KY: Kentucky Educational Television.

Fearon, C., McLaughlin, H., & Eng, T. Y. (2012). Using student group work in higher education to emulate professional communities of practice. *Education + Training, 54*(2/3), 114- 125.

Felix, U. (2002). The web as vehicle for constructivist approaches in language teaching. *ReCAL, 14*(1), 2–15. doi:10.1017/S0958344002000216

Fleming, S., Hiple, D., & Du, Y. (2002). Foreign language distance education: The University of Hawaii experience. In C. A. Spreen (Ed.), *New technologies and language learning: Cases in the less commonly taught* (pp. 13–54). Honolulu, HI: Second Language Teaching &Curriculum Center.

Furstenberg, G. (1997). Teaching with technology: What is at stake? *ADFL Bulletin, 28*(3), 21–25. doi:10.1632/adfl.28.3.21

Garbett, C. (2011). Activity-based costing models for alternative modes of delivering on-line courses. European Journal of Open. *Distance and E-Learning, 1*, 1–14.

Goldberg, D., Looney, D., & Lusin, N. (2015). Enrollments in Languages Other Than English in United States Institutions of Higher Education, Fall 2013. *Modern Language Association*. Retrieved from http://www.mla.org/pdf/2013_enrollment_survey.pdf

Gruba, P. (1999). *The role of digital video media in second language listening comprehension* [Unpublished doctoral dissertation]. University of Melbourne, Australia.

Hall, J. C. (2001). *Retention and wastage in FE and HE*. Edinburgh: The Scottish Council for Research in Education.

Hampel, R., & de los Arcos, B. (2013). Interacting at a distance: A critical review of the role of ICT in developing the learner–context interface in a university language program. *Innovation in Language Learning and Teaching*, 7(2), 158–178. doi:10.1080/17501229.2013.776051

Hara, N., & Kling, R. (2000). Students' distress with a Web-based distance education course. *Information Communication and Society*, 3(4), 557–579. doi:10.1080/13691180010002297

Harasim, L. (2000). Shift happens: Online education as a new paradigm in learning. *The Internet and Higher Education*, 3(1), 41–61. doi:10.1016/S1096-7516(00)00032-4

Holmberg, B. (1995). The evolution of the character and practice of distance education. *Open Learning*, 10(2), 47–53. doi:10.1080/0268051950100207

Holmberg, B., Shelley, M., & White, C. (Eds.). (2005). *Distance education and languages: Evolution and change*. Clevedon, U.K.: Multilingual Matters.

Hurd, S. (2005). Autonomy and the Distance Language Learner. In B. Holmberg, M. A. Shelley, & C. J. White (Eds.), *Languages and distance education: evolution and change* (pp. 1–19). Clevedon: Multilingual Matters.

Hurd, S. (2007). Anxiety and non-anxiety in a distance language learning environment: The distance factor as a modifying influence. *System*, 36(4), 487–508. doi:10.1016/j.system.2007.05.001

Jaggars, S. S. (2014). Choosing between online and face-to-face courses: Community college student voices. *American Journal of Distance Education*, 28(1), 27–38. doi:10.1080/08923647.2014.867697

Johnston, L., & Miles, L. (2004). Assessing contributions to group assignments. *Assessment & Evaluation in Higher Education*, 29(6), 751–768. doi:10.1080/0260293042000227272

Joliffe, A., Ritter, J., & Stevens, D. (2001). *The online learning handbook: Developing and using web-based learning*. Kogan Page: Springer. Joy-Matthews.

Jung, I. (2001). Building a theoretical framework of web-based instruction in the context of distance education. *British Journal of Educational Technology*, 32(5), 525–534. doi:10.1111/1467-8535.00222

Kan, Q. (2013). The use of ICT in supporting Distance Chinese language learning-Review of the Open university's beginner's Chinese course. *Journal of Technology and Chinese Language Teaching*, 4(1), 1–13.

Kan, Q., Stickler, U., & Xu, C. (2013). Chinese-English eTandem Learning: The role of pre- project preparation and collaboration. *Chinese Language Globalization Studies*, 2, 131–143.

Kearsley, G. (2000). *Online education: Learning and teaching in cyberspace*. Toronto, ON: Wadsworth Thomson Learning.

Kim, E., & Schniederjans, M. J. (2004). The role of personality in web-based distance education courses. *Communications of the ACM, 47*(3), 95–98. doi:10.1145/971617.971622

Krashen, S. (1982). *Principles and practice in second language acquisition*. Oxford: Pergamon.

Kurtz, G. (2014). Integrating a Facebook group and a course website: The effect on participation and perception on learning. *American Journal of Distance Education, 28*(4), 253–263. doi:10.1080/08923 647.2014.957952

Laverie, D. A. (2002). Improving teaching through improving evaluation: A guide to course portfolios. *Journal of Marketing Education, 24*(2), 104–113. doi:10.1177/0273475302242003

Levy, M., & Stockwell, G. (2006). *CALL Dimensions: Options and Issues in Computer-Assisted Language Learning*. Mahwah, NJ: Lawrence Erlbaum.

Li, B., Fukada, A., & Hong, W. (2012). Online business Chinese speaking instruction: A Speak Everywhere speaking program for Practical Business Chinese. *Global Business Language, 17*, 93–105.

Li, B., & Hong, W. (2014, June). 初级汉语远程教学的实践与展望 (Developing elementary–level Distance Chinese language courses---findings and future directions). *Proceedings for the 12th International Conference of Chinese Pedagogy*, Harbin, China (pp. 417- 424).

Longcamp, M., Boucard, C., Gilhodes, J. C., Anton, J. L., Roth, M., Nazarian, B., & Velay, J. L. (2008). Learning through hand- or typewriting influences visual recognition of new graphic shapes: Behavioral and functional imaging evidence. *Journal of Cognitive Neuroscience, 20*(5), 802–815. doi:10.1162/jocn.2008.20504 PMID:18201124

Lou, Y., Abrami, P. C., & d'Apollonia, S. (2001). Small group and individual learning with technology: A meta-analysis. *Review of Educational Research, 71*(3), 449–521. doi:10.3102/00346543071003449

Lynch, R., & Dembo, M. (2004). The relationship between self-regulation and online learning in a blended learning context. *International Review of Research in Open and Distance Learning, 5*(2), 1–16.

MacDonald, L., & Caverly, D. (2001). Techtalk: Expanding the online discussion. *Journal of Developmental Education, 25*(2), 38.

MacKnight, C. B. (2000). Critical thinking and collaborative inquiry. *Journal of Interactive Instruction, 12*(4), 3–11.

Major, C. H. (2010). Do virtual professors dream of electric students? University faculty experiences with online distance education. *Teachers College Record, 112*(8), 2154–2208.

McDonough, K., & Trofimovich, P. (2008). *Using priming methods in second language research*. London: Routledge.

Megginson, J., & Surtees, M. (2004). *Human resource development* (3rd ed.). London: Kogan Page.

Meishar-Tal, H., Kurtz, G., & Pieterse, E. (2012). Facebook groups as LMS: A case study. *International Review of Research in Open and Distance Learning, 13*(4), 33–48.

Moore, M. G. (1989). Three types of interaction. *American Journal of Distance Education, 3*, 1–7.

Moore, M. G., & Kearsley, G. (1996). *Distance education: A systems view*. Belmont, CA: Wadsworth Publishing.

Morgan, Y. Y. K. (2012). Attitudes toward Hanzi production ability among Chinese teachers and learners [Doctoral dissertation]. Retrieved from http://docs.lib.purdue.edu/dissertations/AAI3545325/

Muilenburg, L. Y., & Berge, Z. L. (2005). Student barriers to online learning: A factor analytic study. *Distance Education, 26*(1), 29–48. doi:10.1080/01587910500081269

Nandu, S. (2013). Transforming MOOCs and MOORFAPS into MOOLOS. *Distance Education, 34*(3), 253–255. doi:10.1080/01587919.2013.842524

Nault, D. (2006). Going global: Rethinking culture teaching in ELT contexts. *Language, Culture and Curriculum, 19*(3), 314–328. doi:10.1080/07908310608668770

Navarro, P. (2000). The promise – and potential pitfalls – of cyberlearning. In R. A. Cole (Ed.), *Issues in web-based pedagogy: A critical primer* (pp. 281–297). Westport, CT: Greenwood Press.

Northrup, P. T. (2002). Online learners' preferences for interaction. *The Quarterly Review of Distance Education, 3*(2), 219–226.

Olivera, E., & Straus, S. G. (2004). Group-to-individual transfer of learning: Cognitive and social factors. *Small Group Research, 35*(4), 440–465. doi:10.1177/1046496404263765

Osman, G., & Herring, S. C. (2007). Interaction, facilitation, and deep learning in cross-cultural chat: A case study. *The Internet and Higher Education, 10*(2), 125–141. doi:10.1016/j.iheduc.2007.03.004

Owens, J., Hardcastel, L., & Richardson, B. (2009). Learning from a distance: The experience of remote students. *Journal of Distance Education, 23*(3), 57–74.

Oxford, R. L. (1990). *Language Learning Strategies: What Every Teacher Should Know*. Boston: Heinle & Heinle.

Palloff, R. M., & Pratt, K. (1999). *Building learning communities in cyberspace: Effective strategies for online classroom*. San Francisco, CA: Jossey-Bass.

Patrovic, N., Jeremic, V., Cirocic, M., Radojicic, Z., & Milenkovic, N. (2014). Facebook Versus Moodle in practice. *American Journal of Distance Education, 28*(2), 117–125. doi:10.1080/08923647.2014.896581

Rennie, F., & Morrison, T. (2012). *E-Learning and social networking handbook - resources for higher education*. London: Routledge.

Seaton, J. X., & Schwier, R. (2014). An exploratory case study of online instructors: Factors associated with instructor engagement. *International Journal of E-Learning & Distance Education, 29*(1), 1–16.

Sherry, L. (1996). Issues in distance learning. *International Journal of Distance Education, 1*(4), 337–365.

Shield, L., Hauck, M., & Kötter, M. (2000). Taking the distance out of distance learning. In P. Howarth & R. Herrington (Eds.), *EAP learning technologies* (pp. 16–27). Leeds, England: University Press.

Simonson, M., Smaldino, S., Albright, M., & Zvacek, S. (2009). *Teaching and learning at a distance: Foundations of distance education* (4th ed.). Boston: Allyn & Bacon.

Spangle, M., Hodne, G., & Schierling, D. (2002). Approaching value-centered education through the eyes of an electronic generation: Strategies for distance learning. *Paper presented at the Annual Meeting of the National Communication Association*, New Orleans, USA.

Sun, M., Chen, Y., & Olson, A. (2013). Developing and implementing an Online program: A case study. In B. Zou Chen, M. Xing, C. Xiang, Y. Wang, & M. Sun (Eds.), *Computer- assisted foreign language teaching and learning: Technological advances* (pp. 160–187). Hershey, PA, USA: IGI Global. doi:10.4018/978-1-4666-2821-2.ch010

Swain, M. (1985). Communicative competence: some roles of comprehensible input and comprehensible output in its development. *Input in second language acquisition*, 15, 165- 179.

Tan, L. H., Laird, A. R., Li, K., & Fox, P. T. (2005). Neuroanatomical correlates of phonological processing of Chinese characters and alphabetic words: A meta-analysis. *Human Brain Mapping*, 25(1), 83–91. doi:10.1002/hbm.20134 PMID:15846817

Tee, M. Y., & Karney, D. (2010). Sharing and cultivating tacit knowledge in an online learning environment. *Computer-Supported Collaborative Learning*, 5(4), 385–413. doi:10.1007/s11412-010-9095-3

Tian, J., & Wang, J. (2010). Taking language learning outside the classroom: Learners' perspectives of eTandem learning via Skype. *Innovation in Language Learning and Teaching*, 4(3), 181–197. doi:10.1 080/17501229.2010.513443

Tricker, T., Rangecroft, M., Long, P., & Gilroy, P. (2001). Evaluating distance education courses: The student perception. *Assessment & Evaluation in Higher Education*, 26(2), 165–177. doi:10.1080/02602930020022002

Wang, C. (2012). Pre-service teachers' perceptions of learning a foreign language online: Preparing teachers to work with linguistic, cultural, and technological diversity. *International Journal of Computer-Assisted Language Learning and Teaching*, 2(1), 30–45. doi:10.4018/ijcallt.2012040103

Wang, C. (2015). From preservice to inservice: Can practicing foreign language learning online help teachers transfer linguistic, cultural, and technological awareness into teaching English language learners? *International Journal of Computer-Assisted Language Learning and Teaching*, 5(2), 1–21. doi:10.4018/ ijcallt.2015040101

Wang, Y., & Chen, N. S. (2013). Engendering interaction, collaboration, and reflection in the design of online learning assessment in language learning: A reflection from the course designers. In B. Zou Chen, M. Xing, C. Xiang, Y. Wang, & M. Sun (Eds.), *Computer- assisted foreign language teaching and learning: Technological advances* (pp. 16–38). Hershey, PA, USA: IGI Global. doi:10.4018/978-1-4666-2821-2.ch002

Wang Szilas, J., Berger, C., & Zhang, F. (2013). eTandem language learning integrated in the curriculum: reflection from students' perspective. *Proceedings of the European Distance and E-learning Network 2013 Annual Conference* (pp. 93-102). Olso: The Joy of Learning.

Wetzel, C. D., Radtke, P. H., & Stem, H. W. (1994). *Instructional Effectiveness of Video Media*. Hillsdale, NJ: Lawrence Erlbaum.

White, C. (2003). *Language learning in distance education*. Cambridge: Cambridge University Press. doi:10.1017/CBO9780511667312

White, C. (2004). Independent Language Learning in Distance Education: Current Issues. *Proceedings of the Independent Learning Conference 2003.*

White, C. (2005). Towards a learner-based theory of distance language learning: The concept of the learner–context interface. In B. Holmberg, M. Shelley, & C. White (Eds.), *Distance education and languages: Evolution and change* (pp. 55–71). Clevedon, UK: Multilingual Matters.

White, C. (2006). The distance learning of foreign languages. *Language Teaching*, *39*(4), 247–264. doi:10.1017/S0261444806003727

White, C. (2008). Language learning strategies in independent language learning: An overview. In T. Lewis & S. Hurd (Eds.), *Language learning strategies in independent settings* (pp. 3–24). Clevedon, UK: Multilingual Matters.

Williams, K. C., Cameron, B. A., & Morgan, K. (2012). Supporting online group projects. *North American College Teachers of Agriculture Journal*, *56*, 15–20.

Xu, P., & Jen, T. (2005). "Penless" Chinese language learning: A computer-assisted approach. *Journal of the Chinese Language Teachers Association*, *40*(2), 25–42.

Yao, S., & Hong, W. (2015, July). 初级网络课程的考评 (The Evaluation in Elementary-level Distance Chinese Courses---challenges and solutions.) *Proceedings for the 13th International Conference of Chinese Pedagogy*, Hohhot, China (pp. 201-206).

Zaid, M. A. (1999). Cultural Confrontation and Cultural Acquisition in the EFL Classroom. *International Review of Applied Linguistics in Language Teaching*, *37*(2), 111–126. doi:10.1515/iral.1999.37.2.111

Section 3
Web Collaboration across Languages

Chapter 7
Creating a Micro–Immersion Environment Through Telecollaboration

Tasha N. Lewis
Loyola University Maryland, USA

ABSTRACT

This chapter offers an innovative approach for implementing telecollaborative activities in order to enable students to connect with peers in real-time, with the goal of creating a micro-immersion experience called a "Virtual Language Exchange". This chapter describes and compares two intermediate Spanish classes participating in Virtual Language Exchanges via Skype: one paired with peers from the target language and culture, and one paired with peers from within the class itself. Students from both groups participate in meaningful interactions in the target language in order to complete the assigned task-based activities. The chapter argues that finding new ways to bring the target language to life by using technology, like the Virtual Language Exchange experience described here, can benefit students' foreign language development in multiple ways.

INTRODUCTION

The use of technology for educational purposes is nothing new nowadays. Technology has become exceedingly commonplace in many educational fields over the years because it has the ability to empower its users in multiple ways. Currently, in the field of foreign language education in particular, Computer Assisted Language Learning (CALL) technology is frequently expected. CALL affords teachers and students alike an opportunity to directly connect with the target language and culture in new and exciting ways. CALL technology is remarkable because it is quite versatile in its application; it can be used inside as well as outside of the classroom for the benefit of both teachers and students.

This chapter reports the use of an Internet-based videoconferencing software in two separate foreign language classrooms for the purpose of creating an environment in which language learners must use the target language in order to complete an assignment. Although the two classes participating in this

DOI: 10.4018/978-1-5225-0177-0.ch007

study are partnered with different people, (i.e., one group is paired with native speakers of the target language and the other group with peers from within the class itself) so that a comparison can be made, the study offers both teachers and researchers an innovative approach to bringing the target language to life through the use of technology. The information provided in this chapter is twofold. First, it is meant to link current theories of second language acquisition (i.e., the communicative language approach, task-based language learning/teaching and intercultural communicative competence) with the use of technology for language learning purposes, more specifically, the CALL practice of telecollaboration. Second, it is meant to serve as a model for implementing and using telecollaboration in foreign language classrooms in non-traditional ways in order to create an immersion-like environment.

BACKGROUND

Telecollaboration

Internet-mediated Intercultural Foreign Language Education (Belz & Thorne, 2006) as well as Online Intercultural Exchange (O'Dowd, 2007b) are terms that have been used interchangeably with telecollaboration. Telecollaboration, the preferred term of this chapter, should be understood as an Internet-based intercultural exchange between people of distinct cultural backgrounds with the goal of developing language skills as well as intercultural communicative competence through structured tasks conducted in an institutional context.

The main objective of telecollaboration is not solely to practice and improve foreign language skills; telecollaboration is meant to connect foreign language learning with learning about culture (i.e., another culture as well as one's own culture) (Belz, 2006). More specifically, it is a mediated situation in which participants are given the opportunity to increase their intercultural communicative competence through discovering another culture while at the same time reflecting upon their own (Byram, 1997). The simple act of interaction and information exchange over the Internet provides language learners in this situation with a chance to expand their ever-growing intercultural communicative competence (Belz & Thorne, 2006). Learning management systems, e-mail, social networking sites, wikis, blogs, video conferencing software, media sharing websites, Second Life, etc. are all specific examples of how telecollaboration has made its way into the realm of education. These prevalent examples demonstrate how telecollaboration is versatile since it can be used inside or outside of the classroom as well as synchronously or asynchronously. Telecollaboration has been particularly useful in the field of second language acquisition because it is a way to bring two cultures closer together in a virtual environment that would otherwise be located very far apart. In recent years, research has especially supported the use of telecollaboration for the development of intercultural communicative competence in language learners (e.g., Chun, 2011; Hauck & Youngs, 2008; Levy, 2007; Müller-Hartmann, 2006; O'Dowd, 2003, 2007a; Schenker, 2012) despite some of its limitations, which will be further addressed throughout this section (e.g., Belz, 2002; O'Dowd & Ritter, 2006; Schenker, 2012; Ware, 2005; Ware & Kramsch, 2005).

The asynchronous use of e-mail in foreign language classrooms has been examined in terms of its ability to provide a unique space for second language learners to demonstrate their intercultural communicative competence (O'Dowd, 2003; Schenker, 2012). According to O'Dowd (2003), Spanish second language learners showed more intercultural communicative competence when they were given an opportunity to talk about their cultural identity. As learners shared more information about themselves, they also asked more about the target culture in the second language. However, when learners were not able to gather the information requested about the target culture, negative attitudes emerged and stereotypes were referenced. Likewise, Schenker (2012) observed a similar situation when German second language learners participated in e-mail exchanges with native speakers. Although this asynchronous method of communication helped students learn about the target culture and demonstrate their intercultural communicative competence, several study specific challenges were also observed (e.g., miscommunications, scheduling conflicts, and time constraints) and could not be ignored.

A comparison of asynchronous and synchronous telecollaborative exchanges has also been the focus of investigation (Chun, 2011; Hauck & Youngs, 2008). Chun (2011) compared the development of second language pragmatic competence and the intercultural communicative competence of advanced German language learners in both asynchronous and synchronous exchanges. She found that learners were more engaged and showed more intercultural communicative competence overall in the synchronous environment as opposed to the asynchronous environment. However, students still benefited from the asynchronous online discussions, even more so if they felt satisfied with their online interactions. Hauck and Youngs (2008) assert that the diverse possibilities afforded by telecollaboration create varied learning environments that allow for different levels of interaction. They insist that it is the task design itself, and not the method of telecollaboration, that ultimately affects students' motivation to learn language and culture. Regardless of the telecollaborative exchange method chosen for their study, asynchronous or synchronous, what really affected the second language learners' experience was their ability to make the mode of communication as efficient as possible.

Language learners have also been shown to benefit both linguistically as well as culturally when participating solely in synchronous virtual language exchanges (Lewis, 2013). The telecollaborative language exchanges reported by Lewis gave learners a particular opportunity to notice gaps in their linguistic knowledge and negotiate meaning in the target language, all the while learning about the target culture. Students reported that the virtual language exchange was a good way of practicing their speaking skills and learning about another culture. Moreover, students showed better oral proficiency outcomes after having participated in the exchange experience.

Although telecollaboration in its many manifestations undoubtedly enables language learners to have authentic contact with the target language and culture for the purposes of developing second language competence, it is not without obvious limitations. Issues concerning student motivation and participation (Belz, 2002; Hauck & Youngs, 2008; Ware, 2005), miscommunication (O'Dowd & Ritter, 2006, Schenker, 2012; Ware & Kramsch, 2005), as well as varied expectations and norms between teachers and students (Schenker, 2012; Ware, 2005) have been reported. Suggestions for how to overcome these types of limitations have been mentioned as well; however, they have varied greatly based on the specifics of each telecollaborative exchange. Nevertheless, the overall advantage that telecollaboration affords in the acquisition of a second language and culture seems to far outweigh its drawbacks because it provides a direct opportunity to use the target language in a real life situation where cultural communication can take place.

TASK-BASED LANGUAGE LEARNING/TEACHING

In light of Hauck and Youngs' (2008) suggestion that telecollaboration is most successful when the task design is thoroughly planned, the telecollaborative language exchange described in this chapter requires participants to complete a level-appropriate task-based activity before, during and after their virtual language exchange. The structured tasks explained here ensure that students are using authentic language to fulfill meaningful tasks in the target language, which is what second language educators and researchers call a task-based approach to language teaching/learning (Candlin, 1987; Ellis, 2003; Nunan, 1989, 2004; Prabhu, 1987; Skehan, 2001; Willis, 1996).

The task-based language teaching/learning approach was first introduced when the Bangalore/Madras Communication Teaching Project was initiated (Prabhu, 1987). For this project, it was thought that second language skills would be best strengthened if learners were presented with interactive conditions in which they needed to use communication tools to navigate situational demands. Prahbu firmly believed that the development of linguistic competence was less reliant on explicit teaching and deliberate practice. As a result, the main objective of the project was to provide a communicative situation for managing meaning by means of a task instead of specifically practicing grammatical competence. Similarly, Candlin (1987) associates task-based language learning with the expanding approach of communicative language teaching, which is the idea that learners should ultimately strive for communicative competence (Hymes, 1972). According to Candlin, a task would be considered communicative if there was a focus on the procedure as well as the goal while using the target language. The procedure would at the very least offer learners an opportunity to negotiate, interact, engage with comprehensible input, and produce target language in order to complete a particular assignment.

According to Willis (1996), task-based language teaching is an ideal approach because it offers appropriately fundamental conditions for successful language learning. Learners are motivated by the exposure to authentic language to use their target language listening, speaking, reading and writing skills in order to complete a specific task. In addition, the task-based approach to language teaching/learning creates moments where learners essentially need to focus on form.

As a result of the growing popularity of the task-based approach for language teaching/learning in the 1990s, applied linguistics researchers later attempted to clarify what constitutes a task. Skehan (2001) defined task as an activity related to a realistic situation in which meaning is essential and where a problem must be solved and its outcome evaluated. Ellis (2003) further emphasized that a task must include a workplan, a primary focus on meaning, real-world processes of language use, the use of any of the four skills (i.e., listening, speaking, reading, writing), and a clearly defined communicative outcome. Tasks can be used in multiple ways. They can be focused, meant for practicing a particular feature of language, or they can be unfocused, wherein the procedure is designed to avoid practicing a particular feature of language, during a communicative language exchange. Examples include information/reasoning/opinion gap activities, questions/answers, dialogues, role plays, matching activities, communication strategies, pictures, picture stories, puzzles, problems, discussions, and decisions (Nunan, 2004).

Despite the fact that there is not one universally accepted model for language teaching (Brandl, 2008), the use of tasks for language learning purposes effectively creates conditions for a communicative environment. Tasks fundamentally allow there to be more of a focus on the learner (as opposed to the teacher) who must use the target language and authentic materials for meaningful interaction (communicative language teaching as described by Wesche and Skehan, 2002). Language leaners can successfully acquire and use the target language at any level with the implementation of communicative tasks.

Language Learning Contexts

In addition to the multiple conditions for creating a communicative environment, the actual act of language learning can occur in many contexts. For instance, it is possible for someone to learn a second language in a place where a different language is the language of majority (e.g., learning German in the U.S. where English is the majority language) or it is possible to learn a second language in an environment where the language being learned is the language used on a daily basis (e.g., learning Italian in Italy). Some environments are preferred over others for particular reasons; however, there is a general widespread belief among teachers and learners alike that second language learning is most successful when it takes place in an immersion context. Regardless of the lack of consistent empirical evidence supporting the advantages of acquiring language by immersing oneself in a target language environment (e.g., Collentine & Freed, 2004; DeKeyser, 1991; Freed, Segalowitz, & Dewey, 2004; Huebner, 1995; Lafford, 1995; Lapkin, Hart, & Swain, 1995, Liskin-Gasparro, 1998; Pérez-Vidal, 2011; Serrano, Llanes, & Tragant, 2011, among others), it is commonly assumed that target language contexts are able to provide learners with optimal conditions for advancing linguistic as well as cultural competence. Typical classroom contexts, irrespective of teaching approach employed, are frequently seen as deficient primarily because they are artificially constructed target language environments. Consequently, language learners are time and again encouraged to study abroad; however, not all students are easily afforded this type of opportunity. Despite the underlying negative tone for second language acquisition occurring in a classroom context, the various technologies offered today by CALL have the ability to bring the target language and culture that much closer to learners who are not able to study abroad.

Telecollaboration in particular is one way in which a target language can be brought to life for the benefit of a learners' foreign language development. More specifically, it is synchronous telecollaboration that enables learners to have direct real-time contact with peers who are native speakers of the target language, thus bringing language and culture into the confines of a classroom environment. Synchronous telecollaboration creates a simulated immersion environment without the need to physically travel. Moreover, when given a task to complete, this micro-immersion context naturally presents language learners with a situation where meaningful interaction in the target language must take place. Learners are exposed to an authentic use of the target language while the focus rests on the learners' needs. The micro-immersion environment, as described here, by its very nature, is an ideal communicative context for task-based teaching/learning to occur when typical immersion is not possible. This chapter offers an innovative approach to implementing telecollaborative activities in an intermediate Spanish class located in the U.S., thus enabling students to connect with peers in real-time to create a micro-immersion experience called a "Virtual Language Exchange".

History of the Virtual Language Exchange

The specific Virtual Language Exchange described in this chapter is the result of an evolving telecollaborative program at Loyola University Maryland (see Lewis & Schneider, 2015 for details). The Virtual Language Exchange had modest beginnings; it was first conceived of by a Spanish instructor who created a telecollaborative exchange in her own class between her American students in Beginning Spanish II who were learning Spanish and her former student from Spain who was learning English. The original idea was that this cultural activity, which took place during class time in the Language Learning Center, would help her students practice particular vocabulary in Spanish while integrating culture into their experience. In subsequent semesters, the same Virtual Language Exchange was offered to Intermediate Spanish II, again taking place in the Language Learning Center, but was optional outside of class cultural activity in which students could choose to participate. In both cases, the instructor reserved a room in the Language Learning Center that was equipped with a large screen television connected to a computer with a webcam so that she could log on to Skype. During the prearranged Virtual Language Exchange time, students were seated in front of the television so that they could all clearly see their language partner and vice versa. Students were expected to come prepared with questions for the language partner and as they each asked a question, the instructor would help mediate the conversation and facilitate comprehension.

Not long after these few experiences, the same instructor heard about a Virtual Dual Immersion Program organized by the Association of Jesuit Universities in Latin America (AUSJAL) and the Association of Jesuit Colleges and Universities (AJCU), in which audio and video technology as well as telecollaboration is used for language learning purposes by means of virtual student exchanges. After inquiring more, three Virtual Language Exchange sessions were organized and opened to all students studying beginning and intermediate Spanish as an optional cultural activity or a way to gain extra speaking practice. Students who had participated in these exchanges where asked to take a short survey immediately following their exchange experience while still in the Language Learning Center. The feedback from these surveys was very useful for future iterations of the virtual interactions.

The Virtual Language Exchanges subsequently grew in to curriculum-wide program known as the Virtual Language Exchange Program with 32 sessions offered in a semester at its peak. Again, with the support of the AJCU and the AUSJAL Virtual Dual Immersion Project, the main objective of the program was to bring together students from different linguistic and cultural backgrounds in order to develop foreign language skills as well as intercultural communicative competence. The language exchanges took place outside of class time in the Language Learning Center and were all organized by one coordinator (i.e., the director of the Language Learning Center). All students enrolled in Intermediate Spanish I were required to participate in at least one Virtual Language Exchange during the semester, and students enrolled in Intermediate Spanish II had the option of participating in a Virtual Language Exchange as one of the options available for their required cultural activity throughout the semester.

THE VIRTUAL LANGUAGE EXCHANGE

Virtual Language Exchange is Loyola University Maryland's term for telecollaboration. It is an event that is intended to connect students from Loyola University Maryland with students from a partner university in a country that is home to the target language, in this case Spanish, via Skype. The overarching goal is to pair native English speaking students who are learning Spanish with native Spanish speaking students who are learning English thus providing all of the participants with an opportunity to communicate with native speakers of each of the respective target languages. Both groups of students benefit from the exchange because the exchange is evenly divided for half of the conversation to be in English (i.e., for the benefit of the non-native English speakers) and half in Spanish (i.e., for the benefit of the non-native Spanish speakers). The conversations are synchronous and multimodal, because they involve video as well as audio, and they take place in the computer lab on campus. Students are ideally paired individually with one student from the target country. However, sometimes this is not possible and two students on either end of the conversation are paired with one student from the other country. Whether in twos or threes, each student has their own headset and microphone plugged into a computer for the duration of the language exchange.

In order to pedagogically prepare for the Virtual Language Exchange, instructors at Loyola University Maryland are asked to design and execute their own pre-Virtual Language Exchange activity with students during class time prior to having students sign up for the Virtual Language Exchange. This activity is meant to prepare students to have a conversation in the target language. During the conversation, students are expected to gather information from their partner, with the aid of a handout identifying areas of inquiry, so that they could later complete a follow-up task summarizing the information that was obtained during the exchange. The task-based activity for the students at Loyola University Maryland is not the same as the activity that the students from the partner institution have to complete. Each side of the exchange has their own task to complete, which is assigned by their respective instructors. A detailed description of the task-based activity for this particular study is provided in a later section.

Preparing for a Virtual Language Exchange at Loyola University Maryland begins approximately 30 minutes prior to session start time. The Language Learning Center staff begins by logging all of the computers on to Skype using generic usernames created for the Virtual Language Exchange and testing the audio through the Skype call testing service. As students begin to arrive at the Language Learning Center, the staff checks the students in and directs them each to a computer ready for the exchange. The instructor (or computer lab student assistant leading the exchange) has 5 minutes to welcome students, give some brief instructions about the exchange and ask if there are any questions before the Virtual Language Exchange begins. At the scheduled call time, students initiate the calls and for the next 20 minutes converse in the agreed-upon start language. Students gather the information they need to complete the task-based activity then are notified to switch to the other language. The instructors, prior to starting the Virtual Language Exchange, agree upon the order of languages so that all students are conversing in the same language at the same time. With 5 minutes remaining in the 50-minute session, students are prompted to wrap up their conversations, exchange contact information with their partner if they desire, and end the call.

There are fundamental components to executing a successful Virtual Language Exchange. They are: a partner institution, student participants, a designated coordinator/liaison, a written plan/agreement, an on-site facilitator, technological resources, and a task-based activity for students. The partner institution should ideally be of the same education level (i.e., higher education with higher education, K-12 with k-12) and it is most convenient if the time difference is not too great. A designated coordinator or liaison helps plan the session and manage the logistics. He or she is also responsible for all correspondence with the partner institution prior to the Virtual Language Exchange. These two parties create a written agreement detailing all of the pertinent information in order to have a successful exchange (i.e., time, date, number of participants, name of facilitators, Skype usernames, student pairs, duration of session, first/second language to be spoken, who will initiate the call, etc.). The facilitator is present during the actual Virtual Language Exchange. This can be the same person as the coordinator, but it need not be. The facilitator supervises the session. He or she indicates when to begin and end the Skype calls, when to switch languages, and should any technical/logistic difficulties arise, he or she would address them.

Since the Virtual Language Exchange is rooted in technology, it requires certain indispensable hardware/software. Most obvious is a computer for each student with an Internet connection (preferably Ethernet) and a video chat program such as Skype. The coordinators agree upon which video chat program their students will use prior to the Virtual Language Exchange. Headsets equipped with earphones and a microphone as well as a webcam (built-in or not) is needed for each student. At Loyola University Maryland, all Virtual Language Exchanges take place in the Language Learning Center in one of the computer labs with staff on hand in case there is a need for immediate technological support. Lastly, a device called a splitter is convenient to have if there is a need to pair students on one end of the conversation because there are an uneven number of participants. A splitter allows two headsets to connect into one computer so that all three participants can join the conversation.

STUDY DESIGN

Two Virtual Language Exchanges were organized for this study following the example of the large-scale Virtual Language Exchange Program as described above. These two Virtual Language Exchanges served to explore in depth two different approaches to completing a particular task-based activity in an immersion-like environment. The specific research questions guiding this study were:

1. What are students' attitudes towards and motivation for participating in a Virtual Language Exchange? How might these attitudes and motivations change over the course of the semester with multiple Virtual Language Exchange experiences? How might student attitudes and motivations differ with regards to type of Virtual Language Exchange (i.e., with native speakers versus with non-native speakers)?
2. How do students approach the designated task-based activity for the Virtual Language Exchange over the course of the semester? Might there be any obvious differences based on Virtual Language Experience?

METHODOLOGY

Participants

Two sections of approximately 20 students each of Intermediate Spanish II at Loyola University Maryland took part in this study. All of the students from Loyola University Maryland were non-native speakers of Spanish and the majority spoke English as their first language. The instructor for both of the Intermediate Spanish II sections that were selected for this study was the same. This instructor was very familiar with the larger Virtual Language Exchange Program as described above and had served as coordinator as well as facilitator in the past. The students at the partner institution for this study were from the Universidad Centroamericana UCA de Nicaragua in Managua. Approximately 20 native Spanish speaker students learning English as a second language participated in the Virtual Language Exchange with the students from Loyola University Maryland. Only the information pertaining to the Loyola University Maryland side of the exchange will be reported in this study.

Facilities and Equipment

The Virtual Language Exchanges for both sections of Intermediate Spanish II took place in the Language Learning Center lab on campus. Twenty computers equipped with headsets, microphones, webcams, and Skype were used. Each student was assigned to a computer and in the case that there were more than 20 students, each additional student was paired with a classmate and asked to use the extra headset that was connected to a splitter for a 3-way conversation.

Procedure

The participants in the first section of Intermediate Spanish II, designated the native speaker (NS) group, experienced Skype chat sessions with native Spanish speakers studying English as a second language at the Universidad Centroamericana UCA de Nicaragua. Before the semester began, the NS group was scheduled to have four Virtual Language Exchanges during four separate 50-minute class periods over the course of the semester. However, due to unanticipated circumstances, two Virtual Language Exchanges needed to be cancelled. For the two Virtual Language Exchanges that took place with the partner institution, the two Virtual Language Exchanges that will be analyzed in this chapter, students were expected to divide the session, speaking both English and Spanish, equally. For the two Virtual Language Exchanges with the partner institution that had to be cancelled, a replacement telecollaborative activity (like the one the second group experienced) was used in substitution. All of the Virtual Language Exchanges were evenly spaced throughout the semester taking place as a culminating activity upon the completion of a chapter in the textbook. Participants in the NS group were required to complete the tasks described below for each of the Virtual Language Exchanges.

The participants in the second section of Intermediate Spanish II, designated the non-native speaker (NNS) group, experienced Skype chat sessions with individuals from their own class section. Before the semester began, the NNS group was scheduled to have four Virtual Language Exchanges during four separate 50-minute class periods over the course of the semester. Unlike the NS group, no unexpected circumstances arose during the Virtual Language Exchanges and they all proceeded as planned. During the Virtual Language Exchanges students were expected to divide the session equally among the pair speaking Spanish the whole time. All of the Virtual Language Exchanges were evenly spaced throughout the semester also taking place after the completion of a chapter in the textbook just as was done with the NS group. In fact, the NNS group's Virtual Language Exchanges all took place on the same day as the NS group. Participants in the NNS group were also required to complete the same tasks as the NS group, described below, for each of the Virtual Language Exchanges.

Additionally, all of the participants from Loyola University Maryland were required to take a 10-question survey prior to beginning the first Virtual Language Exchange as well as after having completed the last Virtual Language Exchange. The surveys were deployed by the instructor to each student's computer so that they could be answered anonymously and their responses recorded in the software program Qualtrics. The questions included in the survey were intended to investigate students' motivation for learning about the target language and culture as well as their attitudes regarding the target language and culture. The survey included the following questions for students to answer using a 6-point Likert scale (strongly disagree to strongly agree):

Q1: Learning Spanish is really great.

Q2: I wish I could speak Spanish perfectly.

Q3: Studying Spanish is important because it will allow me to meet and converse with more and varied people.

Q4: I never feel quite sure of myself when I am speaking in my Spanish class.

Q5: I feel anxious if someone asks me something in Spanish.

Q6: I have a positive attitude toward Spanish speaking people and their culture.

Q7: The more I learn about native Spanish-speakers, the more I like them.

Q8: I would like to get to know native Spanish-speakers better.

Q9: I admire Spanish speaking people and their culture.

Q10: Most native Spanish-speakers are considerate of the feelings of others.

Task-Design

The Loyola University Maryland students participating in this study each completed a pre-designed 5-part task-based activity for each of the Virtual Language Exchanges (see Appendix for sample task-based activity). These activities were created in order to enhance the students' telecollaborative language exchange experiences and facilitate the conversations. Each of the task-based activities centered around a chapter theme and included the following parts:

- **Pre-Session Activities (Completed prior to the Virtual Language Exchange):**
  - Review of vocabulary and grammatical structures separately.
  - Formulation of intended questions combining vocabulary and grammatical structures.
- **Session Activity (Completed during the Virtual Language Exchange):**
  - Space to take notes.
- **Post-Session Activities (Completed after the Virtual Language Exchange):**
  - Auto-reflection and auto-evaluation of foreign language use.
  - Summary and reflection of the experience.

The instructor asked students to complete the first two parts of the task-based activity two days before the Virtual Language Exchange was to take place so that the instructor could look over the students' work and make comments where necessary. The first section was meant to have students review in isolation the vocabulary and grammar pertaining to the chapter that had just been studied. The second section served to have students put the vocabulary and grammatical structures from the first section into context with questions intended for their partner. The third section provided students with a space to take notes during the conversation and jot down the main points, as well as a place to make comparisons between the cultures of the two participants. Students completed the fourth and fifth sections of the task-based activity after having participated in the Virtual Language Exchange, outside of class time. These sections were meant to have students reflect on their experience as well as auto-evaluate themselves for vocabulary and grammar usage, and allow students to recap the conversation and write a detailed summary of what they talked about in regards to the chapter theme, all the while focusing on culture and using the vocabulary and grammar of interest to express themselves. The two auto-evaluations in the fourth part required students to circle the statements that they thought represented the tasks they did (a) especially well on, as well as the tasks they (b) struggled with:

QA: Using the appropriate vocabulary,

QB: Using the appropriate grammatical structures[1],

QC: Understanding my partner,

QD: Asking conversational questions,

QE: Circumlocution,

QF: Other?

All students submitted the entire task-based activity for assessment during the class period following the Virtual Language Exchange.

EXPLORATORY FINDINGS AND GENERAL DISCUSSION

Survey

Various independent *t*-tests were conducted on the student survey responses for the students paired with native speakers (NS group) and the students paired with non-native speakers (NNS group) prior to as well as after having participated in the Skype sessions in order to better understand the students' motivation for learning about the target language and culture in addition to their attitudes regarding the target language and culture (see Table 1). Although the tests were two-tailed, because they were exploratory in nature, no Bonferroni or other correction procedure was employed. A significant difference between each group's responses on Q3 can be seen ($t[37] = 2.231$, $p = .032$). Students in the NS group demonstrate more motivation for learning about the target language and culture as they feel that studying Spanish is important because it will allow them to meet and converse with more and varied people. The results from Q10 approached significance with the NS group having a more positive attitude towards Spanish speaking people and their culture. In addition, although not statistically significant, the participants in the NS group tend to more strongly agree that most native Spanish-speakers are considerate of the feelings of others (Q9). These results confirm that the students in both groups, NS group and NNS group, are not that different prior to participating in the Virtual Language Exchange. The only really noticeable difference is that the students in the NS group show more motivation for learning the target language so that they can have contact with native speakers. Perhaps this extra motivation comes from the fact that the students in the NS group knew that they would have contact with native speakers and were enthusiastic about using the target language in a real-life context.

Similar to the pre-Virtual Language Exchange survey analysis, an independent *t*-test was conducted for the NS and NNS groups' responses on the survey after having participated in the Virtual Language Exchange (see Table 2). There was a significant difference between each group's responses on Q2 ($t[33] = 2.189$, $p = .036$), Q3 ($t[33] = 2.409$, $p = .022$), and Q5 ($t[31] = 2.132$, $p = .041$). After the Virtual Language Exchange experience participants in the NS group demonstrated more motivation to learn the target language perfectly and again they show more motivation to learn about the language because they believe it will allow them to meet and converse with more and varied people. Interestingly, the participants in the NNS group seem to feel less anxious if someone asks them a question in the target language. The results from Q6 and Q10 approach significance with the NS group having a more positive attitude towards native speakers and their culture and believing that native speakers are considerate of the feelings of others. The NS group also tends to show more of a positive attitude towards native speakers of

Table 1. Results of survey responses for NS group vs. NNS group before the Virtual Language Exchange

Question	Group	N	Mean	SD
Q1	NS	20	4.15	1.09
	NNS	19	3.63	1.61
Q2	NS	20	5.20	1.06
	NNS	19	4.84	1.30
Q3	NS	20	5.00	0.92
	NNS	19	4.21	1.27
Q4	NS	20	4.50	1.32
	NNS	19	4.53	1.54
Q5	NS	20	4.35	0.99
	NNS	19	4.11	1.59
Q6	NS	20	4.80	1.06
	NNS	19	4.42	1.35
Q7	NS	20	4.30	0.86
	NNS	19	3.84	1.26
Q8	NS	20	4.05	0.94
	NNS	19	3.79	1.18
Q9	NS	20	4.60	0.94
	NNS	19	4.00	1.29
Q10	NS	20	4.70	0.57
	NNS	19	4.21	1.03

the target language due to learning about them (Q7), although this is not a statistically significant result. Overall, it appears that the NS group experiences more motivation to learn the target language perfectly possibly because they have had real-life contact with native speakers and have enjoyed the experience. It is not so surprising that the NNS group shows less pressure about being asked a question in the target language because they have not had this real-life situation to deal with during these Virtual Language Exchanges. The participants who have had conversations with peers from their own class are probably unaware of what they might feel like if they were in a situation where they had to converse with native speakers. Consequently, they feel less anxious about the thought of being in this situation.

As a consequence of the need to maintain the anonymity of the respondents both before and after Virtual Language Exchange surveys, it was not possible to match up a participant's before and after responses to one another. Due to this limitation, when examining changes within the NS and NNS groups from before and after the Virtual Language Exchange, it was not possible to use a dependent *t*-test to analyze the data. Instead, independent *t*-tests were used. Given that this less than ideal statistical test was used to analyze the before and after Virtual Language Exchange change findings, these results should be interpreted with caution. The NS group showed a slight increase in agreement for Q6 after the Virtual Language Exchange, although this finding only approaches significance. In addition, the NS group also showed an increasing trend for Q2 and Q7 as time went on. Taken together, these slight increases in responses after the Virtual Language Exchange suggest that students in the NS group have

Table 2. Results of survey responses for NS group vs. NNS group after the Virtual Language Exchange

Question	Group	N	Mean	SD
Q1	NS	18	4.39	1.04
	NNS	17	4.06	1.43
Q2	NS	18	5.67	0.59
	NNS	17	5.18	0.73
Q3	NS	18	5.28	0.67
	NNS	17	4.53	1.12
Q4	NS	18	4.67	1.14
	NNS	17	4.47	1.12
Q5	NS	17	4.53	1.01
	NNS	16	3.63	1.41
Q6	NS	18	5.33	0.77
	NNS	17	4.88	0.78
Q7	NS	18	4.72	0.75
	NNS	17	4.29	0.92
Q8	NS	17	4.47	0.94
	NNS	16	4.19	0.75
Q9	NS	18	4.78	1.11
	NNS	17	4.47	0.94
Q10	NS	18	4.89	0.96
	NNS	17	4.29	0.85

a more positive attitude towards the target language and culture possibly because of having conversed with native speakers a couple of times via Skype. This experience appears to have also affected the students' motivation for learning the target language because they have actually put the language to use in order to complete the assigned task. Overall, the NS group participants seem to have the desire to further perfect their target language speaking skills after having conversed with a native speaker peer. Conversely, the NNS group showed no significant change in responses after the two Virtual Language Exchange experiences. Participants did, however, rate Q4 and Q5 lower and Q1, Q2, Q6, Q7, Q8, and Q9 higher on the second survey. Q10 remained the same. These results suggest that although the Virtual Language Exchange with other non-native speaking peers had no visible effect on motivation to learn about the target language and culture and no visible effect on attitude towards the target language and culture, the experience itself slightly helped students deal with feelings of self-consciousness and anxiety when speaking the target language. Moreover, it is no surprise that there is no change in their opinion about the considerateness of native speakers because the NNS group did not have any contact with native speakers of the target language.

Although it is important to examine possible difference between the NS and NNS groups before and after the Virtual Language Exchange, a more general and useful comparison may be to simply examine all of the students before and after the Virtual Language Exchange regardless of group membership. To accomplish this an independent *t*-test was conducted comparing all students' answers to the survey questions before and after the Virtual Language Exchange. Overall, participants were found to gain a more positive attitude toward Spanish speaking people and their culture (Q6) over time (t[72] = -2.075, p =.042). The results from Q2, Q7 and Q8 approach significance with participants showing a more favorable attitude towards the target language and culture as well as a desire to further their target language speaking skills.

Overall, it appears that the Virtual Language Exchange is a helpful experience for all participants in some way or another; whether it be to increase a student's desire to further their knowledge of the target language or to develop a more positive attitude towards the target language and culture. However, it is those participants who have direct contact with native speakers of the target language that seem to benefit the most. These students in particular tend to show more positive feelings about the experience. The survey results confirm that acculturation is important and that students are undeniably affected by being directly exposed to the target language and culture through Virtual Language Exchanges.

Activities

The topic for the first Virtual Language Exchange task-based activity focused on the various stages of life as well as love and friendship. Students were expected to have already studied the vocabulary pertaining to family, love and friend relationships as well as to have mastered the use of the preterit versus the imperfect, *ser* versus *estar* (both 'to be'), and the future. The theme for the second Virtual Language Exchange task-based activity was university life. Students were expected to have learned vocabulary pertaining to the university experience, as well as to know how to use the subjunctive mood. Again, each task-based assignment included five parts:

- **Pre-Session Activities**
  - Review of vocabulary and grammatical structures separately.
  - Formulation of intended questions combining vocabulary and grammatical structures.
- **Session Activity**
  - Space to take notes.
- **Post-Session Activities**
  - Auto-reflection and auto-evaluation of foreign language use.
  - Summary and reflection of the experience.

As one would expect, all student responses for the first pre-session activity in both Virtual Language Exchanges were very similar. The lists of vocabulary were all comparable in amount and kinds of words listed as well as the type of grammatical structures written for review. Students made extensive lists of pertinent vocabulary from the chapter being studied and regurgitated conjugation lists having to do with the grammatical structures that they had been learning. The responses for the second pre-session activity for both of the Virtual Language Exchanges were also similar. Students demonstrated their ability to focus on certain forms; however, typical grammar mistakes as well as poor vocabulary choices were also made. All of the student questions related to the themes of chapters covered and many of them were the same across the two groups.

A closer analysis of the second post-session activity revealed a few qualitative differences between the first and second Virtual Language Exchanges for each group as well as a few differences between the groups. When commenting on the actual experience of the Virtual Language Exchange, many participants in the NNS group reported feeling preoccupied with grammar during the conversation. Nonetheless, multiple students wrote that they really liked the experience and that it was fun. One student even stated that she had never had a conversation in the target language for more than a few minutes before, but that this experience finally gave her an opportunity to use the language in a new and interesting way. Another student said that using the target language in this format felt natural. Some students even reflected on what they could do to better prepare for the next Virtual Language Exchange, such as prepare more questions or practice circumlocution for when their partner does not understand what they are saying. One student expressed a desire to have this same experience, but with a partner from the target language and culture. In general, the participants from the NNS group demonstrated difficulty expressing any intercultural communicative competence as they only reported factual information about the first conversation. For the second Virtual Language Exchange, the NNS group did not comment as much on the grammatical difficulties experienced. Instead, many reported having a more natural and more fluid conversation the second time around. From a teacher's perspective, there also appeared to be a noticeable improvement in grammar usage when analyzing the written summaries, as one would have hoped, given that this is one of the main objectives of taking a language course.

After the first Virtual Language Exchange many of the participants in the NS group wrote that it was very interesting to speak with a real native speaker. Some felt that the situation was difficult, but that they had learned new things. One student even said that the experience was more fun than they expected. However, many participants reported being preoccupied with a comparison of language ability (i.e., that the native Spanish speaker could speak better English than the non-native Spanish speaker could when speaking Spanish). Fortunately, some students felt that they should not have been so nervous and that better preparation before the next Virtual Language Exchange would help ease their nerves. Almost all of the student summaries for the NS group expressed some sort of intercultural communicative competence in regards to a cultural aspect that was new to them. For the second Virtual Language Exchange, the participants from the NS group overwhelmingly reported feeling more confident and comfortable when speaking with their partner and many reported a more fluid conversation. Students said that they had better comprehension skills during the second Virtual Language Exchange and that they were able to use the target language more. One student even stated that he received more help from he partner when speaking the target language, and he appreciated that. Again from a teacher's perspective, the NS group written summaries appeared to include more target language expressions that are not typical of Intermediate Spanish II student language use (e.g., *montón* 'a lot', *genial* 'brilliant', etc.).

Overall, the student summaries and reflections on the Virtual Language Exchange experience reveal that regardless of group, the Virtual Language Exchange resulted in a positive experience. Students reported that this daunting telecollaborative situation felt more natural as time went on and that the conversations became more fluid. However, one noticeable difference between the NS and NNS groups is that the NS group described feeling more at ease and more confident in their language use over time. Perhaps this change in reported self-confidence and comfort level is a direct effect of being paired with native speakers in that the target language learners are receiving direct feedback, whether positive or negative, from native speakers who are able to give them their undivided attention for twenty minutes straight in the target language, or, perhaps it is the case that the NNS group participants feel the same way, but not enough in order to report it. Nevertheless, in analyzing the trends of what the students in both groups did report, it is clear that all of the students enjoyed working on their speaking skills in this particular telecollaborative format.

Several chi-square analyses were also conducted on the responses for QA through QD the fourth part of the task-based assignment, the auto-evaluations, in order to look for differences in the students' answers from the first Virtual Language Exchange to the second Virtual Language Exchange, but no significant results were found (see Table 3).[2] What is interesting from these results, however, is that across the two

Table 3. Results of auto-evaluation responses for both of the Virtual Language Exchanges for the NS and NNS groups

Question	Session	Auto-Evaluation	Group	
			NS	NNS
QA	1			
		Well	13	9
		Poorly	3	3
		Not Selected	0	0
	2			
		Well	15	10
		Poorly	1	2
		Not Selected	0	0
QB	1			
		Well	8	2
		Poorly	7	10
		Not Selected	1	0
	2			
		Well	5	4
		Poorly	8	8
		Not Selected	3	0
QC	1			
		Well	7	8
		Poorly	8	2
		Not Selected	1	2
	2			
		Well	8	9
		Poorly	6	3
		Not Selected	2	0
QD	1			
		Well	11	12
		Poorly	4	0
		Not Selected	1	0
	2			
		Well	11	10
		Poorly	4	1
		Not Selected	1	1

groups the subjective opinion about their foreign language abilities overwhelmingly reveals that students have much more confidence in their use of appropriate vocabulary and relatively little confidence in their correct use of grammar throughout the entire experience. It appears that the mere experience of speaking, whether it is with a NS or another NNS, does not improve one's self-perceived use of grammar in particular as one might naively assume. Perhaps grammar is so intimidating to students that no matter what their language learning experience, they will always feel that their grammar skills are not up to par.

IMPLICATIONS FOR LEARNING AND TEACHING

It is evident, based on the information reported in this chapter regarding the telecollaborative Virtual Language Exchanges for Intermediate Spanish II students conversing with either native speakers or non-native speakers of the target language and culture, that both teachers and students, regardless of group membership (i.e., NS group or NNS group), benefit from the experience. It is believed that these results go beyond level and institution and are relevant to all foreign language educators and researchers worldwide. If there continues to be an underlying assumption that foreign languages are best learned in a target language environment, then teachers must find innovative ways to transport their students "virtually" to the language that they are learning when studying abroad is not an option. Telecollaboration in particular gives teachers an opportunity to bring the target language and culture to life within the walls of a traditional classroom where physical distance from the target language and culture is no longer problematic. The use of an assigned task helps guide students through the experience and affords each student an opportunity to work on multiple skills (i.e., reading, writing, listening, speaking) at the same time. Micro-immersion environments allow students to put what they have already learned to real-life use in relevant ways all the while encouraging students to continue improving their foreign language skills while simultaneously giving them an extended opportunity to do so.

In light of the study described here which includes a telecollaborative experience between two non-native speakers, it is worth proposing a change to Byram's (1997) definition of telecollaboration. Telecollaboration should be more broadly understood as Internet-based intercultural exchanges between *second language learners* (as opposed to between people of different cultural backgrounds) with the goal of developing language skills as well as intercultural communicative competence through structured tasks conducted in an institutional context. Even if language learners are not able to converse with native speakers of the target language and culture, telecollaboration offers students a chance to reflect on and speak about one's own culture, which is part of developing intercultural communicative competence (i.e., effectively and appropriately communicating about culture in general).

LOOKING TO THE FUTURE

It is hoped that the Virtual Language Exchange, in its varied formats, will continue to be an option for teachers and students of Spanish at Loyola University Maryland in the future. It provides an essential opportunity to bring the target language and culture to life without the need for travel and its positive aftereffects are far reaching. It is believed that the simple experience of a Virtual Language Exchange can benefit all of those involved in infinite ways.

In the future, the foreign language education community as a whole would benefit from more detailed reports of telecollaborative experiences. Since technology is ever changing, there is a need to continuously document how technology is being used to benefit the development of foreign language. Doing so has two consequences: it allows others to replicate a telecollaborative environment while addressing potential challenges and it adds to the growing body of research dedicated to outcomes based on the experience. It is hoped that teachers, who are at the forefront of the language learning process, share their successes as well as their struggles with telecollaboration for the greater good of benefiting foreign language learners everywhere.

CONCLUSION

The Virtual Language Exchange began with one teacher's intention of finding new ways to bring the target language to life for students studying Spanish as a foreign language. The observations made throughout this study suggest that telecollaboration has a lot to offer teachers and students alike. For the teacher in this case, it granted all of her students an opportunity to use their foreign language skills for an extended period of time when, typically, each student is only offered a few moments to use all of their skills during any given class period. The act of participating in the experience itself appeared to motivate students to further improve their foreign language skills and, in some cases, it also positively affected students' attitudes towards the target language and culture. All of the participants of this study have shown in one way or another that, regardless of the native language of the partner involved in the conversation, telecollaboration benefits the development of a foreign language immensely.

The strength of telecollaboration in general lies in the opportunity for different types of language learners to explore the target language through meaningful face-to-face exchanges and to experience culture, whether it is one's own or another's, from beginning to end by utilizing level-appropriate task-based assignments before, during and after the telecollaborative experience. Furthermore, the micro-immersion experience, whether done with other non-native speakers or native speakers of the target language and culture, engages students to integrate and hone all four skills (i.e., reading, writing, listening, speaking), while strengthening intercultural and communicative competence using computer-mediated communication.

REFERENCES

Belz, J. A. (2002). Social dimensions of telecollaborative foreign language study. *Language Learning & Technology*, *6*(1), 60–81.

Belz, J. A. (2006). At the intersection of telecollaboration, learner corpus analysis and L2 pragmatics: Considerations for language program direction. In J. A. Belz & S. L. Thorne (Eds.), *Internet-mediated intercultural foreign language education* (pp. 207–246). Boston: Thomson Heinle.

Belz, J. A., & Thorne, S. L. (2006). Introduction. In J. A. Belz & S. L. Thorne (Eds.), *Internet-mediated intercultural foreign language education* (pp. viii–xxv). Boston: Thomson Heinle.

Brandl, K. (2008). *Communicative language teaching in action: Putting Principles to Work*. Upper Saddle River, NJ: Prentice Hall.

Byram, M. (1997). *Teaching and assessing intercultural communicative competence*. Clevedon, UK: Multilingual Matters.

Candlin, C. N. (1987). Towards task-based language learning. In C. N. Candlin and D. Murphy (Eds.), Lancaster practical papers in English language education (Vol. 7, pp. 5-22). Englewood Cliffs, NJ: Prentice Hall.

Chun, D. M. (2011). Developing intercultural communicative competence through online exchanges. *CALICO Journal, 28*(2), 392–419. doi:10.11139/cj.28.2.392-419

Collentine, J., & Freed, B. F. (2004). Learning context and its effects on second language acquisition: Introduction. *Studies in Second Language Acquisition, 26*(02), 153–171. doi:10.1017/S0272263104262015

DeKeyser, R. M. (1991). Foreign language development during a semester abroad. In B. F. Freed (Ed.), *Foreign langauge acquisition and the classroom* (pp. 104–118). Lexington, MA: D. C. Heath.

Ellis, R. (2003). *Task-based language learning and teaching*. Oxford, UK: Oxford University Press.

Freed, B. F., Segalowitz, N., & Dewey, D. P. (2004). Context of learning and second language fluency in French: Comparing regular classroom, Study Abroad, and intensive domestic immersion programs. *Studies in Second Language Acquisition, 26*(02), 275–301. doi:10.1017/S0272263104262064

Hauck, M., & Youngs, B. L. (2008). Telecollaboration in multimodal environments: The impact on task design and learner interaction. *Computer Assisted Language Learning, 21*(2), 87–124. doi:10.1080/09588220801943510

Huebner, T. (1995). The effects of overseas language programs: Report on a case study of an intensive Japanese course. In B. F. Freed (Ed.), *Second language acquisition in a study abroad context* (pp. 171–193). Amsterdam: Benjamins. doi:10.1075/sibil.9.11hue

Hymes, D. H. (1972). On communicative competence. In J. B. Pride & J. Holmes (Eds.), *Sociolinguistics: Selected readings* (pp. 269–293). Harmondsworth, UK: Penguin Books.

Lafford, B. A. (1995). Getting into, through and out of a survival situation: A comparison of communicative strategies used by students studying Spanish-abroad and 'at home. In B. F. Freed (Ed.), *Second language acquisition in a study abroad context* (pp. 97–121). Amsterdam: Benjamins. doi:10.1075/sibil.9.08laf

Lapkin, S., Hart, D., & Swain, M. (1995). A Canadian interprovincial exchange: Evaluating the linguistic impact of a three-month stay in Quebec. In B. F. Freed (Ed.), *Second language acquisition in a study abroad context* (pp. 67–94). Amsterdam: Benjamins. doi:10.1075/sibil.9.06lap

Levy, M. (2007). Culture, culture learning and new technologies: Towards a pedagogical framework. *Language Learning & Technology, 11*(2), 104–127.

Lewis, T. (2013). DBR and task-based learning: The ongoing experience of designing a task-based telecollaboration. In C. Pardo Ballester & J. Rodríguez (Eds.), Design-based research in CALL (Vol. 11, pp. 211-233). San Marcos, TX: CALICO.

Lewis, T. N., & Schneider, H. (2015). Integrating international video chat into the foreign language curriculum. *International Journal of Computer-Assisted Language Learning and Teaching, 5*(2), 74–87. doi:10.4018/IJCALLT.2015040105

Liskin-Gasparro, J. E. (1998). Linguistic development in an immersion context: How advanced learners of Spanish perceive SLA. *Modern Language Journal, 82*(2), 159–175. doi:10.1111/j.1540-4781.1998.tb01189.x

Müller-Hartmann, A. (2006). Learning how to teach intercultural communicative competence via telecollaboration: A model for language teacher education. In J. A. Belz & S. Thorne (Eds.), *Internet-mediated intercultural foreign language education* (pp. 63–84). Boston: Thomson Heinle.

Nunan, D. (1989). *Designing tasks for the communicative classroom*. Cambridge, UK: Cambridge University Press.

Nunan, D. (2004). *Task-based language teaching*. Cambridge, UK: Cambridge University Press. doi:10.1017/CBO9780511667336

O'Dowd, R. (2003). Understanding the "other side": Intercultural learning in a Spanish-English e-mail exchange. *Language Learning & Technology, 7*(2), 118–144.

O'Dowd, R. (2007a). Evaluating the outcomes of online intercultural exchange. *ELT Journal, 61*(2), 144–152. doi:10.1093/elt/ccm007

O'Dowd, R. (Ed.). (2007b). *Online intercultural exchange: An introduction for foreign language teachers*. Clevedon, UK: Multilingual Matters.

O'Dowd, R., & Ritter, M. (2006). Understanding and working with 'failed communication' in telecollaborative exchanges. *CALICO Journal, 23*(3), 1–20.

Pérez-Vidal, C. (2011). Language acquisition in three different contexts of learning: Formal instruction, study abroad, and semi-immersion (CLIL). In Y. Ruíz de Zarobe, J. M. Sierra, & F. Puerto (Eds.), *Content and foreign language integrated learning: Contributions to multilingualism in European contexts* (pp. 103–127). New York: Peter Lang.

Prabhu, N. S. (1987). *Second language pedagogy*. Oxford, UK: Oxford University Press.

Schenker, T. (2012). Intercultural competence and cultural learning through telecollaboration. *CALICO Journal, 29*, 449–470. doi:10.11139/cj.29.3.449-470

Serrano, R., Llanes, A., & Tragant, E. (2011). The effect of context of second language learning: Intensive and semi-intensive courses vs. study abroad in Europe. *System, 39*, 133–143. doi:10.1016/j.system.2011.05.002

Skehan, P. (2001). The role of focus on form during task-based instruction. In Mª L. and A. I. Celaya (Eds.), Trabajos en lingüística aplicada (pp. 11-24). Barcelona, Spain: AESLA.

Ware, P. D. (2005). "Missed" communication in online communication: Tensions in a German-American telecollaboration. *Language Learning & Technology, 9*(2), 64–89.

Ware, P. D., & Kramsch, C. (2005). Toward an intercultural stance: Teaching German and English through telecollaboration. *Modern Language Journal*, *89*(2), 190–205. doi:10.1111/j.1540-4781.2005.00274.x

Wesche, M. B., & Skehan, P. (2002). Communicative, task-based, and content-based language instruction. In R. B. Kaplan (Ed.), *The Oxford handbook of applied linguistics* (pp. 207–288). New York: Oxford University Press.

Willis, J. (1996). *A framework for task-based learning*. London: Longman.

KEY TERMS AND DEFINITIONS

CALL (Computer Assisted Language Learning): Computer applications used for language teaching and learning.

Intercultural Communicative Competence: The abilities needed to communicate effectively and appropriately about culture with people of a possibly different linguistic and cultural background.

Micro-Immersion: An artificial context in which second language learners have direct contact with peers who speak the target language for an extended period of time.

Skype: A synchronous multimodal video conferencing software.

Task-Based Activity: An assigned activity that allows second language learners to have meaningful interaction using the target language in order to complete an objective.

Telecollaboration: An Internet-based intercultural exchange between second language learners with the goal of developing language skills as well as intercultural communicative competence through structured tasks conducted in an institutional context.

Virtual Language Exchange: A synchronous multimodal event that takes place via Skype intended for second language learners to practice the target language with peers (native or non-native speakers).

ENDNOTES

[1] The particular grammatical structures of focus for each session were spelled out in the statement (e.g., Using the preterit and imperfect to speak about the past as well as the future).

[2] QE was eliminated from the analysis because students seemed confused about its definition. A few students actually wrote on their handouts that they did not understand what circumlocution meant and many students did not select this option in either auto-evaluation as an applicable option to them.

APPENDIX

Sample of Task-Based Activity

Figure 1.

SESIÓN 1:
VEJEZ Y JUVENTUD, AMOR Y AMISTAD

SN 104

Objetivos de la conversación:
- Conocer a tu compañero; su situación familiar, sus amigos, etc.
- Describir la familia y los amigos de ti y de tu compañero

PASO I. Pre-sesión (30 minutos)

Antes de reunirte con tu pareja, debes anticipar el vocabulario y las funciones gramaticales que emplearás durante tu conversación

Escribe palabras de vocabulario aquí que necesitarás para tu conversación:

Modelo: *los miembros de la familia, los amigos, nacer, amoroso*

_____

_____

_____

_____

_____

_____

_____

_____

_____

_____

Escribe formas gramaticales que has estudiado en capítulo 2 y 4 que van a ser útiles en tu conversación:

Modelo: *ser, estar*

(soy, eres, es…, estoy, estás, está…)

_____

_____

_____

_____

_____

Figure 2.

PASO II. Pre-sesión
(30 minutos)

la familia	el/la novio/a	los amigos
la juventud	la vejez	
el amor	la amistad	la vida

Piensa en los temas de la caja de arriba y prepárate a **describirle a tu compañero cómo es tu familia, cómo son tus amigos y si tienes novio/a.**
Completa las siguientes frases según tu experiencia y opiniones:

Descripción del presente:
En mi familia hay…

Descripción del pasado:
Cuando yo era niño/a…

Narración de un evento en el pasado:
Una vez cuando yo era niño/a…

Hablar del futuro:
En el futuro…

Antes de tu conversación, escribe preguntas basadas en los mismos temas para conocer mejor a tu compañero:

1. _____

2. _____

3. _____

4. _____

5. _____

6. _____

7. _____

8. _____

9. _____

10. _____

Figure 3.

PASO III. Durante la sesión
(20 minutos en español)

A. ¿Qué ha dicho tu pareja?

Toma **apuntes** (no escribas oraciones completas) aquí de palabras, expresiones, u otra información que quieres recordar. ¡Recuerda! Es un **diálogo**—¡no debes pasar mucho tiempo escribiendo durante tu conversación!

B. En general, haz algunas comparaciones entre tu vida y la vida tu compañero en cuanto a la vida familiar y la amistad.

C. ¿Puedes resumir los puntos básicos de tu conversación? Escribe aquí los temas claves.

➢

➢

➢

➢

Figure 4.

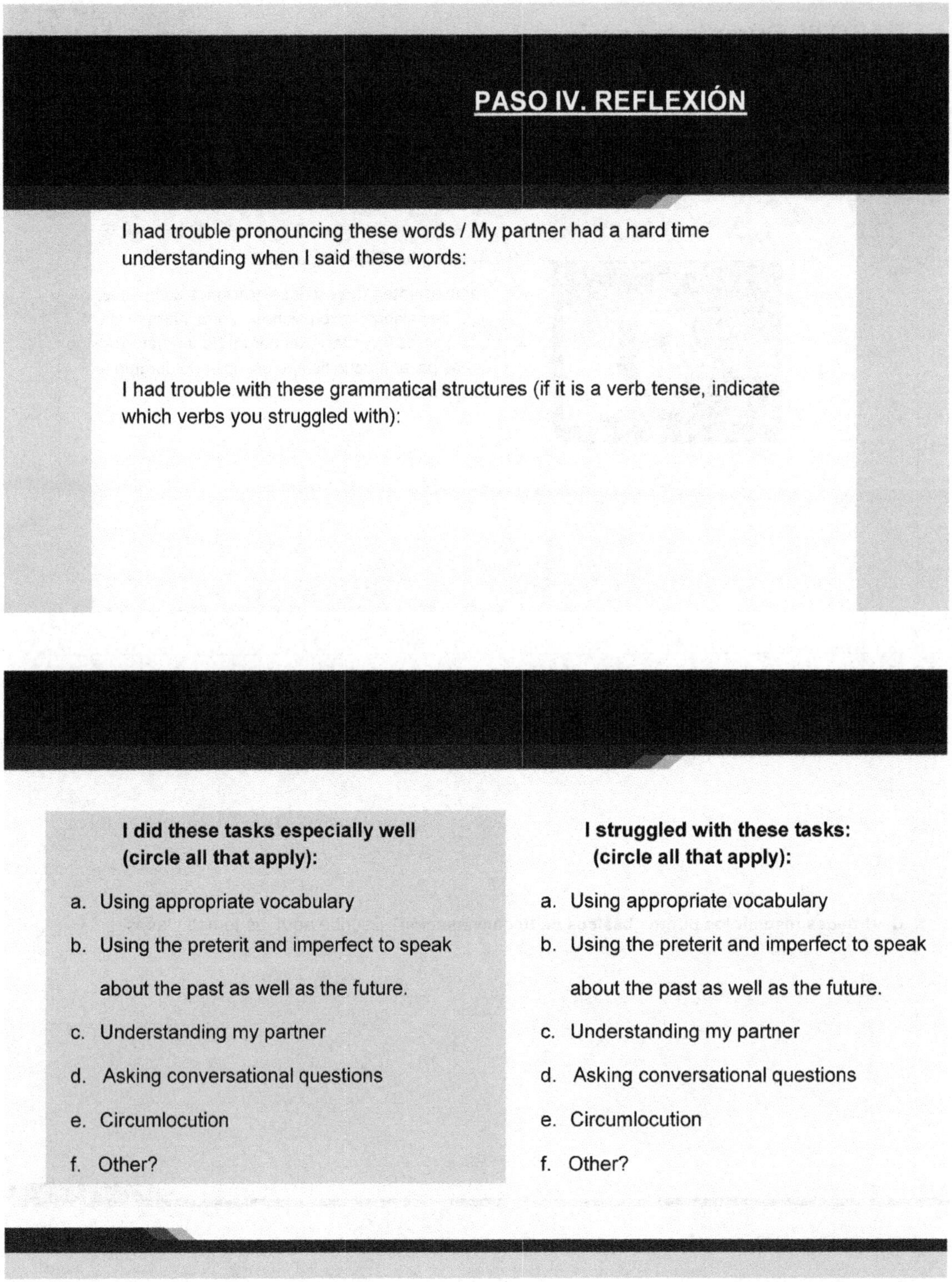

PASO IV. REFLEXIÓN

I had trouble pronouncing these words / My partner had a hard time understanding when I said these words:

I had trouble with these grammatical structures (if it is a verb tense, indicate which verbs you struggled with):

I did these tasks especially well (circle all that apply):	**I struggled with these tasks: (circle all that apply):**
a. Using appropriate vocabulary	a. Using appropriate vocabulary
b. Using the preterit and imperfect to speak about the past as well as the future.	b. Using the preterit and imperfect to speak about the past as well as the future.
c. Understanding my partner	c. Understanding my partner
d. Asking conversational questions	d. Asking conversational questions
e. Circumlocution	e. Circumlocution
f. Other?	f. Other?

Figure 5.

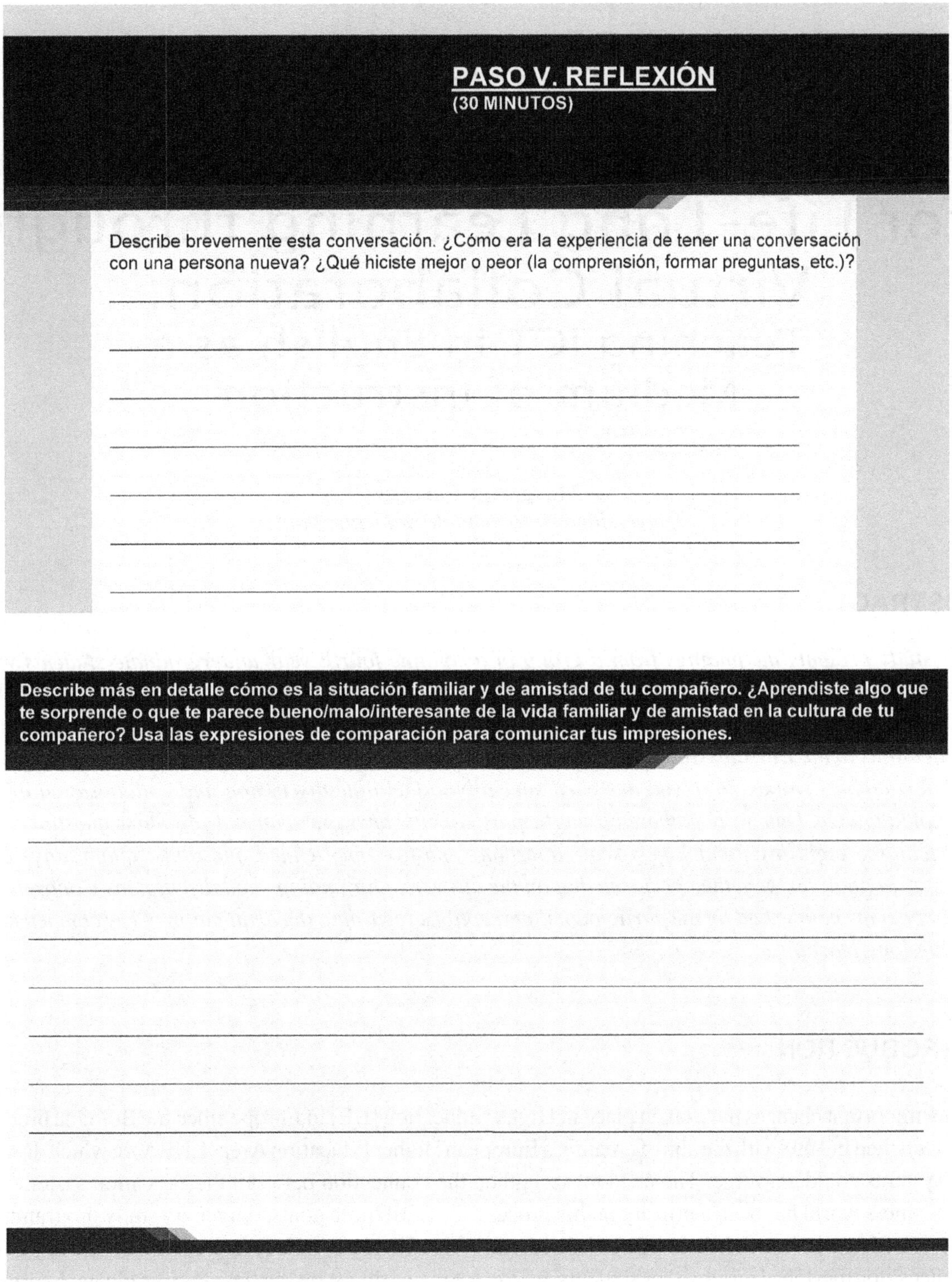

PASO V. REFLEXIÓN
(30 MINUTOS)

Describe brevemente esta conversación. ¿Cómo era la experiencia de tener una conversación con una persona nueva? ¿Qué hiciste mejor o peor (la comprensión, formar preguntas, etc.)?

_____

_____

_____

_____

_____

_____

Describe más en detalle cómo es la situación familiar y de amistad de tu compañero. ¿Aprendiste algo que te sorprende o que te parece bueno/malo/interesante de la vida familiar y de amistad en la cultura de tu compañero? Usa las expresiones de comparación para comunicar tus impresiones.

_____

_____

_____

_____

_____

_____

_____

_____

Chapter 8

Developing Key Competences for Life–Long Learning through Virtual Collaboration:
Teaching ICT in English as a Medium of Instruction

Margarita Vinagre
Universidad Autónoma de Madrid, Spain

ABSTRACT

This study presents the findings from a group of forty-nine fourth year undergraduate students who were trained in a blended learning environment over two months in order to acquire base knowledge and hands-on experience about information and communication technologies (ICT) and their possible applications to the EFL classroom. The course was taught in English as a Medium of Instruction (EMI) and participants worked in a wiki designed specially to facilitate discussion and collaboration in the foreign language. Data were gathered from the participants' answers to an end-of-course questionnaire that featured eight five-point Likert-scale questions and five open-ended questions; quantitative and qualitative analyses were then performed upon the answers. Our findings and discussions elaborate on the impact the course had on the participants' perceptions regarding the acquisition of key competences for life-long learning.

INTRODUCTION

Many important changes have taken place in Higher Education (HE) in Europe since the Bologna process was launched in 1998 with the aim of creating a European Higher Education Area (EHEA) in which diverse HE systems could converge. The need to strengthen the connection between the education system and the business world has been a priority in this process. To fulfil these goals, university study programmes have included a series of reference points that are described in terms of learning outcomes and key competences[1] for life-long learning that students are expected to achieve by the time they graduate. Learning

DOI: 10.4018/978-1-5225-0177-0.ch008

outcomes refer to what students are expected to know, understand, and be able to demonstrate after the learning experience. According to the European Commission (2007), these transferable competences are a combination of knowledge, skills, attitudes, and values that are particularly necessary for personal fulfilment and development, social inclusion, active citizenship, and employment. The development of these competences, which are a major factor in innovation, productivity, and competitiveness, also guarantees greater flexibility in the labour force by allowing it to adapt more quickly to the constant changes of an increasingly interconnected world.

Many studies and reports have provided frameworks with descriptions of key competences for life-long learning (European Commission's Framework of Reference, 2007); the OECD's Definition and Selection of Competencies (DeSeCo) Project, 2005 and the Tuning Higher Education Project (González & Wagenaar, 2005; Villa & Poblete, 2008). These key competences have also been described by many authors (Marin et al., 2011; Penttilä et al. 2012; Shuman et al., 2005). In this study we shall adopt the European Commission's proposal (2007) which considers the information in Table 1 as key competences for life-long learning[2].

To date, research on key competence development in educational environments has highlighted that only a limited number of these competences have been assessed. Thus, a report by Eurydice (2009) emphasized that only three competences, namely communication in the mother tongue, communication in foreign languages, and basic competences in mathematics, science, and technology, are commonly assessed in national tests. By contrast, in many European countries, other core competences such as learning to learn or social competences were not formally assessed (Eurydice, 2009). These lesser assessed competences included digital competence, learning to learn competences, social competences, sense of initiative and entrepreneurship, and cultural awareness. Similarly, the European Commission (2010) itself found that, in comparison with subject knowledge, the challenge of assessing key competences across the curriculum was "acute and ongoing". Current efforts to address this issue include efforts by Alsina, Boix, Burset, Buscà, Colomina, García, Maurí, Pujolà & Sayós, (2011), Blömeke, Zlatkin-Troitschanskaia,

Table 1. European reference framework (2007): Key competences for life-long learning

Competence	Knowledge, Skills, and Attitudes
Communication in foreign languages: This involves the capacity for listening, speaking, reading, and writing in the foreign language, together with mediation and intercultural understanding.	• Ability to communicate in a second (foreign) language • Appreciation for diversity and multiculturality
Basic competences in science and technology: These competences refer to the mastery, use, and application of knowledge and methodologies that explain the natural world. These involve an understanding of the changes caused by human activity and each individual's responsibility in this process.	• Capacity for analysis and synthesis, abstract, and analytical thinking • Grounding in base knowledge (knowledge and understanding of the subject area) • Ability to make reasoned decisions • Research skills • Ability to act on the basis of ethical reasoning
Digital competence involves the confident and critical use of information society technology and, thus, basic skills in information and communication technology (ICT).	• ICT digital skills • Information management skills (ability to retrieve and analyze information from different sources)
Learning to learn refers to the ability to pursue and organise one's own learning, either individually or in groups, in accordance with one's own needs, whilst being aware of methods and opportunities.	• Ability to plan and manage time • Ability to identify, pose and resolve problems • Critical and self-critical abilities • Capacity to learn and stay up-to-date with learning • Capacity to apply knowledge in practical situations • Ability to work autonomously

Kuhn & Fege, (2013) and Watts, Marín, García & Aznar, (2012). Similar concerns have also been present in Higher Education institutions in the United States since the year 2000. An example of this is the MIT's CDIO Project (*Conceive, Design, Implement & Operate*), which aims to provide solutions to solve the mismatch between what is taught at universities and the needs of the labour market. In order to address this issue, the European Commission (2010) calls on educators to implement new methodological techniques that facilitate the development of core competences, "especially digital and entrepreneurial competences in order to encourage initiative rather than simple reproduction of received knowledge and to better adapt to learners and employers' needs" (p.5). The development of these lesser assessed competences and their respective knowledge, skills, and attitudes (e.g. capacity to work autonomously, effective team-work, entrepreneurial spirit, and participation in international or multicultural groups) can be difficult in many educational settings given the number of contact hours and the limitations posed by face-to-face learning environments. In this respect, the European Commission (2010) suggests that this can be solved by integrating technologies and "more cross curricular and innovative approaches, such as learning by doing or project based learning" (p. 26). Virtual collaboration is such an approach, since it is project-based and encourages experiential learning by providing students with first-hand experience that is directly related to successful professional practices in the global workplace. It also offers educators an opportunity to develop students' base knowledge and competences by transcending the traditional-learning classroom (Vinagre, 2005). Computer networks offer the promise of increasing student-student and student-teacher interaction, not only locally but also globally, through resources such as the Web 2.0. Whereas students have traditionally been limited to fifty minutes of classroom interaction three times a week, they can now consult one another and their teacher outside of class. Moreover, they can interact and carry out tasks with peers around the world so that they can glimpse other ways of seeing the world.

BACKGROUND

Virtual Collaboration for Competence Development

The ability to integrate new technologies in the classroom has become an essential part of learning in the 21st century. One approach to teaching that facilitates this process is virtual collaboration. This refers to the application of online communication tools to bring together learners with the aim of developing their base knowledge and competences through collaborative tasks and project work. Authors such as Graham & Misanchuk (2004) discuss the benefits of virtual group collaboration, concluding that it encourages negotiation of meaning, re-conceptualization of previous knowledge, motivation to learn, high-quality decision-making and reasoning, general cognitive development, creativity, reduction of anxiety, and the creation of learning communities. Other authors such as Kaye (1989) claim that computer-mediated collaboration fosters more evenly distributed turn-taking and also more thoughtful inputs when compared to face-to-face collaborative learning. Authors such as Pallof & Pratt (2005) suggest that virtual collaboration has been shown to contribute to better learning outcomes, including development of critical thinking skills, co-creation of knowledge and meaning, reflection, and transformative learning. These authors also mention that different learning styles and cultures can be accommodated more easily because effective collaborative learning values diversity (p.5-6). Furthermore, competences gained from experiencing collaborative learning are highly transferable to work environments (Shaw, 2006).

The theoretical principles that underlie virtual collaboration are not new. These principles are based on socio-constructivist approaches to learning (Daniels, 2008; Vygotsky,1987) that emphasize the importance of social interaction for the construction of shared knowledge. Current literature often associates them with the pedagogical paradigms of situated and distributed learning (Brown, Collins & Duguid, 1989), as well as with activity theory (Engeström, Miettinen & Punamäki, 1999). In such approaches, learning takes place as a result of socially situated interactions that are conducive to the creation of knowledge and development of competences. This process requires active participation, interaction and reflection, and technologies are considered to be mediating tools in this process. In a collaborative learning environment, knowledge is shared among learners as they work towards common goals. They take an active role in the learning process as they participate in discussions, search for information, and exchange opinions and feedback with their peers. Knowledge is co-created and learners depend on each other's contributions to complete their goals (Vinagre, 2010). According to Palloff & Pratt (2005) collaborative learning processes help students achieve richer knowledge generation through shared goals, shared exploration, and a shared process of meaning building.

Recent research on virtual collaboration in foreign language learning has shown its potential to support learner autonomy (Fuchs, Hauck & Müller-Hartmann, 2012), foster foreign language awareness and accuracy (Sauro, 2009; Vinagre & Muñoz, 2011), and develop higher order thinking skills (Von der Emde, Schneider, & Kötter, 2001). This mode of learning can also encourage the development of learners' socio-pragmatic skills (Kinginger, 2000; Vinagre, 2008), intercultural competence (Vinagre, in press), electronic literacies (Hauck, 2010), and multiple literacies (Guth & Helm, 2011). Despite all these benefits, research has also highlighted the limited impact of virtual collaboration in university contexts to date (Belz & Müller-Hartmann, 2003; Guth, Helm & O'Dowd, 2012).

Virtual Collaboration in Wikis

Wikis have gained popularity as an interactive tool for virtual collaboration (Bower, Woo, Roberts & Watters, 2006; Bruns & Humphreys, 2005). Authors such as Parker & Chao (2007) have claimed that wikis bring together many desirable qualities such as "including a virtual presence, a variety of interactions, easy participation, valuable content, connections to a broader subject field, personal and community identity and interaction, democratic participation, and evolution over time" (p.58). Most authors agree on the collaborative nature of wikis and numerous studies have emphasized that wikis can facilitate reflection and collaboration (Lee, 2010; Lund, 2008). Minocha & Thomas (2007) have added that, besides facilitating collaborative learning, wikis are good media for collaborative work (p.198). Other authors have elaborated on this tool's suitability to foster student interaction. In this respect, Huang & Nakazawa (2010) and Li (2012) have described them as enhancers of peer interaction and group work as opposed to competition. According to Boulos, Maramba & Wheeler (2006), they are excellent resources for the learners' own construction of knowledge, since they provide an opportunity to engage in knowledge building at the same time they foster metacognition (higher-order thinking skills). Additional inherent benefits of wikis are mentioned by Wheeler, Yeomans, & Wheeler (2008), who suggest that wikis have the ability to keep learners connected, so that they feel closer to one another and more engaged in the learning task. Wikis are also considered highly democratic by authors such as Lee (2010), since they disperse individual power and all participants have an equal status and the right to contribute or edit entries. They are unique in that they serve as a platform for scaffolding, foster student-centered learning, allow for the incorporation of multiple perspectives, and facilitate the development of learning communities.

English as a Medium of Instruction

In order to foster the development of those competences related to communicating in the foreign language, some educational institutions have favoured the implementation of programmes and courses which are taught using English as a Medium of Instruction (EMI). This practice has received wide recognition from researchers and professionals, since providing curriculum content in a foreign language can lead to both increased subject knowledge and enhanced L2 proficiency (Coyle, 2005; Dalton-Puffer, 2007; Marsh, Maljers & Hartiala, 2001; Stohler, 2006; Wilkinson, 2004). The term EMI has been used to refer to those contexts in which non-language content subjects are taught through English. UNESCO's Education Position Paper (2003) explains it as follows:

The language of instruction is the medium of communication for the transmission of knowledge. This is different from language teaching itself where the grammar, vocabulary, and the written and the oral forms of a language constitute a specific curriculum for the acquisition of a second language other than the mother tongue. Learning another language opens up access to other value systems and ways of interpreting the world, encouraging inter-cultural understanding and helping reduce xenophobia. This applies equally to minority and majority language speakers. (p. 16)

We are increasingly becoming a multilingual and multicultural society in which linguistic diversity is part of everyday life. For this reason, becoming effective communicators in foreign languages has become one of the main priorities of educational policies all over the world. A recent report by the European Commission on lifelong language learning (2012) mentions as one of its main aims "spreading the benefits of multilingualism to everybody throughout their lives, starting in childhood" (p.27). In order to reach this target, challenges such as how to encourage people to learn and what are the best ways to teach and learn languages have to be met. EMI environments originated as an answer to those challenges. In this study, we have understood EMI as a synonym for Content and Language Integrated Learning (CLIL). The term CLIL was adopted by European experts in 1996 as a generic umbrella term to refer to diverse methodologies that can lead to a bilingual education where attention is given to both the subject and the language of instruction. It is used to describe any educational situation in which an additional language is used for the teaching and learning of subjects other than the language itself (Marsh 2006, p. 29).

Despite its broad use, we decided to use the term EMI since, according to some authors (Smit & Dafouz 2012, p. 4-5), it is becoming more widely used and popular in Higher Education settings. EMI programmes can offer a variety of benefits: strengthen bilingualism, foster multilingualism and multiculturality, increase the potential mobility of citizens, revive endangered languages, and encourage internationalization (Eurydice 2012; Dearden, 2015; Wong, 2009).

In this exploratory study we decided to use wikis as an online asynchronous tool to integrate virtual collaboration in an EMI course in order to discover the potential of this teaching approach for the development of key competences for life-long learning. More specifically, we looked for answers to the following research questions:

RQ1: What were the students' perceptions regarding the development of key competences while working collaboratively online?

RQ2: According to the students, which key competences were required for successful virtual collaboration?

Rationale

During the first semester of 2014, a course entitled *Information and Communication Technologies* (ICT) was offered in EMI at a Spanish University as an optional course for the B.A. in English Studies. The course aimed to foster a critical stance towards the academic literature underlying computer supported collaborative learning and to involve participants in exploring different ICT tools and their possible applications in EFL (English as a Foreign Language), teaching and learning contexts in order to help them move from theory to classroom practice. The course was delivered by a team of two instructors, one of whom is also the author of this paper.

CONTEXT AND PARTICIPANTS

Forty-nine fourth year undergraduate students enrolled in the course. Teachers and students met twice a week but tasks were completed mostly online, working in small groups outside the classroom. The students were mostly Spanish speakers, with the exception of four students whose mother tongues were Arabic, Chinese, Swedish, and Romanian respectively. As regards gender, thirty-three participants were female and sixteen were male. The level of experience with the use of the technology was very similar and they had no previous experience in computer-supported collaborative learning, although some were familiar with the use of some ICT tools (blogs, skype) and social networks (e.g. facebook, whatsapp).

Activities and Tools

Over the course of two months, the students worked on a wiki in small groups of four or five, where they had to carry out a series of collaborative tasks. These were designed following O'Dowd & Ware's (2009) 'collaborative task' category, which requires learners not only to exchange and compare information but also to work together to produce a joint product or conclusion (p. 178). In this study, students were asked to review articles on virtual collaboration and explore different ICT tools (blogs, wikis, skype, podcasts, and google drive) and activities (webquests and treasure hunts). They also had to become familiar with different models of virtual collaboration and finally suggest how they could be integrated into the EFL classroom. These tasks were aimed at fostering information exchange, comparison, discussion, and reflection (see questions for reflection in Appendix A) that would result in the creation of a wiki space totalling six pages that had to be designed and edited jointly by all group members, and whose content also had to be agreed upon by them. As a final task, the students had to give a final group presentation in class in which they would present their wikis to the rest of their classmates. A summary of the tasks is provided in Table 2.

Method

At the end of the semester, after the completion of their respective wiki projects, 39 students responded to an online questionnaire where they were asked to express their opinions about the project (see Appendix B). The questionnaire was designed as a tool to gather information about how much the students felt they had learned in the form of base knowledge and key competences for life-long learning. We

Table 2. Description of tasks

	Unit (Presented in Class)	Activity (in Small Groups in a Wiki)
1	Introduction to Computer Supported Collaborative Learning (CSCL or telecollaboration)	Study and discussion of relevant aspects and resources presented in class. Design a wiki space. Upload a summary of what you have learned about CSCL on the wiki and invite your group's member to discuss your contribution.
2	Exploring CSCL	Working in groups: select, read, upload, summarize and review one article about CSCL on your wiki page. Comment upon and discuss the articles with your group members using the wiki discussion facility. Answer questions for reflection in the wiki. Wikipage 1
3	Web 2.0 tools in EFL teaching and learning (1): Blogs & Google Drive	Create a blog and post a comment. Design a questionnaire using Google drive and invite your group's members to answer it. Discuss with your group members in the wiki possible applications of these tools to the EFL classroom. Upload a summary of your ideas to your group's wiki pages. Wikipage 2
4	Web 2.0 tools in EFL teaching and learning (2): Skype, Podcasts (iTunesU)	Explore podcasts of your interest in iTunes U. Use Skype to get in touch with your group's members in order to discuss how to use these ICT tools in the EFL classroom. Upload a summary of your ideas on your group's wiki pages. Wikipage 3
5	ICT-based activities: Webquests & Treasure hunts	Analyze the webquests and treasure hunts provided by the teachers. Discuss with your group members in the wiki how they can be integrated in the EFL classroom. Upload a summary of your ideas on your group's wiki pages. Wikipage 4
6	CSCL Exchanges (1): Models of CSCL exchanges: -eTandem: principles of application -eTwinning: principles of application -Cultura: principles of application	Comparison, analysis and critical evaluation of authentic data and samples taken from projects. Discuss with your group members in the wiki how these exchanges can be integrated in the EFL classroom. Upload a summary of your ideas on your group's wiki pages. Answer questions for reflection in the wiki. Wikipage 5
7	CSCL Exchanges (2): How to organise an exchange for language and culture learning -General guidelines: organisation, tools, chronogram, topics to discuss, peer-feedback (focus on form) -Language learning diary -Tasks	Decide with your group members how to organize your own exchange for language and culture learning. You will need to include guidelines, activities and tools you would use and justify your decisions. Answer questions for reflection in the wiki. Wikipage 6
8	Final oral presentations: present your wiki to your classmates and comment on what you have learned on this course and your experience working collaboratively online	

elicited responses from 8 Likert-scale questions and 5 open-ended questions. We coded the first part of the questionnaire quantitatively and then we explored their answers to the open-ended questions.

RESULTS AND DISCUSSION

Quantitative Data

Figure 1 illustrates how much participants considered they had learned about base knowledge (knowledge and understanding of the subject area) during the course. Answers to question 1 show that the vast majority of students (37, 95%) thought they could easily explain what virtual collaboration meant.

Figure 1. Students' perceptions of base knowledge

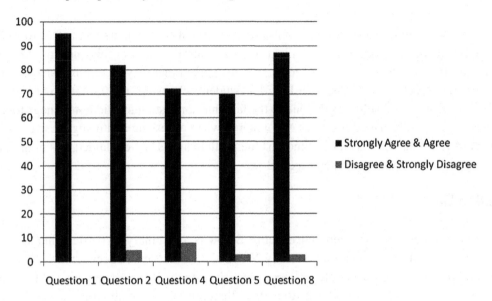

Similarly for questions 2 and 8, the majority of students (32, 82% and 34, 87% respectively) agreed that they had learned about different models of virtual collaboration and where to find web activities that they could integrate in the EFL classroom. Finally, for questions 4 & 5, the majority of students (28, 72% and 27, 70% respectively) indicated that they knew how to use web pages in order to find partners in other countries and that they could organize a virtual project and negotiate all aspects of the project with their partners.

Figure 2 shows the students' perceptions regarding their level of confidence in the use of the ICT tools introduced during the course. As can be seen, for question 6 the majority of students (36, 92%)

Figure 2. Students' confidence in the use of the ICT tools explored during the course

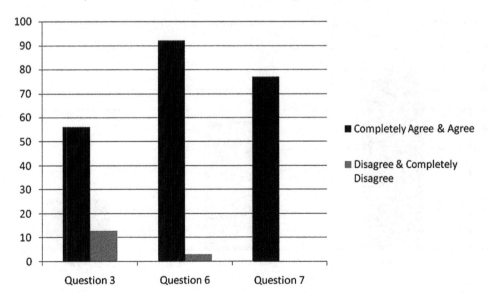

agreed that they had learned how to choose the most adequate ICT tools (email, blogs, wikis, skype and podcasts) to suit potential students' learning objectives and the main objectives of a virtual collaborative project. In question 7, most students (30, 77%) said that they felt confident using the ICT tools that they had explored in class. However, 9 (23%) students chose 'neutral' to answer this question. Similarly, the answers to question 3 show that only 22 (56%) students agreed that they were familiar with the use of synchronous and asynchronous tools, with 12 (31%) students choosing 'neutral' and 5 (13%) disagreeing. We believe that these results may be due to the fact that some students did not manage to use blogs and podcasts successfully. The difficulties encountered when accessing and using these tools together with time constraints caused frustration amongst the participants. They explained this in their answers to the open-ended question 9 as we shall see below.

Qualitative Data

The questionnaire included five open-ended items. Below is a summary of participants' comments to the three questions that are relevant for this study. We used their answers to question 9 ("If there is a tool that you didn't feel confident using please specify which and why") to corroborate and triangulate the information obtained in those closed questions that elicited information about the students' perceived knowledge and familiarity with the use of the ICT tools introduced during the course (questions 3, 6 and 7). Then, we analyzed their answers to questions 10 ("What competences have you developed while working collaboratively online") and 11("What competences are required in order to work collaboratively online in a successful manner") to elicit information about which key competences they perceived they had developed and were relevant for this mode of learning. The students were not prompted in their answers in any way and they were not familiar with the list of the key competences introduced in Table 1.

As can be seen in Figure 3, answers to question 9 revealed that some students (7, 18% and 5, 13% respectively) thought that blogs (blogger) and podcasts (iTunesU) were not user-friendly and that they had difficulty accessing them. Finally, 2 students (5%) mentioned that Skype is a tool that they would use for personal purposes but did not feel comfortable using in an EFL context.

Figure 3. Students' perceptions of the ICT tools they found most difficult to use

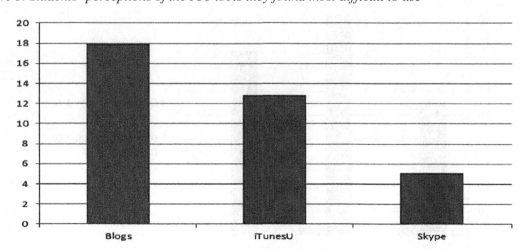

As regards the participants' answers to the open questions 10 and 11, we have categorized key competences according to the European Reference Framework (see Figure 4).

As noted in Figure 4, 32 (82%) students said that they had developed social competences in the form of team work abilities and interpersonal skills. Another 24 (61.5%) students said that they had developed digital competences and information management skills, and 23 (59%) students said that they had developed basic competences in science and technology in the form of base knowledge of the subject, research skills, capacity for analysis and synthesis, and decision-making abilities. Other students (11, 28%) said that they had developed *learning to learn* competences in the form of organization and planning, problem-solving, critical and self-critical skills, and autonomous work. Fewer students (10, 26%) said that they had developed entrepreneurial skills in the form of adapting to new situations, creativity, leadership, project management, initiative, and will to succeed, while 7 (18%) said that they had developed linguistic skills and appreciation for diversity during the course. The fact that linguistic skills were mentioned is interesting since the foreign language was not explicitly taught during the course. Finally, the capacity to work in an international context was mentioned by only 1 member of the team composed of international students. It is interesting that the student was aware of having developed specific intercultural competences as a result of collaborating successfully in an international team.

As regards those key competences that participants thought they needed in order to work successfully in virtual collaboration (question 11), the vast majority of students (32, 82%) mentioned that they had needed social competences in the form of team work abilities and interpersonal skills. Nineteen (48.7%)

Figure 4. Key competences developed and required in virtual collaboration

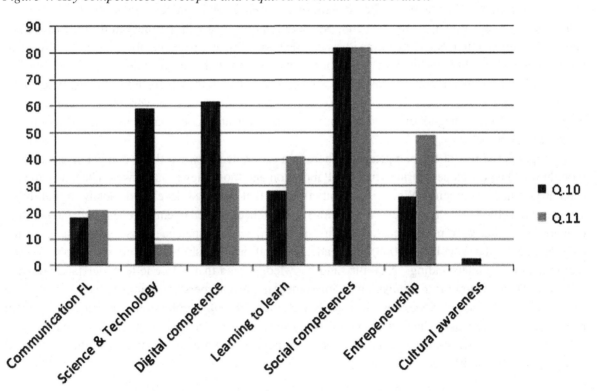

students also mentioned that effective virtual collaboration required entrepreneurial skills in the form of adapting to new situations, creativity, leadership, project management, initiative, and will to succeed whilst 16 (41%) claimed learning to learn competences were required in the form of organization and planning, problem-solving, critical and self-critical skills, autonomous work, and capacity to learn. Twelve (30.7%) students claimed they needed digital competences and information management skills, while 8 (20.5%) students mentioned the same of linguistic skills and appreciation of diversity. Finally, 3 (8%) students mentioned basic competences in science and technology in the form of capacity for synthesis and analysis and research skills.

In summary, for research question 1, the vast majority of students perceived social competences (team work abilities and interpersonal skills) as the competences they developed the most during the course, followed by digital competence (information management skills) and base knowledge of the subject area together with research skills, capacity for analysis and synthesis and decision-making abilities (basic competences in science and technology). As regards research question 2, social competences were also perceived as the most necessary to succeed in virtual collaboration by the vast majority of students. However, many students emphasized the need for entrepreneurial (in the form of adapting to new situations, creativity, leadership, project management, initiative and will to succeed) and learning to learn competences (in the form of organization and planning, problem-solving, critical and self-critical skills, and autonomous work) in order to succeed in virtual collaboration.

According to these findings, social competences were the competences most developed by participants and most necessary to succeed at virtual collaboration. This would be consistent with the nature of collaborative tasks. These require not only information exchange, discussion, and comparison but also working together in a team in order to achieve a consensus and produce a joint product or conclusion. These competences refer to managing personal relationships with partners in different contexts, and they require an understanding of the ideas and feelings of other group members based on a sense of tolerance and flexibility. For successful collaboration one needs to be responsible for one's own performance and that of other members, making relevant contributions to the group and following procedures in order to achieve a joint goal. However, individual members should also be capable of presenting and defending their ideas, negotiating, and proposing alternatives after considering the arguments offered by other team members.

As regards the rest of the competences, there is a difference between those competences students thought they had developed during virtual collaboration and those they thought were necessary to succeed at virtual collaboration. Whereas students thought that they had developed mostly digital, basic science and technology competences, it was those competences related to entrepreneurship and learning to learn skills that were most necessary for its success. These competences, also known as systemic competences (Villa & Poblete, 2008), are leadership abilities and skills that concern whole systems (combination of understanding, sensibility and knowledge), and that help one to understand complex relations. They require prior acquisition of instrumental and interpersonal competences and they are more difficult to acquire since they are usually developed through professional practice and critical reflection on this practice. The findings in this study suggest that experiencing and reflecting on virtual collaboration can have similar effects in the development of systemic competences to those achieved though professional practice.

CONCLUSION

This study presents some limitations that need to be considered. A questionnaire is a subjective assessment tool and since findings rely on the participants' perceptions, it is not possible to categorically state that any competence development actually took place. Moreover, cross-program and cross-institutional studies with larger sample sizes are required in order to ensure that results are significant. Despite these limitations, we were able to gain some insight from the students' perspectives based on their own experience which is essential in more flexible ICT based learning environments. The findings in this study indicate that virtual collaboration, when integrated in a classroom where content is taught through EMI, has the potential to foster the acquisition not only of base knowledge of the subject, but also of a variety of key competences for life-long learning. These included mostly social and digital competences, entrepreneurial and learning to learn skills, which also happen to be among the lesser assessed competences according to the European Commission (2010). Many of these competences are usually developed through work experience and, in this respect, virtual collaboration can equip students with the competences that they will need when they enter the labour market whilst still in education and training. Students also mentioned that they had developed linguistic skills in the foreign language, although this was a non-language subject. These findings seem to support current research in EMI and Content and Language Integrated Learning (CLIL) which suggests that implementing these approaches into the classroom can offer significant gains in the foreign language (Admiraal, Westhoff & de Boot, 2006). Therefore in future research projects, it would be worth exploring the impact that engaging students in virtual collaboration in either of these two environments has for foreign language development. Another aspect worth exploring in future studies is whether participants who experience virtual collaboration with peers from diverse cultural backgrounds develop certain specific interpersonal competences that those working in same-culture groups do not develop. Therefore, in future editions of this course we intend to connect students who are geographically distant from each other and are native speakers of the foreign language being used as a medium of instruction. Finally, experiential learning that engages students fully in the collaborative process with all that it entails (i.e. information exchange, discussion, negotiation, solving problems, providing feedback, and reaching a consensus) can facilitate more collaboration in return and increase the participants' awareness of the benefits it offers.

ACKNOWLEDGMENT

I would like to thank the book editors and the two anonymous reviewers for their insightful comments. This research was funded by the Spanish Ministry of Economy and Competitiveness (EDU2014-54673-R).

REFERENCES

Admiraal, W., Westhoff, G., & de Boot, K. (2006). Evaluation of bilingual secondary education in the Netherlands: Pupils' language proficiency in English. *Educational Research and Evaluation, 12*(1), 75–93. doi:10.1080/13803610500392160

Alsina, J., Boix, R., Burset, S., Buscà, F., Colomina, R., García, M., & Sayós, R. et al. (2011). *Evaluación por competencias en la Universidad: Las competencias transversales. Cuadernos de docencia universitaria 18*. Barcelona: Octaedro.

Belz, J. A., & Müller-Hartmann, A. (2003). Teachers negotiating German-American telecollaboration: Between a rock and an institutional hard place. *Modern Language Journal, 87*(1), 71–89. doi:10.1111/1540-4781.00179

Blömeke, S., Zlatkin-Troitschanskaia, O., Kuhn, C., & Fege, J. (Eds.). (2013). *Modeling and measuring competencies in higher education*. Rotterdam: Sense Publishers. doi:10.1007/978-94-6091-867-4

Boulos, M. N. K., Maramba, I., & Wheeler, S. (2006). Wikis, blogs and podcasts: A new generation of Web-based tools for virtual collaborative clinical practice and education. *BMC Medical Education, 6*(41). PMID:16911779

Bower, M., Woo, K., Roberts, M., & Watters, P. (2006). Wiki pedagogy - A tale of two wikis. *Proceedings of the 2006 7th International Conference on Information Technology Based Higher Education and Training* (pp. 209-220).

Brown, J. S., Collins, A., & Duguid, P. (1989). Situated cognition and the culture of learning. *Educational Researcher, 18*(1), 32–42. doi:10.3102/0013189X018001032

Coyle, D. (2005). Developing CLIL. Towards a theory of practice. *APAC Monographs, 6*, 5–29.

Dalton-Puffer, C. (Ed.). (2007). Empirical perspectives on CLIL classroom discourse. Frankfurt: Peter Lang.

Daniels, H. (2008). *Vygotsky and research*. Abingdon: Routledge.

Dearden, J. (2015). *British Council Report, English as a medium of instruction– a growing global phenomenon*. Oxford: University of Oxford.

Engeström, Y., Miettinen, R., & Punamäki, R. (1999). *Perspectives on activity theory*. Cambridge: Cambridge University Press. doi:10.1017/CBO9780511812774

European Commission. (2007). *Key competences for lifelong learning. European Framework of Reference*. Luxembourg: European Commission.

European Commission. (2010). *New skills for new jobs: Action now*. Retrieved from http://ec.europa.eu/social/main.jsp?catId=568&langId=en&eventsId=232&furtherEvents=yes

European Commission. (2012). *Europeans and their languages*. Retrieved from http://ec.europa.eu/public_opinion/archives/ebs/ebs_386_en.pdf

Eurydice. (2006). *Content and language integrated learning (CLIL) at schools in Europe*. Brussels: European Commission.

Eurydice. (2009). *National testing of pupils in Europe: Objectives, organisation and use of results*. Brussels: European Commission.

Fuchs, C., Hauck, M., & Müller-Hartmann, A. (2012). Promoting learner autonomy through multiliteracy skills development in cross-institutional exchanges. *Language Learning & Technology, 16*(3), 82–102.

González, J., & Wagenaar, R. (Eds.). (2003). *Tuning Educational Structures in Europe I.* Universidad de Deusto and Universidad de Groningen.

Guth, S., & Helm, F. (2011). Developing multiliteracies in ELT through telecollaboration. *ELT Journal, 66*(1), 42–51. doi:10.1093/elt/ccr027

Guth, S., Helm, F., & O'Dowd, R. (2012). *University Language Classes Collaborating Online. A Report on the Integration of Telecollaborative Networks in European Universities.* INTENT Project Final Report.

Hauck, M. (2010). Telecollaboration: At the interface between multimodal and intercultural communicative competence. In S. Guth & F. Helm (Eds.), *Telecollaboration 2.0* (pp. 219–244). Bern: Peter Lang.

Kinginger, C. (2000). Learning the pragmatics of solidarity in the networked foreign language classroom. In J. K. Hall & L. S. Verplaeste (Eds.), *Second and foreign language learning through classroom interaction* (pp. 23–46). Mahwah, NJ: Erlbaum.

Marin-Garcia, J., Aznar-Mas, L., & González-Ladrón-de-Gevara, F. (2011). Innovation types and talent management for innovation. *Working Papers on Operations Management, 2*(2), 25-31.

Marsh, D., Maljers, A., & Hartiala, A. K. (Eds.). (2001). Profiling European CLIL classrooms: languages open doors. University of Jyväskylä, Jyväskylä.

O'Dowd, R., & Ware, P. (2009). Critical issues in telecollaborative task design. *Computer Assisted Language Learning, 22*(2), 173–188. doi:10.1080/09588220902778369

OECD. (2005). *The definition and selection of key competencies.* Executive summary. DeSeCo Project. Retrieved from http://www.oecd.org/fr/edu/apprendre-au-dela-de-l-ecole/definitionandselectionofcompetenciesdeseco.htm

Palloff, R. M., & Pratt, K. (2005). *Collaborating online: Learning together in community.* San Francisco, CA: Jossey-Bass.

Penttilä, T., & Kairisto-Mertanene, L. (2012). Innovation competence barometer ICB - a tool for assessing students' innovation competences as learning outcomes in higher education. *Proceedings of INTED2012*, 6347–6351.

Sauro, S. (2009). Computer-mediated corrective feedback and the development of L2 grammar. *Language Learning & Technology, 13*(1), 96–120.

Shaw, S. (2006). New reality: Workplace collaboration is crucial. *Eedo Knowledgeware Whitepaper.* Retrieved through personal subscription.

Shuman, L. J., Besterfield-Sacre, M., & McGourty, J. (2005). The ABET "Professional skills" - Can they be taught? Can they be assessed? *The Journal of Engineering Education, 94*(1), 41–55. doi:10.1002/j.2168-9830.2005.tb00828.x

Smit, U., & Dafouz, E. (2012). Integrating content and language in higher education. An introduction to English-medium policies, conceptual issues and research practices across Europe. In Smit, U. & E. Dafouz (Eds.), Integrating Content and Language in Higher Education. Gaining Insights into English-Medium Instruction at European Universities. Special Issue of AILA Review, 25, 1-12. doi:10.1075/aila.25.01smi

Stohler, U. (2006). The acquisition of knowledge. *Vienna English Working Papers,* 3(6), 41-46.

Teodorescu, T. (2006). Competence versus competency: What is the difference? *Performance Improvement,* 45(10), 27–30. doi:10.1002/pfi.4930451027

UNESCO. (2003). *Education position paper: Education in a multilingual world.* Paris: United Nations Educational, Scientific and Cultural Organization.

Villa, A., & Poblete, M. (Eds.). (2008). *Competence-based Learning. A Proposal for the Assessment of Generic Competences.* Bilbao: Universidad de Deusto.

Vinagre, M. (2005). Fostering language learning by e-mail: An English-Spanish exchange. *Computer Assisted Language Learning,* 18(5), 369–388. doi:10.1080/09588220500442749

Vinagre, M. (2008). Politeness strategies in collaborative e-mail exchanges. *Computers & Education,* 50(3), 1022–1036. doi:10.1016/j.compedu.2006.10.002

Vinagre, M. (2010). *Teoría y práctica del aprendizaje colaborativo asistido por ordenador.* Madrid: Síntesis.

Vinagre, M. (forthcoming). Promoting intercultural competence in culture and language studies: Outcomes of an international collaborative project. In Martín-Monje, E., Elorza, I & García Riaza, B. (Eds.), Technological advances in specialized linguistic domains: Learning on the move (pp. 37-52). London: Routledge.

Vinagre, M., & Muñoz, B. (2011). Computer-mediated corrective feedback and language accuracy in telecollaborative exchanges. *Language Learning & Technology,* 15(1), 72–103. Retrieved from http://llt.msu.edu/issues/february2011/vinagremunoz.pdf

Von Der Emde, S., Schneider, J., & Kötter, M. (2001). Technically speaking: Transforming language learning through virtual learning environments (MOOs). *Modern Language Journal,* 85(2), 210–225. doi:10.1111/0026-7902.00105

Vygotsky, L. S. (1987). Thinking and speech. In *L. S. Vygotsky, collected works.* New York: Plenum.

Watts, F., Marín, J. A., García, A., & Aznar, L. E. (2012). Validation of a rubric to assess innovation competence. *Working Papers on Operations Management,* 3(1), 61-70.

Wheeler, S., Yeomans, P., & Wheeler, D. (2008). 'The good, the bad and the wiki: Evaluating student-generated content for collaborative learning'. *British Journal of Educational Technology,* 39(6), 987–995. doi:10.1111/j.1467-8535.2007.00799.x

Wilkinson, R. (Ed.). (2004). *Integrating content and language. Meeting the challenge of multilingual higher education*. Maastricht: Universitaire Pers Maastricht.

Wong, R. (2010). The effectiveness of using English as the sole medium of instruction in English classes: Student responses and improved English proficiency. *Porta Linguarum, 13*, 119–130.

KEY TERMS AND DEFINITIONS

Asynchronous Tools: These web-based tools allow users to communicate at their own convenience and based on their own schedule. Users do not communicate in real time, rather, they send or post messages to each other and check them when it is convenient to them. E-mail, wikis, blogs and discussion boards are all asynchronous online tools.

Collaborative Learning: A way of learning in which students at various performance levels work together in small groups towards a common goal. Reaching this goal is a joint endeavour and all group members are responsible for their own performance and that of others.

Key Competences for Life-Long Learning: These competences, also known as core or transversal competences, are a combination of knowledge, skills and attitudes particularly necessary for personal fulfillment and development, social inclusion, active citizenship and employment. They provide added value for the labour market.

Systemic Competences: Complex competences (knowledge, skills and attitudes) concerning whole systems. They are a combination of understanding, sensibility and knowledge and require prior acquisition of instrumental and interpersonal competences.

Virtual Collaboration: An approach to collaboration that integrates online tools as mediators in the interaction among group members (see collaborative learning).

Wikis: A web 2.0 asynchronous tool that can facilitate collaborative writing. It allows for multiple users to edit the same document, offers great flexibility in the management of information and can enhance social interaction.

ENDNOTES

[1]   Although some authors (Teodorescu, 2006) suggest that there are differences between the terms competence and competency, most dictionaries define them as synonyms and most studies use both terms interchangeably. In this paper, we have adopted the term competence since it is the term used by the European Commission in its European Reference Framework.

[2]   The European Commission's proposal also includes an eighth competence, namely *Communication in the mother tongue*, which we have excluded from this study since the participants' mother tongue was not used during the course.

APPENDIX A

Questions for Reflection, Unit 2

1. Why are we interested in using technologies within the paradigm known as computer supported collaborative learning?
2. What are the main theoretical principles underlying its application?
3. What are the objectives that can be achieved via virtual collaborative projects that are difficult to achieve in a face-to-face setting?
4. How can we justify the integration of collaborative virtual exchanges in the foreign language classroom?

Questions for Reflection, Unit 6

1. What are the main differences between the different models of virtual collaboration?
2. What are the positive and negative aspects of each model?
3. How would you summarize the main differences between the Cultura, e-Tandem and eTwinning models of virtual collaboration? Which one is most suitable for your students' needs and your pedagogical objectives?

Web pages provided for analysis:
   http://www.slf.ruhr-uni-bochum.de/etandem/etindex-es.html
   http://cultura.mit.edu/archives-2/
   http://www.etwinning.net/es/pub/index.htm
   http://interculture.wikispaces.com
   http://schoolsonline.britishcouncil.org/
   http://esleflstudents.edublogs.org/
   http://isabelperez.com/students.htm#Projects

Questions for Reflection, Unit 7

1.   How can we find classes-partners in other countries?
2.   How can we integrate these initiatives in the foreign language classroom?
3.   How long should a virtual collaborative project last?
4.   What are the pedagogical objectives that need to be considered when implementing a project of this kind?
5.   What topics should be discussed by the participants?
6.   What types of tasks are most appropriate for virtual collaboration?
7.   Should there be a focus on form? Why and how should it be integrated into the project?
8.   What aspects should be included in the project's guidelines?
9.   How can a project be evaluated? What aspects should be assessed?
10. What ICT tools (synchronous and/or asynchronous) should be used and why?
11. What criteria should be considered when making this decision?

APPENDIX B

Table 3. End- of-course questionnaire

		Completely Disagree	Disagree	Neither Agree nor Disagree	Agree	Completely Agree
1.	I can easily explain what CSCL or virtual collaboration means					
2.	I know the different models of online collaboration and the differences between them					
3.	I am familiar with the use of asynchronous and synchronous ICT tools					
4.	I know how to use web pages in order to find partners in other countries					
5.	I can organize a collaborative project of this kind and negotiate all aspects of the exchange					
6.	I know how to use the most adequate ICT tools (blogs, wikis, skype, etc.) to achieve the students' learning objectives					
7.	I feel confident using the ICT tools that we have explored in class					
8.	I know where to find web activities that I could integrate in the EFL classroom					
9.	If there is a tool that you don't feel confident using please specify which and why					
10.	What competences have you developed while working collaboratively online?					
11.	What competences are needed in order to work collaboratively online in a successful manner?					
12.	I would like to know about your experience on this course					
13.	I would like to hear any comments, ideas or opinions that might help improve this experience					

Chapter 9
Translanguaging in Multilingual Chat Interaction:
Opportunities for Intercomprehension between Romance Languages

Sílvia Melo-Pfeifer
University of Hamburg, Germany

ABSTRACT

In this contribution, intercomprehension between Romance Languages (RL) will be analyzed as a particular setting of multilingual interaction in the globalized and digital world. Intercomprehension is a multilingual practice where interlocutors collaboratively achieve meaning through the use of typologically related languages and other semiotic resources, exploiting the similarities existing across languages and the opportunities of transfer they offer. The communicative contract underlying this particular typology of multilingual interaction stresses that each interlocutor should master at least one RL and use it productively and, at the same time, try to understand the RL of the other speakers. Through the analysis of multilingual exchanges in chat-rooms of the platform Galanet, the need to take a more open stance towards the communicative contract will be evinced. Particularly, three behaviors related to the breakdown of the communicative contract – and respective consequences – will be critically analyzed: the use of a taboo language (English), the use of other linguistic resources not included in the contract and the production of utterances in target languages. These communicative behaviors will justify the need to enrich the understanding of intercomprehension by adopting a translingual lens and, thus, by abandoning a still prevalent monoglossic orientation in research dealing with this multilingual communicative context.

1. INTRODUCTION

Language education in the digital era is being confronted with the idea that linguistic borders are liquid and inadequate to explain linguistic phenomena or communication in super-diverse contexts (Canagarajah, 2013; Makony & Pennycook, 2007; Pennycook, 2010). From this perspective, language education should not be bound to a particular (foreign) language, but should engage with diversity and plurality in order

DOI: 10.4018/978-1-5225-0177-0.ch009

to achieve a holistic comprehension of the world's linguistic organization, management, manipulation, and dispensation:

Assumptions about the existence of languages and, ipso facto, multilingualism, are so deeply embedded in predominant paradigms of language studies that they are rarely questioned. Multilingualism, furthermore, viewed from this perspective, is an indomitably good thing; the task of linguists, sociolinguists, applied linguists and educational linguists is to enhance our understanding of multilingualism, to overcome the monolingual blinkers of Anglo- or Eurocentric thought, to encourage both understanding of and the practice of multilingualism. (Makoni & Pennycook, 2011, p. 439)

Furthermore, real linguistic practices are becoming semiotically more complex in the digital era. This is due to the multiplication of communicative resources, which introduces new sense-containers, i.e., new features able to create meaning (Jewitt, 2009), and creates new possibilities of meaning construction. Such complexity can be grasped through concepts such as translanguaging (Garcia & Wei, 2014), which refer to transemiotic communicative practices that crisscross several linguistic resources (or "bits of languages", according to Blommaert, 2010) and other semiotic codes, such as symbols or images.

In this contribution one specific context where translanguaging is particularly visible will be presented and analyzed: the chat conversations produced within the Galanet project (platform presently moved to http://miriadi.net/elgg/miriadi/home). This European project (developed between 2001 and 2004, but still producing new on-line sessions) aimed at creating multilingual contact situations across speakers from different Romance Languages (Catalan, French, Italian, Portuguese, Romanian, and Spanish). The Galanet platform includes several communicative tools (e-mail, discussion forum, and chat rooms) in order to provide opportunities for engaging with the project's philosophy: speaking a Romance Language (RL) and trying to understand the language(s) of the other RL speakers. This communicative philosophy is known as intercomprehension between RL. Intercomprehension, from this interactional perspective, is a multilingual communicative practice between speakers who do not make use of a common language during conversation, resorting instead to the use of their Mother Tongues to the use of their Mother Tongues (or other reference/known languages) in trying to understand each other. Intercomprehension between RL is based on the assumption that they are part of a linguistic *continuum*, and that a positive and systematic exploitation of similarities and differences between these languages can support language acquisition on the one hand, and be an alternative to monolingual communication on the other hand (Araújo e Sá, De Carlo & Melo-Pfeifer, 2010). Galanet multilingual chats thus foster intercomprehension through the simultaneous practice of several RL, both productive and receptive: productive, because participants may use and adapt the already known RL to communicate; and receptive, because those languages are used to access meaning in new, unknown languages, by means of cross-linguistic transfer. Seen dialogically, both productive and receptive orientations to intercomprehension foster co-construction of meaning and collaborative achievement in multilingual interaction in RL.

The research questions in this contribution are:

- How does using a translanguaging lens enrich the concept of intercomprehension between RL (from an interactional perspective)?
- Which dynamics and accomplishments characterize multilingual interaction in chat-rooms?
- How do interlocutors in multilingual RL chat sequences challenge linguistic contracts and language policing?

This contribution will unfold in three parts. In the first part, we draw on state of the art developments that relate to multilingual interaction and their main theoretical developments, in order to understand the Galanet project and the main tenets of the RL interactions being analyzed in the empirical section. The theoretical overview will highlight the importance and the consequences of analyzing instances of communicative contract breakdown. In the second part, we will present the Galanet project and platform, its communicative and multilingual foundations, and the dynamics following the contract breakdown. Finally, we will explore the consequences of the empirical study relating to the development of inter-comprehension as a valuable concept in foreign language education.

2. DIFFERENT GEOMETRIES OF MULTILINGUAL INTERACTION

Communication in the globalization (Kramsch, 2014) and digital era is still oriented by monolingual and monoglossic perspectives, ideologies, and norms (Canagarajah, 2013 and 2014; García, 2014; Pennycook, 2010). Indeed, common assumptions underlying communication are still permeated by monolingual communicative scenarios and the use of a single language, be it English or any other. The most basic assumption is that communication is possible when interlocutors make use of a common language, even if their competences in that language are very uneven. As stressed by S. Canagarajah:

We believe that for communication to be efficient and successful we should employ a common language with shared norms. These norms typically come from the native speaker's use of the language. We also believe that languages have their own unique systems and should be kept free of mixing with other languages for meaningful communication. I consider these assumptions as constituting a monolingual orientation to communication. (2013, p. 1)

Two analytical tendencies for multilingual interaction ruled by monoglossic and heteroglossic norms will be illustrated. For argumentative purposes, they will be called here "covert multilingual interaction", i.e., interactions where multilingualism is not acknowledged by speakers, and "overt multilingual interaction", i.e., interaction where multilingualism is acknowledged as a basic ingredient of the communicative context, respectively.

In unbalanced, monolingual scenarios, many studies have been concerned with the strategies deployed by interlocutors to achieve comprehension and solve communicative problems and clashes. Such situations cover interaction between so-called native and non-native speakers or between experts and non-experts, and describe how the most proficient speaker can foster communication and serve as a linguistic guide throughout the interaction. In such situations, even if the less proficient speaker of the language being used to communicate tries to reverse their non-expert status and calls for a more comprehensive and balanced status of the use of languages, communication is still very asymmetrical, and the more one speaker knows the language, the more power and voice they have. In such cases of "covert multilingual communication", multilingualism is suppressed in order to preserve the monolingual communicative contract and maintain the *status quo* of the interlocutors. Such preservation of the monolingual contract is carried out through the recall of linguistic and communicative norms – the native-like norms – by both the "expert" and the "non-expert" speaker. Common interactional features include asking for and providing linguistic assistance (missing lexical items, correction of syntax and intonation, for example), and engaging in repair sequences, in order to avoid or solve incomprehension.

Even if such situations are very uneven in terms of the management and sharing of linguistic repertoires, some features may help to ensure effective communication: first, the distribution and mutual acceptance of roles; second, the will to attend to a common goal; and third, the articulated use of linguistic, para-linguistic and non-linguistic resources. From this perspective, despite the uneven distribution of voice, linguistic, and communicative resources and communicative power, success in communication may still be attained through a "collaborative disposition", i.e., "the attitudes and skills multilinguals bring from their home communities" (Canagarajah, 2014, p. 90), such as language awareness, social values, and learning strategies. As the same author further explains:

Multilinguals bring a set of language assumptions, social orientation, and strategies of negotiation/learning that help them develop performative competence and engage in translingual practices. (2014, p. 91)

This perspective is more visibly present in studies dealing with explicit multilingual interaction, ruled by more flexible and open linguistic norms (classified by Canagarajah, 2014 within the Language Awareness subcategory, in his Cooperative Disposition model; see also Araújo e Sá & Melo, 2007 relating Language Awareness and Multilingual Interaction). In these studies, usually concerned with the management of two languages in the communication process, a more traditional perspective analyzed the interactive organization of linguistic resources, using heuristic concepts such as code-switching or code-mixing to describe instances of linguistic alternation (these concepts being used also in the study of "covert multilingual interaction"). This tradition led to a somewhat structuralist view of multilingual interactions, with a large emphasis on explaining the grammar of linguistic resources, dispensation, and allocation, relying on several contextual ingredients (interlocutors, themes, competences, etc.). A more recent perspective on bilingual interaction, however, abandons this focus on the code (or codes), and places the interlocutors at the heart of the linguistic management and co-achievements. This perspective is illustrated by concepts such as "translanguaging" (García & Wei, 2014) or "translingual practices" (Canagarajah, 2013). In this kind of interaction, the "native-like" norm is permanently re-negotiated and rebalanced by the acceptance of "alloglot interlocutor-like" norms or even by the recognition that any norm is just locally valid and temporarily binding. This acceptance includes, on the one hand, recognition of dynamic and multilayered communicative norms that go beyond linguistic resources and, on the other, collaborative manipulation and adjustment *of* and *to* those locally and temporarily required norms (Canagarajah, 2013; Pennycook, 2010).

The next section, following developments in the study of multilingual interactions, a critical stance toward intercomprehension is adopted, questioning its normative and monoglossic assumptions. This critical stance will be fundamental to understanding the empirical research in parts 3 and 4.

2.1. Intercomprehension between Romance Languages as a Particular Case of Multilingual Interaction

In order to understand the general context of Galanet and the multilingual interactions analyzed, it should first be explained how and where intercomprehension as a research field was born, which principles underlie it and how those principles can be questioned.

Intercomprehension is a concept introduced in Europe to challenge the routines of language teaching and learning (Capucho, 2008; Capucho et al, 2007; Doyé & Meissner, 2010; Meissner et al, 2011) as well as the increasing monolingualism of the European foreign language education curriculum. It also challenges monolingual ideologies in communication, namely the idea that a *lingua franca* is always necessary when speakers do not share a common language (Melo-Pfeifer, Araújo e Sá & Santos, 2012). Even if the concept particularly stresses the value of intercomprehension in communication, most of the research carried out tries to understand the processes underlying receptive multilingualism, i.e., the comprehension of oral and written texts in several languages of a same linguistic family, within a cognitive tradition (Melo-Pfeifer, 2011).

The mainstream definition states that intercomprehension, from an interactional perspective, relates to a situation where a speaker uses one language and understands the (different) language used by the other(s) interlocutor(s). Such a situation of cross-comprehension is possible through lexical, grammatical, semantic and pragmatic similarities that exist across languages, namely when occurring between RLs (or other linguistic families). However, even if it can be called a "fluid language practice" (García & Leiva, 2014: 200), intercomprehension is still embedded within a monoglossic standpoint, as the languages used to communicate are said to keep separate, one being used productively and the other being targeted receptively. Therefore, even if this concept already challenges monolingual communicative norms and dismisses old assumptions related to the use of a single language, a critical stance may still be necessary to take a step towards a more heteroglossic and integrated use of linguistic and other semiotic resources in communication.

Within a heteroglossic perspective that highlights "social tensions inherent to language" (Bailey, 2011: 499), intercomprehension is a concept that illustrates how translanguaging works in a "radical" multilingual environment, i.e., in communicative settings where several languages are accepted as valid meaning-containers and meaning-makers, and where several interlocutors mobilize, share and co-construct their multilingual resources. Such a complex linguistic and communicative setting helps to understand intercomprehension between RLs not just in terms of the multiplicity of linguistic resources being used, but also and foremost in terms of the complex geometry of these resources in action and use (Blackledge & Creese, 2014). The main studies on translanguaging and translingual practice have dealt with multilingual communicative situations where two or three "traditional codes" overlap and merge to achieve social meaning. Focusing on intercomprehension between RL where potentially all RL, dialects, codes, and registers can be used, may thus enlarge the scope of phenomena observed through a "translanguaging" lens, as heteroglossic elements (intra- and inter- language variation and relationships, mobility, flux and voices) are much more visible and variable.

From that interactional and intersubjective perspective, intercomprehension defies and even resists the commonly accepted monolingual alignment of speakers during interaction. Indeed, intercomprehension in RL postulates the following six principles (Melo-Pfeifer, 2015, p. 102):

- Languages belonging to this family are part of a linguistic *continuum* that has no clear borders, making RL necessarily heteroglossic and carrying other voices;
- This linguistic *continuum* allows interlocutors to effectively engage in conversations;
- In multilingual communication, interlocutors develop creative and supplementary strategies to collaboratively achieve social meaning;
- Performing multilingual RL communication dynamically engages interlocutors in the co-construction of context, forms and meaning, community solidarity and linguistic well-being;

- The so-called productive and receptive skills in RL are dialogically dependent and can be deployed through several linguistic resources at the same time;
- Intercomprehension between RLs is multisemiotic and multimodal and should not be jaded by and analyzed through a linguistic hegemonic perspective.

This understanding of intercomprehension legitimates a socio-constructivist stance that posits the co-construction of meaning as the center of the conversational analysis: meaning making is thus a social practice that involves ecological and contextual cues (Canagarajah, 2013, p. 12; also Bono & Melo-Pfeifer, 2011), as meaning is not given in advance but results from situated interactional cooperation and work.

To sum up: from an interactional perspective, intercomprehension between RL is a particular geometry of overt multilingual communication, where a lexical item or an utterance, prompts the recall of its equivalents in other bordering languages, allowing for a permanent interplay and merging of semiotic resources and their use for meaning-making purposes. In this situation, the communicative contract is permanently multilingual, the emergence of all RL being allowed from the beginning, all interlocutors being experts in some of the languages in use. Originally, the interactional perspective of intercomprehension stresses a monoglossic view of this sort of multilingual interaction (where languages are kept separate within the same linguistic family, divided into productive and receptive resources) and is deeply concerned with the maintenance of the multiplicity of the linguistic resources during interaction. However, a more heteroglossic perspective of intercomprehension is needed in order to: i) grasp the complexity of use of intersected and multilayered semiotic resources; and ii) avoid essentializing intercomprehension as merely an alternate and juxtaposed use of languages belonging to a same linguistic family. The empirical study here presented, based on the analysis of violations of the linguistic contract by speakers, will provide evidence for the importance of adopting a more open and heteroglossic perspective of both intercomprehension between RL and multilingual interaction as a whole.

3. THE GALANET PROJECT AS AN INNOVATIVE PEDAGOGICAL MODEL FOR MULTILINGUAL LANGUAGE EDUCATION

3.1 The Platform

Galanet was an on-line platform developed within the scope of a homonymous European project (funded by the European Commission, between 2001 and 2004, and coordinated by Christian Degache). The goal was to provide plurilingual intercomprehension opportunities among individuals through synchronous chat as well as through asynchronous modes such as forums. The Galanet venue allowed university students from RL countries to collaborate. For instance, collaboration consisted of the production of a "press dossier" on an intercultural theme previously negotiated between the participants. Galanet thus fosters intercomprehension by directly proposing a multilingual collaborative scenario, based on interaction between participants from different countries as a starting point to the co-creation of a final document.

Figure 1 illustrates the design of the virtual spaces and their organization.

The platform can be described as being visually organized around two metaphors: time and space. In terms of the temporal metaphor, a Galanet session happens in 4 interdependent and sequential phases (Araújo e Sá, De Carlo & Melo-Pfeifer, 2010), as can be seen in Figure 1 (left side) and Table 1. These 4 phases lead up to the multilingual end-product already mentioned.

Figure 1. Visualization of the Galanet home page

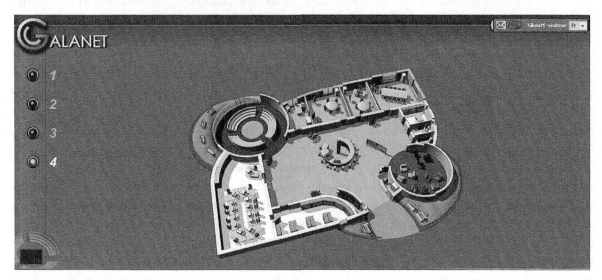

Table 1. The chronological development of a session

Phase	Activities
breaking the ice and choice of theme	- Participants create profiles, introduce themselves to one another, share ideas about projects and what they hope to accomplish as well as their motivations for ideas about projects; - Participants come up with different categories of discussion, share their opinions, and determine which category or theme they will focus and reflect upon;
brainstorming	- Participants brainstorm to come up with sub-categories of their topics to develop a more "press dossier" with specific editorial parameters.
collecting documents and debate	- Participants look for, present, and discuss materials make references to illustrate each sub-category.
elaborating and publishing the press dossier	- Each team prepares a concise summary of debates, a written synthesis of each debate, consolidating the press dossier, and incorporates addition of diverse aspects to the discussion.

(Araújo e Sá, De Carlo & Melo-Pfeifer, 2010).

In terms of virtual spaces, the platform visually reproduces different work settings: welcome desk (center), private bureau, library (bottom left) and resource center (next to the library), forum (top left), meeting room (top right), and open chat spaces (bottom right). All these spaces have a different function within a session:

- Areas for engaging with other participants in synchronous or asynchronous on-line multilingual conversations (discussion forums, chats and e-mail);
- Areas to deepen knowledge about a particular RL or about the functioning of on-line and multilingual communication (library);
- Areas for developing particular competences, usually written or oral receptive skills in several RL, depending on the "reference language" (resource center);
- Areas for accomplishing collaborative tasks and producing the "press dossier" (meeting room).

Since the interactions that will be analyzed in this contribution took place in the discussion chat rooms of this platform, a closer look at their design may help to understand the nature of the interactions, providing contextual cues. The platform has three chat rooms (Figure 2), and all participants are aware that interactions will be chronologically saved and stored in a database, and, thus, available to other participants.

In the initial phase of Galanet, the design team was only concerned with the RL repertoires and goals of the students, other languages being given lower status and functions, limiting the expression of a fully multilingual identity. This is visible, for example, in the fact that all participants have to define their starting and target RL in order to get accepted in a session. Only when editing their linguistic profile could participants' full linguistic repertoires be filled in and consequently accessed by other participants. This concern with RL-only is related to the concept of intercomprehension as it was understood at the time of the creating the platform. This concept, as mentioned in section 2, was embedded in a political ideology of fighting linguistic hegemony and the use of a *lingua franca* (namely English) in multilingual encounters, and aimed at understanding the functioning of partial linguistic receptive abilities between RL. Thus, these concerns had a deep impact on both the design of the platform and its initial presuppositions, consequently also affecting how participants behaved.

3.2 Session and Participants

During the Canosession (presented here, the second intercomprehension session in the Galanet platform, held between February and May 2004), 13 teams from 6 different countries (Argentina, Belgium, France, Italy, Portugal and Spain) participated in the session (236 participants in total, students and tutors counted together). The participants identify themselves by means of a nickname and are organized in teams, by

Figure 2. The three chat rooms

universities and countries. It must also be stated that during Canosession these university students used the platform mostly in a blended-learning format, being accompanied by the university teacher/tutor in foreign language courses. This author accompanied the Portuguese teams, being a tutor in the French course. One hour of regular class time was allocated for use of the platform within the classroom, but the students could use it to communicate with other university students whenever they wanted to.

There were two Portuguese teams (34 participants), four French teams (62 participants), two Spanish teams (70 participants) and two Italian teams (34 participants). Argentina and Belgium had one team each, with 14 and 8 participants respectively. In terms of linguistic profiles, French is a common *lingua franca*, as it is shared by all the teams involved in the project, alongside the official language of each country. Furthermore, it is also a target language for all teams, except the French ones. So, every team has at least a bilingual profile and seeks to develop intercomprehension skills in the other languages of the platform.

All the participants, both students and tutors, declared having some degree of proficiency in different "linguistic mobile resources" (Blommaert, 2010) acquired at school or in other contexts. The communicative situations in this project (and being elicited by it) can be described as multi-plurilingual (see Ehrhart, 2010), as plurilingual individual repertoires co-exist in a multilingual virtual social space (Melo-Pfeifer, 2015).

The linguistic contract in this first intercomprehension Session in Galanet states that each interlocutor should speak their language(s) and try to understand the other RL. These communicative rules will generate several "resistance acts", namely:

- Using English in some utterances, the *lingua franca* of multilingual encounters (see Melo-Pfeifer, 2014 for a full account);
- Employing other linguistic resources available in the individual repertoires, not belonging to a RL but specified in the full linguistic profile;
- Defying the "receptive clause" of the contract and producing utterances not only in the "reference languages" (the languages participants already "master") but also in the so-called "target languages", i.e. in the languages participants are expected to make an effort to understand.

The chosen theme in the chosen session was "Ridiamo per le stesse cose?... Y a-t-il un humour romanophone?" ("Do we laugh at the same things?... Is there a Romance Language humour?"), and the examples discussed in this contribution originate from discussions around this intercultural theme.

4. METHODOLOGY: ANALYSIS OF MULTILINGUAL CHAT SEQUENCES

Chat sessions were automatically saved on the platform, a fact that all participants were aware of during their interactions. In order to be studied, all chat sessions were printed and all 25 instances of linguistic contract violation through the introduction of a non-RL were analyzed. Furthermore, we also analyzed instances of use of languages being declared "target RL". The aim was to uncover the tensions between intercomprehension principles, as described in the communicative and linguistic contract, and the actual behaviours of the participants.

Such episodes illustrate how:

1. Individual agency defies the pre-given communicative; and
2. Such rebelliousness impacts other speakers' attitudes and linguistic behaviors (such as "language policing").

In other words, the analyzed episodes will highlight the tensions within and between individual *repertoires* and communicative *codes* and the communicative contract.

The analysis will focus on the three "acts of resistance" (and subsequent acts of "language policing") previously presented: use of English, use of non-romance linguistic resources, and production in a target RL. This will allow us to grasp the connections between intercomprehension and translanguaging. All the excerpts will be reproduced with the orthography as used by participants.

4.1 *"Ciao Sono Benedetto da Cervaro Italy How Do You Do?"*: Using a Taboo Language (English)

As already noted, using English in RL interactions is seen as some sort of "communicative depravity", since one of the aims of the project is to fight against linguistic hegemony within multilingual interaction. As English is frequently said to diminish linguistic resources in such situations, any utterance made in English is usually and immediately remarked upon and even censored. The rule of avoiding English is so important that "language policing" (Blommaert et al, 2009) is taken up by some participants (usually tutors, but not exclusively), who recall the linguistic contract for chat communication. In this context, language policing is, following Blommaert et al (2009), any discursive action of production of linguistic "order", executed by chat participants, in order to ensure the maintenance of the linguistic contract.

Because of its potential for face-threatening, language policing is usually performed through play and surrounded by humor and several other face protecting discursive strategies. One such episode of linguistic challenge and policing is transcribed in Table 2.

In this excerpt, Benedetto, a student from Italy, introduces himself in Italian, but mixes English in his initial production. Djose, an Italian tutor, promptly takes on the role of linguistic moderator and reminds Benedetto of the communicative contract: not only should communication happen exclusively in RL, but also that English is a proscribed language (*"Benedetto qui nos si parla ingles"*). Because of this "linguistic fine", potentially perceived as face-threatening, other participants greet Benedetto in Italian: ValeriaT answers Benedetto's question ("How do you do?") and ElenaT tells the new interlocutor they are welcome in the chat room. So, language policing is perceived as endangering participants' contributions and thus as a potential source of silencing. In order to minimize these dangers and to keep speakers' discursive engagement, other participants produce positive appraisals towards contributions.

Table 2. Language policing in Romance language chat rooms

Original	English Translation
[Benedetto] Ciao sono benedetto da Cervaro Italy how do you do? Mi piace il calcio e sono tifoso della lazio. (IT and EN)	[Benedetto] Hello! I am benedetto from Cervaro Italy *how do you do?* I like football and I am a great fan of lazio.
[djose] Benedetto qui nos si parla ingles (IT)	[djose] Benedetto we don't speak English here
[ValeriaT] ciao benedetto io sono valeria di campobasso e invece sono juventina col cuore (IT)	[ValeriaT] Hi benedetto I am valeria from campobasso and instead I am a fan of Juventus
[ElenaT] Ciao Benedetto, benvenuto ! (IT)	[ElenaT] Hi Benedetto, welcome !

In other excerpts (see Melo-Pfeifer, 2014 for a full account), Floquet, a member of the Belgian team, reminds a Portuguese student who produced an utterance in English, about the language policy in the platform and about the censorship she will be facing if she keeps using a forbidden language ("aie quelqu'un qui parle anglais dans ce projet, il vas se faire éjecter:-)" / "aie anyone who speaks English in this project will get themselves ejected:-)"). The menace of suppression as punishment has both symbolic and ironic value, since the use of English, the acknowledged language of global communication, threatens the speakers' voice and presence in the chat room. The action of "contract resistance" by that Portuguese student and the act of "language policing" (even if smiling) by Floquet, illustrates the tensions in a multilingual setting, where linguistic ideologies, on the one hand, and individual practices and aspirations, on the other, collide.

In some situations, English is used to overcome linguistic and communicative problems (Melo-Pfeifer, 2014). In the excerpt presented in Table 3, occurring between three Portuguese speakers (Qalbu, Carla and Xander), a French tutor (ChristianD), a Spanish Tutor living in France (Colombia), and a Spanish student (LauraA), the use of the Spanish word "cosquillas" (tickles) is linguistically opaque. It instigates the emergence of several discursive strategies to remediate it: interlocutors mobilize several languages (French, Spanish, and English) and even onomatopoeias ("guili-guili") to overcome the lexical problem.

In this example, strategies such as giving synonyms of the opaque word in several RL ("cosquillas = chatouilles = soletico") or even providing an onomatopoeia ("guili-guili=cosquillas") are combined with the translation of the unknown word into Portuguese ("cócegas") and English ("tickles"). The pragmatic and utilitarian function of this translation into English in this particular situation could be discussed, as the problem had already been solved by other participants. However, it is claimed here that the "communicative habitus" of multilingual interaction prompts Xander, a Portuguese student, to use English as a remediation strategy with the other Portuguese student, as this language is often assumed to be a problem-safe or a problem solving instrument. In this situation, unlike the previous one, language policing is not activated, perhaps because solving a problem is seen as a collective mission, to be solved by all means, "côute qui côute". So, English as a "mal necessaire" is tolerated in order to return to the discussion.

In other situations, however, even if communication is not severely impaired by the misunderstanding of certain vocabulary, English is perceived as a guaranteed platform of understanding. This perception is illustrated in Table 4, which displays a potential communicative clash between Spanish (JavierT and PauV) and Portuguese (Xander) students.

Table 3. English as a remediation tool in multilingual interaction

Original	English Translation
[LauraA] pero que te hacen para reirte? cosquillas? chistes? (ES)	[LauraA] but what do they do to you to make you laugh?
[qalbu] que é cosquillas?????????? (PT and ES)	Cosquillas (tickles)? jokes?
[ChristianD] chatouilles (FR)	[qalbu] what is cosquillas??????????
[colombia] des guili-guili=cosquillas (FR and ES)	[ChristianD] chatouilles
[ChristianD] cosquillas = chatouilles = soletico (ES, FR and IT)	[colombia] some guili-guili=cosquillas
[qalbu] je ne comprends pas (FR)	[ChristianD] cosquillas = chatouilles = soletico
[qalbu] CÓCEGAS?? (PT)	[qalbu] I don't understand
[carla] cocegas (PT)	[qalbu] CÓCEGAS (TICKLES)??
[xander] tickles (EN)	[carla] cocegas
[ChristianD] je sais pas en portugais (FR) "cosquillas"? (ES)	[xander] tickles
[qalbu] brigado (PT)	[ChristianD] I don't know in Portuguese
[ChristianD] cocegas, grazie (PT and IT)	"cosquillas"?[qalbu] thanks
	[ChristianD] cocegas, thanks

Table 4. Overcoming communicative clashes through English

Original	English Translation
[xander] que es "mosqueó" ???? (ES)	[xander] what is "mosqueó" ????
[JavierT] yo entiendo mejor hablando a un chino que a un portugués, en serio (ES)	[JavierT] I understand a chinese [person] better than a Portuguese [person], really
[PauV] enfadarse (ES)	[PauV] annoyed
[PauV] mosqueae=enfadar (ES)	[PauV] mosqueae=to bother
[JavierT] un poco menos que enfadarse (ES)	[JavierT] a bit less than annoy
[xander] porque no te gusta los portugueses???? (ES)	[xander] why don't you like Portuguese people????
[xander] hablas ingles? (ES)	[xander] do you speak English?

In this excerpt, Spanish could be said to play the role of *lingua franca* and this monolingual orientation is not questioned. The Portuguese student adapts his linguistic resources and uses Spanish instead of his mother tongue. Because participants are sensitive to the thematic path in this excerpt, and perhaps because English is perceived as a more neutral linguistic resource to keep on discussing a delicate issue ("porque no te gusta los portugueses????"/"Why don't you like portuguese people????"), a second stance of monolingual orientation is suggested by Xander ("hablas ingles?"/"Do you speak English?"), who can see his face threatened by two factors. The first factor is linguistic and is related to the use of a foreign language, the language being used to depreciate Portuguese; the second factor is thematic and is related to the unsympathetic statements towards Portuguese people and language being made by the Spanish conversational partners (despite the obvious linguistic similarities between Portuguese and Spanish, JavierT choses to underline the comprehension problems between those languages and refers to Chinese as easier to understand than Portuguese). In this case, then, the suggestion of using English as language of communication, even if perceived on the Galanet platform as taboo, is an attempt to introduce a new balance in face, voice and power between participants.

4.2 "*La Hacemos Romana Pues*": Attempting to Expand the Semiotic Resources Allowed

It has already been mentioned that speakers did not abide by the rules of the communicative and linguistic contract. Another instance of violating the contract and exposing its fragilities is the use of non-RL that integrate the multilingual repertoires of the participants, such as Arabic, Chinese, English, Flemish, Fulani and German. The following example illustrates the attempt to expand the linguistic resources allowed and, once again, the language policing of other participants but also shows acts of "self-defense" (Table 5).

In this excerpt, qalbu, a Portuguese participant that uses an Arabic nickname ("qalbu" means "heart" in Arabic), introduces this language in the chat conversation. Even if this introduction is not subjected to direct language policing, its use requires an explanation, which can be said to be an indirect act of language policing ("Why do you always say salame-alekum?"). An explanation is provided by another team member: Qalbu is studying Arabic and this language can be considered a part of his linguistic repertoire. The explanation is accepted and prompts no further questions.

In other cases, the use of German prompts explicit language policing by means of three different discursive strategies. One is recalling of the RL contract. Another argument used by "language police officers" is the fact that German is a difficult language, making it difficult to understand for other participants. Finally, the prohibition is extended to English, as neither language is a RL.

Table 5. The use of a non-Romance language (Arabic)

Original	English Translation
[qalbu] salame-alekum	[qalbu] salame-alekum
[guidiguidi] obrigada	[guidiguidi] thank you
[AvataraA] hola qalbu	[AvataraA] hello qalbu
[AvataraA] de donde eres?	[AvataraA] where are you from?
[lusitana] alekum salam, 9	[lusitana] alekum salam, 9
[lusitana] ;)	[lusitana] ;)
[guidiguidi] portugal	[guidiguidi] portugal
[ChristianD] Pourquoi qalbu dis-tu toujours salame-alekum?	[ChristianD] Why do you always say salame-alekum?
[carla] hola,salut, olá a todos!	[carla] hola,salut, hello everybody!
[guidiguidi] nao sabe dizer outra coisa	[guidiguidi] He doesn't know anything else to say
[tita] salut	[tita] hello
[AvataraA] hola carla	[AvataraA] hello carla
[carla] qalbu dit ça parce qui'il etufe arabe	[carla] qalbu says that because he studies arabic

Observing violations of the RL-Only rule makes it clear that "resisting" and "language policing" go hand in hand: resisting is related to the extended linguistic repertoires that speakers bring to the communicative effort and that they wish to show off; language policing is related to the linguistic contract but also to individual interests. In this chat conversation, claiming that a language is difficult or that one does not understand it, as it reveals attitudes and stereotypes towards languages, should not be considered a valid argument to exclude a language. In the specific case of German, as it is not a taboo language and is not seriously seen as threatening the multilingual nature of the communicative situation, linguistic boundaries, and stereotypes related to difficulty are combined to ensure its restriction.

In other situations, instead of language policing, violations of the linguistic contract may prompt several requests to expand the linguistic resources being used, as well as a discussion about linguistic biographies and relationships between languages (example in Table 6). In this situation, Mokab and SilviaM actively use more linguistic resources than the allowed Mother Tongue (Portuguese) and even their other reference RL (French). Annelisa, in turn, attached to the French team but who has Flemish as a Mother Tongue (not included with the linguistic contract), uses Italian to greet the participants already in the chat room ("ciao a tutti!").

In this situation, the presence of members of the French team with Flemish as a Mother Tongue prompts the Portuguese interlocutors to elicit the production of utterances in a language not included in the linguistic contract and, furthermore, to produce speech acts in that same language, through imitation and adaptation of the resources. Both Portuguese participants actively use the recently-learnt Flemish resources, merging them into Portuguese ("*Kits para ti também:)))*") or approximating the newly received Germanic resources ("*ik ben 22 jaar.*") to productive resources available in languages of the same "forbidden" linguistic family ("*Ich bin 26 jahre alt*"). This disrespect for the linguistic philosophy of the Galanet project (increased by the use of English in "PLEASE!!!") does not seem to worry the participants. Indeed, Annalisa attends to Mokab's and SilviaM's requests ("ecrit un petit peu en flamand!" and "Escreve algo em Flamand....", respectively) and introduces herself in Flemish. Only when a German translation of "ik ben 22 jaar" is provided by SilviaM do attitudes of language policing emerge ("ohlala mais tu réponds en allemand! c'est pas la meme chose hè"), started and finished by humoristic speech chunks close to orality ("ohlala" and "hè"). This episode shows once more that both challenging the communicative contract and language policing (in this case by recalling linguistic borders between different Germanic languages) are more easily performed through play and humour.

Table 6. The use of non-RL (Flemish and German)

Original	English Translation
[Annalisa] ciao a tutti! (IT)	[Annalisa] Hello everybody!
[SilviaM] Olá Annalisa! (PT)	[SilviaM] Hello Annalisa!
[mokab] Olá Annalisa! De onde vens? (PT)	[mokab] Hello Annalisa! Where are you from?
[Annalisa] de belgica! (PT)	[Annalisa] from Belgium!
[Annalisa] y tu? (ES)	[Annalisa] and you?
[SilviaM] Oh eu adora a Bélgica!!!!!! (PT)	[SilviaM] Oh I love Belgium!!!!!!
[SilviaM] Sou de Aveiro! (PT)	[SilviaM] I am from Aveiro!
[mokab] J'adore ce pays! On peut parler en français! (FR)	[mokab] I love that country! We can speak in French!
[Annalisa] bien sur! (FR)	[Annalisa] of course!
[SilviaM] De que parte da Bélgica es? (PT)	[SilviaM] Which part of Belgium are you from?
[Annalisa] de flandre, c'est le nord (FR)	[Annalisa] from Flanders, it's the north
[SilviaM] Alors, tu parle le flamand????? (FR)	[SilviaM] so, you speak Flemish?????
[mokab] Je viens d'Aveiro, une belle ville portugaise. Tu as déja visité mon pays? (FR)	[mokab] I am from Aveiro, a beautiful Portuguese city. Have you already visited my country?
[Annalisa] oui (FR)	[Annalisa] yes
[SilviaM] Juste un peu, juste un peu.... (FR)	[SilviaM] just a little bit, just a little bit....
[SilviaM] Escreve algo em Flamand.... (PT and FR)	[SilviaM] write something in Flemish....
[Annalisa] non j ai de la famillen qui habite en algarve (FR)	[Annalisa] no I didn't. I have family that lives in Algarve
[Annalisa] ok!	[Annalisa] ok!
[mokab] ecrit un petit peu en flamand! PLEASE!!! (FR and EN)	[mokab] write a little bit of Flemish! PLEASE!!!
[SilviaM] Escreve flamanego:(Vá lá!!!!!(PT)	[SilviaM] Write Flemish:(Come on!!!!!
[Annalisa] hallo alles kits? (FL)	[Annalisa] hallo alles kits?
[Annalisa] ik ben 22 jaar. en jij? (FL)	[Annalisa] ik ben 22 jaar. en jij?
[SilviaM] Kits para ti também:))) (FL and PT)	[SilviaM] Kits to you too:)))
[mokab] Qu'est-ce que ça veut dire? (FR)	[mokab] What does that mean?
[SilviaM] Ich bin 26 jahre alt (DE)	[SilviaM] I am 26 years old
[Annalisa] ohlala mais tu réponds en allemand! C'est pas la meme chose hè (FR)	[Annalisa] ohlala but you answer in German! It is not the same thing hè
[mokab] Ik ben 24 jaar! Chouette, je sais parler déjà un petit peu de flamand! (FL and FR)	[mokab] Ik ben 24 jaar! Cool, I can already speak a little bit of Flemish!
[Annalisa] parfait! (FR)	[Annalisa] perfect!

4.3 "*Parla Avec Noi? (J'essai d'écrire en Italien)*": Defying the Multilingual Receptive Contract

The communicative contract used in the Galanet platform imposes another restriction, as already revealed: the differentiation of receptive and productive skills according to the linguistic profile. In the following examples (Table 7), all participants violate the communicative contract, as they do not abide by the rule of exclusively speaking their own language(s) while attempting to understand those of the other participants.

In this excerpt, the Portuguese participants (Mokab and SilviaM) and the Italian student, clearly ignore the rule of producing only in the RL reference language(s). Moreover, production in the target languages is made discursively explicit, as the participants visibly proclaim lack of expertise in the language they attempt to use ("Oppps.... mi ctalán es un atentado al catalan de verdad....." and "no, yo sé un poquito de espanol") or they overtly signal their approximation to the languages of the other participants ("Andrea, que passa? parla avec noi? (J'essai d'écrire en italien;)").

Related to these attempts to expand the semiotic resources (previous section) is the constant demand for producing in languages not included in the linguistic contract: Catalan. Even if it is a RL, it was not included in this particular session in the project, and its use leads all the participants to partially switch

Table 7. Producing in the RL target languages

Original	English Translation
[mokab] Elia, diz alguma coisa ao italiano? mas em catalão! (PT)	[mokab] Elia, say something to the Italian? But in Catalan!
[EliaC] si voleu puc parlar en català perque el italià tampoc ho he estudiat (CAT)	[EliaC] if you want I can speak Catalan, because I haven't studied Italian
[SilviaM] parla catalá.... (CAT)	[SilviaM] speak Catalan....
[Andreag] tu puedes parlar en espanol (ES and IT)	[Andreag] You can speak Spanish
[SilviaM] NOOO: kiero catalá.... (ES and CAT)	[SilviaM] NOOO: I what Catalan....
[EliaC] jo parlo el que vosaltres volgueu (CAT)	[EliaC] I speak what you wish me to
[mokab] Catalá no lo sei! (CAT and ES)	[mokab] I don't know Catalan!
[SilviaM] io volgueu catalá...(CAT)	[SilviaM] I want Catalan...
[EliaC] yo hablo lo que vosotros querais (ES)	[EliaC] I speak whatever you want
[SilviaM] Oppps.... mi ctalán es un atentado al catalan de verdad.... (ES)	[SilviaM] Oppps.... My Catalan is an offense to real Catalan....
[EliaC] llavors, Silvia tu has estudiat català? (CAT)	[EliaC] So, Silvia have you studied Catalan?
[SilviaM] no, nunc.... Pero hecho trabajos de comprensión del catalan.... (CAT and ES)	[SilviaM] no, never.... But I did some works of Catalan comprehension....
[EliaC] mokab, el català es una llengua molt facil d'entendre, no et preocupis segur que ho entens tot (CAT)	[EliaC] mokab, Catalan is a very easy to understand language, don't worry, you will surely understand everything
[Andreag] no, yo sé un poquito de espanol (ES)	[Andreag] no, I know a little bit of Spanish
[SilviaM] Se puede comprender muy muy bien.... que idioma encantador, chica!!!! (ES)	[SilviaM] It can be understood very very well.... what a charming language, girl!!!!
[SilviaM] Me encantaria poder hablar catalan... (ES)	[SilviaM] I would love to be able to speak Catalan...
[EliaC] a mi méagraderia parlar portugues i italia... (CAT)	[EliaC] I would love to speak Portuguese and Italian...
[EliaC] la veritat que quan comences a estudiar idiomas no pots parar..o almenys això em passa a mi (CAT)	[EliaC] the truth is that when you start learning languages, you can't stop... At least that is the case with me
[SilviaM] Eu tambem sou assim! é o feitiço das línguas... (PT)	[SilviaM] I'm like that as well! It is the languages' feitiço (spell)...
[EliaC] feitiço?? (PT)	[EliaC] feitiço??
[SilviaM] hechizo (ES)	[SilviaM] Spell
[SilviaM] se escribe así? (ES)	[SilviaM] do you write it like this?
[EliaC] si, muy bien (ES)	[EliaC] yes, very good
[SilviaM] Yupppiiiiiiii!	[SilviaM] Yupppiiiiiiii!
[SilviaM] Algunas palabras las escribo como me suenan.... (ES)	[SilviaM] Some words I write the way they sound to me....
[mokab] Andrea, que passa? parla avec noi? (J'essai d'écrire en italien;) (IT and FR)	[mokab] Andrea, what is wrong? Speak with us? (I try to write Italian;)

to Catalan or to include Catalan fragments in their written discourse (for example: "io volgueu catalá..."), in no way embarrassed by the lack of correctness or by the partial skills in the language. So, EliaC, as a (self-) recognized expert in this language, uses both Catalan and Spanish to communicate, sometimes translating from one language to the other in order to promote comprehension ("jo parlo el que vosaltres volgueu" and "yo hablo lo que vosotros querais"). Because the production in this new target language sparks off written communicative difficulties, the Portuguese participants constantly mobilize different resources, namely Portuguese, thereby returning to the communicative contract (to their reference language). This in turn generates new linguistic opacity ("feitiço??"), the resolution coming once more from "contract violation", as Spanish is not supposed to be used by a Portuguese speaker ("hechizo"), to solve the linguistic problem afflicting the Catalan participant. Furthermore, the use of uncertain knowledge in the foreign language ("se escribe así?") stimulates further change in the linguistic resources being used.

In this excerpt, it is clear that violating the communicative contract enhances translanguaging by expanding the semiotic resources allowed. Violations become a valuable means of improving intercomprehension (as unforeseen linguistic resources are introduced, discussed and shared), improving linguistic well-being (since every speaker feels accepted with their linguistic resources, but also linguistic doubts and problems), and including play and humour (visible through the use of semiotic resources such as onomatopoeias, punctuation and smileys) in an overt multilingual scenario. At the same time, constant language policing is performed by the very speakers who do not conform to the communicative rules. In this last episode, for example, the poor self-evaluation of written communicative competence in the RL being used can be understood as forms of language policing and recalling of the linguistic contract, by suggesting that only "mastered" RL should be productively used. And again, the use of humour (smileys or interjections) helps to mitigate such face-threatening acts (confession of lack of proficiency and admission of communicative contract violation) and is used to facilitate the co-construction of meaning.

5. SYNTHESIS AND FURTHER RESEARCH PERSPECTIVES

5.1 Conclusion

In the Galanet communicative situations, all RL share the discursive floor and are admitted as valid linguistic resources (alongside electronic communication codes). From this perspective, Galanet affords overt multilingual communicative scenarios where several resources are welcome and where participants are challenged to overcome a monolingual *modus* and a monolingual *habitus* in international communicative settings. Intercomprehension thus enlarges communicative experiences and defies monolingual assumptions that still prevail when speakers of different languages meet and are expected to work together.

Intercomprehension in RL in chat communication, even if helping to overcome a "monolingual orientation to communication", imposes other orientations on communication that participants resist. One is the exclusion of non-Romance languages from the participants' linguistic repertoires; the other is the reduction of the "productive spectrum". Both issues are related to borders and dichotomies: Romance and non-Romance languages, on the one hand, receptive and productive skills, on the other. Participants are far from seeing the borders between these dichotomies as unchangeable and untouchable, as borders between languages and skills are challenged and crossed, even when they are subject to discursive actions of linguistic policing.

Galanet's linguistic contract explains that participants (usually university students) should use their "reference" RL (sometimes identified as "Mother Tongue") and try to simply understand those of others. The communicative contract thus imposes a multilingual orientation that is monoglossic in nature (based on the separation of languages and on a focus on productive skills in one language and receptive skills in the others). It also limits (or even forbids) the use of languages belonging to other linguistic families. However, as in the multilingual exchanges analyzed here, participants do not always abide by these rules (Bono & Melo-Pfeifer, 2011). They actively engage in the production of utterances in RL meant to be the "target Romance Languages" and they use other linguistic resources available in their plurilingual repertoires, such as German, English or Flemish (Melo-Pfeifer, 2014). These instances of violation of the communicative contract illustrate individual and collective agency during interactions. Secondly, they demonstrate students' perceptions of the full potential of translanguaging, which does not recognize legitimacy in reducing the possibilities of mobilization of semiotic resources available. And thirdly, they highlight speakers' efforts to "de- and re-authenticate" (Rampton, 2014, p. 297) the communicative situation by using translanguaging as an act of "multilingual performance" (following from García & Leiva, 2014) and "border demolition".

Another aspect must be pointed out: contrary to translanguaging as it is perceived in bilingual education (García & Leiva, 2014; García & Wei, 2014), in intercomprehension between RL issues such as power and empowerment, hierarchies, voice, emancipation and social equity or proficiency in the languages being used are absent or do not seem to be relevant to participants: all participants feel they are experts in some language and partially proficient in others. Power, voice, equity, proficiency and expertise are a given and ensured through the communicative contract. However, when intercomprehension meets translanguaging, the interdependence of resources is made visible by the resistance against the linguistic contract, so that participants mobilize their resources without diglossic functional separation. Translanguaging in chatrooms as analyzed here, becomes an act of struggle against the involuntary and imposed truncation of linguistic repertoires, and a clear disapproval of linguistic or skill borders as they are imposed by the communicative contract. Thus, translanguaging in RL chat rooms, where only RL are admitted, releases speakers from two constraints: being "RL multilinguals only" and being "multilingual receptive competent only".

In these multilingual exchanges, a translingual lens to intercomprehension shows how speakers draw on all their semiotic resources to maximize understanding and achievement, solve communicative problems and promote an environment of multilingual well-being. This point of view, as put forth in the theoretical section, goes beyond a monoglossic perspective on intercomprehension *between* RL and shows how languages are used in a dynamic and functionally interwoven way to co-construct meaning *across* RL. In this context, translanguaging, resorting to linguistic and other semiotic resources such as smileys and punctuation, is a way to scaffold RL production and reception not only in terms of linguistic issues (solving and avoiding opacity), but also to perform pragmatic and symbolic intentions such as avoiding potentially face-threatening acts. From this perspective, a more heteroglossic view of intercomprehension is needed in order to fully understand how speakers make a full-use of their semiotic repertoires in multilingual interaction.

5.2 Implications for Foreign Language Education and Research Agenda

In terms of the introduction of multilingual perspectives and stances in language education in formal contexts, a more realistic perspective of language practices should be aimed for, since such practices are becoming more complex and demanding by not abiding by monolingual and monoglossic norms:

We have to consider what pedagogies can open up to the classroom as a space for social negotiations, ecological affordances, and practice-based learning. Rather than asking what we can offer "deficient" multilingual students, we have to ask how we can let students bring into the classroom the dispositions and competencies they have already developed richly outside the classroom. This involves turning the classroom into a site for translingual socialization. Teachers have to permit, as much as they can, the conditions, resources, and affordances students find outside the classroom for the development of their performative competence. (Canagarajah, 2014, p. 99)

The introduction of overt multilingual communicative scenarios in language classrooms could have a double effect: i) enlarge students' knowledge about the richness of human communication and its unexploited possibilities; and ii) expand students' awareness of how communication works in hyper-complex linguistic settings, where meaning has to be collectively constructed and achieved (even if meaning always has to be achieved, being a process and a product, not a given). This introduction would also aid perceptions of the imposed nature of every communicative convention and the effects of those impositions on everyday performances and interlocutors' behaviors (and particularly on language policing attitudes, related to the use of a native-like norm or of an essentialized linguistic code).

Finally, a research agenda for the analysis of multilingual interaction would include the need to study how intercomprehension, as a particular form of multilingual interaction, and translanguaging, as an ethical and heuristic lens to look at it, works beyond pedagogical scenarios in real life situations. Such scenarios can encompass written interaction in different platforms (such as YouTube) or in social networks, as well as oral interaction in different media (such as Skype) and in different professional settings. This broadening of the situations taken into consideration would allow researchers to find patterns and identify and understand individual creative solutions and strategies of translanguaging. Furthermore, a study of speakers' representations towards multilingual interaction, specifically an analysis of their narrated experiences of participating in such multilingual encounters, would help to:

- Evaluate the impact of social representations and interlocutors' previous experiences on the assessment of multilingual interaction; and
- Establish a research agenda that articulates the analysis of discursive practices and the perception of those practices by social actors.

REFERENCES

Araújo e Sá, M. H., De Carlo, M., & Melo-Pfeifer, S. (2010). O que diriam sobre os portugueses? [What would you say about Portuguese people?]: Intercultural curiosity in multilingual chat-rooms. *Language and Intercultural Communication, 10*(4), 277–298. doi:10.1080/14708471003611257

Araújo e Sá, M. H., & Melo, S. (2007). On-line plurilingual interaction in the development of Language Awareness. *Language Awareness, 16*(1), 7–20.

Bailey, B. (2011). Heteroglossia. In M. Martin-Jones, A. Blackledge & A. Creese (Eds.), *The Routledge Handbook of Multilingualism* (pp. 439-453). Oxon: Routledge

Blackledge, A., & Creese, A. (2014). Heteroglossia as Practice and Pedagogy. In A. Blackledge & A. Creese (Eds.), *Heteroglossia as Practice and Pedagogy* (pp. 1-20). London: Springer.

Blommaert, J. (2010). *The Sociolinguistics of Globalization*. Cambridge: Cambridge University Press. doi:10.1017/CBO9780511845307

Blommaert, J., Kelly-Holmes, H., Lane, P., Peppänen, S., Moriarty, M., Pietikäinen, S., & Piirainen-Marsh, A. (2009). Media, multilingualism and language policing: An introduction. *Language Policy, 8*(3), 203–207. doi:10.1007/s10993-009-9138-7

Bono, M., & Melo-Pfeifer, S. (2011). Language negotiation in multilingual learning environments. *The International Journal of Bilingualism, 15*(3), 291–309. doi:10.1177/1367006910379299

Canagarajah, S. (2013). *Translingual Practice. Global Englishes and Cosmopolitan Relations*. Oxon: Routledge.

Canagarajah, S. (2014). Theorizing a competence for translingual practice at the context zone. In S. May (Ed.), *The Multilingual Turn* (pp. 291-309). Oxon: Routledge.

Capucho, F. (2008). L'intercompréhension est-elle une mode? Du linguiste citoyen au citoyen plurilingue. *Revue Pratiques*, 139-140, 238–250. doi:10.4000/pratiques.1252

Capucho, F., Martins, A., Degache, Ch., & Tost, M. (Eds.), (2007). *Diálogos em Intercompreensão*. Lisboa: Universidade Católica Portuguesa.

Doyé, P., & Meissner, F.-J. (Eds.). (2010). *Lernerautonomie durch Interkomprehension: Projekte und Perspektiven / L'autonomisation de l'apprenant par l'intercompréhension: projets et perspectives / Promoting Learner Autonomy through intercomprehension: projects and perspectives*. Tübingen: Narr.

Ehrhart, S. (2010). Pourquoi intégrer la diversité linguistique et culturelle dans la formation des enseignants au Luxemburg. In S. Ehrhart, Ch. Hélot & A. Nevez (Eds.), *Plurilinguisme et Formation des Enseignants: une approche critique* (pp. 221-238). Bern: Peter Lang.

García, O. (2014). Countering the Dual: Transglossia, Dynamic Bilingualism and Translanguaging in Education. In R. Rubdy & L. Alsagoff (Eds.), *The global-local interface, language choice and hybridity* (pp. 100-118). Bristol: Multilingual Matters.

García, O., & Wei, Li (2014). *Translanguaging. Language, Bilingualism and Education*. Hampshire: Palgrave MacMillan.

García, O., & Leiva, C. (2014). Theorizing and enacting translanguaging for social justice. In A. Blackledge & A. Creese (Eds.), *Heteroglossia as Practice and Pedagogy* (pp. 199–216). London: Springer. doi:10.1007/978-94-007-7856-6_11

Jewitt, C. (2009). An introduction to multimodality. In C. Jewitt (ed.), *The Routledge Handbook of Multimodal Analysis* (pp. 14-27). London: Routledge.

Kramsch, C. (2014). Teaching Foreign Languages in an Era of Globalization: Introduction. *Modern Language Journal*, *98*(1), 296–311. doi:10.1111/j.1540-4781.2014.12057.x

Makony, S., & Pennycook, A. (2007). *Disinventing and reconstituting Languages*. Clevedon: Multilingual Matters.

Makony, S., & Pennycook, A. (2011). Disinventing multilingualism. From monological multilingualism to multilingua francas. In M. Martin-Jones, A. Blackledge & A. Creese (Eds.), *The Routledge Handbook of Multilingualism* (pp. 439-453). Oxon: Routledge.

Meißner, F.-J. Capucho, F. Degache, Ch. Martins, A. Spita, D., & Tost, M. (Eds.), (2011). *Intercomprehension. Learning, teaching, research. Apprentissage, enseignement, recherche. Lernen, Lehren, Forschung*. Tübingen: Narr.

Melo-Pfeifer, S. (2011). De la dissociation à l'articulation de compétences: apports théoriques au concept d'Intercompréhension. In F.-J.Meißner, F. Capucho, Ch. Degache, A. Martins, D. Spita & M. Tost (eds.), *Intercomprehension: Learning, teaching, research / Apprentissage, enseignement, recherche / Lernen, Lehren, Forschung* (pp. 219-242). Tübingen: Narr Verlag.

Melo-Pfeifer, S. (2014). Intercomprehension between Romance Languages and the role of English: A study of multilingual chat rooms. *International Journal of Multilingualism*, *11*(1), 120–137. doi:10.1080/14790718.2012.679276

Melo-Pfeifer, S. (2015). An interactional perspective on intercomprehension between Romance Languages: Translanguaging in multilingual chat rooms. *Fremsprachen Lehren und Lernen, 44*(2), 100–113.

Melo-Pfeifer, S., Araújo e Sá, M. H., & Santos, L. (2012). As "línguas que não sabemos que sabíamos" e outros mitos: um olhar sobre o percurso da Didática de Línguas a partir da intercompreensão. Cadernos do Lale, Série Reflexões (Vol. 4, pp. 33–55). Aveiro: Universidade de Aveiro.

Pennycook, A. (2010). *Language as a local practice*. London: Routledge.

Rampton, B. (2014). Dissecting heteroglossia: interaction ritual or performance in crossing and stylization? In A. Blackledge & A. Creese (Eds.), *Heteroglossia as Practice and Pedagogy* (pp. 275-300). London: Springer. 10.1007/978-94-007-7856-6_15

Chapter 10
French–Chinese Dialogical Interaction via Web Collaborative Blog–Writing:
Code–Switching to Extend Online Tandem Language Learning

Ya Rao
Paul Valery University, France

Congcong Wang
University of Northern Iowa, USA

Jacob Bender
University of Iowa, USA

ABSTRACT

This qualitative study explores how a French-Chinese web collaborative blog-writing project provides a space for understanding the various metalinguistic approaches that foreign language learners' use to facilitate foreign language learning and intercultural communication. It adopts a multilingual-plurilingual approach, an interlingual approach and a web collaboration approach as a framework. Qualitative data was collected from the blogs and online interactions of 22 French Foreign Language (FFL) learners in China, and 24 Chinese Foreign Language (CFL) learners in France. The findings reveal the increased development of FFL and CFL learners' metalinguistic awareness, plurilingual competence, and bilingual skills that is accomplished through web collaboration. Implications regarding web-based tandem language learning and peer-assisted web collaboration are discussed.

INTRODUCTION

Prior to 2000, language education in European countries was primarily focused on the study of one's maternal language and English. But post-2000, the Common European Framework of Reference for Languages (CEFR, now known as the Council of Europe, 2001) proposed that all language learners

DOI: 10.4018/978-1-5225-0177-0.ch010

should possess plurilingual skills and be given opportunities to interact with a growing and increasingly culturally diverse population. Armand and Dagenais (2005) stress that recent foreign language education should focus on systematically preparing students to become bilingual or multilingual stakeholders in their personal lives and fields, as well as in a local-global context. Due to a renewed respect for foreign and regional languages learning, interest in multiculturalism and multilingualism increased (Filippetti, 2014). Thus, plurilingual competence has since become a major goal of language education in Europe.

To help learners develop plurilingual competence, plurlingual environments and pluralistic opportunities are important, which assist learners to develop linguistic and cultural sensibilities and awareness. In the development of plurilingual and pluralist competencies, metalinguistic awareness is central to foreign language learning (Ildikó, 2005). Mediating the gap between the target language and mother tongue, metalinguistic awareness enables learners to discover knowledge about both language practices and systems comparatively. However, the literature shows that metalinguistic awareness has been understudied within tandem and bilingual learning contexts (Reder, Marec-Breton, Gombert, & Demont, 2013). Therefore, this qualitative study explores how French Foreign Language (FFL) learners and Chinese Foreign Language (CFL) learners develop plurilingual competence and metalinguistc awareness through web collaborations.

LITERATURE REVIEW

Plurilingual Competence

Plurilingual competence refers to the ability to manage multiple language codes in communication, according to the need or necessity of the situation (Coste, Moore, and Zarate; 2009). It is associated with the learner's ability to gather, juggle, connect, and manage his/her language repertoire by understanding bits and pieces of one language, and modify as well as build new languages based on prior knowledge (Coste, 2001). Plurilingual competence reflects how individuals utilize multiple language resources to mediate their communication in a new language situation, as well as consider the social appropriateness of language use (Moore, 2006; Pretceille, 2006). A learner's negotiation and management of coexisting different language and culture systems contributes to the construction of a constantly renewed repertoire. Therefore, the development of plurilingual and pluricultural competence requires learners to have a broad vision between the different systems of languages and cultures. Teaching plurilingualism can be closely tied to students' metalinguistic awareness (Candelier, 2008).

Based on reflexivity and metalinguistic awareness, a pluralist approach can be recognized and conducted by the learner during language activities in a school context (Ildikó, 2005). Pluralistic approaches refer to activities involving multiple linguistic and cultural varieties across and within languages. Geographical and organizational differences exist among these linguistic and cultural varieties, e.g., regional languages, standardized official languages, and Creoles. Social characteristics of language are related to personal contexts, such as family language versus school language. The goal of pluralist approaches is to develop a metalinguistic awareness, as well as metalanguage skills for each individual learner (Castelloti Moore 2005). However, some learners who try to master two or more languages simultaneously may encounter linguistic and sociolinguistic difficulties if they lack plurilingual competence.

This pluralist approach differs from the traditional learning or teaching model wherein a language seems to be an autonomous and separated system. On the contrary, when learners interact and work with native speakers during face-to-face foreign language learning, they must step back, reflect, and try to explain linguistic and cultural phenomena associated with their interaction. Learners consider the passages and transfer of learning resources. "Passage" in this context refers to the act of placing one language into another language, while "transfer" refers to a situation in which learners use their current knowledge and expertise to perform in a new situation. Based on prior knowledge about grammatical structures and vocabulary, new language is thereby constructed. These passages and transfer scenarios stimulate students to employ multiple language and cultural resources to learn a new language.

Correspondingly, learning a foreign language in this manner is a step towards the "other" with an awareness of diversity. This change in language code during a conversation is called "bilingual speech." This change has also been described as *translanguaging*: transferring or crossing meaning across languages (García, 2011). Multilingual people alternate languages to mark their social and cultural identity, to offer meaning, and to complete or provide more information about the content of the message.

According to Rodi (2009), translanguaging among plurilingual speakers occurs with a reason and purpose. Those who utilize multiple languages create "their own linguistic systems in contact with their own rules" (Rodi, 2009, p. 5). Dillon (2009) found that when children from the ages of 10 to 12 are balanced bilinguals (e.g., Irish-English), they are more capable of exhibiting increased metalinguistic awareness and translanguaging skills. These back and forth processes of generating passages and transferring knowledge in written dual language interaction promote metalinguistic awareness and construction of new language based on the different components of one's plurilingual repertoire. In a study by Kotter (2003), German and North American English speakers who engaged in group-to-group online collaborative language exchange during face-to-face discourse similarly found that learners who had good metalinguistic skills were successful in second language acquisition. Additional studies on task-based collaborative language exchange can similarly prompt metalinguistic awareness of language forms. University peers who engage in this cross-linguistic exchanges were able to overcome most communication issues through negotiation of meaning on collaborative tasks, and had time to provide somewhat superficial feedback, which, in turn, incidentally influenced the peers' ability to focus on and monitor language form (Bower & Kawaguchi, 2011; Kabata & Edasawa, 2011; Ware & O'Dowd, 2008).

METALINGUISTIC AWARENESS

Language learning is a metacognitive process, which involves learners' awareness of their own language use (Gombert, 1996). As a subdomain of metacognition, metalinguistic activity is related to the learner's cognition and language awareness (Gombert, 1990). According to Bialystok (2001), metalinguistics is multifaceted and related to metalinguistic awareness, ability, and skills. Metalinguistic *knowledge* however is the "knowledge that is made explicit during language acquisition" (p. 127). Metalinguistic *ability* is the ability to use one's prior knowledge about language and apply it to learn more about a language's function (Araujo, 1992; Bialystok, 2001). Metalinguistic awareness can include phonemic and syntactic awareness.

According to Blasco (2013), through a metalinguistic analysis of learners' own interlingual interactions, learners can:

1. Gain depth of language understanding through an analysis of their native language as contrasted to the target language;

2. Engage in disciplinary and intercultural decompartmentalisation as the deconstruct and co-construct knowledge about the target language; and

3. Gain greater awareness of the specific rules of each language to avoid erroneous transfers. In understanding the types of linguistic metacognition that can occur during interlingual web collaboration (as are proposed in this study), six meta-processes associated with multiple facets of metalinguistic awareness are essential (Gombert, 1990, 1996; Marot, 2002):

    a. **Metaphonological Awareness:** Focuses on meaningful segmentation units of oral language such as syllables and phonemes (Marot, 2002). Learners in web collaboration during negotiation of meaning will attempt to purposefully and appropriately manipulate language sounds in the target language.

    b. **Metasemantic Awareness**: Refers to the conscious ability to recognize the meaning of words within the context of interaction (Gombert, 1992). Learners during web collaboration may reveal their metasemantic awareness by engaging in semantic correction and self-correction to clarify meaning.

    c. **Metasyntatic Awareness**: Refers to how the interlocutor pays attention to grammar rules and word order. This type of awareness often plays a role in learning how to read and speak. Metasyntactic awareness lends to understanding how word order affects meaning. It may be demonstrated through the types of corrective feedback that peer learners provide one another about word order that may affect meaning during online chat or web collaboration.

    d. **Metapragmatic Awareness:** Focuses on the types of utterances that occur within particular language contexts. Metapragmatic awareness includes a monitoring of speech tone, atmosphere, honorifics, and nonverbal management of language. The context which may include the social space (e.g., web collaboration) and the topic (e.g., preparing to write an article together, or informal socializing on blog space) can impact how the language is produced. Speech tone, atmosphere, and/or nonverbal management, honorifics, etc. are considered. The relationship between the social context and language use contribute to the understanding of utterances.

    e. **Metatextual Awareness:** Includes the analysis of text structure by learners. For example, Learners rely on the text to understand meaning. During web collaboration, learners pay attention to the coherence and cohesion of the text for their peer with whom they are collaborating. Learners monitor the text, text structure utilizing strategies that lead to understanding. Genette and Lewin (1997) note the importance of understanding through awareness of intertexuality, or the idea of quotation marks to highlight information from another person within a text. They describe paratextual awareness as an understanding of how the titles, subtitles, footnotes, forward, can be utilized to guide the reader. Asynchronous web collaboration provides for opportunities to monitor the text message before it is sent out. Similarly, language peers may have to guess, based on context clues (which is also associated with metapragmatic awareness) of the intended meaning in a peer's message. Peer learners choose strategies that make understanding text easier. Some strategies may appear unorthodox but they move language forward, e.g., the use of code-switching, translanguaging in text to ensure meaning of the entire text, etc.

    f. **Metalexical Awareness:** Promotes the construction of the internal lexicon of the subject. New words are added to the knowledge base. Then, sense-making and co-construction of new knowledge occurs. Metalexical awareness can be seen in the memorization of words that are stored for later use. Similarly, the storing of particular memorized phrases leads to language automaticity in responding and frees up space for language acquisition and advance language ability development (Winstead, 2004). Finally, textual awareness applies to the overall understanding of text. This awareness focuses on coherence and cohesion of the text, the control of the text structure, as well as strategies utilized to increase understanding of the entire text, (e.g., context clues).

In foreign language teaching, the teacher's role is not only to teach students to speak and write the target language but also to think about the relationship between the mother tongue and the foreign language in order to achieve better learning. One of the best ways to learn about a language can be made through the metalinguistic method. It creates a distance between the speaker's speech and him/herself as the utterance subject, as well as between his/her speech and the world as an utterance subject (Kim, 2003).

Bilingual and Plurilingual Repertoires: Code-Switching

Since the 1980s, many authors have contributed to research on bilingualism and multilingualism that reveals how plurilingual repertoire evolves and changes based on the context (Grosjean, 1984; Lüdi,1993, 1995, 2004, 2013; Py, 1996, 2003; Beacco, 2004: Coste, Moore & Zarate 1997, 2009; Candelier, 2007; Castellotti and Moore, 2011). Coste, Moore, and Zarate (1997) put forward the idea of plurilingual repertoire, an idea that demonstrates that languages are always evolving based on constantly changing circumstances and interactions.

According to Lüdi (1995), bilinguals may be confirmed bilingual or budding bilingual, i.e. language learners. Both types of bilingual or multilingual speakers must choose the language varieties according to the communication situation.

In any bilingual or multilingual linguistic community, bilingual speech or code-switching very commonly exist. Code-switching generally refers to "a switch from one language to another in a communication situation" (Lüdi & Py, 2013, p. 146). It can be applied to a single word as well as to minutes of speech (Scotton & Ury, 1977). Language codes can designate any language that is different, or even two registers within the same language.

When learners are more proficient in switching between languages, code-switching is more likely to be a voluntary approach associated with developing comradery during social communication (Winstead, 2013). The choice of code-switching in bilingual or multilingual contexts may be voluntary or involuntary, such as when trying to fill a gap in language communication. Voluntary code-switching is often purposeful and cognitive, and learners share social co-identity in the dual language exchange context (Bullock, 2009; Cashman, 2006; Ellwood, 2008) (see Figure 1 for types of code-switching).

Based on Poplack (1988) and Lüdi and Py's (2013) work, the researchers of this study propose to distinguish types of code-switching depending on the context in which the language change occurs. According to Poplack (1988), inter-sentential and intra-sentential types correspond to fluid and extra-sentential type, as well as the marked switching. It is sometimes difficult to distinguish between three types of switching because they may overlap in the same speaking slot. By adapting it to the analysis of our data set, we propose a code-switching diagram as shown in Figure 2.

Unlike some researchers who consider code-switching to be an indication of a linguistic gap or ineffective teaching of language, Lüdi (1999) argues that code-switching is "a community phenomenon, which

Figure 1. Types of code-switching
Source: (Ludi & Py, 2013, p. 145)

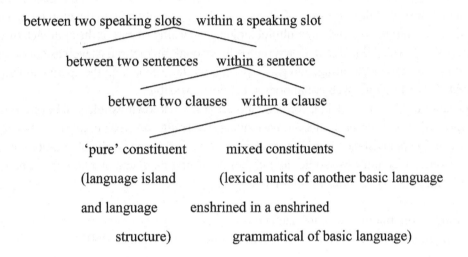

code switching

between two speaking slots   within a speaking slot

between two sentences   within a sentence

between two clauses   within a clause

'pure' constituent   mixed constituents

(language island   (lexical units of another basic language

and language   enshrined in a enshrined

structure)   grammatical of basic language)

Figure 2. Types of code switching

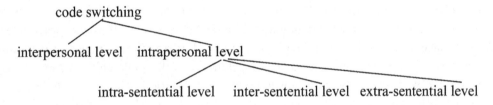

code switching

interpersonal level   intrapersonal level

intra-sentential level   inter-sentential level   extra-sentential level

presupposes language proficiency involved and thus represents an indication of a bilingual proficiency" (p.12). Through the mobilization strategies of bilingual communicative skill, learners can gain more language and intercultural knowledge.

In this study, bilingual speech is defined as a phenomenon in which speakers use two languages during a communication. The researchers consider the practice of bilingual speech as a linguistic, cultural, and social practice. During bilingual or multilingual speech interactions, the interlocutors build their linguistic, cultural, and social identity. It is in this constructional process that researchers observe the characteristics of a diverse community of speakers, which accommodates the existence of different linguistic and cultural systems. To typify different types of language contact phenomena such as code-switching, borrowing, layer, and interference, transcodic marks are often utilized (Lüdi, 1993). As defined in this study, "transcodic marks" refer to the relatively simultaneous activation of two linguistic systems in the case of speech or bilingual communication.

In order to gain a deeper understanding of learners' practices of bilingual speech and particular language contact phenomena that typify their bilingual speech, the researchers of this study established a web collaborative program to observe learners' social interation.

WEB COLLABORATION FOR SOCIAL INTERACTION

Over the past decade, foreign language educators have been using networked technologies to support social interaction, discussion, debate, and/or intercultural exchanges. More recently, television-based research demonstrated through web 2.0 tools have demonstrably helped develop language skills, all by integrating communicative and intercultural language learning as part of the approach by task. The chief characteristic of Web 2.0 is that it allows multi-directional interaction, as well as encourages collaboration through sharing, negotiating, and participating, while overcoming the spatial and temporal hurdle. With Web 2.0 technology, web collaboration becomes possible.

According to O'Dowd (2011), web collaboration (also known as telecollaboration) utilizes online chat and/or videos to promote collaborative language learning and cross-cultural study via various online forums, e.g., Skype. Distance is no longer an issue in virtual space. Web collaboration can pull students together from one country to another to collaborate during language practice or online projects. Based on social media, web collaborations aim to:

1. Promote collaboration on Internet, and
2. Maintain supportive learning practice in communities (Wenger, 2005).

However, Belz (2003) affirms that learners in these online collaborative endeavours face intercultural issues centered around the challenges self-decenterednesss, opening up to each other, exchanging personal information, and experiencing empathy. Distance courses use digital artifacts of communication such as messaging, chat, and forum to develop dialogues, organize debates, as well as encourage intercultural exchange to advance language learning. Dooly and O'Dowd (2012) further note that by adding goal-oriented collaborative projects, communicative competence as well as intercultural competence can be achieved. Harris's (1998) study also indicates how web collaboration structures include interpersonal exchanges, information collection and analyses, and the employ of problem solving activities and strategies. O'Dowd and Waire (2009) identified three main categories of tasks that blend intercultural web collaboration projects:

1. Information Exchange (type of epistolary exchanges).
2. Comparison and Analysis tasks (tasks geared towards developing intercultural competence).
3. Collaboration and Product Creation tasks (a text, a translation, an advertisement, etc.).

Web collaboration approaches have various potential. Some web collaboration sites promote primarily language exchange and communication for participants. These sites include but are not limited to the following: eTandem Europa (http://www.cisi.unito.it/tandem/etandem/etindex-en.html) and Entre2classes (http://www.entre2classes.com/). The other web collaboration sites were organized by language classes involving two partner teachers and two groups of students from two different cultures. For example, the Cultura project (http://cultura.mit.edu) offers a combination of questionnaires and forums to enhance language skills and intercultural communication competence. On other sites, collaborative projects are designed formally by instructors. The curriculum uses a combination of goal-oriented tasks for language development, such as Global School Net's Projects & Programs (www.gsn.org/project/index.html), Kidproj (an appearance of Kidlink, http://www.kidlink.org/drupal/project/) and Galanet (http://www.galanet.eu/).

However, when collaboration approaches are overburdened by too many school tasks or goals, it often leads to a reductive evolution of language pedagogy (Springer, 2014). Instead, researchers suggest that class projects adopt more meaningful approaches that promote learning communities and are not just task-based (Springer, 2014; Wenger, 2005).

Therefore, web collaboration requires the implementation of a common task by geographically distant classes, which combines the pedagogy of the project and the use of Web 2.0 to facilitate collaboration and co-construct learning. This shared learning approach allows students to develop cross-cutting, social, personal, intercultural, and language skills. With its focus on developing communicative competence and intercultural skills, web collaboration is an effective approach that tends to build social relationships and personalities in the spirit of sharing.

THEORETICAL FRAMEWORK

As the literature indicated, web collaboration allows language learners to develop plurilingual competence as well as interlingual skills. The researchers of this current study adopted these theories as a foundation for research design.

Multilingualism theories, including the theoretical constructs of competence and metalinguistic development (Gombert, 1996), are essential to understanding bilingual speech and code-switching (Lüdi, 1995). The multilingual-plurilingual approach provides method to explore how learners engage in specific metaprocesses when negotiating meaning, as well as how they may consciously or unconsciously drift between and among languages. These theories also provides insights to understand the linguistic and extralinguistic factors involved in language choices during web collaboration.

In addition, an interlingual approach offers a comparison of the language as a way to learn a new language. It also helps learners self-recognize their understanding of their native language. When learning a foreign language, comparisons about language grammar may enhance learners' understanding of new terms, e.g., conjugations, nouns, adjectives. This approach provides insights about how language learners may compare their heritage language, second language, and/or target language in order to decode meaning of a new language by activating their prior knowledge. Similarly, interlingual situations and contexts provide foreign language learners with opportunities to develop learning strategies as well as corrective feedback that might enhance their comprehension.

Since web-based tandem language learning provides learners with opportunities to consciously or unconsciously go back and forth between their two language systems, this method may prompt various metalinguistic skills (e.g., metasemantic, metapragmatic, metatextual). Web collaboration may metacognitively engage learners in linguistic comparison of written traces of communication. Self-regulated and peer-assisted language exchanges allow learners to engage in metacognition during bilingual learning (Springer, 2014; Winstead, 2013). Situated plurilingual competence destabilizes the dominant paradigms about how languages are taught (Castelloti & Moore). For instance, teachers who have taught languages in a traditional way are now being asked to guide language learners through plurilingual face-to-face collaborative situations.

However, the existing literature indicates that metalinguistic awareness has been less studied within tandem and bilingual learning contexts (Reder, Marec-Breton, Gombert, & Demont, 2013). In addition, major concerns include the development of personal, social, and cut-crossing competences that promote the autonomy of the interlocutors who work collaboratively on bilingual-plurilingual projects. Thus, engaging students in multilingual-contact in foreign language learning is a step towards acknowledging the linguistic assets of the other in ways that promote alternative teaching and learning approaches.

To fill the gap in literature, this study adopted a multilingual-plurilingual approach, interlingual approach and web collaboration approach as a framework to explore web-based tandem language learning. It also aims to explore whether foreign language learners develop plurilingual competence and metalinguistc awareness through a web collaborative blog writing project.

Purpose of the Study

This qualitative study explored whether Chinse Foreign Language learners and French Foreign Language learners develop metalinguistic awareness and bilingual skills to engage in online foreign language interaction. It also explores whether learners develop plurilingual competence and co-construct language and cultural knowledge during web collaboration.

Research Questions

The research questions of this study include:

1. Do FFL and CFL students mobilize metalinguistic awareness through a web collaborative blog-writing project? If so, how do FFL and CFL students develop metalinguistic awareness through target language online learning and collaboration with native-speaking peers?
2. Do FFL and CFL students develop French-Chinese bilingual skills through web collaboration? If so, how do they develop French-Chinese bilingual skills?
3. What facilitate CFL and FFL learners' language exchange in communicating with native-speaking peers and learning the target languages?

Methodology

This study adopted a qualitative approach to explore how the web collaborative blog-writing project between foreign language learners and native speakers helps learners develop plurilingual competence and metalinguistic awareness.

Participants

This study required remote cooperation between CFL and FFL participants who are multilingual speakers and college students in France and China. Twenty-two native French-speaking CFL students in France and 24 native Chinese-speaking FFL students in China participated in this study. They participated in written dialogical exchanges through web collaboration, in which they self-regulated their teaching and learning activities.

All French students were from the University of Strasbourg and studied Chinese as a minor at their 2nd and 3rd year. The Chinese students were enrolled in a French program organized by the French Alliance of Qingdao located in China. At the beginning of the exchange program, the French students reached A1 to A2 levels of Chinese proficiency while the Chinese students reached A2 level of French proficiency.

According to the Common European Framework, A2 is the upper-most basic level of language ability. Learners at the A2 level are at the upper level of basic. They are able to understand sentences, utilize everyday expression, exchange information, and describe information. Learners at the B1 level have just met the intermediate threshold. They are independent learners who are able to read articles and reports as well as write comments on contemporary issues.

Context and Background of Study

This web collaboration project is composed of three parts:

1. Active learning scenarios of a 16-week collaboration through participants' blog writing in the target languages and web interactions;
2. A partnership between the French Alliance of Qingdao and the Chinese department at the University of Strasbourg; and
3. A platform[1] for language exchanges and participants' blog publications (See Figure 3 for the Interface of the French-Chinese Exchange Blog).

Figure 3. The interface of the French-Chinese exchange blog

The web-collaborative educational scenarios allowed participants to perform essay-writing tasks in the target languages through collaboration and exchange with native speakers without language restrictions. Blog comments also supported their task-based and informal exchanges during this process.

The Chinese department at the University of Strasbourg assigned a Chinese language instructor to facilitate French students' online learning. These French students spent 1 hour a week in web collaboration, which includes 30-minute online practice as part of their Chinese speaking course and another 30-minute practice outside the regular Chinese as foreign language class. They participated in the program for 24 weeks. The Chinese instructor was in charge of training students, developing collaborative program, answering questions, and solving technology issues.

Similarly, during a 16-week web collaboration program, FFL students spent two hours a week in blog-writing and online interaction. A French language teacher was assigned by the French Alliance of Qingdao to facilitate FFL students' online learning, such as encouraging students to post comments and guiding students at an appropriate pace of blog-writing. This collaboration lasted for one and half years. Data were collected over the course of two semesters in a single academic year.

Data Sources

Data sources for this study include Blogs (e.g., Wordpress, BBpress, and Facebook), peer comment posts, pre- and- post tasks, and writing tasks.

Blogs

Blog posts include FFL and CFL students' Wordpress, BBpress, and Facebook posts. The writing tasks include participants' blog writing by using the target languages. For instance, FFL students were asked to write essays in French and post them to their blogs. Similarly, CFL students were likewise asked to write essays in Chinese and post them to their blogs. Table 1 shows that FFL and CFL participants contributed 81 essays in total. Blog posts functioned as the main data source by which to analyze participants' perceptional representations of the language.

Peer Comment Posts

After essays were published on foreign language participants' blogs, their native-speaking peers were invited to post comments on those essays. In total, FFL and CFL participants made 480 comment posts in response to peers' essay posting. These total blog comment posts include 225 comments, 14 BBpress messages, and 231 Facebook posts.

Table 1. Number of contributions collected

Communication Tools	Data Type	Total Contributions
Blogs (Wordpress, BBpress, Facebook)	Essays (Wordpress)	81
	Comments (225) Messages (BBpress 14; Facebook 231)	480

Pre- and Post-Tasks

The exchange project includes pre- and post-tasks as well as two tasks which involve target language writing and communication. The pre-task was a preparatory stage which aims to provide FFL and CFL learners with preparation for all the individual and collaborative work throughout the year.

Writing Tasks

The writing tasks aim to develop participants' co-construction competence of the target languages and cultural knowledge through peer-assisted learning. These tasks allow participants work with native-speaking group members to build their linguistic and cultural repertoires. Over the first week of the course, French-native speaking participants became familiar with their Chinese-native speaking partners. They also learned communication tools, scenario steps, and techniques regarding how to switch the French keyboard to a Chinese keyboard. Similarly, Chinese-native speaking learners learned how to switch the Chinese keyboard to the French keyboard.

From the first session, CFL and FFL participants were divided into several groups. Each group has four to five members according to their affinities. Group members were trained to prepare for a group essay-writing task. The writing task required the members of each group to collectively write an essay by using the target languages. Groups of native speakers from each of the countries were encouraged to support the learning of their respective peers as they wrote essays in the target languages. Participants commented and interacted via their blogpost.

Data Collection

The data collected is based on the written and asynchronous interactions (blogs) of the participants through three platforms: Wordpress, BBpress, and Facebook. With the participants' prior consent, the researchers collected all of the participants' blog essays and comment posts throughout the year. Table 1 above reflects how the data was collected from three communication (tools) platforms, the data type, and the total number of student contributions collected and analyzed. Participants were not restricted in their language use despite the goal of submitting a collaboratively written article in the target languages on their blog forum. Thus, code-switching and translanguaging (that is, using other languages for communication) was permitted.

Data Analysis

The researchers utilized a directed approach to analyze the content from French-Chinese blog web collaboration data based on a metalinguistic theoretical frame established in the language field (Gombert, 1990, 1996; Marot, 2002), all while remembering that "With a directed approach, analysis starts with a theory or relevant research findings as guidance for initial codes" (Hsieh & Shannon, 2005; Potter & Levine-Donnerstein, 1999). Based on this theoretical frame, this deductive approach was utilized to analyze data and answer the three research questions. The researchers intended to capture all the possible occurrences of metalinguistic awareness identified by six key elements that served as the initial coding scheme: metaphonological, metasemantic, metasyntactic, metapragmatic, metalexical, and metatextual awareness. Next, the blog messages best representing these predetermined codes were highlighted. Data were categorized by themes, e.g., "metalinguistic awareness", and coded for analysis. For example, data that reflected "code-switching" were picked out and categorized separately. According to the context in which code-switching occurred, the specific data regarding the "code-switching" type were analysed in context. Operational definitions for the key concepts are provided in the theoretical framework mentioned above.

RESULTS AND DISCUSSION

As a qualitative study, the themes and patterns emerging from the data are used to answer the three research questions.

In response to the first research question, "Do FFL and CFL students mobilize metalinguistic awareness through a web collaborative blog-writing project? If so, how do FFL and CFL students develop metalinguistic awareness through target language online learning and collaboration with native-speaking peers?", the analysis of their blog notes and reflections reveal aspects of at least five of the six elements. It was notable that language learners utilized comparison as a way to express their metalinguistic awareness of the target language.

Theme 1: Language Comparisons Reveal Metalinguistic Awareness

As shown in Figure 4, researchers identified 17 occurrences of comments addressing the representation of the Chinese language. Among these comments, 13 of the 17 were written by the French students. 11 French students found that the Chinese language was both challenging and exciting. French participants commented that though they likewise found the Chinese language to be attractive, exciting, and beautiful; but they also wrote that Chinese characters were difficult to write. Here is one of the female participant's perceptions about Chinese (Figure 4).

Figure 4.

AnneC Says:
<u>mars 30th, 2011 at 19 h 41 min</u> <u>edit</u>
我学中文学了六年了、我觉得中文很有意思。语法的中文比法语的很容易，可是汉字很难写也很难记住。汉字很好看，我喜欢练习汉字。我听说惯用左手的人写汉字写得不好...我是左撇子，可是我觉得我写的汉字不错。汉语拼音给外国的中文学生很方便。语音和四声非常难、所以要想学好中文，一定要多练口语。

【English translation: I have studied Chinese for six years, I find that Chinese is very interesting. Chinese of the grammar is easier than French grammar, but the characters are very difficult to write and memorize. Chinese characters are very beautiful. I like practicing writing Chinese characters. I heard that the left-handed do not write Chinese characters well ... I am left-handed, but I think I write Chinese characters well. The Pinyin system is very convenient for foreign students to learn Chinese. Intonation and four tones are really hard, so if you want to study Chinese well, you have to practice speaking a lot. 】

Further analysis of other blog comments similarly reveals that Chinese students also had some difficulty with French, despite noting that it is an "elegant" and "fashionable" language. The major issue cited was about writing grammar, especially verb conjugations.

This example shows that through peer-assisted blog writing and web interaction, CFL and FFL students were able to reflect on their foreign language learning, particularly in comparison with their native language learning. By connecting learners' prior linguistic and cultural knowledge to target language learning, participants demonstrated metalinguistic awareness.

Theme 2: Five Levels of Metalinguistic Awareness

In the data set, several traces of metalinguistic awareness were identified, with the exception of the phonological level, as our experiment focused primarily upon written interaction.

Metalexical Awareness

According to Gombert (1990, 1996), the language learner uses the automated metaprocesses when it encounters an obstacle of linguistic treatment, and decides to control the treatment of the language. Traces of metalexical awareness correspond to these two aforementioned processes in our data set. Linguistic backgrounds can occur in the three following situations:

1.   When the subject encounters a difficulty in reading comprehension and in written exchanges;
2.   When the subject corrects the lexical errors of the speaker and explains the reason for such corrections; and
3.   When the subject explains new words to his interlocutor in their communication.

As an example of metalexical awareness, the data shows a commentary in which a Chinese participant suggested replacing the word "游历" ("Travel around", which is used as a transitive verb to emphasize the broad areas one has traveled) with the more accurate term "旅游" ("Tour visit"). We observed three cases of this same type of metalinguistic awareness (Figure 5).

In this example, Nelly expressed his experience of traveling around many countries, however, he used游历 as an intransitive verb, which is not grammatically correct in Chinese. In addition, Nelly also mis-typed 厉(strict, rigorous), when he should have used 历 (experience). Each Chinese character has its own meaning, while a combination of two different characters may create a completely different meaning; hence, "旅游" and "游历" have different meanings and usage. Thus, how the Chinese language differs from the French language may cause difficulty for foreign language learners. These two posts show that Nelly was unaware of the grammatical and pragmatic difference of the word "travel", while Nelly's Chinese-speaking peer helped him become aware.

Metasynctatic Awareness

The participants paid attention to both the sentence construction of the native speakers' texts and that of their own texts posted in blogs. We find many traces of metasynctatic awareness in the correction and self-correction of the text. Both examples shown in Figure 6 illustrate the two cases of syntactic correction. In the first example, a Chinese speaker corrects an erroneous sentence written by a French student

Figure 5.

Nelly F Says:
mars 30th, 2011 at 21 h 42 min   edit

你们好！(^.^)

我是Nelly！

我真喜欢游厉！

二年的时候我第一游厉可是不想起。这个时代自从每年署假我跟我的家人游厉。我去德国意大利西班牙希腊土耳其埃及可是从未去亚洲。。。我很想在中国和日本因为也学习日文。

游厉的时候我喜欢探胜迹堵会和穿统的寨，发现新文化。

你常常游厉吗？

【English translation: Hello everyone, I am Nelly. I really like to travel around. When (I was in second grade) two year I first travelled around but (I) cannot remember (it). This era since every summer vacation I travel around with my family (Now my family and I travel every summer vacation.) I have been to Germany, Italy, Spain, Greece, Turkey, and Egypt but I have never been to Asia … I really want to go to China and Japan, since I am also studying Japanese. When traveling around, I like to explore ancient monuments block meeting and wear traditional villages, find new cultures. Do you travel around often?】

Commentaire 8: du tongle mar 31, 2011 @ 13:37:16

du tongle Says:
mars 31st, 2011 at 13 h 37 min   edit
你好Nelly :D 很高兴认识你
如果你不介意的话，我想说在这种情况下我们通常会说"旅游" :)

【English translation: Hello Nelly:D I'm very happy to get to know you.

If you don't mind, I would say that in this situation, we usually would say "tour":)】

learning Chinese, and gives her a suggestion and explanation regarding the past tense in the Chinese language. In the second example, a Chinese participant self-corrects his French writing by paying attention to the feminine agreement of the adjective "happy" (Figure 6).

Metasemantic Awareness

Three examples of metasemantic awareness were identified (See Figure 7 for an example). In this comment, a native French-speaking participant corrects a French sentence written by an American female student studying in France. He suggests replacing the word "practice" with the word "improve" in the last sentence of her text: "When I was 17, I went to China for three weeks. I started my Chinese studies at the university after this visit, so I really want to go back and practice my Chinese!" The proposed correction occurs on the semantic level, depending on the context of the use of this word "practice" (Figure 7).

Figure 6.

Jingjing Z Says:
novembre 25th, 2010 at 4 h 48 min edit
Bonjour! Je suis étudiant de Français en Qingdao, il y a quelques petites fautes dans votre composition, au dessous je me permets de faire quelques corrections.

你们好！

我叫萨哈！我今年二十岁。我是西班牙（si vous voulez dire que vous êtes Espagnole：我是西班牙人）。我爸爸在法国工作。我有一个弟弟，他是中学生。

我会说西班牙语，法语和英语。我在学习中文，希腊语和英语！我爱看书，我爱看电影，我还爱吃糖！

我很想去中国！

Julien

你们好！我叫立揚,我今年二十一岁. 我有一个哥哥. 我是法国人. 我来自法国.

我去年在台北. 我刚刚回法国. 我（曾经：avant)在東吳大学读书. 我现在是斯特拉斯堡大学的学生. 我去过一次中国, 兩次香港 和澳门, 因 为我很喜欢旅行.

再见！

【English translation of the underlined text: Hello! I am a student of French in Qingdao, there are a few mistakes in your composition, below I would like to make some corrections.

Hello! My name is Sarah! I am twenty years old this year. I'm Spain. (If you mean that you are Spanish: I am Spanish.) [...]

I was in Taipei last year. I just came back to France. I (ceng jing: once) studied at Soochow University.】

guozheng yu Says:
février 13th, 2011 at 16 h 08 min edit
J'ai une faute. C'est »heureuse ».⊙﹏⊙‖

【English translation: I made a mistake. It is "happy." ».⊙﹏⊙‖】

Metatextual Awareness

The consciousness on language regarding text concerns both text form and its content. A female Chinese student presents a text shaped in the form of a heart and uses the phrase "I like... but I do not like..." throughout the text. In the comments below, shown in Figure 8, a French participant makes a comment regarding the main structure of the text; another participant also finds it interesting and considers it as a poem rather than as a simple text. Presented below is the Chinese student's text (Figure 8).

Metapragmatic Awareness

Given that meta-processes often occur in situations where there exists an inability to understand written messages or uncover linguistic errors, the concept of saving face is considered important during this

Figure 7.

> *Hamza M* Says:
> <u>février 22nd, 2011 at 2 h 39 min</u> edit
> Anne 你好！
>
> 我觉得你的法语很好。
> 我认识一些在Georgetown学习过的学生。
> 他们都说Georgetown大学是一个很好的学校。
>
> <u>P.S : On dit plutôt « pratiquer » et non practiquer. Et dans ta phrase,</u>
> <u>« améliorer » irait mieux. C'est le seul détail qui trahit ta langue maternelle anglaise</u>
> ☺
>
> 加油！

【English translation of the underlined text: Hello Anne ! [...] PS: One usually says "practice" rather than "practiquer". And in your sentence, "improve" would be better. This is the only detail that gives away your native English. ☺. 】

meta-processes. In order to achieve progress in learning foreign languages, many participants usually do not tolerate linguistic errors. However, how does one report errors and give explanations without running into a potential losing of face? In this study, we observed that the metapragmatic awareness allows participants to minimize the problem of losing face in the case of error correction.

In the example below, a French student responds to a Chinese student's presentation about his leisure activities. The Chinese student's presentation is written entirely in French, except for the title of the film, which is in English: *Amelie*. Thus the French participant, Flora, suggests that his Chinese counterpart utilize the French title *Le fabuleux destin d'Amélie Poulain*, instead of the English version, in order to maintain consistency in French. A little smiley emoticon is added by the student at the end of the comment to show sympathy with his interlocutor. This addition of the emoticon shows that this type of language behaviour aims to achieve coherence in language and cultural knowledge, rather a critical attitude regarding the ignorance of the French title of a famous French film (Figure 9).

Another example shows an explanation of the error made by a female French student when writing Chinese. The error involves the fact that Traditional Chinese script is used in Taiwan and Hong Kong; Simplified Chinese script is utilized in mainland China. Mirana recognizes that she used the traditional version rather than the simplified version. By reviewing her comment, it is obvious she takes into account the geographical location of the speaker. Her explanation for her error and the script change reveals that she is utilizing a form of metapragmatic awareness (Figure 10)

Complex Metalinguistic Awareness

The linguistic meta-processes can be mixed by two or more types. In the small conversation below, a Chinese participant asks the meaning of the phrase "on decline" as it is employed by a French participant. The latter helps him understand this word by explaining the meaning in French and using an example related to China. We note that in the first comment when the question arises about the meaning of a word or words, there is a trace of metalexical awareness. Within the second comment, the meaning of the word is illustrated as a level decrease in power or size; the participant also includes an antonym of

Figure 8.

J'aime manger, mais je n'aime pas faire la cuisine.

J'aime faire des photos à d'autres personne, mais je n'aime pas les dire.

J'aime écouter de la musique étrangère, mais je ne connais pas ces paroles.

J'aime lire des histoires, mais je n'aime pas des fins malheureuses.

J'aime faire des voyages, mais je n'aime pas quitter ma famille très longtemps.

J'aime mon prénom français Erica, mais je n'aime pas bien mon non chinois ⊂⊃, parce qu'il fait entendre un peu comme un nom de garçon.

J'aime une vie simple et tranquille.

J'aime une pensée libre.

J'aime tous les choses qui sont très belles.

C'est tout.

ヽ(￣∇￣)ノ

Marion J Says:
<u>mars 15th, 2011 at 15 h 27 min</u> edit
我很喜欢你的介绍！"我喜欢。。。但不喜欢。。。"

Marion ☺

【English translation: I love your presentation! "I like ... but I do not like ..."】

Hamza M Says:
<u>mars 16th, 2011 at 10 h 50 min</u> edit
Salut !
J'aime beaucoup ta présentation ☺ Tu es probablement une poète en herbe !
Très original !

【English translation: Hi! I like your presentation You're probably a budding poet! Very original! 】

Figure 9.

Flora M Says:
<u>janvier 4th, 2011 at 19h 02min</u> edit
salut! en france on appelle le film dont tu parles: « Le fabuleux destin d'Amélie Poulain »^^

【English translation of sentence above: hi! in france the film you mention is called: "Le fabuleux destin d'Amélie Poulain " ^^】

Figure 10.

> *Mirana R* Says:
> février 7th, 2011 at 21h 07min edit
> Désolée, j'ai étudié 2 mois à Taiwan alors j'ai écrit en caractères traditionnels sans faire exprès....

【English translation of sentence above: Sorry, I studied two months in Taiwan so I wrote in traditional characters without meaning to ....】

this word, "en pleine ascension," in reference to China's emergent economic status, to help the Chinese participant better understand the word "en déclin" (in decline). At this level, we see that the author of the second comments mobilized a metasemantic awareness. In addition, the use of emoticons reinforces the explanation of the antonyms "en déclin" and "en pleine ascension", in order to provide a better understanding of the interlocutor regarding these two phrases. Thus, the author engages in metapragmatic awareness (Figure 11).

Choices of Language in Bilingual Interaction

To answer the second research question, "Do FFL and CFL students develop French-Chinese bilingual skills through web collaboration? If so, how do they develop French-Chinese bilingual skills?", data reveal how those bilingual skills are developed.

In order to help improve writing skills in the target language, participants were allowed in this study to choose language freely when posting messages and comments on the blog and forum. Researchers were additionally interested in determining the language choice utilized for scaffolding and negotiating meaning during peer communication. Thus, the corpus of data analysed revealed differences in language choice among Chinese and French language peers. In the data set, the categorization, separation, comparison, and contacting process occurs during the interactions with native speakers. By speaking with

Figure 11.

> *lv rui* Says:
> avril 3rd, 2011 at 13 h 40 min edit
>
> 2 Pardon, je ne comprend bien ta queston, "en déclin??", j'ai consulté dans le dictionnaire, mais pas tres claire.

【English translation: [...] 2 Sorry, I do not understand very well your question, "on decline??", I consulted the dictionary, but it is not very clear. [...]】

> 2
> *Hamza M* Says:
> avril 3rd, 2011 at 15 h 36 min edit
> OK ! Merci pour tes réponses ! 你的回答很好 !
> Pour la deuxième question, « en déclin » signifie quelque chose dont le niveau, la puissance, ou la grandeur diminuent. On dit souvent que la Chine est un pays émergent, en pleine ascension \(^o^)/ : le déclin c'est un peu le contraire ! ☹

【English translation: For the second question, "declining" means something whose level, the power or the size decrease. China is often said that an emerging country, on the rise \(^ o ^) /: the "declining" is the opposite! ☺ [...]】

real interlocutors, students had the opportunity to think about the target language. These thoughts did not come from a book or teacher; their metalinguistic understanding came from personal reflections based on their authentic written interactions with the target language peers. Thus, the practice of writing in the target language and the practice with the native speakers offered them the opportunity to express their thoughts and reconstruct presentations in both the target language and the mother tongue. Furthermore, an admiration and mutual appreciation for one another's language was highly evidenced as noted above.

The researchers found that the posts and comments are mixed in various kinds of languages and combinations, including monolingual messages in Chinese or French, mixed in two languages (Chinese and French), or even four languages (Chinese, English, French, and Japanese). To show general patterns regarding CFL and FFL students' overall language use, the researchers calculated participants' posts and percentage of bilingual-monolingual language use. As shown in Table 2, 20.9% among the total of 225 comments were mixed in two languages.

According to Table 2, monolingual comments (36.4% + 41.8%) appear about four times as much as bilingual comments (21.8%) in the web collaboration learning process. This significant difference among the Chinese students, as well as among the French students, shows that the written exchange on the blog falls within a monolingual logic. In the case of the monolingual, comments in French exist slightly more than the Chinese comments, i.e. 45.7% in French as compared with 35.7% in Chinese. Of the two national groups, French participants used their mother tongue (45.7% vs. 35.5%) more than the Chinese participants, the latter of which equally used the Chinese and French languages (35.7% vs. 37.9%). The proportion of the bilingual messages is higher for Chinese participants than French participants, i.e., 26.4% against 18.8%.

By comparing the contributions between the first and the second semester, the results reveal a significant change in the number of bilingual comments during experimentation, particularly in relation to the number of comments in the native language and target language. Nevertheless, the three types of language using (mother tongue, foreign language, and bilingual) in written interaction increases at different paces (see Figure 12 for Rate of increase of contributions in three languages between semester 1 and semester 2).

Table 2. Number and percentage of comments in Chinese, French and bilingual

	French-Chinese Bilingual Message	Message Only in Chinese	Message Only in French	Total Number (%)
French group				
Total posting	**26** (18.8%)	**49** (35.5%)	**63** (45.7%)	**138** (100%)
Semester 1	3 (7.3%)	13 (31.7%)	25 (61%)	41 (100%)
Semester 2	23 (23.7%)	36 (37.1%)	38 (39.2%)	97 (100%)
Chinese group				
Total posting	**23** (26.4%)	**31** (35.7%)	**33** (37.9%)	**87** (100%)
Semester 1	4 (16.7%)	5 (20.8%)	15 (62.5%)	24 (100%)
Semester 2	19 (30.1%)	26 (41.3%)	18 (28.6%)	63 (100%)
All Members				
Total posting	**49** (21.8%)	**82** (36.4%)	**94** (41.8%)	**225** (100%)
Semester 1	7 (10.8%)	18 (27.7%)	40 (61.5%)	65 (100%)
Semester 2	42 (26.2%)	62 (38.8%)	56 (35%)	160 (100%)

According to Figure 12, at the monolingual level, the rate of increase in native language comments is 52%, as contrasted against 177% in a foreign language for French participants. These figures signify that the French students are more motivated to interact with native Chinese speakers and to practice of the foreign language. Among the Chinese students, the rate of increase in practicing foreign language is 20% while their use of the mother tongue increased by 420%. The comparison of such percentages shows that the motivation to engage in foreign language practice is much lower among Chinese students than that among French students. The increase in the mother tongue contributions during the second semester indicates that during the second semester, their attention has focused more on producing meaning and in the intensity of the interaction, rather than on written expression training in a foreign language.

Factors of Language Change and Choice of Language

To answer the third research question, "What facilitate CFL and FFL learners' language exchange in communicating with native-speaking peers and learning the target languages?", data indicate two factors that drive the transition from one language to another:

1. Language change at intra- and inter-sentential levels; and
2. The choice of the language (e.g., first language, target language, or another language).

The active presence of the two languages (French and Chinese) in the bilingual exchange among participants manifests itself in very different configurations. The code switching occurred between sentences or elements within a sentence in the same speaking slot at the intra-personal level. It also intervened between the speaking slots of participants in the exchange, i.e. the inter-personal code switching.

Figure 12. Rate of increase of contributions in three languages between semester 1 and semester 2

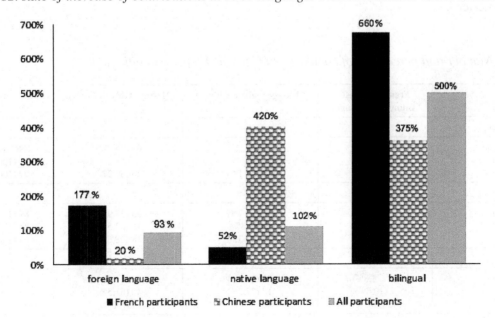

Factors of Language Change at Intra-Personal Level

The code-switching at the intra-personal level includes the inter-sentential level, intra-sentential level, and the extra-sentential. Language change at the inter-sentential level appears when the language change occurs entirely between two sentences or two propositions, wherein each of the sentences or propositions depends upon a different code.

Compared to the intra-sentential switching, inter-sentential switching and extra-sentential switching are the majority of cases in our data set. The major factors that triggered code-switching among both French members and Chinese members occurred primarily during linguistic breakdowns. As a way to address this change, either the topic was changed, or the sentence or phrase was reformulated.

Factors of Language Choice at Interpersonal Level

In order to analyse the choice of language at the interpersonal level, the researchers analyzed comment posts, which revealed some common factors that may influence the choice of language. Data analysis reveals that the choice of language in written interaction on the blog depends on the language environment, the written skill, and the conversation context of the language exchange. Here is a summary table of factors that influence the language choice of comments. The participants' exchange was not limited strictly to French or Chinese. Instead, they may translanguage by utilizing third and fourth languages, such as English, as resources to promote and extend their communication (Table 3).

In most cases, the authors observed a consistency of language choice in their conversation. In general, when the first member author posted his/her comments in a language, the other member authors followed him/her in the same language, unless they encountered a written difficulty or other factors that disrupted the consistency of the language choices. This linguistic compliance, regardless self-awareness or not, ensures that the impact of the linguistic environment on language choice is much stronger than that of two other factors (gap in written production, and conversational context) on the choice of languages for posting comments.

Table 3. Factors of language choice at interpersonal level

Factors Influencing the Choice	Language Choices	Functions
Language environment (Adapt language to that of the previous comment)	Chinese	Search linguistic coherence
	French	
	Foreign language	
	Mother tongue	
	Mixed languages	
Gap in written production	Mother tongue	Bridging the language gap and build a social and community identity
	Mixed languages	
Conversational context (the objective of exchange, foreign language native speaker level, change the subject)	Foreign language	Practicing, verify, and improve in written in a foreign language production
	Mother tongue or mixed languages	More information
	Foreign language and mixed languages Mother tongue and mixed languages	Ensure effective communication, establish a social link that takes into account the written competency in the target language of the other

In some comments shown in Figures 4-12, participants spoke almost exclusively in foreign languages or in mixed languages, except where the interlocutors met the difficulty of writing. While they addressed abstract and interesting topics, sometimes they all chose to communicate in mother tongue to ensure the smooth flow of conversation, shown in Figures 9-11.

Gaps in written expression are the second factor of language choice in bilingual interaction. We noticed that in some situations, the A2 language level did not allow participants to express what they want to say, especially in conversations where participants discussed on societal, economic, linguistic, and educational topics. Thus, with greater topic depth, the language learners could not express themselves fully and had to partially support their language interaction by choosing the mother tongue. The use of the mother tongue did not affect the exchange negatively, quite the opposite; that level of translanguaging assisted the participants in written comprehension.

Language choices of participants was different for French versus Chinese Leaners. The French group revealed a much greater tendency to move from monolingual expression (61% during the first semester) to foreign language (37.1% in Chinese during the second semester) and bilingual and/or plurlilingual (23.7% during the second semester) expression.

Chinese students mainly chose to write comments in the target foreign language (61%) at the start of the exchange. During this period, they focused more on the linguistic aspect than on the situational aspects. Observations reveal that as Chinese progressed in their interaction with others in the program they utilized their mother tongue (41.3%), the target language of French (28.6%), and Bilingual (30.1%) including English in their exchanges. The plurilingual use was seen more among the French (30.1%) when compared to their Chinese counterparts (23.7%) who were learning Chinese. During the exchange, the French used three types of language (mother tongue- 39.2%, foreign- 37.1%, and mixed language- 23.7%). The Chinese participants were less likely using French language (28.6%), the target language, than mother tongue, Chinese (41.3%).

The more that French students became familiar with Chinese students, the more they became interested in the cultural and social aspects of the exchange. This increased interest led to more in-depth discussions. While the topic levels became more advanced and in depth, it was difficult for participants to continue comprehensible communication solely in the foreign language of study. That is when the students utilized their other languages as resources to promote communication flow in ways that allowed for depth of conversation. Thus, bilingual as well as plurilingual communication has become unavoidable in order to ensure that exchange becomes convenient and consistent. It is through these mobilization strategies of bilingual communication skills as resources that they were able to gain more language and intercultural knowledge, and succeed in effective and comprehensible communication.

CONCLUSION AND IMPLICATIONS

This French-Chinese web collaboration project provides a space for FFL and CFL learners to work on their dialogic writing skills with the goal of writing primarily in the target language. This project also aims to explore whether French and Chinese students' web collaboration through blog-writing prepares them with metalinguisc awareness, plurlingual competence and bilingual skills.

Data analysis indicated that more than a third of the foreign language participants demonstrated metalinguistic awareness during online interaction with native speakers. These FFL and CFL students seemed to consciously connect target language learning to their prior knowledge of their mother tongues. Peer feedback through blog-writing not only motivate foreign language learners' target language learning but also help all learners to reflect on their own language use. This indicates that web-based communication platform is a useful way to develop foreign language learners' metalinguistic awareness (Rao, 2015).

During the web collaboration, all participants demonstrated bilingual skills (e.g., code-switching). As an intercultural tool code-switching allows students to manage two or more languages in their written interactions. Code-switching occurred more frequently among native French-speaking students than native Chinese-speaking students. In free interaction, French students seemed to experience a change from relying their communication on French to employing French-Chinese bilingual skills in their web interaction. Their shift from unilingual to bilingual seems to be less obvious among native Chinese-speaking students. This further indicates that web-based free language learning environment and native-speaking peer assistantship contributes to native French-speaking learners' CFL learning. Similarly, CFL learners were also benefited from increasing their bilingual and plurilingual skills. Comparatively, such improvement seemed to be less obvious among native Chinese-speaking learners' FFL learning. This requires future research to further explore what factors may lead to such difference.

The language switching appears both at the inter-individual and intra-individual levels. However, due to the big difference between the two language systems, the occurrence of intra-sentential code-switching was not common. Data reveal three important factors which may trigger French and Chinese speakers' code-switching: conversation context (e.g., Responding to the first speaker, the second speaker tends to adopt the same language choice), linguistic breakdowns, and conversation topics (e.g., the need to change topic or reformulate questions or answers).

Multilingual and multicultural expertise is closely linked with plurilingual competence (Castellotti & Moore, 2011; Lüdi & Py, 2013). Such skills allow speakers to develop connections between languages as well as switch codes from one language to another in order to reach communicative purpose (Lüdi & Py, 2013). Through our observations of online interaction between foreign language learners and native speakers, the researchers found that in such web-based collaborative learning context, FFL and CFL learners developed their metalinguistic awareness to comprehend meaning as well as facilitate target language learning.

Major implications of the study include: Web collaboration in a tandem learning form can be utilized for developing foreign language learners' plurilingual competence and metalinguistic awareness. Since web collaboration costs less human and material resources in comparison with a traditional face-to-face learning, it benefits small foreign language programs and students in remote areas to practice foreign language learning with native-speakers. Web collaboration not only shows a big potential to facilitate students learning in and outside the classroom, but also engage learners in developing intercultural awareness and bilingual skills.

In the future, researchers may conduct a quantitative study to measure whether foreign language learners improve their metalinguistic awareness and bilingual skills through web collaborative blog-writing. It is also suggested that similar web collaborative research should be conducted in different countries and/or among different foreign language learners to explore whether such web-based tandem learning is also effective for other language learners.

REFERENCES

Araújo-Carreira, M. H. (1992). La diversité des langues a l'école: réflexions sur la place d'une langue romane, le portugais. *Repères 6, Langues Vivantes et Français à l'Ecole* (pp. 57-67). Paris: INRP.

Armand, F., & Dagenais, D. (2005). Langues en contexte d'immigration: éveiller au langage et à la diversité linguistique en milieu scolaire. In *Revue de l'Association des études canadiennes* (pp. 110-113).

Belz, J. A. (2003). Linguistics perspectives on the development of intercultural competence in telecollaboration. *Language Learning & Technology, 7*(2), 68–117.

Bialystok, E. (2001). *Bilingualism in development: Language, literacy and cognition.* Cambridge University Press. doi:10.1017/CBO9780511605963

Blasco, J. (2013). *L'apprentissage des langues étrangères au cycle 3: activités réflexives entre langues 1 et 2.* Mémoire de Master, Ecole Interne IUFM Midi-Pyrénées.

Bullock, B. (2009). Themes in the study of code-switching. In The Cambridge Handbook of Linguistic Code-Switching (pp. 1-17).

Candelier, M. (2008). Approches plurielles, didactiques du plurilinguisme: Le même et l'autre. *Cahiers de l'ACEDLE, 5*(1), 65–90.

Cashman, H. (2005). Identities at play: Language preference and group membership in bilingual talk in interaction. *Journal of Pragmatics, 37*(3), 301–315. doi:10.1016/j.pragma.2004.10.004

Castellotti, V., & Moore, D. (2005). Répertoires pluriels, cultures métalinguistiques et usages d'appropriation. In J.C. Beacco, et al. (Eds.), Les cultures éducatives et linguistiquesdans l'enseignement des langues (pp. 107-132). Paris, PUF.

Castellottie, V., & Moore, D. (2011). La compétence plurilingue et pluriculturelle: genèse et évolution d'une notion-concept. In *P. Blanchet, & P. Chardenet (Eds.), Guide pour la recherche en didactique des langues et des cultures: approches contextualisées. In Archives contemporaines* (pp. 241–252). Pages.

Conseil de l'Europe, C. (2001). *Cadre européen commun de référence pour les langues.* Les Éditions Didier, Paris. Retrieved from http://www.coe.int/t/dg4/linguistic/Source/Framework_FR.pdf

Coste, D. (2001). La notion de compétence plurilingue. *Proceedings of the seminar L'enseignement des langues vivantes, perspectives.* Retrieved from: http://eduscol.education.fr/pid25239-cid46534/la-notion-de-competence-plurilingue.html

Coste, D., Moore, D., & Zarate, G. (2009). *Compétence plurilingue et pluriculturelle.* Strasbourg: Conseil de l'Europe.

Dooly, M., & O'Dowd, R. (1996). *Researching online foreign language interaction and exchange: Theories, methods and challenges.* Peter Lang. Gombert, J. É.

Ellwood, C. (2008). Questions of classroom identity: What can be learned from codeswitching in classroom peer group talk. *Modern Language Journal, 92*(4), 538–557. doi:10.1111/j.1540-4781.2008.00786.x

Ellwood, C. (2008). Questions of classroom identity: What can be learned from codeswitching in classroom peer group talk. *Modern Language Journal*, *92*(4), 538–557. doi:10.1111/j.1540-4781.2008.00786.x

Filippetti, A. (2014). *Les langues de France*. Paris: Dalloz.

García, O. (2011). The translanguaging of Latino kindergarteners. Bilingual Youth: Spanish in In *English-Speaking Societies* (pp. 33-55).

Genette, G., & Lewin, J. E. (1997). *Paratexts: Thresholds of Interpretation*. New York: Cambridge Press. doi:10.1017/CBO9780511549373

Gombert, J. É. (1990). *Le développement métalinguistique*. Paris: Presses universitaires de France.

Gombert, J. E. (1992). *Metalinguistic development*. University of Chicago Press. Activités métalinguistiques et acquisition d'une langue. *Acquisition et Interaction en Langue Étrangère*, (8): 41–55.

Grosjean, F. (1982). *Life with two languages: an introduction to bilingualism*. Cambridge, MA: Harvard University Press.

Grosjean, F. (1984). Le bilinguisme: vivre avec deux langues. In Revue Tranel (Travaux neuchâtelois de linguistique), (7), 15-41.

Gumperz, J. J. (1982). Discourse strategies. Cambridge University Press.

Gumperz, J. J. (1989). *Sociolinguistique Interactionnelle: une approche interprétative*. L'Harmattan. Université de la Réunion.

Harris, J. (1998). *Virtual architecture: Designing and directing curriculum-based telecomputing*. Eugene, OR: International Society for Technology in Education.

Kim, J.-O. (2003). *Étude des verbalisations métalinguistiques d'apprenants coréens sur l'imparfait et le passé composé en français* (Doctoral Thesis). Université Paris III- Sorbonne nouvelle. Retrieved from http://www.kimjinok.com/html/theses/intro.html

Lüdi, G. (1992, April 6-11). Statuts et fonctions des marques transcodiques en conversation exolingue. In G. Hilty (Ed.), *Actes du XXè Congrès international de linguistique et philologie romaines*, Université de Zurich (pp. 123-136). Tübingen, Basel: Francke.

Lüdi, G. (1995). Parler bilingue et traitements cognitifs. *Intellectica*, *1*(20), 139–156.

Lüdi, G. (2004). Pour une linguistique de la compétence du locuteur plurilingue. *Revue française de linguistique appliquée*, 9(2), 125-135.

Lüdi, G., & Py, B. (2013). *Etre bilingue. (4ᵉ édition)*. Bern: Peter Lang. doi:10.3726/978-3-0351-0647-3

Marot, T. (2002). *Conscience phonographique et apprentissage du lire-écrire: vers un enseignement systémique et développemental* [PhD thesis]. Université Lyon II.

Moore, D. (2006). *Plurilinguismes et école*. Paris: Didier.

Poplack, S. (1988). Conséquences linguistiques du contact des langues: Un modèle d'analyse variationniste. *Langage & Société*, *43*(1), 23–48. doi:10.3406/lsoc.1988.3000

Rao, Y. (2015). *Apprentissage du chinois (CLE) et du français (FLE) dans une communauté numérique bilingue* [PhD thesis]. Université Aix-Marseille.

Reder, F., Marec-Breton, N., Gombert, J., & Demont, E. (2013). Second-language learners' advantage in metalinguistic awareness: A question of languages' characteristics. *The British Journal of Educational Psychology*, *83*(4), 686–702. doi:10.1111/bjep.12003 PMID:24175689

Rey-Debove, J. (1986). *Le métalangage*. Paris: Le Robert.

Rodi, M. (2009). Compétences plurilingues et acquisitions, *Langage & Pratiques*, 44, 2-12.

Scotton, C. M., & Ury, W. (1977). Bilingual strategies: The social functions of code-switching. *International Journal of the Sociology of Language*, 13, 5–20.

Springer, C. (2009a). *CECR et Perspective Actionnelle: de la tâche pédagogique communicative au projet collaboratif.* Actes du Symposium international Didactique des Langues Étrangères et Maternelles: TIC, aides et méthodes d'apprentissage, Université Mohammed Premier - Oujda (Maroc). Retrieved from http://springcloogle.blogspot.com/2009/02/cecr-et-perspective-actionnellede-la.html/

Springer, C. (2014). *La webcollaboration pour les classes bilingues / FLE*. Synergies Espagne.

Wenger, E. (1998). *Communities of practice. Learning, meaning, and identity. Cambridge.* UK: Cambridge University Press. doi:10.1017/CBO9780511803932

Wenger, E. (2005). *La théorie des communautés de pratique.* (F. Gervais, Trad.) Sainte-Foy, Québec: les Presses de l'université Laval.

Wenger, E., McDermott, R., & Snyder, W. M. (2002). *Cultivating communities of practice: A guide to managing knowledge*. Boston, MA: Harvard Business School Press.

Winstead, L. (2004). Increasing academic motivation and cognition in reading, writing, and mathematics: Meaning-making strategies. *Educational Research Quarterly*, *28*(2), 30–49.

Winstead, L. (2013). Apprehension and motivation among adolescent dual language peers: Perceptions and awareness about self-directed teaching and learning. *Language and Education*, *27*(1), 1–21. doi:10.1080/09500782.2012.669767

Zongo, B. (2004). *Le parler ordinaire multilingue à Paris. Ville et alternance codique*. Paris, L'Harmattan.

ENDNOTE

[1]   Retrieved from http://echange-francochinois.unistra.fr/

Section 4
Less Commonly Taught Languages

Chapter 11

Yiddish in the 21st Century:
New Media to the Rescue of Endangered Languages

Agnieszka Legutko
Columbia University, USA

ABSTRACT

This chapter offers the first scholarly analysis of teaching the Yiddish language in the digital age, and argues that new media have a tremendous potential for rescuing endangered languages. It investigates the pedagogical advantages and disadvantages of using digital technologies in teaching languages, as well as the ensuing challenges for teachers and students. A brief overview of the history of the Yiddish language and culture is followed by examination of such new digital platforms as Yiddishpop.com, Mapping Yiddish New York, The Grosbard Project, Yiddish audio and visual materials available online, such as videos, sound archives, online newspapers and dictionaries, as well as distance learning opportunities.

1. A SHORT HISTORY OF THE YIDDISH LANGUAGE AND CULTURE

1.1. The Language

Yiddish, the vernacular language of the Ashkenazic (Central and East European) Jews, traditionally categorized as a Germanic language, is a fusion language (M. Weinreich, 1973) that combines characteristics from the Semitic, Germanic, and Slavic language families. It emerged in the tenth century in the Rhineland or Bavaria regions (Dovid Katz, 1987; Wexler, 1991) in Germany, but as a result of the migration of its speakers to Central and Eastern Europe in the Middle Ages, it underwent a substantial process of Slavicization. Thus, the modern Yiddish language consists of three main vocabulary components: German, Hebrew-Aramaic, and Slavic (Polish, Russian, Ukrainian, Belarusian, Czech, Slovak, etc.), and its syntax and underlying structure are influenced by Slavic patterns. Yiddish is written in the Hebrew alphabet (right to left); but unlike Hebrew, which uses an abjad writing system (a consonantal script of 22 letters with vowels marked diacritically), Yiddish uses a phonemic orthography, in which all vowels are represented by separate symbols. Several other studies are recommended for more infor-

DOI: 10.4018/978-1-5225-0177-0.ch011

mation on the history and linguistic structure of the Yiddish language (Birnbaum, 1979; M. Weinreich, 1973; J. E. Fishman, 1991; Jacobs, 2005; Dovid Katz, 2004;).

1.2 Literature and Culture

The earliest evidence of written Yiddish dates back to 1096, in the form of lists of names of Jews from Mainz, Germany, who were murdered during the First Crusade (Jacobs, 2005, p. 50). The first written sentence in Yiddish is found in a 1272 prayerbook from Worms; the earliest Yiddish texts feature adaptations of European romance chivalric epics, as well as Biblical and Talmudic explorations and moralistic tractates circulated in manuscripts since 1382 (Dovid Katz, 2004, p. 82). The first Yiddish book was printed in 1543 in Krakow, Poland (Jacobs, 2005, p. 50), and was followed by a surge in Yiddish publications of both religious and secular texts, including such best-sellers as *Tsene-rene,* or the so-called "women's bible," which appeared in over two hundred editions since the earliest extant 1622 edition (Dovid Katz, 2004, p. 87).

The rise of modern Yiddish literature dates back to the mid 19th century with its "golden age" occurring in the 1920s and '30s in Poland, the Soviet Union, and the United States, the three largest Yiddish-speaking centers prior to 1939. Although Yiddish literature developed in a relatively brief period of time, it quickly attained the status of a European literature. By the early 20th century, Yiddish culture flourished worldwide: the Yiddish press published hundreds of titles daily around the globe; Yiddish theater and film enjoyed the time of their highest glory; and networks of Yiddish schools were established in the United States and Europe (Freidenreich, 2010; Eisenstein, 1950; Shneer, 2004). The YIVO (*Yidisher Visnshaftlekher Institute*) Institute for Jewish Research, established in 1925 in Vilnius, Poland (now Lithuania), pioneered Yiddish research and played an important role in creating and promoting the so-called *klal shprakh*, the modern Yiddish standard dialect, which is now the variety taught at schools, universities, and language programs. This creates a certain pedagogical dilemma: for the overwhelming majority of Yiddish native speakers use one of the modern Eastern Yiddish dialects: Northeastern (Lithuanian), Mideastern (Polish), Southeastern (Ukrainian), or the currently emerging Standard Hasidic Yiddish (Dovid Katz, 2015, p. 292), whereas students are taught the *klal shprakh*, which is hardly ever spoken outside the community of academics and Yiddishists.

1.3 Status Struggles

Despite enjoying prominence from the Middle Ages until the Holocaust, Yiddish struggled to achieve a fully respectable status as a national language of the Jewish people. Yiddish, the everyday language of the Ashkenazic Jews, has always been juxtaposed with Hebrew-Aramaic, the so-called *loshn-koydesh*, the "holy tongue," the language of the Torah (the Hebrew Bible), used in liturgy and written rabbinical commentaries, which was reserved for the male intellectual elite (although they also spoke Yiddish, since Hebrew had not been a living language for two millennia until it was revived as a daily spoken vernacular at the turn of the 20th century). Jews have traditionally been multilingual: they were familiar (to varying degrees) with Hebrew-Aramaic, and in case of the Ashkenazic Jews, they spoke Yiddish in everyday life (Dovid Katz, 2004, pp. 45–77). The so-called acculturated Jews (often less observant or entirely secular) also spoke the language of the country in which they resided (Polish, Russian, German, English, etc.). Nonetheless, for centuries, and especially since the 18th-century *Haskalah*, or Jewish Enlightenment,

Yiddish encountered rejection and dismissal as a "corrupt German jargon." It was derided as a "vulgar [language] that has no rules" (D. E. Fishman, 2010, p. 5), an inferior dialect of women and uneducated masses, unworthy of serious rabbinic and secular literary creativity. With the rise of nationalism in Europe and especially Zionism, which raised the question of the national language of the Jews, the competition between Yiddish and Hebrew escalated. Yiddishists advocated the recognition of Yiddish as the primary language of the Jews in Central and Eastern Europe, whereas proponents of Zionism, who focused on building a Jewish society in the land of Israel (then-Palestine), championed the idea of Hebrew as the primary language of the new land, even though they used Yiddish to reach out to the masses (Seidman, 1997; Dovid Katz, 2004; J. E. Fishman, 1991, pp. 11–68). Following the mass Eastern European Jewish emigration to America in the years 1881-1924, about 2.5 million Yiddish speakers settled in the United States. Until the Second World War, Yiddish seemed to be dominating as the national language of the Jews, since it was the language of two-thirds of the world Jewish population (D. E. Fishman, 2010, p. 15). Famously a language without a country, Yiddish received only a temporary recognition and brief government support from the Soviet Union in the 1920s, and nowhere else (D. E. Fishman, 2010, p. 15).

1.4. The Language Genocide: Yiddish in the Post-Holocaust World

The Second World War put an end to the blossoming Yiddish culture. Out of the six million Jews who perished during the Holocaust, more than five million were Yiddish speakers, nearly half of the prewar Yiddish speaking population. Although the estimated number of Yiddish speakers after the Second World War was about seven million (Birnbaum, 1979, p. 40), and about three million in 1991 (J. E. Fishman, 1991, pp. 329–330), the cultural and geographical center where Yiddish thrived for almost a thousand years was irreversibly destroyed. The exodus of the Holocaust survivors to other countries, and the subsequent cultural and linguistic assimilation was a significant factor in the rapid decrease of the number of its speakers. Although literature was created in Yiddish throughout the 20th century (and was recognized by the Nobel Prize in literature awarded to Isaac Bashevis Singer in 1978), the number of its readers continued to plunge. Secondly, the establishment of the State of Israel in 1948, with Hebrew declared the official language of the new state (despite the fact that 46.8 percent of the new Israeli population declared Yiddish as their mother tongue) (J. E. Fishman, 1991, p. 407), with the attendant intense focus on forging a new national Israeli identity, resulting in a formation of hostile policy towards Yiddish (J. E. Fishman, 1991, p. 17), further contributed to the devastating decline in the Yiddish speaking population.

1.5 Yiddish Speakers in the 21st Century

One of the many tragic outcomes of the Holocaust was the loss of secular native Yiddish speakers who engaged with Yiddish culture broadly understood, which has been replaced by the phenomenon referred to as "postvernacularism" (Shandler, 2006), a symbolic use of the language that is no longer used as the vernacular. The flourishing modern Yiddish culture was cut in its prime and has never fully recovered from the trauma of the genocide.

One group that has actively continued to speak Yiddish after the Holocaust and still speaks Yiddish today are the Hasidic and the Ultra-Orthodox Jews (also referred to as the Haredi). They use Yiddish in everyday life and as a language of instruction in schools and in Talmudic studies, but they eschew any contact with secular Yiddish literature and culture, following the pious standards set by the religious leadership. A certain paradox emerges: Yiddish is a thriving language of a community that does not engage with non-religious Yiddish culture. Since the worldwide Hasidic community of over one million is growing at a rate of five percent a year, the predictions are that by 2075, they will number between eight and ten million (Eisenberg, 1995, p. 1-2), which shall permanently remove the endangered status of Yiddish and ensure that the future of Yiddish is Hasidic (Dovid Katz, 2015).

As Katz points out, there is also a certain power imbalance between Yiddish-speaking Hasidim and Haredim ("Powerless Yiddish") and secular Yiddishists ("Yiddishless Yiddish Power") who may be less immersed in the living language itself but are more successful in fund raising and in their focus of contemporary Yiddish culture and academic study (Dovid Katz, 2015, pp. 293–295). Indeed, it is the "secular camp" that has created all of the digital platforms discussed here, since the Ultra-Orthodox Hasidim are yet to exhibit interest in online Yiddish teaching initiatives. Still, the growing online presence of Hasidic blogs in Yiddish and English is worth noting. The secular initiatives are also behind academic Yiddish language instruction. At least fifty colleges and universities around the globe offer Yiddish language courses (most of them are located in the United States, Germany, Canada, and Poland), in addition to about ten several-week-long summer programs in the United States, Europe, and Israel, and several shorter klezmer programs. However, it must be mentioned that the preponderant number of courses are for beginners, the majority of whom do not continue beyond this stage and do not deepen their familiarity with the language. Therefore, intermediate and advanced courses are offered only at a handful of universities. The doctoral programs in Yiddish studies (at Columbia, Harvard, JTS, University of Pennsylvania, University of Michigan, Tel Aviv University, to name but a few) produce advanced researchers but provide very little formal Yiddish teacher training.

1.6. Who Learns Yiddish Today?

Since Yiddish remains a stateless language, theoretically speaking it has no practical application in today's world outside the Hasidic circles. It is not a language of commerce or business, and there is virtually no imaginable situation in which one's survival would depend on knowing Yiddish (most native Yiddish speakers know at least one other language). Of course, the immensely rich, over one-thousand-year-old Yiddish culture, history, and (somewhat younger) literature await explorers, researchers, and translators, but as is the case with humanities today, the general interest lies in the sciences. Furthermore, as Tatjana Soldat-Jaffe observes, "for the vast majority of contemporary [non-Hasidic] Jewry, the function of a Yiddish *mame-loshn* [mother tongue] is now merely a shared cultural memory" (Soldat-Jaffe, 2012, p. 76). The condescendingly narrow approach to Yiddish prevails, as illustrated by numerous press articles presenting Yiddish as a language of humor and curses that now drowns in Yinglish, recycling the concept of the Yiddish revival (Kafrissen, 2012), or depicting Yiddish as an object of nostalgia and sentimentality that "no longer has any validity as a vital cultural idiom" (Isenberg, 1997).

Nonetheless, the interest in learning Yiddish among today's college students brings to mind Marcus Lee Hansen's immigration theory, "the principle of third generation interest," according to which "what the son wishes to forget, the grandson wishes to remember" (Hansen, 1938, p. 9). Many Yiddish students are the grandchildren of the Yiddish-speaking Holocaust survivors who immigrated to America in the postwar years. These students wish to engage with the cultural heritage of their grandparents in contrast to the parent generation, and perceive learning Yiddish as "a powerful way of connecting to our culture and religion" (Samilow, 2016).

A survey conducted on fifteen participants of the *kave-sho*, a monthly Yiddish conversation hour run at Columbia University ("Yiddish Kave Sho," 2015), about their motivation behind engaging with Yiddish seems to confirm the above claim. One of the most popular incentives is to reclaim one's heritage: "This is part of my heritage that I was deprived of as my parents (and grandparents) didn't teach me the language." Another common refrain is that parents (and sometimes grandparents) use(d) Yiddish as the secret language in front of the (grand)children when they did not want them to understand, so the next generation is learning Yiddish to understand the secret language of their childhood and youth. Some people do it for "family reasons:" they want to learn the language of their Yiddish-speaking partner, parent or grandparent for purposes of communication and closer bonding. Infatuation with Yiddish literature, especially with the works by Isaac Bashevis Singer, and academic research interests – from the Holocaust, through German-Jewish literature, to Yiddish in Palestine/Israel were also cited as reasons behind the initial impetus to explore Yiddish. Fascination with klezmer music, as well as with the world of Hasidism – both with Hasidic history and literature, as well as with the world of actual Hasidic Jews, many of whom decide to leave the community and pursue secular college education – was also cited as the stimulus to engage with Yiddish. Finally, Yiddish offers an alternative Jewish identity for people who may not be religious and may decline an affiliation with Israel. Often the reasons overlapped but the message was clear: the millennial generation (14 out of the 15 participants of the *kave sho* were under 30 years of age) is seriously invested in reclaiming Yiddish for themselves. Today, to revise a common Yiddish sentiment, "Yiddish speakers are made *both* in the bedroom and in the classroom" (Shandler, 2006, p. 60).

2. NEW MEDIA IN YIDDISH LANGUAGE TEACHING

There is virtually no research published on new media in Yiddish language teaching. As far as is known, this is the first scholarly attempt to provide an overview of new technology employed in Yiddish pedagogy. However, recent scholarship on Yiddish pedagogy includes unprecedented research into the evolution of secular Yiddish textbooks associated with Yiddish school system in the 20th century (Wiecki, 2009) and several blog posts on the recently launched online Journal of Yiddish Studies, *In geveb*, in its Pedagogy section ("Pedagogy," n.d.).

The integration of technology in the classroom and online learning opportunities appear to be strongly affecting the status of Yiddish in the 21st century. New media is the language of today's students, often referred to as "digital natives," (used interchangeably with "Net generation" and "Millennials," i.e. people born after 1980) who, as Marc Prensky notes, have been surrounded by new technology throughout their entire lives and have a perfect command of the language of computers, video games, social media, and the Internet (Prensky, 2001a, 2001b). Digital natives receive their information fast, prefer graphics to text, enjoy random access (hypertext), multi-tasking and networking, demand instant gratification and rewarding, and prefer games to "serious" work (Prensky, 2001a, pp. 2–3). Prensky's concept of digital natives has been since criticized as lacking empirical evidence and critical analysis, and as creating divides between the natives and the immigrants, that are compared to "hierarchical violence" (Bayne & Ross, 2007; Koutropoulos, 2011). Indeed, the encompassing presence of the Internet extends beyond the millennial generation. Many students of the Silent (1928-1945), Boomer (1946-64), and Gen X (1965-1980) generations also use technology to engage with Yiddish, as illustrated by the online Yiddish literature classes offered by the Workmen's Circle in New York (Borodulin, 2015). Furthermore, as many critics point out, the divide between the digital natives and immigrants – which allegedly reflects the divide between the tech-savvy students and teachers who lag behind (Holton, 2010) – quickly disappears or becomes irrelevant in digitial contexts (also, many of the digital natives become teachers themselves). While further research is still needed and it may yet be too early to obtain conclusive data showing the revolutionary differences in learning styles between the digital natives and earlier generations, the digital native discourse points out to important new characteristics of the millennial generation.

The twenty-first century language pedagogy should take into consideration the needs of students who are said to be multi-tasking and team-oriented (Oblinger, 2003; Tapscott, 1998), and are generally in favor of gaming, interaction and stimulation (i.e. multi-linear, visual, and virtual environments) and whose knowledge acquisition process appears to be heavily digitalized. Furthermore, language teaching should take advantage of the digital disposition of today's students, who are enticed to interactive and collaborative learning and who are drawn to sharable, online projects with a creative component. The advancement of technology not only tremendously enhances language teaching and learning, but also helps save endangered languages by expanding the variety of language teaching materials and activities that can be implemented in the classroom. This preservation is accomplished by establishing a virtual language community, and by offering a wider access for students who seek to engage with the less commonly taught languages but lack local access to language classes or teachers. The increasing number of online learning programs and their popularity demonstrate that new media indeed can come to the rescue of endangered languages.

2.1 YiddishPOP

New digital tools, such as YiddishPOP ("YiddishPOP," n. d.), an animated interactive program for learning Yiddish designed for younger learners but fully appreciated and enjoyed by college students, seems to be a "dream" response to the needs of the digital natives. It offers a stimulating, interactive environment with a gaming experience component (Figure 1). YiddishPOP as well as YouTube videos, images, sound archives, and online projects transform Yiddish language acquisition and the perception of the language itself: it now has an appealing online presence.

YiddishPOP, "an animated educational site for Yiddish language students of all ages," ("YiddishPOP," n. d.) is a spin-off of BrainPOP's subsidiary, BrainPOP ESL ("BrainPOP ESL," n.d.), a comprehensive English as Second Language learning program, launched in 2009 and now used worldwide. YiddishPOP was established in honor and memory of Dr. Naomi Kadar (1949-2010), educator and Yiddish scholar. She together with her team created BrainPOP ESL, which uses animated movies to introduce model conversations, as well as grammar and vocabulary items, and addresses the students' varying needs and learning styles by introducing fun activities such as interactive quizzes and games (memory games, board game simulations, listening comprehension challenges, etc.) that help practice and review the recently acquired language skills. The possibility of incorporating such a program into a language classroom definitely transforms Yiddish language pedagogy, which offers only a handful of traditional textbooks (U. Weinreich, 1949; M. Schaechter, 1986; Zucker, 1994; Estraikh, Katz, & Clifford, 1996; Goldberg, 1996; Bordin, 2000; Margolis, 2012; Kahn, 2012), lacks engaging teaching materials, and might be perceived as somewhat resistant to innovative teaching methodologies (only two of the textbooks have audio materials).

YiddishPOP, currently in BETA, is still expanding and needs improvement in several areas. It has only 15 lessons available online, so it can currently only be used in elementary level classes. It has only one voiced character, which limits students' exposure to various accents and manners of speaking. Since it ambitiously targets students "of all ages," writing skills are barely addressed and the overall level of

Figure 1. YiddishPOP
(Image courtesy of Maya Kadar Kovalsky). The video (in the top left corner) introduces new vocabulary and grammar items, the exercises below include: (starting from left, then bottom row) quizzes, exercises, games, flashcards, grammar overview, listening and speaking practice, writing exercises, and reading practice. Other features include: information for teachers, vocabulary lists, and help on the right-hand sidebar, as well as cultural component. All the videos, games, and exercises can be accessed an unlimited number of times.

difficulty is not demanding enough for college students. Another challenge of using YiddishPOP in college classroom is the fact that YiddishPOP curriculum does not correspond to any of the existing Yiddish textbooks and standard college language syllabi, which often requires "jumping" between the existing lessons. Interestingly, YiddishPOP does not follow the award-winning curriculum of BrainPOP ESL. There is definitely a need for digital initiatives to complement all levels of instruction and it would be incredibly beneficial, if similar platforms were created specifically for college students. Nonetheless, the program offers a wealth of resources, such as lesson plans (though currently for the first 5 lessons only), a cultural component section, as well as vocabulary lists and grammar overview. All in all, YiddishPOP greatly enhances language acquisition and contributes to making language learning not only educational but also enjoyable.

2.2 Mapping Yiddish New York

Cooperative online projects, such as Mapping Yiddish New York (MYNY) ("Mapping Yiddish New York," n. d.), currently under development at Columbia University, as well as class-centered digital assignments, all help create online communities of Yiddish learners, and contribute to a new appreciation of the language learning experience. In 2014, the Columbia University Center for New Media in Teaching and Learning, in collaboration with Yiddish faculty, launched MYNY, dedicated to mapping Yiddish culture in New York over the last 150 years. The MYNY project is presently based on student-generated entries that are contributed to the growing online archive in the form of digital essays created as assignments required in content and language classes under faculty supervision: e.g. *The Taste of Yiddish* (Fall 2014), *Women, Gender, and Yiddish Literature* (Spring 2015), *Yiddish New York* (Spring 2016), and Yiddish language classes taught in the years 2013-2016. The website offers students an opportunity to engage with authentic language materials, such as newspaper advertisements, theater programs for lower levels, and newspaper articles for more advanced levels. The website also allows students to explore the cultural content before they commence language acquisition.

The collaborative aspect of the digital projects has been met with an enthusiastic embrace by the students who requested more digital assignments, and who had expressed appreciation for the wide range of possibilities offered by new media that allowed them to enhance conventional essays by audio and visual materials. This passionate response (Fan, 2015) to the online collaborative projects seems to confirm Prensky's observations about the millennial generation's predisposition to team-work, which results in creative and sharable digital projects. Nonetheless, such projects are not without challenges. Acquiring complex technical skills needed for the digital projects is time consuming and often frustrating. A number of students exhibited a lack of tech-savviness, thus providing evidence for Prensky's critics' observations that not all digital natives possess inborn expertise with new technologies. Students commented on the fact that the focus on the digital component of the assignments often took time away from concentrating more on the content. In terms of the language classes' usage of the MYNY website, the ongoing and seemingly insurmountable challenge is the issue of typing in Yiddish, which is written in the Hebrew alphabet, right-to-left, with Yiddish-specific diacritical marks, especially when juxtaposed with left-to-right Latin characters. This difficulty applies to all applications of new media in Yiddish language classroom, including wikis and blogs. Furthermore, the assessment of students' progress in the context of collaborative digital assignments also requires a new approach and a new grading rubric.

2.3. The Grosbard Project

Another online project that can be used in Yiddish language classes is the Grosbard Project ("The Grosbard Project," n.d.), an online archive of digitalized recordings of the so-called "word concerts" performed by Yiddish actor and word artist, Hertz Grosbard (1892-1994). The website was launched for the "Jewspeak and Its Aftermath: Speech and Orality in Modern Jewish Discourse" Ginor Seminar at the Jewish Theological Seminar, New York (October 18, 2014) and received coverage in the Yiddish *Forverts* (S.-R. Schaechter, 2015). This depository of authentic listening comprehension material, featuring various works of Yiddish literature, from poems, plays, to short stories, artistically recited with great diction and exquisite skill, serves as a powerful resource for the classroom. Students expressed appreciation for the clarity of Grosbard's speech, and they engage with the language by recording their own renditions of selected poems.

Not only is the language learning process enhanced by cultural components (as exemplified by their encounters with a selection of the best works of Yiddish literature), but students also have an opportunity to improve their speaking skills, their fluency, and intonation by listening and imitating Grosbard's masterful performances. Some of the activities incorporating the website in the classroom included students choosing one poem, rehearsing it, and then recording their own rendition of the poem. The results were astounding: in most cases, their rendition of Grosbard's accent and diction were by all discernable measures flawless, and their general level of fluency and intonation slightly improved. The website features the Yiddish texts of the works performed by Grosbard, but it still needs listening comprehension activities for a broader use in language courses and translations in order to reach to audiences beyond college classroom.

2.4. YouTube Videos and Other Online Materials

YouTube videos offer a wealth of Yiddish teaching materials that greatly enhance the language learning process. Using videos in class offers students a possibility to hear all varieties of the language, with the visual component enhancing comprehension, and also engage with the language in a meaningful way, e.g. by creating English subtitles to Yiddish videos and vice versa, as well as by creating their own videos. Examples of such activities include creating Yiddish subtitles for *The Jewish Food Taste Test* (BuzzFeedYellow, n. d.), a short film in which people try Jewish food for the first time, in an intermediate language classroom. The activity involved translation of the English comments on the food, but also required exploration of Jewish food culture, in addition to new media skills needed to insert subtitles onto a film. YouTube also boasts surprising finds, such as Yiddish-dubbed *Seinfeld* episodes (A Mishel, n. d.), or contemporary Hasidic Yiddish pop music by Lipa Schmeltzer (Winkler, 2015), who is referred to as "the Lady Gaga of Hasidic music" (Winer, 2012). The recently launched Yiddish-language web series called *YidLife Crisis* ("YIDLIFE CRISIS," n. d.), created by Jamie Elman and Eli Batalion, and dubbed as "the world's first modern Yiddish online sitcom" (JDOV, 2016), offers yet another way of engaging with newly created Yiddish culture and its exploration of today's religious and cultural Jewish identity. Bringing such materials to the language classroom not only enhances the exploration of the contemporary cultural component, but also enables establishing connections with the surrounding mainstream culture.

Furthermore, the large online sound archives, such as Judaica Sound Archives ("FAU Judaica Sound Archives," n. d.), hosted by Florida Atlantic University Libraries and the Robert and Molly Freedman Jewish Sound Archive ("Robert and Molly Freedman Jewish Sound Archive," n. d.) at the University of Pennsylvania, offer inexhaustible resources for listening comprehension use in class. Established in 2002, Judaica Sound Archives (JSA) is the largest collection of Jewish music recordings, featuring over 72,500 songs (and counting) as of 2014 (Lieberman, 2014), with thousands of recordings available online, on an easily searchable website. Since 95% of the JSA's collection cannot be legally shared online due to U.S. copyright laws, the JSA created a Research Station ("FAU Judaica Sound Archives Research Station," n. d.), offering a special access to the collection for researchers, educators, and students – currently through the thirteen participating institutions – who can listen to digitized music in its entirety in a non-downloading format. Despite these limitations, the JSA is an incredible resource for the classroom, allowing not only for access to authentic Yiddish songs at one's fingertips but also offering insights into the history of Yiddish theater and Yiddish music created around the world. Still, it would be useful to create online listening comprehension activities that could accompany the use of the sound archives in the classroom. The Freedman Jewish Sound archive, currently containing over 4,000 recordings, primarily in Yiddish and Hebrew, is more of a reference resource, as it features over 35,000 entries in the trilingual database catalog, offering information on title, author(s), composer(s), performers, and first lines of songs. Although only a sample of recordings can be heard online, this archive contains a wealth of information about the history of Jewish music, and preserves the authentic recordings.

The above sound archives are not the only Yiddish archival and educational resources available online. Yiddish Book Center, established in 1980, has physically rescued over a million of Yiddish books (Lansky, 2005), and then digitized and uploaded over 12,000 titles that have been downloaded free of charge over 500,000 times. Expanding online access to Yiddish books has been a tremendous step in rescuing the Yiddish literary heritage that can now be easily reached in classrooms worldwide. The Center is also dedicated to Yiddish education, offering Yiddish language courses for undergraduate and graduate students and adults, fellowships for recent college graduates, and translation fellowships. In 2012, the Center created the Yiddish Language Institute, which aims to develop high-quality online Yiddish learning opportunities ("Learn | Explore | Yiddish Book Center," n. d.). As of now, the website offers about 20 online *heymarbet* (homework) worksheets at a beginning level usually featuring a song, accompanied by images or videos and a quiz activity ("Heymarbet - Homework | Yiddish Book Center," n. d.), which can be a great addition to the classroom.

Finally, the oldest running Yiddish newspaper *Forverts* (established in 1897), which in 2013 launched a new daily website ("The Yiddish Daily Forward," n. d.), is an indispensable resource in the Yiddish language classroom. In addition to the news and opinion articles, the website also features a multimedia section that consists of Forward Video Chanel with segments covering history, travel, cooking, interviews, Jews around the world, culture and art, and Forverts Voice, a current Yiddish radio podcast station, with regular Yiddish reports from Los Angeles, Paris, Warsaw, Moscow, Jerusalem, and Melbourne, as well as Yiddish Forward Hour Archive with a weekly New York report. The radio podcasts are accompanied by a Yiddish transcript, whereas the videos have subtitles, which unfortunately cannot be disabled. *Forverts* joined forces with the latest *Comprehensive Yiddish-English Dictionary* (Beinfeld & Bochner, 2013), which became available online ("Comprehensive Yiddish-English Dictionary," n. d.) in 2013; this union allows for the possibility of highlighting an unknown word on the *Forverts* website and seeing a pop-up box with an English definition, which has truly opened up the world of Yiddish not only to college students but also to the general public.

2.5. Distance Learning

These increasingly popular distance learning opportunities not only transpose Yiddish into the 21st century, but also offer a global access to Yiddish language learning to people located in places without formal Yiddish language instruction. The distance learning Yiddish programs, such as the online classes offered by the Workmen's Circle ("Winter-Spring 2016 Yiddish Online Class Descriptions," 2014; Butnick, 2014) in New York and Gratz College ("Yiddish Gratz College," n. d.); at the Medem Bibliotèque Paris Yiddish Center ("Online courses Paris Yiddish Center," n. d.); at eTeacher ("Learn Yiddish Online with eTeacher and the Hebrew University," n. d.) in collaboration with the Hebrew University ("Learn Yiddish - The Hebrew University's Online Languages Program," n. d.); at the Dora Teitelboym Center for Yiddish Culture ("The Dora Teitelboim Institute for Yiddish Education," n. d.) in Florida; at Yiddish Academy ("Learn Yiddish Online Today Using a Fun, Fast Method," n. d.); as well as all-level classes offered by individual teachers ("Learn Yiddish in a live environment - face-to-face on the internet!," n. d.), all attract a diverse group: from high school and college students, to lifelong learners and heritage speakers who wish to reconnect with the language, but either have no local opportunities available to them, or prefer to learn from the comfort of their home (Teitelbaum, 2015). The Workmen Circle, which bills itself as "the largest provider of the Yiddish language classes in the U.S. outside of academic institutions" ("Yiddish Language - The Workmen's Circle," n. d.), in the years 2013-2015 offered eight online courses (in addition to in-person courses), which brought together 220 students from nine countries (Borodulin, 2015). The age of the virtual students spanned between 15 and over 80 (Butnick, 2014), which once more challenges Prensky's notion that digital immigrants intrinsically struggle with technology. Nonetheless, the online learning courses offer limited possibilities for student-student interactions and pair and group work, and due to their virtual character may focus more on speaking, listening, reading skills, and grammar, but less upon writing, which requires scanning and sharing files and/or typing in Yiddish, which is often strenuous.

3. CHALLENGES

3.1 Advantages and Disadvantages of Using New Media in Language Teaching

The pedagogical advantages of using new media in teaching languages are enormous. First and foremost, this is the language of today's students, and thus, in order to establish effective educational process, we need to "speak their language" in a technological sense. Secondly, the recent growth in online Yiddish learning possibilities signals that there is a demand for such opportunities, which can also serve as an incentive for creative pedagogical innovations, employing new media. Thirdly, the enthusiastic response of students to new media use in language class and the cross-generational interest in online Yiddish educational initiatives signal that this is the path worth exploring. Employing new media in language learning appears to be engaging and motivating, which increases the effectiveness of the learning process.

However, there are some disadvantages that need to be taken into consideration. The human interactive aspect of language teaching has been on the decline. An increasing amount of time in the new media language class is spent on the collective staring at the screen, instead of interacting with classmates. This is the key characteristic of "digital natives" who spend most of their waking hours engaged with digital devices, from smart phones and computers to TVs. The battle against this depersonalization of human interactions seems quixotic; still, the contemporary digitalization of language learning process appears to devalue one of the key aspects of language, that is, interpersonal communication.

3.2. New Media Challenges for Teachers and Students

The new media are definitely a challenge for teachers who, in many cases, were not born into the digital world. Even if they have successfully adapted to the world of new technology, this is an ongoing learning process that is time and energy consuming. The time spent on designing and preparing digital projects and assignments, in addition to class preparation, grading, and other teaching obligations, is often at the expense of research and family life. Despite their digital proficiency, students repeatedly express concerns about the amount of time and energy they have to spend on learning new programs and obtaining skills required for the digital publishing of their work. In addition, they admit that the content and quality of their work suffers due to the time-consuming focus on the digital aspects of the assignments. However, these may be just initial impediments and once the skills are obtained, the emphasis in the subsequent assignments will be placed on the content, not only on the digital form. Finally, as mentioned earlier, the problem of typing in Yiddish, which has idiosyncratic diacritical marks that distinguish it from Hebrew, is a recurring obstacle. Macintosh has a free Yiddish keyboard and a recently released *Yiddish Klal* keyboard layout ("Typing in Yiddish on a Mac – Isaac L. Bleaman," n.d.), also available free of charge, but PC computers often require installation of additional programs that need to be purchased.

3.3 The Yiddish Experience as a Model for Other LCTLs

The case of the successful use of new media in Yiddish language teaching and learning can serve as a model for other less commonly taught languages. YiddishPOP is in a sense a unique creation, which requires immense financial and technological investment, in addition to educators' input into the program. However, it serves as an excellent example of innovative new media content that not only helps with the Yiddish language acquisition, but also promotes the language, especially among the younger generations of students.

The online sound archives and digitized book collections are a result of enormous collaborative effort, institutional support, and the investment of substantial financial resources. It is almost impossible to carry out such projects individually, but the examples of the Yiddish Book Center (which was actually started by one person) and other digital collaborations can serve as a model or an inspiration. Furthermore, the examples of new media use (YouTube, wikis, blogs, etc.) in the classroom and associated activities can be applied in other languages as well, as they are mostly teacher-generated. Finally, even creating basic interactive teaching materials, such as grammar and vocabulary exercises, or listening comprehension activities on Google Docs that can be shared with students and other educators, not only cater to the digital interest of today's students and expand the possibility of outreach to other potential students, but also in the long run save time, energy, and paper. Once created, digital materials can be used repeatedly.

4. CONCLUSION

It is indeed a very rewarding and exciting experience to teach Yiddish in the digital era. The opportunities for the enhancement of the language learning process seem endless, and despite the challenges that are mostly associated with the time one needs to spend on mastering the new media world, the promises of the outcome are thrilling and motivating. Still, it is yet to be qualitatively and quantitatively researched as to whether the digital teaching platforms are indeed effective and result in successful language acquisition, fluency, proficiency, and a maintained commitment to the language.

Another aspect of new media that is essential in teaching less commonly taught languages is their promotional potential. Social media can serve as a very efficient way of promoting the less commonly taught language courses and reaching wider audiences. Platforms such as Twitter and Facebook are a great resource for promoting less commonly taught languages. Several Yiddish language programs and Yiddish organizations have their significant Facebook presence, e.g. Columbia University, Oxford University, Bard-YIVO and Vilnius Yiddish Summer Programs, Yiddish Book Center, *In geveb: A Journal of Yiddish*

Studies, etc. There are also many Yiddish-related Facebook pages, such as Yiddish Word-of-the-Week (currently with 3,548 likes), or closed groups like Yiddish Pour Tous (Yiddish for All), which currently has 5,083 members. The Facebook pages and Twitter accounts dedicated to Yiddish have thousands of followers, which signals that social media outreach for less commonly taught languages has a promising potential. All the above does mean that the teachers' job description gets longer and longer, but if the outcome is saving the endangered languages, it seems worth the effort.

REFERENCES

Bayne, S., & Ross, J. (2007). The "Digital Native" and "Digital Immigrant:" A Dangerous Opposition. *Presented at The Annual Conference of the Society for Research into Higher Education (SRHE)*, Brighton, Sussex.

Beinfeld, S., & Bochner, H. (2013). *Comprehensive Yiddish-English Dictionary*. Bloomington, Ind: Indiana University Press.

Birnbaum, S. (1979). *Yiddish: A Survey and A Grammar*. Toronto, Buffalo: University of Toronto Press.

Bordin, H. (2000). *Mit vort un maysim*. Israel.

Borodulin, K. (2015, October 29). Yidish af internets.

Brain, POP. ESL. (n. d.). Retrieved from https://esl.brainpop.com/

Butnick, S. (2014, September 19). Yiddish Goes Virtual With Online Classes. Retrieved from http://www.tabletmag.com/scroll/185004/yiddish-goes-virtual-with-online-classes

BuzzFeedYellow. (n. d.). *The Jewish Food Taste Test*. Retrieved from https://www.youtube.com/watch?v=SqYGGqTC_Us

Comprehensive Yiddish-English Dictionary. (n. d.). Retrieved from http://verterbukh.org/

Eisenberg, R. (1995). *Boychiks in the Hood: Travels in the Hasidic Underground* (1st ed.). San Francisco, CA: Harper.

Eisenstein, M. (1950). *Jewish Schools in Poland, 1919-1939*. New York: King's Crown Press.

Estraikh, G., Katz, D., & Clifford, D. (1996). *Intensive Yiddish: with grammar sections based on Gennady Estraikh's Grammar of the Yiddish Language*. Oxford: Oksforder Yidish Press.

Ethnologue, Y. Eastern. (2015). Retrieved from https://www.ethnologue.com/language/ydd

Fan, K. (2015, October 21). With Over 50 Offerings, Columbia's Language Program Second Largest among Ivies. Retrieved from http://columbiaspectator.com/news/2015/10/21/languages

FAU Judaica Sound Archives Research Station. (n. d.). Retrieved from http://faujsa.fau.edu/jsa/research_station.php

Fishman, D. E. (2010). *The Rise of Modern Yiddish Culture* (1st paperback ed.). Pittsburgh, PA: Univ. of Pittsburgh Press.

Fishman, J. E. (1991). *Yiddish: Turning to Life*. Amsterdam, PA: J. doi:10.1075/z.49

Freidenreich, F. (2010). *Passionate pioneers: The Story of Yiddish Secular Education in North America, 1910-1960*. Teaneck, NJ: Holmes & Meier Publishers.

Goldberg, D. (1996). *Yidish af yidish*. New Haven, CT: Yale University Press.

Hansen, M. L. (1938). *The Problem of the Third Generation Immigrant*. Rock Island, Ill: Augustana Historical Society.

Heymarbet - Homework | Yiddish Book Center. (n. d.). Retrieved from http://www.yiddishbookcenter.org/heymarbet

Holton, D. (2010, March 20). The Digital Natives / Digital Immigrants Distinction Is Dead, Or At Least Dying. Retrieved from https://edtechdev.wordpress.com/2010/03/19/the-digital-natives-digital-immigrants-distinction-is-dead-or-at-least-dying/

Isenberg, N. (1997). Critical Post-Judaism, Or Reinventing a Yiddish Sensibility in a Postmodern Age. *Diaspora: A Journal of Transnational Studies*, 6(1), 86–96.

Jacobs, N. (2005). *Yiddish: A Linguistic Introduction*. Cambridge, UK, New York: Cambridge University Press.

JDOV. (2016, February 11). WATCH: What Exactly Is a "YidLife Crisis?" *Haaretz*. Retrieved from http://www.haaretz.com/jewish/news/1.702593

Judaica Sound Archives. (n. d.). Retrieved from http://faujsa.fau.edu/jsa/home.php

Kafrissen, R. (2012, January 4). Rootless Cosmopolitan: Straw Man. Retrieved from http://rokhl.blogspot.com/2012/01/straw-man.html

Kahn, L. (2012). *Colloquial Yiddish: The Complete Course for the Beginners*. Abingdon, Oxon, New York: Routledge.

Katz, D. (1987). The Proto-Dialectology of Ashkenaz. In D. Katz (Ed.), *Origins of the Yiddish Language* (pp. 47–60). Oxford, New York: Pergamon Press.

Katz, D. (2004). *Words on Fire: The Unfinished History of Yiddish*. New York: Basic Books.

Katz, D. (2011, October 31). Language: Yiddish. In *YIVO Encyclopedia of Jews in Eastern Europe*. Retrieved from http://www.yivoencyclopedia.org/article.aspx/Language/Yiddish

Katz, D. (2015). *Yiddish and Power*. New York: Palgrave Macmillan.

Koutropoulos, A. (2011). Digital Natives: Ten Years After. *Journal of Online Learning and Teaching*, 7(4), 525.

Lansky, A. (2005). *Outwitting History: The Amazing Adventures of a Man Who Rescued a Million Yiddish Books*. Chapel Hill, N.C.: Algonquin Books of Chapel Hill.

Learn | Explore | Yiddish Book Center. (n. d.). Retrieved from http://www.yiddishbookcenter.org/learn-explore

Learn Yiddish in a live environment - face-to-face on the internet! (n. d.). Retrieved from http://learny-iddishlive.com/

Learn Yiddish Online Today Using a Fun, Fast Method. (n. d.). Retrieved from http://yiddishacademy.com/

Learn Yiddish Online with eTeacher and the Hebrew University. (n. d.). Retrieved from http://eteach-eryiddish.com/

Learn Yiddish - The Hebrew University's Online Languages Program. (n. d.). Retrieved February 16, 2016, from http://languages.huji.ac.il/courses/learn-yiddish-level-a

Lieberman, R. P. (2014, November 17). International Yiddish Conference a Hit in Boca. Retrieved February 16, 2016, from http://www.sun-sentinel.com/florida-jewish-journal/news/palm/fl-jjps-yiddish-1119-20141117-story.html

Mapping Yiddish New York. (n. d.). Retrieved from https://myny.ccnmtl.columbia.edu/

Margolis, R. (2012). *Basic Yiddish: A Grammar and Workbook. Milton Park*. Abingdon, Oxon, New York: Routledge.

Mills, K. (2000). Rescuing Yiddish for Future Generations. *Indiana University Research & Creative Activity*. XXIII no. 1.

Mishel, A. (n. d.). *Yiddish & Seinfeld. Dentist Jokes*. Retrieved from https://www.youtube.com/watch?v=_jG6B9Pt_ug

Moseley, C. (2010). Atlas of the World's Langagues in Danger. Paris: UNESCO Publishing; Retrieved from http://www.unesco.org/languages-atlas/en/atlasmap.html

Oblinger, D. (2003). Boomers, Gen-Xers, and Millenials: Understanding the New Students. *EDUCAUSE Review*, July/August) 200.

Paris Yiddish Center. (n.d.). Online courses. Retrieved from http://yiddishweb.com/en/online-courses/

Pedagogy. (n. d.). Retrieved from http://ingeveb.org/pedagogy

Portnoy, E. (2012, August 13). The Disappearing Yiddish Accent. *The Forward*. Retrieved from http://forward.com/culture/160767/the-disappearing-yiddish-accent/

Prensky, M. (2001a). Digital Natives, Digital Immigrants Part I. *On the Horizon*, 9(5), 1–6. doi:10.1108/10748120110424816

Prensky, M. (2001b). Digital Natives, Digital Immigrants Part II. *On the Horizon*, 9(6). doi:10.1108/10748120110424843

Freedman, R., & Freedman, M. (n.d.). Retrieved February 16, 2016, from http://sceti.library.upenn.edu/freedman/index.cfm

Samilow, J. (2016, February 10). Yiddish Is Making a Comeback and for Good Reason. *Haaretz*.

Schaechter, M. (1986). *Yidish tsvey: a lernbikhl far mitndike kursn*. Philadelphia: Institute for Research on Humanities.

Schaechter, S.-R. (2015, February 15). A Delightful Way to Listen to Yiddish Literature. *The Yiddish Daily Forward*. Retrieved from http://yiddish.forward.com/articles/185375/a-delightful-way-to-listen-to-yiddish-literature/?p=all

Seidman, N. (1997). *A Marriage Made in Heaven: The Sexual Politics of Hebrew and Yiddish*. Berkeley: University of California Press.

Shandler, J. (2006). *Adventures in Yiddishland: Postvernacular Language and Culture*. Berkeley and Los Angeles, CA: University of California Press.

Shneer, D. (2004). *Yiddish and the Creation of Soviet Jewish Culture: 1918-1930*. New York: Cambridge University Press.

Soldat-Jaffe, T. (2012). *Twenty-First Century Yiddishism: Language, Identity & the New Jewish Studies*. Brighton, Portland: Sussex Academic Press.

Tapscott, D. (1998). *Growing Up Digital: The Rise of the Net Generation*. New York: McGraw-Hill.

Teitelbaum, P. (2015, May 5). Regards from Agi and a question email.

The Dora Teitelboim Institute for Yiddish Education. (n. d.). Retrieved from http://www.yiddishculture.org/dtf1.html

The Grosbard Project. (n. d.). Retrieved from http://grosbardproject.com/Grosbard_Project/Home.html

The Yiddish Daily Forward. (n. d.). Retrieved from http://yiddish.forward.com/

Typing in Yiddish on a Mac – Isaac L. Bleaman. (n. d.). Retrieved from https://wp.nyu.edu/ibleaman/yiddish/typing/

Weinreich, M. (1973). *History of the Yiddish Language* (1980th ed.). Chicago: University of Chicago Press.

Weinreich, U. (1949). *College Yiddish: Introduction to the Yiddish Language and to Jewish Life and Culture*. New York: YIVO Institute for Jewish Research.

Weinreich, U. (1972). *Explorations in Semantic Theory*. The Hague, Paris: Mouton. doi:10.1515/9783110813142

Wexler, P. (1991). Yiddish - the Fifteenth Slavic Language: A Study of Partial Language Shift from Judeo-Sorbian to German. *International Journal of the Sociology of Language*, *91*, 9–150.

Wiecki, E. (2009). Untervegs: A Journey with the Yiddish Textbook. *European Judaism*, *42*(2), 47–61. doi:10.3167/ej.2009.420207

Winer, S. (2012, August 16). Hasidic Pop Star Dons IDF Togs. *The Times of Israel*. Retrieved from http://www.timesofisrael.com/hasidic-pop-star-dons-idf-togs/

Winkler, J. (2015, July 6). A Day in the Life of Lipa Schmeltzer, Ex-Ultra-Orthodox Celebrity. Retrieved from http://www.tabletmag.com/jewish-arts-and-culture/music/191829/lipa-schmeltzer

Winter-Spring 2016 Yiddish Online Class Descriptions. (2014, December 18). Retrieved from https://circle.org/what-we-do/yiddish-language/winter-spring-2016-yiddish-class-descriptions/

Yiddish, POP. (n. d.). Retrieved from http://www.yiddishpop.com/

Yiddish | Gratz College. (n. d.). Retrieved from http://www.gratz.edu/programs/yiddish

Yiddish Kave Sho. (2015, October7).

Yiddish Language - The Workmen's Circle. (n. d.). Retrieved from https://circle.org/what-we-do/yiddish-language/

YIDLIFE CRISIS. (n. d.). Retrieved from http://www.yidlifecrisis.com/

Young, J. (2014, September 12). *Down with the "Revival": Yiddish is a Living Language*. Retrieved from https://www.yivo.org/down-with-the-revival-yiddish-is-a-living-language

Zucker, S. (1994). *Yiddish: An Introduction to the Language. Literature, and Culture*. Hoboken, NJ: KTAV in conjunction with Workmen Circle.

Chapter 12
Korean Foreign Language Learning:
Videoconferencing with Native Speakers

Byung-jin Lim
University of Wisconsin-Madison, USA

Danielle O. Pyun
Ohio State University, USA

ABSTRACT

This article presents intercultural and linguistic exchanges by foreign language learners in an exploratory study of Internet-based desktop videoconferencing between Korean learners at a university in the United States, and their counterparts at a South Korean college. The desktop videoconferencing project was designed for foreign language learners of Korean to assist in developing linguistic competence, as well as intercultural communicative competence, by providing the learners with the target language and culture through real-time, one-on-one communication. The study shows the emerging themes that recur in a video-chat. It also reports on the Korean language learners' self-rated proficiency in their target language. Challenges and difficulties in video-conferencing are examined, followed by a discussion of the effectiveness of synchronous one-on-one video-conferencing for language learning in general, and in Korean language education in particular.

INTRODUCTION

Since the early 1990s, networked computers have been used in a variety of ways as an inexpensive, cost-effective medium for interactive communication that can be accessed by anyone connected online (Kern, Ware, & Warschauer, 2008; Ortega, 1997). The advantages of networked multimedia in fostering communicative competence in second as well as foreign language have been well documented in a number of studies, particularly in those written from an interactionist perspective (e.g., Blake, 2000; Fernández-García & Martínez-Arbelaiz, 2002; Pellettieri, 2000; Smith, 2004; Toyoda & Harrison, 2002; Tudini, 2003; Yanguas, 2010). In general, studies reported that networked computer mediation provides language learners with:

DOI: 10.4018/978-1-5225-0177-0.ch012

1.   Increased opportunities to produce the target language, and
2.   Opportunities to engage in active negotiation of meaning using various discourse strategies (Blake, 2000; Chun & Plass, 2000; Fernández-García & Martínez-Arbelaiz, 2002; Kelm, 1992; Kern, 1995).

Kern (2015), for example, found that in a group discussion setting, students produced two to four times more sentences in synchronous conferencing sessions than they did in oral discussions. In Fernández-García & Martínez-Arbelaizs' study (2002), it was observed that the negotiations of meaning common in oral interactions (e.g., confirmation, requests for clarification) were also recurrent in the synchronous electronic medium.

Among the variety of network-based communications, often referred to as Computer-Mediated Communication (CMC), synchronous CMC has received much attention for its resemblance to oral communication in terms of the types of discourse functions generated during the interaction (Chun, 1994; Sotillo, 2000). Herring (1996) defines Computer-Mediated Communication (CMC) as "communication that takes place between human beings via the instrumentality of computers" (p.1). This communication can be synchronous or asynchronous depending on the goal of communication. Compared to asynchronous communication such as e-mail correspondence, online face-to-face communication motivates language learners to learn language due to the virtual, yet social presence, perceived proximity, and close to real-time speed and spontaneity of communication (Yamada & Akahori, 2009).

While previous studies have reported that text-based CMC—a hybrid of written and spoken language—bears some similarities to face-to-face communication with regard to its interactive discourse features (Kern, 1995; Blake, 2000; Smith, 2003; Hampel & Baber, 2003), it lacks the use of social cues such as eye-gazing, nodding, and gestures so commonly associated with face-to-face interaction which enhances interpersonal solidarity and comradery (Yamada & Akahori, 2009). In her study of distance language learning via desktop videoconferencing, Wang (2006) found that both parties of the videoconferencing frequently used visual cues to confirm understanding or nonunderstanding and such visual information significantly facilitated communication. In a similar vein, Lee (2007) observed that synchronous videoconferencing, by exposing L2 learners to authentic target language input involving nonverbal cues, fostered oral interaction, as well as intercultural exchanges.

In actual face-to-face communication between language learners, Winstead (2013) reports that although there is initial apprehension, that nevertheless students problem-solve, engage in different discourse functions, and gain confidence and motivation to learn from others as they develop social comradery. CMC-mediated types of interactive learning may possibly produce similar results. Some studies about CMC-mediated interaction reveal that not only did CMC help increase participants' L2 confidence given more opportunities to practice the L2 (Gleason & Suvorov, 2012) but also increased motivation to use the target language with others (Gleason & Suvorov, 2012; Wu, Yen, & Marek, 2011; Sun, 2009).

Based on a search of the literature, the majority of previous research on the use of asynchronous as well as synchronous CMC in language learning has been carried out using text-based media (e.g., Blake, 2000; Smith, 2004; Sotillo, 2000). There is a dearth of studies concerned with oral or oral-visual modes of CMC including asynchronous video (e.g., Hirotani & Lyddon, 2013), asynchronous audio (e.g., Gleason & Suvorov, 2012), and synchronous videoconferencing (e.g., Katz, 2001; Lee, 2007; O'Dowd, 2000; Schenker, 2013; Wang, 2006). Much of the research has been focused on CMC-mediated ESL/EFL (English as a Second Language/English as a Foreign Language) learning (e.g., Gleason & Suvorov, 2012; Smith, 2004; Sotillo, 2000; Wu, Yen, & Marek, 2011), or learning of commonly taught languages such as Spanish and French (e.g., Blake, 2000; Katz, 2001; Lee, 2007; Yanguas, 2010). Little research, however, has been reported regarding the use and impacts of videoconferencing in the teaching and learning of LCTLs, and, in particular, Korean.

When considering the teaching and learning of less commonly taught languages (LCTL) in the digital age, students have less access to these types of language courses, let alone exposure to interactive dialogues with native speakers. In general, those who are in favor of CMC for interactive and communicative activities base their argument on the theoretical foundation called "interactionist approach," which emphasizes the importance of interaction in SLA (Long 1996). Interactionists believe that conversational interaction and comprehensible input generated by those interactions can significantly enhance L2 proficiency.

Long (1996) asserts that through interactional exchanges, learners encounter input or modified input, are pushed to produce output, receive feedback, reformulate output, and negotiate meaning when communication breakdowns occur. According to the interactional approach, it is through this process of interaction that learning occurs. The interactive capability of CMC carries a valuable implication particularly in foreign language contexts where second language (L2) learners as well as foreign language (FL) learners lack sufficient opportunities to interact in the target language. The potential of synchronous videoconferencing to promote language learning and interaction needs to be more equitably investigated in the LCTL learning scenarios.

To fill this gap in the research, the present study aims to describe and analyze the Internet-based videoconferencing mediated interaction through interrogating the cross-cultural and linguistic exchanges made by Korean language learners during one-on-one desktop videoconferencing. Examining learners' interactions and experiences in networked videoconferencing can shed light on its advantages and limitations as a pedagogical tool as well as the ways in which those advantages can be exploited in the foreign language classroom. The following provides an overview of increased interest in Korean as a foreign language and a review of literature on synchronous online interactions in L2 and FL learning which will orientate the reader to the context of this study.

INCREASED INTEREST IN KOREAN AS A FOREIGN LANGUAGE

Interest in Korean courses is on the rise in the United States. According to a recent Modern language Association (MLA) report, Korean enrollments showed the highest percentage increase (44.7%) from 2009 to 2013 when compared with enrollments of languages other than English in U.S. colleges and universities (Goldberg, Looney, & Lusin, 2015). Enrollments in Korean rose significantly at both undergraduate and graduate levels. The report also indicated that enrollments in Korean have increased at every institutional level between 2009 and 2013: 27.6% in two-year institutions, 45.3% in four-year institutions, and 86.6% in graduate programs.

One of the factors contributing to the growing rate of Korean language learners is the widespread access to and consumption of Korean pop culture by non-Koreans worldwide in such areas as music, dramas, and films. Interest in Korean pop media and culture is one of the strong motivators that inspire many to learn the Korean language in Asia (Chan & Chi, 2011). The Korean phenomenon has reached world-wide proportions and high interest in North America as well (Damron & Forsyth, 2012). Based on the authors' anecdotal experience, with the proliferation of Youtube videos and social media, college students of today's digital era come to the Korean classroom often with familiarity with some aspects of Korean culture as well as with the desire to satisfy their curiosity and interest in Korean culture and its people.

Learners who study LCTLs tend to learn the target language out of personal interests and curiosity rather than taking it merely to satisfy their foreign language requirement or solely for an instrumental purpose (Godwin-Jones, 2013). Correspondingly, studies have reported that learner profiles of LCTLs tend to be somewhat different from those of commonly taught languages (Brown, 2009; Godwin-Jones, 2013; Magnan, Murphy, Sahakyan, & Kim, 2012). For instance, based on the results obtained from a survey on college students' goals and expectations for foreign language learning, learners of LCTLs are not only interested in language learning but also learning about the target culture and people of these groups. Magnan et al. (2012) indicated that the importance of learning about target culture and its people is more highly regarded among learners of LCTLs than learners of commonly taught languages. They further recommend that, among the five Cs (Communication, Cultures, Connections, Comparisons, and Communities) of the national standards for foreign language learning, cultures and connections be prioritized for learners of LCTLs including learners of Korean.

Given such characteristics in the profiles of LCTL learners, Godwin-Jones (2013) pointed out that pragmatics, e.g., sociolinguistic elements and politeness, are important areas also associated with culture that need to be incorporated into instruction in the early stages of foreign language learning. Furthermore, this is especially so for second languages that do not share cognates and are culturally distant from the first language as associated with the case of English learners of Korean. Godwin-Jones (2013) recommends CMC mediated learning opportunities to promote greater language contact.

With the interest in social media among today's students, it would seem that having students learning a LCTL enter into contact with native speakers through CMC would be the ideal vehicle for cultural exchange, as well as, of course, as providing valuable opportunities for real use of the target language. (P.14)

Thus, electronic communication tools like CMC-mediated synchronous videoconferencing can significantly contribute to the increased cross-cultural communication and social connection deemed so relevant in the study of LCTLs (Godwin-Jones, 2013; Spreen, 2002).

A REVIEW OF THE LITERATURE: SYNCHRONOUS ONLINE INTERACTIONS IN L2 AND FL LEARNING

One of the widely held beliefs in SLA (Second Language Acquisition) is that language proficiency involves not only linguistic or grammatical competence but, equally important, it also involves communicative, interactive and strategic competence, which deals with the ability to use appropriate, functional, and meaningful language in situated contexts. For the past two decades, there has been a growing interest in the role of CMC as a means to practice interactive competence and communicative strategies. Salaberry (1999) found that CMC generated a high level of interactivity, and that this interaction helped language learners improve the quality of their written and spoken discourse. Kern (1995) also advocated the use of computer networks through which a wide variety of discourse structures were generated. In Chun and Plass's study (2000), networked computers were evaluated as an effective medium to promote L2 learners' communicative competence, by providing L2 learners with ample opportunities to use context-specific knowledge and discourse strategies while negotiating meaning with others.

Similarly, Chun (1994) examined discourse functions and characteristics of real-time networked communication generated by first-year German language students to analyze interaction features. Computer assisted classroom discussion facilitated a number of interactive discourse moves, such as initiative in asking questions, expanding on topics, request for clarification, and providing feedback. Chun concluded that computer assisted communication allowed students to "take a more active role in the discourse management than is typically found in normal classroom discussion" and hence CMC lends itself to be "an effective medium for facilitating the acquisition of interactive competence in second language writing and speaking" (p.28). Blake (2000) in his study of CMC interaction similarly found L2 Spanish learners who participated in synchronous pair chats utilized various types of incidental negotiations (e.g., pronunciation negotiation, lexical negotiation, syntactic negotiation) those to resolve lexical confusions most commonly occurred in networked discussions. Moreover, Blake found that vocabulary breakdowns were a noticeable obstacle to communication and students engaged most frequently in lexical negotiations in their exchanges. Smith (2004) found that ESL learners were able to negotiate the meaning of unknown words, and that overall acquisition of target words were measured by immediate and delayed posttests (Smith, 2004).

Pellettierie (2000) raised the importance of the goal-oriented language tasks to promote increased negotiation of meaning. Non-native speakers of Spanish were asked to complete five communication tasks in dyads. Task-based Spanish online chat communication showed how learner's negotiated meaning to resolve problems when trouble arose. Blake (2000) similarly found that when students were involved in task-based cooperative jigsaw, greater negotiation of meaning and decision-making takes place. Thus, highly goal-oriented tasks during synchronous online chat sessions and discussions can facilitate meaning negotiation, comprehension, and successful communication (Blake, Pellettierie).

Discussion of communicative and interactive capabilities of CMC has dominantly focused on text-based synchronous CMC (often called real-time chat). Another advanced communication technology, which is receiving more recent attention in L2 education, is the use of real-time teleconferencing via video technology. A few recent L2 studies of video teleconferencing are particularly relevant to the present study.

In a study of Interactional modifications is a topic of study about investigated negotiation of meaning in desktop videoconferencing between the teacher and learners of Chinese who completed various speaking tasks. Wang (2006) found participants exhibited various kinds of interactional modifications (g., trigger, indicator, response, reaction to response) as well as evidence of L2 acquisition (e.g., modified output). She noted that participants' low listening proficiency resulted in frequent breakdowns in understanding which in turn triggered negotiation of meaning.

Lee (2007) reported on the use of one-to-one desktop videoconferencing in a foreign language course. College learners of Spanish were connected to native speakers or Spanish instructors at a distance location using a videoconferencing software program in order to collaboratively work on interactive tasks. Lee's data of video-recordings, interviews, and students' reflection logs indicated that desktop videoconferencing fostered L2 oral skills. On the other hand, it was found that students with lower listening proficiency experienced difficulties and anxiety in comprehending L2 input.

Similar to Lee (2007), Katz (2001) found videoconferencing benefitted language learning but that anxiety was an issue for less proficient learners. Katz studied virtual exchanges via videoconferencing were carried out between an American university and a French university. The observed pedagogical benefits of videoconferencing included the increased opportunities to practice L2 listening and speaking skills as well as learning about different cultural perspectives. Katz found that less-proficient students had overcome their affective pressure of shyness and insecurity.

Learning about language culture has also been studied. Schenker (2013), investigated virtual exchanges between German students studying English and U.S. students studying German. The results of post-survey indicated that participants were highly interested in learning about the target culture. Virtual exchanges with members of the target culture served as a platform for integrated learning of language and culture as well as for authentic and personalized communication. A similar line of research was undertaken by O'Dowd (2000), who promoted intercultural exchanges between college foreign language learners in Spain and in the U.S. The interaction was productive in terms of developing intercultural awareness, increasing students' confidence in the target language, and increasing students' sensitivity to body language and presentation skills.

Taken together, previous studies suggest that synchronous CMC helps learners engage in meaningful, constructive and interpretive L2 interaction as well as build cross-cultural knowledge and understanding. Yet, the studies suggest that learners can experience apprehension and nervousness in a new synchronous CMC environment (Katz, 2001; Wang, 2006), as well as about communicating in the target language particularly when they lack confidence in L2 (Lee, 2007; Katz, 2001). Furthermore, the apprehension can increase when faced with technological instability such as bandwidth limitations and latency (Wang, 2006). While previous studies support the usefulness of synchronous CMC for generating meaningful negotiation and furthering understanding of L2 culture, they also warrant careful planning to cope with individual learner needs and technological challenges.

METHODOLOGY

Despite a number of studies noted in the literature about computer-mediated communication (CMC), less is known about Korean language learning and interaction. The current study explores and examines how the foreign language is interactively mediated among language learners of Korean and native speakers of Korean during synchronous face-to-face videoconferencing. In so doing, linguistic and intercultural exchanges are analyzed. The major research questions were addressed:

1. How do students negotiate meaning interactions during the real-time multi-modal videoconferencing?
2. How confident do the learners feel about their proficiency in the target language for videoconferencing?
3. What are their expectations of videoconferencing on their target language learning?

Background of the Study

Previous studies show that CMC furthers the development of foreign language learners' linguistic skills as well as their intercultural communicative competence (Abrams, 2003; Belz, 2003; Warschauer, 1997; Warschauer & Kern, 2000). Especially, Internet-based collaborative exchanges among foreign language learners create more learner-centered and interactive learning environments compared to face-to-face classroom settings (O'Dowd, 2007).

Inspired by these new approaches to using technology for foreign language learning and teaching, the authors began a research project entitled, "Videoconferencing for the learners of Korean in the United States." The videoconferencing project extended over a period of three years (2009~2012). An initial pilot study was conducted in the fall of 2009. This pilot study showed that one-on-one desktop videoconferencing motivated learners of Korean to utilize their classroom knowledge in the videoconferences with native speakers of Korean. This led the researchers to investigate ways in which the Internet-mediated collaborative videoconferencing promotes language learners' development of linguistic skills and intercultural communicative competence by providing the learners with target languages and cultures through interactions with the native speakers of the target languages. Therefore, a series of videoconferencing sessions were conducted between 2010 and 2012 by employing synchronous videoconferencing to two student groups: students studying Korean in the United States and Korean students studying English in South Korea.

The videoconferencing project presented here was conducted during the spring of 2011 with an intermediate Korean class consisting of 21 students at a large Midwestern university in the United States and an English course of 32 students (all native speakers of Korean) at a small college in South Korea.

Participants

All of the participating students of the Korean class in the United States had more than 250 hours of classroom instruction, and their ages ranged from 18 to 24 years old. The 21 learners of Korean consisted of 15 female students and six male students. Of them, the majority (seven students) identified English as their first language; other first languages were Chinese (four students), Hmong (three students), Spanish (two students), Indonesian (one student), Japanese (one student), Russian (one student), Thai (one student), and Vietnamese (one student).

The counterpart South Korean college students were taking an English course, and their ages ranged from 21 to 27 years old. The researchers estimated the Korean students' English proficiency from novice high to advanced low according to the ACTFL Proficiency Guidelines (2012). There were 24 female and eight male students.

Procedures

The videoconferencing sessions were carried out once a week over a 10 week period using Skype on desktop computers in a computer lab. Skype was chosen because most, if not all, of the participating students were familiar with using Skype. In a critical comparison study of the usefulness and practicality of the six CMC chat tools (i.e., CUworld, ICQ, MSN Messenger, Paltalk, Skype, and Yahoo Messenger), language teachers preferred Skype and MSN Messenger over other tools (Eröz-Tuga & Sadler, 2009).

To engage in authentic communication in the target language, the participating students discussed a topic in English one week, and then switched to Korean the following week. According to Little and Brammerts (1996), for successful Internet-mediated language learning, two principles should be observed: the Principle of Learner Autonomy and the Principle of Reciprocity. In particular, the Principle of Reciprocity indicates that both participants in the language exchange should invest an equal amount of time and effort for mutual benefits, including language use in the exchange. This means about the same amount of time should be devoted to each of the two languages exchanged.

Students' participation in the project is a part of course requirements in order to avoid "the pitfalls of poor sustainability and diminishing student motivation" (Mullen, Appel, & Shanklin, 2009, p. 116). This led to an unmatched number of students between the two universities, as there were more students studying English than those studying the Korean language at the time of the study. As a way to resolve this issue, the student pair-up was made by the instructors on the basis of compatibility of interests, linguistic ability and language anxiety of the students. However, due to the unmatched student numbers, one-on-two pair-ups were unavoidable as shown in Figure 1.

L2 Korean learners' participation in the videoconferencing sessions was coordinated by the first author who was also the instructor of the Korean class in the United States. For each weekly videoconferencing session, there is information exchange task, comparison & analysis task, or collaborative task given to the participating students to ensure sustained and interactive conversations (O'Dowd, 2007; O'Dowd & Ritter, 2006). The tasks were arranged by the instructors of the two partner classes. The tasks for Korean communication were chosen to correspond to the content or theme of the lesson the students of Korean were learning, which included holidays, modes of transportation, food, and shopping. For instance, participants were asked to identify and compare similarities or differences between Korean holidays and American holidays in terms of why they are special and how they are celebrated. Since each videoconferencing session engaged in Korean was preceded by several classroom sessions on the lesson (e.g., dialogues, grammar, vocabulary), students were familiar with basic vocabulary and expressions related to the topics of the videoconferencing.

During each conference, the researchers made a brief observation note while assisting students with any questions or technical difficulties. After each conference, the researchers made detailed notes on what was observed in class such as outstanding student exchanges, challenges and difficulties that occurred during the videoconferencing, and any suggestions and/or solutions to the challenges and difficulties within that session.

Figure 1. Students engaged in videoconferencing

Data Collection

Data collection included pre-questionnaire surveys, post-conferencing surveys, students' journal entries, and post-conferencing interviews with the language students of Korean.

Pre-questionnaire surveys that were conducted during the first week of the semester consisted of questions regarding the students' reasons for taking the current Korean course, any requested topics for videoconferencing, and basic demographic information (e.g., age, gender, ethnicity, academic major(s), and primary language used at home).

After their last videoconferencing for the semester was completed, the students were requested to voluntarily participate in the post-conferencing surveys online. As a result, 11 of the 19 Korean language students (58%) submitted their responses while 23 of the 32 Korean college students (72%) responded. The post-conferencing surveys consisted of 17 questions using a five-point Likert scale (see Appendix A); these questions focused on students' preparation for video-conferencing, their attitudes toward video-conferencing, their self-rated proficiency in the target language, and their estimated effects of videoconferencing on their target language learning. The students were asked to rate their agreement on the scale (1= strongly agree; 2= agree; 3=not sure; 4=disagree; 5=strongly disagree).

All participating students wrote a short journal entry in the language used that week after each video-conferencing session; the journal entry was then e-mailed to the instructor within two days. Specifically, students were asked to be as detailed as possible about how they prepared for the videoconferencing, what they talked about with their partners in videoconferencing, whether they had any technical difficulties, and how they would prepare for the next meeting.

In addition, to gain better perspectives of the participating students, at the end of the semester one-on-one follow-up exit interviews with the language students of Korean in the United States were also conducted. Unfortunately, due to scheduling conflicts the college students in South Korea could not participate in this interview process.

The interviews were semi-structured and lasted about 50 minutes per student. Follow up interview questions included:

1. What were the memorable moments in your videoconferencing sessions, and why were they memorable?
2. How did you prepare for each videoconference?
3. How did you like your partner online?
4. Did videoconferencing sessions help you with learning Korean?
5. Did videoconferencing sessions help you with learning about Korean culture and people?
6. What were the difficulties and challenges you faced during videoconferencing?

For further analysis all of the interview sessions were video-taped.

DATA ANALYSIS

In this study, the main aim is to examine the language learners' synchronous videoconferencing interactions in a CMC learning environment. In so doing, the students' journal entry was the primary data source in which students were asked to freely express their feelings about videoconferencing. In total,

133 students' journals were collected, and analyzed following standard qualitative data procedures (Marshall & Rossmann, 1999). Specifically, the line-by-line descriptions from the students' journals were organized and hand-coded by the researchers. Following Miles and Huberman (1994), recurring patterns related to the research questions were located throughout the data. After multiple and repetitive passes through the data, certain patterns or themes emerged, which will be reported in the following sections. With identified themes constructed, the interactional features by learners are illustrated in the forms of the representative descriptions from the students' journals followed by interpretative explanations.

Findings

What are some themes repeatedly occurring in students' interactions during the real-time multimodal videoconferencing?

The emerging themes identified from the data were:

1. Anxiety/nervousness of first encounters with partners;
2. Fun/excitement of connection with partners;
3. Language practice;
4. Awareness in language use; and
5. Intercultural awareness.

Anxiety/Nervousness

Meeting a new person can be overly exciting and overwhelming. The following excerpt captures well one of the Korean language students' anxiety as well as her excitement prior to the first online videoconferencing with her partners. Her partners were just one-click away on the other side of the screen, and yet, it seemed to be quite daunting for her to click the button to see them online. This is similar to what Winstead (2013) found in face-to-face dual language learning that students are initially apprehensive:

For the past semester I have been anticipating this video-conference with a Korean student. I was extremely nervous and excited at the thought of speaking Korean to a person who has the same struggles as me but with English. It took about a good ten minutes before someone came on. Right then, I realized it's nerve-racking to click the video button and actually see them! (Jennifer[1], journal, 3/9/11)

Meeting new people is one thing and carrying on a conversation with them is quite another. In a synchronous videoconferencing environment, silence between the two sides seemed to be quite awkward. But the students immediately came up with ideas to break the ice. For example, the students of Korean read a brief description of K-pop phenomena along with some questions which they prepared during the pre-conference brainstorming sessions with the classmates in the Korean class. In response, the Korean college students answered and then that awkwardness disappeared. They soon found themselves busily engaging in lively conversations with their partners online as they became more comfortable with each other. They even realized that they had a great deal in common:

We didn't open up our conversation until we started talking about Girls' Generation[2]…we also connected a lot talking about international soccer. Because I like the Korean men's national team, we talked for quite a while about the good run they had at the last World Cup, as well as some of the more successful international players like Park Ji-Sung, Park Chu-Young, and Cha Du-Rhee. (Thomas, journal, 3/9/11)

At the very beginning it was a little awkward, but in a very funny way, so that it was not uncomfortable for either of us. We started talking using only Korean, and that made me feel a lot less shy. My partner was very nice and made me feel comfortable right away. I had a great time practicing Korean with my partner! (Rachel, journal, 3/10/11)

Fun/Excitement

Once that brief awkward moment of the first encounter dissipated, the students found that connecting with their partners is fun and exciting in videoconferencing. There were also predictions that the semester was going to be fun because of these exciting moments of connections they had in their first videoconferencing:

The first videoconferencing was a LOT of fun. I met two students and we had many things in common. We have similar goals and interests. I think this will be a fun semester with videoconferencing ^^. It is a great experience meeting these students. (Amy, journal, 3/11/11)

I think skyping is a very good idea, because it is a totally different learning experience. It is also very fun! (Isabelle, journal, 3/9/11)

Overall, XX was really nice and fun to talk to. I am looking forward to next week's video-conference so that I can learn more about him. (Thomas, journal, 3/9/11)

Language Practice

For successful communication to take place in a target language, students may need to force themselves outside of their comfort zone more assertively than they initially thought. The students in this study had to devote a significant amount of time and effort to use the target language in communication. In the following excerpts, the students share their frank thoughts and honest reactions, and also give details about their efforts to achieve successful communication in the target language:

I don't remember specifically what we talked about but I know it was a good conversation mostly because I was able to use my Korean and not feel intimidated. I think it's very crucial the comfort level or setting I practice my Korean in. How confident or relaxed I feel allows me to use my Korean knowledge more comfortably. (Jennifer, interview, 5/12/11)

이것 이외에도 제 능력이 조금 모자란 듣기는 문제가 많아요. *XX* 가 천천히 말해도 잘 이해하기 못했어요. 그리고 *XX* 가 말하는 것에 제가 모르는 단어가 하나라도 있으면 이해할 수 없게 됐어요. 아마 아직 조금 생소해서 너무 초조했으니까 제가 보통때보다 더 잘 듣지 못한 것예요. 듣기 이외에 말도 잘 하지 못했는데요. 제가 보통 한국말로 말하기전에 마음에 많이 생각하는 것이 필요한데요. 그리고 제가 천천히만 말할 수 있어요. 그런데 지금 누군가는 제가 말하는 것을

기다리는데요. 제가 *XX*를 기다리게 하고 싶지 않았어요... 그런데 계속 한국어로 말해 볼 거예요. 안 포기하면 언젠가 꼭 성공할 거라고 믿었어요. *(James, interview, 5/11/11)*

(Translation³: Beside that, I have to pay attention to my listening skills, which needs improving. Because I couldn't fully understand my partner even when she spoke slowly. Furthermore, I couldn't understand her if there were any words that I haven't learned in what she said. This is probably because this video-conference is pretty new to me, and thus I became nervous, and I couldn't understand her well enough compared to what I was used to. Other than listening skills, I was not speaking in Korean well, either. In general, I have to think before I speak in Korean. And I can speak slowly in Korean. But the fact is that somebody was waiting for me to speak in return, and I didn't want to keep her waiting...I will keep speaking in Korean no matter what. I believe someday I will succeed if I don't give up).

Awareness in Language Use

In addition, the language learners of Korean seemed to be fascinated by the ways in which Korean people use the Korean language in a different manner, especially when they are conversing with older people. As a result, the learners of Korean became more observant and attentive to the ways in which the language is used to show respect toward elders in a proper manner:

Elders are highly respected in Korea so you must always show respect to them not only with your physical actions but also with the language you use toward them. (Frank, interview, 5/12/11.)

While engaging in conversation with their partners, the students soon realized that the situation was reversed when they were asked about the ways in which the English language is used with one's elders. The language learners of Korean were able to then reflect on the ways in which English is utilized to show respect to the interlocutors, such as with changes in prosody, lexicon, grammar, or pragmatics of the language:

My partner asked how we change speech styles in English. While it was a bit difficult to answer, I explained about the conditional, vocabulary differences, and some titles that we use. (Thomas, journal, 4/22/11)

At first, I just asked if an older person would get offended or angry if I accidentally used inappropriate speech styles to talk with them. Both of them (my partners) agreed that it would probably happen.... They, then, asked if it would be similar in America. I tried to explain that although there isn't a specific speech style in English, adults can get very offended when certain slang or tones of voice are used with them from younger people. (Linda, interview, 5/11/11)

Intercultural Awareness

The language students of Korean in the United States discovered that most of their Korean partners seemed to have practical experiences with study abroad or short-term trips to foreign countries. They also realized that their Korean partners seemed to have a well-rounded knowledge of other foreign cultures including American culture:

So my partner, XX, loves to travel. She has been to many places around the world...she lived in Australia for 3 years...In Europe, she went to Switzerland, France, Italy, and England. She has been to Mexico... In the US, she has been to Seattle, New York City, California, Boston, Indiana, Minnesota, Las Vegas, and many more...I haven't travelled as much in America but I was able to share experiences from when I went to Washington D.C. and Atlanta. (Jessica, journal, 4/8/11)

My two partners are very knowledgeable about American culture because in Korea, American music, movies, and food are famous and popular, so they all know about them (Mark, journal, 4/9/11)

나의 파트너 *X*와 *Y*는 미국에 가 본 적이 없습니다. 미국에 가고 싶지만 대학생있어서 돈이 없고 시간이도 없습니다. 그런데 미국에 가면 *X*는 로스 엔젤레스하고 뉴역에 가고 싶습니다. 영화에서 그 도시는 보통 나와서 거기에 가고 싶습니다. *Y*는 워싱턴 디시하고 조지 워싱턴 대학교에도 보고 싶습니다. 왜냐하면 *Y*의 교수님은 조지 워싱턴 대학교에서 졸업했습니다. 나의 파트너는 미국의 문화를 다 알고 있습니다. 한국에서 미국의 음악과 영화와 음식과 유명해서, 인기가 많이 있어서 미국의 문화를 다 알고 있습니다. *(James, journal, 4/15/11)*

(Translation: My partners, X and Y, have not yet been to the U.S. They hope to visit the U.S., but since they are now college students, they don't have the time or the money. If he can, X wants to visit Los Angeles and New York City among other places because it is these two cities that you see in the movies all the time. As far as Y is concerned, he wants to look around Washington D.C. and George Washington University. That's because one of his professors graduated from George Washington University in Washington D.C. My two partners are very knowledgeable about American culture because in Korea, American music, movies, and food are famous and popular, so they (my partners) all know about them).

From the conversations and interaction with their partners through the videoconferencing, the students had the opportunity to experience a foreign culture without visiting that country. Their interactions did not end with just simple comparisons of the two cultures. While engaging in videoconferencing, they began to see the differences and similarities between two or more cultures, and thus were able to interpret other cultures by relating them on their own (Byram, 1997):

Our fundamental difference I think we agreed on was that Korean food has much more of an identity than American food. By that I mean, Korean food is usually thought to be strictly Korean whereas American food is more influenced by foreign countries than from within. For instance, originally hamburgers were a German food, pizza is from Italy, and tacos from Mexico. (Thomas, journal, 4/7/11)

One thing I found interesting was that Korean families seldom give gifts to anyone besides younger kids on Christmas. As much as younger kids are the main focus in America, Christmas is often largely dependent on giving and receiving gifts to family and friends of all ages; generally, that's why Christmas is such a stressful time for many Americans. In Korea, it's either a day spent with your girlfriend, if you have one, or your family largely not concerned with any gift giving. And my partner XX being a man has the luxury of even less stress because he does not need to cook the meals at all. This aspect is true of all the holidays. (Mark, journal, 4/8/11)

Her perspective of American families is pretty well informed. However, I disagreed with some – though not many – of her generalizations. She is under the impression that a lot of American families are very religious. While this is true, I don't think that they are as religious as the people she encountered. Where I'm from, there is a lot of religious apathy and the families are more centered around each other than religion. (Rachel, journal, 4/21/11)

In the following sections, based on the post-conferencing online survey, we will report the participating Korean language students' responses regarding their self-rated proficiency in the target languages as well as their estimate of the effects of videoconferencing on their target language learning. The self-assessment information was gathered in order to gain information about students' perception of their own L2 proficiency as well as their expectation of participating in videoconferencing for their target language learning.

How Confident Do the Learners Feel about Their Proficiency in the Target Language?

Previous studies have shown that self-assessment measures a combination of learners' ability to use the language in given contexts and their level of confidence in doing so (Clément, 1986). In her study of self-regulated dual language (English-Spanish) program, Winstead (2013) shows that adolescent students experienced language acquisition with increased target language confidence through self-regulated learning process. "Confidence became a way to measure their [students'] ability to understand their peer in the target language" through the stages of Language Initiation and Language Acquisition in her Alternative Dual Language Model (Winstead, 2013, p. 12).

Figure 2 shows the language students of Korean's self-assessed confidence in their Korean along with their partner's estimates.

As shown with the black bars, all of the Korean language students (n=11) believed that their Korean proficiency was "acceptable" for carrying on conversations with their Korean counterparts. As indicated

Figure 2. Was your Korean acceptable for the video-chat?/Was your partner's Korean acceptable for the video-chat?

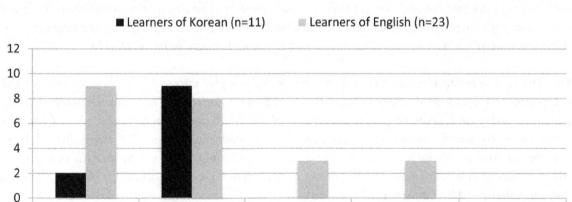

by the grey bars, 17 Korean college students also agreed that their partners' (i.e., the Korean language students') Korean was "acceptable." However, the remaining Korean college students (six students) were not sure about or disagreed with the acceptability of their partner's proficiency in Korean.

It must not have been easy to carry on conversations using only the target language during the videoconferencing. The students came to realize how challenging, and also rewarding, it was to speak the target language with their partners, and also how thankful they felt toward their partners while they were engaged in conversations using the language. For instance:

So during the video-conference I tried to speak Korean as much as I could, but it is very hard for me to form sentences. I feel really embarrassed or scared to speak Korean because I cannot speak fluently. My partner speaks only Korean to me and I thank her so much for that because I am learning so many new words and phrases (Amanda, interview, 5/10/11).

Regarding self-assessed proficiency of their target language, considering they were students of fourth-semester Korean, the Korean language students seemed to be quite confident in their Korean proficiency in that they all believed their Korean was acceptable for carrying on conversations with the native speakers of Korean during the video-chat. Through authentic interaction with native speakers of the target language, learners' increased confidence promotes language gains, which may lead to language acquisition (Gleason & Suvorov, 2012; O'Dowd, 2000; Winstead, 2013; Wu et al., 2011).

What Are Their Expectations of Videoconferencing on Their Target Language Learning?

One of the goals of the videoconferencing project was to develop student's linguistic competence in the target language by meeting with native speakers through online video-chat. The overwhelming majority of the students reported that their linguistic competence improved as a result of videoconferencing.

As shown in Figure 3, most of the learners of Korean (82%, as shown by the black bars) agreed that the videoconferencing improved their Korean. In a similar manner, a majority (61%) of the Korean col-

Figure 3. Has the videoconferencing improved your Korean/English?

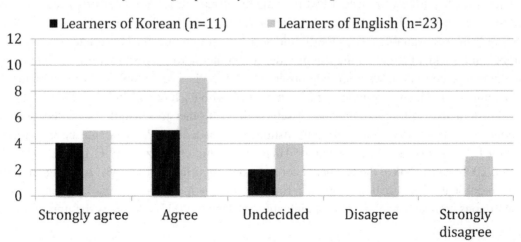

lege students also thought their English improved due to participating in the videoconferencing, and yet, quite a significant number of students (39%, as shown by the grey bars) seemed to think that it had not improved their English, or at least were unsure of the effects. The fact that some Korean college students had a favorable experience with videoconferencing but others did not may be related to the fact that some Korean college students were not paired up with their English counterparts "one-on-one" but rather "one-on-two."

DISCUSSION AND CONCLUSION

Overall, our data show that the language students positively evaluated videoconferencing in contributing to the development of listening and speaking skills. Communication via videoconferencing facilitated learner-centered learning as students were constantly pushed and stimulated to process comprehensible input and thus produce output in L2. As reported in the first stage of Language Apprehension (Winstead, 2013) and anxiety identified in other studies (Lee, 2007; Katz, 2001), the language students similarly showed anxiety as well as excitement in initiating conversation with their partners. In addition, some students were frustrated by their linguistic inability to communicate in the target language.

Through continued authentic interaction with native speakers in videoconferencing, the learners felt comfortable, and thus became more confident in their interactions with the native speakers of the target language, which is similar to the findings in the second stage of Language Initiation (Winstead, 2013). According to the interviews with students, their communication with their Korean partners often involved cultural aspects of the target language or target language community. For instance, participants shared how speech levels and styles are realized differently between L1 and L2 or how the celebration of the same holiday can vary according to cultural contexts. Participants broadened their cultural horizons through first-hand exposure to target language speakers, a finding that lends support to the similar conclusions made in the previous studies (Katz, 2001; Schenker, 2013)

While participating in this videoconferencing study, the students and teachers experienced a series of challenges and difficulties. First, they dealt with quite a few technical difficulties in terms of connectivity, as the CMC tool, Skype, did not always work for every student every time. For instance, some students could not hear their partners or their partners were not able to see them because their computer screens froze. Thus, they had to rely on instant text messaging, instead. It is also noteworthy that the students seemed to be less troubled by the technical challenges as they exhibited their problem solving strategies by utilizing whatever available modes they could access to communicate. This relates to a recent study by Hampel and Stickler (2012) on the use of videoconferencing to support multimodal interactions in distance language education, wherein they observed "the modes were combined to complement each other, to compensate for shortcomings, or in competition with each other" (p. 132). Second, the teachers and the students had to communicate closely with each other to schedule the videoconferencing throughout the semester due to the different institutional academic calendars and the time difference between the U.S. and Korea. Third, as suggested in previous studies (Belz, 2003; O'Dowd, 2007; Müller-Hartmann, 2006; Kern, 2006), the teachers become more important in the CMC learning environment than the traditional educational settings in terms of their involvement in organizing and facilitating the synchronous computer-mediated communication. O'Dowd (2007) addresses the importance of the teachers' role in this kind of computer-mediated communication and divides the teacher's role into four major categories: organizer, intercultural partner, model and coach, and source and resource. In addressing the importance of using a synchronous online environment and training tutors for online language courses for "new classrooms," Hampel and Stickler (2005) suggest "a pyramid of skills" necessary for successful online teaching, which includes "the more general skills of dealing with the technology and using its advantages, the social skills of community building, language teaching skills, and the skills to teach creatively and develop a personal teaching style" (p. 311).

Given the current situation where teachers of the less commonly taught languages including Korean are already facing many challenges and difficulties because of limited resources (Lim, 2011), then, the roles of the teachers of Korean language become immense and thus their burden can be overwhelming in the context of the computer-mediated communication for Korean language instruction. However, as Zhao (2003) puts it, "the effects of any technology on learning outcomes lie in its uses" and the effectiveness of this synchronous multi-modal (i.e., video-, audio-, and textual modes) online communication for Korean language learning can outweigh the challenges. First, as suggested in previous studies (Birdwhistell, 1970; Knapp and Hall, 2006), non-verbal communication plays a major role in second language communicative competence. According to Singelis (1994), the speakers of the same language rely heavily on non-verbal communication for negotiation of meanings, and when it comes to the communication between second language learners, "the reliance on the non-verbal communication may be even greater than normal" (p.275). Multi-modal videoconferencing naturally provides verbal and non-verbal information simultaneously, which makes it easier for learners to engage in conversation and effectively negotiate meanings with their interlocutors because they can go beyond the linguistic context by concomitantly obtaining verbal and non-verbal cues from intonation, tone of voice, gesture, facial expressions, and gaze behaviour.

Second, most college students who study foreign languages severely lack opportunities to actually use their foreign language knowledge for communication in their daily lives (Ho, 2003; Chase and Alexander, 2007; Sun, 2009). By providing students videoconferencing communication opportunities, we can create an environment where students put their foreign language knowledge into practice in and outside of the classroom.

Finally, there is no doubt that this kind of collaborative and learner-centered online communication activity requires expanded roles and responsibilities from the teacher – a problem if the teacher has already been suffering from a lack of resources, time, and little to no support or help from their own institutions (Arnold, 2007; Butler & Sellbom, 2002; Egbert, Paulus, & Nakamichi, 2002; Ertmer, Addison, Lane, Ross, & Woods, 1999; Wilson, 2003). Despite the extra stress, teachers will most likely be willing to integrate technology into classroom curricula; as Miller and Olson (1994) put it "teachers do things for good reasons" (p. 123). Ultimately, we predict that they will find it rewarding to witness their own students' successful and meaningful interactions with the native speakers of the language they are learning.

As an exploratory study of Korean language learning using videoconferencing technology, the current study is mostly descriptive in nature. The authors acknowledge the limitations associated with the study. First, most of the findings reported are based on students' self-assessments and their own descriptions of the interactions in the videoconferencing. Second, the descriptions of the synchronous interactions in the videoconferencing were made mainly by the Korean language students, and thus, the voices of all learners were not fully portrayed. Third, the questionnaires used for students' perception and self-assessments are by no means thorough in offering a comprehensive picture of their language learning experience. Therefore, more comprehensive studies are needed in the uses of technology in language learning, and the effectiveness of the Internet-based technology on Korean language teaching. Along this line, it is our intention that this paper invites further research into effective applications of technology in language learning in general, and more specifically, to the contributions of video-conferencing to learning less commonly taught languages.

REFERENCES

Abrams, Z. I. (2003). The effects of synchronous and asynchronous CMC on oral performance. *Modern Language Journal*, *87*(2), 157–167. doi:10.1111/1540-4781.00184

American Council on the Teaching of Foreign Languages. (2012). *ACTFL proficiency guidelines*. Alexander, VA: Author.

Arnold, N. (2007). Technology-mediated learning 10 years later: Emphasizing pedagogical or utilitarian applications? *Foreign Language Annals*, *40*(1), 161–181. doi:10.1111/j.1944-9720.2007.tb02859.x

Belz, J. A. (2003). Linguistic perspective on the development of intercultural competence in telecollaboration. *Language Learning & Technology*, *7*(2), 68–99.

Birdwhistell, R. L. (1970). *Kinesics and context*. Philadelphia, PA: University of Pennsylvania Press.

Blake, R. (2000). Computer mediated communication: A window on L2 Spanish interlanguage. *Language Learning & Technology*, *4*(1), 120–136.

Brown, A. (2009). Less commonly taught language and commonly taught language students: A demographic and academic comparison. *Foreign Language Annals*, *42*(3), 405–423. doi:10.1111/j.1944-9720.2009.01036.x

Butler, D. L., & Sellbom, M. (2002). Barriers to adopting technology for teaching and learning. *EDUCAUSE Quarterly*, *2*, 22–28.

Byram, M. (1997). *Teaching and assessing intercultural communicative competence*. Clevedon, UK: Multilingual Matters.

Chan, W. M., & Chi, S. W. (2011). Popular media as a motivational factor for foreign language learning: The example of the Korean wave. In W. W. Chan, K. N. Chin, M. Nagami, & T. Suthiwan (Eds.), *Media in foreign language teaching and learning* (pp. 151–188). De Gruyter Mouton. doi:10.1515/9781614510208.151

Chase, C., & Alexander, P. (2007). The Japan-Korea culture exchange project. In R. O'Dowd (Ed.), *Online intercultural exchange: An introduction for foreign language teachers* (pp. 259–263). Clevedon, UK: Multilingual Matters.

Chun, D. M. (1994). Using computer networking to facilitate the acquisition of interactive competence. *System*, *22*(1), 17–31. doi:10.1016/0346-251X(94)90037-X

Chun, D. M., & Plass, J. L. (2000). Networked multimedia environments for second language acquisition. In M. Warschauer & R. Kern (Eds.), *Network-based language teaching: Concepts and Practice* (pp. 20–40). Cambridge University Press. doi:10.1017/CBO9781139524735.009

Clément, L. R. (1986). Second language proficiency and acculturation: An investigation of the effects of language status and individual characteristics. *Journal of Language and Social Psychology*, *5*(4), 271–290. doi:10.1177/0261927X8600500403

Damron, J., & Forsyth, J. (2012). Korean language studies: Motivation and attrition. *Journal of Less Commonly Taught Languages*, *12*, 161–182.

Egbert, J., Paulus, T. M., & Nakamichi, Y. (2002). The impact of CALL instruction on classroom computer use: A foundation for rethinking technology in teacher education. *Language Learning & Technology*, *6*(3), 108–126.

Eröz-Tuga, B., & Sadler, R. (2009). Comparing six video chat tools: A critical evaluation by language teachers. *Computers & Education*, *53*(3), 787–798. doi:10.1016/j.compedu.2009.04.017

Ertmer, P. A., Addison, P., Lane, M., Ross, E., & Woods, D. (1999). Examining teachers' beliefs about the role of technology in the elementary classroom. *Journal of Research on Computing in Education*, *32*(1), 54–71. doi:10.1080/08886504.1999.10782269

Fernandez-Garcia, M., & Martinez-Arbelaiz, A. (2002). Negotiation of meaning in non-native speaker non-native speaker synchronous discussions. *CALICO Journal*, *19*, 279–294.

Gleason, J., & Suvorov, R. (2012). Learner perceptions of asynchronous oral computer- mediated communication: Proficiency and second language selves. *Canadian Journal of Applied Linguistics*, *15*(1), 100–121.

Godwin-Jones, R. (2013). Emerging technologies: The technological imperative in teaching and learning less commonly taught languages. *Language Learning & Technology*, *17*(1), 7–19.

Goldberg, D., Looney, D., & Lusin, N. (2015). *Enrollments in languages other than English in the United States institutions of higher education, fall 2013*. Modern Language Association of America.

Hampel, R., & Baber, E. (2003). Using Internet-based audio-graphic and videoconferencing for language teaching and learning. In U. Felix (Ed.), *Language learning online: Towards best practice* (pp. 171–191). Lisse, The Netherlands: Swets & Zeitlinger.

Hampel, R., & Stickler, U. (2005). New Skills for New Classrooms: Training tutors to teach languages online. *Computer Assisted Language Learning*, *18*(4), 311–326. doi:10.1080/09588220500335455

Hampel, R., & Stickler, U. (2012). The use of videoconferencing to support multimodal interaction in an online language classroom. *ReCALL*, *24*(2), 116–137. doi:10.1017/S095834401200002X

Herring, S. (Ed.). (1996). *Computer-mediated communication: Linguistic, social, and cross-cultural perspectives*. Amsterdam: John Benjamins. doi:10.1075/pbns.39

Hirotani, M., & Lyddon, P. A. (2013). The development of L2 Japanese self-introductions in an asynchronous computer-mediated language exchange. *Foreign Language Annals, 46*(3), 469–490. doi:10.1111/flan.12044

Ho, Y. K. (2003). Audiotaped dialogue journals: An alternative form of speaking practice. *ELT Journal, 57*(3), 269–277. doi:10.1093/elt/57.3.269

Katz, S. (2001). Videoconferencing with the French-speaking world: A user's guide. *Foreign Language Annals, 34*(2), 152–157. doi:10.1111/j.1944-9720.2001.tb02820.x

Kelm, O. R. (1992). The use of synchronous computer networks in second language instruction: A preliminary report. *Foreign Language Annals, 25*(5), 441–545. doi:10.1111/j.1944-9720.1992.tb01127.x

Kern, R., Ware, P., & Warschauer, M. (2008). Network-based language Teaching. In N. Van Deusen-Scholl and N. H. Hornberger (Eds.), Encyclopedia of Language and Education (2nd ed., Vol. 4, pp. 281–292). Springer Science+Business Media LLC. doi:10.1007/978-0-387-30424-3_105

Kern, R. G. (1995). Restructuring classroom interaction with network computers: Effects on quantity and characteristics of language production. *Modern Language Journal, 79*(4), 457–476. doi:10.1111/j.1540-4781.1995.tb05445.x

Kern, R. G. (2006). Perspectives on technology in learning and teaching languages. *TESOL Quarterly, 40*(1), 183–210. doi:10.2307/40264516

Knapp, M., & Hall, J. (2006). *Nonverbal communication in human interaction*. Belmont, CA: Thomson Wadsworth.

Lee, L. (2007). Fostering second language oral communication through constructivist interaction in desktop videoconferencing. *Foreign Language Annals, 40*(4), 635–649. doi:10.1111/j.1944-9720.2007.tb02885.x

Lim, B. J. (2011). Korean language education with one-on-one desktop videoconferencing. *Journal of Korean-American Education, 28*, 16–21.

Little, D., & Brammerts, H. (1996). A guide to language learning in tandem via the Internet. *CLCS Occasional Paper* No. 46. Dublin: Trinity College, Centre for Language and Communication Studies.

Long, M. H. (1996). The role of the linguistic environment in second language acquisition. In W. Ritchie & T. Bhatia (Eds.), *Handbook of second language acquisition* (pp. 413–468). San Diego, CA: Academic Press. doi:10.1016/B978-012589042-7/50015-3

Magnan, S., Murphy, D., Sahakyan, N., & Kim, S. (2012). Student goals, expectations, and the standards for foreign language learning. *Foreign Language Annals, 45*(2), 170–192. doi:10.1111/j.1944-9720.2012.01192.x

Marshall, C., & Rossman, G. B. (1999). *Designing qualitative research* (3rd ed.). Thousand Oaks, CA: Sage Publications.

Miles, M. B., & Huberman, A. M. (1994). *An expanded sourcebook: qualitative data analysis* (2nd ed.). Thousand Oaks, CA: Sage Publications.

Miller, L., & Olson, J. (1994). Putting the computer in its place: A study of teaching with technology. *Journal of Curriculum Studies, 26*(1), 121–141. doi:10.1080/0022027940260201

Mullen, T., Appel, C., & Shanklin, T. (2009). Skype-based tandem language learning and Web 2.0. In M. Thomas (Ed.), *Handbook of Research on Web 2.0 and Second Language Learning* (pp. 101–118). New York, NY: Information Science Reference. doi:10.4018/978-1-60566-190-2.ch006

Müller-Hartmann, A. (2006). Learning how to teach intercultural communicative competence via telecollaboration: A model for language teacher education. In J. A. Belz & S. Thorn (Eds.), *Internet-mediated intercultural foreign language education* (pp. 63–84). Boston, MA: Heinle & Heinle.

O'Dowd, R. (2000). Intercultural learning via videoconferencing: A pilot exchange project. *ReCALL, 12*(1), 49–61. doi:10.1017/S0958344000000616

O'Dowd, R. (2007). Evaluating the outcomes of online intercultural exchange. *ELT Journal, 61*(2), 144–152. doi:10.1093/elt/ccm007

O'Dowd, R., & Ritter, M. (2006). Understanding and working with 'failed communication' in telecollaborative exchanges. *CALICO Journal, 23*, 1–20.

Ortega, L. (1997). Processes and outcomes in networked classroom interaction: Defining the research agenda for L2 computer-assisted classroom discussion. *Language Learning & Technology, 1*(1), 82–93.

Pellettieri, J. (2000). Negotiation in cyberspace: The role of chatting in the development of grammatical competence. In M. Warschauer & R. Kern (Eds.), *Network-based Language Teaching: Concepts and Practices* (pp. 59–86). New York: Cambridge University Press. doi:10.1017/CBO9781139524735.006

Salaberry, M. R. (1999). Call in the Year 2000: Still Developing the Research Agenda. *Language Learning & Technology, 3*(1), 104–107.

Schenker, T. (2013). The Effects of a Virtual Exchange on Students' Interest in Learning About Culture. *Foreign Language Annals, 46*(3), 491–507. doi:10.1111/flan.12041

Singelis, T. (1994). Nonverbal communication in intercultural interactions. In R. Brislin & T. Yoshida (Eds.), *Improving intercultural interactions* (pp. 268–294). Thousand Oaks, CA: Sage.

Smith, B. (2003). Computer-mediated negotiated interaction: An expanded model. *Modern Language Journal, 87*(1), 38–57. doi:10.1111/1540-4781.00177

Smith, B. (2004). Computer-mediated negotiated interaction and lexical acquisition. *Studies in Second Language Acquisition, 26*(03), 365–398. doi:10.1017/S027226310426301X

Sotillo, S. M. (2000). Discourse Functions and Syntactic Complexity in Synchronous and Asynchronous Communication. *Language Learning & Technology, 4*(1), 82–119.

Spreen, C.A. (Ed.), (2002). Preface. In C.A. Spreen (Ed.), New technologies and language learning: Cases in the less commonly taught languages (pp. xiii-xxiv). National Foreign Language Resource Center.

Sun, Y. C. (2009). Voice blog: An exploratory study of language Learning. *Language Learning & Technology, 13*(2), 88–103.

Toyoda, E., & Harrison, R. (2002). Categorization of text chat communication between learners and native speakers and native speakers of Japanese. *Language Learning & Technology*, *6*(1), 82–99.

Tudini, V. (2003). Using native speakers in chat. *Language Learning & Technology*, *7*(3), 141–159.

Wang, Y. (2006). Negotiation of meaning in desktop videoconferencing-supported distance language learning. *ReCALL*, *18*(1), 122–146. doi:10.1017/S0958344006000814

Warschauer, M. (1997). Computer-mediated collaborative learning: Theory and practice. *Modern Language Journal*, *81*(4), 470–481. doi:10.1111/j.1540-4781.1997.tb05514.x

Warschauer, M., & Kern, R. (2000). *Network-based language teaching: Concepts and practice*. Cambridge, UK: Cambridge University Press. doi:10.1017/CBO9781139524735

Wilson, W. (2003). Faculty perceptions and uses of instructional technology. *EDUCAUSE Quarterly*, *2*, 60–62.

Winstead, L. (2013). Apprehension and motivation among adolescent dual language peers: Perceptions and awareness about self-directed teaching and learning. *Language and Education*, *27*(1), 1–21. doi:10.1080/09500782.2012.669767

Wu, W., Yen, L., & Marek, M. (2011). Using online EFL interaction to increase confidence, motivation, and ability. *Journal of Educational Technology & Society*, *14*(3), 118–129.

Yamada, M., & Akahori, K. (2009). Awareness and performance through self and partner's image in videoconferencing. *CALICO Journal*, *27*(1), 1–25. doi:10.11139/cj.27.1.1-25

Yanguas, Í. (2010). Oral computer-mediated interaction between L2 learners: It's about time! *Language Learning & Technology*, *14*(1), 72–93.

Zhao, Y. (2003). Recent developments in technology and language learning: A literature review and meta-analysis. *CALICO Journal*, *21*(1), 7–27.

ENDNOTES

[1]   For identity protection, a pseudonym is used for each participant.

[2]   Girls' Generation is a popular South Korean idol group with eight girl members.

[3]   The authors translated the passage. In the translations, the authors tried to capture as close as possible what the learners of Korean conveyed in the target language.

APPENDIX

Post-Conferencing Questionnaire

Dear Students,

This questionnaire serves to invite your comments on the video-conferencing project in which you participated this semester.

Please *reply in English* to each of the following questions.

Topic/Preparation

1. How did you like the video-conferencing topics this semester?
2. What topics did you find most interesting? Why is that?
3. What topics did you find least interesting? Why is that?
4. What additional topics would you like to have included in the future? Tell me at least *two topics* you would like to add.
5. Was the amount of class time spent on the preparation for video-conferencing sufficient? (Choose one, please)
    (a) strongly agree (b) agree (c) not sure (d) disagree (e) strongly disagree
6. Was the instructor's assistance helpful during this preparation? (Choose one, please)
    (a) strongly agree (b) agree (c) not sure (d) disagree (e) strongly disagree
7. How would you evaluate the preparation procedure for video-conferencing?

Video-Conferencing

8. Did you enjoy this video-conferencing project? Why or why not?
9. What major technical difficulties did you encounter during the conferencing? How did you solve these challenges?

Language Use

10. Do you think your current Korean proficiency was at an acceptable level for you to carry on conversations with your partners during the conferencing? (Choose one, please)
    (a) strongly agree (b) agree (c) not sure (d) disagree (e) strongly disagree
11. Do you think your partner's English proficiency was at an acceptable level for you to carry on conversations with him/her during the conferencing? (Choose one, please)
    (a) strongly agree (b) agree (c) not sure (d) disagree (e) strongly disagree
12. Do you think this video-conferencing project improved your Korean proficiency? (Choose one, please)
    (a) strongly agree (b) agree (c) not sure (d) disagree (e) strongly disagree
13. If you answered 'yes' or 'somewhat yes' to question 10, in what ways did it improve your Korean proficiency?

Follow-Up

14. Would you be interested in continuing the video-conferencing on your own with your partner(s) at the Korean University after this semester? (Choose one, please)
    (a)   strongly agree (b) agree (c) not sure (d) disagree (e) strongly disagree
15. Would you be willing to keep in touch with your partner(s) (e.g., e-mail, phone call)? (Choose one, please)
    (a)   strongly agree (b) agree (c) not sure (d) disagree (e) strongly disagree
16. What improvements would you suggest be done to enhance future video-conferencing projects?
17. Was this video-conferencing project useful? If so (or if not), please specify.

Chapter 13
Globalization and Possibilities for Intercultural Awareness:
Multimodal Arabic Culture Portfolios at a Catholic University

Sawsan Abbadi
Loyola University, USA

ABSTRACT

This case study explores the teaching and learning of Arabic at one Catholic university campus, with a focus upon the complex interactions between language and culture in a postmodern globalized context. Specifically, it examines the use of "multimodal culture portfolios" as a means to engage students both linguistically and culturally in classroom and community discourses. Through their interactions and co-construction of knowledge with other participants, these students are led to think about the multiple communicative contexts that are shaping and being shaped by them. Data collection was conducted through survey questionnaires and students' responses to the assigned culture portfolio. The participants were made up of students enrolled in first year Arabic courses during the 2012 spring semester. The purpose of this exploratory case is to attempt to understand students' investments in Arabic and their cultural knowledge of the Arab world pre and post their enrollment in the Arabic courses. It also seeks to understand their socialization into the culture assignment and the main challenges they faced in accessing, interacting with, and reflecting upon cultural aspects related to the Arab world. This study's findings are significant for enriching the general conversation on intercultural proficiency in classroom discourse, curricular decisions, roles and challenges of teachers, and the involvement in target language communities, particularly in less commonly taught languages such as Arabic.

INTRODUCTION

The multiplicity of communication channels brought about by multiculturalism, globalization, and multimodalism has profoundly affected both language education in general and world language education in particular. In what he called "domesticating the foreign," Lo Bianco (2014) argues that "teachers

DOI: 10.4018/978-1-5225-0177-0.ch013

of different languages need to make multilingual and multicultural realities...central notions in [the] curriculum" (p. 312), especially if they are to accommodate such communicative shifts. Furthermore, he questions the concept of "foreignness" (p. 313) in foreign or world language education, and claims that globalization has shattered the old order of nations, national languages, and "culturally authentic language" (p. 314). It is thus imperative to rethink how we prepare students to participate in this highly globalized and culturally pluralistic world.

Given the increase in globalization and the explosion of communication technologies, there have been many productive debates on the changes and challenges in language education (Cope & Kalantzis, 2010; Kramsch, 2007, 2005; and Kumaravadivelu, 2003). In critiquing national language education policy in the United States and its politically charged ideologies, Blake and Kramsch (2007) referred to the irony of calls to encourage learning world languages as part of the "internationalization" (p. 247) of higher education while the arguments clearly point to the politically charged relations between language learning and the government's need to face "continual threats of terrorism" (p. 247). In the case of Arabic, Gerwin and Osborn (2005) argue against the dangers of aligning language education to such claimed threats:

Japan's attack on Pearl Harbor provides a compelling historical analogy for the September 11 attack itself...The war on terrorism...is open ended and murky on many scores, but the enemy does have a face. The enemy is Muslim, the enemy is Middle Eastern, the enemy is an Arab. (Gerwin & Osborn, 2005, p. 106)

Because of the political nature of language education, Arabic as a foreign language has inherited the pros and cons of attempts to interpret globalization's impact on the fate of the field (Abbadi, 2014, 2013). As a result, a widespread enthusiasm for teaching and learning Arabic has been reinvigorated (Allen, 2007; Leeman & Martinez, 2007; Ryding, 2006; Kramsch, 2005; Allen, 2004; Byrnes et al., 2004; and Edwards, 2000). Thus, it has received more attention and experienced growth in reaction to wider global economic, social, and political events, "transform[ing] [it] from an exotic less commonly taught language into a mainstream one" (Abdallah & Al-Batal, 2011-12, p. 1). With the above ironies in mind, Arabic, along with other less commonly taught languages, has become "a formidable challenge" (Byrnes, 2009, p. 261), demanding a rejuvenated curriculum. As a result, an increase in the quantity and quality of trained teachers and a critical need to redesign the framework and infrastructure of language programs is necessary (Ryding, 2013; Wang, 2009; Al-Batal, 2007; and Allen, 2007).

These demands have become even more pervasive given that political interest in the Arab and Islamic world has not subsided post 9/11. In fact, it has gained more attention currently due to the uprisings in many Arab countries, starting with Tunisia and spreading to Egypt, Libya, Yemen, Syria and Iraq among unsettlements in other regions. However, the interest in learning about the culture of the "Other" and questioning ideological perspectives brought about by media and fast communication has also height-ened interest in the field. Because of these communicative changes, new possibilities have surfaced in the academy to critically explore the macro sociopolitical and cultural contexts of learning and teaching world languages. This means that there is now also space for the micro hybrid contexts of language classrooms to support linguistic and intercultural competence. A more urgent need to transform our classrooms into a *cultural* and *interactional* context (Kramsch, 1993, p. 41) is thus inescapable. Moving beyond classrooms, language teachers need to build crossings between learning in the classroom and the possibilities of carrying its implications and processes to real action outside within wider communities (Fairclough, 2001).

THEORETICAL BACKGROUND: LANGUAGE AND CULTURE

Vygotsky's (1978) theory on learning and development and Halliday's systemic functional linguistics (Halliday & Hasan, 1989) help situate the teaching and learning processes created within a learning environment, i.e., they explain how meanings are created and *mediated* within a social and cultural context (Dixon et al., 2012; Pacheco, 2012; Thoms, 2012; and Magnon, 2007). Such contexts need to prepare learners for interconnecting with wider communities as citizens in a hybrid, global, multicultural, and multilingual world. Although culture is problematic to define and standardize, it has long moved beyond reductionist modernist views that categorized it as stable and fixed. In other words, culture has long been conceptualized as being fluid. Recent research supports the ever-changing nature of culture and its connection to perspectives, attitudes, artifacts, practices, and signs, in addition to other salient and vague aspects of culture (Pacheco, 2012; Rampton, 2006; Kramsch, 2003; Fairclough, 2001; and Kramsch, 1993). Wendy Allen (2014) defines culture by accentuating how it translates into meaningful classroom objectives:

Intercultural competence (IC) lies at the intersection of attitudes, knowledge and skills. It is the ability to interact with others, to understand other perspectives and perceptions of the world, to mediate between different perspectives and to be conscious of one's own and other's evaluation of difference. (Allen, 2014, p. 27)

In current discussions of language teaching and learning at professional, institutional, and personal levels, Scollon and Scollon (2001) explore intercultural communication while Kramsch (1998) describe intercultural learners/speakers, both of which shed significant light on intercultural competence. Moving beyond a mythical view of native speakers, target language, and culture, intercultural awareness proposes a more "reflexive" approach that helps learners focus on their own cultures and perspectives. Intercultural awareness also encourages them to explore the cultures and perspectives of others in order to help them "perceive and cope with difference" (Byram & Fleming, 1998, p. 4). The idea then is to move beyond finding general commonalities across cultures and peoples and rather observe, understand, and gain critical insights into the cultures and languages of the speakers and the targeted learned ones. This movement involves questioning, implicitly and explicitly, the "taken-for-granted" insights of cultures we are "socialized" into and critically interrogating our own "assumptions and values" (Byram & Fleming, 1998, p. 6).

This paper agrees with the need to situate intercultural competence in curricular models with clear objectives that allow for functional tasks and student projects to mediate linguistic and cultural learning beyond classroom contexts to larger community contexts (cf. Page & Benander, 2014; Cadd, 2012). It does not, however, address the significant body of research on intercultural competence. To sum up, the goal is for learners of world languages to develop, transfer, and transform language learning into something experiential. This can be accomplished by mediating differences, questioning their linguistic and cultural socialization, and reflecting on the practices and attitudes of their own cultures and those of the cultures studied.

This exploratory case study focuses on the following questions: What can language teachers do to critically engage with and respond to the politically charged contexts of teaching world languages in general, and Arabic in particular? How can we employ community resources within educational institutions or in their wider communities to problematize students' understanding of language and culture as a social activity, all in order to foster linguistic and cultural proficiency? How can we explicitly, as teachers, make "classroom discourse more explicitly intercultural" (Kramsch, 1998, p. 28)?

METHODOLOGY

This paper draws on data from an exploratory case study at one Catholic university campus on the teaching and learning of Arabic as a world language. It sheds light on the possibilities for intercultural awareness by examining the use of multimodal culture portfolios as a pedagogical tool in Arabic classrooms to implicitly and explicitly interrogate students' understandings of linguistic and cultural difference. The study highlights learning beyond the classroom through engagement with larger communities through projects, experiential learning opportunities, and service as a means to prepare students to lead critical roles as global citizens. A follow-up discussion is provided on becoming an intercultural learner as well as on the importance of fostering a critically engaged "learning community" for Arabic students (Ryding, 1994, p. 23).

The researcher will first introduce the university context and its unique mission as a religious institution in fostering students' educated awareness of culture and society as global citizens with a social responsibility of service to others. The researcher will introduce the new Arabic program that aligns its language and culture objectives to the larger university mission. The researcher will follow this introduction with a description of the learning context and the participants within the larger community.

Research Context

University Context

The study was conducted in the early summer of 2012 at a Catholic university campus in the United States. It is located in a highly dense metropolitan city in the American Midwest, enrolling about 16,000 undergraduate students and employing about 4,000 faculty and staff members. The university has several local and international campuses in Europe and Asia to support its Catholic mission and identity. As part of its mission statement, the university prides itself on and is dedicated to providing a dynamic, transformative understanding of education that joins faith and reason and commits to excellence in integrative education and discursive knowledge. The university welcomes all faiths and traditions, encourages service to others as social agents, and fosters a high sense of social awareness and responsibility.

Given its relation to faith and tradition, the Arabic program is housed within the Department of Modern Languages as one of the critical less commonly taught languages on campus. Professor Marsha (pseudonym), an early supporter of the Arabic program at the college of arts and sciences, noted Arabic has been taught on this campus for over 15 years, offering two years of Arabic courses at the undergraduate level. A third year level has been officially approved in the past few years, however, as it seems that budgets and faculty allocations may have influenced the stability rate of students at the third year level. The program attracts about 80 students every semester based on the budget-approved courses offered.

Due to the program's stable enrollment, the campus has benefited in the past from several adjunct faculty members and Fulbright visitors, not all of whom were necessarily Arabic language or education specialists. Only recently did the department succeed in securing one fulltime position to rebuild the program and establish a new minor in Arabic, with attention paid towards the recent developments in the field of teaching the Arabic language and culture. This initiative has further helped to strengthen the field's interdisciplinary connections to other fields, including political science, international studies, and theology, with particular attention to enhancing Islamic studies. Currently, the newly established Arabic minor hosts around 50 students from a nexus of academic majors and investments in learning Arabic. Building on the larger university's mission, the Arabic program has visibly contributed to promoting students', faculties', and the larger community's engagement through service and experiential learning opportunities.

City/Community Context

The university is located in one of the most diverse and densely populated cities in Midwestern America, IL. According to the city's 2010 census, the racial composition of the city is approximately 45% White, 33% African American, and 29% Latino people, in addition to some smaller groups, including Arab Americans. Religiously, the city is also diverse, enriching the campus body with members of multiple faiths, including Christianity, Islam, Judaism, Hinduism, and Buddhism. In regards to Arabic, Professor Marsha emphasizes the importance of the Arab heritage communities to Illinois at large, a demographic that, according to the Arab American Institute Foundation website (2015, July 25), ranks seventh in terms of total numbers of Arab Americans in the United States. Ethnically, the university also invites students from the larger South Asian heritage who actively participate in Arabic courses for personal, religious, and academic reasons.

Arabic Program

Arabic has been taught at this university for more than 15 years. However, the last few years have witnessed structural changes to improve the quality of the Arabic program under a new grant that allowed for a fulltime position and a doctorate level degree, with a focus on teacher education and curriculum studies. These allowances were made to ensure the program would be rejuvenated, the curriculum revamped, and teaching methods put in place that follow recent research in teaching world languages. The funding also offered the program the unique opportunity to be under the supervision of an external evaluator who supports the program's progress and offers rich consultation. The external evaluator is one of the main scholars and distinguished professors in the field of teaching Arabic in the United States. He is also a well-known author of one of the bestselling Arabic textbooks in teaching Arabic as a foreign language.

As part of the previously mentioned efforts to revitalize the program, a minor in Arabic language and culture was approved in the spring of 2012 with an interdisciplinary focus to serve the wider student population's majors/minors as well as their interests. There are limitations to this mission, however, beginning with the fact that the Arabic program mainly teaches Standard Arabic, offering colloquial Levantine Arabic only through about 15% of its teaching and learning materials. Hence, with limited teaching resources, fulfilling the program's desire to provide a special course or more integrative courses in colloquial spoken Arabic is still a challenge. To make up this deficit, supplementary authentic materials constitute a significant part of the classroom teaching practices to offer different insights and lively engagement with the language and culture. The materials include Arabic newspapers, folkloric games and riddles, songs, music, cartoons, menus, and more. The Arabic program also runs its own website, with an emphasis on students' investments in cultural awareness engagement initiatives. It also encourages community involvement, offering a number of projects on and off campus including voluntary work with new immigrants, Arab refugees, blogs on study abroad experiences, and diverse socializing venues in learning Arabic.

In the Arabic courses in particular, one of the main assignments, which is of particular significance to this study, is the culture portfolio required of all Arabic learners. This activity has been adopted through consultation with the external evaluator and his home institution. It consists of four to five essays in English for first year Arabic learners, and two written in the Arabic language for second year Arabic learners. The entry essays include short critical reviews reflecting on practices, perspectives, and other linguistic and cultural aspects related to Arabic and the Arab world, at least as students themselves observe and understand them. The review also includes the students' conscientious voices reflecting on their own interpretation and negotiation of intercultural and linguistic variations in their native cultures. Those entries are designed around the following activities: attending a lecture related to the Arab world, watching an Arabic movie with English captions, reading an Arabic short story in translation, interviewing or initiating a chat with a native speaker, and reflecting on a topic of interest to be approved by the instructor. One of those choices may be modified with the instructor to reflect on participation in a community service project.

To promote learning and engagement amongst students in class, all responses are posted on Blackboard, a learning management system, so students can read each other's reviews and reflections. Entries are corrected by the teacher with a focus on providing explicit feedback to students on their tools and processes of analysis. Thus, there is a focus on the reasons behind their choices and interpretations and the perspectives consciously or unconsciously employed in interpretations of events. Attention is also given to reflections on their own native linguistic and cultural choices, taken-for-granted assumptions, and possible different/alternative points of view. The main focus for the teacher then is not accuracy of information but rather opening up a space for the students to unravel the mediational and socialization processes involved in dialectically constructing and deconstructing their meanings. Exemplary entries are further announced to students via email, and hard copies are pinned publicly on the walls outside the Arabic office for public viewing. However, verities of such an activity may be available on other campuses beyond the reach of this study.

While some language courses are dedicated to one of the aforementioned cultural activities, like film studies, or some aspect of engagement with native speakers as found in study abroad courses, the culture portfolio is unique in this study for several reasons:

- The culture portfolio allows students to engage with authentic Arab cultural artifacts available on their university campus and in the larger city. In fact, students are encouraged to take advantage of those resources, including making contact with people living in heritage specific neighborhoods. Hence, some activities resemble mini immersion experiences linking micro classroom discourse and macro community-wide discourses.
- It emphasizes students' use of multimodal texts, which enables them to draw on spoken, written, audiovisual, and "post-linguistic" forms (Fairclough, 2001, p. 2) when engaging in various course-related activities. Consequently, students' reflections are supported by several contextualized events that help them construct their responses to and against those texts.
- It also fosters implicit and explicit implementation of tools from critical language awareness (cf. Fairclough, 2001). Thus, students learn about the Arabic language and cultures while engaged in multimodal projects to help them assess their own constructed perspectives of other cultures and

people (Janks, 2010, 1991). At the same time, students become more aware of their deliberate choices, interests, and biases, and how to problematize their representations of themselves and others as a step towards acceptance of cultural differences (Kramsch, 2003, 1993).

- Since the assignments are in English, students are given the chance early on to draw on their linguistic and cultural proficiencies to maximize the use of the resources available in their immediate communities. Naturally and unfortunately, study abroad is not an option for all students, so these assignments can help make up the difference.

- The culture portfolio creates a significantly strong logistic bond between the Arabic program's vision and the university's unique mission towards globalization, social responsibility, and cross-cultural engagement. This bond allows for college and university wide support of Arabic on campuses beyond the short-term interests triggered by global political events.

Study Participants

The researcher is an instructor of Arabic at the campus of study. Due to the sensitive relations with the students, and in order to eliminate any biases or discomfort, the research was conducted in the summer of 2012 to ensure the participants' graduations, so as to ensure that the submission of their final grades in Arabic spring courses were not affected by the research. Hence, participants are considered former students to further protect their rights and the voluntary nature of their participation. Volunteered participants were enrolled in first year Arabic courses in either both the fall of 2011 and spring of 2012, or at least the spring semester of 2012. Any former student of one or more semesters of Arabic between2011-2012 was eligible to volunteer to participate. Participants were given a survey questionnaire and an informed consent sheet upon the conclusion of the semester and were instructed to return the completed surveys during the summer of 2012. Additionally, the participants' responses to all culture portfolio assignments for the whole academic year were collected and analyzed (Figure 1).

With only two senior students and four freshmen, the largest two groups enrolled (at 41% and 37%) were sophomores and juniors. Racially[1], South Asians (Indian, Pakistani, and Sri Lankan) comprised the largest group at about 38%, followed by Caucasians at 31%, and Arab Americans at about 21%. Classroom data mirrors the demographic makeup of the larger community and city in which the university is located.

Academically, the Arabic learners constituted an interesting blend of majors and minors, with the highest percentages in biology 35% and international studies 24%. Other majors and minors included psychology, criminal justice, Spanish, Italian, political science, and history. At the time of the study, only 4% of the students declared enrollment in the newly established minor in Arabic Language and Culture, as the university had just been approved for the initiative to establish it.

It was also shown that 63% of students' enrolled in the Arabic course in the spring of 2012 had voluntarily participated in this study. Unfortunately, without certain of the research limitations imposed by the campus of study, the study could have attracted larger responses among the Arabic learners, and hence provided more important details on Arabic studies within this Catholic institution. One of these limitations includes the institutional regulation prohibiting the researcher from conducting the study with "current" students enrolled during the academic year, so as to minimize students' compulsory participation or an influence on grades. Hence, the researcher had to wait until the end of the semester for the learners to be officially considered former students. Naturally, access to students over the summer was a challenge. The researcher was also the only Arabic instructor in the program during the spring of 2012 and the only instructor working with those learners.

Figure 1.

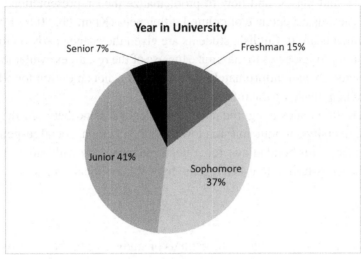

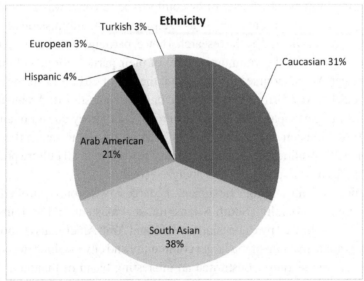

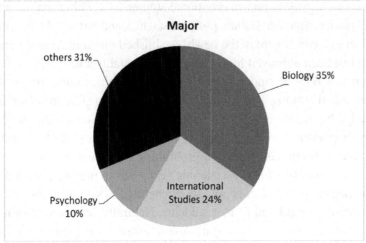

FINDINGS AND DISCUSSION

The exploratory study at this particular Catholic institution helped shed more light on the investments of Arabic learners, specifically in regards to their challenges in learning the language and culture through formal and informal channels. Additionally, the study helped provide feedback to the teacher in regards to curricular choices, both linguistic and cultural, and to foster a supportive yet critical learning community for Arabic students.

Investments in Learning Arabic

In reflecting on the racial diversity of students and their university majors/minors, the survey responses of first year Arabic learners focused on a few major investments, with overlap in several areas for some learners. For example, some students have several overlapping investments at the same time such as both religious and political at the same time. Research on investments in learning Arabic has been the focus of a number of studies all of which support the findings of this current exploration (cf. Belnap, 2006; Husseinali, 2006; and Suleiman, 1991). These investments, which I will detail below, encompass the religious, sociocultural, political, and personal reasons students had for pursuing Arabic studies.

Religious

The Muslim students, who were mostly South Asian with only a few Arab Americans, clearly indicated that they were learning Arabic for religious reasons, namely, to help them read and understand the Quran. Fifteen students, representing 30% of the participants, reiterated that they had some exposure to Arabic through Islamic weekend schools, private religious tutors, and Islamic institutions during the academic year or summer. A number of them emphasized the role of Arabic in their prayers and their interest in understanding what they say or read. A few mentioned the role of elders in their families and communities who encouraged them to read and understand the Quran. Some referred to feeling disappointed in their pronunciation while reading the Quran and felt ashamed of losing the Quranic learning they received as children. Some students also referred to performing or desiring to perform Hajj or Umrah, both pilgrimage trips, emphasizing how Arabic would help them through the religious journey and rituals. There was only one student who did not identify as Muslim, who claimed that he took the course because of his interest in understanding the "parallels and origins" (Meg, survey, May 1, 2012) of religions through language.

Socio-Cultural

A more hybrid group of students clearly referenced understanding the Arab culture and gaining perspective on other people's lives as their primary motivation for taking the courses. Fourteen students, representing 28.5% of the participants, highlighted their interest in learning about a new culture and gaining new perspectives as a way to learn about global affairs and thus become a "multicultural" person. These same students also indicated that they enjoyed sharing what they learnt about new cultures and people with their families, in addition to mentioning a desire to not feel "ignorant" (Crystal, survey, April 27, 2012) about other cultures of the world. They also cited enjoyment in getting to know their own cultures and heritage and attempting to rectify the "limited point of view" (Auburn, survey, May 13, 2012) others may have constructed about Arab cultures. Some participants shared that they were curious about misperceptions as a reaction to global events, which included awareness or a lack thereof of stereotypes, a lumping together of all cultures in media representations, or misunderstandings due to an acquaintance with friends and neighbors of Arab heritage. Some students referred to having some exposure to aspects of Arab culture through travel, even though not necessarily to Arab countries, but to areas where Arab and Muslim cultures have left an imprint such as India, Italy (Islamic influence on southern Italy), and Spain (Islamic and Arabic influence in Al-Andalus). Students' responses also emphasized the cultural aspects they had been exposed to in other disciplines on campus and the impact it had on their investments in learning more about Arabs and Arabic. For instance, students reiterated the value of learning courses about the history of Islam, cultures of the Middle East, Media studies, gender, and Art in Islam on their investments for learning Arabic.

Political

Naturally, reactions to the political events in a post 9/11 context and the current uprisings and crises in many Arab countries informed part of the learners' investment in learning Arabic. Ten students representing 20.5% of the participants highlighted the enormous attention on the Middle East post 9/11 and the media coverage with references to Al-Jazeera. Others referred to the War in Iraq and their interests in joining the Army, or in serving as a humanitarian aid in affected areas. Some students positively referred to their interest in being the exception among Americans in being politically educated about the Arab world, noting that their interest in Arabic became a "passion" (Madeline, survey, April 27, 2012). Others also referred to shocking life-turning events as they witnessed their close friends and neighbors being scrutinized in airports due to their race, dress, or names. They passionately expressed feeling "ashamed" (Auburn, survey, May 13, 2012) by such discrimination, especially as Americans, which led to a willingness to transform this "fear of others" and "backlash...against Arab" (Auburn, survey, May 13, 2012) through education and knowledge of other cultures. Some students also referred to future jobs in the FBI, in the State Department, as translators/interpreters, and in diplomacy and the marketing of Arabic in the midst of the aforementioned global political events.

Personal

The majority of participants, almost 90%, expressed various personal investments related to gaining comfort in talking with heritage family members or friends, being intellectually and cognitively challenged in learning a more demanding language, having a love for Arabic calligraphy and hence the language, and wanting other job opportunities in the future. Usually these investments are categorized in conjunction with one or more of the previous ones explained above.

Culture Portfolios and Becoming Intercultural

The culture portfolios are meant to allow students a personal and collective construction of linguistic and cultural proficiency through critical reflection and engagement with community and authentic artifacts. They are also meant to deliver more deliberate, diverse feedback both from the teacher in the classroom and other participants in the macro contexts of the university and community. The culture portfolios are thus used to develop students' intercultural awareness and in response to this, 47 students representing

96% of participants reported that the culture portfolios were extremely helpful in being engaged in new aspects of culture beyond linguistic forms and classroom contexts. Students recognized a deeper growth in their critical understanding of cultures beyond a standard one-sided view, as they were pushed to take part in several activities in different contexts that fostered hybrid "cultural styles, norms, and mixing of peoples of different lands" (Mumtaaz, survey, May 1, 2012). Almost every student also emphasized that without being pressured to complete such a requirement, especially one that constituted 10% of their course grade, they may have never attempted to reach out and chat with a native Arab, watch an Arabic movie, or read Arabic short stories in translation.

Chat with a Native

In regards to chatting with a native speaker, which was the highest valued activity, participants' comments focused on taking a courageous step in asking to interview someone of a different background or experience. Some also highlighted the friendship created through meeting "a really good Arab friend" (Farrah, survey, May 17, 2012) which continued developing even after the activities were completed. Students were interested in being actively engaged in gathering information directly from a native speaker. This information entailed noticing differences in dialects, picking up slang phrases, observing traditional practices, trying samples of cuisine, hearing stories of immigration and adjustment in a new country among other family stories, and reflecting on personal memories of being an Arab post 9/11. Students reiterated their respect for the struggles of those natives (Aiman, culture entry 1, September, 2015; Ali, culture entry 3, October, 2011; and Auburn, culture entry 5, November, 2011).

In addition to learning more from a native, some students also commented on the benefit of chatting as an interactive chance to experience cultures and be able to compare and contrast them with their own. Some students met each other on campus, while others visited each other's family homes, as they were more fascinated with the new learning opportunity. A number admired their ability to engage in greetings and understand a few Arabic words, in addition to loving the challenge and being open-minded enough to talk to someone in Arabic. They referred to feeling increased hope and being encouraged by their interviewees to continue practicing their learning of Arabic. Many students reflected on learning how to separate being an Arab from being a Muslim among many religious and cultural practices (Mary, culture entry 3, November, 2015; Basima, culture entry 2, February, 2012).

In terms of who the students selected to interview, some chatted with elder members of their family or Arab neighbors in their community. In doing this, they were not only surprised by the cultural knowledge they experienced firsthand, but also by the appreciation of the interviewees and their high regard for being valued, listened to, and asked to speak about their language and cultures. One student wrote after visiting a lonely native elderly in the community: "I did not know I could have such an impact on someone's life even with an assignment like this. This was more than an assignment, but a lesson to me as well" (Dana, culture entry 2, September, 2011).

Movies

Watching a movie in Arabic also captivated the students' attention, as it allowed them to focus on aspects of the language and culture that the classroom setting was not always able to provide due to time, technology arrangements, curriculum requirements, or ability to satisfy diverse students' needs and investments. While the teacher pointed the students to a few titles available in the language lab and university library, they were encouraged to research others on their own, which opened up a space for new knowledge to unfold without prior expectations from the teacher. A student can pursue choices that may be unknown or even new to the teacher allowing both to be active participants of the learning process. The freedom to choose thus allowed them to construct insights "that a textbook cannot provide" (Taha, survey, May, 2012). Movies also creatively introduced students to the Middle East and helped them reflect on the linguistic and cultural knowledge they were introduced to in the classroom without having to "fly to the Middle East" (Farrah, survey, May, 2012). Some students enjoyed the different dialects and pronunciation while others took interest in the "styles of dress" (Nili, culture entry 2, October, 2011), "household interactions" (Crystal, culture entry 3, October, 2011), "wedding customs" (Khan, culture entry 3, November, 2011), and "foods" (Mary, survey, April, 2012). Movies varied in topic from politics and family life to comedy and romance among others depicting different Arab countries and diverse faiths.

Once they viewed the movie, students submitted rubric-defined written reflections and received feedback to help them analyze cultural aspects and critique biases. The goal of this activity was to attempt to understand native perspectives on topics related to social class, politics, religion, gender roles, and ideologies of media representations, in comparison to their own cultures. The teacher's feedback was thus not about the correctness of students' analyses, but rather a dialogic encounter with students' voices to visibly accentuate tools of analysis to construct and deconstruct their interpretations. A large number of students admitted they had never watched an Arabic film and they may never have done so without this requirement. One student commented, "more importantly, I learned not to accept everything that I hear without looking further into it" (Lee, culture entry 1, September, 2011).

Lectures

Participants also noted that attending and/or listening to lectures about the Arab world on and off campus, including multimodal recordings, further developed their interest in Arabic within an interdisciplinary nexus. A large number responded positively to the informative and eye-opening topics they attended to and mentioned that they enjoyed reflecting on their understandings as well as their agreements and disagreements with other speakers through the writing assignment. Lectures covered a large spectrum of topics. The teacher actively announced via emails all possible opportunities to learn more about Arab culture in the community by attending events and speeches organized on campus and by other Middle Eastern organizations in the larger Arab community. However, the majority of topics were political in nature due to current global events in the Arab world such as the Arab countries' uprisings and unsettlements in many regions. Students reflected on their "ignorance" (Zena, culture entry 2, October, 2011), "misconceptions" (Joshua, culture entry 2, October, 2011), and moments of "change of heart" (Hamad, culture entry 2, October, 2011). Since students' own interest dictated the choice of lecture, they continued to feel empowered making decisions, owning their learning, and taking responsibility for their efforts to enhance their Arabic studies linguistically and culturally. Because of these Arabic classes and more specifically because of the culture portfolio, students were able to gain firsthand experience in learning how to be a global citizen of the world, which is part of the university's mission.

Free Choice

The free activity was the one choice that students felt the most capable to adjust to their interests and curiosity. Some went to restaurants, visited Arab families, worked with refugees, listened to songs, cooked an Arabic meal, wrote about Henna and Arabic folkloric dancing, attended weddings and *Eid* celebrations, tried learning calligraphy, attempted wearing Islamic clothing in public as a form of awareness, or researched a topic of their own related to the arts, politics, the economy, media, and/or global events, to name a few. Many participants pointed to enjoying the activities and said that they suggested them to others too. On some occasions, students even mentioned having to provide a rationale to their American friends for engaging in such activities, which allowed them to promote awareness as well as get practice in reflexively negotiating their own cultural attitudes outside the classroom space.

Literature

As with other portfolios, reading an Arabic story in translation provided students with deeper linguistic and cultural insights, despite a number of students reporting it was sometimes hard to understand all of the messages in the text. The reasons for this hardship were due to it being their first encounter with Arabic literature, preconceptions and misconceptions of Arab cultures, and the linguistic challenges of uncovering metaphors and symbolism. Even with these difficulties, students highlighted how the stories helped them "dispel such broad generalizations" (Zena, culture entry 5, April, 2012) and admire the authenticity of the writing due to their abilities to find human connections across cultures, pay attention to ironies, and reflect on events they may have been exposed to in other portfolios. They also noted being attentive to different literary styles, encountering societal values and individual choices, and being surprised by unconventional social topics like love and gender, for example.

As a result of engaging with Arabic literature, most participants shared that their prior image of Arab world cultures was "limited/minimal" (Zena, survey, April, 2012), "lumped" (Crystal, survey, April, 2012), "homogenous" (Khan, survey, May, 2012), and "westernized" (Cary, survey, April, 2012). This was largely due to their reliance on the media and other interdisciplinary university courses in history or political science for information about the Arab world. In some cases, it was also due to their own religious practices or those of friend or family members who were heritage speakers. Very few students had actually travelled to the Middle East or had firsthand exposure to Arab cultures.

When asked how the choices they personally adopted for their culture portfolios had shaped their developing knowledge of the cultures of the Arab world, students responded passionately to their significant level of growth in knowledge as well as awareness of several sensitive issues related to attitudes, values, and perspectives. For instance, a number of students wrote about awareness of political problems in the Middle East, as well as of gaining different perspectives on occupations and their effects on civilians and children, particularly in light of watching movies or talking with immigrants. They also emphasized the diversity of the Arab world in terms of dialects, customs, political concerns, and societal values. References to arts and sciences in early and modern Arab cultures, literary styles, colonization's influence on regions, and religious schisms are but a few of the topics students revisited with new insights in their portfolios, or referred to reading in other participants' portfolios posted on Blackboard.

Challenges and Changes

Given the range of topics highlighted in the portfolios, the verities of students' investments, majors, and backgrounds were naturally reflected in their responses to their favorite assignments, and the challenges and strengths regarding the value of the culture portfolios. Most students, though admitting the time and effort commitment involved, expressed their love for the portfolios and how personally invested they were in their learning.

Despite this investment, the students remarked having a number of difficulties with the portfolio. When asked about the most difficult entry in terms of access and/or reflection, 13 students responded that the short story entry was a challenge. Difficulties included access to "good" literature (Nili, survey, May 30, 2012), especially online, "interpreting the cultural meanings and importance" (Cary, survey, April 30, 2012), and confusion due to "translation" (Hamad, survey, 2012; Suma, survey, 2012). While only five students said the chat with a native speaker was a challenge due to fear and anxiety factors, 10 students mentioned it was in fact the easiest due to easy access to the Arab heritage community available both at the university and in the larger community. Chatting thus became like a mini immersion experience for some, especially those who visited native homes and neighborhoods to conduct interviews. Building friendship, practicing their Arabic, exploring firsthand traditions and artifacts, and reflecting on cultural norms was also mentioned as part of the fun of chatting.

In addition to the short story being a challenge, an almost equal number of students referred to the lecture as either the most difficult entry or the easiest. Of all the participants, 4 students found it the hardest while 3 confirmed it being the easiest. While some noted challenges related to the time of the lectures and commuting, others referred to the large number of lectures available on campus that were facilitated by different interdisciplinary fields and the general campus's interest in nurturing globally aware citizens. As for the films, seven participants found them to be an easy and enjoyable entry due to the interactive aspect and audiovisual engagement with language and culture, particularly in regards to the politically charged global events. A few referred to difficulties such as interpreting cultural norms, attempting to listen while following captions, and time issues. This free activity was highly rated, however, as it fostered students' own investments and research on a more specific and personal basis. Since all entries were in English for first year Arabic students, they were given the chance to socialize with language and culture outside classroom contexts at their own comfort too, which undoubtedly impacted their sense of ease with some of the assignments.

CONCLUSION AND IMPLICATIONS

There is significant research on fostering the growth of an intercultural learner through diverse aspects similar to the culture portfolios highlighted here, although most studies focus on just one aspect, like chatting with natives in study abroad contexts (Cadd, 2012) or using films as a pedagogical tool in language classrooms (Sturm, 2012). Currently, recommendations to provide contextualized learning opportunities away from textbooks in real communities are highly encouraged and becoming more visible (Glynn, 2013).

This contextualization also works to satisfy a great deal of students' curiosity about the *Other* both in terms of linguistics and cultures. As Ryding (1994) suggested, an attractive approach to teaching and learning Arabic needs to be "combined with a lively and informed introduction to Arab culture" (p. 27). Culture portfolios are a mechanism that combines various aspects of content and task-based teaching with direct and indirect applications of critical language awareness as a pedagogical tool to problematize students' understanding and awareness of ideological links between language, culture, identity, and power.

The ideological connection between teaching Arabic as a foreign language in the U.S. and current rapid shifts in the global sociopolitical and cultural contexts between the U.S. and the Arab world is significant. The field of Arabic is at the center of a new "critical juncture" (Duncan, 1991, p. vi), impacting the roles of teachers in the classrooms and the need to move beyond traditional contexts of learning and teaching. With the particular focus on new technologies in contexts of globalization and digital media, new kinds of linguistic and cultural projects are needed that employ multimodality and digital applications for new kinds of learning, as suggested by Cope & Kalantzis (2010) in "New Media: New Learning." Obviously, demands, challenges, and possible tensions as to a teacher's commitment to time and institutional support are part of the issues to be considered here as well.

More research on pedagogical tools that foster becoming an intercultural learner is needed in Arabic classes, particularly with the heightened political, religious, and sociocultural attention being afforded to the field. More research is also needed to support Arabic programs within their home institutions through alignment of missions to attract the humane and financial resources required to sustain the program's growth and teacher development initiatives.

REFERENCES

Abbadi, S. (2013). *Teaching Arabic post 9/11: Late modernity in language classrooms- challenges and possibilities for change* [Doctoral dissertation].

Abbadi, S. (2014). Teaching Arabic post 9/11: Humor and the potential for critical language awareness. *Dirasat: Human and Social Sciences Journal, 41*(1), 322–334. doi:10.12816/0018576

Abdallah, M., & Al-Batal, M. (2011-12). College-level teachers of Arabic in the United States: A survey of their professional and institutional profiles and attitudes. *Al-Arabiyya, 44-45*, 1–28.

Al-Batal, M. (2007). Arabic and national language educational policy. *Modern Language Journal, 91*(2), 268–271. doi:10.1111/j.1540-4781.2007.00543_10.x

Allen, R. (2004). Perspectives on Arabic teaching and learning. *Modern Language Journal, 88*(2), 275–278.

Allen, R. (2007). Arabic—Flavor of the moment: Whence, why, and how? *Modern Language Journal, 91*(2), 258–261. doi:10.1111/j.1540-4781.2007.00543_6.x

Allen, W. (2014). Developing cultural proficiency. *Language and Education, 9*(1), 26–27.

Arab American Institute. (2015). Demographics. Retrieved from http://www.aaiusa.org/pages/demographics/

Belnap, K. (2006). A profile of students of Arabic in U.S. universities. In K. Wahba, Z. Taha, & L. England (Eds.), *Handbook for Arabic language teaching professionals in the 21st century* (pp. 169–178). New Jersey: Lawrence Erlbaum Associates.

Blake, R., & Kramsch, C. (2007). Guest editor's introduction. *Modern Language Journal, 91*(2), 247–249. doi:10.1111/j.1540-4781.2007.00543_2.x

Byram, M., & Fleming, M. (1998). Introduction. In M. Byram & M. Fleming (Eds.), *Language learning in intercultural perspective: Approaches through drama and ethnography* (pp. 1–10). Cambridge: Cambridge University Press.

Byrnes, H. (2009). Perspectives. *Modern Language Journal, 93*(2), 261–263. doi:10.1111/j.1540-4781.2009.00860_1.x

Byrnes, H., Edwards, J. D., Scollon, R., Allen, R., Wesche, M., Allen, W., & Pratt, M. L. (2004). Perspectives. *Modern Language Journal, 88*(2), 266–291. doi:10.1111/j.0026-7902.2004.00229.x

Cadd, M. (2012). Encouraging students to engage with native speakers during study abroad. *Foreign Language Annals, 45*(2), 229–245. doi:10.1111/j.1944-9720.2012.01188.x

Cope, B., & Kalantzis, M. (2010). New media, new learning. In D. Cole & D. Pullen (Eds.), *Multiliteracies in motion: Current theory and practice*. New York: Routledge.

Dixon, L., Zhao, J., Shin, J., Wu, S., Su, J., Brigham, R., & Snow, C. et al. (2012). What we know about second language acquisition: A synthesis. *Review of Educational Research, 82*(1), 5–60. doi:10.3102/0034654311433587

Duncan, G. (1991). Forward. In E. S. Silber (Ed.), *Critical issues in foreign language instruction*. New York, NY: Garland Publishing, Inc.

Edwards, J. D. (2000). Working beyond the academy: The federal government. *ADFL, 32*(1), 48–49. doi:10.1632/adfl.32.1.48

Fairclough, N. (2001). *Language and power* (2nd ed.). London, UK: Longman.

Gerwin, D., & Osborn, T. (2005). What September 11 also teaches us. In T. A. Osborn (Ed.), *Language and cultural diversity in U.S. schools* (pp. 103–116). Westport, CT: Praeger.

Glynn, C. (2013). Stepping out of the textbook and into contextualized language instruction. *Language and Education, 8*(6), 46–47.

Halliday, M., & Hasan, R. (1989). *Language, context and text: A social semiotic perspective*. Oxford: Oxford University Press.

Husseinali, G. (2006). Who is studying Arabic and why? A survey of Arabic students' orientations at a major university. *Foreign Language Annals, 39*(3), 397–414. doi:10.1111/j.1944-9720.2006.tb02896.x

Janks, H. (1991). A critical approach to the teaching of language. *Educational Review, 43*(2), 191–199. doi:10.1080/0013191910430207

Janks, H. (2010). *Literacy and power*. New York, NY: Routlege.

Kramsch, C. (1993). *Context and culture in language teaching*. Oxford: Oxford University Press.

Kramsch, C. (1998). The privilege of the intercultural speaker. In M. Byram & M. Fleming (Eds.), *Language learning in intercultural perspective: Approaches through drama and ethnography* (pp. 16–31). Cambridge: Cambridge University Press.

Kramsch, C. (2003). *Language and culture* (4th ed.). Oxford: Oxford University Press.

Kramsch, C. (2005). Post 9/11: Foreign languages between knowledge and power. *Applied Linguistics, 26*(4), 545–567. doi:10.1093/applin/ami026

Kramsch, C., Howell, T., Warner, C., & Wellmon, C. (2007). Framing foreign language education in the United States: The case of German. *Critical Inquiry in Language Studies*, *4*(2-3), 151–178. doi:10.1080/15427580701389615

Kumaravadivelu, B. (2003). *Beyond methods: Macrostrategies for language teaching.* New Haven, CT: Yale University Press.

Leeman, J., & Martinez, G. (2007). From identity to commodity: Ideologies of Spanish in heritage language textbooks. *Critical Inquiry in Language Studies*, *4*(1), 35–65. doi:10.1080/15427580701340741

Lo Bianco, J. (2014). Domesticating the foreign: Globalization's effects on the place/s of languages. *Modern Language Journal*, *98*(1), 312–325. doi:10.1111/j.1540-4781.2014.12063.x

Magnon, S. (2007). Reconsidering communicative language teaching for national goals. *Modern Language Journal*, *91*(2), 249–252. doi:10.1111/j.1540-4781.2007.00543_3.x

Pacheco, M. (2012). Learning in/through everyday resistance: A cultural historical perspective on community resources and curriculum. *Educational Researcher*, *41*(4), 121–132. doi:10.3102/0013189X12442982

Page, D., & Benander, R. (2014). Helping students change their view of the world: Moving from products and practices to perspectives. *Language and Education*, *9*(1), 28–31.

Rampton, B. (2006). *Language in late modernity: Interaction in an urban school.* Cambridge: Cambridge University Press. doi:10.1017/CBO9780511486722

Ryding, K. (1994). Fostering a learning community for Arabic. *Theory into Practice*, *33*(1), 23–28. doi:10.1080/00405849409543611

Ryding, K. (2006). Teaching Arabic in the United States. In K. Wahba, Z. Taha, & L. England (Eds.), *Handbook for Arabic language teaching professionals in the 21st century* (pp. 13–20). New Jersey: Lawrence Erlbaum Associates.

Ryding, K. (2013). *Teaching and learning Arabic as a foreign language: A guide for teachers.* Washington, D.C.: Georgetown University Press.

Scollon, R., & Scollon, W. (2001). *Intercultural communication: A discourse approach* (2nd ed.). Malden, MA: Blackwell Publishers.

Sturm, J. (2012). Using film in the L2 classroom: A graduate course in film pedagogy. *Foreign Language Annals*, *45*(2), 246–259. doi:10.1111/j.1944-9720.2012.01187.x

Suleiman, Y. (1991). Affective and personality factors in learning Arabic as a foreign language: A case study. *Al-Arabiyya*, *24*, 83–110.

Thoms, J. (2012). Classroom discourse in foreign language classrooms: A review of literature. *Foreign Language Annals*, *45*(1), 8–27. doi:10.1111/j.1944-9720.2012.01177.x

U.S. Census Bureau. (2010). *State & county quickfacts: Chicago, IL.* Retrieved from http://quickfacts.census.gov/qfd/states/17/1714000.html

Vygotsky, L. (1978). *Mind in society: The development of higher psychological processes*. Cambridge, MA: Harvard University Press.

Wang, S. (2009). Preparing and supporting teachers of less commonly taught languages. *Modern Language Journal, 93*(2), 282–287. doi:10.1111/j.1540-4781.2009.00860_8.x

ENDNOTE

[1]   Ethnicity was defined by the students themselves. Hence, "Europeans" does not assume all Europeans are a homogeneous group linguistically or racially. The same applies for other ethnicities as well.

Section 5
Teacher Education and Learning Strategies

Chapter 14
The Role of Multi–Media in Expanding Pre–Service Teachers' Understanding of Culturally and Linguistically Diverse Classrooms and Furthering Their Professional Identities

Latisha Mary
Université de Lorraine, France

Andrea Young
Université de Strasbourg, France

ABSTRACT

This chapter details a qualitative study conducted with pre-service elementary school student teachers enrolled in a Masters course on cultural and linguistic diversity at one university teacher education institute in France. The study aimed to evaluate the impact of the course on the student teachers' understanding of culturally and linguistically diverse classrooms and questioned whether the use of multimedia resources throughout the course could contribute to fostering a greater sense of empathy towards their future culturally and linguistically diverse students. The data analysis reveals that the use of video in particular, in combination with theoretical readings, was highly instrumental in helping the students to understand the concepts linked to second language acquisition and in providing them with strategies for their linguistically and culturally diverse classrooms. The authors question whether the use of multimedia is sufficient to foster a sense of empathy in students and suggest further pedagogical interventions.

DOI: 10.4018/978-1-5225-0177-0.ch014

INTRODUCTION

The power of using multi-media resides in its ability to increase cognitive and emotional interest and attention by creating more coherent and authentic representations of knowledge. (Wankel & Blesinger, 2013, p.6)

According to many researchers and education professionals in Europe and around the world, pre-service teachers are increasingly faced with cultural and linguistic diversity in the classroom for which they are only slightly or not at all prepared. (Cajkler & Hall, 2012; Kuiken, 2014; Murakami, 2008; Schwartz & Mor-Sommerfeld, 2010; Thomauske, 2011). It has thus become necessary to develop intercultural skills and sensitivity to otherness among teachers. In 2005, a bi-national team (France-Scotland) attempted to address this problem within the European project *TESSLA* (Teacher Education for the Support of Second Language Acquisition) by designing, piloting and evaluating a teacher education course. The aim of the course was to sensitize pre-service elementary school teachers to the needs of their culturally and linguistically diverse students and to generate strategies and classroom practices that would support all students in their learning (Hancock et al, 2006).

Since its conception, the course has been adapted and delivered in a variety of contexts (Mary & Young, 2010; Young & Mary, 2010; Young & Mary, 2016). However, the sensitization of student teachers to the needs of their culturally and linguistically diverse pupils through collective reflection, and the development of tools and practices to support their learning, has remained a central concern. One of the objectives in the study described in this chapter was that, through participating in the course, student teachers would not only gain important knowledge but would also acquire the ability to empathize and become agents of change. Previous research has highlighted the fact that many student teachers come to such courses with already established attitudes and ideologies about language (conscious or unconscious) which act as roadblocks to gaining new awareness (Banks, 2001; Commerford, 2005; Garmon, 2004) and that knowledge of content and pedagogy alone are not sufficient in helping teachers to be effective (Horan & Hersi, 2011). In light of this challenge, the didactic model *Problem Based Learning* (Komur & Kogut, 2006) was chosen as the most appropriate approach for the course. It was hoped that this instructional method, based on authentic or real world problems, in conjunction with theoretical reading and the use of multimodal and multimedia resources and tools would provide a rich context in which the students could confront their ideas and engage with their learning within a safe space. This chapter aims to highlight in particular the types of resources used, the reasons underlying the choice of these, the ways in which they were implemented and their role in expanding pre-service teachers' understanding of culturally and linguistically diverse classrooms and in furthering their professional identities.

BACKGROUND

The training of teachers and educators to better take into account the linguistic and cultural diversity present in schools is a challenge teacher educator's face. Teachers and education professionals in general often lack the training necessary (Murakami, 2008; Wiley, 2008; Schwartz et al, 2010; Thomauske, 2011; Cajkler & Hall, 2012; Kuiken, 2014) to assist the increasing number of children for whom the school language is not the language spoken at home. Schools need professionals who have developed the capacity to empathize and an ability to understand others in their differences in order to reduce the gap between students and effectively teach increasingly heterogeneous classes. The barriers schools face are manifold and include future-teachers' limited knowledge of issues related to culture and identity (Santoro & Allard, 2005; Abdellak & Heidenreich, 2004), negative representations with respect to migrant students (Goï & Huver, 2013), and a lack of critical thinking enabling them to analyse school language education policies that can create inequality and marginalization (Gay, 2010; Jokikokko, 2005; 2010).

The European Comenius 2.1 project TESSLA (Teacher Education for the Support of Second Language Acquisition), supported by the Socrates program, was designed to meet these challenges. The specifications of the project included the development of curricula and materials for teachers to understand why and how they need to consider and develop the bilingualism of their students.

The Role of Empathy in Expanding Teachers' Professional Identities

Empathy is thought to contribute to an increased sensitivity to different cultures (Germain, 1998; McAllister & Irvine, 2002; Tiedt & Tiedt, 2010) and is seen as an essential quality to be promoted in teacher education, especially in courses which aim to raise student teachers' awareness of issues concerning diversity and social justice in their classrooms (Dolby, 2012).

The concept of empathy, which has both an affective (feeling what other people feel) and a cognitive (understanding others' situations) component, has also been described as 'taking on another's perspective' as well as being able to respond to another from that perspective (McAllister & Irvine, 2002, p. 433). One educational expert, Dolby (2012) emphasizes the important role that empathy plays for educational communities stating that educators in particular 'need to be able to empathize in order to act in a meaningful way' (p. 69). Dolby highlights the fact that although recent research in the area of neuroscience has shown that most humans possess the biological ability to empathize, other studies point to the fact that individuals are most likely to empathize with others who are most similar or closest to themselves (Bailenson, Iyengar, Yee and Collins, 2008; Ehrlich & Ornstein, 2010). This is in line with Acquah & Commins (2013), who remark that:

several studies have shown that most predominantly white and middle-class pre-service teachers have limited experience outside 'their world'; that is, they have had limited or no experience with persons from different ethnicities or social class prior to enrolling in a diversity course (Larke 1990; Nieto 1998; Ahlquist 1991; Carpenter 2000). This lack of or limited exposure to different ethnicities or social classes tends to reinforce pre-service teachers' stereotypical beliefs. (p. 2).

These findings contribute to our understanding of why this area remains a challenge for teacher educators desirous of raising students' awareness of and sensitivity to the needs of their linguistically and culturally diverse students, who, for the most part, do not share the same background and characteristics of many of their students and their families.

Various attempts have been made by teacher educators in the area of multicultural education to foster empathy in their students. Among the most successful initiatives are those in which students had the opportunity to come into contact with and/or spend time with individuals who were part of a minority group (McAllister & Irvine, 2002, Houser, 2008). Students reported that these experiences allowed them to better understand these individuals in a very personal way which contributed to a more positive vision of them and increased feelings of empathy. However, providing students with such experiences is not always possible, and raises the question of whether teacher educators could draw on alternative strategies/methods, such as the use of multimedia, to increase students' feelings of empathy.

For the purposes of this chapter the concept of using multi-media within the educational context is defined as the use of or combination of more than one means of presenting information with the goal of instruction. Mayer (2003) echoes this definition stating that during multimedia learning 'the student receives an instructional message that is presented in two formats- as words (spoken or printed text) and pictures (animation or illustrations) (p. 126). Brophy (2004) expands on this and describes multimedial narratives as those "in which *educational stories* are told in sound and picture, sometimes connected with text" (p. 133, highlighting by authors). The use of video in instruction in combination with texts and classroom interaction could thus be seen as a possible alternative strategy towards fostering empathy in students as illustrated below.

In one study by Lin and Bradford (2010) which aimed to evaluate the effectiveness of video in raising student empathy towards professors from ethnic minority background, one half of the students in the group watched a video giving general background knowledge of a particular professor (information on his home country and culture), while the other half watched a video giving more personal information on him. After each group watched the videos, the personal information group had more positive personal views of the professor, while the second group, who received general information, showed increased negative stereotypes of this professor. With regards to this study Dolby states that:

while preliminary, their research suggests that personal knowledge and connection – that which decreases the distance between human beings – increases empathy. As students began to know more about the professor as a person, they moved him/her from 'far' to 'near', or from outside of their circle of moral regard, to inside. (Dolby, 2012).

The results of this study also suggest that where personal contact experiences are not possible, the use of videos/multimedia presenting personal information regarding minority language children and their families, can be effective in altering students' perceptions and knowledge of them and can possibly contribute to increased feelings of empathy towards them. Several of the video extracts used in the course described in this chapter allowed the authors to present such personal testimonies. One of these video extracts presented a school project conducted in an elementary school in a multilingual classroom in France (Hélot, Young & Delforge, 2005a; Hélot, Young & Delforge, 2005b; Young, 2008). When showing extracts the authors were able to describe the background and school experiences of two Turkish children and to point out how they suddenly came alive during the project when their home culture and competences in their home language were valued at and by the school. The authors were able to focus attention on the expressions on the children's faces and to "tell their stories," which appeared to have a noticeable impact on the student teachers.

Other videos used during the course presented the web documentary 'Photo de Classe' (http://www.photo-de-classe.org/#/accueil) which featured children from a multilingual school interviewing their parents and/or grandparents about their experiences and feelings as a result of migration to France. The video *In Safe Hands* (Hyder & Rutter, 2001), about refugee children, presented the testimony of a mother who tells the harrowing story of why her family had to leave their country and speaks of the shame she feels at having to rely on the social services of the country to which she has fled. From the same video, a child from Sri Lanka speaks of the anxiety refugee families feel, living in constant fear that they might be forced to leave their new life in the UK, whilst another boy from war-torn Afghanistan explains how he misses his grandparents who had to stay behind. The very personal feelings of sadness and fear expressed by these children and their families seemed to raise the students' awareness of the hardships some of the children in their classroom may have had to face.

Giving Students Real-Life Examples of Good Practice

The use of video in teacher education has also been touted as an effective means of showing student teachers the realities of the classroom. Case studies of classroom practice presented through video provide rich details of classroom life and place the viewer within the action as a result of the distinct visual and aural qualities they provide (Clarke and Hollingsworth, 2000). Brophy (2004) highlights the affordances using videos of classroom practice can provide over the practice of sending students into different schools to observe classroom practices and specifies that viewing video extracts allows teacher educators to focus on one particular practice or aspect of practice and so to ask specific questions about what exactly is being viewed. In addition, video extracts enable teacher educators to choose examples of model practices which may be difficult to observe during random student teacher observations. According to one survey among teacher educators who regularly used video viewing as part of their curriculum (Perry & Talley, 2001), presenting examples of good practice was cited as being the most desired objective for using videos in teacher training classrooms.

The use of multi-media in the classroom has also been advocated as a means of promoting deeper understanding and learning. The rationale supporting this claim as stated in Mayer's (2002) cognitive theory of multimodal learning is, stated simply, that "people learn more from words and pictures than from words alone" (p.31). This element is linked to the nature of information processing and the fact that information processed through multiple channels is processed more deeply. In addition to this, Berk (2009) states that certain forms of multimedia, the use of video in particular, automatically elicit an array of feelings which can have powerful cognitive and emotional impacts on learners. Moreover, various authors have highlighted the ability of multimodal resources and multimedia in enhancing students' "sense-making", increasing their levels of motivation, participation and engagement (Wankel & Blessinger, 2013) and encouraging deeper forms of understanding (Veenema & Gardner, 1996).

Dolby (2012) warns, however, that just "understanding" the material is not enough to motivate people to act, and that teacher educators using multi-media to further students' professional identities need to ensure that the resources used present quality and carefully selected pieces of personal information, and in addition that the methodology chosen engages the learners in reflexion (for example, "social perspective taking", see Rios et al. 2003).

CONTEXT OF THE STUDY: EXPERIENTIAL LEARNING AND THE USE OF MULTI-MEDIA FOR DEEPER UNDERSTANDING AND ENGAGEMENT: THE CASE OF DEVELOPING EMPATHY AND CULTURAL AND LINGUISTIC SENSITIVITY IN THE TESSLA COURSE

Problem Based and Multimodal Learning

In close collaboration with our Scottish colleagues from the University of Edinburgh, the authors developed a training course for students in initial teacher training. The main teaching model chosen by the team, Problem Based Learning (PBL), was supplemented by theoretical lectures, personal narratives and videos of teachers, parents and children interacting in school and family contexts. A wide range of additional resources were used in the course to illustrate the content, to further understanding of the issues and to suit different learning styles. By adopting a multimodal approach including simulation, discussion and group work as recommended by Gellevij et al. (2002); Jewitt et al. (2000, 2001) and Sternberg et al. (1998), it was hoped that the course would have a greater impact on the students' representations and learning than more traditional models.

One of the central goals of the TESSLA course was to provide materials and resources which would enable the students to decentre and to develop a greater capacity for empathy with regard to their linguistically and culturally diverse students. As emphasized above, research supports the idea that in order to adopt another's perspective, students need multiple contact points with different viewpoints and experiences. Therefore, the videos that were integrated into the course were situated within different contexts and presented a variety of perspectives including those of practising teachers, immigrant and refugee children, parents, guest lecturers, and specialists in the area of bilingual education. These particular types of resources have been found to increase empathy in children and adults (Feshbach & Feshbach, 2011).

The course also implemented videos of authentic classroom practice, models of teaching and the effective implementation of these models. This allowed students to see extracts of innovative practices that they would most likely not have been able to see in their local observation assignments as suggested by Brophy (2004). In line with Dolby's (2012) review of research on empathy, Brophy also warns that simply viewing the videos is not sufficient to make a lasting impact on student teachers' future teaching practices. They suggest rather that video extracts need to be embedded in the curriculum and introduced with specific objectives in mind. As the video extracts in this course were selected and implemented in the context of a problem based learning model, they were carefully selected to correspond to the problem situation and to the particular aspect of the problem under discussion in a specific class in order to provide student teachers with complementary visions of the situation and of the possible responses to the problem.

Course Content and Choice of Resources

The resources implemented in the course were chosen in relationship to the course content presented in Table 1.

Among the expected outcomes of the course were: the development of a critical awareness of the nature of linguistic and cultural diversity, knowledge of language development and of the differences between language learning at home and in the school context, knowledge of first language acquisition, bilingual

Table 1. TESSLA course content

1. Introductions: participants, tutor, methodology, PBL approach, course contents, evaluation.
2. Linguistic and cultural diversity.
3. L1/2 acquisition and foreign language learning.
4. Bilingualism.
5. Language sensitive teaching.
6. Identity and home school relationship.
7. Linguistic policies, official documentation and terminology, National, European levels portfolios.
8. Student presentations & peer assessment.

language acquisition, second language acquisition and early foreign language learning, an awareness of the knowledge and skills emergent bilingual children bring to the classroom, and the demands that are placed on these children by the school as well as an examination of how lesson and classroom planning can accommodate these children.

As mentioned above, the didactic model chosen for the course was Problem Based Learning (PBL), an instructional method based on the use of *authentic* or *real world* problems (Kumar & Kogut, 2006; Williams, 2001). Within the PBL model, students work together in small groups to reflect on a problem or set of problems in order to generate various solutions in a collective, collaborative way. The role of the teacher is to facilitate the process and to provide various sources of information and support to the groups. PBL has been shown to be a practice that engages students in critical reflection and promotes active learning. The *real life* problem with which student teachers were presented was the following:

Mme Martin teaches a class of 7 year olds which contains a number of children whose home language (their mother tongue) is different from the language of the school. Mme Martin is really concerned that these children don't seem to be making the same progress as the native speakers of the school language. Some of them don't participate in learning activities. The French/francophone children in the class are losing patience with these children's attempts to communicate. Mme Martin would really like to help these pupils more and would like to help the class as a whole to be more welcoming. She is discussing with you what she might do. (Hancock, A., Hermeling, S., Landon, J. & Young, A., 2006)

In the first half of each course the authors presented new content and materials: theoretical readings illustrated by personal testimonies, video recordings and a wide variety of other resources (music, children's literature, website materials including games and classroom ideas). During the second half of the course, students were expected to engage in discussion around the problem situation and to propose new solutions and strategies to be put into practice in light of the new content and material presented in the first half of the course. During the first course on linguistic and cultural diversity, students were asked to complete the answers to a quiz in groups with the help of various documents and a web quest. They were also asked to identify different languages in a multilingual song "Le Pétrin" (La Tordue, 2002) while they listened to it. For themes 2 through 6, in addition to the reading materials provided, videos were selected to raise students' awareness of the concepts covered in order to present materials from personal, first hand perspectives and to show authentic examples of classroom practices (see Table 2 for list of resources). One of the main criterion in selecting the video extracts involved choosing extracts which gave personalized accounts to illustrate the ways in which individuals experienced their pluri-/bilingualism, which has the potential for fostering a sense of empathy in students.

Online Platform and Access to Online Resources and Digital Classroom Resources (Videos, Web-Conferences) as a Means to Foster Understanding and Empathy Among the Student Teachers

The courses implemented in the teacher education institutions made use of an online platform which provided access to the course objectives and course content, academic articles (first and second language acquisition, bi-plurilingalism, questions around language and identity, language policies and ideologies), links to relevant websites and online resources and interactive discussion forums used for posting and responding to weekly student group reports.

Table 2. List of resources used during the course

Title of Resource	Content/Themes Addressed
Original research footage from the Didenheim project *La diversité linguistique et culturelle à l'école* (Hélot, Young & Delforge, 2005)	Primary classroom activities about languages and cultures co-constructed by parents and teachers.
Original research footage from a multilingual pre-school in Mulhouse (Horvart, Mary & Young, 2014-15)	Pre-primary classroom activities showing how the teacher includes minority language children and families through translanguaging
Raconte-moi ta langue/Tell me how you talk (Feltin, 2008)	Documentary about the Didenheim project and teacher education for diversity, includes interviews with parents, teachers and researchers
Jim Cummins' conference in Strasbourg 28th January 2015 Bilingual Education: International Perspectives on Research and Policy	Clip during which a minority language girl shares personal memories about learning a second language in school.
Comparons nos langues (CRDP de Languedoc-Roussillon-Montpellier, 2005)	Clips showing classroom footage of how to use multiple languages as resources for learning
Tuning into children (BBC Educational Publishing, 1999)	Video sequence of a young Chinese girl making a cake in a nursery setting.
'Sharing stories' from *Progress with Purpose: Supporting Continuity in Children's Learning 3-8 Additional Materials* (LTS, 2003)	Emergent bilingual pupils and a bilingual teaching assistant read and talk about a picture book story first in L2 only, then using L1
In safe hands, (Save the Children & the Refugee Council, 2001)	Documentary about life as a refugee child (interviews with parents, school staff & children)
Photo de classe http://enseigner.tv5monde.com/collection/photo-de-classe_ (TV 5 Monde, 2014)	Web documentary presenting a project and video extracts from one multilingual/multicultural class in which the children interviewed their parents and grandparents on their feelings/experiences concerning their recent migration.

Online resources were provided throughout the course with the aim of engaging student teachers in reflection around the questions of second language acquisition and the needs of their linguistically and culturally diverse pupils. The resources not only presented current information on first and second language acquisition and linguistic diversity, but also provided access to videos and examples of classroom practice, example lesson plans, pedagogical resources, materials, and resources for welcoming and supporting parents (table 2).

METHODOLOGY, DATA COLLECTION

The data collected from the various versions of the course over the past 10 years have included identical pre & post course questionnaires, working group minutes, and post course evaluations (for an analysis see Young & Mary, 2010 and Mary & Young, 2010). Concerning the data collected in the spring term of 2015 the course evaluation by students (see appendix) contained additional questions specifically pertaining to their evaluation of the use of resources (multi-media and written) during the course. The data analysed in this chapter pertains to the students' responses to the course evaluation.

Impact of Multi-Media Resources on the Students Learning and Understanding

This data collected in 2015 was drawn from two classes comprising 18 students total enrolled in the TESSLA course in their first year of their two-year Master of Education degree as part of their initial teacher training and took place from January 2015 to April 2015. The course was part of the core curriculum required to earn a Masters in Education preparing them to teach children from age 2 to 11 years old. During their first semester, students also had courses in subject didactics (Math, French, History etc…), child development and psychology, as well as a foreign language course in either English, German, Spanish, or Italian. At the end of their first year in the Masters programme, the students usually take a national competitive teaching exam. Those who succeed on the exam are taken on as student teachers for the second year of their Masters degree and are then granted official full-time teacher status upon successful completion of their course work and teaching internship. Students whose exam scores are not high enough to qualify as student teachers, continue as full-time students into the second year of the Masters programme with the intention of sitting the exam a second time in the Spring. The university teacher education institute in which the study was conducted was situated in a small city in the East of France. The students were between the ages of 20 and 42, and comprised seventeen female and one male student with a general socio-economic status ranging from average to low. Only two of the students enrolled in the course were from ethnic minority groups.

The 18-hour course was divided into nine 2-hour weekly sessions. As mentioned above, one of the central goals of the TESSLA course was to sensitize student teachers to the needs of their linguistically and culturally diverse pupils so they could develop teaching strategies to support these children in the classroom. A pre-course questionnaire was administered with the aim of providing information on their linguistic and cultural background and experience and their attitudes toward and knowledge of second language acquisition and its role and influence in the classroom. Identical questionnaires were completed at the close of the course to evaluate the impact of the course on the students. In addition, the students completed an anonymous course evaluation (Appendix) during the last session which contained a total of 8 questions regarding their perception of the didactic model chosen for the course (PBL), their evaluation of the resources implemented, what they liked about the course, and their suggestions for improvement. The questionnaire and course evaluation were distributed by the instructor on the last day of the course. The students were allowed as much time as necessary to complete the two documents and were informed that the course evaluation was anonymous, and that their answers would remain confidential. The analysis detailed below focuses in particular on their evaluation of the resources implemented throughout the course (online, video, audio and written; in class and outside of class). The qualitative analysis of these data was undertaken using the « constant comparative method » (Ryan, Bernard & Beck, 2000; Wellington, 2004). Emerging themes and concepts were identified and then refined, compared, and contrasted in order to form a coherent picture in relation to the research questions and course objectives.

Concrete Situations: A Means to Providing Deeper Understanding

With regards to Q5, "Did the use of the different resources (written, audio-visual, paper, internet etc.) during the course and outside of the course (for example, the resources consulted on the online course platform) help you to gain a deeper understanding of the concepts/issues surrounding second language learning and culturally and linguistically diverse classrooms? If Yes/No, please explain", 16 out of the 18 students surveyed stated that the videos in particular helped them to understand the course content better. A large majority (14 out of 18) of the students pointed to the benefits of videos stating that these allowed them to see "concrete" or "real-life classroom situations":

Les vidéos sont très parlantes puisque ce sont des situations réelles qui ont été filmées. Elles permettent de voir concrètement comment cela se passe. Les liens vers les ressources sont également très intéressantes et peuvent être réutilisés plus tard (Student E1).

The videos are very meaningful because they are real situations that were filmed. They allow you to concretely see what really happens. The links to resources are also very interesting and can be reused later.

Oui, car on peut voir différents points de vue qui nous aident à nous faire un avis ou à changer notre propre idée de départ. (Student E3)

Yes, because you can see different perspectives that help you to form an opinion or to change your own initial idea.

Oui, car témoignages (par exemple), vidéos de véritables situations. (Student E14)

Yes, because of the personal accounts (for example), videos of real situations.

Some students (E4, E13), mentioned the ways in which the videos allowed them to reinforce concepts they had read about in the written documents, with one student stating that the videos helped her to see the different dimensions present in certain classroom situations:

La diversité des documents m'a permis d'envisager le problème dans ses différentes dimensions. J'ai particulièrement apprécié les vidéos qui permettent de voir la mise en œuvre et les comportements des enfants (Student E7).

The diversity of materials allowed me to see the problem in its different dimensions. I particularly enjoyed the videos that allowed us to see the implementation [of practices] and the children's behaviour.

Role of Multi-Media Resources in Structuring Thought and Fostering Memorization

Several students (E6, E13) specifically spoke of how the videos supported their understanding specifying that they were able to learn better through visual resources:

Oui, une compréhension via différents supports aide à la mémorisation. (Student E6)

Yes, understanding via various media helps memorization.

Oui, je comprends mieux sur support visuel mais j'ai besoin de lire des textes ensuite pour structurer ma pensée. (Student E13)

Yes, I understand better through visual aids but I need to read texts then to structure my thoughts.

Cela permet de revenir sur des notions qui n'étaient pas forcément comprises en cours. (Student E4)

It allows you to reflect back to notions that you hadn't necessarily understood in class.

Others (7 out of 18) pointed to increased understanding through seeing strategies being put into action, which they felt they could draw on later.

In response to Q6, "Which resources, if any, helped deepen your understanding of the issues related to second language learning/acquisition and culturally and linguistically diverse classrooms?", 12 out of 18 students specified videos as the resource that helped them best understand the concepts and issues related to learning a second language and welcoming linguistic diversity in the classroom. However, 6 students mention gaining a better understanding of these issues through the theoretical readings or a combination of the two resources. This is an interesting finding when contrasted with their responses to Q7 "Which resources did you *like* the most" for which the majority of students indicated the videos. In this same vein, the students who indicated an answer for Q8 (only 5 of them responded to this question) "Are there any resources you didn't like, if so which ones and why?" all five mentioned disliking the use of theoretical texts in the course as they felt these were either "too long" (students E1, E5, E11, E16), "too theoretical/too difficult" (Students E5 & E16) or "too numerous" (E3, E8).

The analysis of the data highlights the use of multi-media resources in the course as a resource, which allows most of the students to gain practical knowledge of teaching strategies to implement in the classroom, and that this was much appreciated by them. However, one particular student specifically stated that for her the only way to gain an accurate idea of the reality of a linguistically and culturally diverse classroom would be direct observation, while another student suggested, as a means to improve the course, being able to "test out" these strategies in a real classroom.

What has emerged through the course evaluation data is that the resources used (audio-visual, online and written) allowed the students to understand different classroom situations with regards to second language learning, acquisition and development and enabled them to gain knowledge of teaching strategies they could draw on in a linguistically and culturally diverse classroom. However, what seems to be absent from many of the students' responses is, in effect, signs of them having gained in empathy towards these students. Banks states that in the 21st century, citizens (and therefore, the teachers responsible for their education) will need to "know, to care and to act" (Banks, 2001, p. 9). The students who followed this course seemed to have learned important concepts and gained effective "tools" to implement in the classroom but in analysing the data the question remains as to whether the course and its resources had a long lasting impact on them on a *personal level*, and whether this would enable them to 'care' about their future linguistically and culturally diverse pupils?

Issues for Reflection

In reflecting on the question of how to not only increase student teachers' *understanding* of the theories and concepts linked to second language acquisition, and awareness of the pedagogical interventions possible in their linguistically culturally diverse classrooms, but also to foster a sense of empathy for their future pupils in these classrooms, several issues have emerged.

The Issue of Time

Over the past ten years, the authors, as teacher-educators, have struggled with shifts in curriculum requirements and procuring the spaces in which students can be provided with knowledge, and also given sufficient time for discussion and reflection. In previous analyses of this course (Young & Mary, 2016), the difficulties of finding spaces in which students can be provided with a sufficient amount of time to discuss the materials and confront their own opinions and points of view in groups is discussed. The results of these analyses indicate that when there is insufficient time for discussion of the problem situation (the basis of PBL) the students are not able to engage with the materials in meaningful ways and therefore demonstrate fewer signs of gaining in empathy. This indicates that the use of multimedia alone in this course is not enough to make a lasting impact on students and cannot replace the benefits of time for discussion. This, however, is a difficult task for teacher educators as they are often faced with an increasingly limited number of hours in the curriculum.

In addition, it appears that in order to have a lasting impact on student teachers, one that would be transformative and allow them to "care" and to "act", sensitization to the questions of intercultural education and equity should not take place in 'isolation' but rather needs to be established through links across the curriculum. Garmon (2004) and Pohan (1996) stress the need to multiply student teachers' experiences throughout their training and academic courses in order to create more opportunities for them to revisit and review their own attitudes and representations. In one case study, Garmon found that it was not a single course that contributed to changes that had occurred in one particular student's attitudes and willingness to change but rather an accumulation of experiences she had encountered, either through course work or direct contact with minority students and individuals with backgrounds different from her own. Burns & Shadoian-Gersing (2010) mirror this point of view:

Improved teaching for diverse student populations is an increasingly important competency for current and future teachers. However, too often these topics are addressed through a sole course, often as an elective. As systems increasingly recognise the need to prepare teachers for a diversifying student population, there must be a systematic effort to integrate this topic and strategies into the curriculum. Moreover, a crucial component of teaching for diversity lies in examining one's own beliefs and how they influence behaviour. Much like any other teacher competency, the requisite skills for teaching and motivating diverse classrooms and attitudinal awareness cannot be simply absorbed through a one-off course during initial education or professional development. Instead, it is important to build on this training throughout teachers' careers, so that they gain transversal exposure to knowledge and perspectives that can have a meaningful impact on how they practice. (p. 290)

Direct Contact with Diversity

Another issue addressed in the literature is the impact that experiences and/or direct contact with diversity has on individuals (Dolby, 2012; Garmon, 2004; McAllister & Irvine, 2002) and the lack of such experiences among student teachers. Acquah & Commins (2013) highlight that:

Several studies have shown that most predominantly white and middle-class pre-service teachers have limited experience outside 'their world'; that is, they have had limited or no experience with persons from different ethnicities or social class prior to enrolling in a diversity course (Larke 1990; Nieto 1998; Ahlquist 1991; Carpenter 2000). This lack of or limited exposure to different ethnicities or social classes tends to reinforce pre-service teachers' stereotypical beliefs. Shultz, Neyhart, and Reck (1996) suggest that pre-service teachers are naive and hold stereotypical beliefs about urban children, for example that they bring attitudes that interfere with their education." (p. 2)

Without a doubt, real immersion experiences in a culture other than the students' own is more effective than vicarious exposure. However, providing students with such experiences remains a challenge for teacher educators.

SOLUTIONS AND RECOMMENDATIONS

One student stated in the course evaluation that in order to understand the issues at stake in diverse classrooms, student teachers need to be immersed in the classroom setting, stating that "nothing replaces direct observation" (Student E10). McAllister & Irvine's study (2002) also showed that many teachers in their programme felt that the "direct contact experience" (e.g. going into communities/families' homes) they had had was vital to nurturing their own feelings of empathy. The authors also point to further studies (Chambers et al., 1998) which show that gaining knowledge alone makes no difference in changing student teachers beliefs. However, when working in contexts where providing quality observations for all student teachers and/or providing them with such direct contact experience with different cultures are not possible, teacher-educators must reflect on ways to simulate these experiences in the classroom or in the surrounding environment, in order to cultivate empathy. As a starting point, it is possible to draw on the success of previous programmes in this area in an attempt to attain this goal. Below are outlined three programmes that have had success in implementing what Dolby (2012) refers to as "exercises in empathy" (p. 98) and which have been shown to have had an impact on students' beliefs and understanding.

Social Perspective Taking

This multi-cultural course implemented at two different universities, with students enrolled in a teacher education degree, was based on the idea that the use of personal narratives in class could have a powerful impact on students. Rios et al. explain that "by engaging narratives of 'others,' we are provided with alternative worldviews that enable us to challenge/trouble our own. Through the use of narratives, readers situate themselves in the other and then determine degrees of connectedness." (Rios, Trent & Castaneda, 2003: p.6).

The social perspective taking activity took place in several stages. At the first stage, students watched two videos of interviews with adult professionals who had been denied their language and culture in school when they were children and who recalled the painful memories they had of these experiences. Students were then asked to take on the role of one of the professionals and to write a letter to the teacher from their perspective. This was followed by a second stage, during which the students were then asked to imagine they were the recipients of these same letters (meaning they then took on the role of the teachers who had denied the children their language and culture) and to write about how they would feel upon receiving the letter and what they would then do. Rios et al. argue that:

By assuming the position of "other," ... students are forced to become consciously aware and awakened to their specific location as they adapt an identity mediated by life experiences different (in many cases) from their own.... Social perspective-taking may move future and current teachers to consider and challenge their understandings as well as their (explicit or implicit) acceptance of teaching philosophies/notions associated with deficit understandings, disadvantage, advantage, privilege, and oppression. (2003, p. 11)

Reflection Paper

As part of her multicultural education course, Dolby (2012) requires her students to attend an event where they will be in the minority among one of the following categories: race, sexual orientation, religion, or national identity. After the event the students must reflect on the experience and write a paper about their feelings during the event stating what they felt, experienced and learned from the activity. Dolby specifically insists on the fact that they are to attend as the minority participant and not to pretend that they are part of the group itself. The students are also told that that they must not attend the event in which they take on a "helping role" (Dolby, 2012: p. 99) in any way.

Empathy through Global Experience

Suarez describes an increase in empathy on the part of in-service second language teachers after having had the experience of language immersion classes and living with a family in Venezuela and/or Mexico. This first-hand experience helped move the teachers from a position of sympathy towards their pupils to one of empathy with them. The students described experiencing feelings of isolation and frustration with monolingual courses and teaching strategies. Having "walked in their students' shoes" (Suarez, 2013: p. 181), they became acutely aware of the difficulties of learning a second language and how exhausting this could be.

FUTURE RESEARCH DIRECTIONS

The exercises in empathy described above present various means of engaging students in reflection and of helping them to decentre. Two of the strategies mentioned require students to engage in these activities outside the classroom and to reflect on these experiences individually. Both of the authors' teacher education departments strongly encourage students to take part in teaching practices/exchanges in foreign countries and both are working actively to continue to develop partnership programs in order to provide these experiences for student teachers. However, in reality only a small percentage of the student teachers choose to/are able to participate in such programs which means that the majority of newly qualified teachers begin their teaching careers without the benefit of such experiences. In the TESSLA course, one of the goals of Problem Based Learning is to allow students with such experiences to share them with others through the group discussions. It is hoped that through this sharing of experiences, students with limited exposure to diversity will be able to benefit vicariously from these. However, when there is a lack of diversity within the working groups or class itself and thus an insufficient number of experiences with diversity and different viewpoints to share, teacher educators must rely on additional stimulus from outside sources to stimulate reflection. It is in this context that the use of videos and the practice of "social perspective taking" could have a strong impact. The data presented in this chapter has highlighted the impact the video extracts had on the student teachers' understanding of the issues but also underlined the lack of identifiable signs of the students having gained in empathy. Combining social perspective taking exercises with the use of video in the course, however, could be an effective means of enabling the students to "put themselves in another's shoes" and to "experience" a situation from another's perspective and possibly foster a greater sense of empathy.

In addition, with the goal of extending students' opportunities to engage in their reflection on diversity and equity in schools, and in line with Garmon's (2004) and Burns & Shadoian-Gersing's (2012) suggestions our teacher education institutions need to provide training in the area of second language acquisition and linguistically and culturally diverse classrooms not only for their graduate students but for the whole of the teaching staff in order to facilitate the weaving of these questions into the entire fabric of the curriculum and not just into one course on multi-cultural/lingual education. Addressing these issues early on in teacher training programs allows students to be aware of certain questions and to pay attention to them throughout their practice and during their encounters with others. Returning to the same questions through the lenses of different disciplines and within different contexts can help broaden student teachers' visions and beliefs.

CONCLUSION

This chapter aimed to describe and analyse the role of multi-media resources in expanding pre-service teachers' understanding of culturally and linguistically diverse classrooms and furthering their professional identities. The data indicated that knowledge about culture, language and identity and how it was acquired, namely through the teaching framework of Problem Based Learning and the use of multi-media resources, and the selection of pertinent video extracts and access to online resources was instrumental in the evolution of the students' essentially mono-cultural, monolingual frameworks. Students stated that the use of video in particular in the course helped them to gain a greater understanding of the issues related to second language acquisition and linguistic and cultural diversity. In order to foster a greater sense of empathy towards students from culturally and linguistically diverse backgrounds practices in which students vicariously experience diversity or in which they try to imagine an experience from another's point of view are proposed. We also suggested that teacher education institutions develop continuing professional development for members of their teaching staff in order to address questions of diversity and multicultural/multilingual education throughout the curriculum.

REFERENCES

Acquah, E. O., & Commins, N. L. (2013). Pre-service teachers' beliefs and knowledge about multiculturalism. *European Journal of Teacher Education, 36*(4), 445–463. doi:10.1080/02619768.2013.787593

Bailison Bailenson, J.N., Iyenger, S., Yee, N., Collins, N.A. (2008). Facial similarity between voters and candidates causes influence. *Public Opinion Quarterly*, 72(5) 2008, 935–961

Banks, J. A. (2001). Citizenship Education and Diversity. *Journal of Teacher Education, 52*(1), 5–16. doi:10.1177/0022487101052001002

Berk, R. A. (2009). Multimedia teaching with video clips: TV, movies, YouTube, and mtvU in the college classroom. *International Journal of Technology in Teaching and Learning, 5*(1), 1–21.

Brophy, J. (2004). *Using Video in Teacher Education*. Bingley: Emerald Group Publishing Limited.

Brush, T., & Saye, J. (2008). *The effects of multimedia-supported problem-based inquiry on student engagement, empathy, and assumptions about history. Interdisciplinary Journal of Problem-Based Learning, 2(1)*. Available at; doi:10.7771/1541-5015.1052

Burns, T., & Shadoian-Gersing, V. (2010). Supporting effective practice: the pending agenda. In T. Burns & V. Shadoian-Gersing (Eds.), *Educating Teachers for Diversity: Meeting the Challenge*. Paris: OECD. doi:10.1787/9789264079731-16-en

Cajkler, W., & Hall, B. (2012). Languages in primary classrooms: A study of new teacher capability and practice. *Language Awareness, 21*(1-2), 15–32. doi:10.1080/09658416.2011.639889

Clarke, D., & Hollingsworth, H. (2000). Seeing is understanding. *Journal of Staff Development, 21*, 40–43.

Commerford, S. A. (2005). Engaging through Learning-Learning through engaging: An alternative approach to professional learning about human diversity. *Social Work Education, 24*(1), 113–135. doi:10.1080/0261547052000325017

Dolby, N. (2012). *Rethinking Multicultural Education for the Next Generation*. New York: Routledge.

Ehrlich, P. R., & Ornstein, R. (2010). *Humanity on a tightrope: Thoughts on empathy, family and big changes for a viable future*. New York: Rowman and Littlefield.

Fechbach, N. D., & Fechbach, S. (2011). Empathy and Education. In J. Decety & W. Ickes (Eds.), *The Social Neuroscience of Empathy*. Massachusetts: MIT Press.

Garmon, M. A. (2004). Changing Preservice Teachers' Attitudes/Beliefs About Diversity What are the Critical Factors? *Journal of Teacher Education, 55*(3), 201–213. doi:10.1177/0022487104263080

Gay, G. (2010). Classroom practices for teaching diversity: an example from Washington State (United States). In T. Burns & V. Shadoian-Gersing (Eds.), *Educating Teachers for Diversity: Meeting the Challenge*. Paris: OECD. doi:10.1787/9789264079731-15-en

Gellevij, M., Meij, H., & Jong, T. (2002). Multimodal versus unimodal instruction in a complex learning context. *Journal of Experimental Education, 70*(3), 215–239. doi:10.1080/00220970209599507

Hancock, A., Hermerling, S., Landon, J., & Young, A. (2006). *Building on language diversity with young children: Teacher education for the support of second language acquisition*. Münster, Germany: LIT Verlag.

Hélot, C., Young, A. & Delforge, O. (2005) *La diversité linguistique et culturelle à l'école* (original version in French).

Hélot, C. Young, A. & Delforge, O. (2005) *Windows on the World: A language awareness project in a French primary school* (English subtitled version).

Horan, D. A., & Hersi, A. A. (2011). Preparing for diversity: the alternatives to 'linguistic course-work' for student teachers in the USA. In S. Ellis & E. McCartney (Eds.), *Applied Linguistics and Primary School Teaching* (pp. 44–52). Cambridge, England: Cambridge University Press. doi:10.1017/CBO9780511921605.007

Houser, N. O. (2008). Cultural plunge: A critical approach for multicultural development in teacher education. *Race, Ethnicity and Education*, *11*(4), 465–482. doi:10.1080/13613320802479034

Hyder, T., & Rutter, J. (2001). *Safe Hands*. London: Save the Children and Refugee Council.

Jewitt, C., Kress, G., Ogborn, J., & Tsatsarelis, C. (2000). Teaching and learning: Beyond language. *Teaching Education*, *11*(3), 327–341. doi:10.1080/713698977

Jewitt, C., Kress, G., Ogborn, J., & Tsatsarelis, C. (2001). Exploring learning through visual, actional and linguistic communication: The multimodal environment of a science classroom. *Educational Review*, *53*(1), 5–8. doi:10.1080/00131910123753

Komur, M., & Kogut, G. (2006). Students' perceptions of problem-based learning. *Teacher Development*, *10*(1), 105–116. doi:10.1080/13664530600587295

Kuiken, F. (2014). Competencies of preschool educators in Amsterdam: A Dutch perspective on language proficiency, language targets and didactic skills. *European Journal of Applied Linguistics*, *2*(1), 101–119. doi:10.1515/eujal-2014-0006

La Tordue. (2002). *Champs libre* (Album, music CD).

Lin, X., & Bransford, J. (2010). Personal background knowledge influences cross-cultural understanding. *Teachers College Record*, *112*(7), 1729–1757.

Mary, L., & Young, A. (2010). Preparing teachers for the multilingual classroom: Nurturing reflective, critical awareness. In S.H. Ehrhart, C., Hélot & A. Le Nevez, (Eds), Plurilinguisme et formation des enseignants: Une approche critique / Plurilingualism and Teacher Education: a critical approach. Frankfurt: Peter Lang.

Mayer, R. E. (2002). Multimedia learning. *Psychology of Learning and Motivation*, *41*, 85–139. doi:10.1016/S0079-7421(02)80005-6

McAllister, G., & Irvine, J.J. (2002). The role of empathy in teaching culturally diverse students: A qualitative study of teachers' beliefs. *Journal of Teacher Education*, *53*(5), 433–443. doi:10.1177/0022487102237397

Murakami, C. (2008). 'Everybody is just fumbling along': An investigation of views regarding EAL training and support provisions in a rural area. *Language and Education*, *22*(4), 265–282. doi:10.1080/09500780802152556

Perry, G., & Talley, S. (2001). Online video case studies and teacher education: A new tool for preservice education. *Journal of Computing in Teacher Education*, *17*(4), 26–31.

Rios, F., Trent, A., & Castaneda, L. (2003). Social Perspective taking: Advancing empathy and advocating justice. *Equity & Excellence in Education*, *36*(1), 5–14. doi:10.1080/10665680303506

Ryan, G. W., Bernard, H. R., & Beck, C. T. (2000). Data management and analysis methods. In N. K. Denzin & Y. S. Lincoln (Eds.), *Handbook off qualitative research* (2nd ed.). Thousand Oaks: Sage.

Schwartz, M., Mor-Sommerfeld, A., & Leikin, M. (2010). Facing bilingual education: Kindergarten teachers' attitudes, strategies and challenges. *Language Awareness*, *19*(3), 187–203. doi:10.1080/0965 8416.2010.491919

Sternberg, R. J., Torff, B., & Grigorenko, E. L. (1998). Teaching triarchically improves school achievement. *Journal of Educational Psychology*, *3*(3), 374–384. doi:10.1037/0022-0663.90.3.374

Suarez, D. (2003). The Development of empathetic dispositions through global experiences. *Educational Horizons*, *81*(4), 180–182.

Thomauske, N. (2011). The relevance of multilingualism for teachers and immigrant parents in early childhood education and care in Germany and in France. *Intercultural Education*, *22*(4), 327–336. doi :10.1080/14675986.2011.617425

Tiedt, P. l., & Tiedt, I. M. (2010). *Multicultural Teaching: Activities, Information, and Resources.* Boston: Allyn and Bacon/Pearson Education.

Veenema, S., & Gardner, H. (1996). Multi-media and multiple intelligences. *The American Prospect*, *29*, 70–75.

Wankel, L. A., & Blessinger, P. (2013). Inventive approaches in Higher Education: An introduction to using multimédia technologies. In L. A. Wankel & P. Blessinger (Eds.), *Increasing Student Engagement and Retention using Multimedia Technologies.* Bingley: Howard House Publishing. doi:10.1108/ S2044-9968(2013)000006D003

Wellington, J. (2000). *Educational Research: Contemporary issues and practical approaches.* London: Continuum.

Williams, B. (2001). Developing critical reflection for professional practice through problem-based learning. *Journal of Advanced Nursing*, *34*(1), 27–34. doi:10.1046/j.1365-2648.2001.3411737.x PMID:11430603

Young, A. S. (2008). Diversity as an asset: Multiple language integration. In M. Dooly & D. Eastment (Eds.), *How we're going about it. Teachers' voices on innovative approaches to teaching and learning languages* (pp. 51–65). Newcastle upon Tyne: Cambridge Scholars Publishing.

Young, A. S., & Mary, L. (2010). Une formation des professeurs des écoles en phase avec le 21ème siècle. In J.-M. Mangiante (Ed.), *Langue et Intégration* (pp. 349–363). Frankfurt: Peter Lang.

Young, A. S., & Mary, L. (2016). Dix ans d'expérimentation dans la formation de (futurs) acteurs de l'éducation pour une meilleure prise en compte de la diversité linguistique et culturelle des élèves: Enjeux, défis et réussites. *Carnet des Ateliers Sociolinguistiques.*

APPENDIX

Student Questionnaire Compiled by Latisha MARY and Andrea YOUNG: Course Evaluation (April 2015)

1. What have you learned from the course?
2. Has your opinion changed?
3. What suggestions do you have to improve the course?
4. What do you think of Problem Based Learning?
5. Did the use of the different resources (written, audio-visual, paper, internet etc.) during the course and outside of the course (for example, the resources consulted on the online course platform) help you to gain a deeper understanding of the concepts/issues surrounding second language learning and culturally and linguistically diverse classrooms?
   a. If Yes, please explain
   b. If No, please explain:
6. Which resources, if any, helped deepen your understanding of the issues related to second language learning/acquisition and culturally and linguistically diverse classrooms.
7. Which resources did you *like* the most? Why?
8. Were there any resources you didn't like, if so which ones and why?'

Chapter 15
Investigating Mobile Assisted English Foreign Language Learning and Teaching in China:
Issues, Attitudes and Perceptions

Haixia Liu
Michigan State University, USA & Beijing Normal University Zhuhai Campus, China

Wenhao Tao
Beijing Normal University Zhuhai Campus, China

William Cain
Michigan State University, USA

ABSTRACT

This study aims to investigate how English as a Foreign Language (EFL) teachers and students in China spontaneously use apps for smartphone and tablets to support their informal language learning. It also seeks to determine EFL teachers' perspectives on informal and formal Mobile Assisted Language Learning (MALL). A total of 240 smartphone and/or tablet users (186 students and 54 EFL teachers) from four colleges in Guangdong China participated in the survey. Twenty-eight teachers selected from the survey participants were interviewed afterwards. Analysis of the survey data showed that all participants were using apps to learn foreign languages informally. Survey data analysis also revealed that the most frequently used apps were based on form-focused behaviorist activities rather than learner-centered constructivist activities. A comparison of usage between EFL teachers and students revealed no significant difference in their choice of apps, yet students expected guidance from EFL teachers in using apps and resources to facilitate language learning. Finally, while the survey data indicated EFL teachers had positive attitudes towards informal MALL, the interviews revealed that many of them held negative sentiments toward MALL in the classroom. We interpret this difference in attitudes as a reflection of the teachers' concerns about learners' self-control and autonomous learning skills, as well as concerns about required teachers' knowledge and perceived changes to teachers' roles. We conclude by discussing the implications of MALL for language teacher education and professional development.

DOI: 10.4018/978-1-5225-0177-0.ch015

INTRODUCTION

Mobile learning (m-learning) can be briefly described as e-learning that uses mobile devices and wireless transmission (Keegan, 2002). Compared to classroom-based computer learning, mobile learning can extend interaction beyond the classroom and thus provide chances for individualized, contextualized, and informal learning (Cheon, Lee, Crooks, & Song, 2012). One of the major subject areas of education that could potentially benefit from learning strategies using mobile technology is second/foreign language learning and teaching. *Mobile Assisted Language Learning* (MALL) is language learning that is assisted or enhanced through the use of a handheld mobile device (Chinnery, 2006). Proponents claim that it is commonplace to integrate mobile technology in language classrooms in many secondary and higher education institutions (Abdous, Camarena & Facer, 2009). In addition, mobile technology, combined with dramatic increases in online resources and abundant educational apps, provide new opportunities for self-directed learning outside of classroom (Godwin-Jones, 2011b).

However, few studies have investigated how smartphone and tablets that boast enhanced capabilities and numerous applications (apps) can facilitate language learning and teaching. Even fewer studies have looked into whether and how language teachers and students in college would spontaneously use such devices and apps to support their language learning out of classroom. Another area of concern is teachers' perception and attitude towards MALL. Previous literature on language teachers' perceptions of and attitudes toward the use of mobile devices for learning and teaching is partial and scarce (Oz, 2015), while studies on how smartphone or tablets with abundant apps can support language learning are even more difficult to find.

Although there is a paucity of research, MALL studies have often been undertaken in some developed areas such as in USA, UK, Taiwan, and Japan (Burston, 2014), and much fewer studies were conducted in China. However, China has witnessed sharp increases in smartphone and tablet users in recent years. The smartphone user penetration rate among mobile phone users in China are rising from 43 percent in 2013 to 48 percent in 2014, with over half of all smartphone users aged between 18 and 34 years old ("Share of mobile," n.d.). China is also forecasted to be the world leader in terms of tablet users in 2015 ("Tablet Users," 2015). Given the scarcity of MALL studies in China, especially as far as new mobile devices such as the iPhone and iPad are concerned, plus the fast increase of smartphone and tablet users in China, the purpose of this study is to identify whether and how language teachers and students at the university level in China are using such devices in informal language learning. If they do, what is their evaluation on facilitating informal MALL using smartphones or tablets? Furthermore, this study seeks to determine how language teachers in China perceive language classrooms facilitated by mobile devices with smartphone features; what, then, are their concerns for MALL to be implemented in classrooms?

LITERATURE REVIEW

Though the concept of MALL has existed for nearly two decades (dating back to 1994), MALL is considered by some to be still "on the fringes" (Burston, 2014, p. 103). Investigating further, our review of early research on MALL (pre-smartphone) revealed three main areas of concern (technical, pedagogical, and attitudinal) when it came to adopting MALL approaches and practices. Our review also suggests the advent of smartphone technology alleviates these earlier concerns.

Technical Issues in MALL

While surveying early model mobile phone usage on language projects, Chinnery (2006) reports many technical issues that have hampered the students' ability to engage with the content, such as problematic display of images or videos, difficult text entry, and small and low-resolution screens. With the advent of smartphones (such as the Apple iPhone in 2007) some of these issues were mitigated with advanced features such as bigger screens, higher resolution, responsive touch screen, enhanced text entry, and etc. The iPhone has been called "a game changer in the mobile area which has led functionality upgrade of other mobile devices from iPhone's competitors (Godwin-Jones, 2011a, p.2). Older non-smartphones were limited due to their operating systems; only a few apps could be loaded and then with limited functionality. Current smartphones, however, run more advanced operating systems (such as Apple's iOS or Google's Android OS), which allow them to also run more sophisticated mobile applications. Apple's iOS is quite popular and accounts for nearly 25 percent of mobile operating systems currently in use in China ("Share of mobile," n.d.).

The Apple App Store has more than 1.4 million apps (Ingraham, 2015), and a good number of which can be used to support language learning. Using "ESL" (English as a Second Language) as a keyword, one study (Kim & Kwon, 2012) searched in both iTunes Store and Google's Android OS and found 499 and 250 applications respectively. A further analysis of those apps showed that they covered most of the basic language skills, including vocabulary, grammar, listening, reading, speaking, and writing, aside from the common function of e-dictionary. The researchers of this study pointed out that while most ESL apps are form-focused, audio-lingual, and test-based, these apps are also effective in providing individual, extracurricular activities that can enhance learners' motivation and autonomy in MALL. Though the underlying concept of many language learning apps is similar to web 1.0, in that they promote teacher-centered content delivery, more language learning apps are now taking the feature of web 2.0, which provides for user-centered collaborative content construction. Along with those applications designed specifically for language learning, smartphones support a number of general-purpose apps can be used in language learning as well, a use category Claire Siskin called "repurposed apps" (Siskin, n.d.). A good example is the use of Global Positioning System (GPS) application in language learning (Ogata, Hui, Yin, Ueda, Oishi & Yano, 2008). Another example is the iTunes U application. This app offers many open courses that are delivered in English and other languages and cover a variety of subjects, which could be good supplements for language learning.

Given that numerous apps exist with the potential for supporting mobile assisted language learning, certain research questions regarding their exact use take shape. What are the apps that are chosen by language teachers and learners? What do they think about the effectiveness of those apps? These particular questions have not been addressed sufficiently in the literature. This chapter includes an overview of pedagogical issues in MALL as well the influence smartphones and tablets on language teaching and learning behavior.

Pedagogical Issues in MALL

One challenge that teachers must confront with mobile devices is how to shift their pedagogy to successfully implement MALL. Mobile technology can support both traditional pedagogical approaches (e.g. content transmission, behaviorist drills) and contemporary approaches (e.g. collaborative learning, constructivist activity). Behaviorist activities can "promote learning as a change in learners' observable actions" while constructivist activities help learners "actively construct new ideas or concepts based on both their previous and current knowledge" (Naismith, Lonsdale, Vavoula & Sharples, 2004, p. 2). Behaviorist learning adopts a transmission model and information is delivered from the tutor to the learner. Many language learning apps, such as vocabulary drills, belong to this category. Constructivist learning frameworks, however, encourage students to actively build knowledge rather than to be passive recipients. For example, using apps that support micro blogging or podcasting to practice foreign languages with others could be considered a form of constructivist learning.

Despite the potential of mobile devices to support different pedagogies, it is unclear whether teachers are inclined to use mobile devices in pedagogically optimal ways (Pegrum, Howitt & Striepe, 2013). Ever-improving technology alone does not necessarily guarantee a change from behaviorist learning to constructivist learning. Indeed, Pattern, Arnedillo-Sanchez and Tangney (2006) conducted a study that found many pedagogical uses of mobile devices were rooted in behaviorist traditions; their conclusions urged educators to consider shifting to constructivist approaches when incorporating mobile devices. Likewise in their comprehensive review of MALL pedagogy, Agnes Kukukska-Hulme and Lesley Shield (2007) pointed out that uses of mobile devices were often uncreative and repetitive, and often failed to take advantage of features such as peer connectivity and advanced communication. This could partially be attributed to the limitations of the older non-smart mobile devices at that time. The current generation of apps in smartphones and tablets, however, offer options for both repetitive pattern drill exercises and communication activities among teachers and learners that can accommodate both behaviorist learning and constructivist learning approaches. Moreover, a well-designed app offers language learners abundant resources, tutorials and even interaction, which is what language teachers generally offer in the classroom. In a case study on the app *Essay Writing Wizard MAX*, Kim & Kwon (2012) found that some applications can effectively facilitate writing using various writing approaches, even giving individual web-based feedback as reference for self-editing. Given the increasing potential for constructivist-type learning with smartphone apps, it is reasonable to assume that such advanced functionality may encourage teachers to revisit the concept of MALL. Moreover, it is also reasonable to assume that if MALL is to be widely adopted among institutions, language teachers may have to rethink their pedagogical strategies in relation to the technologies they use to teach.

Teacher Perceptions about MALL

Advances in technology have created exciting possibilities for education, and yet the integration of mobile devices in teaching and learning is very much related to teachers' attitude towards mobile learning. On the one hand, the literature on mobile devices in education has been mostly positive (Baran, 2014) when reporting their use for developing new literacies (Husbye & Elsener, 2013) or engaging in rich language learning contexts (Shohel & Power, 2010). At the same time, studies concerning teachers' perception and attitudes about the use of mobile devices for classrooms showed varied results.

Earlier studies found that classrooms are one of the most inappropriate contexts for mobile phone use (e.g. Campbell, 2006). Similarly, Wang & Higgins (2006) pointed out that a significant barrier to the use and integration of mobile devices is teachers' attitude that these devices are unacceptable in the context of a language classroom. More recent studies also indicate that teachers' evaluations on mobile learning is low (Serin, 2012) and that teachers perceived the benefits of cell phone usage in classrooms as limited (Thomas & O' Bannon's, 2013). A survey conducted among 38 in-service teachers revealed that the majority did not consider mobile devices as tools in their teaching (Ismail, Azizan & Azman, 2013).

Other studies, however, yielded different results: One study (Uzunboylu & Ozdamli, 2011) indicated teachers' evaluation on mobile learning was above medium levels; another study (Thomas, O'Bannon & Bolton, 2013) found that teachers supported the use of cell phone in the classroom. Advances in technology mean the performance of smartphones and tablets are nearly comparable with full-fledged computers in many aspects, such as multimedia capabilities and network connectivity, yet few studies have investigated how smartphones and tablets would influence in-service language teachers' perceptions and attitudes on MALL in and out of classrooms.

RESEARCH QUESTIONS

The purpose of this study was to investigate the influence smartphones and tablets have on language learning behavior among university language teachers and students. Specifically, the main objectives were: to explore spontaneous use of smartphone or tablets in language learning out of classrooms; to identify the kinds of apps used most often by language teachers and students and the evaluation they gave for those apps; and to examine language teachers' perception and attitudes toward MALL. The following research questions formed the basis for this study:

1. Do college language teachers and college students who own Apple mobile devices (iPhone or iPad) use such devices to assist with their informal language learning?
2. If they do, what kinds of apps do they use for language learning? Is there any difference among different groups in apps usage?
3. If they do, how do they evaluate using Apple mobile devices to assist language learning? What are their expectations in using these devices? What differences, if any, exist among different groups?
4. What are the possible factors that inhibit teachers from actively using apps to facilitate informal language learning?
5. What are teachers' attitudes toward mobile-assisted language classroom?

METHODOLOGY

The overall research design used a mixed-methods approach to data collection and analysis. A survey provided quantitative data for questions 1 to 3 while follow-up interviews provided qualitative data for questions 4 and 5.

Research Context

The survey was conducted at four universities in Zhuhai, Guangdong, China. This is a relatively developed area in China and the four universities investigated are private universities. While all four universities have multimedia classrooms with computers provided for students who take listening classes, none of these universities have employed mobile devices in language classrooms, nor have they offered training on mobile learning and teaching to their language teachers. This study focused on teachers and students who have an iPhone or an iPad to assure that participants' mobile devices would have equal performance in hardware and access to the same or similar apps. In addition, one previous study (Kim & Kwon, 2012) found that apps in both Apple iOS and Google Android OS have the same function if the same company develops them, and Apple iOS provides more ESL related apps. Finally, many students attending those universities observed already owned an iPhone or an iPad. The teacher participants were teaching both general English and courses for English major students.

Participants

A total of 240 students and teachers participated in the survey. Of these, 54 were foreign language teachers and 186 were students (60 were English majors and the remaining 126 were from 14 different majors). There were 135 (56.2%) females and 105 (43.8%) males and the mean age of the participants was 22.83 years (SD=3.11). Twenty-eight teachers from the survey participants also took part in a follow-up interview.

Procedure

A call for participation was made on the official websites of the four universities. The call specified that only language teachers and students who owned an iPhone or an iPad should participate in the study. The call also stated that participation in this study was voluntary and that confidentiality and anonymity were assured. Those interested in participating were asked to click on an URL that linked to an online survey. Interviews with language teachers were also used as the data source in this study. In the final part of the survey, teacher participants could indicate whether they are willing to participate in a 20-30 minute interview. If they were and provided their contact information, researchers of this study would contact them. All interviews were audio recorded and transcribed verbatim.

Instruments

The survey included three sections: Basic Information, Applications and Language Learning, and Evaluation. There were six items in the Basic Information section and participants were asked to provide information on the following: was the person a teacher or student; English major or not; types of Apple mobile devices used; length of usage; whether or not they used those devices to facilitate language learning, and if so, which languages? The Applications and Language Learning section asked participants to answer ten True/False items about the applications they used. "True" was calculated as one point, and "False" was calculated as zero. Finally, the Evaluation section had four items; each item was assessed using a five-point Likert scale, where 1="strongly disagree" and 5="strongly agree". All items in the survey were presented in Chinese, the participants' native language.

The interview portion of the study used semi-structured protocol and covered two areas of interest: factors affecting apps usage in Apple devices in informal language learning, and attitudes and perceptions concerning the use of smartphones in second language classrooms.

Data Analysis

The reliability and validity of the survey data were assessed using Cronbach's alpha (α), which are 0.86 for the second part and 0.82 for the third part of the survey. The values are between 0.80 and 0.90, which are considered good according to Devellis (2003). The data were then analyzed using descriptive statistics (means and frequencies, and percentage) and inferential statistics (One Way ANOVA). The qualitative data from interviews were organized by research questions and coded by theme. After initial coding, the researchers revisited each interview transcript to confirm that the data reflected its initial code.

RESULTS

Research Question 1: Informal Mobile-assisted Language Learning

Forty-five participants of the whole group owned two or more types of Apple devices and most of the subjects had investigated owning an iPhone. The 54 foreign language teachers owned 24 iPads, 48 iPhones, and 6 iPods, whereas the 186 students owned 39 iPads, 153 iPhones, and 15 iPods. Regarding length of usage, most of the teachers owned an Apple device for about 12 to 18 months; 27 students had one for more than 12 months; 87 students had one for 6 to 12 months; and 72 students possessed a device for less than 6 months.

All the participants chose "True" when asked whether they have used Apple devices to facilitate language study. Forty-eight of the teachers chose "English" and 30 of them chose "other foreign language". Types of languages involved were Japanese, Portuguese, French, Spanish, Russian and German. Among the English major students, 57 used their devices to facilitate English learning and 48 used them to facilitate Japanese, Korean and French learning. For non-English major students, 123 used their devices to learn English and 48 used them to learn Korean, Japanese, French and Spanish. Although most college students and teachers did not had access to Apple mobile devices for long (most of them no more than 1 year), they all tried to use them to facilitate their study of English. More than half of them used them to learn another foreign language other than English. Thus, our findings suggest that all of the students and teachers have tried to use Apple mobile devices to facilitate informal language learning.

Research Question 2: Application Usage and Group Differences

There were 10 questions about application usage and language learning. The total score was 10 points and all of the scores calculated in this part were analyzed by SPSS (see Table 1).

In Table 1, we see that the average score of three groups was 4 to 5 points. ANOVA analysis shows that $F=0.333$, $p=0.719>0.05$. Thus, there is no significant difference among these three groups in using applications to facilitate language study.

To understand the actual usage of applications, the percentage of application usage among each group and the total are calculated and arranged in order of reported popularity (see Table 2).

In Table 2, we see that the most frequently used apps are dictionaries, which accounts for 94.2% of the total subjects. All the English major students have used this kind of application. Most of the foreign language teachers (90.9%) and most of the non-English major students (92.9%) have used this kind of application. The second most frequently used apps of the total subjects were used for watching foreign movies and TV episodes, which was noted by 73.9% of all subjects. The third most frequently used apps were those designed for improving language skills (60.9%). Other categories of app use include: reading foreign books, newspapers, magazines and websites (52.2%); playing foreign language computer games (36.2%); listening to foreign language Podcasts (34.8%); and practicing online language tests (33.3%). Subjects who chose these applications only account for half or one third of the total. Apps such

Table 1. One-way ANOVA of Using Applications to Facilitate Language Learning

Group	N	Mean	SD	F	p
Teachers	54	4.833	2.209	0.333	0.719
English Major Students	60	4.250	1.880		
Non English Major Students	126	4.619	1.925		

*p<0.05;
**p<0.01

Table 2. Percentage of Application Usage in Groups

Rank	Statements	Teachers (n=54)	English Major (n=60)	Non- English (n=126)	Total (n=240)
		People who chose "True"(%)			
1	I installed e-dictionary for language learning in my Apple device.	90.9%	100.0%	92.9%	94.2%
2	I installed apps such as Youtube to watch foreign language movies or TV episodes.	81.8%	75.0%	71.4%	73.9%
3	I installed apps that are designed to promote language skills, such as listening, speaking, writing, etc..	45.5%	68.8%	61.9%	60.9%
4	I installed apps such as iBook or PDF reader to read foreign language magazines, newspapers, literatures etc.	63.6%	43.8%	52.4%	52.2%
5	I installed apps that are game-based to facilitate language learning.	54.5%	31.3%	33.3%	36.2%
6	I installed apps such as Podcast to listen to foreign language broadcast.	18.2%	31.3%	40.5%	34.8%
7	I installed apps that are test-based to prepare myself for foreign language tests such as CET, IELTS.	36.4%	18.8%	38.1%	33.3%
8	I installed encyclopedia apps in my Apple device.	18.2%	18.8%	21.4%	20.3%
9	I installed micro-blogging apps such as Facebook or Wechat to practice speaking or writing in foreign languages.	18.2%	31.3%	11.9%	18.1%
10	I installed iTunes U or similar online course apps to promote my language ability by watching online courses.	18.2%	0.0%	11.9%	10.1%

as encyclopedias (20.3%), micro-blogging (18.1%) or iTunes U (10.1%) were the least frequently used and accounted only for 10 to 20% of the total subjects. The findings indicate that Apple mobile devices are not fully utilized and thus their potential remains underdeveloped. The findings also indicate that the main factor underpinning this situation is that fundamental learning and teaching methods have not changed despite the fast development of information technology.

Research Question 3: Evaluation and Expectation on Mobile-assisted Informal Language Learning

The third section of the survey contained four statements aimed at eliciting the participants' evaluations on using Apple devices to facilitate language learning.

In Table 3, we see that the average score was 3.829 for the first statement and 3.614 for the second statement in this part. These two statements concerned the usefulness and ease of use concerning Apple devices. Both statements were evaluated as above 3.5, which are close to 4 points (Agree), indicating subjects generally took a positive attitude toward language learning facilitated by smartphones or tablets such as iPhone or iPad. The third statement is "Learning language through Apple device is going to take place of official classroom teaching". The average score here was 2.524, which is between 2 (Disagree) and 3 (Not sure), indicating the subjects basically took a negative attitude toward this view. The last question asked for their opinion on whether foreign language teachers should guide students to utilize Apple mobile devices for language learning. The average score was 3.814, indicating most subjects agreed that foreign language teachers should give certain guidance or recommendations in using mobile devices to facilitate language learning.

Table 3 is an analysis based on descriptive data. In order to find out differences in the opinions among three groups, inferential data was obtained using One-way ANOVA. Table 4 displays the results:

In Table 4, we see that there is no significant difference among three groups concerning the first three statements. Significant difference, however, is found with the last statement, $p=0.007<0.05$. To understand exactly in which two groups the difference exists, we used LSD to compare each group and found that the difference existed between English major students and non-English major students ($p=0.003$). English major students have a much stronger desire for language teachers to guide them in using resources on Apple devices than non-English major students.

These findings indicate that gaps exist between students' expectations and teachers' actual abilities. Most of the students, especially those who are English majors, hope that foreign language teachers can guide them or make recommendations to them about using Apple device resources. The results from Table 1, however, show that no significant differences existed in the utilization of this device among teachers and students. The findings may also indicate that the teachers did not necessarily know how to make use of the devices better than students and thus were not be able to offer effective guidance.

Table 3. Evaluation and Expectation on Mobile-assisted Language Learning

NO.	Statements	Mean	SD
1	I found that the Apple Device is beneficial to language learning.	3.829	0.613
2	I found that it is convenient to learn language through Apple device.	3.614	0.666
3	Official classroom language teaching will be replaced by technology-assisted language learning such as learning using mobile device (e.g. iPhone or iPad).	2.524	1.042
4	Foreign language teacher should guide students in proper use of apps and online resources to facilitate language learning.	3.814	0.906

Table 4. Group Difference on Evaluation and Expectation

Statements	Mean			One-way ANOVA	
	Teachers	English Major	Non-English Major	F	Sig. (p)
1	3.750	3.625	3.929	1.564	0.217
2	3.583	3.688	3.595	0.124	0.884
3	2.583	2.375	2.524	0.184	0.833
4	4.083	4.313	3.548	5.377	0.007*

*$p<0.05$;
**$p<0.01$

Research Question 4: Factors Affecting Apps Usage

Question 4 aimed to identify factors that lead to less use of certain applications by teachers, such as Podcast, iTunes, iBook etc. Participants' responses in the interviews revealed four major reasons for low frequency usage of some apps.

First, teachers were not fully aware of what apps are available for language learning in Apple devices. For example, most of the teachers (26 out of 28) were ignorant of the iTunes U app. Only 2 teachers have tried it and agreed that "it has many courses which can expand one's knowledge" (Teacher #5) and that "it can promote my teaching" (Teacher #19). As for the Podcast app, only ten teachers said that they knew what a Podcast was, while the other 18 teachers said they had not even heard about it before.

The interviews revealed the teachers' lack of motivation for trying new apps was another factor their usage patterns. Of the ten teachers who had heard about Podcast, most of them have not even tried to use it to promote language teaching. They stated reasons such as "I have not thought of the possibility of applying Podcast in teaching and I do not know how" (e.g. Teacher #8) and they wonder "why use Podcast when there are already plenty of language learning resources" (e.g. Teacher #27). Another teacher (#17) reported:

I do not feel the necessity of trying to use apps such as Podcast to promote our language learning and teaching. The school has a syllabus requiring us how to teach and what to teach and I do not feel it is appropriate to try new apps when the actual effectiveness is still unknown to the public.

Teachers also reported feeling that the time and effort spent in learning new apps would not be rewarded, as pointed out by another teacher (#13):

Learning new apps or related technology would cost me much time and energy. Yet neither my students nor the administrators would appreciate for the effort I make to integrate technology in language learning and teaching.

Software and hardware considerations were two other factors that affected the teachers' app use. Twenty-two teachers thought that many language-learning apps in Apple devices were not appropriate for their own language learning, because the knowledge provided in the apps was "too easy" for them (e.g. teacher # 6, 8, 11, 22, 23). For example, one teacher noted that, "Many of the Podcast programs only offer basic language knowledge and very few of those programs are suitable for me." They also hesitate in using some apps in language teaching as well. As for the courses offered in apps such as iTunes U, teachers (#3) commented "those courses might not be suitable for my students, because their (my students') English proficiency have not reached to such level." Teachers also associated the hardware with certain health concerns. For example, when asked why they did not use iBooks to read, eighteen teachers explained their reason for not using iBooks because it is not appropriate for reading, such as "reading books using iPad or iPhone are bad for one's eyes" (e.g. teacher #7, 8, 19, 20, 25). One teacher (#26) explained that:

While I use those devices (iPhone, iPad) to watch movies or language teaching videos, I seldom use those for reading. Because reading and watching are two different things. I would prefer to read use Kindle than iPad because I feel my eyes get sore reading on iPad for a long time.

Research Question 5: Attitude Toward Mobile-Assisted Formal Language Learning

MALL has not been implemented yet among language classes in the schools of this study. It is of interest, however, how teachers perceive the possibility of applying an iPhone, iPad or similar mobile devices with enhanced abilities in their classroom teaching. For instance, while acknowledging the facilitating function of those devices in language study, only less than one third of the teachers interviewed supported the idea of using such devices in classroom teaching. This attitude is similar to the attitude the teachers gave in survey answers when they were asked whether official classroom language teaching would be replaced by technology-assisted language learning. Teachers who supported MALL gave the following reasons: "iPads can motivate students to learn" (Teacher # 7); "students can learn more autonomously" (Teacher #5); "all the students can participate in classroom activities" (Teacher #16); the devices "can help students to focus on understanding instead of taking notes" (Teacher #19).

However, more than two thirds of the teachers interviewed expressed their disagreement or concern for MALL in classroom. They were mainly concerned about four problems. First, they questioned their ability to monitor students' behavior in class. As Teacher #10 and Teacher #15 noted, "many students do not even listen to lectures where there is no Internet" and "students would be easily distracted" when Internet connections are present. Teacher #20 echoed this sentiment when she described her experiences conducting computer-supported listening classes:

I gave listening tasks to them every class, yet they played computer games or surfed on the Internet instead. It would be very difficult to monitor their behavior when a mobile device such as an iPad is used in classes.

Second, the teachers expressed concern over how to let students learn independently and individually while still keeping them on schedule. Reflecting on her teaching experiences in the past, Teacher #11 stated:

I have tried to let students do some independent learning and the result is not satisfactory due to the big difference among students. Some of my students have much higher English proficiency and better autonomous learning ability, yet many of them could not or would not learn autonomously. I have to resort to giving lectures so at least they can keep on the same track.

Other teachers expressed similar concerns that "most of the students lack self-regulation ability" (Teacher #13) and "it (autonomous learning) is possible for small classes but my class generally contains more than 30 students" (Teacher #12).

Third, teachers were generally concerned that they lacked the necessary knowledge, training, and experience to use mobile devices for language learning. Teachers felt they needed additional training for MALL to be successfully implemented in classroom related workshop, so "at least I know how to use those devices to teach" (Teacher #17). Teacher #14 added that "training on how to implement MALL" and "how to cope with technical problems" were necessary.

Fourth, teachers were concerned that changing the classroom environment technologically would lead to larger changes in teaching and learning. Teachers agreed that traditional language teaching needs to be changed, but many of them were not sure about how to effectively achieve such changes. One of the teachers (#23) explained:

Generally my class would contain vocabulary learning and grammar exercise checking. With MALL, students can learn vocabulary using mobile devices and those devices could also help in checking grammar exercises. Thus how to organize teaching activities in classroom would be a new topic for me.

Other than the concern for their own teaching, teachers also felt that the change of teaching style would be a challenge to students as well. As stated by Teacher #21 and Teacher #20, "what worries me is how students would respond to such a change (MALL) because they are used to learning from teachers' lecture" and "they (students) are expecting to learn from us, not technology tools such as computers."

DISCUSSION

Analysis of the survey data indicates that both language teachers and students are using the Apple devices they own to facilitate informal language learning. Their evaluation and attitudes toward MALL are basically positive as well. Yet a few of the findings from the interview data are intriguing and thus warrant further discussion.

Still Existing Technical Issues

While iPhones and iPads have many enhanced capabilities compared to older mobile devices, technical issues still exist that prevent the use of such devices in educational contexts. For an example, Apple devices can make the display of text and images extremely crisp, yet this function does not mean users have better or even similar reading experiences when compared to reading traditional books. Participants in this study, while using applications such as iBOOK, reported occasional eye irritation after long time reading on those devices, and hence were less willing to use Apple devices for reading.

Another area of concern is the design of apps for language learning. For an example, some teachers in this study attributed their infrequent use of certain apps to the impression that the content included in those apps is either boring or not appropriate for learning or teaching in terms of difficulty. Yet to develop an app by themselves involves knowing a programming language, which would be very time-consuming. This finding confirmed findings in a previous study (Godwin-Jones, 2011a), mainly that apps developers need to rethink how to enhance language learning with the assistance of smartphones or tablets. Projects such as TenseITS (Cui & Bull, 2004) or the personalized context-aware ubiquitous learning system (Chen & Li, 2010) have been cited as good examples of language learning apps.

Prior Language Learning Experience and MALL Pedagogy

Results of this study indicate that the most frequently used apps for MALL are e-dictionary, media/video apps, or apps that targeted certain language skills. By matching apps to the functions they support, we can infer that activities such as vocabulary building (checking a dictionary), watching foreign movies or doing pattern-drill exercises are still the main language learning methods for Chinese students and teachers. These apps, while effective in delivering language knowledge, did not have learners actively participate in the learning process. Conversely, apps that are more constructivist-based, such as micro blogging, podcasting, were less frequently used. Thus, despite the rich online resources and the various apps available, the potential to facilitate language learning with such resources and apps remains untapped.

Moreover, a comparison among language teachers, English major students and non-English major students showed that no significant difference existed among the three groups, indicating that all three groups tended to choose apps that are form-focused and behaviorist-based. This is unsurprising, since both language teachers and students in this study were taught language within the framework of behaviorism and structuralism. It seems natural that previous language learning experiences would influence their choice of application concerning language learning, which Lortie (1975) referred to this phenomenon as "apprenticeship of observation."

Mobile devices are often thought to be particularly suited to supporting social contacts and collaborative learning, which are claimed to be closely related to language learning (Kukulska & Shield, 2008). This study found, however, that based on the attitudes of teachers and students, it will be difficult to change their long-standing and deeply rooted language learning practices. Similarly, most of the language-learning apps were identified as form-focused, which may be attributed to the prior language learning experiences of the app developers themselves.

Mobile devices can help learners break the limits of traditional teaching, to engage in learning anytime and anywhere. If used in the classroom, students and teachers can participate more easily and conveniently in interactive teaching activities. These tools are also ideal carriers of electronic textbooks and are necessary student platforms in a technology-rich classroom environment. Providing such devices, however, does not guarantee effective change. Students and teachers surveyed in this study still rely on traditional language learning methods despite owning an iPad or iPhone, indicating that a change in conceptualizations and approaches to learning is an important factor when adopting technology for educational purposes.

Conflicting Attitudes toward Informal and Formal MALL

Some teacher participants in this study were found to have conflicting attitude toward MALL in different settings. Many held positive attitudes towards informal MALL (out of class) and negative attitudes towards formal MALL (in class). When asked to evaluate their experience of informal language learning using Apple devices, most of the teacher participants responded positively on the benefit (Mean=3.750) and convenience (Mean=3.583) of these devices to facilitate language learning. Based on the Technology Adoption Model (Davis, 1989), attitudes toward technology can be predicted based on perceptions of usefulness and ease of use. Thus the teachers' attitudes toward informal MALL were generally positive. Yet during the interview, two thirds of the teacher participants interviewed stated that they prefer not to use mobile devices in their classroom teaching. This finding reflects similar findings in another study (Van Praag & Sanchez, 2015), mainly that teachers tend to forbid or are unwilling to tolerate mobile devices usage in their classrooms.

A possible explanation for this paradoxical attitude toward MALL is that a language classroom is a complex language-learning environment, with more factors to be considered compared to individual informal learning. A further analysis of the teachers' responses indicated that in classroom teaching, language teachers need to consider factors such as: learners' self-control, autonomous learning, teachers' pedagogical and technological knowledge, change of role in teaching, etc. Numerous studies confirm that those factors are influential and thus their concern is reasonable. Take learners' self-control as an example: One study investigating information behavior in the mobile environment found that undergraduate smartphone users mainly use smartphones for recreational purpose instead of for academic uses (Liu, Huang & Fu, 2014). Previous studies also showed that mobile device can be seen as a nuisance and distraction by teachers (e.g. Campbell, 2006). As far as teachers' knowledge is concerned, there is a substantial body of research discussing the importance of *technology pedagogical content knowledge* (TPACK, Mishra & Koehler, 2006). The TPACK framework describes how the interaction of content, pedagogy and technology can produce the types of flexible knowledge needed for effective technology integration in teaching. Yet such knowledge often needs to be developed through professional development and practice. Changing of teachers' role is an even bigger challenge for most of the language teachers. Teachers used to act as a major resource when students had difficulties such as encountering an unknown word or a difficult concept, but mobile device can easily provide links to supplemental resources and thus present a challenge to teachers' knowledge and expertise (Van Praag & Sanchez, 2015).

IMPLICATIONS

The findings of this study have implications for both language teachers and teacher educators. First, students in this study were found to expect teachers' guidance in using apps and online resources. We believe language teachers in China should develop their awareness of MALL theories, technologies, and methods even though it has not been widely implemented yet in many institutions. Indeed, there is ample support for the concept of "mobile literacy" in educational research literature. As Hockly (2013) suggests, "mobile literacy" is an increasing important skill for both teachers and learners (Hockly, 2013, p.83). Parry (2011) contends that teaching mobile web literacy is as crucial as teaching basic literacy.

A second implication of the study is that language educators should encourage and assist learners' autonomous learning using mobile devices. The study echoes earlier findings that learners are less likely to develop as autonomous learners if they are provided unrestricted access to information without proper guidance and feedback (Murray, 1999). Moreover, Godwin-Jones (2011a) argues that smartphones are "ideal for individualized informal learning" and advocates that students should be encouraged and assisted in their autonomous learning to "combine formal and informal learning" (p.8).

Results from this study concerning language teachers' negative attitudes toward MALL in the classroom should be of interest to teacher educators as well. In the field of teacher education, mobile learning is under-theorized (Kearney & Maher, 2013), yet teachers need to understand the value of mobile technologies and know ways of integrating them into classroom (Schuck, Aubusson, Kearney, & Burden, 2013). The findings of this study indicated that spontaneous MALL is happening now even when MALL has not been widely implemented in many institutions. Yet most language teachers have not been trained and thus are not fully prepared for such change. Abundant online resources and numerous apps on smartphones and tablets have the potential to change the nature and practice of language learning and yet many teachers remain unwilling and unprepared to change their existing mindset. How to develop proper MALL pedagogy among language teachers through professional development programs is consequently an urgent and imperative task teacher educators are facing now.

FUTURE TRENDS

As a sub branch of computer assisted language learning (CALL), MALL is still a young discipline with a promising yet potentially difficult future. We argue that existing and emerging trends in this evolving discipline need to be investigated in future studies. The subjects in this study experienced MALL spontaneously and without formal instructional support or guidance. It is unclear whether teachers' and students' attitudes would be different had they experienced MALL in formal instructional settings. It is also unclear whether teachers' perceptions of and attitudes toward MALL would be different after a certain period of professional development in MALL, or whether such training would lead to teachers actually using mobile devices to facilitate language-learning activities in the classroom. Finally, technology is ever changing, and the mobile devices that can be used in language classroom are evolving as well. While this study focused on the use of smart phones and tablets in language teaching and learning, we suggest future research should investigate whether and how other kinds of mobile technology products, such as robots, can lead to changes in teachers' and students' conception of language learning and their attitudes towards MALL in the future.

CONCLUSION

The development of information and communication technology (ICT) has made teaching environments increasingly digital for the past twenty years. Multi-media computers, projectors, the Internet and interactive whiteboards have become indispensable elements. We believe including mobile devices such as smartphones and tablets in classroom practices can encourage the development of a digital campus. In time the application of ICT in teaching may cause changes in teaching pedagogy, learners' autonomous learning and the relationship among teachers, students and textbooks. However, teachers and students may not adapt to such change very quickly. During the interviews, most of the teachers were doubtful as to how they should adjust themselves to more technology-rich educational contexts, as well as to how they should teach if such devices as iPad are employed in the classroom. Some of them consider that the benefits from information technology to language learning are minimal. We find these doubts and opinions hinder teachers in trying new methods or in abandoning older and familiar teaching practices. The same situation is true of students. Student-centered autonomous learning requires strong student motivation, highly independent consciousness, clear learning targets and the ability to act according to plans. We recommend more studies in the field of MALL concerning the aforementioned issues should be conducted in the future. Only when these issues are addressed can these questions concerning how mobile devices are used in classroom teaching be resolved.

REFERENCES

Abdous, M., Camarena, M., & Facer, B. R. (2009). MALL technology: Use of academic podcasting in the foreign language classroom. *ReCALL*, *21*(01), 76–95. doi:10.1017/S0958344009000020

Baran, E. (2014). A Review of Research on Mobile Learning in Teacher Education. *Journal of Educational Technology & Society*, *17*(4), 17–32.

Burston, J. (2014). The reality of MALL: Still on the fringes. *CALICO Journal*, *31*(1), 103–125. doi:10.11139/cj.31.1.103-125

Campbell, S. (2006). Perceptions of mobile phones in college classrooms: Ringing, cheating, and classroom policies. *Communication Education*, *55*(3), 280–294. doi:10.1080/03634520600748573

Chen, C.-M., & Li, Y.-L. (2010). Personalized context-aware ubiquitous learning system for supporting effective English vocabulary learning. *Interactive Learning Environments*, *18*(4), 341–364. doi:10.1080/10494820802602329

Cheon, J., Lee, S., Crooks, S. M., & Song, J. (2012). An investigation of mobile learning readiness in higher education based on the theory of planned behavior. *Computers & Education*, *59*(3), 1054–1064. doi:10.1016/j.compedu.2012.04.015

Chinnery, G. M. (2006). Going to the MALL: Mobile assisted language learning (Emerging technology). *Language Learning & Technology*, *10*(1), 9–16.

Cui, Y., & Bull, S. (2005). Context and learner modelling for the mobile foreign language learner. *System*, *33*(2), 353–367. doi:10.1016/j.system.2004.12.008

Davis, F. D. (1989). Perceived Usefulness, Perceived Ease of Use, and User Acceptance of Information Technology. *Management Information Systems Quarterly*, *13*(3), 319–340. doi:10.2307/249008

DeVellis, R. F. (2003). *Scale development: Theory and applications* (2nd ed.). Thousand Oaks, CA: Sage Publications, Inc.

Godwin-Jones, R. (2011a). Emerging technologies: Mobile apps for language learning. *Language Learning & Technology*, *15*(2), 2–11.

Godwin-Jones, R. (2011b). Emerging Technologies: Autonomous language learning. *Language Learning & Technology*, *15*(3), 4–11.

Hockly, N. (2013). Mobile learning. *ELT Journal*, *67*(1), 80–84. doi:10.1093/elt/ccs064 PMID:23923690

Husbye, N. E., & Elsener, A. A. (2013). To move forward, we must be mobile: Practical uses of mobile technology in literacy education courses. *Journal of Digital Learning in Teacher Education*, *30*(2), 46–51. doi:10.1080/21532974.2013.10784726

Ingraham, N. (2015). Apple's App Store has passed 100 billion app downloads. *The Verge*. Retrieved from http://www.theverge.com/2015/6/8/8739611/apple-wwdc-2015-stats-update

Ismail, I., Azizan, S. N., & Azman, N. (2013). Mobile phone as pedagogical tools: Are teachers ready. *International Education Studies*, *6*(3), 36–47. doi:10.5539/ies.v6n3p36

Kearney, M., & Maher, D. (2013). Mobile learning in math teacher education: Using iPads to support pre-service teachers' professional development. *Australian Educational Computing*, *27*(3), 76–84.

Keegan, D., & Fern Univ., Hagen (Germany). Inst. for Research into Distance Education. (2002). *The future of learning: From eLearning to mLearning*. ERIC Clearinghouse.

Kim, H., & Kwon, Y. (2012). Exploring smartphone applications for effective mobile-assisted language learning. *Multimedia-Assisted Language Learning*, *15*(1), 31–57.

Kukulska-Hulme, A., & Shield, L. (2007, September). An Overview of Mobile Assisted Language Learning: Can mobile devices support collaborative practice in speaking and listening. Proceedings of the conference EuroCALL'07 Conference Virtual Strand.

Kukulska-Hulme, A., & Shield, L. (2008). An overview of mobile assisted language learning: From content delivery to supported collaboration and interaction. *ReCALL*, *20*(03), 271–289. doi:10.1017/S0958344008000335

Liu, Z. M., Huang, X. B., & Fu, Y. A. (2014). Information behavior in the mobile environment: A study of undergraduate smartphone users in China. *Chinese Journal of Library and Information Science*, *7*(4), 1–15.

Lortie, D. (1975). *Schoolteacher: A sociological study*. Chicago: University of Chicago Press.

Mishra, P., & Koehler, M. J. (2006). Technological Pedagogical Content Knowledge: A Framework for Teacher Knowledge. *Teachers College Record*, *108*(6), 1017–1054.

Murray, D. E. (1999). Access to information technology: Considerations for language educators. *Prospect*, *14*(3), 4–12.

Naismith, L., Lonsdale, P., Vavoula, G., Sharples, M., & Series, N. F. (2004). Literature review in mobile technologies and learning. *Nesta Futurelab Series*. Retrieved from http://citeseerx.ist.psu.edu/viewdoc/citations?doi=10.1.1.136.2203

Ogata, H., Hui, G. L., Yin, C., Ueda, T., Oishi, Y., & Yano, Y. (2008). LOCH: Supporting mobile language learning outside classrooms. *International Journal of Mobile Learning and Organisation*, *2*(3), 271–282. doi:10.1504/IJMLO.2008.020319

Oz, H. (2015). An investigation of preservice English teachers' perceptions of mobile assisted language learning. *English Language Teaching*, *8*(2), 22–34. doi:10.5539/elt.v8n2p22

Parry, D. (2011). Mobile perspectives: On teaching mobile literacy. *EDUCAUSE Review*, *46*(2), 14.

Patten, B., Arnedillo-Sánchez, I., & Tangney, B. (2006). Designing collaborative, constructivist and contextual applications for handheld devices. *Computers & Education*, *46*(3), 294–308. doi:10.1016/j.compedu.2005.11.011

Pegrum, M., Howitt, C., & Striepe, M. (2013). Learning to take the tablet: How pre-service teachers use iPads to facilitate their learning. *Australasian Journal of Educational Technology*, *29*(4).

Schuck, S., Aubusson, P., Kearney, M., & Burden, K. (2013). Mobilising teacher education: A study of a professional learning community. *Teacher Development*, *17*(1), 1–18. doi:10.1080/13664530.2012.752671

Serin, O. (2012). Mobile learning perceptions of the prospective teachers (TPNR Sampling). *Turkish Online Journal of Educational Technology*, *11*(3), 222–233.

Share of mobile phone users that use a smartphone in China from 2013 to 2019. (n. d.). *Statisa*. Retrieved from http://www.statista.com/statistics/257045/smartphone-user-penetration-in-china/

Shohel, M. M. C., & Power, T. (2010). Introducing mobile technology for enhancing teaching and learning in Bangladesh: Teacher perspectives. *Open Learning*, *25*(3), 201–215. doi:10.1080/02680513.2010.511953

Siskin, C. B. (n. d.). Language Learning Applications for Smartphones, or Small Can Be Beautiful. *Edvista*. Retrieved from http://www.edvista.com/claire/pres/smartphones/#repurposed

Tablet Users to Surpass 1 Billion Worldwide in 2015. (2015, Jan. 8). *Emarketer*. Retrieved from http://www.emarketer.com/Article/Tablet-Users-Surpass-1-Billion-Worldwide-2015/1011806#sthash.aHZ-WN7ma.dpuf

Thomas, K., & O'Bannon, B. (2013). Cell phones in the classroom: Preservice teachers' perceptions. *Journal of Digital Learning in Teacher Education*, *30*(1), 11–20. doi:10.1080/21532974.2013.10784721

Thomas, K. M., O'Bannon, B. W., & Bolton, N. (2013). Cell phones in the classroom: Teachers' perspectives of inclusion, benefits, and barriers. *Computers in the Schools*, *30*(4), 295–308. doi:10.1080/07380569.2013.844637

Uzunboylu, H., & Özdamlı, F. (2011). Teacher perception for m-learning: Scale development and teachers' perceptions. *Journal of Computer Assisted Learning*, *27*(6), 544–556. doi:10.1111/j.1365-2729.2011.00415.x

Van Praag, B., & Sanchez, H. S. (2015). Mobile technology in second language classrooms: Insights into its uses, pedagogical implications, and teacher beliefs. *ReCALL*, *27*(03), 288–303. doi:10.1017/S0958344015000075

Wang, S., & Higgins, M. (2006). Limitations of mobile phone learning. *The JALT CALL Journal*, *2*(1), 3–14.

ADDITIONAL READING

Bell, J., Sawaya, S., & Cain, W. (2014). Synchromodal classes: Designing for shared learning experiences between face-to-face and online students. *International Journal of Designs for learning, 5*(1).

Li, L. (2014). Understanding language teachers' practice with educational technology: A case from China. *System, 46*, 105–119. doi:10.1016/j.system.2014.07.016

Uzunboylu, H., & Ozdamli, F. (2011). Teacher perception for m-learning: Scale development and teachers' perceptions. *Journal of Computer Assisted Learning, 27*(6), 544–556. doi:10.1111/j.1365-2729.2011.00415.x

Yusup, Y. (2014). Preliminary study on teachers' use of the iPad in bachelor of education program at a private university in Malaysia. *TechTrends, 58*(2), 14–19. doi:10.1007/s11528-014-0732-y

KEY TERMS AND DEFINITIONS

Android (OS): Android is an operating system for mobile devices developed by Google.

Apple's iOS: OS is short for operating system. Apple's iOS is the operating system developed by Apple Inc. for mobile devices including iPod, iPhone and iPad etc.

Apps: Short form of Applications. Apps refer to software programs designed to run on mobile phones or other handheld mobile devices.

Behaviorist Approach: Also called behaviorism, it refers to a theory of explaining human behavior in terms conditioning and reinforcement activities without reference to thoughts and feelings.

Constructivist Approach: Also called constructivism, it is a theory of how people learn. Constructivism posits that people's knowledge is built on their own personal experience and reflective thinking.

Form-Focused Instruction: An approach in language education that emphasizes the acquisition of linguistic forms such as lexical features, phonological features, grammatical forms, etc.

Learner-Centered Instruction: A teaching method that focuses on students engaging in hard work, reflecting on their learning process, and learning independently or collaboratively.

MALL: Abbreviation for *Mobile Assisted Language Learning*. MALL refers to the use of handheld mobile devices (MP3 and MP4 players, mobile phones, tablets, etc.) to facilitate language-learning activities including accessing information, communicating with teachers and students, etc.

TPACK: Abbreviation for *Technological Pedagogical Content Knowledge*. Proposed in 2006 by Mishra and Koehler, TPACK is a framework to describe knowledge growth in teachers' professional practice and development along three intersecting dimensions: content, pedagogy, and technology.

Chapter 16

Mexican Heritage ELL and Native English Speaker Interaction:
A Case Study of Tandem Language Learning Strategies

Lisa Winstead
California State University, USA

ABSTRACT

This case study explores 1) the potential of a dual language program that provides an English Language Learner (ELL) and a Spanish Learner (SL) with opportunities to engage in authentic as well as mutual language exchange; and, 2) the multiple types of language strategies employed by adolescents to teach and learn language from one another in tandem learning situations. Findings from a transcription analysis of 12 English and Spanish videotaped sessions of one dyad reveal novel and in depth information about strategies utilized in compensatory, administrative, and social ways to extend the flow of communication in tandem learning. Findings indicate that tandem language learning not only provides a space for language learners to engage in plural strategies to promote teaching and learning, but also learner metacognition when peer learners employ interlingual and plurilingual measures to compensate for language gaps. Implications for the study of online tandem language learning are also highlighted..

TANDEM/DUAL LANGUAGE LEARNING: ISSUES AND CHALLENGES

Education in the 21st century includes goals of promoting global awareness and communicative competence (Hymes, 1974; Savignon & Sysoyev, 2005). This awareness is necessary because children from diverse backgrounds should have equitable access to educational resources and language study that contributes to their global communicative awareness. Moreover, minority and plurilingual children have a right to sustain and maintain competence in their primary language. While face-to-face dual language learning is possible, some students may not have access to plurilingual learning opportunities.

DOI: 10.4018/978-1-5225-0177-0.ch016

Dual immersion and bilingual programs allow immigrant children to interact face-to-face equally with content in two languages and have found to been effective in helping EL students achieve high scores on state tests (Thomas & Collier, 2002). English Learners need to be presented with opportunities to learn language in an authentic setting "where they must use that language, and preferably in a friendly and relaxed context" (Brisk & Harrington, 2002, p. 104). Schools that value the bilingual and bicultural capital of immigrants can act as an inclusive bridge to promote participation as well as linguistic and cultural exchange within the classroom.

While face-to-face dual language learning is possible in dual immersion programs in which the status of both the heritage and primary language are valued, limited access and demand for these programs can prevent access to these interactions. Win-win opportunities can emerge for both foreign language and second language learners should EL students, such as Mexicans who speak Spanish, are seen as resources for mutual and temporal language practice. After school or during school language programs can provide a space for this type of learning. Moreover, opportunities for mutual informal language peer language practice is more readily accessible through tandem learning by means of tellecollaboration.

Tandem refers to language exchange between two learners who desire to learn the other's language (Appel & Mullen, 2000). Tandem online exchange provides learners with opportunities to connect with learners from different linguistic backgrounds who might otherwise be separated by borders and oceans. Schools that value the bilingual and bicultural capital of immigrants have the potential to promote linguistic, cultural-exchange, and language-status parity through multiple communicative face-to-face as well as online interactions.

This chapter provides an overview of the challenges (such as restrictive English-only language policies) and benefits for dual language exchange and language parity, including opportunities for win-win tandem learning situations that promote parity and value the cultural and linguistic expertise of heritage language learners as language resources, as well as the implications of computer-mediated tandem language learning in the digital age.

Promoting Parity for Language Minorities

Tandem online learning has often been studied within the realm of foreign language learning; however, it can also play a role in second language and dual language education in ways that meet 21st century goals. Peer face-to-face and tandem online language learning can also be utilized as a way to promote pride in those who teach peers their heritage language. The tandem sharing of language between L1 Spanish heritage language speakers and L1 English speakers can be utilized to foster greater cultural and linguistic sharing among children in schools. Furthermore, tandem language learning between heritage speakers and mainstream students promotes second language proficiency through authentic language practice with native speakers.

Dual language programs provide a space within which to promote equal language status (Winstead, 2013). Promotion of language equality matters because first-world languages in major countries are still considered to be the dominant languages and carry greater status than minority languages, e.g., English over Spanish in the United States, French over Arabic in France (Beardsmore, 2008; Helot, 2003; Winstead, 2013). This is especially the case with transnationals.

Transnationals generally refer to immigrant labor workforces hired in first-world countries (Darder & Uriarte, 2013; Vertovec, 2001). Transnationals maintain their ties to the homeland as they work in the host country (Vertovec, 2004). These workers bring family members who contribute to the plurilingual diversity of schools globally. Plurilingual children come with heritage language and cultural knowledge that can be tapped to promote plurilingual language learning and cultural exchange among mainstream youth. Students gain a sense of pride when they can contribute to society. Winstead (2013) found that English Learners retain a sense of pride when their first language is valued and they are seen as experts in dual language learning processes. Face-to-face and online tandem learning opportunities provide a space for promoting equal language status among Newcomer language learners during dual language exchange.

Restrictive Language Policies

Restrictive language policies in the United States have historically run counter to embracing the cultural and linguistic heritage of immigrants. Furthermore, restrictive language policy in the United States has been historically linked with the rise of Latinos in the United States (San Miguel, 2008). In the 1850s, "Both Texas and California … enacted legislation in this decade mandating English in the schools and restricting the use of Spanish" (San Miguel, p. 43). In 1986, Proposition 63, funded and campaigned by anti-immigrant organizations, made English the official language of government and social functions in California (Padilla et al., 1991). English-only policies passed in more than 23 states across the United States to restrict the primary and heritage language use in schools (Barker, 2001). Propositions 203 and 227, passed respectively in Arizona and California, impact children's heritage language use and bilingual support in classrooms.

Similarly, related is a resurgence of Structured English Immersion (SEI), which utilizes English-only interventions and strategies, are employed in classrooms with newcomer English Learners in California (California Commission on Teacher Credentialing; Clark, 2009) despite research that reveals the importance of primary language support in promoting Latino student achievement (Thomas & Collier, 2002). Teachers who receive English Learner authorizations can work with Newcomers even if they do not speak the primary language of the child or provide support. According to the U.S. Department of Education under Title 1—Improving the Academic achievement of the disadvantaged, educators should meet:

… the educational needs of low-achieving children in our Nation's highest-poverty schools, limited English proficient children, migratory children … in need of reading assistance … (U.S. Department of Education, 2016)

Teachers with English language authorizations have been prepared to work with newcomers utilizing specially designed academic instruction in English; however, many teachers lack the bilingual ability to understand students' prior content knowledge in the first language. Teachers who are proficient in heritage languages can support newcomer language learning and thus provide equitable access to the curriculum, as was mandated by the Supreme Court in Lau versus Nichols, 1978. Studies reveal that when children's primary language and culture is not considered, it affects their identity and well-being in schools (Jagers, 2001; Phinney, Horencyzk, Liebkind, & Vedder, 2001).

In highly Latino-populated states such as Arizona and California, language restrictive measures affect the Newcomers ability to utilize the heritage language as a scaffold for learning English. Monolingual approaches in schools have contributed to heritage language loss and negative feelings towards their own culture (Fitts, Winstead, Weisman, Flores, & Valenciana, 2008; Martinez-Roldan & Malave, 2004). Monolingual deficit discourses are further exhibited in schools that restrict primary language use classrooms (Arellano-Houchin et al., 2001), despite longitudinal research that reveals that bilingual and dual language schooling promote higher achievement among minority children (Thomas & Collier, 2002). Having highly qualified bilingual teachers who can enrich the heritage language is essential to reverse and counter deficit notions about subordinant languages in first-world countries.

Transnational minority language children in socioeconomically challenged areas have less access to heritage language resources in schools that allow them to maintain and promote their multiple literacies or plurilingualism (Skerrett, 2012). Thus, teachers and administrators in K-12 education have an ethical obligation to provide these children with equitable learning opportunities as well as the possibility of retaining their language and sharing of global knowledge with other children in schools. While dual immersion programs have recently become popular in the United States and promote plurilingual learning, the demand for spots in these schools is too competitive (Rogers, 2013; Wilson, 2011) and programs are not necessarily geographically available.

Dual language programs can bridge the gap between mainstream and heritage language population. Correspondingly, online technology has the potential to play a role in bridging the gap between foreign language and second language populations in schools to promote authentic language practice. Innovative technology such as email, Skype, and podcasting provides virtual venues for intercultural exchange through tandem telecollaboration but also extends tandem language learners' oral communicative practice and competence (Goodwin-Jones, 2005; Elia, 2006; O'Dowd, 2015). This type of tandem learning pedagogy should be further expanded to the educational arena to promote the plurilinguistic ability of minority language students (Tse, 2001). When students retain their heritage language and learn the new language through peer interaction, all who participate benefit, and plurilingualism can be retained, enhanced, and advanced.

THEORETICAL PERSPECTIVES

An ethnography of speaking approach, combined with coding speech communities (Hymes, 1974; Dörnyei and Maldarez, 1997; Dörnyei & Scott, 1997; Oxford, Lavine, & Crookall, 1989), provide a framework for describing how peer roles influence the types of language strategies that emerged to extend and move language forward. While a number of strategies identified among the various groups are similar, differences among strategies and the categorization of language learning strategies may differ based on the language learning context (Wharton, 2000) as well as the linguistic level (Lafford, 2004; Winstead, 2013). According to Hymes (1974), "One must discover relevant differences in relation to analysis of context..." which includes the roles played by individuals as they seek to achieve communicative competence (p. 440).

Students who take on social roles and assume responsibility for learning and teaching (Azinezhad et al., 2013) also feel a responsibility to metacognitively think about strategies that promote sociolinguistic understanding during mutual exchanges (Çelik et al., 2013; Winstead, 2013). Social contextual construction is based on the recognition of learner patterns during these interactions (James, 2007). "Aspects of consciousness", including the learner's awareness in recognizing correct language forms and understanding alternative linguistic varieties, become part and parcel of the learner's social understanding (Dörnyei & Scott, 1997). Peers who tandemly learn languages together over a period of time come to evaluate language and adjust language to promote understanding (Winstead, 2013). Rephrasing and clarifying for peers during e-telecollaboration is similarly utilized to promote feedback to enhance meaning (Ware & O'Dowd, 2008).

Social knowing in interactive contexts (James, 2007) also encompasses the learners' conscious use of strategies to extend language, through the use of alternative linguistic approaches that promote mutual understanding (Bialystok, 1983) or the avoidance of topics due to a desire to promote language flow (Dörnyei & Scott, 1997; Winstead). Interlingual approaches, such as voluntary and involuntary code-switching, fill gaps in communication as well as purposefully and socially share language (Ellwood, 2008; García & Wei, 2014; Winstead). Ellwood found that peer language learning among diverse primary language speakers in classroom contexts can contribute to "alternative linguistic varieties", which are utilized by learners to scaffold language which, in turn, promotes collaborative understanding (p. 539).

Peer-assisted academic learning has been similarly studied with respect to the learner and the tutor, who teach language and how this interaction becomes self-regulated, strategy-based, and goal oriented (Spörer & Brunstein, 2009; Zimmerman, 1989). While there is greater depth of research of peer-assisted learning in academic contexts, less literature exists about how strategies emerge cognitively and meta-cognitively among language learners to advance communication.

Researchers suggest that alternatives to traditional language classroom instruction need to be implemented to promote language contact from target linguistic and social cultures, e.g., study abroad, dual language programs, and online tandem learning (Angelova, Gunawardena, & Volk, 2006; Magnan & Back, 2007; Winstead, 2013). It is also recommended that strategies be employed that permit the co-construction meaning, which increases oral ability during language learning situations (Angelova et al.; Azizinezhad, Hashemi, & Darvishi, 2013; Çelik, Aytin, & Bayram, 2013). As such, it is essential to understand how co-constructed learning contributes to researcher understanding about the types of strategies co-language learners employ.

Oxford et al. (1989) identify certain premises associated with various types of language strategies employed that range from compensatory to social in nature during language learning interactions. Cognitive strategies are those utilized to promote practice language through repetition, resources (e.g., dictionaries), and provide feedback. Compensation strategies are those utilized to compensate for a gap in information during communication such as guessing, involuntary code-switching to the first language, rephrasing, or adjusting the message. Metacognitive strategies are utilized for goal-setting, self-monitoring, and self-evaluation. Research reveals that problem-solving is related to a willingness to engage goal-oriented actions (Dörnyei, 2000; Dörnyei and Malderez, 1997; Liem, Lau, and Nie, 2008; Zimmerman, 1989).

Compensatory, cognitive, and metacognitive strategies are useful in identifying major themes and language patterns. In this case study, metacognition is related to making decisions about extending the flow of language communication. Metacognitive strategies are generally associated with purposeful objectives and may include making administrative decision about what is studied or avoided. How the students can act as experts and teachers that metacognitively evaluate their learning situations. For example, a student may make decisions based on the learning situation of whether to avoid or change a topic based on an assessment of the peer's language ability. Similarly, topic change might be necessary due to linguistic breakdown and a desire to promote language flow.

REVIEW OF THE LITERATURE

The first section of the Literature Review focuses on tandem language learning research. The second section provides and overviews research concerning seminal and recent discourse analysis, which contributes to this case study examination of face-to-face tandem language learning and teaching strategies.

Online Tandem Language Learning

Over the last 10 years, technology-assisted language learning literature has provided a basis for understanding how virtual tandem communication can enhance not only language ability on formal and informal levels, but how this form of communication allows students to develop online identities and community with peers with possibly more courage than in face-to-face scenarios. Researchers have examined the positive aspects of dual immersion programs for promoting bilingual achievement and success in ways that level the playing field for minority language students (Block, 2011; Palmer, 2010; Thomas & Collier, 2002).

Information is dearth about how face-to-face and online tandem language learning at the k-12 levels might be also be employed to potentially provide immigrants with opportunities to retain their heritage language in ways that promote acculturation versus assimilation when dual immersion programs are unavailable. Tandem face-to-face learning provides a forum for helping immigrants retain their mother tongue through authentic language exchange and helps them build confidence in themselves and opportunities to learn the target language from their peers in schools (Palmer; Winstead, 2013).

Technology provides virtual space for authentic tandem language communication that can fill the gap that promotes plurilingualism for all students associated with 21st century global awareness. With regard to language learning at the k-12 level, researchers have been specifically concerned with particular pedagogical considerations that will promote learner-centered autonomy, reciprocity (Brammerts, 1996), and cross-cultural understanding that are associated with foreign language program goals (Savignon & Sysoyev, 2005). Similarly, case studies of online bilingual chat and reciprocal online peer tutoring reveal how tandem language learning promote language gains, as well as social opportunities for free and nonthreatening communicative practice (Sykes, 2005).

Synchronous and Asynchronous Tandem Exchange

A plethora of studies about online tandem exchange regarding primarily university-level and foreign language studies in the last 10 years have focused on computer-mediated tandem approaches for foreign language learning at the college level. Despite the preponderance of college and university studies, this research also contributes to our understanding of the ways in which we can employ these approaches in preschool through high school. Among the studies prevalent in the literature, three major categories emerge:

1. Online tandem promotion of primarily social conversational fluency;
2. More purposeful online tandem task-based or purposeful approaches that can engage students in oral collaborative dialogue; and
3. Task-based approaches with peers to promote peer feedback and increased accuracy in the target language.

Synchronous tandem learning via skype conference calls have been found to be beneficial for promoting speaker's social interaction skills, verbal communicative fluency, and promoted gains in the target language (Correa, 2015; Thurston, Duran, Cunningham, Blanch, & Topping, 2009). For example, in their study of nine- to 12-year-old peer learners, Thurston et al. found that Catalonians and Scotts who exchanged in online tandem Spanish and English language tutoring primarily assisted one another with correction of verb conjugations (morph syntax) as well as lexical and orthographic errors. The authors additionally discovered that through this language tutoring process, the Catalonians' Spanish second language proficiency increased, which was similarly the case for the Scottish, whose English reading proficiency increased as well.

Researchers also contend that language should be studied when students are engaged in more purposeful "task-based" project collaboration for the purposes of seeing how students utilize collaborative dialogue in these more formal rather than social types of contexts (Chen & Yang, 2014; Slotte & Tynjälä, 2005; Zeng & Takasuka, 2009). Schenker studied the written and verbal exchanges between U.S. college students studying German and their high school counterparts studying English in Germany. The study revealed that the cross-cultural nature of the exchange in video conferencing, blogs, emails, as well as collaborative essay formats contributed to high student interest.

Chen and Yang (2014) similarly conducted a study of purposeful interaction. In this study seventh-grade Taiwanese students were to interact via online forums as well as Skype with individuals who spoke other varieties of English (e.g., Pakistan, Dubai). While students' struggled with accents, overall they related via surveys that the opportunity promoted language gains.

While collaboration and the verbal production during language learning is key, other researchers are concerned with how peers can help one another during written asynchronous types of learning formats. Alternatively, Sun (2009) conducted a study of asynchronous tandem learning in which college students developed introductory and follow-up blogs as ways to introduce themselves over the course of a semester. Sun found that utilizing introductory blogs as a pedagogical goal promoted interaction as well as greater reflection which, in turn, allowed for increased self-analysis of their verbal speech. As such, Sun found, similar to what Krashen (1987) proposed with the monitor hypothesis, it was found that students that have time to contemplate and evaluate their language over time have greater opportunities to monitor, see weaknesses, and engage in self-correction, as noted by some students in this study. Lee (2009) similarly found that when peers collaboratively working on blogs as well as podcasts, they were able to co-construct knowledge in response to their counterparts online. The author also suggests that collaborative task-based learning contributed to the success of intercultural sharing.

While the two studies above focused primarily on verbal development through asynchronous voice blog and podcasting, other researchers have found that asynchronous communication can also promote increased writing accuracy in the target language (Bower & Kawaguchi, 2011; Kabawa & Edasawa, 2011; Vinagre & Muñoz, 2011). Vinagre and Muñoz studied over a period of three months how Spanish college students studying German and German students studying in Spain could help one another in the development of the target languages through email exchange. They found that students involved in the exchange used a variety of correction strategies that helped students increase accuracy of language form. Bower and Kawaguchi (2011) similarly found that post-chat feedback corrections were beneficial in L2 accuracy. Additionally, they found that students utilized much of the time in the negotiation of meaning for clarification, which helped them understand developmental language gaps.

Kabata and Edasawa (2011) conducted a study about how Japanese and Canadian university students would communicate during asynchronous collaborative projects. The students worked to help one another with language on various school projects in both Japanese and English. Similar to prior studies, learning logs, text messages, and email communication between Japanese and Canadian university students were studied. Kabata and Edasawa found that students provided greater explicit input with regard to different aspects of language forms and grammar. They suggest that because this was a meaningful context-embedded type of learning situation, that incidental learning opportunities could be enhanced. However, students did not explicitly explain why other types of corrections should be made.

How students communicate during classroom and peer-to-peer language exchange and discourse has been the topic of numerous studies. The second half of the literature review is devoted to an overview of seminal and recent discourse analysis, which contributes to this case analysis of face-to-face tandem language learning.

Seminal and Recent Research in Discourse Analysis

Several seminal studies have contributed to the development of the research about classroom discourse, providing various frames of study from which to examine the co-construction of dual language learning among peers. Fanselow (1987), Flanders (1970), and Bellack, Kliebard, Hyman, and Smith (1966) contributed much of the seminal research in classroom discourse analysis about communicative moves and classroom interaction between teacher and student. Flanders (1970) looked at teachers' approaches in identifying student-centered versus teacher-centered classrooms, whereas Fanselow (1987) and Bellack et al. (1966) identified specific units of language communication and pedagogical moves. Fanselow wrote about the importance of not only using linguistic moves or scaffolding types of strategies to teach students, but to utilize powerful nonlinguistic strategies that allow the use of other senses for learning.

The study of communicative strategies in authentic learning contexts reflected a paradigm shift toward the study of authentic social interaction which could promote communicative competence (Hymes, 1972; 1974). Researchers during the 1970s and 1980s became interested in the types of strategies that emerge in natural social language interaction associated with auto- and co-regulated scenarios (Pica & Doughty, 1986; Long, McLean, Adams, & Castaños, 1976; De Avila, Cohen, Intili, 1981). Pica and Doughty (1986) found that when English Learners work with language peers and took responsibility for their own learning, they not only engaged in problem solving and gained social understanding but were also able to engage in greater numbers of speech acts. Language automaticity and structures could be readily acquired through prolonged speech acts during authentic discourse (Lightbown & Spada, 2013). Speech acts are prolonged in particular when students are given specific roles or tasks to fulfil (De Avila, Cohen, & Itili, 1981).

Long et al. (1976) found that when Spanish university students in Mexico worked on specific academic tasks with native English speakers, they were able to extend their speech acts in the target language (Long et al., 1976). The authors organized language learning strategies according to pedagogical moves, social skills, and rhetorical acts. Examples of pedagogical moves that compensate for emergent learner language inadequacies include beginning a new topic, asking for clarification, reformulating a prior assertion—which is similar to rephrasing (see also reformulations in Ware & O'Dowd, 2008)—and providing examples. Furthermore, some examples of social skills include completing another's utterance, inviting others to participate or help, and encouragement. Exemplification, deducing what the speaker will say, and nonlinguistic communication such as drawing and pointing are also included as rhetorical acts (Long et al.).

Self- and co-regulated language learning strategies were similarly identified by Oxford and Nyikos (1989) in their study of 1,200 university foreign language students. Similar to Long et al., they found that language students use "conversational input relational strategies [...] requesting slower speech, asking for pronunciation correction, and guessing what the speaker will say" (p. 293) when communicating with peers. Dörnyei and Scott (1997) created a comprehensive taxonomy that similarly reflects and delineates language learning strategies that have been documented in the literature, including slower speech, translation, response confirmation, and comprehension check. Lafford (2004) who studied language strategies in study abroad situations similarly utilized the same strategies, which, have also been identified by learners in authentic learning abroad while in authentic foreign language settings (Lafford, 2004).

Lafford, who utilized the Dörnyei and Scott (1997) taxonomy, examined two major categories of communication strategies:

1. Interactional strategies utilized in collaborative meaning negotiation, e.g., appeals for help, and
2. Direct strategies, e.g., code-switching, are utilized to increase understanding. Within these two domains, problem-oriented strategies are employed to fill a gap or solve a performance problem.

For interactional strategies, a performance strategy might be employed such as comprehension check. Thus, conferring with the interlocutor. Direct strategies, such as self-repair, is utilized by the learner to correct their own language. For instance, response-repair, or clarification under the heading of direct strategies. Interactional as well as direct strategies allow learners to go around gaps to get a modified version of their point across to the interlocutor.

Lafford (2004) analyzed the communication strategies of 46 U.S. Spanish as foreign language students' communication strategies. Two groups were compared: 20 students who had studied an equivalent of two semesters in the United States (AH group), and 26 students who had similar Spanish study experiences, but additionally engaged in a study abroad program in Alicante, Spain (SH group). Strategies pre- and post-test (after the SA group went to study in Alicante) were compared. Upon pre- and post-test analysis, Lafford found that both groups relied on two major performance strategies: self-repair and accuracy checks. Similarly, they engaged, to a lesser extent, in the use of restructuring of their language to bridge gaps in communication. Notably, the SA group utilized greater self-editing of their language after the study abroad experience whereas the AH group had minimal self-editing change, or greater ability to correct and repair their own speech. While the AH group employed more communication bridging strategies than the SA group. The reduction of communication strategies to support language performance appeared to correspond with their increased interaction and language proficiency achieved in speaking with the home-stay family in Alicante. Winstead (2013) similarly found that once novice Spanish and English learners become more fluent in the target language, there is less need to utilize language strategies for scaffolding. Thus, as communication gaps lessen between speakers, there is less of a need to engage in compensation strategies.

METHODOLOGY

This case study focuses on how a novice EL and SL teach and learn language from one another in an alternative dual language program. Ethnography of speaking approach combined with ideals about speech communities (Dörnyei and Maldarez, 1997; Dörnyei & Scott, 1997; Oxford et al., 1989) provide a framework for describing how peer roles influence the types of tandem language strategies that emerge to extend and move language forward. Hymes' (1974b) ethnography of speaking approach explains the way in which language is communicated as it occurs naturally within the alternative dual language environment, and the roles and status that participants assume within this context. These types of specific communication strategies can be tied to compensation, cognitive, and metacognitive approaches (Oxford et al.).

Research Question

This case study focuses the language strategies that novice adolescent English and Spanish Learners utilize in dual language exchange in order to overcome some language barriers and extend the flow of language communication (Dörnyei & Scott, 1995a; Tarone, 1980). The overarching question posed by this study is, "How do English Learners and Spanish Learners negotiate meaning in a peer-interactive dual language environment when they teach and learn language from one another?"

Study Participants and Context

This case study took place in an alternative dual language program at a rural northern California middle school with 937 students and the following demographics: 58% White, 36% Latino; 2.8% Asian, Pacific Islander, and Filipino; 2.2% African American; and, 1% Native American. Four dyads were recorded throughout the entire course of the program. Ten students participated in the recorded sessions of the afterschool dual language program. The dyad that remained intact throughout the course of the program was chosen for in depth focus and study of language strategies. The pseudonym of Erendira and Cathy identify the English Language Learner and Spanish as a Second Language Learner, respectively. Erendira arrived from Michoacan, Mexico seven months prior to the beginning of the program. In conversations with the parents and the daughter, there was no evidence of the use of loan translations, calquing, and semantic extensions as they are not dominant in the majority language. Cathy, who is White, was born in California and had taken Spanish for seven months before participating in the program and had little prior experience with the language. Both Erendira and Cathy were not fully functioning bilinguals but emergent speakers who volunteered to learn one another's language, English and Spanish respectively. Erendira received ELD and content instruction in the primary language during the day. Cathy was enrolled in the afterschool first year high school Spanish program that was offered to 8th-graders at the middle school.

The researcher provided students with parameters about the dual language program, including the weekly schedule, special bus pick-up information, behavioral expectations (being inclusive and supportive), and the resources they had at their disposal (a facilitative question guide, dictionaries, and realia). The participants understood that the context of teaching and learning was predominantly geared toward oral language exchange. However, they were also afforded opportunities to develop and scaffold their teaching in creative ways (e.g., games, quizzes, and teaching activities). Participants relied on own linguistic repertoire, resources, and strategies to promote communication.

Data Collection

Video data was collected to record the interactions during Spanish and English language sessions. The sessions lasted 35 minutes during each of the 12 language sessions over a period of six weeks. English sessions were rotated with Spanish sessions to promote and ensure equal language status. A math teacher supervised the students involved in the program; however, no instructional support was provided said teacher except for the orientation prior to the course. The video was then analyzed, transcribed, and translated. Just over one hundred pages make up the corpus of data analysis. Audio recordings were utilized to back up language analysis.

Data Analysis

The corpus of bilingual English-Spanish videotaped transcriptions was transcribed verbatim. An independent coding scheme was developed to classify and create typologies of the patterns that emerged from dual language interaction between the two adolescents in a predominantly etic fashion, looking for redundant themes in terms of the strategies used to communicate (Patton, 2002).

While coding for major and redundant themes, the researcher and research assistant analyzed the data across languages recognizing that the roles that the participants assumed as Peer Teacher and Peer Learner influenced the types of language strategies utilized. The hierarchical structure of the language strategies employed was specific to the context of the self- and co-regulated role of peer as teacher or learner. The researcher and research assistant reached an intercoder agreement that stated that Teaching Strategies, Learning Strategies, and Interlingual Strategies best typified the major themes of overall language negotiation and exchange. Subcategories under teaching, learning, and interlingual strategies language exchange were coded and defined in Appendix B. Subcategories as seen in both appendices (A&B) are specific to both teaching and learning strategies identified in the literature (Dörnyei & Scott, 1997).

Inter-Rater Reliability Tested

In order to determine the inter-rater reliability of the strategies based on this coding scheme, the author and research assistant evaluated and tested their ability to comparatively and accurately identify the language codes (strategies). Both independently coded one-fourth of the corpus of the text to determine inter-rater reliability of identification of each strategy in the data subset. Percentages noted in Appendix A represent the level of inter-rater reliability for each language strategy coded based on the following formula: number of language strategies coded correctly / (number of language strategies coded correctly + disagreements) x 100 (Sackett, 1978).

Analysis of Findings

Analysis of the transcription also led the researcher to identify a number of language strategies associated with primarily compensatory and cognitive approaches as identified in Oxford et al. (1989). Both the Peer Learner and the Peer Teacher employed Compensation Strategies. Compensation strategies were utilized by the Peer Teachers to enhance meaning-making and understanding. Language could be compensated through clarification exemplification. Peers Learners incorporated strategies such as Check Meaning to prompt the Peer Teacher to provide information about unknown terminology. Both peer teacher and learning strategies included Slow Speech, Clarification, Checking for Understanding, Guessing, and Translation that surfaced in this study coincide with strategies mentioned in the literature (Dörnyei & Scott, 1997; Lafford, 2004; Long et al., 1976; Oxford et al., 1989; Oxford & Nyikos, 1989;

Tarone, 1980; Winstead, 2013). Analysis revealed how strategies fell into primarily two of the categories: compensatory and cognitive. Interlingual strategies such as voluntary and involuntary code-switching provided unique and depth of information about cognitive, purposeful, and socially motivated interaction. Social code-switching [SOC CODE-SWITCHING], for example, typifies changing language to show comradery and mutual dual language identity. However, involuntary code-switching which was not socially purposeful in nature, was utilized to compensate for gaps in language (See Table 1).

Through their interaction, the Spanish Learner and English Learner dyad employed Teaching and Learning Strategies that would help them negotiate meaning, learn language, and advance language communication flow. Teaching language strategies consisted of administrative moves to keep peers on task, as well as other strategies intended to promote language learning by slowing speech, and correcting and testing language. Thus, novel information about the types of cognitive and administrative strategies associated with learners involved in co-regulated dual language learning similarly emerged (see Table 2).

Cognitive and administrative strategies were employed by the Peer Teacher regardless of the language taught. The cognitive strategies were employed primarily to teach and correct language. Thus the Peer Teacher thought about the language repairs that were needed and offered translations, suggestions, or provided a short explanation or mini-lesson.

The administrative strategies were geared towards ensuring the language learner was on task during language learning interaction. Administrative strategies are also cognitive; however, they are generally more authoritative as a Peer Teacher would make a command to pay attention. Similarly, the Peer Teacher might demand action or encourage (urge) a response or action from the student. At times, nonlinguistic

Table 1. Peer Teacher (PT) & Peer Learner (PL) compensatory teaching, learning, and interlanguage strategies

Compensatory Teaching Strategies	Compensatory Learning Strategies	Compensatory Interlingual Strategies
Linguistic PT Check for understanding PT Check meaning PT Clarification PT Example PT Guess PT Slower speech *Nonlinguistic* PL Gesture PT Point and show PT Point, show, and question	*Linguistic* PL Command check for understanding PL Check meaning PL Dictionary PL Learn language *Nonlinguistic* PL Gesture	PT/PL Translation strategy PT/PL Code switch strategy (involuntary code-switching)

Table 2. Peer teacher cognitive and administrative strategies

Cognitive Strategies	Administrative Strategies
PT Teach/Correct language PT Teach language, cloze (n/a) PT Translation	PT Change topic (Metacognitive strategy) PT Command PT Urging *Nonlinguistic* PT Gesture (encourage response from PL) PT Point and show (encourage response from PL) PT Point, show, and question (prompt a response from PL)

clues such as gesture, point, and show. Gesture point and show was a way to also test the capability of the Peer Learner. Similarly, responses were further prompted after point and show with a question, e.g., what is that?

Changing topic or topic avoidance was an administrative decision intended to promote the continued flow of communication. It was more metacognitive in nature as the Peer Teacher had made a choice not to continue a conversation in the same vein due to linguistic breakdown. Thus, a more difficult topic would be avoided to prevent the halting of the communication flow. Getting out a resource such as dictionary to provide an answer to a question also could prevent would upset the extension of conversation. It appeared that change topic was indicative of a need to continue rather than get stuck.

DISCOURSE ANALYSIS: TEACHING, LEARNING, AND INTERLINGUAL STRATEGIES

Through their interaction, the Spanish Learner and English Learner dyad employed Teaching and Learning Strategies that would help them negotiate meaning, learn language, and advance language communication flow. Teaching Strategies consisted of administrative moves to keep peers on task as well as other strategies intended to promote language learning by slowing speech, correcting and testing language.

Learning strategies similarly employed included the slowing of speech (Slows Speech) incorporated the moves employed by the learner to check for meaning and understanding as well as prompt the Peer Teacher to provide information about unknown terminology. Language Strategies such as Slows Speech, Clarification, Code-Switching, Checking for Understanding, Guessing, and Translation that surfaced in this study coincide with strategies mentioned in the literature (Dörnyei & Scott, 1997; Lafford, 2004; Long et al., 1976; Oxford et al., 1989; Oxford & Nyikos, 1989; Tarone, 1980; Winstead, 2013). Interlingual Strategies in this study also include the use of different types of code-switching which can be voluntary or involuntary. Voluntarily making a choice to purposefully change languages during interaction would be considered cognitive code-switching. Yet voluntary code-switching may be based on social motivation as well. In a social setting such as peer-to-peer situation, social code-switching may occur to show signs of comradery and linguistic sharing within the dual language community. While there is choice and it is cognitive in nature, it is also motivated by social sharing to show linguistic solidarity with peers (Bullock, 2009; Cashman, 2006; Ellwood, 2008).

Teaching Strategies

There are a number of teaching strategies as noted earlier that are also noted as learning strategies (e.g., Comprehension Check, Exemplification, Translation). Those types of strategies that are not listed as either Teaching or Learning strategies are those which are administrative. There is no evidence of a Peer Learner, in this case study, taking an administrative or authoritative type of role when learning language from the Peer Teacher.

Example 1:

1. Cathy (PT): Uhm…Well, we can pretend we're having a phone conversation. Do you want to do that?
2. Erendira (PL): Okay.

3. Cathy (PT): Alright…Uhm…Ring, ring, ring¡!
4. Erendira (PL): *(Laughs).*
5. Cathy (PT): Oh, come on¡! [URGING].
6. Erendira (PL): Ay¡!

Teaching Strategies are employed by the Peer Teacher. Thus, if the language is Spanish, the English Learner takes the lead role. *Urging* is identified as one of the administrative strategies used by the Peer Teacher to keep peers on task and to encourage them to speak in the target language.

In the following Spanish Session, Erendira becomes the Peer Teacher and she utilizes three teaching strategies: Teach Language Cloze, Translation, and Teaches/Corrects Language.

Example 2:

1. Erendira (PT): This is _____ [TEACH LANGUAGE—CLOZE]
2. Cathy (PL): ¿An empty bottle?
3. Erendira (PT): En español es "botella." [TRANSLATION] O.K.? (She writes down b – o – t – e – ll – a on a sheet of paper). [TEACHES/CORRECTS LANGUAGE]
4. Cathy (PL): ¿Botella? [RESPONSE CONFIRM]

Peer Teacher Erendira attempts to use the cloze strategy. However, she has begun to use English instead of Spanish. Realizing the learner has responded in English instead of Spanish (as she used the wrong language in this scenario), she provides Cathy with a translation of the word bottle. She then reinforces her verbal translation by spelling the term. Any type of writing or spelling or correction of either is called the Teach/Correct language strategy. Although Erendira started out in English, she managed to gear the language session towards Spanish. As a consequence, this has given Cathy an opportunity to repeats and confirms the pronunciation of *botella*. This type of repetition to confirm allows the Peer Learner to confirm the appropriate pronunciation as is called a Response Confirm CS.

Because they are incipient bilinguals, it is common for linguistic breakdowns to occur. One of the conscious methods Peer Teachers often implement Topic Avoidance to avoid time that would be lost through correction and explanation (Dörnyei, 1995a). And while language instructors may consider these types of approaches as unorthodox, they are geared toward moving language forward. In the following excerpt, the Peer Teacher is not sure how to say "subject" in Spanish. In this case, she attempts to create a false cognate of the word to see if meaning will occur to the Peer Learner. Cathy is confused yet attempts to advance the conversation despite this linguistic breakdown.

Example 3:

1. Cathy (PL): ¿Qué quiere dice [sic] "subject" en español? [LEARN LANGUAGE] (How do you say "subject" in Spanish?)
2. Erendira (PT): ¿Subject…subjecto¿? ((She says "subjecto" attempting to negotiate meaning by trying to create a *Spanish* cognate.))
3. Cathy (PL): Yeah…*um* ((Cathy scratches her head)) Sometimes *ah* I can remember it. Sometimes I can remember it.
4. ((LINGUISTIC BREAKDOWN— PT Erendira changes the topic))
5. Erendira (PT): ¿Tienes buenos grados? [TOPIC AVOIDANCE] (Do you have good grades?)

6.   Cathy (PL): No sé grados (I don't know "degrees")…Oh. ((Cathy then realizes that the false cognate "grados" is utilized for the word grades or *calificaciones*)). A, pocos A's (A, a few A's).

As the Peer Teacher, Erendira takes action to help restore the flow of communication, she deliberately avoids the prior topic and introduces a new topic—grades. This alternative linguistic detour—employing a false cognate—did not work the first time, but when employed again, it did aid in helping the Peer Learner comprehend in the latter part of the conversation and helped to extend the flow of communication (Ellwood, 2008; Dörnyei & Scott, 1997). Erendira is conscious of her partner's language capabilities and has adjusted language within their zone of proximal development (Dörnyei & Scott, 1997; Vygotsky, 1988, Krashen & Terrel, 1983) through the use of a false cognate. A language instructor probably would not make this kind of move but provide the language equivalent, stop the conversation, and provide additional scaffolding to explain the term which might stymie the language flow. The use false cognate may be included in the types of unorthodox pedagogical moves evinced in natural language learning situations (e.g., study abroad, alternative dual language community) in which the native speaker may be unable to provide translations of appropriate language usage.

Learning Strategies

There are a number of teaching strategies that are strategies that are also employed by the Peer Learner, yet generally to a lesser extent than the Peer Teacher. These strategies include Check Meaning, Exemplification, Translation, and types of Repetitive Strategies. Learning Strategies soley employed by Peer Learners in this study include Learn Language, and Learn Language Cloze.

When Peer Learners want to learn language from their Peer Teacher, they employ the learn language strategy [LEARN LANGUAGE]. The learn language strategy was employed regularly the Peer Learners in all of the English and Spanish sessions. The Peer Learner utilizes this useful phrase to request the translation of a word, *"¿Qué quiere decir _____ en español"* from the Peer Teacher? "What does _____ mean in Spanish?" In this way, the Peer Learner does not necessarily play a passive role in their learning of the language but can also gain language knowledge using active appeals for help (Dörnyei & Scott, 1997). Thus, while the Peer Teacher is the expert and authority, there is room for the Peer Learner to co-facilitate the learning of the target language. In the following case, the Peer Teacher, or expert in the target language, translates for the Peer Learner.

Example 4:

1.   Cathy (PL): Agua…¿Cómo se dice "please" en español? [LEARN LANGUAGE] (Water…How do you say "please" in Spanish?)
2.   Erendira (PT): Por favor. [TRANSLATION] (Please.)

Nakahama, Tyler, and Van Leir (2002) identify the Learn Language Strategy as a comprehension check used in repair negotiation. In this case, however, the emergent Peer Learner consciously utilized this strategy as a way to acquire language she may have forgotten from her Spanish class. Furthermore, Cathy utilizes her Peer Teacher as a language resource, much like a dictionary. Thus, much of the exchange that occur between the Peer Teacher and Peer Learner is interactional based on a number of phrases that have become automatic but also allows the learner to speak in the target language while appealing for help (Dörnyei & Scott, 1997).

Thus, the Learn Language Strategy is not only important for helping the student learn language but in promoting communicative flow. This type of strategy allows the student to come up with a term or phrase that could lead to a variety of topic changes as well. In this case, Cathy as the Peer Learner initiates a conversation about Erendira's family, but she does not know how to say the term "relative" in Spanish.

Example 5:

1. Cathy (PL): ¿Qué quiere decir "relative" en español? [LEARN LANGUAGE] (How do you say "relative" in Spanish?)
2. Erendira (PT): I don't know. [CHECK MEANING]
3. Cathy (PL): Oh, nosotros *fuimos* [APPLICATION] visitar mis papás [EXEMPLIFICATION] (Oh, we went to visit my parents.)
4. Erendira (PT): Oh, tus familiares. [TEACHES/CORRECTS LANGUAGE] [TRANSLATION] (Oh, your relatives.)
5. Cathy (PL): Familiares. [RESPONSE CONFIRM] (Relatives.)

Again, Erendira does not know the meaning of "relative" in Spanish until Cathy uses an alternative phrase such as *mis papas* (my parents). Thus, Peer Learner Cathy has facilitated the flow of communication by utilizing Exemplification. By giving an example, Cathy not only negotiated meaning in a way that Erendira could understand, but it also gave Erendira an opportunity for her to teach language through translation of the term relative (*familiares*). In using this CS, the Peer Learner has provided support for the enhanced flow of communication for the Peer Teacher as well. Also within this excerpt, Cathy's Response and Confirm demonstrated that she understood the new term in the target language and could apply it.[1]

Application

Application is not a language strategy but denotes the ability of the Peer Learner to apply the correct form of the language learned during language sessions. "[…] cognitive psychology shows that learning strategies helps learners assimilate new information into their own existing mental structures or schemata, thus creating increasingly rich and complex schemata" (Oxford and Nyikos, 1989, p. 291). It is a way to document how learning strategies help peers assimilate and acquire language.

As noted in the previous example, the past-tense of infinitive "to go" which is utilized in the first person plural "we went" or *nosotros fuimos* has been employed by Peer Learner Cathy. Cathy had not been taught the past tense of *ir* "to go" in her first-year Spanish class, but has come to know the meaning of *fuimos* (went) in prior language sessions (as noted in transcripts) with her Peer Teacher and now correctly applies the this conversation with Erendira. Thus, Application is not a strategy but shows the ability of the learner to acquire language through multiple exposures and then apply a term or phrase later on separate occasions. Cathy employed the phrase in a prior session and then again in the one noted above.

In another language session, Cathy kept incorrectly said more or less in Spanish. She would say *muchos o pocos* (much or little). Only after Peer Teacher Erendira utilized repetition, slow speech and pronunciation strategies was Cathy able to apply or adopt the correct form of "more or less" (*más o menos*) as evidenced in later language sessions.

Interlingual Strategies

Interlingual Strategies are generally used by either the Peer Learner or the Peer Teacher as they share language. Two types of code-switching were quite common: Cognitive and Involuntary code-switching. In the case of Cognitive Code-switching, the speaker deliberately uses the primary language, as noted blow, when teaching the language partner as a way to ensure understanding.

Example 7:

1. Erendira (PT): ¿Te gustan los "chips"? (Do you like the "chips") [COGNITIVE CODE-SWITCHING]
2. Cathy (PL): Chips [RESPONSE REPHRASE] ((she then nods yes)). [GESTURE]
3. Erendira (PT): Estos te gustan más ((she points to the Munch 'Ems and later to other items)) [POINT/SHOW] (You like these more.)
4. Cathy (PL): Me gusta chocolate. (I like chocolate.) ((She leaves out the article "el" before "chocolate."))

The intersentential switch is denoted as voluntary switch versus borrowing (McClure, 1992). This voluntary switch is not only cognitive but also social in nature. And in some ways, the decision to translanguage may be also considered metacognitive. Due to her exposure to English during this time, Erendira has acquired the word "chips" in her vocabulary.

The researcher asserts that individuals in Mexico who live near the borderlands may switch to "chips" as a borrowed term; however, those who live in the interior of Mexico in states such as Michoacan, where Erendira is from, generally refrain from using borrowed words from English when speaking Spanish (Galindo, 1996; Hidalgo, 1986).[2] Moreover, Erendira is an emergent speaker who, when participating in this program, had been in the United States for less than six months. Thus, the researcher postulates, Erendira concsiously inserts the English word chips during the Spanish Session as she has come to anticipate that her partner may not understand the Spanish term *papitas*, and as a way to avoid a linguistic breakdown (Vygotsky, 1988). Furthermore, the peers were socializing after break. And, they were smiling and laughing. This move is also strategic way of ensuring comprehension within the zone of proximal development of the learner (Savignon & Sysoyev, 2005).

Thus, Peer Teachers appear to be somewhat aware of the language peer's competence and utilize strategies such as code-switching to enhance the flow of communication (Dörnyei & Scott, 1997). Peers who participated in a similar dual language program talked about how their partner's came to know their learning needs better (Winstead, 2013). This recognition of the other person's capability shows that self-directed adolescent peers are thoughtful and strategic not only about language exchange but are also cognizant of what code-switching may be necessary to promote language comprehension as well as move language forward.

Peers would also use nonlinguistic cues to further enhance the flow of communication and facilitate comprehension. In the aforementioned excerpt, Erendira points to the other type of chips that she knows (from prior experience during language sessions) that Cathy likes.[3] For the Peer Teacher, gesturing and pointing to concrete objects and stating their meaning allows for the teaching and immediate understanding of the lexicon at hand. And the visual, which reinforces the language, can also prompt further communication in the target language. When the Peer Teacher, points to chocolates Cathy now responds by saying she likes chocolate *Me gusta [el] chocolate*. Thus, the Peer Teacher facilitates and reinforces the idea of liking something which provides an opportunity for Cathy to extend the conversation and state that she likes chocolate.

In the following instance, the type of code-switching that takes place is not purposeful and is therefore indicated by [INV CODE-SWITCHING]. Erendira understands the question but does not know how to say skating or skates, so she involuntarily code-switches to the Spanish term *patinas* (saying skates instead of *patinar* which means to skate). And, because *patinar, cantar, bailar* are some of the recognizable vocabulary that students have learned in Spanish class, Cathy remembers this term from Spanish class (along with others, *cantar* and *bailar*) and is able to promote the flow of conversation by literally translating the term in response "skate" although sounding a little unsure. In not knowing the term, skates, Erendira alternatively employs a term can communicate, "study."

Example 8:

1. Cathy (PT): *Uh*…What do you like to do after school?
2. Erendira (PL): Patinas…and study. ((She responds in Spanish first, stating skates, patinas, the noun instead of the verb and then answers the words that she can say about what she does after school in English) [INV CODE-SWITCHING] (Skates…and study.)
3. Cathy (PT): Skate? [TRANSLATION]

In the following example, Erendira she asks Cathy about her grade point average. Despite the fact that she is the Peer Teacher in this instance and knows the term for grade point average (*el promedio de calificaciones*), she chooses switch again to English during the Spanish session.

Example 9:

1. Erendira (PT): ¿Cuál es tu GPA? (What is your GPA?) ((She states "GPA" or grade point average using the acronym in English.)) [COGNITIVE CODE-SWITCHING]
2. Cathy (PL): Tres *point, oh yeah*, siete uno cuatro [INV CODE-SWITCHING]. Es (Is)//
3. Erendira (PT): Three point seven one four [TRANSLATION].

Further analysis of the text reveals how Peer Learner (Cathy) uses Involuntary Code-switching when she cannot find the term for point (*punto*) in Spanish. Additionally, she says 'Oh yeah." Dörnyei (1995) describes these as "hesitation devices" that help move conversation, and while hesitation devices were not noted in this study, this provides additional understanding about language flow and communication.

In another espisode, Cathy is the Peer Teacher and Erendira is the Peer Learner. They are talking about their favorite activities and Cathy utilizes Exemplification by offering examples or choices. These choices provide opportunities for further language. If the Peer Learner is not familiar with one term, she may be able to talk about another. Erendira talks about going out with her friends. Erendira has answered one of the options although it appears that she may not truly understand.

Example 10:

1. Cathy (PT): Uh huh…Uh…Okay. What's your favorite activity, like drawing? [EXEMPLIFICATION]
2. Erendira (PL): I like to go with my friends.
3. Cathy (PT): I'm always busy with basketball. So, I don't have much time to talk with my friends except at school here…Okay. Let's see…Uhm. What's like your favorite time of the day—like morning, mid-morning, afternoon, evening? [EXEMPLIFICATION]
4. Erendira (PL): I like tonight?

5.   Cathy (PT): Tonight? [RESPONSE CONFIRM] Night? [TEACHES/CORRECTS LANGUAGE]
6.   Erendira (PL): Yeah.
7.   Cathy (PT): Oh, you like the night-time *en la noche* (at night), that's fun. [SOC CODE-SWITCHING] [TRANSLATION]

Here is another example of a time when Cathy is the Peer Teacher and decides to use employ the Spanish words *en la noche* during the English lesson to share bilingual language ability with her language partner. While this could possibly identified as a Translation strategy; it does occur in midsentence and may be designated as code-switching (McClure, 1992).

This type of voluntary social code-switching tends to become more common as the students' progress in their dual language development and as they share a co- identity as members of their speech community (Bullock, 2009; Cashman, 2006; Ellwood, 2008). Social Code-Switching is generally indicated when a Peer Teacher may not have an academic reason to switch to the Peer Learner's native language during target language sessions. Instead, the Peer Teacher may be motivated to do so as a way to show mutual bilingual growth as well as bilingual, or to encourage responses from the Peer Learner (Santiago-Rivera et al., 2009). While Social Code-Switching and Cognitive Code-Switching are difficult to identify, they are concepts that should be further addressed in the literature with regard to peer teaching and learning environments.

Correcting language by providing a correct response versus stating that a student has said something wrong is also useful practice. For instance, Erendira teaches Cathy the appropriate way to say "more or less." The verbalized modeling of corrected language benefits the student who will hear it and may voluntarily repeat it, as in the case of Cathy. Once the student has applied the correct form in a number of instances then there is a greater chance for appropriate application in the future. Other complementary strategies such as clarification and urging are ways for the student teachers to monitor their partner's progress and understanding.

CONCLUSION

This study reveals the types of strategies that emerged during the verbal interplay between native speakers of Spanish and of English who have fewer opportunities to interact in mainstream school settings. Teacher-less tasks such as language practice between peers encouraged more turn-taking and engaged in more speech acts as peers are prompted by language peers and fill in each other's utterances and repair language can be seen in opportunities in which students teach and correct language, utilize cloze strategies, as well as code-switch (Shannon, 1990; Kramsch, 1987; Pica & Doughty, 1986; Lightbown & Spada, 2013).

The context of the environment including the norms of the program had a bearing on how the Peer Teachers and Peer learners interacted and the status conferred upon the nondominant language learners. In this self-directed alternative dual language community, there were no rules about the appropriate use of grammar or scaffolding but the idea that language learning was to occur and be facilitated by the Peer Teacher. Peer Teachers were given full authority and were considered the experts in the program thereby promoting equal status for those speaking the non-dominant language, Spanish (Jimenez, 2000; Dörnyei & Scott, 1997; Melville, 1983; Hymes, 1974b).

Perhaps more importantly, these roles affected the types of language strategies employed by peers. Strategies were often related to whether the peer was in the Teacher or Learner role and who initiated the strategy. This conferred responsibility also caused solely the Peer Teacher to engage in administrative types of strategies that would promote the flow of communication (e.g., Urging, Topic Avoidance or topic changes). Topic Avoidance emerged as powerful alternative linguistic that helps learners avoid linguistic breakdowns (Dörnyei & Scott, 1997; Dörnyei, 1995).

Thus, in their attempts to teach and learn language, powerful yet sometimes unorthodox language strategies were used to repair language and fill resource gaps in order to enhance the flow of communication (e.g., switching to the primary language during the target language sessions, utilizing a false cognate to facilitate communication) (Ellwood, 2009; Kratzis, Tang, & Koyment, 2009). These incipient bilinguals were, even at emergent levels, could engage in and become aware of their peer's ability and choose language they believed would enhance their conversational ability (Hwang, 2009; Dörnyei & Scott, 1997; Vygotsky, 1988). While some of these "language detours" employed by the Peer Teacher would be considered unorthodox in a formal classroom language setting, it may not be unusual to see these sorts of strategies used between native speakers and language learners in more natural settings such as study abroad environments (Lafford, 2005; Dörnyei & Scott, 1997; Oxford & Nyikos, 1989; Long, McLean, & Castaños, 1976). In these cases, it appears that the goal is not perfect language communication but the idea of moving language forward and not getting stuck in the details (Lafford, 2004; Canale & Swain, 1980; Tarone, 1980).

Despite some use of these unorthodox approaches, the Peer Teachers are conscious of their speech acts, are aware of what may cause linguistic breakdowns, and have become aware of the Peer Learner's capabilities and attempt to compensate for that lexical inaccessibility through this type of language scaffolding (Dörnyei & Scott, 1997). Unlike instructors in classroom settings, Peer Teachers will deviate from what might be an appropriate classroom method or strategy for ensuring that the language learner understands language forms and definitions correctly (e.g., employing the false cognate).

Similarly, important was the opportunity for students to practice language within their zone of proximal development via alternative linguistic detours to extend communication opportunities (Ellwood, 2009; Dörnyei & Scott, 1997; Vygotsky, 1988). Therefore, further research could be conducted about how traditional language approaches could be paired with face-to-face dual language programs or online tandem learning. Teachers may be better able to instruct and teach students how to address linguistic breakdowns by using strategies other than Topic Avoidance or Code-switching which would further enhance communication flow and language acquisition (Dörnyei & Scott, 1997; Cashman, 2005).

The study of tandem learning provides a model from which to further analyze the study of tandem learning and the language strategies utilized by peers in face-to-face as well as online formats. Online tandem language scenarios are inexpensive and can be utilized to promote language practice as well as inform instructor practice in the field. While much of the data in the past has been video and or audio-recorded and transcribed, new online research venues can also provide researcher with opportunities to explore dual language communication through speech recognition technology (Jones, Squires, & Hicks, 2008). Through evaluation of the common patterns of language strategy use and identification possible breakdowns, researchers can gain insights about language gaps and how to support learners in tandem scenarios. Future research should focus on the linguistic breakdowns that stymie tandem language conversations and acknowledge alternative strategies that promote authentic language interaction that benefits heritage language learners who are ELLs in schools.

REFERENCES

Angelova, M., Gunawardena, D., & Volk, D. (2006). Peer teaching and learning: Co-constructing language in a dual language first grade. *Language and Education, 20*(3), 173–190. doi:10.1080/09500780608668722

Appel, C., & Mullen, T. (2000). Pedagogical considerations for a web-based tandem language learning environment. *Computers & Education, 34*(3), 291–308. doi:10.1016/S0360-1315(99)00051-2

Arellano-Houchin, A., Flamenco, C., Merlos, M. M., & Segura, L. (2001). Has California's passage of Proposition 227 made a difference in the way we teach? *The Urban Review, 33*(3), 221–235. doi:10.1023/A:1010366004719

Azizinezhad, M., Hashemi, M., & Darvishi, S. (2013). Application of cooperative learning in EFL classes to enhance the students' language learning. *Procedia: Social and Behavioral Sciences, 93*, 138–141. doi:10.1016/j.sbspro.2013.09.166

Barker, V., Giles, H., Noels, K., Duck, J., Hecht, M. L., & Clément, R. (2001). The English-only movement: A communication analysis of changing perceptions of language vitality. *Journal of Communication, 51*(1), 3–37. doi:10.1111/j.1460-2466.2001.tb02870.x

Beardsmore, H. (2008). Language promotion by European supranational institutions. In O. García (Ed.), *Bilingual Education in the 21st Century* (pp. 197–217). Chichester: Wiley-Blackwell.

Bellack, A. A., Kliebard, H. M., Hyman, R. T., & Smith, F. L. Jr. (1966). *The language of the classroom.* New York: Teachers College.

Bialystok, E. (1983). Some factors in the selection and implementation of communication strategies. In C. Faerch & G. Kaspar (Eds.), *Strategies in interlanguage communication* (pp. 100–118). Harlow, UK: Longman.

Block, N. (2011). The impact of two-way dual immersion programs on initially English-dominant Latino students' attitudes. *Bilingual Research Journal, 34*(2), 125–141. doi:10.1080/15235882.2011.598059

Block, N. C. (2011). Perceived impact of two-way dual immersion programs on Latino students' relationships in their families and communities. *International Journal of Bilingual Education and Bilingualism, 15*(2), 235–257. doi:10.1080/13670050.2011.620079

Bower, J., & Kawaguchi, S. (2011). Negotiation of meaning and corrective feedback in Japanese/English eTandem. *Language Learning & Technology, 15*(1), 41–71.

Brammerts, H. (1996). Language learning in tandem using the internet. In M. Warschauer (Ed.), *Telecollaboration in Foreign Language Learning, Second Language Teaching and Curriculum Center, Universtiy of Hawai'i* (pp. 121–130). Manoa.

Brisk, M. E., & Harrington, M. M. (2000). *Literacy and bilingualism: A handbook for alAl teachers.* Mahwah, N.J.: Lawrence Earlbaum Associates.

Bullock, B. (2009). Themes in the study of code-switching. In The Cambridge Handbook of Linguistic Code-Switching (pp. 1-17).

Canale, M., & Swain, M. (1980). Theoretical bases of communicative approaches to second language teaching and testing. *Applied Linguistics*, *1*(1), 1–47. doi:10.1093/applin/1.1.1

Cashman, H. (2005). Identities at play: Language preference and group membership in bilingual talk in interaction. *Journal of Pragmatics*, *37*(3), 301–315. doi:10.1016/j.pragma.2004.10.004

Çelik, S., Aytin, K., & Bayram, E. (2013). Implementing cooperative learning in the language classroom: Opinions of Turkish teachers of English. *Social and Behavioral Sciences*, *70*, 1852–1859.

Chen, J. J., & Yang, S. C. (2014). Fostering foreign language learning through technology-enhanced intercultural projects. *Language Learning & Technology*, *18*(1), 57–75. Retrieved from http://llt.msu.edu/issues/february2014/chenyang.pdf

Clark, K. (2009). The case for Structured English Immersion. *Educational Leadership*, *66*(7), 42–46.

CTC. (2014). Serving English Learners. State of California Commission on Teacher Credentialing. Retrieved from http://www.ctc.ca.gov/credentials/leaflets/cl622.pdf

Cummins, J. (1979). Cognitive/academic language proficiency, linguistic interdependence, the optimum age question and some other matters. *Working Papers on Bilingualism*, *19*, 121–129.

Darder, A., & Uriarte, M. (2013). The politics of restrictive language policies: A postcolonial analysis of language and schooling. *Postcolonial Directions in Education*, *2*(1), 6–67.

De Avila, E., Cohen, E., & Intili, J. (1981). Multicultural improvement of cognitive abilities. *Final Report to the California State Department of Education*.

Dörnyei, Z. (1995). On the teachability of communication strategies. *TESOL Quarterly*, *29*(1), 55–85. doi:10.2307/3587805

Dörnyei, Z. (2000). Motivation in action: Towards a process-oriented conceptualization of student motivation. *The British Journal of Educational Psychology*, *70*(4), 519–538. doi:10.1348/000709900158281 PMID:11191185

Dörnyei, Z., & Malderez, A. (1997). Group dynamics and foreign language teaching. *System*, *25*(1), 65–81. doi:10.1016/S0346-251X(96)00061-9

Dörnyei, Z., & Scott, M. L. (1997). Communication strategies in a second language: Definitions and taxonomies. *Language Learning*, *47*(1), 173–210. doi:10.1111/0023-8333.51997005

Elia, A. (2006). Language learning in tandem via Skype. *The Reading Matrix*, *6*(3), 269–280.

Fanselow, J. F. (1987). *Breaking rules: Generating and exploring alternatives in language teaching*. White Plains, NY: Longman, Inc.

Fitts, S., Winstead, L., Weisman, E., Flores, S., & Valenciana, C. (2008). Coming to voice: Preparing bilingual-bicultural teachers for social justice. *Equity & Excellence in Education*, *40*(3), 357–371. doi:10.1080/10665680802174916

Flanders, N. A. (1970). *Analyzing teaching behavior*. Menlo Park, CA: Addison-Wesley.

Flores, S. (2005). Teaching Latino children and youth. *High School Journal*, *88*(2), 1–2. doi:10.1353/hsj.2004.0022

Galindo, D. L. (1996). Language use and language attitudes: A study of border women. *Bilingual Review*, *21*, 1, 5–17.

García, O., & Wei, (2014). *Translanguaging: Language, Bilingualism and Education*. New York: Palgrave MacMillan.

Helot, C. (2003). Language policy and the ideology of bilingual education in France. *Language Policy*, *2*(3), 255–277. doi:10.1023/A:1027316632721

Hidalgo, M. (1986). Language contact, language loyalty, and prejudice on the Mexican border. *Language in Society*, *15*(21), 193–220. doi:10.1017/S004740450000018X

Hwang, S. (2009). A Vygotskian approach to heterogeneous communication and multi/cultural literacy: Commentary on David Kellog's "Taking uptaking up, or, a deconstructionist 'ontology of different' and a developmental one." *Mind, Culture, and Activity*, *16*(2), 191–197. doi:10.1080/10749030802590614

Hymes, D. (1972). On communicative competence. In J. B. Pride & J. Holmes (Eds.), *Sociolinguistics (pp. 269-293)*. Harmondsworth: Penguin.

Hymes, D. (1974). Ways of Speaking. In R. Bauman & J. Sherzer (Eds.), *Explorations in the Ethnography of Speaking (pp. 433-451)*. Cambridge: Cambridge University Press.

Jagers, R. (2001). Cultural integrity and social and emotional competence promotion: Work notes on moral competence. *The Journal of Negro Education*, *70*(1/2), 59–71.

Jagers, R. T. (2001). Cultural integrity and social and emotional competence promotion: Work notes on moral competence. *The Journal of Negro Education*, *70*(1/2), 59–71.

James, G. (2007). The affordances of social psychology of the ecological approach to social knowing. *Theory & Psychology*, *17*(2), 265–279. doi:10.1177/0959354307075046

JimenezR.T. (2000).

Jimenez, R. T. (2000, January01). Literacy and the identity development of Latino/a students. *American Educational Research Journal*, *37*(4), 971–1000. doi:10.3102/00028312037004971

Jones, G., Squires, T., & Hicks, J. (2008). Combining speech recognition/natural language processing with 3d online learning environments to create distributed authentic and situated spoken language learning. *Journal of Educational Technology Systems*, *36*(4), 375–392. doi:10.2190/ET.36.4.c

Kabata, K., & Edasawa, Y. (2011). Tandem language learning through a cross-cultural keypal project. *Language Learning & Technology*, *15*(1), 104–121.

Kramsch, C. J. (1987). Theory in to practice. *Teaching Foreign Languages*, *26*(4), 243–250.

Krashen, S., & Terrell, T. (1983). *The natural approach*. Hayward, California: The Alemany Press.

Krashen, S. D. (1987). *Principles and Practice in Second Language Acquisition*. Prentice-Hall International.

Kyratzis, A., Tang, Y., & Koymen, S. B. (2009). Codes, code-switching, and context: Style and footing in peer group bilingual play. *Multilingua*, *28*(2-3), 265–290. doi:10.1515/mult.2009.012

Lafford, B. A. (2004). The effect of the context of learning on the use of communication strategies by learners of Spanish as a second language. *Studies in Second Language Acquisition*, *26*(2), 201–225. doi:10.1017/S0272263104262039

Lam, W. S. E. (2004). Second language socialization in a bilingual chat room: Global and local considerations. *Language Learning & Technology*, *8*(3), 44–65.

Lee, L. (2009). Promoting intercultural exchanges with blogs and podcasting: A study of Spanish–American telecollaboration. *Computer Assisted Language Learning*, *22*(5), 425–443. doi:10.1080/09588220903345184

Levy, M. (1997). *Computer-assisted language learning: Context and conceptualization*. New York: Clarendon Press.

Liem, A. D., Lau, S., & Nie, Y. (2008). The role of self-efficacy, task value, and achievement goals in predicating learning strategies, task disengagement, peer relationship, and achievement outcome. *Contemporary Educational Psychology*, *33*(4), 486–512. doi:10.1016/j.cedpsych.2007.08.001

Lightbown, P. M., & Spada, N. (2013). *How languages are learned*. Oxford: Oxford University Press.

Long, M. H., Adams, L., McLean, M., & Castaños, F. (1976). Doing things with words—verbal interaction in lockstep and small group classroom situations. In J. Fanselow & R. Crymes (Eds.), *On TESOL '76*. Washington, D.C.: TESOL.

Magnan, S., & Back, M. (2007). Social interaction and linguistic gain during study abroad. *Foreign Language Annals*, *40*(1), 43–61. doi:10.1111/j.1944-9720.2007.tb02853.x

Martinez-Roldan, C. M., & Malave, G. (2004). Language ideologies mediating literacy and identify in bilingual contexts. *Journal of Early Childhood Literacy*, *4*(2), 155–180. doi:10.1177/1468798404044514

McClure, E. (1992). The pragmatics of code-switching in Mexican political, literary, and news magazines. *Pragmatics and Language Learning*, *3*, 182–196.

Melville, M. B. (1983). Ethnicity: An analysis of its dynamism and variability focusing on the Mexican/Anglo/Mexican American interface. *American Ethnologist*, *10*(2), 272–289. doi:10.1525/ae.1983.10.2.02a00040

Nakahama, Y., Tyler, A., & Van Lier, L. (2001). Negotiating meaning. *TESOL Quarterly*, *35*(3), 377–405. doi:10.2307/3588028

O'Dowd, R. (2013). Telecollaboration and CALL. In M. Thomas, H. Reinders, & M. Warshauer (Eds.), Contemporary omputer-assisted language learning (pp. 123–140). London: Bloomsbury Academic. Retrieved from http://site.ebrary.com/lib/uon/detail.action?docID=10632566

Oxford, R., Lavine, R. Z., & Crookall, D. (1989). Language learning strategies, the communicative approach, and their classroom implications. *Foreign Language Annals*, *22*(1), 29–39. doi:10.1111/j.1944-9720.1989.tb03139.x

Oxford, R., & Nyikos, S. (1989). Variables affecting choice of language strategy by university students. *Modern Language Journal, 73*(3), 291–301. doi:10.1111/j.1540-4781.1989.tb06367.x

Padilla, A., Lindholm, K., Chen, A., Duran, R., Hakuta, K., Lambert, W., & Tucker, G. R. (1991). The English-only movement: Myths, reality, and implications for psychology. *The American Psychologist, 46*(2), 120–130. doi:10.1037/0003-066X.46.2.120

Palmer, D. (2010). Race, power, and equity in a multiethnic urban elementary school with a dual-language "strand" program. *Anthropology & Education Quarterly, 41*(1), 94–114. doi:10.1111/j.1548-1492.2010.01069.x

Patton, M. Q. (2002). *Qualitative research and evaluation methods*. Thousand Oaks, CA: Sage.

Phinney, J. S., Horencyzk, G., Liebkind, K., & Vedder, P. (2001). Ethnic identity, immigration, and well-being: An interactional perspective. *The Journal of Social Issues, 57*(3), 493–510. doi:10.1111/0022-4537.00225

Pica, T., & Doughty, C. (1986). The role of groupwork in classroom second language acquisition. *Studies in Second Language Acquisition, 7*(2), 233–248. doi:10.1017/S0272263100005398

Rogers, M. (2016). Demand high for dual immersion in Utah. *The Salt Lake Tribune*, http://archive.sltrib.com/story.php?ref=/sltrib/news/54591846-78/language-programs-chinese-dual.html.csp

Sackett, C. P. (1978). *Observing Behavior* (Vol. 2). Baltimore: University Press.

San Miguel, G., Jr. (2008). The schooling of Mexicanos in the southwest, 1848-1891.

Santiago-Rivera, A. L., Altarriba, J., Poll, N., Gonzalez-Miller, N., & Cragun, C. (2009). Therapists' views on working with bilingual Spanish-English speaking clients. *Professional Psychology, Research and Practice, 40*(5), 436–443. doi:10.1037/a0015933

Savignon, S. J., & Sysoyev, P. V. (2005). Cultures and comparisons: Strategies for learners. *Foreign Language Annals, 38*(3), 357–365. doi:10.1111/j.1944-9720.2005.tb02222.x

Schildkarut, D. J. (2001). Official-English and the states: Influences on declaring English the official language in the United States. *Political Research Quarterly, 54*(2), 445–447. doi:10.1177/106591290105400211

Shannon, S. M. (1990). English in the barrio: The quality of contact among immigrant children. *Hispanic Journal of Behavioral Sciences, 12*(3), 256–276. doi:10.1177/07399863900123002

Sinclair, J. M., & Coulthard, M. (1975). *Towards an analysis of discourse*. London: Oxford University.

Skerrett, A. (2012). Languages and literacies in translocation: Experiences and perspectives of a transnational youth. *Journal of Literacy Research, 44*(4), 364–395. doi:10.1177/1086296X12459511

Slotte, V., & Tynjälä, P. (2005). Communication and collaborative learning at work: Views expressed on a cross-cultural eLearning course. *International Journal on E-Learning, 4*(2), 191–207.

Spörer, N., & Brunstein, J. C. (2009). Fostering reading comprehension of secondary school students through peer-assisted learning: Affects on strategy knowledge, strategy use, and task performance. *Contemporary Educational Psychology, 34*(4), 289–297. doi:10.1016/j.cedpsych.2009.06.004

Sun, Y.-C. (2009). Voice blog: An exploratory study of language learning. *Language Learning & Technology, 13*, 88–103.

Sykes, J. M. (2005). Synchronous CMC and pragmatic development: Effects of oral and written chat. *CALICO Journal, 22*, 399–432. Retrieved from https://calico.org/p-5-Calico%20Journal.html

Tarone, E. (1977). Conscious communication strategies in interlanguage. A progress report. In H.D. Brown, C.A., Yoio & R.C. Crymes (Eds.), On TESOL '77 (pp. 194-203). Washington: TESOL.

Tarone, E. (1980). Communication strategies, foreigner talk and repair in interlanguage. *Language Learning, 30*(2), 417–431. doi:10.1111/j.1467-1770.1980.tb00326.x

The Elusive Quest for Equality. InMoreno, J. F. (Ed.), *The Elusive Quest for Equality: 150 Years of Chicano/Chicana Education* (pp. 31–52). Cambridge: Harvard Educational Review.

Thomas, W. P., & Collier, V. P. (2002). A national study of school effectiveness for language minority students' long-term academic achievement. Eric Digest, ED475 048 FL 027 622.

Thurston, A., Duran, D., Cunningham, E., Blanch, S., & Topping, K. (2009). International on-line reciprocal peer tutoring to promote modern language development in primary schools. *Computers & Education, 53*(2), 462–472. doi:10.1016/j.compedu.2009.03.005

Tolbert, C. J., & Hero, R. E. (2001). Dealing with diversity: Racial/ethnic context and social policy change. *Political Research Quarterly, 54*(3), 571–604. doi:10.1177/106591290105400305

Tse, L. (2001). Resisting and reversing language shift: Heritage-language resilience among U.S. native biliterates. *Harvard Educational Review, 71*(4), 676–708. doi:10.17763/haer.71.4.ku752mj536413336

U.S. Department of Education. (2016). Title 1—Improving the academic achievement of the disadvantaged. U.S. Department of Education. Retrieved from http://www2.ed.gov/policy/elsec/leg/esea02/pg1.html

Ventriglia, L. (1982). *Conversations of Miguel and Maria: How children learn English as a Second Language*. Menlo Park, CA: Addison-Wesley.

Vertovec, S. (2001). Transnationalism and identity. *Journal of Ethnic and Migration Studies, 27*(4), 573–582. doi:10.1080/13691830120090386

Vertovec, S. (2004). Migrant transnationalism and modes of transformation. *International Migration Review, 38*(3), 970–1001. doi:10.1111/j.1747-7379.2004.tb00226.x

Vinagre, M., & Muñoz, B. (2011). Computer-mediated corrective feedback and language accuracy in telecollaborative exchanges. *Language Learning & Technology, 15*(1), 72–103.

Vygotsky, L. S. (1988). Interaction in learning and development. In P. A. Richard-Amato (Ed.), *Making it happen: Interaction in the second language classroom*. White Plains, NY: Longman.

Ware, P., & O'Dowd, R. (2008). Peer feedback on language form in telecollaboration. *Language Learning & Technology, 12*(1), 43–63.

Wharton, G. (2000). Language learning strategy use of bilingual foreign language learner in Singapore. *Language Learning, 50*(2), 203–243. doi:10.1111/0023-8333.00117

Wilson, D. M. (2011). Dual language programs on the rise: "Enrichment" model puts content learning front and center for ELL students. *Harvard Education Letter*, 27(2). Retrieved from https://www.berkeleyparentsnetwork.org/recommend/schools/berkeley/immersion

Winstead, L. (2013). Apprehension and motivation among adolescent dual language peers: Perceptions and awareness about self-directed teaching and learning. *Language and Education*, 27(1), 1–21. doi:1 0.1080/09500782.2012.669767

Wong-Fillmore, L. (1983). The language learner as an individual: implications of research on individual difference for the ESL teacher. In J. Lindfors, et al. (1983). *On TESOL, 82*. ERIC Clearinghouse: FL013682.)

Zeng, G., & Takatsuka, S. (2009). Text-based peer-peer collaborative dialogue in a computer-mediated learning environment in the EFL context. *System*, 37(3), 434–446. doi:10.1016/j.system.2009.01.003

Zimmerman, B. J. (1989). A social cognitive view of self-regulated academic learning. *Journal of Educational Psychology*, 81(3), 329–339. doi:10.1037/0022-0663.81.3.329

ENDNOTES

[1]   While the term has been applied in this case, it is only considered application if it is remembered by the l Learner and correctly applied in a future language session.

[2]   The researcher who has lived in Mexico asserts that there is a tendency for those in outlying and more rural areas deep within Mexico to use the Spanish language with less input from the English language. However, those who are closer to the United States border as well as touristic locations tend to utilize and insert more English words in their language (Galindo, 1996; Hidalgo, 1986).

[3]   After the first language session, students would take a 15 minute break and would eat snacks during this time. Thus, what happened during the break also became a topic for conversation.

[4]   Not all strategies are used in every section of the corpus of transcribed text, e.g., cloze strategy. Twenty-five percent of the text was randomly selected for coding purposes. Thus, the above provides results for the majority of the strategies utilized during peer interaction. Coding strategies were ultimately reconciled with a research assistant.

APPENDIX 1

Inter-Rater Reliability Percentages of Teaching, Interlanguage Communication, and Learning Strategies4 APPLICATION (identified not an actual strategy but the correct application of a term or phrase after using a particular strategy)

Teaching Strategies

[CHANGE T] 57%
[COMMAND] 57%
[CFU] 100%
[CHECK MEANING] 89%
[CLARIFICATION] 83%
[EXAMPLE] 43%
[GUESS] 50%
[SLOWER SPEECH] 100%
[TEACH/CORRECT L] 100%
[TRANSLATION] 86%
[URGING] 100%

Learning Strategies

[CHECK MEANING] 100%
[COMMAND CFU] 100%
[DICTIONARY] 100%
[LEARN L] 86%

Interlingual Strategies

[CODE SWITCH] STRATEGIES 85%

Nonlinguistic Strategies Utilized by Both PL and PT to Teach and Learn Language

[GESTURE] 100%
[POINT/SHOW] 100%
[POINT/SHOW Q] 100%

Repetition Strategies Utilized by Both PL and PT to Teach and Learn Language

[REPEAT CONF] 85%
[REPEAT M] 93%
[RESTATE] 88%

APPENDIX 2

Teaching, Intercommunication, and Learning Strategies: Abridged Definitions of the Dual Language Coding Method (DLCM)
APPLICATION (not necessarily a strategy but reveals the correct application of a term or phrase after being instructed by the Peer Teacher. Appropriate linguistic application of words, or a corrected form utilized by the Peer Learner at least three times is documented as application)

Teaching Strategies

Administrative

[CHANGE T]: The PT changes topic in order to extend the flow of conversation.
[COMMAND]: The PT or PL commands the peer to stay on task. For example, "You need to speak Spanish."
[URGING]: The PT urges participation or a response from a reticent PL. "Aw, come on." "You must have done something." This strategy may also be associated with an affective approach to learning (Oxford & Nyikos, 1989).

Compensatory Teaching Strategies

[CFU]: The PT checks to see if the PL understands. For example, *"¿Comprendes?"* "Do you understand?"
[CHECK MEANING]: The PT checks for meaning. For example, if the PL does not understand he/she might state, "Huh?" "What?" or "I don't know" which generally elicits further explanation or comment from the P
[CLARIFICATION]: The PT simplifies or clarifies language for the PL. For example, "L.A. means Los Angeles." (Also noted as reformulations in e-telecollaboration, see Ware & O'Dowd, 2008).
[EXAMPLE]: The PT provides examples to prompt a PL response. For example, "Do you know the months, like January, February....?"
[GUESS]: The PT or PL attempts to find meaning or guess the answer to a question he/she does not understand.
[HELP OUTSIDE]: The PT or PL requests helps from other interactive dyads or groups in the room.
[HINT]: The PT hints for a desired response by possibly giving the first letter or syllable of a word or explaining the context of a particular word.
[READ]: The PT reads out loud from book.
[SLOWER SPEECH]: The PT slows speech to modify input for the PL as a way to increase understanding.
[TEACH/CORRECT L]: The PT teaches or corrects language. For example, the PT may correct written (spelling), verbal language (pronunciation), or repeat to correct language that was inappropriately used (improper syntax) or by repeating the word or phrase the learner mispronounced or misspoke.
[TEACH L – CLOZE]: The PT has PL provide a word to complete a sentence.
[TEST]: The PT gives written or verbal test.
[TRANSLATION]: Translation by either the PT or PL to move communication forward.

Repeat Strategies

[REPEAT M]: The PT repeats multiple times the same word or phrases uttered prior to increase understanding and meaning.
[REPEAT CONF]: The PT or PL repeats a word or phrase to confirm what was just heard.
[RESTATE]: The PT restates or rephrases a sentence or question in order to help PL comprehension.

Visual Strategies

Ways in which the PT or PL uses visuals through writing, drawing or body language to demonstrate meaning. It should be noted that the pointing, showing, and gestures would have to be documented from a video recording for text analysis.

[DRAWING]: Use of drawing to elicit responses or to demonstrate their ideas.
[POINT/SHOW Q]: The PT may point to an object to see if the PL knows that terminology in the target language. The PL may point to an object to learn the meaning of that object in the target language. For example, *"¿Qué es esto?"* "What is this?"
[POINT/SHOW]: The participant may point or show only without providing a question.
[GESTURE]: The participant motions with hands or body to negotiate meaning and increase comprehension.

Intercommunication Strategies

Voluntary Code-Switching

[COGN CODE SWITCH]: Purposeful code switch conducted between languages. Emergent learners during language sometimes acquire the language of the other and although, for example, an SL could utilize only English during the English Session with an EL, the PT instead cognitively chooses to include a word in Spanish. Depending on the depth of thought this may be a cognitive but possibly a metacognitive strategy as well depending on the forethought of the PT.
[SOC CODE-SWITCHING]: Social Code-Switching is generally indicated when a Peer Teacher has no real reason to switch to the Peer Learner's native language during the session in the target languages, but may be motivated to do so as a way to show mutual bilingual growth and solidarity and encourage responses from the Peer Learner (Santiago-Rivera et al., 2009). This is a social strategy.

Involuntary Code-Switching

[INV CODE-SWITCHING]: With involuntary code-switching the PT or PL cannot think of the word in the target language. The PT or PL would then involuntarily switches to a word in their primary language to fill the gap. This is a compensatory strategy.

Learning Strategies

[COMMAND CFU]: Command to check for understanding. The PL requests or demands an explanation.

[DICTIONARY]: PL or PT uses a dictionary during the conversation as a language reference.

[HELP OUTSIDE]: PT or PL requests help from others outside their language group or dyad.

[LEARN L]: In order to learn language, the PL utilizes a useful phrase. For example, the PL may request a translation of word, *"¿Qué quiere decir _____ en español"?* "What does _____ mean in Spanish?"

[LEARN L – CLOZE]: The PL prompts the PT to fill in a word he/she may not know to complete a sentence.

[NOTEBOOK]: The PL retrieves target language information from a notebook as a language reference.

[REPEAT CONF]: The PT or PL repeats a word or phrase to confirm meaning.

[TEXTBOOK]: The PL uses a textbook from the target language as a language reference.

[TRANSLATION]: Translation by either the PT or PL to move communication forward.

APPENDIX 3

Transcription Conventions

Words that occur before dyadic exchange relate excerpts of exchange that occurred during language sessions.

((Double parentheses)) used to describe what is happening during the dialogue the context of what is happening and possible code-switching.

// describes truncated words

[Square Brackets] indicate the strategies employed by the participants.

…indicates pause, hesitation.

Chapter 17
The Impact of Blog Peer Feedback on Improving Iranian English Foreign Language Students' Writing

Mohsen Shahrokhi
Shahreza Branch, Islamic Azad University, Iran

Shima Taheri
Shahreza Branch, Islamic Azad University, Iran

ABSTRACT

The present study is an attempt to investigate (a) whether using blog peer feedbacks have any statistically significant effect on improving Iranian students' EFL writing skill, and (b) whether participants at different proficiency levels react differently to blog peer feedbacks, as far as their writing improvement is concerned. To this end, sixty Iranian female English Foreign Language (EFL) learners were selected based on their performance on the Oxford Placement Test (OPT) and were then divided into two groups. The first thirty-participant group was taught through the conventional face-to-face method; the second thirty-participant group, which consisted of the same proficiency level members as the first group, received blog peer feedbacks as the treatment. After three months of instruction, a post-test was administered and the results were subjected to statistical analysis. The ensuing analysis revealed that using blog peer feedbacks can have a statistically significant impact upon improving the writing skills of EFL learners.

INTRODUCTION

Communications technology, also called telecommunications technology, consisting of electromagnetic devices and systems for communicating over long distances, has been used for many years. Over the last century, developments in telecommunications have made possible new communicative modalities that blend the presuppositions of spoken and written language (Ramazani, 2006).

DOI: 10.4018/978-1-5225-0177-0.ch017

From the very beginning, the Internet was a community that offered many possibilities for networking, linking people worldwide, and for publishing information for the online community. In recent years, the term "social media software" that facilitates user-centered interactions has come to describe a new phenomenon within the online world. The social media application that has gained the most attention in recent years is weblogging. Originally, weblogs were mainly created to link together pages on the Web that the weblog author considered interesting or noteworthy.

These lists of links included the weblog author's comments on the content of the linked websites. A community of weblog-owners networked around a certain topic, linking and exchanging information.

These new communities demand specific ways of teaching and learning knowledge and skills, which help the learner to interact in these contexts. With weblogs in particular, new communities of discourse writing have emerged; the question is what kind of approach for composition instruction could support learners in acquiring their respective literacies.

Blogs are often a user's "home" on the web, easier to create and edit than web pages, and can host a variety of multimedia and display a user's profile, sometimes containing contact information such as email and text messaging addresses. Blogs provide an updatable template for writing, and their ubiquity on the web makes them a source of reading on innumerable topics.

Consequently, blogs provide an opportunity for students to communicate in a foreign language outside of classroom. Because of the atemporal nature of weblogging, students do not have to learn writing in a specific classroom at a special time of day. So, they can write their comments in a comfortable situation with an increasing amount of time.

LITERATURE REVIEW

There are many advantages in using the Internet, as seen in Fox's (1998), Singhal's (1997), and Warschauer's (1997) studies. First, taking part in the Internet activities is intrinsically motivating for students, since they consider it as a trendy and useful tool, enabling them to be connected with the world. As English is currently the main language of the Internet, learners develop an appreciation for the usefulness of learning the language. Using the net also gives students control over their learning, enabling them to go at their own pace and choose their paths according to their individual needs. It helps in promoting learner independence and the development of learning strategies, provided that learners receive appropriate guidance (Moras, 2001).

Secondly, the World Wide Web (WWW) gives students instant access to a wide range of native-language materials, from newspaper and magazine articles to radio broadcasts and informal chat rooms, and also to material prepared specially for learners, such as grammar, pronunciation and vocabulary exercises and tests. Apart from retrieving information from the Internet, learners can also create their own materials and share them with partner classes or with the general public. This possibility can also generate a great deal of interest for learners, as learners communicate with a real audience (Moras, 2001). Because the internet is primarily text driven, it appeals to shy students, giving them time to think and participate in exchanges in a chat room, e-mail, or class conferencing.

Another positive outcome of the Internet use is improving reading and writing skills. Furthermore, because the language that is used on the Internet tends to be lexically and syntactically more complex than oral discourse, students can potentially gain a broader range of English. Communication with native speakers forces students to practice specific skills such as negotiation, persuasion, clarification meaning, and requesting information.

Finally, the Internet allows learners to participate in the culture of the target language and to see real language in context, away from course books and the classroom (Moras, 2001). An integral part of the internet are weblogs, which are useful for different purposes, including teaching and learning a new language.

Incorporating Weblog into Foreign Language Classes

As far as blogs in language teaching are concerned, a number of different uses have been documented. For example, Catera and Emeigh (2005) asked students of English as a second language at two community colleges to each set up their own blog. Students were assigned partners at their own and another college, and were asked to post personal entries relating to their own lives, answers to comprehension or interpretation questions posted by tutors, commentaries to class reading, or paragraphs of their own writing on which peers could comment.

A further project reported by Ducate and Lomicka (2005) aimed to foster intercultural awareness. It accompanied a spring break trip of American students of French to France and a return visit of the French students to the USA a few weeks later. Students were asked to post entries about both their pre-visit perceptions, and their experiences and observations during the visit, with the aim of fostering a conversation between the French and the Americans and to gain a better understanding of other perspectives. Another project that was similarly focused on cultural issues asked students to write contributions to a collaborative class blog about issues of German culture and society, based upon films that students were viewing in class (Schuetz, 2005).

A different way of using blogs is reported by Foale and Carson (2006, p. 16). They created or, rather, asked their students at a Japanese university to create what they call a "student driven self-access language learning resource". A small (paid) team of students was responsible for writing about anything they liked in the foreign language, and to further update the blog with links to interesting material found on the web.

Pedagogical Benefits of Using Weblog

It is increasingly acknowledged by researchers that creating opportunities for language learners to use technology in their learning can be beneficial in different ways (Zhao, 2007). In fact, a growing number of instructors around the world are seeking to enhance the quality and efficiency of their language instruction through innovative activities and experiences made available by technology. In this regard, it has been claimed that the internet in general and weblogging in particular play an increasingly important role in the learning and instruction of many subjects, including second or foreign languages. For instance, Ngai et al. (2007) argue that web-based teaching materials serve as a platform to facilitate teaching and learning, and to provide new approaches for conducting classes and delivering course materials. Moreover, application of web-based activities and integration of technology in language instruction were found to have a positive effect on learners' attitudes and their motivation for learning a second or foreign language (Chen, 2004; Garcia & Arias, 2000).

An earlier pilot study (Chan & Ridgway, 2005) on the use of blogs demonstrated that blogs could support communication between tutor and students.

As Dippold (2009) states, as a freestanding or integrated tool, blogs offer the educational community a number of advantages. They allow writers to reach a much wider audience than just a tutor (Goodwin-Jones, 2003), encourage and facilitate the exchange of resources and thoughts (Williams & Jacobs, 2004), and enable students' work to be evaluated and assessed by peers (Ward, 2004).

Moreover, through exposure to a multitude of opinions and through awareness of writing for a wider audience, blogs also foster critical thinking, because learners need to reflect on the possible reactions of others to their postings (Williams & Jacobs, 2004; Oravec, 2003; Ducate & Lomicka, 2005). In higher education, blogs have been used as a tool for collaboration and self-reflection on course content (Xie & Sharma, 2005; Williams & Jacobs, 2004; Baggetun & Wasson, 2006), peer feedback (Cooper & Boddington, 2005), and as a resource bank (Martindale & Wiley, 2005).

Significance of Using Weblog in Teaching Writing

A weblog encourages students to read, write, and converse more often. Weblogs offer opportunities for authentic expression in the external world (Kajder & Bull, 2003). Weblogs can motivate students to write and get them to understand that there is an audience for them, and that consequently their communication through words needs to be effective because their peers and the world are reading.

Blogs can remedy student disengagement with academic writing. Multiple studies have shown that blogs motivate many students to write well in the target language (Rodzvilla, 2002; Stiler & Philleo, 2003; Liaw, Chen, & Huang, 2008). Through blogs, one can write and also comment on what one writes in expectation of discussion, and a joint-search for common interests and individual differences. By responding on blogs, students can get feedback from other audiences throughout cyberspace. Moreover, students have an opportunity to read things in which they are interested and write things they truly wish to write, thereby determining their own texts in language education and combining text with conversations in a personal and stimulating way.

Many researchers, such as Downs (2004) and Hall (2006), have claimed that students' writing skills improve when they blog. Another study conducted by Kavaliauskienê and Vaičiūnienê (2006) indicates that the experience of writing on blogs for an audience provides opportunities to help students improve their knowledge of English. Nadzrah (2005) found that blogs let students compose writing with specific purposes that can encourage them to enhance their writing in the language constructively. Abu Bakar, Latif, and Ya'acob (2010) also indicate that through blogging, students are able to express and share thoughts, ideas, and information with the wider public. Furthermore, blogs provide a safer and more relaxed environment for language learners, especially for the shy or less confident ones (Hanson-Smith, 2001). Blog also enables individuals to express their thoughts at their own pace and in their own space so that, in contrast to traditional classroom settings, blog learners do not have to compete with their classmates for the instructor's attention (Bloch, 2004).

Blogs also expand the opportunities for student interaction and the horizons of that "learning space" (Williams & Jacobs, 2004, p. 232; Blackstone, Spiri & Naganuma, 2007) exponentially, and provide student writers with a far greater audience both within and outside the classroom. As Pinkman (2005) writes, blogging becomes communicative and interactive when participants assume multiple roles in the writing process, as writers who write and post, as readers/reviewers who respond to other writers' posts, and as writer-readers who, returning to their own posts, react to criticism of their own posts. Dieu (2004) reaffirms this model by stating that blogging gives learners the chance to "maximize focused exposure to language in new situations, peer collaboration, and contact with experts" (p. 26).

To summarize, given the fact that blogging exposes students to a wider audience for their writing, we can hypothesize that students might attend more carefully to online writing opportunities than they would to papers submitted to an instructor. In the case of the writing prompts that ask students to read and reflect upon specific texts, it might be expected that students will read these texts more carefully when they know their interpretations will be online and therefore accountable to a larger audience.

Learning English Context in Iran

In Iran, educational policies are decided primarily by the central government. All of the decisions made by the central government are passed down through provincial organizations for implementation at lower levels, which have less authority in decision-making. All major educational policies concerning the school systems, the curriculum standards, the compilation of textbooks, the examination system, and so on, are under the jurisdiction of the Ministry of Education (Ghorbani, 2009).

According to Jahangard (2007), students' aural and oral skills are not emphasized in Iranian prescribed EFL textbooks. They are not tested in the university entrance examination, nor in the final exams during the three years of senior high school and one year of pre-university education. Writing is not generally regarded as an important skill in most Iranian EFL classrooms. In most high schools in Iran, the teaching of writing is confined to a focus on the sentence level, with typical exercises including sentence transformation and sentence building. Although textbooks include some writing activities that instruct beyond the sentence level (such as the writing of letters and narratives), these activities are considered optional due to the constraints imposed by large class sizes. In fact, Iranian high school students have few opportunities to practice writing in English or to receive feedback from their teachers. Similarly, writing is not a focus of Iranian EFL classes at the tertiary level, where more emphasis is placed on grammar and reading. It is not compulsory for undergraduates to study writing except those majoring in English, who are required to take Academic Writing courses. Non-English majors are required to take General English (GE) and/or English for Specific Purposes (ESP) for the first year of their undergraduate studies, depending on the nature of their specialties.

As a reaction to most high school and undergraduate university students' dissatisfaction with English education in Iran, private language institutes in 1989 started to provide ELT programs for interested students. Davari and Aghagolzadeh, (2015, p. 14) report that "accompanied by a wave of economic privatization, private language institutes, formerly closed down, resumed their operations, and new private English language institutes were established". The authors add that "a perceived failure of the public education system, characterized by a traditional teacher-centered approach and a grammar-translation method, led to a flourishing private sector" (Davari & Aghagolzadeh, 2015, p. 14). The private language institutes provide a variety of English language education programs aiming at serving students with different English language proficiencies, ranging from beginners to advanced levels. Normally, students who enroll for a language program sit for a general English placement test before the commencement of the program, which would be selected based on the placement test results.

Statement of the Problem

With the astonishing advances in communications brought about mainly by computer and internet, good writing skills have become more and more essential for communication in both academic and real life. According to Olshtain (2001, p. 206), "the skill of writing enjoys special status —it is via writing that a person can communicate a variety of messages to a close or distant, known or unknown reader or readers. Such communication is extremely important in the modern world, whether the interaction takes the form of traditional paper-and-pencil writing or the most technologically advanced electronic mail". For Graham and Perin (2007, p. 3), "writing well is not just an option for young people —it is a necessity. Along with reading comprehension, writing skill is a predictor of academic success and a basic requirement for participation in civic life and in the global economy".

Lin and Chien (2009, p. 79) put it clearly that "free writing, at the beginning of our second millennium, is one of the primary methods that human beings use to convey their thoughts and communicate with each other".

However, writing is not a simple process, even in one's mother language, and it is very challenging for almost all students. According to Celce-Murcia and Olshtain (2000, p. 141), even "a skilled writer, who writes often and for a variety of purposes, does not necessarily find the writing process easy. Many such writers report on the difficulties they encounter in sitting down to initiate a writing task or to carry out the final reformation of something that has already been written in draft form".

For students, the need to write clearly, quickly and convincingly has never been more essential than in today's exceedingly competitive, technology-driven global economy. They need to write proposals, reports, letters, e-mails, and briefings that persuade both individuals and groups of readers. Weblogging provides an opportunity for students to communicate in a foreign language outside of class. Because of the nature of this technology, students do not have to be in a specific classroom at a special time of day. Hence, they can write their comments or homework in a stress-free environment with an increasing amount of time. However, few studies have tried to examine and quantify the effectiveness of blogs in improving foreign language writing skills. These concerns matter because, for students in Iran, as EFL learners, the writing skill is the most challenging skill. Most of the students at the EFL learners' level, after studying English for many years, still have problems writing a paragraph or discovering the writing problems of a text.

Furthermore, when the teacher asks them to provide a summary of a passage or edit a text, most of them fail to do so. Thus, poor vocabulary knowledge, poor grammar, failing in writing consistently, and inability to write or edit a short passage are among the concerns of Iranian English teachers. As a new genre of writing, blogs emerged since the late 1990s onwards. Although they are often considered merely as online diaries in which writers write about their daily lives, the genre is much more varied, with many blogs built around a particular theme and writers presenting themselves as subject experts in that field.

Recently, blogs have also made their entry into higher education in general and language teaching in particular, where they have been used as a tool for collaboration and self-reflection on course content and as a resource bank, but also as a tool for peer feedback on writing. According to Wu (2006), using blogs in TEFL has tremendous advantages for both EFL teachers and students; they have the potential to be a truly transformational technology in that they provide a teaching and learning stage where students enjoy a high level of independence and good opportunities for greater interaction with peers, and for the teacher to conduct his/her teaching with higher efficiency.

In contrast to traditional classroom settings, blogs can be very effective in many ways: first, they can help students to communicate and collaborate with each other in the target language outside the confines of the classroom; second, they grant students the freedom to choose where and when students want to work; third, they allow students to express their thoughts at their own pace and in their own space; fourth, they support cooperative and autonomous learning; fifth, they encourage ownership and responsibility on the part of students through their own self-publishing (Goodwin-Jones, 2003; Edwards & Mehring, 2005; Anderson, 2006; Jones, 2006; Mynard, 2007; Sun, 2009).

However, class time is always limited for giving and taking feedback among students, moreover some students, especially the shy or the less confident ones, avoid giving critical feedback to their classmates inside the classroom. To overcome these problems, Hall (2006) claims that weblogs should be the primary vehicle for students to reflect and give each other feedback on what was presented in class. Supporting this claim, Doris (2009) declares that weblogs are potentially valuable tools for peer feedback. Ertmer (2007) states that despite students' preferences for instructor feedback, online peer feedback are very valuable; and more importantly, online peer feedback not only reinforces students' learning but enables them to achieve higher understanding. Therefore, this study's concern is to check the likely advantages of weblogs for tackling some problems encountered by Iranian EFL learners in writing skills.

Objectives of the Study

Normally, peer feedbacks aim at highlighting the strengths and weaknesses of writing tasks that have been remained unnoticed by peer author. Moreover, peer feedback can provide an opportunity for the feedback provider to practice writing skills and recycle writing abilities, and to improve editing skills as well. As such, the aim of this study was to discuss students' experience of receiving and providing peer feedback using blog as integrated into the EFL classroom. Consequently, the following research questions were formulated to achieve the purposes of current studies.

Research Questions

The present study is an attempt to investigate the following questions:

1. Do blog peer feedbacks improve Iranian EFL students' writing performance?
2. Do conventional in-class feedbacks improve Iranian EFL students' writing performance?
3. Is the writing performance of Iranian EFL students receiving blog peer feedback significantly different from those who received conventional in-class feedbacks?
4. What is the effect of using blog peer feedbacks on improving the writing skills of Iranian EFL students with different proficiency levels?

Research Hypotheses

Based on research questions mentioned above, the following hypotheses were formulated to be tested in thid study:

- **H0 1:** Blog peer feedbacks do not improve Iranian EFL students' writing performance.
- **H0 2:** Conventional in-class feedbacks do not improve Iranian EFL students' writing performance.
- **H0 3:** The writing performance of Iranian EFL students receiving blog peer feedback is not significantly different from those who received conventional in-class feedbacks.
- **H0 4:** Students' English proficiency level does not have any significant effect on their writing improvement through using weblog peer feedbacks.

METHODOLOGY

Method

This study was a quantitative one and adopted an experimental design. The two independent variables of the study were blog peer feedbacks and conventional in-class feedbacks; the dependent variable of the study was English writing skill. The study measured the effect of treatment on the experimental groups through the administration of a pre-test and a post-test. The study involved an experimental and a control group as explained in the following section. In order to identify the participants' language proficiency as it was a covariate of the study, the participants were selected based on their performance on a general language proficiency test, namely, the Oxford Placement Test.

Participants

Initially, 60 EFL learners were selected from Shokooh-e-pouyan Language Center in Shahreza, Isfahan, Iran, based on convenience sampling. They were female students within the age range of 13-18, studying at teenagers' levels. To identify their level of language proficiency at the beginning of study, the Oxford Placement Test (OPT) was administered and participants were then divided into two thirty-participant groups (experimental and control groups) consisting of higher-intermediate (High), intermediate (Mid), and lower-intermediate (Low) proficient participants respectively. At the beginning and before the treatment started, in order to check the participants' initial writing proficiency, California Basic Educational Skills Test (CBEST, 2005) as a pre-test was run.

The control group consisting of ten high, ten mid, and ten low proficient participants received conventional in-class feedback and instruction; in addition to in-class instruction, the experimental group received blog peer feedbacks as treatment. The blog peer feedback group was trained to work on blog environment and was asked to write comment and also to revise their classmates' writings that were uploaded on the Language Center weblog during a three-month instruction. In the control group, the writing feedbacks and instructions in this three-month period were provided directly in the classroom or on students' paper within the class and just by the teacher.

INSTRUMENTS

The Oxford Placement Test (OPT)

The OPT (Allen, 1992) was administered to assess the current language proficiency of the groups. As a proficiency test, it was expected to be norm-referenced and was intended to "measure global language abilities" (Brown, 2005, p. 2). One characteristic of a proficiency test, as a norm-referenced test, is that it should produce "scores which fall into a normal distribution" (p. 5), which allows relative interpretations of the test scores in terms of "how each student's performance relates to the performances of all other students" (p. 4). The second characteristic of the test is that "the test must provide scores that form a wide distribution, so that interpretations of the differences among students will be as fair as possible" (p. 8). In other words, a proficiency test tends to test overall general language proficiency. The test consisted of one-hundred items with different question formats comprising grammar, vocabulary, and reading texts.

The OPT was administered to measure the participants' English proficiency level. The reason why the researchers of the study decided to utilize OPT as the students' measure of proficiency was due to the fact that the test was a standard test of proficiency, and its validity and reliability had been established. The test was used to divide the participants into three levels: high, mid and low proficiency levels. According to the scoring chart of the OPT, those students whose score was above 70, were selected as upper intermediate (high proficiency group), those between 50 and 70 were intermediate (mid proficiency group), and those below 50 were selected as low proficiency group.

Pre- and Post-Tests

In order to check the participants' initial writing proficiency, CBEST writing pre-test whose validity and reliability had been established was given to all the participants (i.e., before conducting the treatment). The pre-test consisted of 2 writing topics, and participants had to write only on one of the topics. After collecting the writing pre-tests they were scored according to the CBEST scale. For the post-test, three months later the same procedure was followed (i.e., after conducting the treatment).

Language Center Weblog

The weblog used in the current study for commenting and giving feedback was accessible at http://shokouhepouyan.persianblog.ir. All students were trained how to write comments on the blog. Each session students' writings were uploaded on the blog by the teacher. Therefore, peer students could write their feedbacks about their classmates' writing on that blog. The feedbacks that were provided indirectly were saved and were accessible to peer authors.

Procedures

At the beginning of the study, an OPT was given to 60 female students to determine their English language proficiency. Having obtained the OPT results, they were divided into control and experimental groups each one consisting of three levels respectively: high, mid and low proficiency levels. There were ten students at each proficiency level in the two groups.

Then the participants in both groups were asked to perform a writing task as a pre-test to measure their level of writing skill. The participants received the required information about the style of writing they had to write.

Before implementing the treatment, both groups were instructed how to write a paragraph as the essential component of any writing genre. Paragraphs were described to participants as a collection of sentences that are combined to express a specific idea, main point, topic, and so on. A number of paragraphs are then combined to write a report, an essay, or even a book. A few sample paragraphs were reviewed by participants along with the teacher to provide models for students including the following paragraph:

Students require more recreational time in order to better focus on lessons in class. In fact, studies have shown that students who enjoy a recess of more than 45 minutes consistently score better on tests immediately following the recess period. Clinical analysis further suggests that physical exercise greatly improves the ability to focus on academic materials. Longer periods of recess are clearly required to allow students the best possible chances of success in their studies. Clearly, physical exercise is just one of the necessary ingredients for improving student scores on standardized tests. (Beare, 2014)

The above paragraph was used to explain three sections of the paragraph, namely: the Beginning, which introduces your idea; the Middle, which explains your idea; and the End, which make your point again, and is a transition to next paragraph.

In general, the participants learned that the purpose of a paragraph is to express one point, idea, or opinion. Accordingly, based on the model paragraphs, a few ideas were highlighted in order to clarify the nature of writing an idea, including the following one:

- For example: Students require more recreational time in order to better focus on lessons in class.

The four types of sentences namely, topic sentence, supporting sentences, concluding sentence, and transitional sentence that make up the structure of a paragraph were taught to participants as follows:

1. **Topic Sentence:** One sentence which states your idea, point, or opinion. This sentence should use a strong verb and make a bold statement (Beare, 2014). For example: Students require more recreational time in order to better focus on lessons in class.
2. **Supporting Sentences:** Supporting sentences (notice the plural) provide explanations and support for the topic sentence (main idea) of your paragraph (Beare, 2014). For example: In fact, studies have shown that students who enjoy a recess of more than 45 minutes consistently score better on tests immediately following the recess period. Clinical analysis further suggests that physical exercise greatly improves the ability to focus on academic materials.

Further explanations were provided to the participants to emphasize that supporting sentences provide the evidence for your topic sentence. The participants were notified that supporting sentences that include facts, statistics, and logical reasoning are much more convincing that simple statements of opinion.

3. **Concluding Sentence:** The concluding sentence restates the main idea (found in your topic sentence) and reinforces the point or opinion (Beare, 2014). For example: Longer periods of recess are clearly required to allow students the best possible chances of success in their studies.
4. **Transitional Sentence:** The transitional sentence prepares the reader for the following paragraph (Beare, 2014).For example: Clearly, physical exercise is just one of the necessary ingredients for improving student scores on standardized tests.

Once the participants learned how to write a paragraph, they were assigned a writing task for every session. The two groups were treated differently as for the feedbacks they received as explained below.

The instruction in the control group included receiving conventional in-classroom pen and paper method as a way of teaching writing and receiving feedbacks about their writing problems within the class directly by the teacher; they mainly had to prepare a writing task assigned and revised by the teacher. For every writing task the students were provided with a title as a writing task. The students could ask any question in the classroom regarding the title before writing. They could spend further time on their writing task at home before handing in their final draft to the teacher in the following session. Once the teacher collected the students' writing task, she checked them and provided the required feedbacks on the students' writing paper sheets. A variety of feedbacks were provided by the teacher depending on the students' performance including feedbacks on grammar, word choice, punctuation, and spelling. A check list (see Appendix) including different items was used by the teacher as the criterion of students' writing evaluation to give the appropriate feedback. Finally, the revised paper sheets were returned to students, who were then requested to rewrite their assignments based on the feedback received.

The current study was followed with training of the treatment group. The researchers trained the participants regarding the activities they had to do on weblog and a pilot task was performed to make sure they can handle leaving comments and feedbacks on weblog writing tasks. Like the control group, for every writing task the students were provided with a title as a writing task. The students could ask any question in the classroom regarding the title before writing. They could spend further time on their writing task at home before handing in their final draft to the teacher in the following session. After collecting the assignments, the teacher checked the student's writing tasks and uploaded them on the weblog. Before posting the feedback on the weblog, the peer students of the group had to write about their peers' writing problems in the form of a comment and it was possible for them to revise their comments as well. Then, the teacher posted her own feedback for students' writing task on the weblog as well. There was, however, no in-class feedback provided by peers or the teacher. The students in the experimental group had to rewrite the final version of their assignment before the next assignment.

Both groups participated in class three times a week (90 minutes) regularly within 20 sessions and they wrote their writings according to class instructions. About three months after administrating pre-test, the development of the learners in the two groups was tested using the post-test. The results of post-test were analyzed to see (a) whether using blog peer feedbacks have any statistically significant effect on improving Iranian students' EFL writing skill, and (b) whether participants at different proficiency levels react differently to blog peer feedbacks as far as their writing improvement is concerned. To answer research questions, the CBEST writing pre-test and post-test were conducted to check whether there is any development after 3 months of instruction or not, and to see whether there is any difference between the writing performance of students in control and experimental groups. The CBEST results were submitted to Statistical Package for Social Sciences (SPSS) for detailed statistical analyses.

DATA ANALYSIS AND RESULTS

The Results of the Pre-Test

Before starting the treatment, the writing proficiency of the participants in the weblog group were compared with that of the participants in the conventional group to make sure that they had the same writing ability level. Table 1 presents the descriptive statistics for the pre-test, and Figure 1 illustrates the means graphically.

As it can be seen in Table 1, there is a slight difference between the means of the two groups. However, in order to make sure that this difference is not statistically significant, an independent-sample *t*-test was employed. Table 2 indicates the results of the *t*-test.

It can clearly be seen in Table 2, that the amount of t-observed is not high enough to be considered statistically significant (t-observed=.763, p=.449). Therefore, it can be concluded that the conventional group's writing abilities were the same as their counterparts in weblog group.

Table 1. Descriptive statistics of the pre-test

Groups	No.	Min	Max	Mean	SD
Weblog	30	2	5	2.73	.230
Conventional	30	2	5	2.50	.202

Figure 1. Graphical representation of the means of the pretest

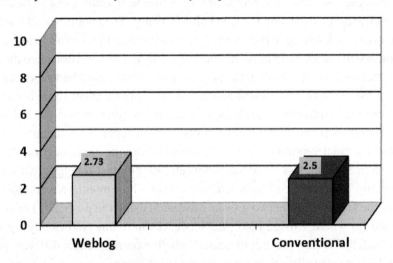

Table 2. The results of the independent-sample t-test for the pre-test

T	Df	Sig.	Mean Difference
.763	58	.449	.23

Investigating the First and Second Hypotheses

As displayed in Table 3, the comparison of the pre-test and post-test results of the experimental group reveals that the integration of web log peer feed backs has improved the writing performance of participants, as the mean score of the group has increased remarkably from 2.73 to 7.72. The difference is big enough to be considered significant.

Table 3. Experimental group performances on pre-test and post-test

Test	N	Min	Max	Mean	SD
Pre-test	30	2	5	2.73	.230
Post-test	30	8	10	7.72	.245

Table 4. Control group performances on pre-test and post-test

test	N	Min	Max	Mean	SD
Pre-test	30	2	5	2.50	.202
Post-test	30	7	9	6.62	.191

As for the control group, the comparison of the group performance on pre-test and post-test reveals that the group performance has improved significantly. The mean score of the group on pre-test has registered 2.50 and improved to 6.62., as displayed in Table 4.

Based on the comparisons made above, it was deduced that both in-class conventional feedbacks and weblog peer feedbacks have affected positively the participants' performance and have improved their writing skills. Therefore, the first hypothesis, "blog peer feedbacks do not improve Iranian EFL students' writing performance,". and the second hypothesis, "conventional in-class feedbacks do not improve Iranian EFL students' writing performance," could be rejected. It is further concluded that compared to conventional in-class feedback, weblog peer feedback is more helpful and influential on participants' writing skill improvement.

Investigating the Third Hypothesis

Having made sure that the two groups were homogeneous, the researchers started conducting the treatment. After the treatment the participants were tested once again with the post-test to find out if the treatment produced any changes, either positive or negative, in the participants' writing performance. Figure 2 displays the means of both groups on the post-test.

According to Tables 3 and 4 and Figure 2, the means are different. To find out whether or not the difference is statistically significant, another independent-sample *t*-test was implemented. Table 5 reports the results of this *t*-test.

Figure 2. Graphical representations of the means for the post-test

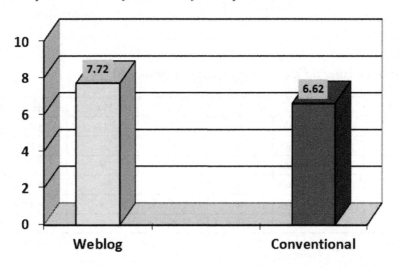

Table 5. The results of the independent-sample t-test for the post-test

Groups	t	df	Sig.	Mean Difference
Weblog Conventional	3.570	58	.001	1.11

Table 5 clearly shows that the amount of t-observed is high enough to be considered statistically significant (t-observed= 3.570, p=.001); in other words, the weblog group outperformed the conventional group. Therefore, the third hypothesis which maintains that, "the writing performance of Iranian EFL students receiving blog peer feedback is not significantly different from those who received conventional in-class feedbacks" can safely be rejected, and it can be claimed that weblog peer feedback helps students learn writing significantly (p<.01) better than that with traditional classroom teaching.

Investigating the Fourth Hypothesis

Once that it was approved that using weblog was helpful in enhancing writing ability, the researchers tried to find out whether it produces the same effect on students' writing performance with different language proficiency levels. To find this, the results of the post-test for each group pair, that is, weblog and conventional, for each proficiency level, that is, high, mid, and low, had to be compared. Table 6 depicts the descriptive statistics for these comparisons, and Figure 3 illustrates the means graphically.

By investigating Table 6 and Figure 3, one can see that there are differences between each group pair. In order to find out if these differences are statistically significant or not, a series of independent-sample *t*-tests were conducted. Table 7 presents the results of these *t*-tests.

The following conclusions can be drawn with regard to the information given in Table 5:

- The amount of *t*-observed for the high groups is not considered statistically significant (*t*-observed= 1.789, p=.090).
- The amount of t-observed for the mid groups is considered statistically significant (t-observed= 3.803, p=.001).

Table 6. Descriptive statistics for the post-test regarding proficiency level

Proficiency Level	Group	N	Min	Max	Mean	SD
High	Weblog	10	8	10	8.70	.675
High	Traditional	10	7	9	8.17	.650
Mid	Weblog	10	6	9	7.70	.823
Mid	Traditional	10	5	8	6.30	.823
Low	Weblog	10	6	8	6.80	.633
Low	Traditional	10	5	6	5.40	.516

Figure 3. Graphical representations of the means for the posttest regarding proficiency level

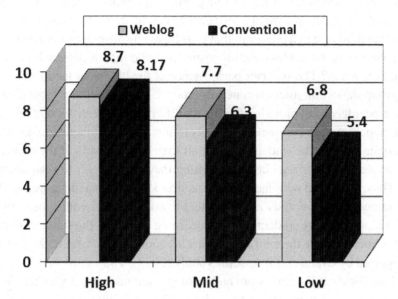

Table 7. The results of the independent-sample t-tests for the post-test regarding proficiency level

Groups' Proficiency	T	df	Sig.	Mean Difference
High	1.789	18	.090	.53
Mid	3.803	18	.001	1.40
Low	5.422	18	.000	1.40

- The amount of t-observed for the low groups is considered statistically significant (t-observed= 5.422, p=.000).

All in all, it can be said that the effect of using weblog peer feedback is not the same for different language proficiency levels. Therefore, the fourth null hypothesis, which states that, "students' English proficiency level does not have any significant effect on their writing improvement through using weblog peer feedbacks," can be retained with regard to students with high proficiency level, but it can be rejected regarding the other two proficiency levels, that is, mid and low.

DISCUSSION AND CONCLUSION

The results indicated that although in-class conventional feedback was not improving the participants' writing performance as much as weblog peer feedback did, both types can be used as instructional aids by EFL teachers to help students develop their writing skills. Therefore, as the first and second questions of the study sought as to whether the two methods of providing feedback improved EFL writing performance, the analysis of data provided confirmatory results to the first and second questions.

Now to address the third research question, that is, is there any difference between the writing performance of students who received in-class writing instruction and that of those who received the weblog integrated writing instruction? The superior performance of the blog peer feedback group compared to the conventional group shows that students generally enjoyed working with blogs and receiving feedback from peers because peer feedback provided them with different perspectives on their performance and afforded them the opportunity to compare their tasks to their fellow students' tasks. Carrying out peer feedback process online allows the students to read all their peers' essays at their own pace, place and time whereas in a typical face-to-face classroom setting they may not get to read others' essays due to time constraints. Thus, compared with face-to-face feedback, blogs provide more flexibility.

The results obtained from this study are consistent to some extend with those of Gedera's (2011), according to which blogs facilitate student-centered learning and allow the students to explore and share their learning experiences outside the confines of the classroom. Furthermore, the results of the present study are also supported by Grami and Alkazemi's study (2012). They show that students are willing to learn beyond the boundaries of the classroom and weblogs can indeed be a very useful alternative. The fact that students no longer write for instructors whose job eventually is to assess their work opens the door for new ways of thinking from students' perspective. Therefore, it would be advisable to encourage students to maintain online interactions via weblogs. The online blogging is an enriching experience and students were generally positive about it. Among many advantages of blogging, collaborative learning was really helpful in making students realize the complexity of various aspects of ESL writing.

To address the fourth research question, which states, what is the effect of using blog peer feedbacks on improving the writing skill of Iranian EFL students with different proficiency level? After three-months of treatment, a post-test was administered. For students at a high proficiency level those who used blog peer feedback only did not benefit much, but at the other two proficiency levels, using blog peer feedback produced a positive result in students' writing performance. The reason could be the fact that blog peer feedback, due to the advantageous nature of writing comments on weblogs, provides opportunity for students to examine many more model paragraphs than the conventional group did. In contrast, students who were taught through conventional method did not benefit much from that method in all proficiency groups. This may indicate that the use of routine method of feedback (teacher feedback on paper) is perhaps not that much useful for the Iranian EFL learners to know about their problems with writing, and that is why students after passing some English courses in institutes, still cannot write accurately.

Implications of the Study

This study could have some potential pedagogical implications for the teachers, students and syllabus designers. The results are useful for language teachers as they can find the possibility to promote the students' positive attitude toward academic English writing through weblogs as this study demonstrated. It is possible to create a lively, challenging and non-threatening atmosphere for writing is a tedious and demanding skill to some EFL learners. Another point which is worth mentioning is that with regard to interactive nature of weblogs peer feedbacks the students would be more motivated to improve their writing skill in an interesting and exciting environment as available on weblogs. Therefore, interested teachers can try the experience of on-line teaching and help their students improve and put to use their English language knowledge especially writing skill. Last but not least, considering the situation of EFL in Iran, syllabus designers and material developers had better use the benefits of blog peer feedbacks in their course designs.

REFERENCES

Abu Bakar, N., Latif, H., & Ya'acob, A. (2010). ESL Students feedback on the use of blogs for language learning. *The Southeast Asian Journal of English Language Studies, 16*(1).

Anderson, H. (2006). Wisconsin TESOL: Literacy for all. *Teaching English as a Second/Foreign Language Newsletter, 6*(1), 1-9. Retrieved From https://www.uwec.edu/esl/minors/Newsletters/Oct06.pdf

Baggetun, R., & Wasson, B. (2006). Self-regulated learning and open writing. *European Journal of Education, 41*(3-4), 453–472. doi:10.1111/j.1465-3435.2006.00276.x

Beare, K. (2014). Paragraph writing. Retrieved from http://esl.about.com/od/writingintermediate/a/paragraphs.htm

Blackstone, B., Spiri, J., & Naganuma, N. (2007). Blogs in English Language Teaching and Learning: Pedagogical Uses and Student Responses. *Reflections on English Language Teaching, 6*(2), 1-20. Retrieved from http://www.nus.edu.sg/celc/publications/RETL62/01to20blackstone.pdf

Bloch, J. (2004). Second language cyber rhetoric: A study of Chinese L2 writers in an online use net group. *Language Learning & Technology, 8*(3). Retrieved from http://llt.msu.edu/vol8num3/bloch/default.html

Brown, J. D. (2005). Testing in language programs: A comprehensive guide to English language assessment (New Ed.). New York: McGraw-Hill College.

Campbell, A. (2003). Weblogs for use with ESL classes. *The Internet TESL Journal, 9*(2). Retrieved from http://iteslj.org/ Techniques/Campbell- Weblogs.html

Cassidy, S. (2006). Developing employability skills: Peer assessment in higher education. *Journal of Education and Training, 48*(7), 508–517. doi:10.1108/00400910610705890

Catera, E., & Emigh, R. (2005). Blogs, the Virtual Soapbox. *Essential Teacher, 2*(3), 46–49.

Celce-Murcia, M., & Olshtain, E. (2000). *Discourse and context in language teaching*. New York: Cambridge University Press.

Chan, K. K., & Ridgway, J. (2005). Blog: a tool for reflective practice in teacher education? *Paper presented at the 3rd International Conference on Education and Information Systems: Technologies and Applications*, Orlando, 333-337.

Chen, P. (2004). *EFL student's learning style preferences and attitudes toward technology-integrated instruction* [Ph.D. Dissertation]. University of South Dakota.

Cooper, C., & Boddington, L. (2005). *Assessment by blog: Ethical case studies assessment for an undergraduate management Class*. Retrieved from http://incsub.org/ blogtalk/?page_id=62

Davari, H., & Aghagolzadeh, F. (2015). To teach or not to teach? Still an open question for the Iranian education system. In C. Kennedy (Ed.), *English language teaching in the Islamic Republic of Iran: Innovations, trends and challenges* (pp. 13–22). UK: British Council.

Dieu, B. (2004). Blogs for language learning. In *Essential Teacher* (pp. 26-30).

Dippold, D. (2009). Peer feedback through blogs: Student and teacher perceptions in an advanced German class. *ReCALL*, *21*(1), 1–33. doi:10.1017/S095834400900010X

Doris, D. (2009). Peer feedback through blogs: Student and teacher perceptions in an advanced German class. *ReCALL*, *21*(1), 17–36.

Downs, S. (2004). Educational blogging. *Educational Review*, *39*(5), 14–26.

Ducate, L., & Lomicka, L. (2005). Exploring the blogosphere: Use of blogs in the foreign language classroom. *Foreign Language Annals*, *38*(3), 410–421. doi:10.1111/j.1944-9720.2005.tb02227.x

Edwards, J., & Mehring, J. (2005). Just-in-time teaching. *Hawai TESOL, 15*(1), 1-12. Retrieved from http://www.hawaiitesol.org/Word%202005%20Sept.pdf

Ertmer, P. (2007). Using peer feedback to enhance the quality of student online postings: An exploratory study. *Journal of Computer-Mediated Communication*, 12(2). Retrieved from http://jcmc.indiana.edu/vol12/issue2/ertmer.html

Foale, C., & Carson, L. (2006). Creating a student driven self-access language learning resource.*Proceedings of the Joint BAAL/IRAAL Conference*, Cork.

Fox, G. (1998). The Internet: making it work in the ESL classroom. *The Internet TESL Journal*, 4(9).

Garcia, M. R., & Arias, F. V. (2000). A comparative study in motivation and learning through print-oriented and computer-oriented tests. *Computer Assisted Language Learning*, *13*(4), 457–465. doi:10.1076/0958-8221(200012)13:4-5;1-E;FT457

Gedera, D. S. P. (2011). Integration of weblogs in developing language skills of ESL learners. *International Journal of Technology in Teaching and Learning*, *7*(2), 124–135.

Ghorbani, M. R. (2009). ELT in Iranian high schools in Iran, Malaysia and Japan: Reflections on how tests influence use of prescribed textbooks. *The Journal of Reflections on English Language Teaching*, *8*(2), 131–139.

Goodwin-Jones, R. (2003). Blogs and wikis: Environments for on-line collaboration. *Language Learning and Technology journal*, *7*(2), 12-16.

Graham, S., & Perin, D. (2007). Writing next: Effective strategies to improve writing of adolescents in middle and high schools. A report to Carnegie Corporation of New York, Washington, DC: *lliance for Excellent Education*. (pp. 1-66). Retrieved from [REMOVED HYPERLINK FIELD]www.all4ed.org/files/archive/publications/WritingNext/WritingNext.pdf

Grami, G. M. A., & Alkazemi, B. Y. (2011). Towards a framework for building a tool to assist L2 writing based on search engines capabilities: The Case of English Phrases and Collocations. *Proceedings of the 3rd CSEDU* (pp. 225-231). Netherlands: Noordwijkerhout.

Hall, J. (2006). A story of using weblogs in English teacher training. In K. Bradford-Watts, C. Ikeguchi, & M. Swanson (Eds.), *Proceedings of the JALT 2005 Conference* (pp. 723-734). Tokyo.

Hanson-Smith, E. (2001). Computer-assisted language learning. In R. Carter & D. Nunan (Eds.), *The Cambridge guide to teaching English to speakers of other languages* (pp. 107–113). Cambridge, UK: Cambridge University Press. doi:10.1017/CBO9780511667206.016

Hewett, B. L. (2000). Characteristics of interactive oral and computer-mediated peer group talk and its influence on revision. *Computers and Composition, 17*(3), 265–288. doi:10.1016/S8755-4615(00)00035-9

Jones, S. (2006). *Blogging and ESL Writing: A case study of how students responded to the use of weblogs as a pedagogical tool for the writing process approach in a community college ESL writing class* [Unpublished PhD. Dissertation]. Faculty of the Graduate School of the University of Texas at Austin, TX, USA.

Kajder, S., & Bull, G. (2003). Scaffolding for struggling students. *Learning and Leading with Technology, 31*(9), 32–35.

Kavaliauskienê, G., & Vaičiünienê, V. (2006). Communication Interaction Using Information and Communication Technology. *Studies about Languages (Kalb Studijos), 8*, 8894. Retrieved from www.ceeol.com

Liaw, S. S., Chen, G. D., & Huang, H. M. (2008). Users' attitudes toward Web-based collaborative learning systems for knowledge management. *Computers & Education, 50*(3), 950–961. doi:10.1016/j.compedu.2006.09.007

Lin, G. H., & Chien, P. C. (2009). An investigation into the effectiveness of peer feedback. *Journal of Applied Foreign Languages Fortune Institute of Technology, 3*, 79–87.

Liu, J., & Sadler, R. W. (2003). The effect and affect of peer review in electronic versus traditional modes on L2 writing. *Journal of English for Academic Purposes, 2*(3), 193–227. doi:10.1016/S1475-1585(03)00025-0

Martindale, T., & Wiley, D. (2005). Using blogs in scholarship and teaching. *TechTrends, 49*(2), 55–61. doi:10.1007/BF02773972

Moras, S. (2001). *Computer-assisted language learning (Call) and the Internet.* Karen's Linguistics Issues.

Mynard, J. (2007). A blog as a tool for reflection for English language learners. *The Philippine ESL Journal, 1*, 77-90. Retrieved from http://www.philippine-esl-journal.com/August-2008-Vol1.pdf

Nadzrah, A. (2005). *Computers for teaching English as a second language in Malaysia: case study.* University of Adelaide.

Ngai, E. W. T., Poon, J. K. L., & Chan, Y. H. C. (2007). Empirical examination of the adoption of Web CT using TAM. *Computers & Education, 48*(2), 250–267. doi:10.1016/j.compedu.2004.11.007

Nicol, D. & MacFarlane-Dick, D. (2006). Formative assessment and self-regulated learning: A model and seven principles of good feedback practice. *Studies in Higher Education, 31*(2), 199-218.

Olshtain, E. (2001). Functional tasks for mastering the mechanics of writing and going just beyond. In M. Celce-Murcia (Ed.), *Teaching English as a second or foreign language* (3rd ed., pp. 206–217). USA: Heinle& Heinle.

Oravec, J. A. (2003). Blogs as an emerging genre in higher education. *Journal of Computing in Higher Education, 14*(2), 21–44. doi:10.1007/BF02940937

Pinkman, K. (2005). Using blogs in the foreign language classroom: Encouraging learner independence. *The JALT CALL Journal, 1*(1), 12–24.

Ramazani, Z. (2006). *A Study of the Role of Using E-mail in Improving High School Students' EFL Reading Skill* [Unpublished Master's Thesis]. Shahreza Branch, Islamic Azad University Isfahan, Iran.

Rodzvilla, J. (2002). *We've got blog: How weblogs are changing our culture.* Cambridge, MA: Perseus Publishing.

Rollinson, P. (2005). Using peer feedback in the ESL writing class. *English Language Teaching Journal, 59*(1), 23–30. doi:10.1093/elt/cci003

Schuetz, D. (2005). *Cultural models and cultural self-awareness*: *A Discourse-analytical approach to the language of students' online journal entries* [PhD Thesis]. Pennsylvania State University.

Singhal, M. (1997). The Internet and foreign language education: Benefits and challenges? *The Internet TESL Journal, 3*(6), 57–62.

Stiler, G. M., & Philleo, T. (2003). Blogging and blog spots: An alternative format for encouraging reflective practice among pre-service teachers. *Academic Research Library, 123*(4), 789–798.

Sun, Y. (2009). Voice blog: An exploratory study of language learning. *Language Learning & Technology, 13*(2), 88–103.

Tuzi, F. (2004). The impact of e-feedback on the revisions of L2 writers in an academic writing course. *Computers and Composition, 21*(2), 217–235. doi:10.1016/j.compcom.2004.02.003

Ward, J. M. (2004). Blog assisted language learning (BALL): Push button publishing for the pupils. *TEFL Web Journal, 3*(1), 1–15.

Ware, D., & Warschauer, M. (2006). Electronic feedback and second language writing. In K. Hyland & F. Hyland (Eds.), *Feedback in second language writing: Context and issues* (pp. 105–121). London: Cambridge University Press. doi:10.1017/CBO9781139524742.008

Warschauer, M. (1997). The Internet for English Teaching: Guidelines for teachers. *TESL Reporter, 30*(1), 27–33.

Williams, J., & Jacobs, J. (2004). Exploring the use of blogs as learning spaces in the higher education sector. *Australasian Journal of Educational Technology, 20*(2), 232–247.

Wu, W. (2006). The effect of blog peer review and teacher feedback on the revisions of EFL writers. *Journal of Education and Foreign Languages and Literature, 3*, 125–139.

Xie, Y., & Sharma, P. (2005). *Students lived experiences of using blogs in a class*: An exploratory study. Retrieved from http://eric.ed.gov/ERICDocs/data/ericdocs2/content_storage

Yang, M., Badger, R., & Yu, Z. (2006). A comparative study of peer and teacher feedback in a Chinese EFL writing class. *Journal of Second Language Writing, 15*(3), 179–200. doi:10.1016/j.jslw.2006.09.004

Zhao, Y. (2007). Social studies teachers' perspectives of technology integration. *Journal of Technology and Teacher Education, 15*(3), 311–333.

KEY TERMS AND DEFINITIONS

Blog: A blog is an online journal that can be updated frequently by an individual and used for personal, educational, and commercial purposes.

English Foreign Language: Learning or teaching English as a foreign language by native speakers of other languages.

Language Proficiency: The level competence of a foreign language learner that enables him/her to perform both in written and oral forms.

Peer Feedback: The use of classmates or learners at the same proficiency level in commenting on other learners' writing performances.

t-Test: A statistical procedure used to indicate whether the mean scores of two independent groups are significantly different or not.

Writing Skill: The ability to write correctly and communicatively in a language, and be able to edit it.

APPENDIX

Table 8. Students' writing task evaluation checklist

No.	Item	Accepted	Failed
1	Paragraphs start with a topic sentence.		
2	The first sentence is indented.		
3	The student stays on topic.		
4	Details are used to support the topic.		
5	The paragraphs include 5-8 complete sentences.		
6	The paragraphs have a summary or closing sentence.		
7	The same words are not used over and over.		
8	Words are spelled correctly.		
9	Each sentence begins with a capital letter.		
10	Each proper name begins with a capital letter.		
11	Periods, exclamation marks, question mark, commas are used correctly.		
12	The students' print or handwriting is clear enough to read.		

Compilation of References

Abbadi, S. (2013). *Teaching Arabic post 9/11: Late modernity in language classrooms- challenges and possibilities for change* [Doctoral dissertation].

Abbadi, S. (2014). Teaching Arabic post 9/11: Humor and the potential for critical language awareness. *Dirasat: Human and Social Sciences Journal, 41*(1), 322–334. doi:10.12816/0018576

Abdallah, M., & Al-Batal, M. (2011-12). College-level teachers of Arabic in the United States: A survey of their professional and institutional profiles and attitudes. *Al-Arabiyya, 44-45*, 1–28.

Abdous, M., Camarena, M., & Facer, B. R. (2009). MALL technology: Use of academic podcasting in the foreign language classroom. *ReCALL, 21*(01), 76–95. doi:10.1017/S0958344009000020

Abrams, Z. I. (2003). The effects of synchronous and asynchronous CMC on oral performance. *Modern Language Journal, 87*(2), 157–167. doi:10.1111/1540-4781.00184

Abu Bakar, N., Latif, H., & Ya'acob, A. (2010). ESL Students feedback on the use of blogs for language learning. *The Southeast Asian Journal of English Language Studies, 16*(1).

Acquah, E. O., & Commins, N. L. (2013). Pre-service teachers' beliefs and knowledge about multiculturalism. *European Journal of Teacher Education, 36*(4), 445–463. doi:10.1080/02619768.2013.787593

ACTFL. (2016, February 24). Why can't tech replace teachers? Here's what happens when you put Adele's "Hello" through Google Translate. *ACTFL.* Retrieved from https://twitter.com/search?q=Why%20can%E2%80%99t%20tech%20replace%20teachers%3F%20&src=typd

Admiraal, W., Westhoff, G., & de Boot, K. (2006). Evaluation of bilingual secondary education in the Netherlands: Pupils' language proficiency in English. *Educational Research and Evaluation, 12*(1), 75–93. doi:10.1080/13803610500392160

Aguaded-Gómez, J. I. (2011). Media Education: An International Unstoppable Phenomenon. The Work of the UN, Europe and Spain in the Field of Edu-communication. *Comunicar, 37*, (7-8).

Alanis, I. (2010). A Texas two-way bilingual program: Its effects on linguistic and academic achievement. *Bilingual Research Journal, 24*(3), 225–248.

Al-Batal, M. (2007). Arabic and national language educational policy. *Modern Language Journal, 91*(2), 268–271. doi:10.1111/j.1540-4781.2007.00543_10.x

Al-Hashash, S. (2007). Bridging the gap between ESL and EFL: Using computer assisted language learning as a medium. *Indian Journal of Applied Linguistics, 33*(1), 5–38.

Alleman, J., & Brophy, J. (2001). *Social studies excursions, K-3. Book 1: Powerful units on food, clothing, and shelter.* Portsmouth, NH: Heinemann.

Alleman, J., & Brophy, J. (2002). *Social studies excursions, K-3. Book 2: Powerful units on communication, transportation, and family living*. Portsmouth, NH: Heinemann.

Alleman, J., & Brophy, J. (2003). *Social studies excursions, K-3. Book 2: Powerful units on childhood, money, and government*. Portsmouth, NH: Heinemann.

Allen, I. E., & Seaman, J. (2011). *Going the distance: Online education in the United States*. Babson Survey Research Group and Quahog Research Group, LLC.

Allen, J. (2008). Why learning to write Chinese is a waste of time: A modest proposal. *Foreign Language Annals, 41*(2), 237–251. doi:10.1111/j.1944-9720.2008.tb03291.x

Allen, J. R. (2009). Why learning to write Chinese is a waste of time. *Foreign Language Annals, 41*(2), 237–251.

Allen, R. (2004). Perspectives on Arabic teaching and learning. *Modern Language Journal, 88*(2), 275–278.

Allen, R. (2007). Arabic—Flavor of the moment: Whence, why, and how? *Modern Language Journal, 91*(2), 258–261. doi:10.1111/j.1540-4781.2007.00543_6.x

Allen, W. (2014). Developing cultural proficiency. *Language and Education, 9*(1), 26–27.

Almeida, M. E. B. (2006). Technology and distance education: Approaches and contributions of digital and interactive learning environments. *Revista Educação e Comunicação, São Paulo, 1*(16), 1–23.

Al-Saleem, B. I. A. (2012). The interactive whiteboard in English as a foreign language (EFL) classroom. *European Scientific Journal, 8*(3).

Alsina, J., Boix, R., Burset, S., Buscà, F., Colomina, R., García, M., & Sayós, R. et al. (2011). *Evaluación por competencias en la Universidad: Las competencias transversales. Cuadernos de docencia universitaria 18*. Barcelona: Octaedro.

Alvarez, B. (2011). Flipping the classroom: Homework in class, lessons at home. *Learning First*. Retrieved from http://www.learningfirst.org/flipping-classroom-homework-class-lessons-home

American Council on the Teaching of Foreign Languages. (2012). *ACTFL proficiency guidelines*. Alexander, VA: Author.

Amish American. (2016, February 2). *Amish American: Iowa Amish*. Retrieved from http://amishamerica.com/iowa-amish/

Anderson, H. (2006). Wisconsin TESOL: Literacy for all. *Teaching English as a Second/Foreign Language Newsletter, 6*(1), 1-9. Retrieved From https://www.uwec.edu/esl/minors/Newsletters/Oct06.pdf

Anderson, L. W., & Krathwohl, D. R. (Eds.), (2001). *A taxonomy for learning, teaching and assessing: A revision of Bloom's taxonomy of educational objectives*. New York: Longman.

Andre, M. (2004). A survey of teachers to assess teacher training. In *Romanowski et al. (Org.). Local knowledge and universal knowledge: research, teaching and teacher action* (pp. 205–218). Curitiba: Champagnat.

Andrews, R., & Haythornthwaite, C. (2007). Introduction to E-learning research. In R. Andrews & C. Haythornthwaite (Eds.), *The SAGE Handbook of E-learning Research* (pp. 1–53). London, England: SAGE Publications, Ltd.

Angelova, M., Gunawardena, D., & Volk, D. (2006). Peer teaching and learning: Co-constructing language in a dual language first grade. *Language and Education, 20*(3), 173–190. doi:10.1080/09500780608668722

Antenos-Conforti, E. (2009). Microblogging on Twitter: Social networking in intermediate Italian classes. In L. Lomicka & G. Lord (Eds.), *The next generation: Social networking and online collaboration in foreign language learning* (pp. 59–90). San Marcos, TX: Computer Assisted Language Instruction Consortium.

Aponte, R., & Pressagno, R. (2009). The communications revolution and its impact on the family: Significant, growing, but skewed and limited in scope. *Marriage & Family Review*, *45*, 576–586.

Appel, C., & Mullen, T. (2000). Pedagogical considerations for a web-based tandem language learning environment. *Computers & Education*, *34*(3), 291–308. doi:10.1016/S0360-1315(99)00051-2

Arab American Institute. (2015). Demographics. Retrieved from http://www.aaiusa.org/pages/demographics/

Araújo e Sá, M. H., & Melo, S. (2007). On-line plurilingual interaction in the development of Language Awareness. *Language Awareness*, 16(1), 7–20.

Araújo e Sá, M. H., De Carlo, M., & Melo-Pfeifer, S. (2010). O que diriam sobre os portugueses? [What would you say about Portuguese people?]: Intercultural curiosity in multilingual chat-rooms. *Language and Intercultural Communication*, *10*(4), 277–298. doi:10.1080/14708471003611257

Araújo-Carreira, M. H. (1992). La diversité des langues a l'école: réflexions sur la place d'une langue romane, le portugais. *Repères 6, Langues Vivantes et Français à l'Ecole* (pp. 57-67). Paris: INRP.

Arellano-Houchin, A., Flamenco, C., Merlos, M. M., & Segura, L. (2001). Has California's passage of Proposition 227 made a difference in the way we teach? *The Urban Review*, *33*(3), 221–235. doi:10.1023/A:1010366004719

Arispe, K., & Blake, R. J. (2012). Individual factors and successful learning in a hybrid course. *System*, *4*(40), 1–27.

Armand, F., & Dagenais, D. (2005). Langues en contexte d'immigration: éveiller au langage et à la diversité linguistique en milieu scolaire. In *Revue de l'Association des études canadiennes* (pp. 110-113).

Arms, W. (2012). The 1990s: The formative years of digital libraries. *Library Hi Tech*, *30*(4), 579–591.

Arnold, N. (2007). Technology-mediated learning 10 years later: Emphasizing pedagogical or utilitarian applications? *Foreign Language Annals*, *40*(1), 161–181. doi:10.1111/j.1944-9720.2007.tb02859.x

Aydin, S. (2014). Twitter as an educational environment. *Turkish Online Journal of Distance Education*, *15*(1), 10–21.

Azizinezhad, M., Hashemi, M., & Darvishi, S. (2013). Application of cooperative learning in EFL classes to enhance the students' language learning. *Procedia: Social and Behavioral Sciences*, *93*, 138–141. doi:10.1016/j.sbspro.2013.09.166

Baggetun, R., & Wasson, B. (2006). Self-regulated learning and open writing. *European Journal of Education*, *41*(3-4), 453–472. doi:10.1111/j.1465-3435.2006.00276.x

Bailey, B. (2011). Heteroglossia. In M. Martin-Jones, A. Blackledge & A. Creese (Eds.), *The Routledge Handbook of Multilingualism* (pp. 439-453). Oxon: Routledge

Bailison Bailenson, J.N., Iyenger, S., Yee, N., Collins, N.A. (2008). Facial similarity between voters and candidates causes influence. *Public Opinion Quarterly*, 72(5) 2008, 935–961

Bañados, E. (2006). A blended-learning pedagogical model for teaching and learning EFL successfully through an online interactive multimedia environment. *CALICO Journal*, *23*(3), 533–550.

Banks, J. A. (2001). Citizenship Education and Diversity. *Journal of Teacher Education*, *52*(1), 5–16. doi:10.1177/0022487101052001002

Baran, E. (2014). A Review of Research on Mobile Learning in Teacher Education. *Journal of Educational Technology & Society*, *17*(4), 17–32.

Barboza, D. (2011, February 22). Workers Sickened at Apple Supplier in China. *The New York Times*. Retrieved from http://www.nytimes.com/2011/02/23/technology/23apple.html?_r=0

Bárcena, E., & Martín-Monje, E. (2014). Introduction. LMOOCs: An emerging field. In E. Martín-Monje & E. Bárcena (Eds.), *Language MOOCs: Providing Learning, Transcending Boundaries* (pp. 1–15). Warsaw: De Gruyter Open.

Barker, V., Giles, H., Noels, K., Duck, J., Hecht, M. L., & Clément, R. (2001). The English-only movement: A communication analysis of changing perceptions of language vitality. *Journal of Communication, 51*(1), 3–37. doi:10.1111/j.1460-2466.2001.tb02870.x

Barreto, R. G. (2004). Technology and education: Work and teacher training. *Educação & Sociedade, Campinas, 25*(89), 1–15.

Barros, D. M. V., & Amaral, S. F. (2006). Emotional intelligence in learning mediated virtual space. *Educação Temática Digital, Campinas, 8*(2), 152–161.

Bartlett-Bragg, A. (2006). Reflections on pedagogy: Reframing practice to foster informal learning with social software. Retrieved from http://matchsz.inf.elte.hu/tt/docs/Anne20Bartlett-Bragg.pdf

Bastos, M. T., Raimundo, R. L. G., & Travitzki, R. (2013). Gatekeeping Twitter: Message diffusion in political hashtags. *Media Culture & Society, 35*(2), 260–270. doi:10.1177/0163443712467594

Bates, A. W. (1997). The impact of technological changes on open and distance learning. *Distance Education, 18*(1), 93–109. doi:10.1080/0158791970180108

Baxter, L. (1984). An investigation of compliance-gaining on politeness. *Human Communication Research, 10*, 427–456.

Bayne, S., & Ross, J. (2007). The "Digital Native" and "Digital Immigrant:" A Dangerous Opposition. *Presented atThe Annual Conference of the Society for Research into Higher Education (SRHE)*, Brighton, Sussex.

Beadle, M., & Santy, J. (2008). The early benefits of a problem-based approach to teaching social inclusion using an online virtual town. *Nurse Education in Practice, 8*(3), 190–196. doi:10.1016/j.nepr.2007.07.004 PMID:17855168

Beardsmore, H. (2008). Language promotion by European supranational institutions. In O. García (Ed.), *Bilingual Education in the 21ˢᵗ Century* (pp. 197–217). Chichester: Wiley-Blackwell.

Beardsmore, H. (2008). Language promotion by European supra-national institutions. In O. García (Ed.), *Bilingual education in the 21st century: A global perspective* (pp. 197–217). Chichester: Wiley-Blackwell.

Beare, K. (2014). Paragraph writing. Retrieved from http://esl.about.com/od/writingintermediate/a/paragraphs.htm

Beaumont, C. (2008, June 27). Bill Gate's dream: A computer in every home. *The Telegraph.* Retrieved from http://www.telegraph.co.uk/technology/3357701/Bill-Gatess-dream-A-computer-in-every-home.html

Beauvois, M. (1999). Computer-mediated communication: Reducing anxiety and building community. In D. J. Young (Ed.), Affect in foreign language and second language learning: A practical guide to creating a low-anxiety classroom atmosphere (pp. 144-165). Boston, MA: McGraw Hill College.

Beauvois, M. H., & Eledge, J. (1995-1996). Personality types and megabytes: Student attitudes toward computer mediated communication (CMC) in the language classroom. *CALICO Journal,* 13(2 & 3), 27-45.

Beaven, T., Codreanu, T., & Creuzé, A. (2014). Motivation in a MOOC, Issues for course designers. In E. Martín-Monje & E. Bárcena (Eds.), *Language MOOCs: Providing Learning, Transcending Boundaries* (pp. 48–66). Warsaw: De Gruyter Open.

Beaven, T., Hauck, M., Comas-Quinn, A., Lewis, T., & de los Arcos, B. (2014). MOOCs: Striking the right balance between facilitation and self-determination. *MERLOT Journal of Online Learning and Teaching, 10*(1), 31–43.

Becker, B. K., & Egler, C. A. G. (1992). *Brazil: a new regional power in the world economy.* New York, New York: Cambridge University Press Archive.

Beck, V. S. (2010). Comparing online and face-to-face teaching and learning. *Journal on Excellence in College Teaching, 21*(3), 95–108.

Beinfeld, S., & Bochner, H. (2013). *Comprehensive Yiddish-English Dictionary.* Bloomington, Ind: Indiana University Press.

Bejarano, P. A. C., & Chapeton, C. M. (2013). The role of genre-based activities in the writing of argumentative essays in EFL. *Profile Journal, Colombia, 15*(1), 26–85.

Beldarrain, Y. (2006). Distance education trends: Integrating new technologies to foster student interaction and collaboration. *Distance Education, 27*(2), 139–153. doi:10.1080/01587910600789498

Bell, T.R. (2015). The flipped German classroom. *Proceedings of the Central States Conference in the Teaching of Foreign Languages Report* (pp. 17-38).

Bellack, A. A., Kliebard, H. M., Hyman, R. T., & Smith, F. L. Jr. (1966). *The language of the classroom.* New York: Teachers College.

Bello, T. (1999). New avenues to choosing and using videos. *TESOL Matters, 9*(4), 20.

Belnap, K. (2006). A profile of students of Arabic in U.S. universities. In K. Wahba, Z. Taha, & L. England (Eds.), *Handbook for Arabic language teaching professionals in the 21st century* (pp. 169–178). New Jersey: Lawrence Erlbaum Associates.

Belz, J. A. (2002). Social dimensions of telecollaborative foreign language study. *Language Learning & Technology, 6*(1), 60–81.

Belz, J. A. (2003). Linguistic perspective on the development of intercultural competence in telecollaboration. *Language Learning & Technology, 7*(2), 68–99.

Belz, J. A. (2003). Linguistics perspectives on the development of intercultural competence in telecollaboration. *Language Learning & Technology, 7*(2), 68–117.

Belz, J. A. (2006). At the intersection of telecollaboration, learner corpus analysis and L2 pragmatics: Considerations for language program direction. In J. A. Belz & S. L. Thorne (Eds.), *Internet-mediated intercultural foreign language education* (pp. 207–246). Boston: Thomson Heinle.

Belz, J. A., & Müller-Hartmann, A. (2003). Teachers negotiating German-American telecollaboration: Between a rock and an institutional hard place. *Modern Language Journal, 87*(1), 71–89. doi:10.1111/1540-4781.00179

Belz, J. A., & Thorne, S. L. (2006). Introduction. In J. A. Belz & S. L. Thorne (Eds.), *Internet-mediated intercultural foreign language education* (pp. viii–xxv). Boston: Thomson Heinle.

Bennett, B., Kern, J., Gudenrath, A., & McIntosh, P. (2011). *The flipped class revealed.* The Daily Riff.

Bennett-Smith, M. (2012, August 12). Wang Shangkun, Chinese teen who sold kidney to buy iPad, too weak to face alleged harvesters in trial. *The World Post.* Retrieved from http://www.huffingtonpost.com/2012/08/10/wang-shangkun-kidney-ipad_n_1764335.html

Benson, P. (2011). *Teaching and researching autonomy* (2nd ed.). London, UK: Longman.

Berge, Z. L. (1999). Interaction in post-secondary, Web-based learning and teaching. *Educational Technology, 39*(1), 5–11.

Bergmann, J., Overmyer, J., & Wilie, B. (2012). The flipped class: Myths versus reality. *The Daily Riff*. Retrieved from http://www.thedailyriff.com/articles/the-flipped-class-conversation-689.php

Bergmann, J., & Sams, A. (2012). *Flip your classroom: Reach every student in every class every day*. International Society for Technology in Education.

Berk, R. A. (2009). Multimedia teaching with video clips: TV, movies, YouTube, and mtvU in the college classroom. *International Journal of Technology in Teaching and Learning, 5*(1), 1–21.

Berlin, L. (2003). Entrepreneurship and the rise of Silicon Valley: The career of Robert Noyce, 1956—1990. *Enterprise and Society, 4*(4), 586–591.

Bernard, R. M., Abramia, P. C., Loub, Y., & Borokhovski, E. (2004). A methodological morass? How we can improve quantitative research in distance education. *Distance Education, 25*(2), 175–198. doi:10.1080/0158791042000262094

Bialystok, E. (1983). Some factors in the selection and implementation of communication strategies. In C. Faerch & G. Kaspar (Eds.), *Strategies in interlanguage communication* (pp. 100–118). Harlow, UK: Longman.

Bialystok, E. (2001). *Bilingualism in development: Language, literacy and cognition*. Cambridge University Press. doi:10.1017/CBO9780511605963

Bilbatua, L., & Herrero de Haro, A. (2014). Teachers' attitudes towards computer-assisted language learning in Australia and Spain. *Círculo De Lingüística Aplicada a La Comunicación, 57*(57), 3–44.

Birdwhistell, R. L. (1970). *Kinesics and context*. Philadelphia, PA: University of Pennsylvania Press.

Birnbaum, S. (1979). *Yiddish: A Survey and A Grammar*. Toronto, Buffalo: University of Toronto Press.

Blackledge, A., & Creese, A. (2014). Heteroglossia as Practice and Pedagogy. In A. Blackledge & A. Creese (Eds.), *Heteroglossia as Practice and Pedagogy* (pp. 1-20). London: Springer.

Blackstone, B., Spiri, J., & Naganuma, N. (2007). Blogs in English Language Teaching and Learning: Pedagogical Uses and Student Responses. *Reflections on English Language Teaching, 6*(2), 1-20. Retrieved from http://www.nus.edu.sg/celc/publications/RETL62/01to20blackstone.pdf

Blake, R. (2000). Computer mediated communication: A window on L2 Spanish interlanguage. *Language Learning & Technology, 4*(1), 120–136.

Blake, R. J. (2009). The use of technology for second language distance learning. *Modern Language Journal, 93*(1), 822–835. doi:10.1111/j.1540-4781.2009.00975.x

Blake, R., Cetto, M., Padro-Ballester, C., & Wilson, N. L. (2008). Measuring oral proficiency in distance, face-to-face, and blended classrooms. *Language Learning & Technology, 12*(3), 114–127.

Blake, R., & Delforge, A. (2007). Online Language Learning: The Case of Spanish Without Walls. In B. Lafford & R. Salaberry (Eds.), *The art of teaching Spanish: Second language acquisition from research to praxis* (pp. 127–147). Georgetown: Georgetown University Press.

Blake, R., & Kramsch, C. (2007). Guest editor's introduction. *Modern Language Journal, 91*(2), 247–249. doi:10.1111/j.1540-4781.2007.00543_2.x

Blasco, J. (2013). *L'apprentissage des langues étrangères au cycle 3: activités réflexives entre langues 1 et 2*. Mémoire de Master, Ecole Interne IUFM Midi-Pyrénées.

Blattner, G. (2014, October). Communicative competence in L2: The invisible culture is invisible in textbooks. *Paper presented at the FFLA*, Miami, FL.

Blattner, G., & Lomicka, L. (2012). A sociolinguistic study of practices in different social forums in an intermediate French class. *International journal on instructional technologies and distance education 9*(9), 3-24.

Blattner, G., & Williams, L. F. (2009). Teaching and Learning Linguistic and Social Dimensions of French-Language Discussion Fora. In L. Abraham, & L. Williams (Eds.), Electronic Discourse in Foreign Language Learning and Teaching (pp. 263-289). Series: Language Learning & Language Teaching. Amsterdam: John Benjamins.

Blattner, G., Dalola, A., & Lomicka, L. (2015). Tweetsmart: A pragmatic analysis of well-known native speaker Tweeters. In E. Dixon, & M. Thomas (Eds.), Researching Language Learner Interactions Online: From Social Media to MOOCs (pp. 213-235). San Marcos, TX: CALICO.

Blattner, G. (2011). Web 2.0 Technologies and Foreign Language Teaching. In V. Wang (Ed.), *Encyclopedia of E-Leadership, Counseling and Training* (pp. 89–107). Hershey, PA, USA: IGI Global.

Blattner, G., Dalola, A., & Lomicka, L. (2016). Twitter in foreign language classes: Initiating learners into contemporary language variation. In V. Wang (Ed.), *The Handbook of Research on Learning Outcomes and Opportunities in the Digital Age* (pp. 769–797). Hershey, PA, USA: IGI Global. doi:10.4018/978-1-4666-9577-1.ch034

Blattner, G., & Fiori, M. (2009). Facebook in the Language Classroom: Promises and Possibilities. *Instructional Technology and Distance Learning, 6*(1), 17–28.

Blattner, G., & Fiori, M. (2011). Virtual social network communities: An investigation of language learners' development of socio-pragmatic awareness and multiliteracy skills. *CALICO Journal, 29*(1), 24–43. doi:10.11139/cj.29.1.24-43

Blinn-Pike, L. (2009). Technology and the family: An overview from the 1980s to the present. *Marriage & Family Review, 45*(6-8), 567–575.

Bliuc, A. M., Goodyear, P., & Ellis, R. A. (2007). Research focus and methodological choices in studies into students' experiences of blended learning in higher education. *The Internet and Higher Education, 10*(4), 231–244. doi:10.1016/j.iheduc.2007.08.001

Bloch, J. (2004). Second language cyber rhetoric: A study of Chinese L2 writers in an online use net group. *Language Learning & Technology, 8*(3). Retrieved from http://llt.msu.edu/vol8num3/bloch/default.html

Block, N. (2011). The impact of two-way dual immersion programs on initially English-dominant Latino students' attitudes. *Bilingual Research Journal, 34*(2), 125–141. doi:10.1080/15235882.2011.598059

Block, N. C. (2011). Perceived impact of two-way dual immersion programs on Latino students' relationships in their families and communities. *International Journal of Bilingual Education and Bilingualism, 15*(2), 235–257. doi:10.1080/13670050.2011.620079

Blömeke, S., Zlatkin-Troitschanskaia, O., Kuhn, C., & Fege, J. (Eds.). (2013). *Modeling and measuring competencies in higher education*. Rotterdam: Sense Publishers. doi:10.1007/978-94-6091-867-4

Blommaert, J. (2010). *The Sociolinguistics of Globalization*. Cambridge: Cambridge University Press. doi:10.1017/CBO9780511845307

Blommaert, J., Kelly-Holmes, H., Lane, P., Peppänen, S., Moriarty, M., Pietikäinen, S., & Piirainen-Marsh, A. (2009). Media, multilingualism and language policing: An introduction. *Language Policy, 8*(3), 203–207. doi:10.1007/s10993-009-9138-7

Bloom, B. (1984). The 2 sigma problem: The search for methods of group instruction as effective as one-to-one tutoring. *Educational Researcher, 13*(6), 4–16. doi:10.3102/0013189X013006004

Boltz, W. (1986). Early Chinese writing. *World Archaeology, 17*(3), 420–436.

Bono, M., & Melo-Pfeifer, S. (2011). Language negotiation in multilingual learning environments. *The International Journal of Bilingualism, 15*(3), 291–309. doi:10.1177/1367006910379299

Bordin, H. (2000). *Mit vort un maysim.* Israel.

Borodulin, K. (2015, October 29). Yidish af internets.

Boulos, M. N. K., Maramba, I., & Wheeler, S. (2006). Wikis, blogs and podcasts: A new generation of Web-based tools for virtual collaborative clinical practice and education. *BMC Medical Education, 6*(41). PMID:16911779

Bourdon, S. (2002). The integration of qualitative data analysis software in research strategies: Resistances and possibilities. *Forum Qualitative Sozial Forschung, 3*(2), 1–10.

Bower, M., Woo, K., Roberts, M., & Watters, P. (2006). Wiki pedagogy - A tale of two wikis. *Proceedings of the 2006 7th International Conference on Information Technology Based Higher Education and Training* (pp. 209-220).

Bower, B. L. (2001). Distance education: Facing the faculty challenge. *Online Journal of Distance Learning Administration, 4*(2).

Bower, J., & Kawaguchi, S. (2011). Negotiation of meaning and corrective feedback in Japanese/English eTandem. *Language Learning & Technology, 15*(1), 41–71.

Bown, J. (2006). Locus of learning and affective strategy use: Two factors affecting success in self-instructed language learning. *Foreign Language Annals, 39*(4), 640–659. doi:10.1111/j.1944-9720.2006.tb02281.x

Boyer, S., & Veeramachaneni, K. (2015). Transfer learning for predictive models in massive open online courses. In C. Conati, N. Heffernan, A. Mitrovic, & M. F. Verdejo (Eds.), Artificial Intelligence in Education, LNCS (Vol. 9112, pp. 54-63). Switzerland: Springer International. doi:10.1007/978-3-319-19773-9_6

Brady, J. (2013, Spetember 2). Amish community not anti-technology just more thought. *NPR: All Tech Considered.* Retrieved from http://www.npr.org/sections/alltechconsidered/2013/09/02/217287028/amish-community-not-anti-technology-just-more-thoughful

Brain, P. O. P. ESL. (n. d.). Retrieved from https://esl.brainpop.com/

Brame, C. (2013). Flipping the classroom. Vanderbilt University Center for Teaching. Retrieved from http://cft.vanderbilt.edu/guides-sub-pages/flipping-the-classroom/

Brammerts, H. (1996). Language learning in tandem using the internet. In M. Warschauer (Ed.), *Telecollaboration in Foreign Language Learning, Second Language Teaching and Curriculum Center, Universtiy of Hawai'i* (pp. 121–130). Manoa.

Brandl, K. (2008). *Communicative language teaching in action: Putting Principles to Work.* Upper Saddle River, NJ: Prentice Hall.

Bransford, J. D., Brown, A. L., & Cocking, R. R. (2000). *How people learn: Brian, mind, experience, and school.* Washington, D.C.: National Academy Press.

Braul, B. (2006). *ESL teacher perceptions and attitudes toward using computer-assisted language learning (CALL): recommendations for effective CALL practice* [MA dissertation]. Department of Secondary Education, Edmonton, Alberta, Canada.

Breault, R. A. (2003). Dewey, FreJre, and a pedagogy for the oppressor. *Multicultural Education, 10*(3), 2–6.

Breen, M., & Littlejohn, A. (Eds.), (2000). *Classroom decision-making: Negotiation and process syllabuses in practice.* Cambridge, UK: Cambridge University.

Brinbaum, Y., & Cebolla-Boado, H. (2007). The school careers of ethnic minority youth. *Ethnicities, 7*(3), 445–473.

Brinbaum, Y., & Kieffer, A. (2009). Trajectories of immigrants' children in secondary education in France: Differentiation and polarization. *Population-E, 64*(3), 507–554.

Brindley, G., & Nunan, D. (1992). *Draft Bandscales for Listening. IELTS research projects: project 1 NCELTR.* MacQuarie University.

Brisk, M. E., & Harrington, M. M. (2000). *Literacy and bilingualism: A handbook for alAl teachers.* Mahwah, N.J.: Lawrence Earlbaum Associates.

Brophy, J. (2004). *Using Video in Teacher Education.* Bingley: Emerald Group Publishing Limited.

Brown, D. B. (2014). *Mobile learning for communicative language teaching: An exploration of how higher education language instructors design communicative mall environments* [Doctoral dissertation]. The University of Memphis, Memphis, TN, USA.

Brown, J. D. (2005). Testing in language programs: A comprehensive guide to English language assessment (New Ed.). New York: McGraw-Hill College.

Brown, A. (2009). Less commonly taught language and commonly taught language students: A demographic and academic comparison. *Foreign Language Annals, 42*(3), 405–423. doi:10.1111/j.1944-9720.2009.01036.x

Brown, J. S., Collins, A., & Duguid, P. (1989). Situated cognition and the culture of learning. *Educational Researcher, 18*(1), 32–42. doi:10.3102/0013189X018001032ʹ

Brown, P., & Levinson, S. C. (1987). *Politeness: Some universals in language usage.* New York: Cambridge University Press.

Brush, T., & Saye, J. (2008). *The effects of multimedia-supported problem-based inquiry on student engagement, empathy, and assumptions about history. Interdisciplinary Journal of Problem-Based Learning, 2(1).* Available at; doi:10.7771/1541-5015.1052

Buckley, F. (2011). Online discussion forums. *European Political Science, 10*(3), 402–415. doi:10.1057/eps.2010.76

Bullock, B. (2009). Themes in the study of code-switching. In The Cambridge Handbook of Linguistic Code-Switching (pp. 1-17).

Burns, T., & Shadoian-Gersing, V. (2010). Supporting effective practice: the pending agenda. In T. Burns & V. Shadoian-Gersing (Eds.), *Educating Teachers for Diversity: Meeting the Challenge.* Paris: OECD. doi:10.1787/9789264079731-16-en

Burston, J. (2003). Proving IT works. *CALICO Journal, 20*(2), 219–226.

Burston, J. (2014). The reality of MALL: Still on the fringes. *CALICO Journal, 31*(1), 103–125. doi:10.11139/cj.31.1.103-125

Burt, M. (1999). *Using videos with adult English language learners.* East Lansing, MI: National Center for Research on Teacher Learning.

Butler, D. L., & Sellbom, M. (2002). Barriers to adopting technology for teaching and learning. *EDUCAUSE Quarterly*, 2, 22–28.

Butler, K. (2010). Tweeting your own horn. *District Administration, 46*(2), 41–44.

Butnick, S. (2014, September 19). Yiddish Goes Virtual With Online Classes. Retrieved from http://www.tabletmag.com/scroll/185004/yiddish-goes-virtual-with-online-classes

BuzzFeedYellow. (n. d.). *The Jewish Food Taste Test*. Retrieved from https://www.youtube.com/watch?v=SqYGGqTC_Us

Byram, M. (1997). *Teaching and assessing intercultural communicative competence*. Clevedon, UK: Multilingual Matters.

Byram, M., & Fleming, M. (1998). Introduction. In M. Byram & M. Fleming (Eds.), *Language learning in intercultural perspective: Approaches through drama and ethnography* (pp. 1–10). Cambridge: Cambridge University Press.

Byrnes, H. (2009). Perspectives. *Modern Language Journal, 93*(2), 261–263. doi:10.1111/j.1540-4781.2009.00860_1.x

Cadd, M. (2012). Encouraging students to engage with native speakers during study abroad. *Foreign Language Annals, 45*(2), 229–245. doi:10.1111/j.1944-9720.2012.01188.x

Cajkler, W., & Hall, B. (2012). Languages in primary classrooms: A study of new teacher capability and practice. *Language Awareness, 21*(1-2), 15–32. doi:10.1080/09658416.2011.639889

Campbell, A. (2003). Weblogs for use with ESL classes. *The Internet TESL Journal, 9*(2). Retrieved from http://iteslj.org/ Techniques/Campbell- Weblogs.html

Campbell, S. (2006). Perceptions of mobile phones in college classrooms: Ringing, cheating, and classroom policies. *Communication Education, 55*(3), 280–294. doi:10.1080/03634520600748573

Canagarajah, S. (2014). Theorizing a competence for translingual practice at the context zone. In S. May (Ed.), *The Multilingual Turn* (pp. 291-309). Oxon: Routledge.

Canagarajah, S. (2013). *Translingual Practice. Global Englishes and Cosmopolitan Relations*. Oxon: Routledge.

Canale, M., & Swain, M. (1980). Theoretical bases of communicative approaches to second language teaching and testing. *Applied Linguistics, 1*(1), 1–47. doi:10.1093/applin/1.1.1

Candelier, M. (2008). Approches plurielles, didactiques du plurilinguisme: Le même et l'autre. *Cahiers de l'ACEDLE, 5*(1), 65–90.

Candlin, C. N. (1987). Towards task-based language learning. In C. N. Candlin and D. Murphy (Eds.), Lancaster practical papers in English language education (Vol. 7, pp. 5-22). Englewood Cliffs, NJ: Prentice Hall.

Capucho, F., Martins, A., Degache, Ch., & Tost, M. (Eds.), (2007). *Diálogos em Intercompreensão*. Lisboa: Universidade Católica Portuguesa.

Capucho, F. (2008). L'intercompréhension est-elle une mode? Du linguiste citoyen au citoyen plurilingue. *Revue Pratiques*, 139-140, 238–250. doi:10.4000/pratiques.1252

Carroll, B (2003). Going hybrid: Online course components increase flexibility of on-campus courses. *Online Classroom*, February, 4-7.

Cashman, H. (2005). Identities at play: Language preference and group membership in bilingual talk in interaction. *Journal of Pragmatics, 37*(3), 301–315. doi:10.1016/j.pragma.2004.10.004

Cassidy, S. (2006). Developing employability skills: Peer assessment in higher education. *Journal of Education and Training, 48*(7), 508–517. doi:10.1108/00400910610705890

Castellotti, V., & Moore, D. (2005). Répertoires pluriels, cultures métalinguistiques et usages d'appropriation. In J.C. Beacco, et al. (Eds.), Les cultures éducatives et linguistiquesdans l'enseignement des langues (pp. 107-132). Paris, PUF.

Castellottie, V., & Moore, D. (2011). La compétence plurilingue et pluriculturelle: genèse et évolution d'une notion-concept. In *P. Blanchet, & P. Chardenet (Eds.), Guide pour la recherche en didactique des langues et des cultures: approches contextualisées. In Archives contemporaines* (pp. 241–252). Pages.

Castrillo de Larreta-Azelain, D. (2013). Learners' attitude toward collaborative writing in e- language learning classes: A twitter project for German as a foreign language. *Revista Española de Lingüística Aplicada, 26*, 127–138.

Catera, E., & Emigh, R. (2005). Blogs, the Virtual Soapbox. *Essential Teacher, 2*(3), 46–49.

Caulfield, J. (2011). *How to design and teach a hybrid course: Achieving student-centered learning through blended classroom, online, and experiential activities.* Sterling, VA: Stylus.

Caulfield, M. (2013). *xMOOC Communities Should Learn From cMOOCs.* Retrieved from EduCause Review website: http://www.educause.edu/blogs/mcaulfield/xmooc-communities-should-learn-cmoocs

Caulfield, J. (2011). *How to design and teach a hybrid course: Achieving student-centered learning through blended classroom, online and experiential activities.* Sterling, Virginia: Publishing, LLC.

CBS News. (2014, February 24). Mark Zuckerberg on "connecting the world," and why he bought WhatsApp. Retrieved from http://www.cbsnews.com/news/mark-zuckerberg-on-connecting-the-world-and-why-he-bought-whatsapp-in-speech-at-world-mobile-congress/

Celce-Murcia, M., & Olshtain, E. (2000). *Discourse and context in language teaching.* New York: Cambridge University Press.

Çelik, S., Aytin, K., & Bayram, E. (2013). Implementing cooperative learning in the language classroom: Opinions of Turkish teachers of English. *Social and Behavioral Sciences, 70*, 1852–1859.

Chan, K. K., & Ridgway, J. (2005). Blog: a tool for reflective practice in teacher education? *Paper presented at the3rd International Conference on Education and Information Systems: Technologies and Applications*, Orlando, 333-337.

Chang, R., Hung, Y., & Lin, C. (2015). Experiential online development for educators: The example of the Carpe Diem MOOC. *British Journal of Educational Technology, 46*(3), 528–541. doi:10.1111/bjet.12275

Chan, W. M., & Chi, S. W. (2011). Popular media as a motivational factor for foreign language learning: The example of the Korean wave. In W. W. Chan, K. N. Chin, M. Nagami, & T. Suthiwan (Eds.), *Media in foreign language teaching and learning* (pp. 151–188). De Gruyter Mouton. doi:10.1515/9781614510208.151

Chao, C. (2007). Theory and research: New emphases of assessment. In J. Egbert & E. Hanson-Smith (Eds.), *CALL environments: Research, practice, and critical issues* (2nd ed., pp. 227–240). Alexandria, VA: TESOL.

Chappell, B. (2016, March 9). A.I. program from Google beats human world champ in game of Go. *NPR: The Two-Way.* Retrieved from http://www.npr.org/sections/thetwo-way/2016/03/09/469788814/ai-program-from-google-beats-human-world-champ-in-game-of-go

Chase, C., & Alexander, P. (2007). The Japan-Korea culture exchange project. In R. O'Dowd (Ed.), *Online intercultural exchange: An introduction for foreign language teachers* (pp. 259–263). Clevedon, UK: Multilingual Matters.

Chen, P. (2004). *EFL student's learning style preferences and attitudes toward technology-integrated instruction* [Ph.D. Dissertation]. University of South Dakota.

Chen, C. (2011). Online Chinese teaching and learning: A case study. *Journal of Technology and Chinese Language Teaching, 2*(2), 50–68.

Chen, C. M., Wang, J. Y., & Chen, Y. C. (2014). Facilitating English-language reading performance by a digital reading annotation system with self-regulated learning mechanisms. *Journal of Educational Technology & Society, 17*(1), 102–114.

Chen, C.-M., & Li, Y.-L. (2010). Personalized context-aware ubiquitous learning system for supporting effective English vocabulary learning. *Interactive Learning Environments, 18*(4), 341–364. doi:10.1080/10494820802602329

Chen, J. J., & Yang, S. C. (2014). Fostering foreign language learning through technology-enhanced intercultural projects. *Language Learning & Technology, 18*(1), 57–75. Retrieved from http://llt.msu.edu/issues/february2014/chenyang.pdf

Chenoweth, N., Ushida, E., & Murday, K. (2006). Student learning in hybrid French and Spanish courses: An overview of language online. *CALICO Journal, 24*(1), 115–146.

Cheon, J., Lee, S., Crooks, S. M., & Song, J. (2012). An investigation of mobile learning readiness in higher education based on the theory of planned behavior. *Computers & Education, 59*(3), 1054–1064. doi:10.1016/j.compedu.2012.04.015

Cherng, R. J., Chang, C., & Chen, J. (2009). A new look at gender inequality in Chinese: A study of Chinese speakers' perception of gender-based characters. *Sex Roles, 61*, 427–443.

Chik, A. (2014). Digital gaming and language learning: Autonomy and community. *Language Learning & Technology, 18*(2), 85–100.

Chinnery, G. M. (2006). Going to the MALL: Mobile assisted language learning (Emerging technology). *Language Learning & Technology, 10*(1), 9–16.

Chun, D. M. (1994). Using computer networking to facilitate the acquisition of interactive competence. *System, 22*(1), 17–31. doi:10.1016/0346-251X(94)90037-X

Chun, D. M. (2011). Developing intercultural communicative competence through online exchanges. *CALICO Journal, 28*(2), 392–419. doi:10.11139/cj.28.2.392-419

Chun, D. M., & Plass, J. L. (2000). Networked multimedia environments for second language acquisition. In M. Warschauer & R. Kern (Eds.), *Network-based language teaching: Concepts and Practice* (pp. 20–40). Cambridge University Press. doi:10.1017/CBO9781139524735.009

Clarke, D., & Hollingsworth, H. (2000). Seeing is understanding. *Journal of Staff Development, 21*, 40–43.

Clark, K. (2009). The case for Structured English Immersion. *Educational Leadership, 66*(7), 42–46.

Clément, L. R. (1986). Second language proficiency and acculturation: An investigation of the effects of language status and individual characteristics. *Journal of Language and Social Psychology, 5*(4), 271–290. doi:10.1177/0261927X8600500403

Cohen, E., & Allen, A. (2013). Toward an ideal democracy: The impact of standardization policies on the American Indian/Alaska native community and language revitalization efforts. *Educational Policy, 27*(5), 743–769.

Cole, J. E., & Kritzer, J. B. (2009). Strategies for success: Teaching an online course. *Rural Special Education Quarterly, 28*(4), 36–40.

Collentine, J., & Freed, B. F. (2004). Learning context and its effects on second language acquisition: Introduction. *Studies in Second Language Acquisition, 26*(02), 153–171. doi:10.1017/S0272263104262015

Collins, P. T. (2011). An insider's view to meeting the challenges of blended learning solutions. T + D, 65(12), 56-61.

Collis, B., & Moonen, J. (2001). *Flexible Learning in a Digital World: experiences and expectations.* London: Kogan Page.

Colpaert, J. (2014). Conclusion. Reflections on present and future: Towards an ontological approach to LMOOCs. In E. Martín-Monje & E. Bárcena (Eds.), *Language MOOCs: Providing Learning, Transcending Boundaries* (pp. 161–170). Warsaw: De Gruyter Open. doi:10.2478/9783110420067.10

Commerford, S. A. (2005). Engaging through Learning-Learning through engaging: An alternative approach to professional learning about human diversity. *Social Work Education, 24*(1), 113–135. doi:10.1080/0261547052000325017

Comprehensive Yiddish-English Dictionary. (n. d.). Retrieved from http://verterbukh.org/

Conlin, J. (2014). The *Gazette Littéraire de l'Europe* and Anglo-French cultural diplomacy. *Études Épistémè.* Retrieved from http://episteme.revues.org/310

Consalvo, M. (2009). Convergence and globalization in the Japanese videogame industry. *Cinema Journal, 48*(3), 135–141.

Consani, M. A. (2008). Technological mediation in education: concepts and applications [Master's thesis]. Universidade de São Paulo, São Paulo, Brazil.

Conseil de l'Europe, C. (2001). *Cadre européen commun de référence pour les langues.* Les Éditions Didier, Paris. Retrieved from http://www.coe.int/t/dg4/linguistic/Source/Framework_FR.pdf

Cooper, C., & Boddington, L. (2005). *Assessment by blog: Ethical case studies assessment for an undergraduate management Class.* Retrieved from http://incsub.org/ blogtalk/?page_id=62

Cope, B., & Kalantzis, M. (2010). New media, new learning. In D. Cole & D. Pullen (Eds.), *Multiliteracies in motion: Current theory and practice.* New York: Routledge.

Cordova, S. T. (2008). Use of visual aids in teaching of veterinary medicine. *Revista Eletrônica Lato Sensu, São Paulo, 3*(1), 1–15.

Coste, D. (2001). La notion de compétence plurilingue. *Proceedings of the seminar L'enseignement des langues vivantes, perspectives.* Retrieved from: http://eduscol.education.fr/pid25239-cid46534/la-notion-de-competence-plurilingue.html

Coste, D., Moore, D., & Zarate, G. (2009). *Compétence plurilingue et pluriculturelle.* Strasbourg: Conseil de l'Europe.

Coyle, D. (2005). Developing CLIL. Towards a theory of practice. *APAC Monographs, 6*, 5–29.

Crawford, J. (2004). *Educating English learners: Language diversity in the classroom.* Los Angeles: Bilingual Education Services.

Crossette, B. (2001). Diplomatically, French is a faded rose in an English garden. *The New York Times.* Retrieved from http://www.nytimes.com/2001/03/25/world/diplomatically-french-is-a-faded-rose-in-an-english-garden.html

Crystal, D. (2000). *Language Death.* New York, NY: Cambridge University Press. doi:10.1017/CBO9781139106856

CTC. (2014). Serving English Learners. State of California Commission on Teacher Credentialing. Retrieved from http://www.ctc.ca.gov/credentials/leaflets/cl622.pdf

Cubillos, (2007). A comparative study of hybrid versus traditional instruction in foreign languages. *NECTFL Review, 38*, 20-38.

Cubillos, J. H. (1998). Technology: A step forward in the teaching of foreign languages? In J. Harper, M. Lively, & M. Williams (Eds.), *The coming of age of the profession: Issues and emerging ideas for the teaching of foreign languages* (pp. 37–52). Boston: Heinle and Heinle.

Cui, Y., & Bull, S. (2005). Context and learner modelling for the mobile foreign language learner. *System, 33*(2), 353–367. doi:10.1016/j.system.2004.12.008

Cummins, J. (1979). Cognitive/academic language proficiency, linguistic interdependence, the optimum age question and some other matters. *Working Papers on Bilingualism, 19*, 121–129.

Cviko, A., McKenney, S., & Voogt, J. (2014). Teacher roles in designing technology-rich learning activities for early literacy: A cross-case analysis. *Computers & Education, 72*, 68–79. doi:10.1016/j.compedu.2013.10.014

D'Cunha, R. (2014, March 7). Semiotics and the #Hashtag. Digital Marketing Blog. Retrieved from http://www.gravy-train.co.uk/blog/semiotics-hashtag/

Dalby, A. (2003). *Language in danger: The loss of linguistic diversity and the threat to our future.* New York, NY: Columbia University Press.

Dalton-Puffer, C. (Ed.). (2007). Empirical perspectives on CLIL classroom discourse. Frankfurt: Peter Lang.

Damron, J., & Forsyth, J. (2012). Korean language studies: Motivation and attrition. *Journal of Less Commonly Taught Languages, 12*, 161–182.

Daniel, J. (2012). Making sense of MOOCs: Musings in a maze of myth, paradox and possibility. *Journal of Interactive Media in Education.* Retrieved from http://www-jime.open.ac.uk/jime/article/viewArticle/2012-18/html

Daniels, H. (2008). *Vygotsky and research.* Abingdon: Routledge.

Danker, B. (2015). Using flipped classroom approach to explore deep learning in large classrooms. *The IAFOR Journal of Education, 3*(1), 171–186.

Darder, A., & Uriarte, M. (2013). The politics of restrictive language policies: A postcolonial analysis of language and schooling. *Postcolonial Directions in Education, 2*(1), 6–67.

Davari, H., & Aghagolzadeh, F. (2015). To teach or not to teach? Still an open question for the Iranian education system. In C. Kennedy (Ed.), *English language teaching in the Islamic Republic of Iran: Innovations, trends and challenges* (pp. 13–22). UK: British Council.

Davidson, N., & Worsham, T. (1992). *Enhancing thinking through cooperative learning.* New York: Teachers College Press.

Davies, R. S., Dean, D. L., & Ball, N. (2013). Flipping the classroom and instructional technology integration in a college-level information systems spreadsheet course. *Educational Technology Research and Development, 61*(4), 563–580. doi:10.1007/s11423-013-9305-6

Davis, F. D. (1989). Perceived Usefulness, Perceived Ease of Use, and User Acceptance of Information Technology. *Management Information Systems Quarterly, 13*(3), 319–340. doi:10.2307/249008

Dawson, S., Joksimović, S., Kovanović, V., Gašević, D., & Siemens, G. (2015). Recognizing learner autonomy: Lessons and reflections from a joint x/cMOOC. *Proceedings of HERDSA conference.* Retrieved from http://www.sfu.ca/~dgasevic/papers_shared/herdsa15.pdf

Dawson, M. (2010). Television between analog and digital. *Journal of Popular Film & Television, 38*(2), 95–100.

De Avila, E., Cohen, E., & Intili, J. (1981). Multicultural improvement of cognitive abilities. *Final Report to the California State Department of Education.*

de Freitas, S., Morgan, J., & Gibson, D. (2015). Will MOOCs transform learning and teaching in higher education? Engagement and course retention in online learning provision. *British Journal of Educational Technology, 46*(3), 455–471. doi:10.1111/bjet.12268

de Larreta-Azelain, M. (2014). Language teaching in MOOCs: The integral role of the instructor. In E. Martín-Monje & E. Bárcena (Eds.), *Language MOOCs: Providing learning, transcending boundaries* (pp. 67–90). Warsaw: De Gruyter Open. doi:10.2478/9783110420067.5

Dearden, J. (2015). *British Council Report, English as a medium of instruction– a growing global phenomenon.* Oxford: University of Oxford.

Dehaene, S. (2009). *Reading in the Brain: The Science and Evolution of a Human Invention.* New York, NY: VIKING.

DeKeyser, R. M. (1991). Foreign language development during a semester abroad. In B. F. Freed (Ed.), *Foreign langauge acquisition and the classroom* (pp. 104–118). Lexington, MA: D. C. Heath.

Delors, J. et al.. (2004). *Education: The treasure within. Report to UNESCO of the International Commission on Education for the XXI. 9* (p. 80). São Paulo: Cortez.

Demski, J. (2013). 6 expert tips for flipping the classroom. *Campus Technology, 25*(5), 32–37.

Dennen, V. P., & Jiang, W. (2012). Twitter-based knowledge sharing in professional networks: The organization perspective. In V. P. Dennen & J. B. Myers (Eds.), *Virtual professional development and informal learning via social networks* (pp. 241–255). Hershey, PA: IGI. doi:10.4018/978-1-4666-1815-2.ch014

Derderian-Aghajanian, A., & Wang, C. C. (2012). How culture affects on English Language Learners' (ELL's) outcomes, with Chinese and Middle Eastern immigrant students. *International Journal of Business and Social Science, 3*(5), 172–180.

DeVellis, R. F. (2003). *Scale development: Theory and applications* (2nd ed.). Thousand Oaks, CA: Sage Publications, Inc.

Dieu, B. (2004). Blogs for language learning. In *Essential Teacher* (pp. 26-30).

Dillon, M. (2009). *Contemporary China: An introduction.* New York, NY: Routledge.

Dippold, D. (2009). Peer feedback through blogs: Student and teacher perceptions in an advanced German class. *ReCALL, 21*(1), 1–33. doi:10.1017/S095834400900010X

Dixon, E., & Thomas, M. (Eds.). (2015). *Researching Language Learner Interactions Online: From Social Media to MOOCs.* San Marcos, TX: CALICO.

Dixon, L., Zhao, J., Shin, J., Wu, S., Su, J., Brigham, R., & Snow, C. et al. (2012). What we know about second language acquisition: A synthesis. *Review of Educational Research, 82*(1), 5–60. doi:10.3102/0034654311433587

Dolby, N. (2012). *Rethinking Multicultural Education for the Next Generation.* New York: Routledge.

Dong, H. (2014). *A history of the Chinese language.* New York, NY: Routledge.

Dooly, M., & O'Dowd, R. (1996). *Researching online foreign language interaction and exchange: Theories, methods and challenges.* Peter Lang. Gombert, J. É.

Dörnyei, Z. (1995). On the teachability of communication strategies. *TESOL Quarterly, 29*(1), 55–85. doi:10.2307/3587805

Dörnyei, Z. (2000). Motivation in action: Towards a process-oriented conceptualization of student motivation. *The British Journal of Educational Psychology*, *70*(4), 519–538. doi:10.1348/000709900158281 PMID:11191185

Dörnyei, Z., & Malderez, A. (1997). Group dynamics and foreign language teaching. *System*, *25*(1), 65–81. doi:10.1016/S0346-251X(96)00061-9

Dörnyei, Z., & Scott, M. L. (1997). Communication strategies in a second language: Definitions and taxonomies. *Language Learning*, *47*(1), 173–210. doi:10.1111/0023-8333.51997005

Dornyei, Z., & Ushioda, E. (2009). Motivation, language identiteis and the L2 self: A theoretical overview. In Z. Dornyei & E. Ushioda (Eds.), *Motivation, language identity and the L2 self* (pp. 1–8). Bristol: Multilingual Matters.

Downs, S. (2004). Educational blogging. *Educational Review*, *39*(5), 14–26.

Doyé, P., & Meissner, F.-J. (Eds.). (2010). *Lernerautonomie durch Interkomprehension: Projekte und Perspektiven / L'autonomisation de l'apprenant par l'intercompréhension: projets et perspectives / Promoting Learner Autonomy through intercomprehension: projects and perspectives*. Tübingen: Narr.

Ducate, L., & Lomicka, L. (2005). Exploring the blogosphere: Use of blogs in the foreign language classroom. *Foreign Language Annals*, *38*(3), 410–421. doi:10.1111/j.1944-9720.2005.tb02227.x

Duncan, G. (1991). Forward. In E. S. Silber (Ed.), *Critical issues in foreign language instruction*. New York, NY: Garland Publishing, Inc.

Dunlap, J. C., & Lowenthal, P. R. (2009). Tweeting the night away: Using Twitter to enhance social presence. *Journal of Information Systems Education*, *202*, 129–135.

Dunne, K., & Palvyshyn, M. (2013). Endangered species? Less commonly taught languages in the linguistic ecology of Australian higher education. *Babel*, *47*(3), 4–15.

Dunne, K., & Palvyshyn, M. (2013). Endangered Species? Less Commonly Taught Languages in the Linguistic Ecology of Australian Higher Education. *Babel*, *47*(3), 4–15.

Dziuban, C., & Moskal, P. (2013). Distributed learning impact evaluation. Retrieved from http://cdl.ucf.edu/research/rite/dl-impact-evaluation/

Dziuban, C., Hartman, J., Juge, F., Moskal, P., & Sorg, S. (2006). Blended learning enters the mainstream. In C. J. Bonk & C. R. Graham (Eds.), *Handbook of blended learning: Global perspectives, local designs* (pp. 195–208). San Francisco, CA: Pfeiffer.

Easton, S. S. (2003). Clarifying the instructor's role in online distance learning. *Communication Education*, *52*(2), 87–105. doi:10.1080/03634520302470

Ebrey, P. B. (2006). *China: A cultural social political society*. Boston: Wadsworth Publishing.

Eder, D. J. (2007). Bringing Navajo storytelling practices into schools: The importance of maintaining cultural integrity. *Anthropology & Education Quarterly*, *38*(3), 278–296.

Educause Learning Initiative. (2012). 7 things you should know about flipped classrooms. *ELI Publications*. Retrieved from http://www.educause.edu/library/resources/7-things-you-should-know-about-flipped-classrooms

Edwards, J., & Mehring, J. (2005). Just-in-time teaching. *Hawai TESOL*, *15*(1), 1-12. Retrieved from http://www.hawaiitesol.org/Word%202005%20Sept.pdf

Edwards, J. D. (2000). Working beyond the academy: The federal government. *ADFL*, *32*(1), 48–49. doi:10.1632/adfl.32.1.48

Edwards, L. (2003). Koscielniak, Bruce. Johannz Gutenberg and the amazing printing press. *School Library Journal*, *49*(9), 184.

Egbert, J., & Hanson-Smith, E. (2007). *CALL environments: Research, practice, and critical issues.* Alexandria, Virginia: Teachers of English to Speakers of Other Languages, Inc.

Egbert, J. L., & Jessup, L. M. (1996). Analytic and systemic analyses of computer-supported language learning environments. *TESL-EJ*, *2*(2), 1–24.

Egbert, J., Hanson-Smith, E., & Chao, C. (2007). Foundations for teaching and learning. In J. Egbert & E. Hanson-Smith (Eds.), *CALL environments: Research, practice, and critical issues* (2nd ed., pp. 1–14). Alexandria, VA: TESOL.

Egbert, J., Paulus, T. M., & Nakamichi, Y. (2002). The impact of CALL instruction on classroom computer use: A foundation for rethinking technology in teacher education. *Language Learning & Technology*, *6*(3), 108–126.

Ehrhart, S. (2010). Pourquoi intégrer la diversité linguistique et culturelle dans la formation des enseignants au Luxembourg. In S. Ehrhart, Ch. Hélot & A. Nevez (Eds.), *Plurilinguisme et Formation des Enseignants: une approche critique* (pp. 221-238). Bern: Peter Lang.

Ehrlich, P. R., & Ornstein, R. (2010). *Humanity on a tightrope: Thoughts on empathy, family and big changes for a viable future.* New York: Rowman and Littlefield.

Eisenberg, R. (1995). Boychiks in the Hood: Travels in the Hasidic Underground (1st ed.). San Francisco, CA: Harper.

Eisenstein, M. (1950). Jewish Schools in Poland, 1919-1939. New York.

Elia, A. (2006). Language learning in tandem via Skype. *The Reading Matrix*, *6*(3), 269–280.

Ellis, R. (2003). *Task-based language learning and teaching.* Oxford, UK: Oxford University Press.

Ellwood, C. (2008). Questions of classroom identity: What can be learned from codeswitching in classroom peer group talk. *Modern Language Journal*, *92*(4), 538–557. doi:10.1111/j.1540-4781.2008.00786.x

Ene, E., & Connor, U. (2014). Technological applications for language teaching: ICT and equipment use in teaching & learning foreign languages. National Foreign Languages 2020 Project, Hanoi, Vietnam.

Engeström, Y., Miettinen, R., & Punamäki, R. (1999). *Perspectives on activity theory.* Cambridge: Cambridge University Press. doi:10.1017/CBO9780511812774

Eröz-Tuga, B., & Sadler, R. (2009). Comparing six video chat tools: A critical evaluation by language teachers. *Computers & Education*, *53*(3), 787–798. doi:10.1016/j.compedu.2009.04.017

Ertmer, P. (2007). Using peer feedback to enhance the quality of student online postings: An exploratory study. *Journal of Computer-Mediated Communication*, 12(2). Retrieved from http://jcmc.indiana.edu/vol12/issue2/ertmer.html

Ertmer, P. A., Addison, P., Lane, M., Ross, E., & Woods, D. (1999). Examining teachers' beliefs about the role of technology in the elementary classroom. *Journal of Research on Computing in Education*, *32*(1), 54–71. doi:10.1080/08886504.1999.10782269

Estraikh, G., Katz, D., & Clifford, D. (1996). *Intensive Yiddish: with grammar sections based on Gennady Estraikh's Grammar of the Yiddish Language.* Oxford: Oksforder Yidish Press.

Ethnologue, Y. Eastern. (2015). Retrieved from https://www.ethnologue.com/language/ydd

European Commission. (2007). *Key competences for lifelong learning. European Framework of Reference.* Luxembourg: European Commission.

European Commission. (2010). *New skills for new jobs: Action now*. Retrieved from http://ec.europa.eu/social/main.js p?catId=568&langId=en&eventsId=232&furtherEvents=yes

European Commission. (2012). *Europeans and their languages*. Retrieved from http://ec.europa.eu/public_opinion/ archives/ebs/ebs_386_en.pdf

Eurydice. (2006). *Content and language integrated learning (CLIL) at schools in Europe*. Brussels: European Commission.

Eurydice. (2009). *National testing of pupils in Europe: Objectives, organisation and use of results*. Brussels: European Commission.

Evers, T. (2015). 2014-2015 Virtual Charter Schools. Retrieved from http://sms.dpi.wi.gov/sites/default/files/imce/sms/ pdf/cs_2015_VirtualSchs.pdf

Fairclough, N. (2001). *Language and power* (2nd ed.). London, UK: Longman.

Fan, K. (2015, October 21). With over 50 offerings, Columbia's language program second largest among Ivies. Retrieved from http://columbiaspectator.com/news/2015/10/21/languages

Fanselow, J. F. (1987). *Breaking rules: Generating and exploring alternatives in language teaching*. White Plains, NY: Longman, Inc.

Farrell Whitworth, K. (2009). The discussion forum as a locus for developing L2 pragmatic awareness. In L. Abraham & L. Williams (Eds.), *Electronic Discourse in Foreign Language Learning and Teaching* (pp. 263–289). Amsterdam: John Benjamins. doi:10.1075/lllt.25.20whi

FAU Judaica Sound Archives Research Station. (n. d.). Retrieved from http://faujsa.fau.edu/jsa/research_station.php

Fazenda, C.A.I. (1993). *Interdisciplinaridade: história, teoria e pesquisa* (2nd ed.). Campinas, SP: Loyola.

Fazey, M. (1999). *Guidelines to help instructors help their learners get the most out of video lessons*. Unpublished manuscript. Lexington, KY: Kentucky Educational Television.

Fearon, C., McLaughlin, H., & Eng, T. Y. (2012). Using student group work in higher education to emulate professional communities of practice. *Education + Training, 54*(2/3), 114- 125.

Fechbach, N. D., & Fechbach, S. (2011). Empathy and Education. In J. Decety & W. Ickes (Eds.), *The Social Neuroscience of Empathy*. Massachusetts: MIT Press.

Fedorov, A. (2001). A Russian Perspective. *Educommunication (Belgium), 55*, 92–95.

Feldscher, K. (2015, September 25). Obama wants 1 million Americans learnning Chinese by 2020. *Washington Examiner*. Retrieved from http://www.washingtonexaminer.com/obama-wants-1-million-americans-learning-chinese-by-2020/ article/2572865

Felix, U. (2002). The web as vehicle for constructivist approaches in language teaching. *ReCAL, 14*(1), 2–15. doi:10.1017/ S0958344002000216

Feng, A. (2009). English in China convergence and divergence in policy and practice. *AILA Review, 22*(1), 85.

Ferguson, H. (2010). Join the flock! *Learning and Leading with Technology, 37*(8), 12–15.

Fernandez-Garcia, M., & Martinez-Arbelaiz, A. (2002). Negotiation of meaning in non-native speaker non-native speaker synchronous discussions. *CALICO Journal, 19*, 279–294.

Filippetti, A. (2014). *Les langues de France*. Paris: Dalloz.

Finardi, K. (2014). The slaughter of Kachru's five sacred cows in Brazil: Affordances of the use of English as an international language. *Studies in English Language Teaching*, 2(4), 401.

Fishman, D. E. (2010). The Rise of Modern Yiddish Culture (1st paperback ed.). Pittsburgh, PA: Univ. of Pittsburgh Press.

Fishman, J. E. (1991). Yiddish: Turning to Life. Amsterdam, PA: J. doi:10.1075/z.49

Fitts, S., Winstead, L., Weisman, E., Flores, S., & Valenciana, C. (2008). Coming to voice: Preparing bilingual-bicultural teachers for social justice. *Equity & Excellence in Education*, 40(3), 357–371. doi:10.1080/10665680802174916

Flanders, N. A. (1970). *Analyzing teaching behavior*. Menlo Park, CA: Addison-Wesley.

Fleming, S., Hiple, D., & Du, Y. (2002). Foreign language distance education: The University of Hawaii experience. In C. A. Spreen (Ed.), *New technologies and language learning: Cases in the less commonly taught* (pp. 13–54). Honolulu, HI: Second Language Teaching &Curriculum Center.

Flores, S. (2005). Teaching Latino children and youth. *High School Journal*, 88(2), 1–2. doi:10.1353/hsj.2004.0022

Flores, S., & Murillo, E. (2001). Power, language, and ideology: Historical and contemporary notes on the dismantling of bilingual education. *The Urban Review*, 33(3), 183–206.

Foale, C., & Carson, L. (2006). Creating a student driven self-access language learning resource.*Proceedings of the Joint BAAL/IRAAL Conference*, Cork.

Foertsch, J., Moses, G., Strikwerda, J., & Litzkow, M. (2002). Reversing the lecture/homework paradigm using eTEACH® web-based streaming video software. *The Journal of Engineering Education*, 91(3), 267–274. doi:10.1002/j.2168-9830.2002.tb00703.x

Fornara, F. (2015, June). Micro-Input: Effects of an Instructor Model on L2 Student Practice on Twitter. Paper presented at the Computer-Assisted Language Consortium Conference, Boulder, CO, USA.

Fox, G. (1998). The Internet: making it work in the ESL classroom. *The Internet TESL Journal*, 4(9).

Freed, B. F., Segalowitz, N., & Dewey, D. P. (2004). Context of learning and second language fluency in French: Comparing regular classroom, Study Abroad, and intensive domestic immersion programs. *Studies in Second Language Acquisition*, 26(02), 275–301. doi:10.1017/S0272263104262064

Freedman, R., & Freedman, M. (n.d.). Retrieved February 16, 2016, from http://sceti.library.upenn.edu/freedman/index.cfm

Freidenreich, F. (2010). *Passionate pioneers: the story of Yiddish secular education in North America, 1910-1960*. Teaneck, NJ: Holmes & Meier Publishers.

Freire, P. (2005). *Teachers as cultural workers: Letters to those who dare teach*. Boulder, CO: Westview Press.

Friedman, J., & Chartier, R. (1996). Gutenberg revisited from the east. *Late Imperial China*, 17(1), 1–9.

Frommer, J. G. (1998). Cognition, context, and computers: Factors in effective foreign language learning. In J. Muyskens (Ed.), *New ways of learning and teaching: Focus on technology and foreign language education* (pp. 199–223). Boston: Heinle and Heinle.

Fuchs, C., Hauck, M., & Müller-Hartmann, A. (2012). Promoting learner autonomy through multiliteracy skills development in cross-institutional exchanges. *Language Learning & Technology*, 16(3), 82–102.

Fulton, K. P. (2012). Ten reasons to flip. *Phi Delta Kappan*, 94(2), 20–24. doi:10.1177/003172171209400205

Furstenberg, G. (1997). Teaching with technology: What is at stake? *ADFL Bulletin*, 28(3), 21–25. doi:10.1632/adfl.28.3.21

Galindo, D. L. (1996). Language use and language attitudes: A study of border women. *Bilingual Review, 21*, 1, 5–17.

Galla, C. K. (2009). Indigenous language revitalization and technology: From tradition to contemporary domains. In J. Reyhner & L. Lockard (Eds.), *Indigenous language revitalization: Encouragement, guidance & lessons learned* (pp. 167–182). Flagstaff, AZ: Northern Arizona University Press.

Gallardo del Puerto, F., & Gamboa, E. (2009). The evaluation of computer-mediated technology by second language teachers: Collaboration and interaction in call. *Educational Media International, 46*(2), 137–152.

Garbett, C. (2011). Activity-based costing models for alternative modes of delivering on-line courses. European Journal of Open. *Distance and E-Learning, 1*, 1–14.

García, O. (2011). The translanguaging of Latino kindergarteners. Bilingual Youth: Spanish in In *English-Speaking Societies* (pp. 33-55).

García, O. (2014). Countering the Dual: Transglossia, Dynamic Bilingualism and Translanguaging in Education. In R. Rubdy & L. Alsagoff (Eds.), *The global-local interface, language choice and hybridity* (pp. 100-118). Bristol: Multilingual Matters.

García, O., & Wei, (2014). *Translanguaging: Language, Bilingualism and Education*. New York: Palgrave MacMillan.

García, O., & Wei, Li (2014). *Translanguaging. Language, Bilingualism and Education*. Hampshire: Palgrave MacMillan.

Garcia, M. R., & Arias, F. V. (2000). A comparative study in motivation and learning through print-oriented and computer-oriented tests. *Computer Assisted Language Learning, 13*(4), 457–465. doi:10.1076/0958-8221(200012)13:4-5;1-E;FT457

García, O., & Leiva, C. (2014). Theorizing and enacting translanguaging for social justice. In A. Blackledge & A. Creese (Eds.), *Heteroglossia as Practice and Pedagogy* (pp. 199–216). London: Springer. doi:10.1007/978-94-007-7856-6_11

García, O., & Wei, L. (2014). *Translanguaging: Language, bilingualism and education*. New York, NY: Palgrave Macmillan.

Garmon, M. A. (2004). Changing Preservice Teachers' Attitudes/Beliefs About Diversity What are the Critical Factors? *Journal of Teacher Education, 55*(3), 201–213. doi:10.1177/0022487104263080

Garrison, D. R., & Kanuka, H. (2004). Blended learning: Uncovering its transformative potential in higher education. *The Internet and Higher Education, 7*(2), 95–105. doi:10.1016/j.iheduc.2004.02.001

Gascoigne, C., & Parnel, J. (2014). Hybrid language instruction: Finding the right fit. *Proceedings of theCentral States Conference on the Teaching of Foreign Languages Report* (pp. 53- 64).

Gay, G. (2010). Classroom practices for teaching diversity: an example from Washington State (United States). In T. Burns & V. Shadoian-Gersing (Eds.), *Educating Teachers for Diversity: Meeting the Challenge*. Paris: OECD. doi:10.1787/9789264079731-15-en

Gedera, D. S. P. (2011). Integration of weblogs in developing language skills of ESL learners. *International Journal of Technology in Teaching and Learning, 7*(2), 124–135.

Gee, J. P., & Hayes, E. R. (2011). *Language and learning in the digital age*. New York, NY: Routledge.

Gellevij, M., Meij, H., & Jong, T. (2002). Multimodal versus unimodal instruction in a complex learning context. *Journal of Experimental Education, 70*(3), 215–239. doi:10.1080/00220970209599507

Genette, G., & Lewin, J. E. (1997). *Paratexts: Thresholds of Interpretation*. New York: Cambridge Press. doi:10.1017/CBO9780511549373

Gerwin, D., & Osborn, T. (2005). What September 11 also teaches us. In T. A. Osborn (Ed.), *Language and cultural diversity in U.S. schools* (pp. 103–116). Westport, CT: Praeger.

Ghorbani, M. R. (2009). ELT in Iranian high schools in Iran, Malaysia and Japan: Reflections on how tests influence use of prescribed textbooks. *The Journal of Reflections on English Language Teaching, 8*(2), 131–139.

Gibbs, W. (2002) Saving dying languages. *Scientific American,* August, 79-85. Retrieved from http://www.language-archives.org/documents/sciam.pdf

Giovanangeli, A. (2009). Competing desires and realities: Language policies in the French-language classroom. *PORTAL: Journal of Multidisciplinary International Studies, 6*(1), 1–14.

Gleason, J., & Suvorov, R. (2012). Learner perceptions of asynchronous oral computer- mediated communication: Proficiency and second language selves. *Canadian Journal of Applied Linguistics, 15*(1), 100–121.

Glynn, C. (2013). Stepping out of the textbook and into contextualized language instruction. *Language and Education, 8*(6), 46–47.

Godev, C. (2014). First-year hybrid Spanish courses: How instructors manage their time. *Hispania, 97*(1), 21–31. doi:10.1353/hpn.2014.0020

Godwin-Jones, R. (2011a). Emerging technologies: Mobile apps for language learning. *Language Learning & Technology, 15*(2), 2–11.

Godwin-Jones, R. (2011b). Emerging Technologies: Autonomous language learning. *Language Learning & Technology, 15*(3), 4–11.

Godwin-Jones, R. (2013). Emerging technologies: The technological imperative in teaching and learning less commonly taught languages. *Language Learning & Technology, 17*(1), 7–19.

Goetz, J., Kiesler, S., & Powers, A. (2003, October). Matching robot appearance and behavior to tasks to improve human-robot cooperation. *Proceedings of the 12th IEEE International Workshop on Robot and Human Interactive Communication ROMAN '03* (pp. 55-60). IEEE.

Goldberg, D., Looney, D., & Lusin, N. (2015). Enrollments in Languages Other Than English in United States Institutions of Higher Education, Fall 2013. *Modern Language Association.* Retrieved from http://www.mla.org/pdf/2013_enrollment_survey.pdf

Goldberg, D., Looney, D., & Lusin, N. (2015, February 15). Enrollments in languages other than English in United States institutions of higher education. *The Modern Language Association.* Retrieved from https://www.mla.org/content/download/31180/1452509/2013_enrollment_survey.pdf

Goldberg, D. (1996). *Yidish af yidish.* New Haven, CT: Yale University Press.

Goldberg, D., Looney, D., & Lusin, N. (2015). *Enrollments in languages other than English in the United States institutions of higher education, fall 2013.* Modern Language Association of America.

Golonka, E. M., Bowles, A. R., Frank, V. M., Richardson, D. L., & Freynik, S. (2014). Technologies for foreign language learning: A review of technology types and their effectiveness. *Computer Assisted Language Learning, 27*(1), 70–105. doi:10.1080/09588221.2012.700315

Gombert, J. É. (1990). *Le développement métalinguistique.* Paris: Presses universitaires de France.

Gombert, J. E. (1992). *Metalinguistic development.* University of Chicago Press. Activités métalinguistiques et acquisition d'une langue. *Acquisition et Interaction en Langue Étrangère,* (8): 41–55.

González, J., & Wagenaar, R. (Eds.). (2003). *Tuning Educational Structures in Europe I.* Universidad de Deusto and Universidad de Groningen.

Goodrich, M. A., & Schultz, A. C. (2007). Human-robot interaction: A survey. *Foundations and Trends in Human-Computer Interaction, 1*(3), 203–275.

Goodwin-Jones, R. (2003). Blogs and wikis: Environments for on-line collaboration. *Language Learning and Technology journal, 7*(2), 12-16.

Graham, S., & Perin, D. (2007). Writing next: Effective strategies to improve writing of adolescents in middle and high schools. A report to Carnegie Corporation of New York, Washington, DC: *lliance for Excellent Education.* (pp. 1-66). Retrieved from [REMOVED HYPERLINK FIELD]www.all4ed.org/files/archive/publications/WritingNext/WritingNext.pdf

Graham, C. R. (2006). Blended learning systems: definition, current trends, future directions. In C. J. Bonk & C. R. Graham (Eds.), *Handbook of Blended Learning: Global perspectives, local designs.* San Francisco, CA: Pfeiffer Publishing.

Grami, G. M. A., & Alkazemi, B. Y. (2011). Towards a framework for building a tool to assist L2 writing based on search engines capabilities: The Case of English Phrases and Collocations. *Proceedings of the 3rd CSEDU* (pp. 225-231). Netherlands: Noordwijkerhout.

Grenoble, L., & Whaley, L. (Eds.). (1998). *Endangered languages: Current issues and future prospects.* New York, NY: Cambridge University Press. doi:10.1017/CBO9781139166959

Grgurovic, M. (2011). Blended learning in an ESL class: A case study. *CALICO Journal, 29*(1), 100–117. doi:10.11139/cj.29.1.100-117

Grinevald, C. (1998). Language endangerment in South America. In L. Grenoble & L. Whaley (Eds.), *Endangered languages: Current issues and future prospects.* New York, NY: Cambridge University Press. doi:10.1017/CBO9781139166959.007

Grosjean, F. (1984). Le bilinguisme: vivre avec deux langues. In Revue Tranel (Travaux neuchâtelois de linguistique), (7), 15-41.

Grosjean, F. (1982). *Life with two languages: an introduction to bilingualism.* Cambridge, MA: Harvard University Press.

Grosse, C. (2010). Corporate recruiter demand for foreign language and cultural knowledge. *Global Business Languages, 3*(1), 2.

Grosse, C. U. (2004). The competitive advantage of foreign languages and cultural knowledge. *Modern Language Journal, 88*(3), 351–373.

Gruba, P. (1999). *The role of digital video media in second language listening comprehension* [Unpublished doctoral dissertation]. University of Melbourne, Australia.

Gualerzi, D., & Nell, E. (2010). Transformational growth in the 1990s: Government, finance and high-tech. *Review of Political Economy, 22*(1), 97–117.

Gumperz, J. J. (1982). Discourse strategies. Cambridge University Press.

Gumperz, J. J. (1982). *Discourse strategies.* New York: Cambridge University Press.

Gumperz, J. J. (1989). *Sociolinguistique Interactionnelle: une approche interprétative. L'Harmattan.* Université de la Réunion.

Gunaratne, S. (2001). Paper, printing and the printing press: A horizontally integrative macrohistory analysis. *Gazette, 63*(6), 459–479.

Guth, S., Helm, F., & O'Dowd, R. (2012). *University Language Classes Collaborating Online. A Report on the Integration of Telecollaborative Networks in European Universities*. INTENT Project Final Report.

Guth, S., & Helm, F. (2011). Developing multiliteracies in ELT through telecollaboration. *ELT Journal, 66*(1), 42–51. doi:10.1093/elt/ccr027

Haboud, M. (2009). Teaching foreign languages: A challenge to Ecuadorian bilingual intercultural education. *International Journal of English Studies, 9*(1), 63–80.

Hakuta, K. (1990). Language and cognition in bilingual children. In A. Padilla, C. Valdez, & H. Fairchild (Eds.), *Bilingual education: Issues and strategies* (pp. 47–59). Newbury Park, California: Sage Publications.

Hale, K. (1992) Endangered languages. *Linguistic Society of America*, 68(1). Retrieved from http://www.jstor.org/pss/416368

Halili, S.H. & Zainuddin Z. (2015). Flipping the classroom: What we know and what we don't. *The Online Journal of Distance Education and E-learning, 3*(1), 28-35.

Halliday, M., & Hasan, R. (1989). *Language, context and text: A social semiotic perspective*. Oxford: Oxford University Press.

Hall, J. (2006). A story of using weblogs in English teacher training. In K. Bradford-Watts, C. Ikeguchi, & M. Swanson (Eds.), *Proceedings of the JALT 2005 Conference* (pp. 723-734). Tokyo.

Hall, J. C. (2001). *Retention and wastage in FE and HE*. Edinburgh: The Scottish Council for Research in Education.

Halverson, L. R., Graham, C. R., Spring, K. J., & Drysdale, J. S. (2012). An analysis of high impact scholarship and publication trends in blended learning. *Distance Education, 33*(3), 381–413. doi:10.1080/01587919.2012.723166

Hammond, K. J., & Richey, J. L. (2014). *The sage returns: Confucian revival in contemporary China*. Albany, New York, NY: State University of New York Press.

Hampel, R., & Baber, E. (2003). Using Internet-based audio-graphic and videoconferencing for language teaching and learning. In U. Felix (Ed.), *Language learning online: Towards best practice* (pp. 171–191). Lisse, The Netherlands: Swets & Zeitlinger.

Hampel, R., & de los Arcos, B. (2013). Interacting at a distance: A critical review of the role of ICT in developing the learner–context interface in a university language program. *Innovation in Language Learning and Teaching, 7*(2), 158–178. doi:10.1080/17501229.2013.776051

Hampel, R., & Stickler, U. (2005). New Skills for New Classrooms: Training tutors to teach languages online. *Computer Assisted Language Learning, 18*(4), 311–326. doi:10.1080/09588220500335455

Hampel, R., & Stickler, U. (2012). The use of videoconferencing to support multimodal interaction in an online language classroom. *ReCALL, 24*(2), 116–137. doi:10.1017/S095834401200002X

Hanada, T. (2003). Cultural diversity as social demand: The Korean minority and Japanese broadcasting. *Gazette, 65*(4-5), 389–400.

Hancock, A., Hermerling, S., Landon, J., & Young, A. (2006). *Building on language diversity with young children: Teacher education for the support of second language acquisition*. Münster, Germany: LIT Verlag.

Hanna, B. E., & de Nooy, J. (2003). A funny thing happened on the way to the forum: Electronic discussion and foreign language learning. *Language Learning & Technology, 7*(1), 71–85.

Hanna, B. E., & de Nooy, J. (2009). *Learning Language and Culture via Public Internet Discussion Forums*. New York, NY: Palgrave Macmillan. doi:10.1057/9780230235823

Hansen, M. H. (1999). *Lessons in being Chinese: Minority education and ethnic identity in southwest China*. Seattle, Washington: University of Washington Press.

Hansen, M. L. (1938). *The Problem of the Third Generation Immigrant*. Rock Island, Ill: Augustana Historical Society.

Hanson-Smith, E. (2001). Computer-assisted language learning. In R. Carter & D. Nunan (Eds.), *The Cambridge guide to teaching English to speakers of other languages* (pp. 107–113). Cambridge, UK: Cambridge University Press. doi:10.1017/CBO9780511667206.016

Han, Y. J. (2015). Successfully flipping the ESL classroom for learner autonomy. *NYC TESOL Journal, 2*(1), 98–109.

Hara, N., & Kling, R. (2000). Students' distress with a Web-based distance education course. *Information Communication and Society, 3*(4), 557–579. doi:10.1080/13691180010002297

Harasim, L. (2000). Shift happens: Online education as a new paradigm in learning. *The Internet and Higher Education, 3*(1), 41–61. doi:10.1016/S1096-7516(00)00032-4

Harris, J. (1998). *Virtual architecture: Designing and directing curriculum-based telecomputing*. Eugene, OR: International Society for Technology in Education.

Harris, P., Connolly, J., & Feeney, L. (2009). Blended learning: Overview and recommendations for successful implementation. *Industrial and Commercial Training, 41*(3), 155–163. doi:10.1108/00197850910950961

Hassal, T. (2008). Pragmatic performance: What are learners thinking? In E. Alcón Soler & A. Martínez Flor (Eds.), *Investigating pragmatics in foreign language learning, teaching and testing* (pp. 72–93). Buffalo: Multilingual Matters.

Hattem, D. (2012). The Practice of microblogging. *The Journal of Second Language Teaching and Research, 1*(2), 38–70.

Hauck, M. (2010). Telecollaboration: At the interface between multimodal and intercultural communicative competence. In S. Guth & F. Helm (Eds.), *Telecollaboration 2.0* (pp. 219–244). Bern: Peter Lang.

Hauck, M., & Youngs, B. L. (2008). Telecollaboration in multimodal environments: The impact on task design and learner interaction. *Computer Assisted Language Learning, 21*(2), 87–124. doi:10.1080/09588220801943510

Hawkins, J. A. (1994). *A performance theory of order and constituency*. New York, NY: Cambridge University Press.

Hayashi, K., & Lee, E. (2007). The potential of fandom and the limits of soft power: Media representations on the popularity of a Korean melodrama in Japan. *Social Science Japan Journal, 10*(2), 197–216.

Hebrard, J. (2000). The goal of the school is culture, not the same life. *Presença pedagógica, Belo Horizonte, 6*(33), 5-17.

Hélot, C. Young, A. & Delforge, O. (2005) *Windows on the World: A language awareness project in a French primary school* (English subtitled version).

Hélot, C., Young, A. & Delforge, O. (2005) *La diversité linguistique et culturelle à l'école* (original version in French).

Helot, C. (2003). Language policy and the ideology of bilingual education in France. *Language Policy, 2*(3), 255–277. doi:10.1023/A:1027316632721

Helot, C., & Young, A. (2005). The notion of diversity in language education: Policy and practice at primary level in France. *Language, Culture and Curriculum, 18*(3), 242–257.

Henshaw, F. (2014). *Do's and Don'ts of Flipped, Hybrid and Online Courses. American Association of Teachers of Spanish and Portuguese (AATSP)*. Conference Talk.

Hermosilla, J. (2014). Hybrid Spanish programs: A challenging and successful endeavor. *Hispania, 97*(1), 1–4. doi:10.1353/hpn.2014.0010

Herring, S. (Ed.). (1996). *Computer-mediated communication: Linguistic, social, and cross-cultural perspectives*. Amsterdam: John Benjamins. doi:10.1075/pbns.39

Hewett, B. L. (2000). Characteristics of interactive oral and computer-mediated peer group talk and its influence on revision. *Computers and Composition, 17*(3), 265–288. doi:10.1016/S8755-4615(00)00035-9

Heymarbet - Homework | Yiddish Book Center. (n. d.). Retrieved from http://www.yiddishbookcenter.org/heymarbet

Hidalgo, M. (1986). Language contact, language loyalty, and prejudice on the Mexican border. *Language in Society, 15*(21), 193–220. doi:10.1017/S004740450000018X

Hill, F., Bordes, A., Sumite, C., & Weston, J. (2016, January). The Goldilocks Principle: Reading children's books with explicit memory representations. *Proceedings of the International Conference on Learning Representations ICLR '16*. Retrieved from http://arxiv.org/pdf/1511.02301v3.pdf

Hirotani, M., & Lyddon, P. A. (2013). The development of L2 Japanese self-introductions in an asynchronous computer-mediated language exchange. *Foreign Language Annals, 46*(3), 469–490. doi:10.1111/flan.12044

Ho, A., Chuang, I., Reich, J., Coleman, C., Whitehill, J., Northcutt, C., . . . Petersen, R. (2015). *HarvardX and MITx: Two Years of Open Online Courses Fall 2012-Summer 2014*. Retrieved from Social Science Research Network website: http://ssrn.com/abstract=2586847

Hockly, N. (2013). Mobile learning. *ELT Journal, 67*(1), 80–84. doi:10.1093/elt/ccs064 PMID:23923690

Hoffman, E. (2014). Beyond the flipped classroom: Redesigning a research methods course for e3 instruction. *Contemporary Issues in Education Research, 7*(1), 51–62. doi:10.19030/cier.v7i1.8312

Hokanson, S. G. (2000). Distance education in foreign languages. *Rocky Mountain Review of Language and Literature, 54*(2), 85–93. doi:10.2307/1348122

Holland, D., Fox, G., & Daro, V. (2008). Social movements and collective identity: A decentered dialogic view. *Anthropological Quarterly, 81*(1), 95–125.

Holmberg, B. (1995). The evolution of the character and practice of distance education. *Open Learning, 10*(2), 47–53. doi:10.1080/0268051950100207

Holmberg, B., Shelley, M., & White, C. (Eds.). (2005). *Distance education and languages: Evolution and change*. Clevedon, U.K.: Multilingual Matters.

Holton, D. (2010, March 20). The Digital Natives / Digital Immigrants Distinction Is Dead, Or At Least Dying. Retrieved from https://edtechdev.wordpress.com/2010/03/19/the-digital-natives-digital-immigrants-distinction-is-dead-or-at-least-dying/

Holton, D. (2012). *What's the "problem" with MOOCs?* Retrieved from EdTechDav website: https://edtechdev.wordpress.com/2012/05/04/whats-the-problem-with-moocs/

Honeycutt, B., & Garrett, J. (2014). Expanding the definition of a flipped learning environment. *Instructional Design: Faculty focus*.

Hopper, K. (2003). *Reasons to go hybrid. Distance Education Report*, 7(24), 7.

Horan, D. A., & Hersi, A. A. (2011). Preparing for diversity: the alternatives to 'linguistic coursework' for student teachers in the USA. In S. Ellis & E. McCartney (Eds.), *Applied Linguistics and Primary School Teaching* (pp. 44–52). Cambridge, England: Cambridge University Press. doi:10.1017/CBO9780511921605.007

Houser, N. O. (2008). Cultural plunge: A critical approach for multicultural development in teacher education. *Race, Ethnicity and Education*, 11(4), 465–482. doi:10.1080/13613320802479034

Houston, M., & Lin, L. (2012). Humanizing the classroom by flipping the homework versus lecture equation. In Society for Information Technology and Teacher Education International Conference (pp. 1177-1182).

Ho, Y. K. (2003). Audiotaped dialogue journals: An alternative form of speaking practice. *ELT Journal*, 57(3), 269–277. doi:10.1093/elt/57.3.269

Hubbard, P. (Ed.). (2009). Computer Assisted Language Learning: Vol. 1-4. (*Critical Concepts in Linguistics Series*). London, UK: Routledge.

Huebner, T. (1995). The effects of overseas language programs: Report on a case study of an intensive Japanese course. In B. F. Freed (Ed.), *Second language acquisition in a study abroad context* (pp. 171–193). Amsterdam: Benjamins. doi:10.1075/sibil.9.11hue

Hurd, S. (2005). Autonomy and the Distance Language Learner. In B. Holmberg, M. A. Shelley, & C. J. White (Eds.), *Languages and distance education: evolution and change* (pp. 1–19). Clevedon: Multilingual Matters.

Hurd, S. (2007). Anxiety and non-anxiety in a distance language learning environment: The distance factor as a modifying influence. *System*, 36(4), 487–508. doi:10.1016/j.system.2007.05.001

Husbye, N. E., & Elsener, A. A. (2013). To move forward, we must be mobile: Practical uses of mobile technology in literacy education courses. *Journal of Digital Learning in Teacher Education*, 30(2), 46–51. doi:10.1080/21532974.2013.10784726

Husseinali, G. (2006). Who is studying Arabic and why? A survey of Arabic students' orientations at a major university. *Foreign Language Annals*, 39(3), 397–414. doi:10.1111/j.1944-9720.2006.tb02896.x

Hwang, S. (2009). A Vygotskian approach to heterogeneous communication and multi/cultural literacy: Commentary on David Kellog's "Taking uptaking up, or, a deconstructionist 'ontology of different' and a developmental one." *Mind, Culture, and Activity*, 16(2), 191–197. doi:10.1080/10749030802590614

Hwang, W. Y., Chen, H. S., Shadiev, R., Huang, R. Y. M., & Chen, C. Y. (2014). Improving English as a foreign language writing in elementary schools using mobile devices in familiar situational contexts. *Computer Assisted Language Learning*, 27(5), 359–378. doi:10.1080/09588221.2012.733711

Hyder, T., & Rutter, J. (2001). *Safe Hands*. London: Save the Children and Refugee Council.

Hymes, D. (1972). On communicative competence. In J. B. Pride & J. Holmes (Eds.), *Sociolinguistics (pp. 269-293)*. Harmondsworth: Penguin.

Hymes, D. (1974). Ways of Speaking. In R. Bauman & J. Sherzer (Eds.), *Explorations in the Ethnography of Speaking (pp. 433-451)*. Cambridge: Cambridge University Press.

Hymes, D. H. (1972). On communicative competence. In J. B. Pride & J. Holmes (Eds.), *Sociolinguistics: Selected readings* (pp. 269–293). Harmondsworth, UK: Penguin Books.

Hyun, J. H. (2008). A comparative analysis of transplants and industrial location of Japanese and Korean automotive industries in Europe. *International Journal of Business, 13*(3), 215–235.

Infoplease (n. d.). Most widely spoken languages in the world. *Infoplease*. Retrieved from http://www.infoplease.com/ipa/A0775272.html

Ingraham, N. (2015). Apple's App Store has passed 100 billion app downloads. *The Verge*. Retrieved from http://www.theverge.com/2015/6/8/8739611/apple-wwdc-2015-stats-update

Instituto Brasileiro de Geografia e Estatística. (2007). *Brazilian statistics*. Retrieved from www.ibge.gov.br

Isaacson, W. (2011). *Steve Jobs*. New York, NY: Simon & Schuster, Inc.

Isenberg, N. (1997). Critical Post-Judaism, Or Reinventing a Yiddish Sensibility in a Postmodern Age. *Diaspora: A Journal of Transnational Studies, 6*(1), 86–96.

Ishihara, T., Itoko, T., Sato, D., Tzadok, A., & Takagi, H. (2012). Transforming Japanese archives into accessible digital books.*Proceedings of the 12th ACM/IEEE-CS Joint Conference on Digital Libraries* (pp. 91-100).

Ismail, I., Azizan, S. N., & Azman, N. (2013). Mobile phone as pedagogical tools: Are teachers ready. *International Education Studies, 6*(3), 36–47. doi:10.5539/ies.v6n3p36

Jacobs, N. (2005). *Yiddish: A Linguistic Introduction*. Cambridge, UK, New York: Cambridge University Press.

Jacot, M. T., Noren, J., & Berge, Z. L. (2014). The flipped classroom in training and development: Fad or the future? *Performance Improvement, 53*(9), 23–28.

Jagers, R. (2001). Cultural integrity and social and emotional competence promotion: Work notes on moral competence. *The Journal of Negro Education, 70*(1/2), 59–71.

Jaggars, S. S. (2014). Choosing between online and face-to-face courses: Community college student voices. *American Journal of Distance Education, 28*(1), 27–38. doi:10.1080/08923647.2014.867697

James, G. (2007). The affordances of social psychology of the ecological approach to social knowing. *Theory & Psychology, 17*(2), 265–279. doi:10.1177/0959354307075046

Janks, H. (1991). A critical approach to the teaching of language. *Educational Review, 43*(2), 191–199. doi:10.1080/0013191910430207

Janks, H. (2010). *Literacy and power*. New York, NY: Routlege.

Janson, A., Ernst, S. J., Lehmann, K. &Leimeister, J. M. (2014). Creating awareness and reflection in a large-scale IS lecture—the application of a peer assessment in a flipped classroom scenario. *Proceedings of the 4th Workshop on Awareness and Reflection in Technology-Enhanced Learning (ARTEL 2014) to be held in the context of EC-TEL* (pp. 35-50).

Jarvis, H., & Achilleos, M. (2013). From Computer Assisted Language Learning (CALL) to Mobile Assisted Language Use (MALU). *Tesl-Ej, 16*(4), n4.

Jarvis, H., & Krashen, S. (2014). Is CALL obsolete? Language acquisition and language learning revisited in a digital age. *TESL-EJ, 17*(4), n4.

JDOV. (2016, February 11). WATCH: What Exactly Is a "YidLife Crisis?" *Haaretz*. Retrieved from http://www.haaretz.com/jewish/news/1.702593

Jewitt, C. (2009). An introduction to multimodality. In C. Jewitt (ed.), *The Routledge Handbook of Multimodal Analysis* (pp. 14-27). London: Routledge.

Jewitt, C., Kress, G., Ogborn, J., & Tsatsarelis, C. (2000). Teaching and learning: Beyond language. *Teaching Education*, *11*(3), 327–341. doi:10.1080/713698977

Jewitt, C., Kress, G., Ogborn, J., & Tsatsarelis, C. (2001). Exploring learning through visual, actional and linguistic communication: The multimodal environment of a science classroom. *Educational Review*, *53*(1), 5–8. doi:10.1080/00131910123753

Jianli, W. (2012). Teachers' changing role in learning in higher education in China. *International Journal of E-Education, E-Business. E-Management and E-Learning*, *2*(3), 223–226.

Jimenez, R. T. (2000, January01). Literacy and the identity development of Latino/a students. *American Educational Research Journal*, *37*(4), 971–1000. doi:10.3102/00028312037004971

JimenezR.T. (2000).

Jochum, C. J. (2013). Analyzing student perceptions of a blended Spanish grammar course. *Tarptautinis psichologijos žurnalas: Biopsichosocialinis požiūris*, *12*, 105-116.

Jochum, C. J. (2011). Blended Spanish instruction: Perceptions and design. *Journal of Instructional Psychology*, *38*(1), 40–46.

Johnson, G. B. (2013). Student perception of flipped classroom [Master's thesis]. The University of British Columbia, Canada.

Johnston, L., & Miles, L. (2004). Assessing contributions to group assignments. *Assessment & Evaluation in Higher Education*, *29*(6), 751–768. doi:10.1080/0260293042000227272

Joksimović, S., Kovanović, V., Jovanović, J., Zouaq, A., Gašević, D., & Hatala, M. (2015). What do cMOOC participants talk about in Social Media? A Topic Analysis of Discourse in a cMOOC. *Paper presented at the5th International Conference on Learning Analytics & Knowledge* (pp. 156-165). New York, NY: ACM.

Joliffe, A., Ritter, J., & Stevens, D. (2001). *The online learning handbook: Developing and using web-based learning*. Kogan Page: Springer. Joy-Matthews.

Jones, S. (2006). *Blogging and ESL Writing: A case study of how students responded to the use of weblogs as a pedagogical tool for the writing process approach in a community college ESL writing class* [Unpublished PhD. Dissertation]. Faculty of the Graduate School of the University of Texas at Austin, TX, USA.

Jones, G., Squires, T., & Hicks, J. (2008). Combining speech recognition/natural language processing with 3d online learning environments to create distributed authentic and situated spoken language learning. *Journal of Educational Technology Systems*, *36*(4), 375–392. doi:10.2190/ET.36.4.c

Judaica Sound Archives. (n. d.). Retrieved from http://faujsa.fau.edu/jsa/home.php

Jung, I. (2001). Building a theoretical framework of web-based instruction in the context of distance education. *British Journal of Educational Technology*, *32*(5), 525–534. doi:10.1111/1467-8535.00222

Jung, S., & Shim, D. (2014). Social distribution: K-pop fan practices in Indonesia and the 'Gangnam style' phenomenon. *International Journal of Cultural Studies*, *17*(5), 485–501.

Kabata, K., & Edasawa, Y. (2011). Tandem language learning through a cross-cultural keypal project. *Language Learning & Technology*, *15*(1), 104–121.

Kachka, P. (2012). Educator's voice: What's all this talk about flipping. Retrieved from https://tippie.uiowa.edu/faculty-staff/allcollege/kachka.pdf

Kafrissen, R. (2012, January 4). Rootless Cosmopolitan: Straw Man. Retrieved from http://rokhl.blogspot.com/2012/01/straw-man.html

Kahn, L. (2012). *Colloquial Yiddish: The Complete Course for the Beginners*. Abingdon, Oxon, New York: Routledge.

Kajder, S., & Bull, G. (2003). Scaffolding for struggling students. *Learning and Leading with Technology, 31*(9), 32–35.

Kane, D. (2006). *The Chinese language: Its history and current usage*. Singapore: Tuttle Publishing.

Kan, Q. (2013). The use of ICT in supporting Distance Chinese language learning-Review of the Open university's beginner's Chinese course. *Journal of Technology and Chinese Language Teaching, 4*(1), 1–13.

Kan, Q., Stickler, U., & Xu, C. (2013). Chinese-English eTandem Learning: The role of pre- project preparation and collaboration. *Chinese Language Globalization Studies, 2*, 131–143.

Kasper, L. (2000). New technologies, new literacies: Focus discipline research and ESL learning communities. *Language Learning & Technology, 4*(2), 105–128.

Katz, D. (2011, October 31). Language: Yiddish. In *YIVO Encyclopedia of Jews in Eastern Europe*. Retrieved from http://www.yivoencyclopedia.org/article.aspx/Language/Yiddish

Katz, D. (1987). The Proto-Dialectology of Ashkenaz. In D. Katz (Ed.), *Origins of the Yiddish Language* (pp. 47–60). Oxford, New York: Pergamon Press.

Katz, D. (2004). *Words on Fire: The Unfinished History of Yiddish*. Basic Books.

Katz, D. (2015). *Yiddish and Power*. Palgrave Macmillan.

Katz, S. (2001). Videoconferencing with the French-speaking world: A user's guide. *Foreign Language Annals, 34*(2), 152–157. doi:10.1111/j.1944-9720.2001.tb02820.x

Kavaliauskienê, G., & Vaičiûnienê, V. (2006). Communication Interaction Using Information and Communication Technology. *Studies about Languages (Kalb Studijos), 8*, 8894. Retrieved from www.ceeol.com

Kawai, Y. (2009). Neoliberalism, nationalism, and intercultural communication: A critical analysis of Japan's neoliberal nationalism discourse under globalization. *Journal of International and Intercultural Communication, 2*(1), 16–43.

Kearney, M., & Maher, D. (2013). Mobile learning in math teacher education: Using iPads to support pre-service teachers' professional development. *Australian Educational Computing, 27*(3), 76–84.

Kearsley, G. (2000). *Online education: Learning and teaching in cyberspace*. Toronto, ON: Wadsworth Thomson Learning.

Keegan, D., & Fern Univ., Hagen (Germany). Inst. for Research into Distance Education. (2002). *The future of learning: From eLearning to mLearning*. ERIC Clearinghouse.

Kehoe, A., & Gee, A. (2011). Social tagging: A new perspective on textual aboutness. Methodological and historical dimensions of corpus linguistics. In P. Rayson, S. Hoffman, & G. Leech (Eds.), Studies in Variation Contacts and Change in English (pages). Helsinki: Research Unit for Variation, Contacts, and Change in English. Retrieved from http://www.helsinki.fi/varieng/series/volumes/06/kehoe_gee/

Kelm, O. R. (1992). The use of synchronous computer networks in second language instruction: A preliminary report. *Foreign Language Annals, 25*(5), 441–545. doi:10.1111/j.1944-9720.1992.tb01127.x

Kenney, M., Breznitz, D., & Murphree, M. (2013). Coming back home after the sun rises: Returnee entrepreneurs and growth of high tech industries. *Research Policy, 42*(2), 391–407.

Kern, R., Ware, P., & Warschauer, M. (2008). Network-based language Teaching. In N. Van Deusen-Scholl and N. H. Hornberger (Eds.), Encyclopedia of Language and Education (2nd ed., Vol. 4, pp. 281–292). Springer Science+Business Media LLC. doi:10.1007/978-0-387-30424-3_105

Kern, R. G. (1995). Restructuring classroom interaction with network computers: Effects on quantity and characteristics of language production. *Modern Language Journal*, *79*(4), 457–476. doi:10.1111/j.1540-4781.1995.tb05445.x

Kern, R. G. (2006). Perspectives on technology in learning and teaching languages. *TESOL Quarterly*, *40*(1), 183–210. doi:10.2307/40264516

Kerr, D. (2014, August 13). Apple halts use of two harmful chemicals in iPhone assembly: The tech giant bans the use of benzene and n-hexane in the final assembly of its devices and lowers the maximum use in early production phases. *CNET*. Retrieved from http://www.cnet.com/news/apple-halts-use-of-two-harmful-chemicals-in-iphone-assembly/

Khan, S. (2011). Salman Khan talk at TED 2011 [Video webcast]. Retrieved from http://youtube/gM95HHI4gLk

Khan, M. T., Humayun, A. A., Sajjad, M., & Khan, N. A. (2015). Languages in danger of death and their relationship. *Journal of Information. Business and Management*, *7*(2), 239–254.

Khan, S. (2012). *The one world schoolhouse: Education reimagined*. New York: Twelve.

Kim, J.-O. (2003). *Étude des verbalisations métalinguistiques d'apprenants coréens sur l'imparfait et le passé composé en français* (Doctoral Thesis). Université Paris III- Sorbonne nouvelle. Retrieved from http://www.kimjinok.com/html/theses/intro.html

Kim, E., & Schniederjans, M. J. (2004). The role of personality in web-based distance education courses. *Communications of the ACM*, *47*(3), 95–98. doi:10.1145/971617.971622

Kim, H., & Kwon, Y. (2012). Exploring smartphone applications for effective mobile-assisted language learning. *Multimedia-Assisted Language Learning*, *15*(1), 31–57.

Kinginger, C. (2000). Learning the pragmatics of solidarity in the networked foreign language classroom. In J. K. Hall & L. S. Verplaeste (Eds.), *Second and foreign language learning through classroom interaction* (pp. 23–46). Mahwah, NJ: Erlbaum.

King, J. (2009). Language is life: The worldview of second language speakers of Māori. In J. Reyhner & L. Lockard (Eds.), *Indigenous language revitalization: Encouragement, guidance & lessons learned* (pp. 97–108). Flagstaff, AZ: Northern Arizona University Press.

Kinney, D. P., & Robertson, D. F. (2003). Technology makes possible new models for delivering developmental Mathematics instruction. *Mathematics and Computer Education*, *37*(3), 315–328.

Knapp, M., & Hall, J. (2006). *Nonverbal communication in human interaction*. Belmont, CA: Thomson Wadsworth.

Koller, D. (2011, December 11). *Death knell for the lecture: Technology as a passport to personalized education. The New York Times*. Retrieved from http://www.nytimes.com/2011/12/06/science/daphne-koller-technology-as-a-passport-to-personalized-education.html?pagewanted=all&_r=0

Komur, M., & Kogut, G. (2006). Students' perceptions of problem-based learning. *Teacher Development*, *10*(1), 105–116. doi:10.1080/13664530600587295

Kop, R., Fournier, H., & Mak, S. (2011). A pedagogy of abundance or a pedagogy to support Human beings? Participant support on Massive Open Online Courses. *International Review of Research in Open and Distance Learning (Special Issue - Emergent Learning, Connections. Design for Learning)*, *12*(7), 74–93.

Kordon, K. (2011). Using English as a foreign language in international and multicultural consulting: Asset or hindrance? *Gruppendynamik Und Organisationsberatung, 42*(3), 285–305.

Koutropoulos, A. (2011). Digital Natives: Ten Years After. *Journal of Online Learning and Teaching, 7*(4), 525.

Kovanović, V., Joksimović, S., Gašević, D., Siemens, G., & Hatala, M. (2015). What public media reveals about MOOCs: A systematic analysis of news reports. *British Journal of Educational Technology, 46*(3), 510–527. doi:10.1111/bjet.12277

Kramsch, C. (1993). *Context and culture in language teaching.* Oxford: Oxford University Press.

Kramsch, C. (1998). The privilege of the intercultural speaker. In M. Byram & M. Fleming (Eds.), *Language learning in intercultural perspective: Approaches through drama and ethnography* (pp. 16–31). Cambridge: Cambridge University Press.

Kramsch, C. (2003). *Language and culture* (4th ed.). Oxford: Oxford University Press.

Kramsch, C. (2005). Post 9/11: Foreign languages between knowledge and power. *Applied Linguistics, 26*(4), 545–567. doi:10.1093/applin/ami026

Kramsch, C. (2014). Teaching Foreign Languages in an Era of Globalization: Introduction. *Modern Language Journal, 98*(1), 296–311. doi:10.1111/j.1540-4781.2014.12057.x

Kramsch, C. (2014). The challenge of globalization for the teaching of foreign languages and cultures. *Electronic Journal of Foreign Language Teaching, 11*(2), 2249–2254.

Kramsch, C. J. (1987). Theory in to practice. *Teaching Foreign Languages, 26*(4), 243–250.

Kramsch, C., Howell, T., Warner, C., & Wellmon, C. (2007). Framing foreign language education in the United States: The case of German. *Critical Inquiry in Language Studies, 4*(2-3), 151–178. doi:10.1080/15427580701389615

Krashen, S. (1982). *Principles and practice in second language acquisition.* Oxford: Pergamon.

Krashen, S. D. (1987). *Principles and Practice in Second Language Acquisition.* Prentice-Hall International.

Krashen, S., & Terrell, T. (1983). *The natural approach.* Hayward, California: The Alemany Press.

Krathwohl, D. R., Bloom, B. S., & Masia, B. B. (1973). *Taxonomy of educational objectives, the classification of educational goals. Handbook II: Affective domain.* New York: David McKay Co., Inc.

Kuiken, F. (2014). Competencies of preschool educators in Amsterdam: A Dutch perspective on language proficiency, language targets and didactic skills. *European Journal of Applied Linguistics, 2*(1), 101–119. doi:10.1515/eujal-2014-0006

Kukulska-Hulme, A., & Shield, L. (2007, September). An Overview of Mobile Assisted Language Learning: Can mobile devices support collaborative practice in speaking and listening. Proceedings of the conference EuroCALL'07 Conference Virtual Strand.

Kukulska-Hulme, A., & Shield, L. (2008). An overview of mobile assisted language learning: From content delivery to supported collaboration and interaction. *ReCALL, 20*(03), 271–289. doi:10.1017/S0958344008000335

Kumaravadivelu, B. (2003). *Beyond methods: Macrostrategies for language teaching.* New Haven, CT: Yale University Press.

Kurtz, G. (2014). Integrating a Facebook group and a course website: The effect on participation and perception on learning. *American Journal of Distance Education, 28*(4), 253–263. doi:10.1080/08923647.2014.957952

Kyratzis, A., Tang, Y., & Koymen, S. B. (2009). Codes, code-switching, and context: Style and footing in peer group bilingual play. *Multilingua*, *28*(2-3), 265–290. doi:10.1515/mult.2009.012

La Tordue. (2002). *Champs libre* (Album, music CD).

Lafford, B. A. (1995). Getting into, through and out of a survival situation: A comparison of communicative strategies used by students studying Spanish-abroad and 'at home. In B. F. Freed (Ed.), *Second language acquisition in a study abroad context* (pp. 97–121). Amsterdam: Benjamins. doi:10.1075/sibil.9.08laf

Lafford, B. A. (2004). The effect of the context of learning on the use of communication strategies by learners of Spanish as a second language. *Studies in Second Language Acquisition*, *26*(2), 201–225. doi:10.1017/S0272263104262039

Lage, M. J., Platt, G. J., & Treglia, M. (2000). Inverting the classroom: A gateway to creating an inclusive learning environment. *The Journal of Economic Education*, *31*(1), 30–43. doi:10.1080/00220480009596759

Lai, C. (2015). Modeling teachers' influence on learners' self-directed use of technology for language learning outside the classroom. *Computers & Education*, *82*, 74–83. doi:10.1016/j.compedu.2014.11.005

Lakarnchua, O., & Wasanasomsithi, P. (2014). L2 student writers' perception of microblogging. *Electronic Journal of Foreign Language Teaching*, *11*(2), 327–340.

Lam, A. (2007). The multi-agent model of language choice: National planning and individual volition in China. *Cambridge Journal of Education*, *37*(1), 67–87.

LaMance, R. A. (2012). *Say hello to hybrid: Investigating student and instructor perceptions of the first hybrid language courses at UT* [Master's Thesis]. University of Tennessee.

Lamb, M. (2004). Integrative motivation in a globalizing world. *Synergy*, *32*(1), 3–19.

Lamprecht, S. (2014). SU Engineer helped to land Philae on comet. *Stellenbosch University*. Retrieved from http://www.sun.ac.za/english/Lists/news/DispForm.aspx?ID=1996

Lam, W. S. E. (2004). Second language socialization in a bilingual chat room: Global and local considerations. *Language Learning & Technology*, *8*(3), 44–65.

Lankshear, C., & Knobel, M. (2006). *New literacies: Everyday practices & classroom learning* (2nd ed.). New York, NY: Open University Press and McGraw Hill.

Lansky, A. (2005). *Outwitting History: The Amazing Adventures of a Man Who Rescued a Million Yiddish Books*. Chapel Hill, N.C.: Algonquin Books of Chapel Hill.

Lapkin, S., Hart, D., & Swain, M. (1995). A Canadian interprovincial exchange: Evaluating the linguistic impact of a three-month stay in Quebec. In B. F. Freed (Ed.), *Second language acquisition in a study abroad context* (pp. 67–94). Amsterdam: Benjamins. doi:10.1075/sibil.9.06lap

Laverie, D. A. (2002). Improving teaching through improving evaluation: A guide to course portfolios. *Journal of Marketing Education*, *24*(2), 104–113. doi:10.1177/0273475302242003

Lawler, A. (2004). The slow deaths of writing. *Science*, *305*(5680), 30–33.

Learn | Explore | Yiddish Book Center. (n. d.). Retrieved from http://www.yiddishbookcenter.org/learn-explore

Learn Yiddish - The Hebrew University's Online Languages Program. (n. d.). Retrieved February 16, 2016, from http://languages.huji.ac.il/courses/learn-yiddish-level-a

Learn Yiddish in a live environment - face-to-face on the internet! (n. d.). Retrieved from http://learnyiddishlive.com/

Learn Yiddish Online Today Using a Fun, Fast Method. (n. d.). Retrieved from http://yiddishacademy.com/

Learn Yiddish Online with eTeacher and the Hebrew University. (n. d.). Retrieved from http://eteacheryiddish.com/

Learner, A. (n. d.). Teacher resources and professional development across the curriculum. Retrieved from http://www.learner.org/series/destinos/

Lee, L. (2009). Exploring native and nonnative interactive discourse in text-based chat beyond classroom settings. In L. Abraham, & L. Williams (Eds.), Electronic Discourse in Foreign Language Learning and Teaching (pp. 263-289). Series: Language Learning & Language Teaching. Amsterdam: John Benjamins. doi:10.1075/lllt.25.10lee

Leeds-Hurwitz, W. (1990). Notes in the history of intercultural communication: The Foreign Service Institute and the mandate for intercultural training. *The Quarterly Journal of Speech, 76,* 262–281.

Lee, L. (2007). Fostering second language oral communication through constructivist interaction in desktop videoconferencing. *Foreign Language Annals, 40*(4), 635–649. doi:10.1111/j.1944-9720.2007.tb02885.x

Lee, L. (2009). Promoting intercultural exchanges with blogs and podcasting: A study of Spanish–American telecollaboration. *Computer Assisted Language Learning, 22*(5), 425–443. doi:10.1080/09588220903345184

Leeman, J., & Martinez, G. (2007). From identity to commodity: Ideologies of Spanish in heritage language textbooks. *Critical Inquiry in Language Studies, 4*(1), 35–65. doi:10.1080/15427580701340741

Leu, D. J., Kinzer, C. K., Coiro, J. L., & Cammack, D. W. (2004). Toward a theory of new literacies emerging from the Internet and other information and communication technologies. In R. B. Ruddell & N. J. Unrau (Eds.), *Theoretical Models and Processes of Reading* (5th ed., pp. 1570–1613). Newark, DE: International Reading Association.

Levy, M. (1997). *Computer-assisted language learning: Context and conceptualization.* New York: Clarendon Press.

Levy, M. (2007). Culture, culture learning and new technologies: Towards a pedagogical framework. *Language Learning & Technology, 11*(2), 104–127.

Levy, M., & Stockwell, G. (2006). *CALL Dimensions: Options and Issues in Computer-Assisted Language Learning.* Mahwah, NJ: Lawrence Erlbaum.

Lewis, T. (2013). DBR and task-based learning: The ongoing experience of designing a task-based telecollaboration. In C. Pardo Ballester & J. Rodríguez (Eds.), Design-based research in CALL (Vol. 11, pp. 211-233). San Marcos, TX: CALICO.

Lewis, T. Comas-Quinn, & Hauck, M. (2015). Clustering, collaboration, and community: Sociality at work in a cMOOC. In E. Dixon & M. Thomas (Eds.), Researching language learner interactions online: From social media to MOOCs (pp. 45-61). San Marcos, TX: CALICO.

Lewis, T. N., & Schneider, H. (2015). Integrating international video chat into the foreign language curriculum. *International Journal of Computer-Assisted Language Learning and Teaching, 5*(2), 74–87. doi:10.4018/IJCALLT.2015040105

Liaw, S. S., Chen, G. D., & Huang, H. M. (2008). Users' attitudes toward Web-based collaborative learning systems for knowledge management. *Computers & Education, 50*(3), 950–961. doi:10.1016/j.compedu.2006.09.007

Li, B., Fukada, A., & Hong, W. (2012). Online business Chinese speaking instruction: A Speak Everywhere speaking program for Practical Business Chinese. *Global Business Language, 17,* 93–105.

Li, B., & Hong, W. (2014, June). 初级汉语远程教学的实践与展望 (Developing elementary–level Distance Chinese language courses---findings and future directions). *Proceedings for the 12th International Conference of Chinese Pedagogy,* Harbin, China (pp. 417- 424).

Lieberman, R. P. (2014, November 17). International Yiddish Conference a hit in Boca. Retrieved February 16, 2016, from http://www.sun-sentinel.com/florida-jewish-journal/news/palm/fl-jjps-yiddish-1119-20141117-story.html

Liem, A. D., Lau, S., & Nie, Y. (2008). The role of self-efficacy, task value, and achievement goals in predicating learning strategies, task disengagement, peer relationship, and achievement outcome. *Contemporary Educational Psychology*, *33*(4), 486–512. doi:10.1016/j.cedpsych.2007.08.001

Lightbown, P. M., & Spada, N. (2013). *How languages are learned*. Oxford: Oxford University Press.

Lim, B. J. (2011). Korean language education with one-on-one desktop videoconferencing. *Journal of Korean-American Education*, *28*, 16–21.

Lin, G. H., & Chien, P. C. (2009). An investigation into the effectiveness of peer feedback. *Journal of Applied Foreign Languages Fortune Institute of Technology*, *3*, 79–87.

Lin, X., & Bransford, J. (2010). Personal background knowledge influences cross-cultural understanding. *Teachers College Record*, *112*(7), 1729–1757.

Liskin-Gasparro, J. E. (1998). Linguistic development in an immersion context: How advanced learners of Spanish perceive SLA. *Modern Language Journal*, *82*(2), 159–175. doi:10.1111/j.1540-4781.1998.tb01189.x

Little, D., & Brammerts, H. (1996). A guide to language learning in tandem via the Internet. *CLCS Occasional Paper* No. 46. Dublin: Trinity College, Centre for Language and Communication Studies.

Liu, C. L., Jaeger, S., & Nakagawa, M. (2004). Online recognition of Chinese characters: The state-of-the-art. *IEEE Transactions on Pattern Analysis and Machine Intelligence*, *26*(2), 198–213.

Liu, J., & Sadler, R. W. (2003). The effect and affect of peer review in electronic versus traditional modes on L2 writing. *Journal of English for Academic Purposes*, *2*(3), 193–227. doi:10.1016/S1475-1585(03)00025-0

Liu, M., Abe, K., Cao, M., Liu, S., Ok, D. U., Park, J. B., & Sardegna, V. G. et al. (2015). An analysis of social network websites for language learning: Implications for teaching and learning English as a Second Language. *CALICO Journal*, *32*(1), 114–152.

Liu, M., Navarrete, C. C., & Wivagg, J. (2014). Potentials of mobile technology for K-12 education: An investigation of iPod Touch use for English language learners in the United States. *Journal of Educational Technology & Society*, *17*(2).

Liu, Z. M., Huang, X. B., & Fu, Y. A. (2014). Information behavior in the mobile environment: A study of undergraduate smartphone users in China. *Chinese Journal of Library and Information Science*, *7*(4), 1–15.

Li, Y., & Li, W. (2014). *The Language Situation in China* (Vol. 2). Boston, MA: Walter de Gruyter Inc.

Liyanagunawardena, T., Adams, A., & Williams, S. (2013). MOOCs: A systematic study of the published literature 2008-2012. *International Review of Research in Open and Distance Learning*, *14*(3). Retrieved from http://www.irrodl.org/index.php/irrodl/article/view/1455/2531

Lo Bianco, J. (2014). Domesticating the foreign: Globalization's effects on the place/s of languages. *Modern Language Journal*, *98*(1), 312–325. doi:10.1111/j.1540-4781.2014.12063.x

Lomicka, L., & Lord, G. (2012). A tale of tweets: Analyzing microblogging among language Learners. *System*, *40*(1), 48–63. doi:10.1016/j.system.2011.11.001

Longcamp, M., Boucard, C., Gilhodes, J. C., Anton, J. L., Roth, M., Nazarian, B., & Velay, J. L. (2008). Learning through hand- or typewriting influences visual recognition of new graphic shapes: Behavioral and functional imaging evidence. *Journal of Cognitive Neuroscience*, *20*(5), 802–815. doi:10.1162/jocn.2008.20504 PMID:18201124

Long, M. H. (1996). The role of the linguistic environment in second language acquisition. In W. Ritchie & T. Bhatia (Eds.), *Handbook of second language acquisition* (pp. 413–468). San Diego, CA: Academic Press. doi:10.1016/B978-012589042-7/50015-3

Long, M. H., Adams, L., McLean, M., & Castaños, F. (1976). Doing things with words—verbal interaction in lockstep and small group classroom situations. In J. Fanselow & R. Crymes (Eds.), *On TESOL '76*. Washington, D.C.: TESOL.

López-Pérez, M. V., Pérez-López, M. C., & Rodríguez-Ariza, L. (2011). Blended learning in higher education: Students' perceptions and their relation to outcomes. *Computers and Education*, *56*(3), 818–826. doi:10.1016/j.compedu.2010.10.023

Lortie, D. (1975). *Schoolteacher: A sociological study*. Chicago: University of Chicago Press.

Louie, K. (2008). *The Cambridge companion to modern Chinese culture*. UK: Cambridge University Press.

Lou, Y., Abrami, P. C., & d'Apollonia, S. (2001). Small group and individual learning with technology: A meta-analysis. *Review of Educational Research*, *71*(3), 449–521. doi:10.3102/00346543071003449

Lüdi, G. (1992, April 6-11). Statuts et fonctions des marques transcodiques en conversation exolingue. In G. Hilty (Ed.), *Actes du XXè Congrès international de linguistique et philologie romaines*, Université de Zurich (pp. 123-136). Tübingen, Basel: Francke.

Lüdi, G. (2004). Pour une linguistique de la compétence du locuteur plurilingue. *Revue française de linguistique appliquée*, *9*(2), 125-135.

Lüdi, G. (1995). Parler bilingue et traitements cognitifs. *Intellectica*, *1*(20), 139–156.

Lüdi, G., & Py, B. (2013). *Etre bilingue. (4ᵉ édition)*. Bern: Peter Lang. doi:10.3726/978-3-0351-0647-3

Lundberg, M. (2009). Regional national autonomy and minority language rights in the PRC. *International Journal on Minority and Group Rights*, *16*(3), 399–422.

Lung, R. (2008). Translation officials of the Tang central government in medieval China. *Interpreting*, *10*(2), 175.

Lynch, R., & Dembo, M. (2004). The relationship between self-regulation and online learning in a blended learning context. *International Review of Research in Open and Distance Learning*, *5*(2), 1–16.

MacDonald, L., & Caverly, D. (2001). Techtalk: Expanding the online discussion. *Journal of Developmental Education*, *25*(2), 38.

Mackness, J. (2013). *cMOOCs and xMOOCs - key differences*. Retrieved from https://jennymackness.wordpress.com/2013/10/22/cmoocs-and-xmoocs-key-differences/

Mackness, J., Mak, S., & Williams, R. (2010). The ideals and reality of participating in a MOOC. In L. Dirckinck-Holmfeld, V. Hodgson, C. Jones, M. De Laat, D. McConnell, & T. Ryberg (Eds.), *Proceedings of the 7th International Conference on Networked Learning* (pp. 266-275). Lancaster, UK: University of Lancaster Press.

MacKnight, C. B. (2000). Critical thinking and collaborative inquiry. *Journal of Interactive Instruction*, *12*(4), 3–11.

Maffi, L. (Ed.). (2001). *On biocultural diversity: Linking language, knowledge, and the environment*. Washington, DC: Smithsonian Institution Press.

Maffi, L., & Woodley, E. (2010). *Biocultural diversity conservation*. Washington, DC: Earthscan LLC.

Magnan, S., & Back, M. (2007). Social interaction and linguistic gain during study abroad. *Foreign Language Annals*, *40*(1), 43–61. doi:10.1111/j.1944-9720.2007.tb02853.x

Magnan, S., Murphy, D., Sahakyan, N., & Kim, S. (2012). Student goals, expectations, and the standards for foreign language learning. *Foreign Language Annals, 45*(2), 170–192. doi:10.1111/j.1944-9720.2012.01192.x

Magnon, S. (2007). Reconsidering communicative language teaching for national goals. *Modern Language Journal, 91*(2), 249–252. doi:10.1111/j.1540-4781.2007.00543_3.x

Major, C. H. (2010). Do virtual professors dream of electric students? University faculty experiences with online distance education. *Teachers College Record, 112*(8), 2154–2208.

Makony, S., & Pennycook, A. (2011). Disinventing multilingualism. From monological multilingualism to multilingua francas. In M. Martin-Jones, A. Blackledge & A. Creese (Eds.), *The Routledge Handbook of Multilingualism* (pp. 439-453). Oxon: Routledge.

Makony, S., & Pennycook, A. (2007). *Disinventing and reconstituting Languages*. Clevedon: Multilingual Matters.

Manjinder. (2012). Before we flip classrooms, let's rethink what we're flipping to. *TechEdBlog*. Retrieved from http://techedblog.tumblr.com/post/34356480070/before-we-flip-classrooms-lets-rethink-what-were

Mapping Yiddish New York. (n. d.). Retrieved from https://myny.ccnmtl.columbia.edu/

Margolis, R. (2012). *Basic Yiddish: A Grammar and Workbook. Milton Park.* Abingdon, Oxon, New York: Routledge.

Marin-Garcia, J., Aznar-Mas, L., & González-Ladrón-de-Gevara, F. (2011). Innovation types and talent management for innovation. *Working Papers on Operations Management, 2*(2), 25-31.

Marot, T. (2002). *Conscience phonographique et apprentissage du lire-écrire: vers un enseignement systémique et développemental* [PhD thesis]. Université Lyon II.

Marsh, D., Maljers, A., & Hartiala, A. K. (Eds.). (2001). Profiling European CLIL classrooms: languages open doors. University of Jyväskylä, Jyväskylä.

Marshall, C., & Rossman, G. B. (1999). *Designing qualitative research* (3rd ed.). Thousand Oaks, CA: Sage Publications.

Martin-Barbero, J., & Barcelos, C. (2000). Comunicação e mediações clutrais [Communication and cultural mediations (Interview)]. Revista Brasileira de Ciências da Comunicação, 23(1), 151-163.

Martindale, T., & Wiley, D. (2005). Using blogs in scholarship and teaching. *TechTrends, 49*(2), 55–61. doi:10.1007/BF02773972

Martinez-Roldan, C. M., & Malave, G. (2004). Language ideologies mediating literacy and identify in bilingual contexts. *Journal of Early Childhood Literacy, 4*(2), 155–180. doi:10.1177/1468798404044514

Marwedel, P., & Engel, M. (2014). *Flipped classroom teaching for a cyber-physical system course-An adequate presence-based learning approach in the internet age. Proceedings of the 10th European Workshopon Microelectronics Education (EWME),* (pp. 11-15). IEEE. doi:doi:10.1109/EWME.2014.6877386 doi:10.1109/EWME.2014.6877386

Mary, L., & Young, A. (2010). Preparing teachers for the multilingual classroom: Nurturing reflective, critical awareness. In S.H. Ehrhart, C., Hélot & A. Le Nevez, (Eds), Plurilinguisme et formation des enseignants: Une approche critique / Plurilingualism and Teacher Education: a critical approach. Frankfurt: Peter Lang.

Matsunaga, M., & Torigoe, C. (2008). Looking at the Japan-residing Korean identities through the eyes of the "outsiders within": Application and extension of co-cultural theory. *Western Journal of Communication, 72*(4), 349–373.

Matsuura, H., Fujieda, M., & Mahoney, S. (2004). The officialization of English and ELT in Japan: 2000. *World Englishes, 23*(3), 471–487.

Mayer, R. E. (2002). Multimedia learning. *Psychology of Learning and Motivation, 41*, 85–139. doi:10.1016/S0079-7421(02)80005-6

Mayer, V. (2004). Fractured categories: New writings on Latinos and stereotypes - A review essay. *Latino Studies, 2*(3), 445–452.

McAllister, G., & Irvine, J. J. (2002). The role of empathy in teaching culturally diverse students: A qualitative study of teachers' beliefs. *Journal of Teacher Education, 53*(5), 433–443. doi:10.1177/002248702237397

McAuley, A., Stewart, B., Siemens, G., & Cormier, D. (2010). *The MOOC model for digital practice.* Retrieved from http://www.davecormier.com/edblog/wp-content/uploads/MOOC_Final.pdf

MCC Costa. (2001). *Educomunicar é Preciso!* Retrieved from http://www.ups.br/educomradio/café/café.asp?editora=TSUPH&cod=377

McCarthy, J. (2016, February 17). Should India's internet be free of charge or free of control? *NPR: All Tech Considered.* Retrieved from http://www.npr.org/sections/alltechconsidered/2016/02/11/466298459/should-indias-internet-be-free-of-charge-or-free-of-control

McClure, E. (1992). The pragmatics of code-switching in Mexican political, literary, and news magazines. *Pragmatics and Language Learning, 3*, 182–196.

McDonough, K., & Trofimovich, P. (2008). *Using priming methods in second language research.* London: Routledge.

McHale, T. (1995). Digital spearheads the revolution: 1. *Electronic Buyers' News*, 38.

McKeachie, W., & Svinicki, M. (2006). *McKeachie's teaching tips: Strategies, research, and theory for college and university teachers.* (12th ed.). Boston: Houghton-Mifflin.

McKIrdy. E. (2015, February 4). China's online users more than double entire U.S. population. Retrieved from http://www.cnn.com/2015/02/03/world/china-internet-growth-2014/

Megginson, J., & Surtees, M. (2004). *Human resource development* (3rd ed.). London: Kogan Page.

Meishar-Tal, H., Kurtz, G., & Pieterse, E. (2012). Facebook groups as LMS: A case study. *International Review of Research in Open and Distance Learning, 13*(4), 33–48.

Meißner, F.-J. Capucho, F. Degache, Ch. Martins, A. Spita, D., & Tost, M. (Eds.), (2011). *Intercomprehension. Learning, teaching, research. Apprentissage, enseignement, recherche. Lernen, Lehren, Forschung.* Tübingen: Narr.

Mello, L. (2011). Communication management and the dialogue in education: An educommunication theme. In T. Bastiaens & M. Ebner (Eds.), *Proceedings of World Conference on Educational Media and Technology 2011* (pp. 2490-2496). Waynesville, NC: Association for the Advancement of Computing in Education (AACE).

Melo-Pfeifer, S. (2011). De la dissociation à l'articulation de compétences: apports théoriques au concept d'Intercompréhension. In F.-J.Meißner, F. Capucho, Ch. Degache, A. Martins, D. Spita & M. Tost (eds.), *Intercomprehension: Learning, teaching, research / Apprentissage, enseignement, recherche / Lernen, Lehren, Forschung* (pp. 219-242). Tübingen: Narr Verlag.

Melo-Pfeifer, S., Araújo e Sá, M. H., & Santos, L. (2012). As "línguas que não sabemos que sabíamos" e outros mitos: um olhar sobre o percurso da Didática de Línguas a partir da intercompreensão. Cadernos do Lale, Série Reflexões (Vol. 4, pp. 33–55). Aveiro: Universidade de Aveiro.

Melo-Pfeifer, S. (2014). Intercomprehension between Romance Languages and the role of English: A study of multilingual chat rooms. *International Journal of Multilingualism, 11*(1), 120–137. doi:10.1080/14790718.2012.679276

Melo-Pfeifer, S. (2015). An interactional perspective on intercomprehension between Romance Languages: Translanguaging in multilingual chat rooms. *Fremsprachen Lehren und Lernen, 44*(2), 100–113.

Melville, M. B. (1983). Ethnicity: An analysis of its dynamism and variability focusing on the Mexican/Anglo/Mexican American interface. *American Ethnologist, 10*(2), 272–289. doi:10.1525/ae.1983.10.2.02a00040

Meskill, C., & Anthony, N. (2005). Foreign language learning with CMC: Forms of online instructional discourse in a hybrid Russian class. *System, 33*(1), 89–105. doi:10.1016/j.system.2005.01.001

Metcalf, A. C. (2005). *Go-betweens and the colonization of Brazil: 1500-1600.* Austin, TX: University of Texas Press.

Meuth Alldredge, J. R. (2011). An analysis of social, environmental, and cultural problems in a northern Amazonian indigenous community. In E. T. Bodah (Ed.), *Conversas entre educadoras: novos dialogos / Conversations among educators: new dialogues.* Pullman, WA: Thaines & Bodah Center for Education and Development.

Miles, M. B., & Huberman, A. M. (1994). *An expanded sourcebook: qualitative data analysis* (2nd ed.). Thousand Oaks, CA: Sage Publications.

Miller, L., & Olson, J. (1994). Putting the computer in its place: A study of teaching with technology. *Journal of Curriculum Studies, 26*(1), 121–141. doi:10.1080/0022027940260201

Mills, K. (2000). *Rescuing Yiddish for Future Generations. " Indiana University Research & Creative Activity.* XXIII.

Mills, N. (2011). Situated learning through social networking communities: The development of joint enterprise, mutual engagement, and a shared repertoire. *CALICO Journal, 28*(2), 345–368. doi:10.11139/cj.28.2.345-368

Milman, N. B. (2012). The flipped classroom strategy: What is it and how can it best be used? *Distance Learning, 9*(3), 85–87.

Ministério da Educação do Brasil. (2010). Retrieved from http://mec.gov.br

Mishel, A. (n. d.). *Yiddish & Seinfeld. Dentist Jokes.* Retrieved from https://www.youtube.com/watch?v=_jG6B9Pt_ug

Mishra, P., & Koehler, M. J. (2006). Technological Pedagogical Content Knowledge: A Framework for Teacher Knowledge. *Teachers College Record, 108*(6), 1017–1054.

Mitchell, A., & Honore, S. (2007). Criteria for successful blended learning. *Industrial and Commercial Training, 39*(3), 143–149. doi:10.1108/00197850710742243

Mithun, M. (1998). The significance of diversity in language endangerment and preservation. In L. Grenoble & L. Whaley (Eds.), *Endangered Languages: Language Loss and Community Response.* New York, NY: Cambridge University Press. doi:10.1017/CBO9781139166959.008

Modiano, M. (2001). Linguistic imperialism, cultural integrity, and EIL. *ELT Journal, 55*(4), 339–346.

Moore, D. (2006). *Plurilinguismes et école.* Paris: Didier.

Moore, M. G. (1989). Three types of interaction. *American Journal of Distance Education, 3,* 1–7.

Moore, M. G., & Kearsley, G. (1996). *Distance education: A systems view.* Belmont, CA: Wadsworth Publishing.

Moore, R. (2007). An investigation of how culture shapes curriculum in early care and education programs on a Native American Indian reservation: "The drum is considered the heartbeat of the community. *Early Childhood Education Journal, 34*(4), 251–258.

Moras, S. (2001). *Computer-assisted language learning (Call) and the Internet.* Karen's Linguistics Issues.

Moreno, J. B. (2012). Only English? How bilingual education can mitigate the damage of English-only. *Duke Journal of Gender Law & Policy, 20*(1), 197–220.

Morgan, Y. Y. K. (2012). Attitudes toward Hanzi production ability among Chinese teachers and learners [Doctoral dissertation]. Retrieved from http://docs.lib.purdue.edu/dissertations/AAI3545325/

Moseley, C. (2010). Atlas of the World's Langagues in Danger. Paris: UNESCO Publishing; Retrieved from http://www.unesco.org/languages-atlas/en/atlasmap.html

Muhanna, W. (2012). Using online games for teaching English vocabulary for Jordanian students learning English as a foreign language. *Journal of College Teaching & Learning, 9*(3), 235–244.

Muilenburg, L. Y., & Berge, Z. L. (2005). Student barriers to online learning: A factor analytic study. *Distance Education, 26*(1), 29–48. doi:10.1080/01587910500081269

Muldrow, K. (2013). A new approach to language instruction: Flipping the classroom. *Language and Education, 8*, 28–31.

Mullen, T., Appel, C., & Shanklin, T. (2009). Skype-based tandem language learning and Web 2.0. In M. Thomas (Ed.), *Handbook of Research on Web 2.0 and Second Language Learning* (pp. 101–118). New York, NY: Information Science Reference. doi:10.4018/978-1-60566-190-2.ch006

Müller-Hartmann, A. (2006). Learning how to teach intercultural communicative competence via telecollaboration: A model for language teacher education. In J. A. Belz & S. Thorne (Eds.), *Internet-mediated intercultural foreign language education* (pp. 63–84). Boston: Thomson Heinle.

Murakami, C. (2008). 'Everybody is just fumbling along': An investigation of views regarding EAL training and support provisions in a rural area. *Language and Education, 22*(4), 265–282. doi:10.1080/09500780802152556

Murday, K., Ushida, E., & Chenoweth, N. A. (2008). Learners' and teachers' perspectives on language online. *Computer Assisted Language Learning, 21*(2), 125–142. doi:10.1080/09588220801943718

Murray, G. (2014). The social dimensions of learner autonomy and self-regulated learning. *Studies in self-access learning journal, 5*(4), 320-341.

Murray, D. E. (1999). Access to information technology: Considerations for language educators. *Prospect, 14*(3), 4–12.

Mynard, J. (2007). A blog as a tool for reflection for English language learners. *The Philippine ESL Journal, 1*, 77-90. Retrieved from http://www.philippine-esl-journal.com/August-2008-Vol1.pdf

Nadzrah, A. (2005). *Computers for teaching English as a second language in Malaysia: case study.* University of Adelaide.

Naismith, L., Lonsdale, P., Vavoula, G., Sharples, M., & Series, N. F. (2004). Literature review in mobile technologies and learning. *Nesta Futurelab Series.* Retrieved from http://citeseerx.ist.psu.edu/viewdoc/citations?doi=10.1.1.136.2203

Nakahama, Y., Tyler, A., & Van Lier, L. (2001). Negotiating meaning. *TESOL Quarterly, 35*(3), 377–405. doi:10.2307/3588028

Nakayama, S. (2002). From PC to mobile internet—overcoming the digital divide in Japan. *Asian Journal of Social Science, 30*(2), 239–247.

Nandu, S. (2013). Transforming MOOCs and MOORFAPS into MOOLOS. *Distance Education, 34*(3), 253–255. doi:10.1080/01587919.2013.842524

Nault, D. (2006). Going global: Rethinking culture teaching in ELT contexts. *Language, Culture and Curriculum, 19*(3), 314–328. doi:10.1080/07908310608668770

Navarro, P. (2000). The promise – and potential pitfalls – of cyberlearning. In R. A. Cole (Ed.), *Issues in web-based pedagogy: A critical primer* (pp. 281–297). Westport, CT: Greenwood Press.

Neuman, W., Park, Y., & Panek, E. (2012). Tracking the flow of information into the home: An empirical assessment of the digital revolution in the United States, 1960-2005. *International Journal of Communication*, 6, 1022–1041.

Neumeier, P. (2005). A closer look at blended learning: Parameters for designing a blended learning environment for language teaching and learning. *ReCALL*, *17*(2), 163–178. doi:10.1017/S0958344005000224

Ngai, E. W. T., Poon, J. K. L., & Chan, Y. H. C. (2007). Empirical examination of the adoption of Web CT using TAM. *Computers & Education*, *48*(2), 250–267. doi:10.1016/j.compedu.2004.11.007

Ng, E. M. W. (Ed.). (2009). *Comparative blended learning practices and environments*. China: Hong Kong Institute.

Nicol, D. & MacFarlane-Dick, D. (2006). Formative assessment and self-regulated learning: A model and seven principles of good feedback practice. *Studies in Higher Education,* 31(2), 199-218.

Ning, L. (2009). China's leadership in the world ICT industry: A successful story of its "attracting-in" and "walking-out" strategy for the development of high-tech industries? *Pacific Affairs*, *82*(1), 67–91.

Northrup, P. T. (2002). Online learners' preferences for interaction. *The Quarterly Review of Distance Education*, *3*(2), 219–226.

Norton, B. (1997). Language, identity, and the ownership of English. *TESOL Quarterly*, *31*(3), 409–429.

Nunan, D. (1989). *Designing tasks for the communicative classroom*. Cambridge, UK: Cambridge University Press.

Nunan, D. (2004). *Task-based language teaching*. Cambridge, UK: Cambridge University Press. doi:10.1017/CBO9780511667336

Nutta, J., Feyten, C., Norwood, A., Meros, J., Yoshii, M., & Ducher, J. (2002). Exploring new frontiers: What do computers contribute to teaching foreign languages in elementary school? *Foreign Language Annals*, *35*(3), 293–306.

O'Brien, S. A. (2016, Feburary 10). Mark Zuckerberg reacts to board member's India comments. *CNN Money*. Retrieved from http://money.cnn.com/2016/02/10/technology/mark-zuckerberg-andreessen-india-facebook/index.html

O'Dowd, R. (2000). Intercultural learning via videoconferencing: A pilot exchange project. *ReCALL*, *12*(1), 49–61. doi:10.1017/S0958344000000616

O'Dowd, R. (2003). Understanding the "other side": Intercultural learning in a Spanish-English e-mail exchange. *Language Learning & Technology*, *7*(2), 118–144.

O'Dowd, R. (2007a). Evaluating the outcomes of online intercultural exchange. *ELT Journal*, *61*(2), 144–152. doi:10.1093/elt/ccm007

O'Dowd, R. (Ed.). (2007b). *Online intercultural exchange: An introduction for foreign language teachers*. Clevedon, UK: Multilingual Matters.

O'Dowd, R., & Ritter, M. (2006). Understanding and working with 'failed communication' in telecollaborative exchanges. *CALICO Journal*, *23*(3), 1–20.

O'Dowd, R., & Ware, P. (2009). Critical issues in telecollaborative task design. *Computer Assisted Language Learning*, *22*(2), 173–188. doi:10.1080/09588220902778369

Oblender, T. E. (2002). A hybrid course model: One solution to the high online drop-out rate. *Learning and Leading with Technology*, *29*(6), 42–46.

Oblinger, D. (2003). Diana Oblinger, "Boomers, Gen-Xers, and Millenials: Understanding the 'New Students. *EDUCAUSE Review*, July/August) 200.

O'Dowd, R. (2013). Telecollaboration and CALL. In M. Thomas, H. Reinders, & M. Warshauer (Eds.), Contemporary omputer-assisted language learning (pp. 123–140). London: Bloomsbury Academic. Retrieved from http://site.ebrary.com/lib/uon/detail.action?docID=10632566

OECD. (2005). *The definition and selection of key competencies*. Executive summary. DeSeCo Project. Retrieved from http://www.oecd.org/fr/edu/apprendre-au-dela-de-l-ecole/definitionandselectionofcompetenciesdeseco.htm

Ogata, H., Hui, G. L., Yin, C., Ueda, T., Oishi, Y., & Yano, Y. (2008). LOCH: Supporting mobile language learning outside classrooms. *International Journal of Mobile Learning and Organisation, 2*(3), 271–282. doi:10.1504/IJMLO.2008.020319

Okimori, T. (2014). Korean and Japanese as Chinese-characters cultural spheres. *Acta Linguistica Asiatica, 4*(3), 43–70.

Oliff, P., Palacios, V., Johnson, I., & Leachman, M. (2013). Recent Deep State Higher Education Cuts May Harm Students and the Economy for Years to Come. *Center on Budget and Policy Priorities*. Retrieved from http://www.cbpp.org/research/recent-deep-state-higher-education-cuts-may-harm-students-and-the-economy-for-years-to-come

Oliveira, M. R. N. S. (2001). From the myth of technology to the technological paradigm: Technological mediation in didactic and pedagogic practices. *Revista Brasileira de Educação, Caxambu, 2*(18), 1–16.

Olivera, E., & Straus, S. G. (2004). Group-to-individual transfer of learning: Cognitive and social factors. *Small Group Research, 35*(4), 440–465. doi:10.1177/1046496404263765

Olshtain, E. (2001). Functional tasks for mastering the mechanics of writing and going just beyond. In M. Celce-Murcia (Ed.), *Teaching English as a second or foreign language* (3rd ed., pp. 206–217). USA: Heinle& Heinle.

Oravec, J. A. (2003). Blogs as an emerging genre in higher education. *Journal of Computing in Higher Education, 14*(2), 21–44. doi:10.1007/BF02940937

Ortega, L. (1997). Processes and outcomes in networked classroom interaction: Defining the research agenda for L2 computer-assisted classroom discussion. *Language Learning & Technology, 1*(1), 82–93.

Osman, G., & Herring, S. C. (2007). Interaction, facilitation, and deep learning in cross-cultural chat: A case study. *The Internet and Higher Education, 10*(2), 125–141. doi:10.1016/j.iheduc.2007.03.004

Ostler, N. (2005). *Empires of the word: A language history of the world*. New York: HarperCollins.

Otto, S., & Pusack, J. (2009). Computer-assisted language learning authoring issues. *Modern Language Journal, 93*(Suppl.), 784–801.

Oviedo, A., & Wildemeersch, D. (2008). Intercultural education and curricular diversification: The case of the Ecuadorian Intercultural Bilingual Education Model (MOSEIB). *Compare: A Journal of Comparative Education, 38*(4), 455–470. doi:10.1080/03057920701860137

Owens, J., Hardcastel, L., & Richardson, B. (2009). Learning from a distance: The experience of remote students. *Journal of Distance Education, 23*(3), 57–74.

Oxford Chinese Dictionary. (2010). *Oxford Chinese dictionary*. New York, NY: Oxford University Press, Inc.

Oxford, R. L. (1990). *Language Learning Strategies: What Every Teacher Should Know*. Boston: Heinle & Heinle.

Oxford, R., Lavine, R. Z., & Crookall, D. (1989). Language learning strategies, the communicative approach, and their classroom implications. *Foreign Language Annals, 22*(1), 29–39. doi:10.1111/j.1944-9720.1989.tb03139.x

Oxford, R., & Nyikos, S. (1989). Variables affecting choice of language strategy by university students. *Modern Language Journal, 73*(3), 291–301. doi:10.1111/j.1540-4781.1989.tb06367.x

Oz, H. (2015). An investigation of preservice English teachers' perceptions of mobile assisted language learning. *English Language Teaching, 8*(2), 22–34. doi:10.5539/elt.v8n2p22

Pacheco, M. (2012). Learning in/through everyday resistance: A cultural historical perspective on community resources and curriculum. *Educational Researcher, 41*(4), 121–132. doi:10.3102/0013189X12442982

Padilla, A., Lindholm, K., Chen, A., Duran, R., Hakuta, K., Lambert, W., & Tucker, G. R. (1991). The English-only movement: Myths, reality, and implications for psychology. *The American Psychologist, 46*(2), 120–130. doi:10.1037/0003-066X.46.2.120

Page, D., & Benander, R. (2014). Helping students change their view of the world: Moving from products and practices to perspectives. *Language and Education, 9*(1), 28–31.

Palloff, R. M., & Pratt, K. (1999). *Building learning communities in cyberspace: Effective strategies for online classroom.* San Francisco, CA: Jossey-Bass.

Palloff, R. M., & Pratt, K. (2005). *Collaborating online: Learning together in community.* San Francisco, CA: Jossey-Bass.

Palmer, D. (2010). Race, power, and equity in a multiethnic urban elementary school with a dual-language "strand" program. *Anthropology & Education Quarterly, 41*(1), 94–114. doi:10.1111/j.1548-1492.2010.01069.x

Pammi, S., Khemiri, H., Petrovska-Delacretaz, D., & Chollet, G. (2013). Detection of nonlinguistic vocalizations using ALISP sequencing. *2013 IEEE International Conference on Acoustics, Speech and Signal Processing*, 7557-7561.

Paris Yiddish Center. (n.d.). Online courses. Retrieved from http://yiddishweb.com/en/online-courses/

Parry, D. (2011). Mobile perspectives: On teaching mobile literacy. *EDUCAUSE Review, 46*(2), 14.

Patrovic, N., Jeremic, V., Cirocic, M., Radojicic, Z., & Milenkovic, N. (2014). Facebook Versus Moodle in practice. *American Journal of Distance Education, 28*(2), 117–125. doi:10.1080/08923647.2014.896581

Patten, B., Arnedillo-Sánchez, I., & Tangney, B. (2006). Designing collaborative, constructivist and contextual applications for handheld devices. *Computers & Education, 46*(3), 294–308. doi:10.1016/j.compedu.2005.11.011

Patterson, J. (2004). For quality and cost-effectiveness build a hybrid program. *Distance Education Report, 8*(21), 1–2.

Patton, M. Q. (2002). *Qualitative research and evaluation methods.* Thousand Oaks, CA: Sage.

Pedagogy. (n. d.). Retrieved from http://ingeveb.org/pedagogy

Pegrum, M., Howitt, C., & Striepe, M. (2013). Learning to take the tablet: How pre-service teachers use iPads to facilitate their learning. *Australasian Journal of Educational Technology, 29*(4).

Pellettieri, J. (2000). Negotiation in cyberspace: The role of chatting in the development of grammatical competence. In M. Warschauer & R. Kern (Eds.), *Network-based Language Teaching: Concepts and Practices* (pp. 59–86). New York: Cambridge University Press. doi:10.1017/CBO9781139524735.006

Pennycook, A. (2010). *Language as a local practice.* London: Routledge.

Penttilä, T., & Kairisto-Mertanene, L. (2012). Innovation competence barometer ICB - a tool for assessing students' innovation competences as learning outcomes in higher education. *Proceedings of INTED2012*, 6347–6351.

Perez, B., McCarty, T. L., Watahomigie, L. J., Torres-Guzman, M. E., Dien, T., Chang, J.-M., & Nordlander, A. et al. (Eds.). (2004). *Sociocultural contexts of language and literacy*. New Jersey: Taylor & Francis.

Pérez-Vidal, C. (2011). Language acquisition in three different contexts of learning: Formal instruction, study abroad, and semi-immersion (CLIL). In Y. Ruíz de Zarobe, J. M. Sierra, & F. Puerto (Eds.), *Content and foreign language integrated learning: Contributions to multilingualism in European contexts* (pp. 103–127). New York: Peter Lang.

Perifanou, M. A. (2009). Language micro-gaming: Fun and informal microblogging activities for language learning. *Communications in Computer and Information Science, 49*(1), 1–14. doi:10.1007/978-3-642-04757-2_1

Perry, M. (2013). Chart of the day: The college textbook bubble. *AEI.org*. Retrieved from https://www.aei.org/publication/chart-of-the-day-the-college-textbook-bubble/

Perry, M. (2015). Monday night links. *AEI.org*. Retrieved from http://www.aei.org/publication/monday-night-links-10/

Perry, G., & Talley, S. (2001). Online video case studies and teacher education: A new tool for preservice education. *Journal of Computing in Teacher Education, 17*(4), 26–31.

Peters, J. D. (2013). Writing. In A. Valdivia & E. Scharrer (Eds.), *The International Encyclopedia of Media Studies: Media Effects/Media Psychology* (1st ed.). New Jersey: Blackwell Publishing Ltd.

Phillipson, R. (1998). Globalizing English: Are linguistic human rights an alternative to linguistic imperialism? *Language Sciences, 20*(1), 101–112.

Phinney, J. S., Horencyzk, G., Liebkind, K., & Vedder, P. (2001). Ethnic identity, immigration, and well-being: An interactional perspective. *The Journal of Social Issues, 57*(3), 493–510. doi:10.1111/0022-4537.00225

Pica, T., & Doughty, C. (1986). The role of groupwork in classroom second language acquisition. *Studies in Second Language Acquisition, 7*(2), 233–248. doi:10.1017/S0272263100005398

Pinkman, K. (2005). Using blogs in the foreign language classroom: Encouraging learner independence. *The JALT CALL Journal, 1*(1), 12–24.

Pitta, D. A. (Ed.). (2009). Rosetta stone language training software: Spanish. Journal of Consumer Marketing, 26(5). Retrieved from edu/doi/full/ doi:10.1108/jcm.2009.07726eab.001

Pohl, M. (2000). *Learning to think, thinking to learn: Models and strategies to develop a classroom culture of thinking*. Cheltenham, Vic.: Hawker Brownlow.

Poon, J. (2013). Blended learning: an institutional approach for enhancing students' learning experiences, *Journal of Online Learning and Teaching, 9(2),* 271-288.

Poplack, S. (1988). Conséquences linguistiques du contact des langues: Un modèle d'analyse variationniste. *Langage & Société, 43*(1), 23–48. doi:10.3406/lsoc.1988.3000

Portnoy, E. (2012, August 13). The Disappearing Yiddish Accent. *The Forward*. Retrieved from http://forward.com/culture/160767/the-disappearing-yiddish-accent/

Power, T., & Erling, E. (2014). Supporting development through improving English language teaching and learning in Bangladesh. *The Open University / UKAID*. Retrieved from http://oro.open.ac.uk/41532/1/Power2014ba.pdf

Prabhu, N. S. (1987). *Second language pedagogy*. Oxford, UK: Oxford University Press.

Pratto, F., Liu, J., Levin, S., Sidanius, J., Shih, M., Bachrach, H., & Hegarty, P. (2000). Social dominance orientation and the legitimization of inequality across cultures. *Journal of Cross-Cultural Psychology, 31*, 369–409.

Pratto, F., & Stewart, A. L. (2011). *Social dominance theory. The Encyclopedia of Peace Psychology.* New Jersey: Wiley-Blackwell.

Prensky, M. (2001). Digital natives, digital immigrants part 1. *On the Horizon, 9*(5), 1–6.

Prensky, M. (2001a). Digital Natives, Digital Immigrants Part I. *On the Horizon, 9*(5), 1–6. doi:10.1108/10748120110424816

Prensky, M. (2001b). Digital Natives, Digital Immigrants Part II. *On the Horizon, 9*(6). doi:10.1108/10748120110424843

Presby, L. (2001). Seven tips for highly effective online courses. *Syllabus, 14*(11), 17.

Pufahl, I., & Rhodes, N. (2011). Foreign language instruction in U.S. schools: Results of a national survey of elementary and secondary schools. *Foreign Language Annals, 44*(2), 258–288.

Raguseo, C. (2010). Twitter Fiction: Social Networking and Microfiction in 140 Characters. *The Electronic Journal for English as a Second Language, 13(4).* Retrieved from http://www.tesl-ej.org/wordpress/issues/volume13/ej52/ej52int/

Ramazani, Z. (2006). *A Study of the Role of Using E-mail in Improving High School Students' EFL Reading Skill* [Unpublished Master's Thesis]. Shahreza Branch, Islamic Azad University Isfahan, Iran.

Rampton, B. (2014). Dissecting heteroglossia: interaction ritual or performance in crossing and stylization? In A. Blackledge & A. Creese (Eds.), *Heteroglossia as Practice and Pedagogy* (pp. 275-300). London: Springer. 10.1007/978-94-007-7856-6_15

Rampton, B. (2006). *Language in late modernity: Interaction in an urban school.* Cambridge: Cambridge University Press. doi:10.1017/CBO9780511486722

Ramsey, M., Ong, T., & Chen, H. (1998). Multilingual input system for the web-an open multimedia approach of keyboard and handwriting recognition for Chinese and Japanese.*Proceedings IEEE International Forum on Research and Technology Advances in Digital Libraries -ADL'98,* 188-194.

Rao, Y. (2015). *Apprentissage du chinois (CLE) et du français (FLE) dans une communauté numérique bilingue* [PhD thesis]. Université Aix-Marseille.

Read, T. (2014). The archetectonics of language MOOCs. In E. Martín-Monje & E. Bárcena (Eds.), *Language MOOCs: Providing learning, transcending boundaries* (pp. 91–105). Warsaw: De Gruyter Open.

Reder, F., Marec-Breton, N., Gombert, J., & Demont, E. (2013). Second-language learners' advantage in metalinguistic awareness: A question of languages' characteristics. *The British Journal of Educational Psychology, 83*(4), 686–702. doi:10.1111/bjep.12003 PMID:24175689

Reese, M. R. (2016, March 1). Google translate sings: "Hello" by Adele [Video file]. Retrieved from https://www.youtube.com/watch?v=GMi4MtyDg40

Reinders, H., & Wattana, S. (2014). Can I say something? The effects of digital gameplay on willingness to communicate. *Language Learning & Technology, 18*(2), 101–123.

Reinhardt, J., & Sykes, J. (2014). Digital game and play activity in L2 teaching and learning. *Language Learning & Technology, 18*(2), 2–8.

Reinhardt, J., & Zander, V. (2011). Social network¬ing in an intensive English program classroom: A language socialization perspective. *CALICO Journal, 28*(2), 326–344. doi:10.11139/cj.28.2.326-344

Rennie, F., & Morrison, T. (2012). *E-Learning and social networking handbook - resources for higher education.* London: Routledge.

Report, S. (2005, June 14). "You've got to find what you love," Jobs says. *Stanford News.* Retrieved from http://news.stanford.edu/news/2005/june15/jobs-061505.html

Rey-Debove, J. (1986). *Le métalangage.* Paris: Le Robert.

Riasati, M. J., Allahyar, N., & Tan, K. E. (2012). Technology in language education: Benefits and barriers. *Journal of Education and Practice, 3*(5), 25–30.

Richardson, W. (2007). Teaching in a Web 2.0 World. *Kappa Delta Pi Record, 43*(4), 150–151.

Rios, F., Trent, A., & Castaneda, L. (2003). Social Perspective taking: Advancing empathy and advocating justice. *Equity & Excellence in Education, 36*(1), 5–14. doi:10.1080/10665680303506

Rivers, W., Robinson, J., Harwood, P., & Brecht, R. (2013). Language votes: Attitudes toward foreign language policies. *Foreign Language Annals, 46*(3), 329–338.

Rodi, M. (2009). Compétences plurilingues et acquisitions, *Langage & Pratiques,* 44, 2-12.

Rodriguez, C. (2012). MOOCs and the AI-Stanford like Courses: Two Successful and Distinct Course Formats for Massive Open Online Courses. *European Journal of Open, Distance and E-Learning, II,* 1–13.

Rodzvilla, J. (2002). *We've got blog: How weblogs are changing our culture.* Cambridge, MA: Perseus Publishing.

Roehl, A., Reddy, S. L., & Shannon, G. J. (2013). The flipped classroom: An opportunity to engage millennial students through active learning strategies. *Journal of Family and Consumer Sciences, 105*(2), 44–49. doi:10.14307/JFCS105.2.12

Rogers, J. (2015). American higher education is one of the greatest bubbles of our time. *BusinessInsider.com.* Retrieved from http://www.businessinsider.com/jim-rogers-higher-education-is-a-bubble-2015-1

Rogers, K. (2013). Did the college textbook bubble burst? *Fox Business.* Retrieved from http://www.foxbusiness.com/personal-finance/2013/10/10/college-textbooks-next-bubble-to-burst/

Rogers, M. (2013). Wired for teaching. Inside Higher Education. Retrieved from https://www.insidehighered.com/news/2013/10/21/more-professors-using-social-media-teaching-tools

Rogers, M. (2016). Demand high for dual immersion in Utah. *The Salt Lake Tribune,* http://archive.sltrib.com/story.php?ref=/sltrib/news/54591846-78/language-programs-chinese-dual.html.csp

Rollinson, P. (2005). Using peer feedback in the ESL writing class. *English Language Teaching Journal, 59*(1), 23–30. doi:10.1093/elt/cci003

Rubdy, R., & McKay, S. (2013). "Foreign workers" in Singapore: Conflicting discourses, language politics and the negotiation of immigrant identities. *International Journal of the Sociology of Language, 222,* 157–185.

Rubio, F. (2015). The role of interaction in MOOCs and traditional technology-enhanced courses. In E. Dixon & M. Thomas (Eds.), *Researching language learner interaction online: From social media to MOOCs* (pp. 63–88). San Marcos, TX: CALICO.

Rubio, F., & Thoms, J. (Eds.). (2012). *Hybrid language teaching and learning: Exploring theoretical, pedagogical and curricular issues. AASC.* Boston: Heinle.

Rüschoff, B., & Ritter, M. (2001). Technology-enhanced language learning: Construction of knowledge and template-based learning in the foreign language classroom. *Computer Assisted Language Learning, 14*(3-4), 219–232. doi:10.1076/call.14.3.219.5789

Russell, S., & Norvig, P. (1995). Artificial Intelligence: A Modern Approach. New Jersey: Englewood Cliffs.

Russell, V. (2012). Learning complex grammar in the virtual classroom: A comparison of processing instruction, structured input, computerized visual input enhancement, and traditional instruction. *Foreign Language Annals, 45*, 42–71.

Ru, X., Lu, X., & Li, P. (Eds.). (2010). The China Society Yearbook: Vol. 4. *Chinese Academy of Social Sciences Yearbooks: Society*. Netherlands: Brill Academic Publishers.

Ryan, G. W., Bernard, H. R., & Beck, C. T. (2000). Data management and analysis methods. In N. K. Denzin & Y. S. Lincoln (Eds.), *Handbook off qualitative research* (2nd ed.). Thousand Oaks: Sage.

Ryang, S. (2012). The denationalized have no class: The banishment of Japan's Korean minority—a polemic. *CR (East Lansing, Mich.), 12*(1), 159–187.

Ryding, K. (1994). Fostering a learning community for Arabic. *Theory into Practice, 33*(1), 23–28. doi:10.1080/00405849409543611

Ryding, K. (2006). Teaching Arabic in the United States. In K. Wahba, Z. Taha, & L. England (Eds.), *Handbook for Arabic language teaching professionals in the 21ˢᵗ century* (pp. 13–20). New Jersey: Lawrence Erlbaum Associates.

Ryding, K. (2013). *Teaching and learning Arabic as a foreign language: A guide for teachers*. Washington, D.C.: Georgetown University Press.

Sackett, C. P. (1978). *Observing Behavior* (Vol. 2). Baltimore: University Press.

Sadler, P. M., & Good, E. (2006). The impact of self and peer grading on student learning. *Educational Assessment, 11*(1), 1–31. doi:10.1207/s15326977ea1101_1

Saine, P. (2012). iPods, iPads, and the SMARTBoard: Transforming literacy instruction and student learning. *New England Reading Association Journal, 47*(2), 74.

Salaberry, M. R. (1999). Call in the Year 2000: Still Developing the Research Agenda. *Language Learning & Technology, 3*(1), 104–107.

Saldaña, J. (2009). *The coding manual for qualitative researchers*. Los Angeles, CA: SAGE.

Samilow, J. (2016, February 10). Yiddish Is Making a Comeback and for Good Reason. *Haaretz*.

Sams, A. (2011). The flipped class: Shedding light on the confusion, critique, and hype. The Daily Rift. Retrieved from http://www.thedailyriff.com/articles/the-flipped-class-shedding-light-on-the-confusioncritique-and-hype-801.php

San Miguel, G., Jr. (2008). The schooling of Mexicanos in the southwest, 1848-1891.

Sang-Hun, C., & Markoff, J. (2016, March 9). Master of Go board game is walloped by Google computer program. *The New York Times*. Retrieved from http://www.nytimes.com/2016/03/10/world/asia/google-alphago-lee-se-dol.html?_r=0

Santiago-Rivera, A. L., Altarriba, J., Poll, N., Gonzalez-Miller, N., & Cragun, C. (2009). Therapists' views on working with bilingual Spanish-English speaking clients. *Professional Psychology, Research and Practice, 40*(5), 436–443. doi:10.1037/a0015933

Santos, D. M. D. (1997). *Learning English as a foreign language in Brazilian elementary schools: Textbooks and their lessons about the world and about learning* [Master's thesis]. University of Oklahoma, Norman, OK.

Sasaki, M. (2008). The 150-year history of English language assessment in Japanese education. *Language Testing, 25*(1), 63–83.

Sauro, S. (2009). Computer-mediated corrective feedback and the development of L2 grammar. *Language Learning & Technology, 13*(1), 96–120.

Savignon, S. J., & Sysoyev, P. V. (2005). Cultures and comparisons: Strategies for learners. *Foreign Language Annals*, *38*(3), 357–365. doi:10.1111/j.1944-9720.2005.tb02222.x

Schaechter, S.-R. (2015, February 15). A Delightful Way to Listen to Yiddish Literature. *The Yiddish Daily Forward*. New York. Retrieved from http://yiddish.forward.com/articles/185375/a-delightful-way-to-listen-to-yiddish-literature/?p=all

Schaechter, M. (1986). *Yidish tsvey: a lernbikhl far mitndike kursn*. *Philadephia*. Institute for Research on Humanities.

Schandorf, M. (2013). Mediated gesture: Paralinguistsic communication and phetic text. *Convergence*, *19*(3), 319–344.

Schaun, A. (2002). *Educomunicação: reflexões e princípios*. Rio de Janeiro, Brazil: Mauad.

Schenker, T. (2012). Intercultural competence and cultural learning through telecollaboration. *CALICO Journal*, *29*, 449–470. doi:10.11139/cj.29.3.449-470

Schenker, T. (2013). The Effects of a Virtual Exchange on Students' Interest in Learning About Culture. *Foreign Language Annals*, *46*(3), 491–507. doi:10.1111/flan.12041

Schildkarut, D. J. (2001). Official-English and the states: Influences on declaring English the official language in the United States. *Political Research Quarterly*, *54*(2), 445–447. doi:10.1177/106591290105400211

Schmidt, R. (1993). Awareness and second language acquisition. *Annual Review of Applied Linguistics*, *13*, 206–226. doi:10.1017/S0267190500002476

Schmidt, R. (2001). Attention. In P. Robinson (Ed.), *Cognition and second language instruction* (pp. 3–32). Cambridge: Cambridge University Press. doi:10.1017/CBO9781139524780.003

Schuck, S., Aubusson, P., Kearney, M., & Burden, K. (2013). Mobilising teacher education: A study of a professional learning community. *Teacher Development*, *17*(1), 1–18. doi:10.1080/13664530.2012.752671

Schuetz, D. (2005). *Cultural models and cultural self-awareness: A Discourse-analytical approach to the language of students' online journal entries* [PhD Thesis]. Pennsylvania State University.

Schwartz, M., Mor-Sommerfeld, A., & Leikin, M. (2010). Facing bilingual education: Kindergarten teachers' attitudes, strategies and challenges. *Language Awareness*, *19*(3), 187–203. doi:10.1080/09658416.2010.491919

Schwieter, J. W. (2011). Preparing students for class: A hybrid enhancement to language learning. *College Teaching Methods and Styles Journal*, *4*(6), 41–50.

Scida, E. E., & Saury, R. E. (2013). Hybrid courses and their impact on student and classroom performance: A case study at the University of Virginia. *CALICO Journal*, *23*(3), 517–531.

Scollon, R., & Scollon, W. (2001). *Intercultural communication: A discourse approach* (2nd ed.). Malden, MA: Blackwell Publishers.

Scott, K. (2015). The pragmatics of hashtags: Inference and conversational style on Twitter. *Journal of Pragmatics*, *81*, 8–20. doi:10.1016/j.pragma.2015.03.015

Scotton, C. M., & Ury, W. (1977). Bilingual strategies: The social functions of code-switching. *International Journal of the Sociology of Language*, 13, 5–20.

Scullen, M. E. (2014, November 14). Flipping and blending the language classroom: Experiment or new standard? Pearson online webinar.

Seaton, D., Coleman, C., Daries, J., & Chuang, I. (2015). Enrollment in MITx MOOCs: Are we educating educators? *EduCause Review*. Retrieved from http://er.educause.edu/articles/2015/2/enrollment-in-mitx-moocs-are-we-educating-educators

Seaton, J. X., & Schwier, R. (2014). An exploratory case study of online instructors: Factors associated with instructor engagement. *International Journal of E-Learning & Distance Education*, *29*(1), 1–16.

Secretaria de Educação Fundamental. (1997). *Parâmetros curriculares nacionais: meio ambiente, saúde*. Retrieved from http://portal.mec.gov.br/seb/arquivos/pdf/livro01.pdf

Seidman, N. (1997). *A Marriage Made in Heaven: The Sexual Politics of Hebrew and Yiddish*. Berkeley: University of California Press.

Selyukh, A., & Domonoske, C. (2016, February 19). Apple, the FBI and iPhone encryption: A what's at stake. *NPR*. Retrieved from http://www.npr.org/sections/thetwo-way/2016/02/17/467096705/apple-the-fbi-and-iphone-encryption-a-look-at-whats-at-stake

Serin, O. (2012). Mobile learning perceptions of the prospective teachers (TPNR Sampling). *Turkish Online Journal of Educational Technology*, *11*(3), 222–233.

Serrano, R., Llanes, A., & Tragant, E. (2011). The effect of context of second language learning: Intensive and semi-intensive courses vs. study abroad in Europe. *System*, *39*, 133–143. doi:10.1016/j.system.2011.05.002

Shandler, J. (2006). *Adventures in Yiddishland: Postvernacular Language and Culture*. Berkeley and Los Angeles, CA: University of California Press.

Shannon, S. M. (1990). English in the barrio: The quality of contact among immigrant children. *Hispanic Journal of Behavioral Sciences*, *12*(3), 256–276. doi:10.1177/07399863900123002

Share of mobile phone users that use a smartphone in China from 2013 to 2019. (n. d.). *Statisa*. Retrieved from http://www.statista.com/statistics/257045/smartphone-user-penetration-in-china/

Sharpe, R., Benfield, G., Roberts, G., & Francis, R. (2006). The undergraduate experience of blended e-learning: A review of UK literature and practice. York, UK: The Higher Education Academy. Retrieved from http://www.heacademy.ac.uk/assets/documents/teachingandresearch/Sharpe_Benfield_Roberts_Francis.pdf

Shaughnessey, E. L. (2006). The beginnings of writing in China. In C. Woods (Ed.), Visible Language: Inventions of writing in the Middle East and beyond. Chicago: University of Chicago Press; Retrieved from https://oi.uchicago.edu/sites/oi.uchicago.edu/files/uploads/shared/docs/oimp32.pdf

Shaw, S. (2006). New reality: Workplace collaboration is crucial. *Eedo Knowledgeware Whitepaper*. Retrieved through personal subscription.

Shearer, R., Gregg, A., Joo, K., & Graham, K. (2014). Transactional Distance in MOOCs: A critical analysis of dialogue, structure, and learner autonomy. *Paper presented at the 55th Adult Education Research Conference*, Middletown, PA, Penn State Harrisburg.

Sherry, L. (1996). Issues in distance learning. *International Journal of Distance Education*, *1*(4), 337–365.

Shield, L., Hauck, M., & Kötter, M. (2000). Taking the distance out of distance learning. In P. Howarth & R. Herrington (Eds.), *EAP learning technologies* (pp. 16–27). Leeds, England: University Press.

Shim, D. (2006). Hybridity and the rise of Korean popular culture in Asia. *Media Culture & Society*, *28*(1), 25–44.

Shimizu, K., Yashima, T., & Zenuk-Nishide, L. (2004). The influence of attitudes and affect on willingness to communicate and second language communication. *Language Learning, 44*(1), 119–152.

Shneer, D. (2004). *Yiddish and the Creation of Soviet Jewish Culture: 1918-1930*. Cambridge University Press.

Shohel, M. M. C., & Power, T. (2010). Introducing mobile technology for enhancing teaching and learning in Bangladesh: Teacher perspectives. *Open Learning, 25*(3), 201–215. doi:10.1080/02680513.2010.511953

Shuman, L. J., Besterfield-Sacre, M., & McGourty, J. (2005). The ABET "Professional skills" - Can they be taught? Can they be assessed? *The Journal of Engineering Education, 94*(1), 41–55. doi:10.1002/j.2168-9830.2005.tb00828.x

Shweiki Media. Social Networking: College Students and Social Media Statistics. Retrieved from http://www.shweiki.com/blog/2014/02/social-networking-college-students-social-mediastatistics/

Siemens, G. (2005). Connectivism: A learning theory for the digital age. *Instructional Technology & Digital Learning, 2*(1).

Simonson, M., Smaldino, S., Albright, M., & Zvacek, S. (2009). *Teaching and learning at a distance: Foundations of distance education* (4th ed.). Boston: Allyn & Bacon.

Simplified Spelling Board. (1920). *Handbook of Simplified Spelling*. New York, NY: Simplified Spelling Board. Retrieved from https://archive.org/stream/handbooksimplif00boargoog#page/n6/mode/2up

Simpson, E. J. (1972). *The classification of educational objectives in the psychomotor domain*. Washington, DC: Gryphon House.

Sinclair, J. M., & Coulthard, M. (1975). *Towards an analysis of discourse*. London: Oxford University.

Singelis, T. (1994). Nonverbal communication in intercultural interactions. In R. Brislin & T. Yoshida (Eds.), *Improving intercultural interactions* (pp. 268–294). Thousand Oaks, CA: Sage.

Singhal, M. (1997). The Internet and foreign language education: Benefits and challenges? *The Internet TESL Journal, 3*(6), 57–62.

Sink, D. L. (2008). Instructional design models and learning theories. In E. Biech (Ed.), *The ASTD handbook for workplace learning professionals* (pp. 195–212). Alexandria, VA: ASTD Press.

Siskin, C. B. (n. d.). Language Learning Applications for Smartphones, or Small Can Be Beautiful. *Edvista*. Retrieved from http://www.edvista.com/claire/pres/smartphones/#repurposed

Sitter, V., Carter, C., Mahan, R., Massello, C., & Carter, T. (2009). Faculty and student perceptions of a hybrid course design. *Proceedings of the ASCUE*, Myrtle Beach. ASCUE.

Skehan, P. (2001). The role of focus on form during task-based instruction. In Mª L. and A. I. Celaya (Eds.), Trabajos en lingüística aplicada (pp. 11-24). Barcelona, Spain: AESLA.

Skerrett, A. (2012). Languages and literacies in translocation: Experiences and perspectives of a transnational youth. *Journal of Literacy Research, 44*(4), 364–395. doi:10.1177/1086296X12459511

Sloman, M. (2007). Making sense of blended learning. *Industrial and Commercial Training, 39*(6), 315–318. doi:10.1108/00197850710816782

Slotte, V., & Tynjälä, P. (2005). Communication and collaborative learning at work: Views expressed on a cross-cultural eLearning course. *International Journal on E-Learning, 4*(2), 191–207.

Smit, U., & Dafouz, E. (2012). Integrating content and language in higher education. An introduction to English-medium policies, conceptual issues and research practices across Europe. In Smit, U. & E. Dafouz (Eds.), Integrating Content and Language in Higher Education. Gaining Insights into English-Medium Instruction at European Universities. Special Issue of AILA Review, 25, 1-12. doi:10.1075/aila.25.01smi

Smith, K., & Kampf, C. (2004). Developing writing assignments and feedback strategies for maximum effectiveness in large classroom environments. *Proceedings of the International Professional Communication Conference IPCC '04* (pp. 77-82). IEEE. doi:doi:10.1109/IPCC.2004.1375279 doi:10.1109/IPCC.2004.1375279

Smith, B. (2003). Computer-mediated negotiated interaction: An expanded model. *Modern Language Journal, 87*(1), 38–57. doi:10.1111/1540-4781.00177

Smith, B. (2004). Computer-mediated negotiated interaction and lexical acquisition. *Studies in Second Language Acquisition, 26*(03), 365–398. doi:10.1017/S027226310426301X

Soares, I. D. O., ... (2000). *O projeto Educom: Formação de professores on line numa perspectiva educomunicativa.* Retrieved from http://www.ups.br/educomradio/cafe/textos/educom_puc.doc

Soares, I. D. O. (2001). *Caminhos da educomunicação.* São Paulo, Brazil: Salesiana.

Soares, I. D. O. (2008). The right to screens: From media education to educommunication in Brazil. *Comunicar, 30*(30), 87–92. doi:10.3916/c30-2008-01-013

Sokolic, M. (2014). What constitutes an effective language MOOC? In E. Martín-Monje & E. Bárcena (Eds.), *Language MOOCs: Providing learning, transcending boundaries* (pp. 16–32). Warsaw: De Gruyter Open.

Soldat-Jaffe, T. (2012). *Twenty-First Century Yiddishism: Language, Identity & the New Jewish Studies.* Sussex Academic Press.

Solmaz, O. (in press). Autonomous Language Learning on Twitter: Performing Affiliation with Target Language Users through #Hashtags. In *The Handbook of Research on Digital Tools for Self-Directed Language Learning.*

Sotillo, S. (2009). Learner noticing, negative feedback, and uptake in synchronous computer mediated environments. In L. Abraham & L. Williams (Eds.), *Electronic Discourse in Foreign Language Learning and Teaching* (pp. 87–110). Amsterdam: John Benjamins. doi:10.1075/lllt.25.08sot

Sotillo, S. M. (2000). Discourse Functions and Syntactic Complexity in Synchronous and Asynchronous Communication. *Language Learning & Technology, 4*(1), 82–119.

Souza, C. (2013). *The combination of educommunication and community media as a development communication strategy: a case study of the Centre of Community Media São Miguel on Air in São Paulo, Brazil.* (Master's thesis). Malmö University, Malmö, Sweden.

Spangle, M., Hodne, G., & Schierling, D. (2002). Approaching value-centered education through the eyes of an electronic generation: Strategies for distance learning. *Paper presented at the Annual Meeting of the National Communication Association,* New Orleans, USA.

Spencer, D., Wolf, D., & Sams, A. (2011). Are you ready to flip? Retrieved from http://www.thedailyriff.com/articles/are-youready-to-flip-6891.php

Spörer, N., & Brunstein, J. C. (2009). Fostering reading comprehension of secondary school students through peer-assisted learning: Affects on strategy knowledge, strategy use, and task performance. *Contemporary Educational Psychology, 34*(4), 289–297. doi:10.1016/j.cedpsych.2009.06.004

Spreen, C.A. (Ed.), (2002). Preface. In C.A. Spreen (Ed.), New technologies and language learning: Cases in the less commonly taught languages (pp. xiii-xxiv). National Foreign Language Resource Center.

Springer, C. (2009a). *CECR et Perspective Actionnelle: de la tâche pédagogique communicative au projet collaboratif.* Actes du Symposium international Didactique des Langues Étrangères et Maternelles: TIC, aides et méthodes d'apprentissage, Université Mohammed Premier - Oujda (Maroc). Retrieved from http://springcloogle.blogspot.com/2009/02/cecr-et-perspective-actionnellede-la.html/

Springer, C. (2014). *La webcollaboration pour les classes bilingues / FLE.* Synergies Espagne.

Stanek, C. (2013). The educational system of Brazil. *IEM Spotlight., 10*(1), 1–10.

Steinfeld, A., Fong, T., Kaber, D., Lewis, M., Scholtz, J., Schultz, A., & Goodrich, M. (2006, March). Common metrics for human-robot interaction. *Proceedings of the 1st ACM SIGCHI/SIGART conference on Human-robot interaction.* Retrieved from https://www.ri.cmu.edu/pub_files/pub4/steinfeld_aaron_m_2006_1/steinfeld_aaron_m_2006_1.pdf

Sternberg, R. J., Torff, B., & Grigorenko, E. L. (1998). Teaching triarchically improves school achievement. *Journal of Educational Psychology, 3*(3), 374–384. doi:10.1037/0022-0663.90.3.374

Stiler, G. M., & Philleo, T. (2003). Blogging and blog spots: An alternative format for encouraging reflective practice among pre-service teachers. *Academic Research Library, 123*(4), 789–798.

Stohler, U. (2006). The acquisition of knowledge. *Vienna English Working Papers, 3*(6), 41-46.

Stracke, E. (2007). A road to understanding: A qualitative study into why learners drop out of a blended language learning (BLL) environment. *ReCALL, 19*(1), 57–78. doi:10.1017/S0958344007000511

Strahler, S. R. (2015). Are Illinois Public Universities Doomed? *Chicago Business.* Retrieved from http://www.chicagobusiness.com/article/20150815/ISSUE01/308159989/are-illinois-public-universities-doomed

Strauss, A., & Corbin, J. (1998). *Basics of qualitative research: techniques and procedures for developing grounded theory* (2nd ed.). London, UK: SAGE.

Street, W. (2015). Wall St. cheat sheet: 7 reasons why we buy Japanese instead of American cars. Chatham: Newstex. Retrieved from http://search.proquest.com.lib-proxy.fullerton.edu/docview/1683369226?pq-origsite=summon

Sturm, J. (2012). Using film in the L2 classroom: A graduate course in film pedagogy. *Foreign Language Annals, 45*(2), 246–259. doi:10.1111/j.1944-9720.2012.01187.x

Stutzmann, B., Colebech, D. Khalid, A., Chin, C. & Sweigart, J. (2013). Flipped classroom or flipped out?: Professors attitudes towards online learning. SoTL Commons Conference Paper.

Suarez, D. (2003). The Development of empathetic dispositions through global experiences. *Educational Horizons, 81*(4), 180–182.

Suleiman, Y. (1991). Affective and personality factors in learning Arabic as a foreign language: A case study. *Al-Arabiyya, 24,* 83–110.

Sun, R. (2014). AMAs: China's Chopsticks Brothers win International song award. *The Hollywood Reporter.* Retrieved from http://www.hollywoodreporter.com/earshot/amas-2014-chinas-chopsticks-brothers-751585

Sun, M., Chen, Y., & Olson, A. (2013). Developing and implementing an Online program: A case study. In B. Zou Chen, M. Xing, C. Xiang, Y. Wang, & M. Sun (Eds.), *Computer- assisted foreign language teaching and learning: Technological advances* (pp. 160–187). Hershey, PA, USA: IGI Global. doi:10.4018/978-1-4666-2821-2.ch010

Sun, Y. C. (2009). Voice blog: An exploratory study of language Learning. *Language Learning & Technology, 13*(2), 88–103.

Sun, Y.-C. (2009). Voice blog: An exploratory study of language learning. *Language Learning & Technology, 13*, 88–103.

Survival International. (2012). *Brazilian indians*. Retrieved from http://www.survivalinternational.org/tribes/brazilian

Swain, M. (1985). Communicative competence: some roles of comprehensible input and comprehensible output in its development. *Input in second language acquisition*, 15, 165- 179.

Sykes, J. M. (2005). Synchronous CMC and pragmatic development: Effects of oral and written chat. *CALICO Journal, 22*, 399–432. Retrieved from https://calico.org/p-5-Calico%20Journal.html

Sykes, J. M., Oskoz, A., & Thorne, S. L. (2013). Web 2.0, synthetic immersive environments, and mobile resources for language education. *CALICO Journal, 25*(3), 528–546.

Symmons, J. (2013). An Exploration of Professors' Use of Twitter in Higher Education. Retrieved from http://www.dr.library.brocku.ca/bitstream/handle/10464/4960/Brock_Symmons_Janet2013.pdf?sequence=1

Tablet Users to Surpass 1 Billion Worldwide in 2015. (2015, Jan. 8). *Emarketer.* Retrieved from http://www.emarketer.com/Article/Tablet-Users-Surpass-1-Billion-Worldwide-2015/1011806#sthash.aHZWN7ma.dpuf

Tabor, S. W. (2007). Narrowing the distance: Implementing a hybrid learning model for information security education. *Quarterly Review of Distance Education, 8*(1), 47–57.

Taguchi, N. (2011). Teaching pragmatics: Trends and issues. *Annual Review of Applied Linguistics, 31*, 289–310. doi:10.1017/S0267190511000018

Talbert, R. (2012). Inverted classroom. *Colleagues, 9*(1). Retrieved from http://scholarworks.gvsu.edu/colleagues/vol9/iss1/7

Tang, J. (1999). The changing face of library and information science education in China in the 1990s. *Asian Libraries, 8*(1), 17–22.

Tan, L. H., Laird, A. R., Li, K., & Fox, P. T. (2005). Neuroanatomical correlates of phonological processing of Chinese characters and alphabetic words: A meta-analysis. *Human Brain Mapping, 25*(1), 83–91. doi:10.1002/hbm.20134 PMID:15846817

Tapscott, D. (1998). *Growing Up Digital: The Rise of the Net Generation*. New York: McGraw-Hill.

Tarone, E. (1977). Conscious communication strategies in interlanguage. A progress report. In H.D. Brown, C.A., Yoio & R.C. Crymes (Eds.), On TESOL '77 (pp. 194-203). Washington: TESOL.

Tarone, E. (1980). Communication strategies, foreigner talk and repair in interlanguage. *Language Learning, 30*(2), 417–431. doi:10.1111/j.1467-1770.1980.tb00326.x

Tee, M. Y., & Karney, D. (2010). Sharing and cultivating tacit knowledge in an online learning environment. *Computer-Supported Collaborative Learning, 5*(4), 385–413. doi:10.1007/s11412-010-9095-3

Teitelbaum, P. (2015, May 5). Regards from Agi and a question.

Teixeira, A., & Mota, J. (2014). A proposal for the methodological design of collaborative language MOOCs. In E. Martín-Monje & E. Bárcena (Eds.), *Language MOOCs: Providing learning, transcending boundaries* (pp. 33–47). Warsaw: De Gruyter Open. doi:10.2478/9783110420067.3

Tenopir, C. (1999). Electronic reference and reference librarians: A look through the 1990s. *RSR. Reference Services Review, 27*(3), 276–280.

Teodorescu, T. (2006). Competence versus competency: What is the difference? *Performance Improvement, 45*(10), 27–30. doi:10.1002/pfi.4930451027

Terras, M., & Ramsay, J. (2015). Massive open online courses (MOOCs): Insights and challenges from a psychological perspective. *British Journal of Educational Technology, 46*(3), 472–487. doi:10.1111/bjet.12274

Thaines, E., & Bodah, B. (2008). *E.E. from Brazil to the U.S.: an invitation to the practical diversity on environmental education.* Passo Fundo, Brazil: Berthier.

Thaines, E., & Rodrigues, L. D. (2007). Educação ambiental: potencialidades e desafios da pratica pedagogica no cotidiano escolar. In *Teoria e pratica pedagogica.* Passo Fundo, Brazil: Universidade de Passo Fundo.

The Dora Teitelboim Institute for Yiddish Education. (n. d.). Retrieved from http://www.yiddishculture.org/dtf1.html

The Elusive Quest for Equality. InMoreno, J. F. (Ed.), *The Elusive Quest for Equality: 150 Years of Chicano/Chicana Education* (pp. 31–52). Cambridge: Harvard Educational Review.

The Grosbard Project. (n. d.). Retrieved from http://grosbardproject.com/Grosbard_Project/Home.html

The New York Times. (2010, December 1). Translanguaging: An approach to bilingualism where speakers switch from one language to another. Retrieved from http://schott.blogs.nytimes.com/2010/12/01/translanguaging/?_r=0

The Yiddish Daily Forward. (n. d.). Retrieved from http://yiddish.forward.com/

Theisen, T. (2013). New spaces new realities: Expanding learning any time, any place. *Foreign Language Annals, 46*(2), 141–142.

Thiong'o, N. (1986). *Decolonizing the mind: The politics of language in African literature.* Nairobi, Kenya: Oxford Publishing Company.

Thomas, W. P., & Collier, V. P. (2002). A national study of school effectiveness for language minority students' long-term academic achievement. Eric Digest, ED475 048 FL 027 622.

Thomas, K. M., O'Bannon, B. W., & Bolton, N. (2013). Cell phones in the classroom: Teachers' perspectives of inclusion, benefits, and barriers. *Computers in the Schools, 30*(4), 295–308. doi:10.1080/07380569.2013.844637

Thomas, K., & O'Bannon, B. (2013). Cell phones in the classroom: Preservice teachers' perceptions. *Journal of Digital Learning in Teacher Education, 30*(1), 11–20. doi:10.1080/21532974.2013.10784721

Thomauske, N. (2011). The relevance of multilingualism for teachers and immigrant parents in early childhood education and care in Germany and in France. *Intercultural Education, 22*(4), 327–336. doi:10.1080/14675986.2011.617425

Thompson, C. (2011). How Khan Academy Is Changing the Rules of Education. *Wired.* Retrieved from http://www.wired.com/magazine/2011/07/ff_khan/

Thoms, J. (2012). Classroom discourse in foreign language classrooms: A review of literature. *Foreign Language Annals, 45*(1), 8–27. doi:10.1111/j.1944-9720.2012.01177.x

Thurston, A., Duran, D., Cunningham, E., Blanch, S., & Topping, K. (2009). International on-line reciprocal peer tutoring to promote modern language development in primary schools. *Computers & Education, 53*(2), 462–472. doi:10.1016/j.compedu.2009.03.005

Tian, J., & Wang, J. (2010). Taking language learning outside the classroom: Learners' perspectives of eTandem learning via Skype. *Innovation in Language Learning and Teaching, 4*(3), 181–197. doi:10.1080/17501229.2010.513443

Tiedt, P. l., & Tiedt, I. M. (2010). *Multicultural Teaching: Activities, Information, and Resources*. Boston: Allyn and Bacon/Pearson Education.

Tolbert, C. J., & Hero, R. E. (2001). Dealing with diversity: Racial/ethnic context and social policy change. *Political Research Quarterly, 54*(3), 571–604. doi:10.1177/106591290105400305

Toven-Lindsey, B., Rhoads, R., & Lozano, J. (2015). Virtually unlimited classrooms: Pedagogical practices in massive open online courses. *The Internet and Higher Education, 24*, 1–12. doi:10.1016/j.iheduc.2014.07.001

Toyoda, E., & Harrison, R. (2002). Categorization of text chat communication between learners and native speakers and native speakers of Japanese. *Language Learning & Technology, 6*(1), 82–99.

Toyoshima, N. (2008). Longing for Japan: The consumption of Japanese cultural products in Thailand. *Sojourn: Journal of Social Issues in Southeast Asia, 23*(2), 252–282.

Tricker, T., Rangecroft, M., Long, P., & Gilroy, P. (2001). Evaluating distance education courses: The student perception. *Assessment & Evaluation in Higher Education, 26*(2), 165–177. doi:10.1080/02602930020022002

Trotman, W. (2010). The Handbook of Language Teaching. *ELT Journal, 64*(3), 342–344. doi:10.1093/elt/ccq028

Trubitt, L., & Overholtzer, J. (2009). Good communication: The other social network for successful IT organizations. *EDUCAUSE Review, 44*(6), 90–98.

Tse, L. (2001). Resisting and reversing language shift: Heritage-language resilience among U.S. native biliterates. *Harvard Educational Review, 71*(4), 676–708. doi:10.17763/haer.71.4.ku752mj536413336

Tucker, C. (2012). Flipped classroom: Beyond the videos. *CatlinTucker.com*. Retrieved from http://catlintucker.com/2012/04/flipped-classroom-beyond-the-videos/

Tudini, V. (2003). Using native speakers in chat. *Language Learning & Technology, 7*(3), 141–159.

Tunison M., & Noonan, B (2001). On-line learning: Secondary students' first experience. *Revue Canadienne de l'Education [Canadian Journal of Education], 26*(4), 495–511.

Tuzi, F. (2004). The impact of e-feedback on the revisions of L2 writers in an academic writing course. *Computers and Composition, 21*(2), 217–235. doi:10.1016/j.compcom.2004.02.003

Typing in Yiddish on a Mac – Isaac L. Bleaman. (n. d.). Retrieved from https://wp.nyu.edu/ibleaman/yiddish/typing/

U.S. Census Bureau. (2010). *State & county quickfacts: Chicago, IL*. Retrieved from http://quickfacts.census.gov/qfd/states/17/1714000.html

U.S. Department of Education. (2016). Title 1—Improving the academic achievement of the disadvantaged. U.S. Department of Education. Retrieved from http://www2.ed.gov/policy/elsec/leg/esea02/pg1.html

U.S. Department of State. (n.d.). U.S. Department of State: Office of the Historian. Retrieved from https://history.state.gov/milestones/1945-1952/japan-reconstruction

UNESCO. (2003). *Education position paper: Education in a multilingual world*. Paris: United Nations Educational, Scientific and Cultural Organization.

University of Michigan. (2014, June). Additional Q&A About Tuition. Public Affairs & Internal Communications. Retrieved from https://publicaffairs.vpcomm.umich.edu/key-issues/tuition/additional-qa-about-tuition/

Uzunboylu, H., & Özdamlı, F. (2011). Teacher perception for m-learning: Scale development and teachers' perceptions. *Journal of Computer Assisted Learning, 27*(6), 544–556. doi:10.1111/j.1365-2729.2011.00415.x

Valdez, E. O. (2001). Winning the battle, losing the war: Bilingual teachers and post-proposition 227. *The Urban Review*, *33*(3), 237–253.

Valenciana, C. (2006). Unconstitutional deportation of Mexican Americans during the 1930's: A family history and oral history. *Multicultural Education Journal*, *13*(3), 4–9.

Valenza, J. K. (2012). The flipping librarian. *Teacher Librarian*, *40*(2), 22–25.

van Lier. (1996). *Interaction in the language curriculum: Awareness, autonomy, authenticity*. New York, NY: Longman.

Van Praag, B., & Sanchez, H. S. (2015). Mobile technology in second language classrooms: Insights into its uses, pedagogical implications, and teacher beliefs. *ReCALL*, *27*(03), 288–303. doi:10.1017/S0958344015000075

vanCompernolle, R. A. (2011). Use and variation of French diacritics on an Internet dating site. *French Language Studies*, *21*(02), 131–148. doi:10.1017/S0959269510000293

vanCompernolle, R. A., & Williams, L. (2007). De l'oral a l'électronique: La variation orthographique comme ressource sociostylistique et pragmatique dans le français électronique. *Glottopol*, *10*, 56–69.

vanCompernolle, R. A., & Williams, L. (2010). Orthographic variation in electronic French: The case of l'accent aigu. *French Review (Deddington)*, *83*, 820–833.

VanPatten, B. (1996). *Input processing and grammar instruction: Theory and research*. Norwood, NJ: Ablex.

VanPatten, B. (2000). Processing instruction as form–meaning connections: Issues in theory and research. In J. F. Lee & A. Valdman (Eds.), *Form and Meaning in Language Teaching* (pp. 43–68). Boston: Heinle & Heinle.

Vaughan, N. D. (2007). Perspectives on blended learning in higher education. *International Journal on E-Learning*, *6*(1), 81-94.

Vecsey, C. (2007). Alfred A. Cave. Prophets of the Great Spirit: Native American revitalization movements in Eastern North America. *The American Historical Review*, *112*(4), 1163–1164.

Veenema, S., & Gardner, H. (1996). Multi-media and multiple intelligences. *The American Prospect*, *29*, 70–75.

Vellenga, H. (2004). Learning pragmatics from ESL and EFL textbooks: How likely? *TESL-EJ, 8*(2). Retrieved from http://www.tesl-ej.org/wordpress/issues/volume8/ej30/ej30a3

Ventriglia, L. (1982). *Conversations of Miguel and Maria: How children learn English as a Second Language*. Menlo Park, CA: Addison-Wesley.

Vertovec, S. (2001). Transnationalism and identity. *Journal of Ethnic and Migration Studies*, *27*(4), 573–582. doi:10.1080/13691830120090386

Vertovec, S. (2004). Migrant transnationalism and modes of transformation. *International Migration Review*, *38*(3), 970–1001. doi:10.1111/j.1747-7379.2004.tb00226.x

Vertovec, S. (2004). Migrant transnationalsim and modes of transformation. *International Migration Review*, *38*(3), 970–1001.

Villa, A., & Poblete, M. (Eds.). (2008). *Competence-based Learning. A Proposal for the Assessment of Generic Competences*. Bilbao: Universidad de Deusto.

Vinagre, M. (forthcoming). Promoting intercultural competence in culture and language studies: Outcomes of an international collaborative project. In Martín-Monje, E., Elorza, I & García Riaza, B. (Eds.), Technological advances in specialized linguistic domains: Learning on the move (pp. 37-52). London: Routledge.

Vinagre, M. (2005). Fostering language learning by e-mail: An English-Spanish exchange. *Computer Assisted Language Learning, 18*(5), 369–388. doi:10.1080/09588220500442749

Vinagre, M. (2008). Politeness strategies in collaborative e-mail exchanges. *Computers & Education, 50*(3), 1022–1036. doi:10.1016/j.compedu.2006.10.002

Vinagre, M. (2010). *Teoría y práctica del aprendizaje colaborativo asistido por ordenador.* Madrid: Síntesis.

Vinagre, M., & Muñoz, B. (2011). Computer-mediated corrective feedback and language accuracy in telecollaborative exchanges. *Language Learning & Technology, 15*(1), 72–103. Retrieved from http://llt.msu.edu/issues/february2011/vinagremunoz.pdf

Vogel, P. (2015, October 2). Myths and Facts About the College Debt Crisis. Media Matters for America. Retrieved from http://mm4a.org/1WC9ii2

Von Der Emde, S., Schneider, J., & Kötter, M. (2001). Technically speaking: Transforming language learning through virtual learning environments (MOOs). *Modern Language Journal, 85*(2), 210–225. doi:10.1111/0026-7902.00105

Voos, R. (2003). Blended learning – what is it and where might it take us? Sloan-C View, 2 (1), 3-5. Retrieved from http://www.sloan-c.org/publications/view/v2n1/blended1.htm

Vygotsky, L. (1978). *Mind in society: The development of higher psychological processes.* Cambridge, MA: Harvard University Press.

Vygotsky, L. S. (1987). Thinking and speech. In *L. S. Vygotsky, collected works.* New York: Plenum.

Vygotsky, L. S. (1988). Interaction in learning and development. In P. A. Richard-Amato (Ed.), *Making it happen: Interaction in the second language classroom.* White Plains, NY: Longman.

Wang Szilas, J., Berger, C., & Zhang, F. (2013). eTandem language learning integrated in the curriculum: reflection from students' perspective. *Proceedings of the European Distance and E-learning Network 2013 Annual Conference* (pp. 93-102). Olso: The Joy of Learning.

Wang, Q. (2014). A study of the relationship between foreign language teachers' TPACK and their self-efficacy on technology integration. *Computer-Assisted Foreign Language Education, 4,* 003.

Wang, C. (2012). Pre-service teachers' perceptions of learning a foreign language online: Preparing teachers to work with linguistic, cultural, and technological diversity. *International Journal of Computer-Assisted Language Learning and Teaching, 2*(1), 30–45. doi:10.4018/ijcallt.2012040103

Wang, C. (2015). From preservice to inservice: Can practicing foreign language learning online help teachers transfer linguistic, cultural, and technological awareness into teaching English language learners? *International Journal of Computer-Assisted Language Learning and Teaching, 5*(2), 1–21. doi:10.4018/ijcallt.2015040101

Wang, C. (2015). From preservice to inservice: Can practicing foreign language learning online help teachers transfer linguistic, cultural, and technological awareness into teaching English Language Learners? *International Journal of Computer-Assisted Language Learning and Teaching, 5*(2).

Wang, J., & Postiglione, G. (2008). China's minorities without written scripts: The case of education access among the Dongxiang. *Journal of Asian Pacific Communication, 18*(2), 166.

Wang, L. (2005). The advantages of using technology in second language education: Technology integration in foreign language teaching demonstrates the shift from a behavioral to a constructivist learning approach. *T.H.E. Journal* [Technological Horizons in Education], *32*(10), 38.

Wang, M. (2014). An empirical study on foreign language anxiety of non-English major students: Take the sophomores in Inner Mongolia University of technology as an example. *Studies in Literature and Language*, *9*(3), 128–135.

Wang, S. (2009). Preparing and supporting teachers of less commonly taught languages. *Modern Language Journal*, *93*(2), 282–287. doi:10.1111/j.1540-4781.2009.00860_8.x

Wang, S., & Higgins, M. (2006). Limitations of mobile phone learning. *The JALT CALL Journal*, *2*(1), 3–14.

Wang, S., & Vasquez, C. (2014). The Effect of Target Language Use in Social Media on Intermediate-level Chinese Language Learners' writing performance. *CALICO Journal*, *31*(1), 78–102. doi:10.11139/cj.31.1.78-102

Wang, Y. (2006). Negotiation of meaning in desktop videoconferencing-supported distance language learning. *ReCALL*, *18*(1), 122–146. doi:10.1017/S0958344006000814

Wang, Y., & Chen, N. S. (2013). Engendering interaction, collaboration, and reflection in the design of online learning assessment in language learning: A reflection from the course designers. In B. Zou Chen, M. Xing, C. Xiang, Y. Wang, & M. Sun (Eds.), *Computer- assisted foreign language teaching and learning: Technological advances* (pp. 16–38). Hershey, PA, USA: IGI Global. doi:10.4018/978-1-4666-2821-2.ch002

Wang, Y., & Phillion, J. (2009). Minority language policy and practice in China: The need for multicultural education. *International Journal of Multicultural Education*, *11*(1).

Wankel, L. A., & Blessinger, P. (2013). Inventive approaches in Higher Education: An introduction to using multimédia technologies. In L. A. Wankel & P. Blessinger (Eds.), *Increasing Student Engagement and Retention using Multimedia Technologies*. Bingley: Howard House Publishing. doi:10.1108/S2044-9968(2013)000006D003

Ward, J. M. (2004). Blog assisted language learning (BALL): Push button publishing for the pupils. *TEFL Web Journal*, *3*(1), 1–15.

Ware, D., & Warschauer, M. (2006). Electronic feedback and second language writing. In K. Hyland & F. Hyland (Eds.), *Feedback in second language writing: Context and issues* (pp. 105–121). London: Cambridge University Press. doi:10.1017/CBO9781139524742.008

Ware, P. D. (2005). "Missed" communication in online communication: Tensions in a German-American telecollaboration. *Language Learning & Technology*, *9*(2), 64–89.

Ware, P. D., & Kramsch, C. (2005). Toward an intercultural stance: Teaching German and English through telecollaboration. *Modern Language Journal*, *89*(2), 190–205. doi:10.1111/j.1540-4781.2005.00274.x

Ware, P., & O'Dowd, R. (2008). Peer feedback on language form in telecollaboration. *Language Learning & Technology*, *12*(1), 43–63.

Warf, B. (2013). Contemporary digital divides in the United States. *Tijdschrift voor Economische en Sociale Geografie*, *104*(1), 1–17.

Warhol, L. (2011). Native American language policy in the United States. *Heritage Briefs Collection*. Retrieved from http://www.cal.org/heritage/pdfs/briefs/native-american-language-policy.pdf

Warschauer, M. (1997). Computer-mediated collaborative learning: Theory and practice. *Modern Language Journal*, *81*(4), 470–481. doi:10.1111/j.1540-4781.1997.tb05514.x

Warschauer, M. (1997). The Internet for English Teaching: Guidelines for teachers. *TESL Reporter*, *30*(1), 27–33.

Warschauer, M. (1998). Technology and indigenous language revitalization: Analyzing the experience of Hawai'i. *Canadian Modern Language Review*, *55*(1), 139–159. doi:10.3138/cmlr.55.1.139

Warschauer, M. (2004). *Of digital divides and social multipliers: Combining language and technology for human development. Information and communication technologies in the teaching and learning of foreign languages: State of the art, needs and perspectives* (pp. 46–52). Moscow: UNESCO Institute for Information Technologies in Education.

Warschauer, M., Donaghy, K., & Kuamoÿo, H. (1997). Leokī: A powerful voice of Hawaiian language revitalization. *Computer Assisted Language Learning, 10*(4), 349–362. doi:10.1080/0958822970100405

Warschauer, M., & Kern, R. (2000). *Network-based language teaching: Concepts and practice.* Cambridge, UK: Cambridge University Press. doi:10.1017/CBO9781139524735

Watts, F., Marín, J. A., García, A., & Aznar, L. E. (2012). Validation of a rubric to assess innovation competence. *Working Papers on Operations Management, 3*(1), 61-70.

Weinreich, M. (1973). History of the Yiddish Language (1980th ed.). Chicago: University of Chicago Press.

Weinreich, U. (1949). *College Yiddish: Introduction to the Yiddish Language and to Jewish Life and Culture.* New York: YIVO Institute for Jewish Research.

Weinreich, U. (1972). *Explorations in Semantic Theory.* The Hague, Paris: Mouton. doi:10.1515/9783110813142

Wellington, J. (2000). *Educational Research: Contemporary issues and practical approaches.* London: Continuum.

Wenger, E. (2005). *La théorie des communautés de pratique.* (F. Gervais, Trad.) Sainte-Foy, Québec: les Presses de l'université Laval.

Wenger, E. (1998). *Communities of practice. Learning, meaning, and identity. Cambridge.* UK: Cambridge University Press. doi:10.1017/CBO9780511803932

Wenger, E., McDermott, R., & Snyder, W. M. (2002). *Cultivating communities of practice: A guide to managing knowledge.* Boston, MA: Harvard Business School Press.

Wenzhong, H., Grove, C., & Enping, Z. (2010). *Encountering the Chinese: A modern country, an ancient culture.* Boston: Intercultural Press.

Wesche, M. B., & Skehan, P. (2002). Communicative, task-based, and content-based language instruction. In R. B. Kaplan (Ed.), *The Oxford handbook of applied linguistics* (pp. 207–288). New York: Oxford University Press.

Wetzel, C. D., Radtke, P. H., & Stem, H. W. (1994). *Instructional Effectiveness of Video Media.* Hillsdale, NJ: Lawrence Erlbaum.

Wexler, P. (1991). Yiddish - the Fifteenth Slavic Language: A Study of Partial Language Shift from Judeo-Sorbian to German. *International Journal of the Sociology of Language, 91*, 9–150.

Wharton, G. (2000). Language learning strategy use of bilingual foreign language learner in Singapore. *Language Learning, 50*(2), 203–243. doi:10.1111/0023-8333.00117

Wheeler, S., Yeomans, P., & Wheeler, D. (2008). 'The good, the bad and the wiki: Evaluating student-generated content for collaborative learning'. *British Journal of Educational Technology, 39*(6), 987–995. doi:10.1111/j.1467-8535.2007.00799.x

White, C. (2003). *Language learning in distance education.* Cambridge: Cambridge University Press. doi:10.1017/CBO9780511667312

White, C. (2004). Independent Language Learning in Distance Education: Current Issues. *Proceedings of the Independent Learning Conference 2003.*

White, C. (2005). Towards a learner-based theory of distance language learning: The concept of the learner–context interface. In B. Holmberg, M. Shelley, & C. White (Eds.), *Distance education and languages: Evolution and change* (pp. 55–71). Clevedon, UK: Multilingual Matters.

White, C. (2006). The distance learning of foreign languages. *Language Teaching, 39*(4), 247–264. doi:10.1017/S0261444806003727

White, C. (2008). Language learning strategies in independent language learning: An overview. In T. Lewis & S. Hurd (Eds.), *Language learning strategies in independent settings* (pp. 3–24). Clevedon, UK: Multilingual Matters.

Wiecki, E. (2009). Untervegs: A Journey with the Yiddish Textbook. *European Judaism, 42*(2), 47–61. doi:10.3167/ej.2009.420207

Wikipedia. (2015, November 2). OpenCourseWare. Retrieved from https://en.wikipedia.org/wiki/OpenCourseWare

Wilkinson, R. (Ed.). (2004). *Integrating content and language. Meeting the challenge of multilingual higher education.* Maastricht: Universitaire Pers Maastricht.

Williams, B. (2001). Developing critical reflection for professional practice through problem-based learning. *Journal of Advanced Nursing, 34*(1), 27–34. doi:10.1046/j.1365-2648.2001.3411737.x PMID:11430603

Williams, J., & Jacobs, J. (2004). Exploring the use of blogs as learning spaces in the higher education sector. *Australasian Journal of Educational Technology, 20*(2), 232–247.

Williams, K. C., Cameron, B. A., & Morgan, K. (2012). Supporting online group projects. *North American College Teachers of Agriculture Journal, 56*, 15–20.

Willis, J. (1996). *A framework for task-based learning.* London: Longman.

Wilson, D. M. (2011). Dual language programs on the rise: "Enrichment" model puts content learning front and center for ELL students. *Harvard Education Letter, 27*(2). Retrieved from https://www.berkeleyparentsnetwork.org/recommend/schools/berkeley/immersion

Wilson, W. (2003). Faculty perceptions and uses of instructional technology. *EDUCAUSE Quarterly, 2*, 60–62.

Winer, S. (2012, August 16). Hasidic Pop Star Dons IDF Togs. *The Times of Israel.* Retrieved from http://www.timesofisrael.com/hasidic-pop-star-dons-idf-togs/

Winke, P., Goertler, S., & Amuzie, G. L. (2010). Commonly taught and less commonly taught language learners: Are they equally prepared for CALL and online language learning? *Computer Assisted Language Learning, 23*(3), 199–219. doi:10.1080/09588221.2010.486576

Winkler, J. (2015, July 6). A Day in the Life of Lipa Schmeltzer, Ex-Ultra-Orthodox Celebrity. Retrieved from http://www.tabletmag.com/jewish-arts-and-culture/music/191829/lipa-schmeltzer

Winstead, L., & Gautreau, C. (2014). Cultural Universals as an integrated pedagogical approach for preservice teachers. *Russian-American Education Forum: An Online Journal, 6*(2). Retrieved from http://www.rus-ameeduforum.com/content/en/?task=art&article=1001066&iid=19

Winstead, L. (2004). Increasing academic motivation and cognition in reading, writing, and mathematics: Meaning-making strategies. *Educational Research Quarterly, 28*(2), 30–49.

Winstead, L. (2013). Apprehension and motivation among adolescent dual language peers: Perceptions and awareness about self-directed teaching and learning. *Language and Education, 27*(1), 1–21. doi:10.1080/09500782.2012.669767

Winter-Spring 2016 Yiddish Online Class Descriptions. (2014, December 18). Retrieved from https://circle.org/what-we-do/yiddish-language/winter-spring-2016-yiddish-class-descriptions/

Witten, H. (2013). World languages. In J. Bretzman (Ed.), *Flipping 2.0: Practical strategies for flipping your class* (pp. 265–280). New Berlin, WI: The Bretzman Group.

Wong-Fillmore, L. (1983). The language learner as an individual: implications of research on individual difference for the ESL teacher. In J. Lindfors, et al. (1983). *On TESOL, 82.* ERIC Clearinghouse: FL013682.)

Wong, L., Chai, C., & Ping, G. (2011). The Chinese input challenges for Chinese as second language learners in computer-mediated writing: An exploratory study. *TOJET: The Turkish Online Journal of Educational Technology, 10*(3), 233–248.

Wong, R. (2010). The effectiveness of using English as the sole medium of instruction in English classes: Student responses and improved English proficiency. *Porta Linguarum, 13,* 119–130.

World Wildlife Foundation. (2012) *Amazon: world's largest tropical rainforest and river basin.* Retrieved from http://www.worldwildlife.org/what/wherewework/amazon/index.html#

Wusan, D. (2014). Ancient Chinese thought of character formation and modern logo design. *Leonardo, 47*(2), 183–185.

Wu, W. (2006). The effect of blog peer review and teacher feedback on the revisions of EFL writers. *Journal of Education and Foreign Languages and Literature, 3,* 125–139.

Wu, W., Yen, L., & Marek, M. (2011). Using online EFL interaction to increase confidence, motivation, and ability. *Journal of Educational Technology & Society, 14*(3), 118–129.

Xie, Y., & Sharma, P. (2005). *Students lived experiences of using blogs in a class*: An exploratory study. Retrieved from http://eric.ed.gov/ERICDocs/data/ericdocs2/content_storage

Xu, P., & Jen, T. (2005). "Penless" Chinese language learning: A computer-assisted approach. *Journal of the Chinese Language Teachers Association, 40*(2), 25–42.

Yamada, M., & Akahori, K. (2009). Awareness and performance through self and partner's image in videoconferencing. *CALICO Journal, 27*(1), 1–25. doi:10.11139/cj.27.1.1-25

Yang, M., Badger, R., & Yu, Z. (2006). A comparative study of peer and teacher feedback in a Chinese EFL writing class. *Journal of Second Language Writing, 15*(3), 179–200. doi:10.1016/j.jslw.2006.09.004

Yanguas, Í. (2010). Oral computer-mediated interaction between L2 learners: It's about time! *Language Learning & Technology, 14*(1), 72–93.

Yao, S., & Hong, W. (2015, July). 初级网络课程的考评 (The Evaluation in Elementary-level Distance Chinese Courses--challenges and solutions.) *Proceedings for the 13th International Conference of Chinese Pedagogy*, Hohhot, China (pp. 201-206).

Yap, C. (2013). Preserving the original layout of ancient Chinese texts using html5: Using Shuowen Jiezi as an example. *International Journal of Humanities and Arts Computing, 7*(supplement), 111–119.

Ye, L. (2013). Shall we delay teaching characters in teaching Chinese as a foreign language? *Foreign Language Annals, 46*(4), 610–627.

Yeung, A. S., Chen, Z., & Li, B. (2015). Maximizing the benefit of technology for language learning. In C. Koh (Ed.), *Motivation, Leadership and Curriculum Design* (pp. 185–199). Singapore: Springer. doi:10.1007/978-981-287-230-2_15

Yiddish | Gratz College. (n. d.). Retrieved from http://www.gratz.edu/programs/yiddish

Yiddish Kave Sho. (2015, October7).

Yiddish Language - The Workmen's Circle. (n. d.). Retrieved from https://circle.org/what-we-do/yiddish-language/

Yiddish, P. O. P. (n. d.). Retrieved from http://www.yiddishpop.com/

YIDLIFE CRISIS. (n. d.). Retrieved from http://www.yidlifecrisis.com/

Young, J. (2014, September 12). Down with the "Revival": Yiddish is a Living Language. Retrieved from https://www.yivo.org/down-with-the-revival-yiddish-is-a-living-language

Young, A. S. (2008). Diversity as an asset: Multiple language integration. In M. Dooly & D. Eastment (Eds.), *How we're going about it. Teachers' voices on innovative approaches to teaching and learning languages* (pp. 51–65). Newcastle upon Tyne: Cambridge Scholars Publishing.

Young, A. S., & Mary, L. (2010). Une formation des professeurs des écoles en phase avec le 21ème siècle. In J.-M. Mangiante (Ed.), *Langue et Intégration* (pp. 349–363). Frankfurt: Peter Lang.

Young, A. S., & Mary, L. (in press). Dix ans d'expérimentation dans la formation de (futurs) acteurs de l'éducation pour une meilleure prise en compte de la diversité linguistique et culturelle des élèves: Enjeux, défis et réussites. *Carnet des Ateliers Sociolinguistiques.*

Young, A., & Helot, C. (2003). Language awareness and/or language learning in French primary schools today. *Language Awareness, 12*(3 & 4), 234–246.

Zaid, M. A. (1999). Cultural Confrontation and Cultural Acquisition in the EFL Classroom. *International Review of Applied Linguistics in Language Teaching, 37*(2), 111–126. doi:10.1515/iral.1999.37.2.111

Zappavigna, M. (2015b). Searchable talk: The linguistic functions of hashtags in tweets about Schapelle Corby, *Global Media Journal, 9*(1). Retrieved from http://www.hca.westernsydney.edu.au/gmjau/?p=1762

Zappavigna, M. (2012). *Discourse of Twitter and Social Media, Continuum Discourse Series*. London: Continuum.

Zappavigna, M. (2015a). Searchable talk: The linguistic functions of hashtags. *Social Semiotics, 25*(3), 274–291. doi:10.1080/10350330.2014.996948

Zappe, S., Leicht, R., Messner, J., Litzinger, T., & Lee, H. (2009). *"Flipping" the classroom to explore active learning in a large undergraduate course*. American Society for Engineering Education.

Zarotsky, V., & Jaresko, G. S. (2000). Technology in education—Where do we go from here? *Journal of Pharmacy Practice, 13*(5), 373–381.

Zeng, G., & Takatsuka, S. (2009). Text-based peer-peer collaborative dialogue in a computer-mediated learning environment in the EFL context. *System, 37*(3), 434–446. doi:10.1016/j.system.2009.01.003

Zhang, Y. (1933). *Kangxi Zidian* (Tong ban ying yin). Shanghai: Shanghai wu yin shu guan.

Zhang, X. (2010). The formation of East Asian world during the 4th and 5th centuries: A study based on Chinese sources. *Frontiers of History in China, 5*(4), 525–548.

Zhang, Z., & Wang, Y. (2015). English language usage pattern in China mainland doctors: AME survey-001 initial analysis results. *Quantitative Imaging in Medicine and Surgery, 5*(1), 174.

Zhao, Y. (2007). Social studies teachers' perspectives of technology integration. *Journal of Technology and Teacher Education, 15*(3), 311–333.

Zhao, Y. (2013). Recent developments in technology and language learning: A literature review and meta-analysis. *CALICO Journal*, *21*(1), 7–27.

Zhou, M. (2003). *Multilingualism in China: The politics of writing reforms for minority languages 1949-2002* (Vol. 89). New York, NY: Walter de Gruyter.

Zhu, G. (2014). The right to minority language instruction in schools: Negotiating competing claims in multinational china. *Human Rights Quarterly*, *36*(4), 691–721.

Zimmerman, B. J. (1989). A social cognitive view of self-regulated academic learning. *Journal of Educational Psychology*, *81*(3), 329–339. doi:10.1037/0022-0663.81.3.329

Zongo, B. (2004). *Le parler ordinaire multilingue à Paris. Ville et alternance codique.* Paris, L'Harmattan.

Zucker, S. (1994). Yiddish: An Introduction to the Language. Literature, and Culture. Hoboken, NJ: KTAV in conjunction with Workmen Circle.

Zuo, X. (2007). China's policy towards minority languages in globalizing age. *Transnational Curriculum Inquiry*, *4*(1), 80–91.

漢典. (2016, March 18). 妭. Retrieved from http://www.zdic.net/z/17/js/597B.htm

About the Contributors

Congcong Wang (Ph.D. in Language, Literacy, and Technology, Washington State University) is an editor, researcher, translator, bilingual writer, and online course developer. She is the associate leader of the Chinese Language Teachers Association-EdTech SIG and the vice-president of the Iowa Chinese Language Teachers Association. She has a master's degree in Bilingual/ELL Education and B.A. in English. Her research focuses primarily upon computer-assisted language learning, cross-cultural psychology, and teachers' awareness development and cultural studies. Her qualitative and quantitative research has appeared in the *International Journal of Computer-Assisted Language Learning and Teaching*, and the *Journal of Personality and Social Psychology*. She presents regularly at conferences such as ACTFL, NCOLCTL, CLTA, and NAR bicentennial. Across the United States and China, she has developed a variety of technology-enhanced face-to-face, hybrid, and online courses offered in synchronous and asynchronous formats for four universities and over 10 programs. She has taught a wide array of university courses, including Beginning to Advanced Chinese language, culture, literature, media, history, and instructional technology, as well as EFL/ESL education at the K-12 level. At the University of Northern Iowa, she relishes working with her colleagues in Languages and Literatures who have given her great support in developing this book. In addition to academic publications, she has also published short stories in Chinese, traditional and digital art works, a children's book, and translations. With an interest in bridging cultures and introducing Asian artists to western audiences, she has performed many Chinese-English translations of international research projects, poetry, interviews, documentaries, commercials, and non-profit organizations. She reviews translated poetry for the *North American Review*, the oldest literary magazine in the United States. She enjoys her collaboration with diverse researchers on international research projects and technology-assisted learning programs for student-athletes, migrant students, preservice teachers, and international scholars.

Lisa Winstead is the Spanish Bilingual Authorization Coordinator and Associate Professor in the Department of Elementary and Bilingual Education at California State University, Fullerton. She received her doctorate in Curriculum and Instruction with an emphasis in language, literacy and culture at the University of the Pacific. She has a master's in International Relations. She has also studied at Waseda University in Japan and Lyon II University in France. These experiences in addition to her high school experience in Mexico, and work as a bilingual reporter for (ABC, Sacramento) Progreso, have influenced her research. Her research interests include heritage and bilingual education, migrant education, second language acquisition, and technological approaches that provide access to language learners globally in socially just and responsive ways. She teaches courses at CSU Fullerton, including Second Languages, Latinos in Education, and Bilingual Methods in Spanish, to prepare teachers who will serve in dual immersion programs. She is also involved in the translation of French and Spanish manuscripts to assist researchers around the world in gaining publication access. Her publications in scholarly peer-reviewed journals include "Apprehension and motivation among adolescent dual language peers" in Language and Education, "Coming to voice: Preparing bilingual-bicultural teachers for social justice" in Equity and Excellence in Education, and "A journey to medieval China: Using technology-enhanced instruction to develop content and digital literacy skills" in The Social Studies Journal. These and other research are regularly presented at regional, national, and international conferences, including the International Symposium on Bilingualism, the National Association for Bilingual Education, the Children's Identity and Citizenship in Europe, and the American Educational Research Association. She is thankful for the support of her colleagues and students during this process.

* * *

Jacob Bender is the copy-editor of the *Handbook of Research on Foreign Language Education in the digital Age.* He is a PhD candidate in English literature at the University of Iowa. He possesses an English MA from the University of Utah and a BA from BYU-Idaho. His research explores the intersection between Irish and Latin American literature in the 20th century. He has previously worked as a Writing Fellow for the Office of Vice-President of Research at Utah, a grant writer, a reporter and copy-editor in Mexico, an ELL teacher in China, a missionary in Puerto Rico, and as a writing center consultant. He has published multiple articles and has professionally copy-edited two books, as well as science articles by Chinese researchers. He has a rich college level teaching experience in Rhetoric and English at UI, Salt Lake Community College, and LDS Business College, where he worked extensively with minority, international, first-generation, and other "non-traditional" students so-called, which he found immensely rewarding.

***

Sawsan Abbadi (Ed.D.) is a faculty member of the Arabic program in the Department of Modern Languages and Literatures at Loyola University Chicago. She received her M.Ed from the University of Massachusetts, Amherst (2004). She serves in the Department of Teacher Education and Curriculum Studies with concentration on Bilingual, Multicultural, ESL Program. She received her Ed.D from the University of Massachusetts, Amherst (2011) with concentration on Language, Literacy, and Culture Program. Her doctoral thesis is entitled "The Teaching and Learning of Arabic post 9/11: Late Modernity and Possibilities for Change in Language Classrooms." In discourses of postmodernity, globalization, and new technological and social conditions, this thesis explores complexities of language teaching and learning, with a focus on Arabic in college contexts post 9/11. Dr. Abbadi taught Arabic in a number of prestigious college campuses in the U.S. and presented different stages of her work in diverse national conferences.

Josh R. Meuth Alldredge received a B.A. degree in Politics from Whitman College. Pursuing his commitment to community development through education, he conducted ethnographic research in an indigenous village in the Brazilian Amazon to explore barriers and opportunities in sustainable development. After publishing his findings, Josh worked with village leadership to co-design and secure grant funding for indigenous youth education in agro-ecological production. Later, Josh worked to expand higher education opportunities for indigenous youth in Bolivia through the Princeton in Latin America Fellowship. Now in Colorado, he works with Head Start to increase access to early education for low-income families, and serves with the Launch High School board to develop entrepreneurship-based education for alternative thinkers.

Geraldine Blattner (PhD – Pennsylvania State University) is Associate Professor of French and Linguistics at Florida Atlantic University. She is the Director of the French basic language program and the ESL Program for Academic Readiness (PAR). She is also the coordinator of the French, German, Italian, and Linguistics teaching assistants. Her research focuses on technology-enhanced foreign language teaching and learning, and on sociolinguistic and pragmatic variation in French-language computer-mediated discourse. Her recent publications investigate how social media such as Facebook and Twitter can culturally enhance foreign language classes and develop mutliliteracy skills in a second language.

Brian W. Bodah holds a Ph.D. in biological and agricultural engineering from Washington State University. He currently serves as the Director of and Agriculture Faculty for WSU Pierce County Extension. His past research includes a variety of research projects studying the heritability of drought tolerance through the use of pea, nutrient, and sediment mitigation in irrigated agriculture through the use of vegetative filter strips, and the development of a portable rainfall simulator capable of mimicking the small drop sizes and low intensities of natural rainfall patterns in the Palouse region of Eastern Washington State. Dr. Bodah has worked with and organized sustainable agriculture in the United States and the Brazilian Amazon, and is involved with conservation themed education in both countries.

Eliane Bodah earned her Ph.D. in Horticulture from Washington State University in 2014. She is an Assistant Professor at Seattle University. Dr. Bodah has melded aspects from the field of biology and ideas of sustainability towards education as well. She became a consultant for the United Nations in 2008, and cofounder of the Thaines and Bodah Center for Education and Development advising international students in both Brazil and the U.S. She has taught a variety of courses, including primarily English as a Second Language in public and private Brazilian schools. Dr. Bodah is currently working as a NIH postdoctoral fellow at the University of Washington. She has co-authored several international publications on education and teaching methods, including the bilingual book "EE from Brazil to the US" with Dr. Brian Bodah.

Clara Burgo is an Assistant Professor of Spanish at Loyola University Chicago. Her teaching and research interests include Sociolinguistics, Spanish for Heritage Speakers, and Spanish Teaching Methods. She has published several articles on Spanish Heritage Language Pedagogy and Variationist Sociolinguistics.

William Cain is Assistant Director for the CEPSE/COE Design Studio and a doctoral candidate in Educational Psychology & Educational Technology at Michigan State University. His research interests focus on how people teach, learn, and collaborate over distances in real-time. William has written extensively on topics such as technology-mediated group dynamics, synchronous hybrid learning, and robotic telepresence. He has been awarded the AT&T/MSU Award of Excellence twice for his work on Blended and Hybrid course designs.

Amanda Dalola (PhD – University of Texas at Austin) is an Assistant Professor of French and Linguistics at the University of South Carolina. Her research interests include phonetics, sociophonetics, and lab phonology, as well as technology and social media use in the L2 classroom. She is the current Facebook moderator for Gaspard le Gamecoq (USC French program) and Français Interactif (UT French program), and has served as a developer for French Online (UT).

Carolin Fuchs is Assistant Professor in the Department of English at City University of Hong Kong. Her primary research interests include telecollaborative and technology-mediated language learning and language teacher education. Specifically, her work focuses upon computer-mediated communication and negotiation, multiliteracies, language play, intercultural learning, social media, networked technologies, and LMOOCs. Prior to joining City U in fall 2015, Carolin was a Lecturer in the TESOL/Applied Linguistics Program at Teachers College, Columbia University, in New York City. She has also worked at the Middlebury Institute of International Studies at Monterey, the Pennsylvania State University, and the University of California at Berkeley.

Emanuelle Goellner holds a B.S. degree in Biology from the University of Passo Fundo. She has an M.S. in engineering, with a concentration on infrastructure and the environment. Her PhD studies are on agricultural and environmental microbiology at the Federal University of Rio Grande do Sul, Brazil. She also works with water resources management, solid waste management, environmental sanitation, and corporate environmental management. Emanuelle also has a specialization in teaching for higher education.

Wei Hong is Professor of Applied Linguistics and the Director of Chinese Language Program in the School of Languages and Cultures at Purdue University, USA. Since 2007, she has been also serving as the Director of the Confucius Institute. She has been teaching and publishing in pragmatics, Business Chinese, Chinese as a foreign language and advising Ph.D. students. Dr. Hong works closely with the business community, K-12 schools, and academia in the State of Indiana in promoting Chinese language education. In 2010, Dr. Hong was elected to the Board of Advisors of Chinese Language Teachers Association in the U.S.

Agnieszka Legutko is Lecturer in Yiddish and Director of the Yiddish Language Program at Columbia University. She specializes in modern Yiddish literature, language, and culture, women and gender studies, and spirit possession in Judaism. Her publications have appeared in several journals and essay collections on Yiddish literature and culture, such as *Cwiszn, Bridges, Lilith, Jewish Quarterly*, and *Silent Souls? Women in Yiddish Culture*. Her research interests include trauma, memory, performance, and the body represented in modern Jewish culture, as well as digital technology and language pedagogy. In her work, she explores the possibilities offered by digital humanities in Yiddish literature and culture, and especially new media integration in the Yiddish language instruction. She received her Ph.D. with distinction in Yiddish Studies from Columbia University and is currently completing a manuscript exploring the trope of dybbuk possession in modern Jewish culture and developing a number of Yiddish-related digital projects.

Tasha N. Lewis has been an Assistant Professor of Spanish at Loyola University Maryland since 2011, where she teaches Spanish language courses as well as various other linguistics courses. She also served as the Core Spanish-Language Coordinator from 2011 to 2015. She received her MA from California State University, Long Beach in Spanish, and her PhD from the University of California, Davis in Spanish Linguistics with a special Designated Emphasis in Second Language Acquisition. Her research interests include foreign language pedagogy, telecollaboration, second language acquisition, the relationship between speech and gesture, as well as the relationship between language and thought, and finally, the relationship between language and cognition.

Bailu Li is a PhD candidate of Applied Linguistics at Purdue University, USA. She also teaches Chinese at all levels and Business Chinese as a senior graduate instructor. Over the past 3 years, she has been the chief developer and main instructor for elementary Chinese distance courses at Purdue. She is currently conducting a new project that compares the learning outcomes of oral and written proficiency between distance and classroom students. Her research interests include technology-advanced language teaching and learning, experiential learning in Chinese classroom, and Chinese multimedia study.

Lara Lomicka (PhD – Pennsylvania State University) is Professor of French at the University of South Carolina, where she currently serves as Graduate Director for Languages. She also serves as an Associate Editor for Language Learning & Technology and at JALT journal. In 2009 her teaching was nationally recognized by the American Council on the Teaching of Foreign Languages (ACTFL) and Cengage Publishers, as she received the Excellence in Foreign Language Instruction Using Technology award. In 2011 she was honored as a Chevalier dans l'ordre des palmes academiques. She was the Calico software editor for a number of years and will be the incoming Calico Vice President in May 2016. Her research interests include teacher education, intercultural learning, social media, study abroad, service learning, and computer assisted language learning.

Byung-jin Lim (Ph.D. in Linguistics, Indiana University-Bloomington) is an Assistant Professor of Korean in the Department of East Asian Languages & Literature at the University of Wisconsin-Madison where he directs the Korean language program. His research interests include Korean linguistics, second/foreign language acquisition, computer-mediated communication, and Korean language textbook development. He is the author of *Perceiving Syllables and Contrasts: Second Language Learning Perspectives* (Korea University Press, 2015) and articles that have appeared in academic journals including *Journal of Korean Language Education, Language and Speech*, and *Japanese/Korean Linguistics*.

Haixia Liu received her MA degree from Sun Yat-sen University in China in 2005. She has worked in the School of Foreign Language, Beijing Normal University at Zhuhai since her graduation. She is currently a PhD student in the Department of Counseling, Education Psychology and Special Education at the College of Education, Michigan State University and an associate professor in Beijing Normal University Zhuhai Campus. Her research interests include second language acquisition, teacher adoption of technology, computer-assisted language learning, language teachers' educational technology professional development, and comparative education.

Latisha Mary gained her Ph.D. from the University of Exeter in 2010 for research into children's identity, self-esteem and personal, social, and citizenship education. She has been working in the area of foreign language didactics and teacher education in France since 2001 and is currently a lecturer of English and applied linguistics at the *Ecole Supérieure du Professorat et de l'Education* at the University of Lorraine where she is involved in initial primary teacher education. Her research and teaching interests include early language learning, teacher education for the support of second language acquisition, bi-/plurilingual education, language awareness, intercultural education, and the role of self-efficacy and affect in language learning. She is a member of the research laboratory ATILF (CNRS): Équipe Didactique des langues et sociolinguistique.

Alcindo Neckel holds a B.S. degree in geography from the University of Passo Fundo, a M.S. of engineering with focus on infrastructure and the environment from that same university, and a Ph.D. in geography from the Federal University of Rio Grande do Sul, Brazil. His research area is environmental analysis. He is currently working on a second Ph.D. degree in geography and environmental sciences at the Atlantic International University. He is a professor of the graduate program in architecture and urbanism at Southern IMED University. He is also a researcher at the IMED foundation, where he is a leader of the following groups: society, environment and urban environmental impacts, and governance in sustainable cities.

Sílvia Melo-Pfeifer is associate professor in the Department of Education, at the University of Hamburg (Germany). She is also a member of CIDTFF (Research Center for Didactics and Technology in Teacher Education, Portugal). Among her research interests are: multilingual interaction, plural approaches to teaching and learning of foreign languages and heritage language education. She is currently a research member of the European projects SPIRAL ("School-teacher Professionalization: Intercultural Resources and Languages") and Koinos ("European Portfolio of Plurilingual Literacy Practices").

Jacques du Plessis grew up in South Africa. He was in the South African Navy for 2 years, concurrently starting his tertiary education at the University of South Africa. He then transferred to the University of Pretoria. In 1984, he transferred to the USA to do his BA (Linguistics, French minor). In 1992 he completed his MA (Linguistics and Language Acquisition) at BYU. He received a PhD from Utah State University in Instructional Technology. He has been teaching Afrikaans at the university level since 1985. Since 2002, he has been on the faculty of the University of Wisconsin, Milwaukee. He developed the first fully online foreign language course at UWM. As part of his research, Jacques developed one of the pioneering Open Course Ware sites for foreign languages in 2004: www.openlanguages.net/Afrikaans. Currently he is developing web-based foreign language learning tools for the blind. Dr. du Plessis is currently the president of the National Council for Less Commonly Taught Languages.

Danielle O. Pyun (Ph.D. in Foreign and Second Language Education, The Ohio State University) is an Associate Professor of Korean in the Department of East Asian Languages and Literatures at the Ohio State University. She teaches Korean language and culture courses and her research areas are Korean-as-a-foreign language pedagogy and second language acquisition. Her publications include a co-authored book *Colloquial Korean: The Complete Course for Beginners* (Routledge, 2009), and research articles that have appeared in various journals including *Foreign Language Annals*, *System* and *the Canadian Modern Language Review*.

Ya Rao is currently an associated teacher and researcher at Paul Valéry University. She has 7 years of experience in teaching university Chinese in France. She has a Ph.D. in Language Education, and is affiliated with the Laboratory Intersite Research Institute of Cultural Studies in Montpellier. She is currently a board member for the Association of Research and Teaching Chinese in Paris. Rao's work is dedicated to the study of Chinese as a Foreign Language with Web 2.0 tools, and upon the construction of knowledge within learning communities. She has published on Intercultural Awareness in Chinese Foreign Language Learning, and on Community Learning in web collaboration.

Mohsen Shahrokhi is an assistant professor in Applied Linguistics at Shahreza Branch of Islamic Azad University, Isfahan, Iran. His research interests include Sociolinguistics, Pragmatics, and issues concerning teaching and learning English as a foreign language. He has taught both graduate and undergraduate courses to students of TEFL and English Language Translation Studies. He has also supervised many MA theses in TEFL and English Language Translation Studies. A number of his research papers have been published in international refereed journals and his latest paper entitled 'The impact of visualization and verbalization techniques on vocabulary learning of Iranian high school EFL learners: A gender perspective' has been published by Ampersand journal, Elsevier (Science Direct). He has also contributed to books and handbooks, including a chapter entitled 'The Impact of Mobile Assisted Language Learning (MALL) on Phrasal Verbs of Iranian Intermediate EFL Students' in 'Handbook of Research on Mobile Learning in Contemporary Classrooms' published by IGI Global, USA; and another chapter entitled 'A Cross-Cultural Study of External Request Modifications in Persian' in 'Bridging the Gap of Cross-Cultural Communication' published by University of Malaya Press (UM Press), Malaysia.

Shima Taheri is an M.A graduate in Teaching English as a Foreign Language. Her research interest includes Computer Assisted Language Learning (CALL).

Wenhao Tao, PhD, is Professor and Dean of the School of Foreign Languages at Beijing Normal University at Zhuhai. He is also the Vice Director of Translation and Interpretation Association of Guandong Province, Member of Teaching Instruction Committee of English Majors of Guandong Province and Educational Inspector of Zhuhai Municipal Government. His research interests include cognitive linguistics, applied linguistics, psycholinguistics, second language acquisition and TESOL, computer assisted language learning, and teacher professional development.

Margarita Vinagre holds a Ph.D. in English Linguistics from the University of Seville and an M. Phil in Applied Linguistics from Trinity College Dublin. Currently she works as an Associate Professor at Autónoma Universidad de Madrid. Her main research interests focus on the integration of technologies in the foreign language classroom, and more specifically, on the development of intercultural and linguistic competences in virtual collaboration. She has published widely on these topics and has coordinated research projects on virtual collaboration and language learning with Trinity College Dublin, the Open University UK, Dublin City University, Dublin Institute of Technology and High School Utrecht. She is currently the principal investigator on a research project in collaboration with the Universities of Hawaii and Columbia.

Sijia Yao earned her PhD in Comparative Literature from Purdue University in May 2016. She will start to teach Chinese language and literature in the University of Nebraska–Lincoln in August 2016. Her publications explore both Chinese language teaching and Chinese literature. She taught various levels of Chinese courses as well as world literature courses. Since she joined the distance Chinese research team in 2013, Sijia has been exploring better on-line assessment, and developing such course materials as Fun Hanzi, Fun Reading, Cultural Video, and Grammar Lectures. Her scholarly interest ranges from teaching Chinese as a foreign language (CFL) and distance Chinese education, to Chinese Studies (literature, film, culture) and Women's Studies.

Andrea Young gained her Ph.D. from Aston University in 1994 for research into motivation and attitudes towards foreign language learning. She has been a lecturer in language education at the *Ecole Supérieure du Professorat et de l'Education* at the University of Strasbourg since 1998. Her research and teaching interests include teacher education for the support of second language acquisition, home/school educational partnerships, teacher language awareness, plurilingual and intercultural education. She has been involved in a number of European projects in these areas, notably with the European Centre for Modern Languages in Graz. Her recent publications include: "Unpacking teachers' language ideologies: attitudes, beliefs and practiced language policies in schools in Alsace, France," *Language Awareness*, 23:1-2 and "Looking through the language lens: Monolingual taint or plurilingual tint?" in Conteh, J. & Meier, G. (eds.) *The multilingual turn in languages education: opportunities and challenges for individuals and societies.*

Index

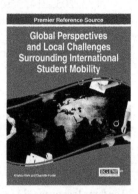
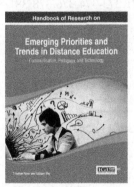
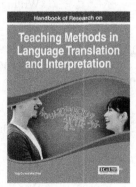
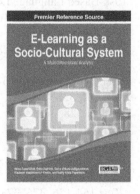

CPSIA information can be obtained
at www.ICGtesting.com
Printed in the USA
LVOW04*1422280217

525680LV00017B/398/P